Introductory Readings in Ancient Greek and Roman Philosophy

Introductory Readings in Ancient Greek and Roman Philosophy

Edited by
C.D.C. Reeve and Patrick Lee Miller

With a General Introduction by
Lloyd P. Gerson

Hackett Publishing Company, Inc.
Indianapolis/Cambridge

Printed in the United States of America

12 11 10 09 08 07 06   1 2 3 4 5 6 7

For further information, please address:

Hackett Publishing Company, Inc.
P.O. Box 44937
Indianapolis, IN 46244-0937

www.hackettpublishing.com

Cover design by Brian Rak
Text design by Meera Dash
Composition by Scribe
Printed at Dickinson Press, Inc.

Library of Congress Cataloging-in-Publication Data

Introductory readings in ancient Greek and Roman philosophy / edited by C.D.C. Reeve and Patrick Lee Miller ; with a general introduction by Lloyd P. Gerson.
p. cm.
Includes bibliographical references.
ISBN-13: 978-0-87220-830-8 (pbk.)
ISBN-10: 0-87220-830-3 (pbk.)
ISBN-13: 978-0-87220-831-5 (cloth)
ISBN-10: 0-87220-831-1 (cloth)
1. Philosophy, Ancient—History—Sources. I. Reeve, C.D.C., 1948– II. Miller, Patrick L. (Patrick Lee), 1970–
B504.I58 2006
180—dc22

2006041318

The paper used in this publication meets the minimum requirements of American National Standard for Information Sciences—Permanence of Paper for Printed Library Materials, ANSI Z39.48–1984.

∞

Contents

---

* Translations by Richard D. McKirahan, Jr., unless otherwise noted.

* Translations by Terence Irwin and Gail Fine, unless otherwise noted.

General Introduction

Lloyd P. Gerson

Ancient philosophy extends roughly from 600 BCE to 600 CE. During this very long period, philosophy as we know it today was invented, and its fundamental problems or areas of concern established. The history of philosophy from 600 CE up to the present is more or less constituted by a series of engagements with the ancient philosophical agenda.

Before We Begin

A student of ancient Greek and Roman philosophical writings has to be as attuned to the historical circumstances surrounding them as to the philosophical arguments they contain. In this regard, there is nothing special about these writings; we could say as much about those produced at any other time and place. There are, however, special problems about these writings and our ability to study them. These derive from the complex path leading from the moment they were first set down to *now*, when a modern English translation of some version of that original text is published.

Almost all of these texts were originally written on papyrus, although there are a few examples that were carved in stone. Papyrus is the writing material named after the Egyptian plant from which it comes. After its surface was prepared, it was then rolled up into a fairly standard size. The ancient Greek word *biblos* is the term for this plant and writing surface. It survives in our words *bibliography* and *Bible*. Early in the Christian era the supply of papyrus became unreliable, and authors shifted to sheepskin or goatskin, which was cut into sheets and bound with some sort of covering; hence, the origin of the modern book. The technique was supposedly developed in Pergamum, a city in Asia Minor. The English word *parchment* comes from the Latin word for this city. Both of these materials are subject to decay and decomposition, so that we have extremely few samples of writings that actually date back to the ancient period.

These papyrus rolls and sheepskin books were each unique exemplars of the author's work, potentially available for copying. As philosophers rose and fell in popularity, their works might be widely copied or not at all. The great libraries of the ancient world were the preserve of such works as had been copied on demand by whoever sponsored the library. The manuscript copies of the original works (or copies of earlier copies, and so on) that are available to us mainly go back no further than the ninth century CE, and most are from several centuries later than that.

Beginning with the invention of the printing press around 1450, scholars began to make "editions" of the works of the ancient authors based on an examination of some or all of the manuscripts then known. Not surprisingly, manuscripts sometimes differ in their "readings," that is, in what the copyist put down. Modern editors have to try to figure out which manuscript retains the best reading—the one most accurately representing what the author of the work actually wrote. This is a demanding technical job, especially for authors of philosophical works in which exact wording often makes all the difference.

These Renaissance editions are the starting point for the classical scholarship that is the backbone of the study of ancient philosophy. Only through editions like these can we hope to understand what the authors were trying to say. Since the late fifteenth century, many, many successive editions of single works have appeared, frequently based on more manuscripts or on more accurate reading of existing manuscripts. Most scholars today use editions of ancient works that go back no further than the nineteenth century, though there are some exceptions.

From this brief account, it should be evident already that there are numerous pitfalls in working back from a contemporary English translation of, say, a work of Aristotle to what Aristotle intended to convey. In addition, there is a problem of a different and even more serious nature, namely, that with two notable exceptions, we do not possess all the works of any ancient philosopher.[1] In some cases, we possess only fragments of their works. In many cases, we possess nothing more than a name and a reference to the philosopher's "school" affiliation. An educated guess would be that we possess something less than 10 percent of the true body of ancient philosophical writings from our period of study. For example, the indispensable ancient historian of philosophy, Diogenes Laertius (c. 200 CE) tells us that the writings of Epicurus are contained in 300 rolls. At about a dozen ordinary book pages per roll, that would make 3,600 pages. What we possess is a mere 100 pages, much of it fragmentary. Another example: We are told that the great Stoic Chrysippus wrote over 700 rolls. But though a substantial number of fragments are extant, no single complete work of his survives. This sad story can be retold again and again for nearly all of the ancient philosophers. Even our fragmentary evidence is often suspect, moreover, since it frequently comes to us as quotations from hostile later writers, who were not above taking a quotation out of context or misquoting it, either inadvertently or mischievously.

What Is Ancient Philosophy About?

A remarkable feature of ancient philosophy is that, though its agenda of problems, questions, and methods grew and to a certain extent mutated through time, there is something like an ongoing dialogue among its practitioners. This is certainly in part because they had, broadly speaking, a common culture and all knew a common language—Greek. It is also because they did not make a sharp separation between thinking about philosophical issues and thinking about what their predecessors thought about these same issues. It is no doubt a much more daunting task today than it was, say, 2,000 years ago to understand the history of a contemporary philosophical problem along with the various solutions offered. As a guide to those encountering ancient philosophical texts for the first time, a few orienting concepts are useful. In fact, there is one in particular that is arguably the central focus of ancient philosophical speculation—the concept of nature. Thinking about it will give us a way of beginning to understand how subsequent philosophers appropriated, expanded, and frequently rejected the legacy of their early predecessors.

The ancient Greek word for nature—*physis*—has its origin in a biological metaphor, since it comes from the verb "to grow." It was well established as a word for the world and all its parts, excluding everything "artificial," like utensils, articles of clothing, or artistic products. The question with which ancient Greek philosophy begins is that of whether nature in this sense is understandable by us. To this simple question, an answer had been widely assumed to be correct perhaps eons before philosophy began. That answer was: no. Nature, it was supposed, was itself a kind of artifact of some unfathomable powers. Regularities or orderliness in nature provided no clues to how we could understand it; at best, they provided clues to the whims of unseen forces.

---

1. The two exceptions are Plato and Plotinus.

It would be a serious mistake to leap to the conclusion, however, that the beginning of philosophy coincided with the complete rejection of unseen powers within and "beyond" nature. On the contrary, the overwhelming majority of ancient Greek philosophers found that *as philosophers* they were compelled to recognize such powers as essential to explaining nature. And they generally had no difficulty in designating one or more of these powers as "divine." But what set philosophers apart was the idea that nature's orderliness was no fluke. Nature (*physis*), they thought, was a *kosmos* (a unified and orderly arrangement of parts) with a *logos* (a rational account, including an explanation of its orderliness).

The idea that nature is orderly and apt for understanding immediately inspires a host of questions. Here is one: If nature is a cosmos, how come it does not *look* like a unified and orderly arrangement of parts? How come it appears immensely diverse and often bizarrely *disordered?* Such a question led—inevitably, one might think—to the idea that the unity and orderliness of nature must be nonapparent or hidden beneath the surface. The consideration of this idea, taken along with the original one that *physis* is a cosmos, provided the core subject matter for philosophy and the wellspring of most philosophical problems. At the same time, it was the core subject matter and wellspring of science (especially *natural* science). The term *cosmology* (*kosmos* plus *logos*) nicely captures the meeting point of philosophy and science. The eventual split between the two came gradually to the fore in our period of study. Its history is part not just of ancient philosophy, but of philosophy more generally.

When we suppose that in order to understand nature we have to suppose it to have a nonapparent structure or arrangement, we immediately introduce a distinction between the way things appear and the way they really are. Such a distinction is part of the tool kit of every speaker of a natural language, whether ancient Greek or English. For example, we easily understand what it means to say, "the dog appears about to attack, but he's really just being friendly." By contrast, we also use the word *appear* in a way that does not suppose that reality differs from appearance, as in, "that thing moving in the corner appears to be alive because it really is!" Commonsense generally starts out with the assumption that things are as they appear. Philosophy challenges commonsense by claiming that nature could not be a cosmos if that was literally and unqualifiedly the case. The point is the same whether we call "nature" the reality behind the appearances or identify nature with the appearances and call the reality behind it something else.

It is not a big stretch, conceptually speaking, from this position to a consideration of the following question: how do we human beings, who are seeking an understanding of nature, fit into this picture? On the one hand, we ought to be counted as part of nature; on the other, we seem to be somehow standing outside of nature when we try to think about it or represent it. Both alternatives yield numerous problems and lines of investigation. On the first alternative, a human being has itself an order; it is a *microcosmos*, a "miniature cosmos"; on the second, our standing outside of nature and representing it in some way seems to open up the possibility that our representations are themselves a sort of artifact and not a part of nature. So, understanding or cognition in general appears to be something other than just naturally interacting with our environment the way other animals do. Yet insofar as we are a part of nature, perhaps we can come to understand it by examining ourselves or engaging in introspection. So, we might be able to explore nature by exploring the microcosmos.

These two perspectives on human beings and their attempts to understand nature are potentially in conflict: if we try to understand nature by engaging in introspection or by "looking into ourselves" as the philosopher Heraclitus put it, will not the results inevitably be just more representations? Will we not merely have discovered a peculiar type of artifact rather than nature's order itself? So, in a way, attempts to understand the order in nature raise problems regarding understanding itself and its very possibility. Throughout our period of study, there is an ongoing debate not just about what the precise order in nature consists of but also about what understanding that order is supposed to be and, indeed, how that is even possible.

One sort of strategy for explaining nature begins by supposing that underlying the apparent diversity in nature is a uniformity of material or elemental "stuff" out of which things are made. A related idea is that underlying it is a set of laws according to which everything operates. It is easy to see that the first idea helps support the second, since if everything is really made out of the same material, there is no reason to believe that a law that operates *here* operates differently *there*. In the early history of ancient Greek philosophy—the period traditionally given the name "Presocratic"—various hypotheses were offered both for the underlying elemental "stuff" and for the laws according to which we could understand how it came to look like nature.

Again, a host of problems emerge even from such rudimentary speculations. For example, if nature arises from some "elements," where do the elements come from? Or are they so different from nature as we know it that their origin needs no explanation (or at least no explanation of the same sort)? Compare the following conversation between a child and a parent:

Child: "Who made me?"
Parent: "God made you."
Child: "Who made God?"
Parent: "No one made God."

If this is held to be a good answer, it is because God, owing somehow to what he is, is not thought to be in need of a similar or, indeed, any explanation. This general issue about explanation deeply shapes the sorts of explanations canvassed in ancient philosophy.

If we posit ultimate explanations, however, it remains very puzzling how a living thing, say, is supposed to come to be from not-living ones. It is difficult to know where even to begin to formulate laws for this. One possible response is to say: the things that supposedly appear in nature are really nothing but the elements as they appear to us under certain conditions or according to certain laws—so that honey is neither sweet nor bitter "in itself," for example, but only appears so depending on the condition of the one who tastes it. Along with this line of thinking goes the argument that "honey" itself is just a word loosely applicable to a collection of certain appearances of the elements to certain individuals. Otherwise, it seems one is obliged to show that things and their natures are as real as any of the elements out of which they are generated.

Turning back to the "problem of the microcosm," we are naturally led to ask whether our efforts to understand nature split into two: what we do with our five senses and what we do with our minds or intellects. For if we conclude that the honey tastes sweet to one person and bitter to another but is in itself neither sweet nor bitter, we are obviously using our senses and our minds differently: our senses tell us the way things appear, while our minds tell us the way things really are. Having recognized such a distinction, it is but a step to the conclusion that our senses in fact have nothing or very little to contribute to our understanding. This is a conclusion that is on the face of it extraordinarily implausible. But perhaps it is no more counterintuitive than the alternative conclusion that the honey really is *both* sweet and bitter at the same time!

Such considerations of various possibilities and their pluses and minuses—what the ancients called "dialectic"—led generally to some very deep questions both about what exactly we mean when we say that something is "real" and about how our senses and our minds do or do not work together. And it is once again easy to see that these two issues are closely connected. For if you think that "real" and "nonsensible" go together, then you are, of course, going to conclude that your senses have very little to do in revealing what is real. If, on the other hand, you suppose that "real" and "sensible" go together—indeed, that associating real and nonsensible is a step backward into obscurantism and not a step toward enlightenment—then apart from the problems you face with the reality of time and the existence of things we cannot sense, we have the problem of explaining what, if anything, intellect or mind contributes to what our senses do reveal. What, in short, does it mean to understand what something is, over and above seeing it, remembering it, and recognizing it again at some later date, all of which can be attributed to the functioning of our five senses? After all, we do not need to suppose anything more than this to explain how animals cope with the world. If the real does not extend beyond what we can sense, then what, exactly, is understanding supposed to be understanding *of*?

By beginning with some quite elementary reflections on our encounter with the world around us, then, an array of philosophical issues almost inevitably spills out. One very human response to all of this is to say: Let's just back off from this precipice and leave nature the way we found it. We don't have to think these thoughts in order to live in the world. Indeed, those who find philosophy a sort of pointless exercise might say something like this. Yet as Aristotle observes, the desire to understand is a deeply human one. Of course, it is hardly controversial to acknowledge that those who like this sort of thing . . . well, like *this sort of thing*, and that is really all there is to say about it. But the ancient Greek philosophers went somewhat further than that.

The word *philosophy* comes from the ancient Greek words for "love" (*philia*) and "wisdom" (*sophia*). *Wisdom* is just another word for the understanding we have been talking about. Hence philosophers were not just people who happened to like to tie themselves up in intellectual knots and then figure out clever ways of escaping. They were people who thought that a way of life focused on a search for understanding was an intrinsically satisfying one, and that the *achievement* of understanding was bound to be life-enhancing—and by "achievement" they meant correct answers to the questions they posed. So, though the search for answers was itself pleasant enough, a life entirely devoted to such a search would not make much sense unless the searcher could reasonably hope to succeed, or at least make some valuable progress along the way. No doubt, many contemporary thinkers (including philosophers) would question whether such answers are possible or whether their achievement would be properly described as seriously life-enhancing. Nonetheless, a genuine appreciation of what the ancient Greek philosophers were doing depends on appreciating their assumption that philosophy was serious business, and that those who are unwilling or unable to partake in it for whatever reason are not just to be thought of as "opting" for another activity, but as substantially discounting their own humanity.

This position might strike one as extraordinarily implausible. After all, one does not need to be a chemist to reap the benefits of chemistry. Here is one way that (for the ancient Greek philosophers, at any rate) philosophy differs from chemistry and science generally: the products of the scientist's laboratory are readily or at least potentially available to all, whereas the "product" of the philosopher's success—wisdom—is not, and this for a very mundane and human reason. If some chemists have figured out how to combine chemicals to make a compound that eliminates rashes, they will not have a very difficult time convincing you that they have done so, especially if they cure your rash with it. On the other hand, if others tell you that they understand this or that profound philosophical matter, they cannot so readily "show you the goods." Of course, they can tell you what they understand or what they think they understand, but the plain hard truth is that whatever they say, it would not be difficult for you to find someone else who will with equal earnestness tell you the opposite.

One possible response to this state of affairs is to take the "pox on both your houses" approach and say that there is no such thing as understanding about these matters or that everyone has his or her own "personal" understanding. We have already seen that this possibility is one canvassed early on in our period of study. But another approach—the one favored by almost all the philosophers represented in this volume—is to recognize that though the various expressions of purported understanding, especially when they are backed up by clear argument, can assist one in attaining understanding, they are no substitute for that attainment. One might be lucky enough to benefit from the fruits of someone else's wisdom, say, by taking their good practical advice or by living in a society based on laws that were wisely instituted, but even that is somewhat problematic. After all, people generally seek out advice from those who will give them the advice they want; human nature being what it is, people do not generally seek out or follow advice that goes against their own inclinations. In addition, even if one is lucky enough to live under good laws, that seems to be a long way from knowing why they are good laws or why obeying them is or is not in one's interest. So, understanding really is not something directly transmittable. Once one realizes this, one need not be shocked by the sheer contrariness of so much of the history of philosophy. The disagreements among philosophers do not in themselves indicate that the attainment of wisdom is impossible; they might well indicate only that people must achieve or fail to achieve wisdom for themselves.

Underlying the above remarks is the best reason we know for studying the history of philosophy: it provides the most efficient way to test-drive some of the most prominent and well-respected claims to wisdom that have ever been made. There is nothing in principle to prevent someone completely ignorant of the history of philosophy from attaining wisdom. Yet, the challenge to say exactly what one thinks is right or wrong in a historical philosophical argument and to explain why is, practically speaking, an indispensable tool of personal enlightenment. Facing up to the challenges posed in the history of philosophy is a sure way to enhance one's own critical powers.

Returning to the theme of nature, it is correct to see the fifth and fourth centuries BCE as the great flowering of Greek philosophy, provided we bear in mind that if we take the long view, philosophy was still then, if not in its infancy, at least in its young adulthood. In fact, with Plato—disciple or student of Socrates and teacher of Aristotle—we see ancient Greek philosophy acquiring not only its maturity but also, in large measure, its future "agenda." It is something of an exaggeration—but a useful one nonetheless—to say that virtually all Greek philosophy after Plato engages with him at some level and in some way. This engagement includes attacks on various claims he made that occur within the ambit of fundamental agreement on principles (like Aristotle's), to attacks against these various principles (like the Stoics), to defenses against all manner of attacks (like Plotinus), to efforts to extend or develop Platonism in the light of competing contemporary claimants to wisdom (like the later Neoplatonists).

It is illuminating to think of Plato as himself engaged with what was by his time some 200 years of philosophy, and to see him as trying to embrace what was good and reject what was bad in his predecessors' efforts to attain wisdom. Regarding nature, Plato argued both for its objective reality and for the distinction between what the senses tell us about it and what the intellect does. But he also argued that what the intellect tells us about nature is more fundamental. That is, what is intelligible can explain what is sensible but not vice versa. If we choose to call what is sensible "real," then we should call what is intelligible "really real," though what this means, minimally, is that the latter serves to explain everything about the former that is explicable. It does not mean that the sensible world is illusory.

Aristotle, to a large extent, endorsed Plato's general view that the intelligible explains the sensible, though he limits the concept of nature to what is changeable. He also made an important distinction between the natural and the artificial, a distinction that deeply informs his approach to the former. Insofar as nature needs any explanation at all, we need to go outside of nature to find it. There are two key points here: one, that in saying this Aristotle is not exactly refuting Plato, who had a more capacious concept of nature; and two, Aristotle opens up the possibility that many things about nature do not need an "external" explanation at all. The whole problem of what does and what does not require an explanation is thus laid open. Aristotle's nuanced investigation of the different types of explanation follows.

Both Plato and Aristotle responded to the Presocratic insights about the relationship between the microcosm and the macrocosm. They both developed complex accounts about how cognition of intelligible reality (as opposed to nonhuman responses to the natural environment) was possible. Both applied these accounts to the fundamental moral problem: what is a person? In developing solutions to it, moreover, both assumed that being subjects of cognitive states was a deep feature of our personhood. Both then proceeded to try to connect human desire with what is really—not just apparently—good. Motivating this discussion is the obvious fact that we do make mistakes about what we desire. With an account of the human person in place, however, one can reason, so Plato and Aristotle thought, toward an understanding of what is good for any person, or what fulfills human nature, in much the way that one does in the case of what is good for a particular species of plant. This quasi-scientific approach to ethics will inform the entire history of our period of study.

The so-called Hellenistic period (roughly, from the death of Alexander the Great in 323 BCE to the founding of the Roman Empire in 27 BCE) saw the rise to prominence of a number of philosophical schools, all of which have their roots in the works of Plato and Aristotle. These are, principally, Stoicism, Epicureanism, and Skepticism (first, Skepticism within Plato's own Academy, and then, much later, more radical Skepticism found throughout the ancient world). All of these schools represent reflective responses to the prevailing Presocratic/Platonic/Aristotelian tradition. They represent challenges to the specific accounts given of nature, including human nature, and even to the way problems had been formulated. Questions were raised, both by Stoics and by Epicurus, the founder of the Epicurean school, about the supposed supernaturalism of previous accounts, that is, about the claims that the intelligibility of nature required a commitment to immaterialism, or the existence of entities other than physical bodies and their attributes. Stoic and Epicurean naturalism (though very different in many respects) are both congenial to a scientific orientation to explanation and hence to a scientific basis for philosophy. Both schools were committed to the principle that whatever unique features human beings may possess, these did not require nonnaturalistic explanations. Accordingly, human destiny and human happiness were to be understood entirely within a naturalistic framework. This did not mean, however, that there ceased to be problems about just what this framework is and how to articulate it. Nor did it mean that Stoics and Epicureans foreswore the by then already ancient Presocratic insight regarding the bipolarity of the concept of nature: endowment (the way things are) and achievement (the way they ought to be). It would be fair to say that the Stoic and Epicurean perspectives spring from a concept of nature more limited than Aristotle's, according to which whatever is intelligible about nature arises from its very materiality, and is in no way independent of that.

In its challenge to the very possibility of knowing nature and its principles, Skepticism served to put in question the entire idea of philosophy as a kind of precious knowledge. For the Skeptic maintained that philosophy had been understood as the pursuit of wisdom about divine and human matters. But if it can be shown that claims for success in this pursuit are nothing but dogmatic pretension, then the very idea of philosophy will be undermined. The Skeptics were extremely careful to avoid the *dogmatic* assertion of their view, or to claim that philosophy was literally impossible. This would have left them open to the charge of a sort of self-refutation. Rather, they were content to persuade others by the application of skeptical "medicine," that is, particular types of refutation crafted to meet particular dogmatic claims. Success in this regard was to lead to a renunciation of philosophy as a necessary means to or as constitutive of a good life. What, after all, is the point of trying to arrive at true beliefs if there is no way of telling the difference between true ones and false ones?

Between the earliest Presocratics, their "dogmatic" successors (including Plato, Aristotle, Stoics, and Epicureans), and the Skeptics, there is to be found a type of dialectic—literally, a conversation. That conversation has its deepest origin in the questions regarding what it means to be a human being living in the world. Perhaps the desire to understand or explain the world around us really is as genuine and natural as any other human desire. Regarding this desire, there is one assumption that the Skeptics shared with their dogmatic predecessors, namely, that if it is necessarily fruitless, its presence in us probably does more harm than good and should be suppressed, just as we should suppress weird desires to eat nonfood items. Skeptics made the ancient Greek philosophers think even more deeply about the way of life that philosophy was supposed to be.

Let us pause for a moment and note that with the Skeptic Aenesidemus, who probably lived sometime in the first century BCE, we are not even halfway through the history of ancient philosophy. A great deal of hard thinking about the issues and problems we have sketched remains to be done. Skepticism certainly does not bring an end to philosophy or to its "dogmatic" development. But as we shall see, it does add a powerful new element to the conversation when Greek philosophy meets the new revealed religion, namely, Christianity.

Ancient Greek philosophy after the Hellenistic period is a complex story of debate among the various schools, attempts to appropriate the wisdom of the "ancients" (especially Pythagoras, Plato, Aristotle, and the Stoics) in ways that bolstered the positions of philosophers against their opponents, and new confrontations with forces in the Roman Empire, especially Christianity. Just to anticipate, this dynamic stew of ideas is heading toward the period that marks the end of "pagan" Greek philosophy. Ultimately, efforts to consolidate the best of Greek wisdom in defense against attacks by Byzantine Christians failed. The Christian victors in this confrontation had to decide just how much of this wisdom they could safely incorporate into their own theological and philosophical constructs.

An additional and extremely important part of the complex intellectual climate in the beginning of the first century BCE and extending right through to and beyond our period of study is the growth of Roman philosophy, alongside Greek philosophy. In part, Roman philosophy is just an extension of Greek philosophy into the Roman world and the Latin language. This is the case, for example, with Lucretius, the Epicurean, and with Seneca, the Stoic. But it is also undoubtedly true that these philosophers, and many others, did make original contributions to philosophy. As Christianity began to rise up in the Roman Empire, however, the engagement of Roman philosophers with the new religion was different from that of Greek philosophers. But by the Middle Ages, philosophy in both the Latin West and in the Romanized Greek culture of the Byzantine Empire had largely become a product of Christianity's victory over competing philosophies and religions in late classical antiquity.

By the first century CE, we find in the extant texts a variety of standard philosophical problems focusing the attention of members of the schools. These included the problem of whether philosophy itself constituted a desirable way of life or whether it was to be understood in a more technical manner. An increasing sophistication about natural science and mathematics impinged on reflection regarding the philosophical understanding of nature. For example, the idea of laws of nature when applied to the microcosm yields the obvious question: how can human beings act freely without supposing that they are exempt from such laws? And if they are not exempt, what exactly becomes of freedom and the moral point of view? For if we are not free, what is the point of trying to figure out how people ought to act or of holding them responsible for not so acting? This is a problem that, like almost all others of the period, has its roots in the writings of Plato and Aristotle. Yet during the Christian era, this problem seems to take on a new urgency with the increasing competition of the philosophical schools for disciples (and here it is useful to consider Christianity as a new competitor on the scene).

All this competition inspired close study of the works of the founders of each school, and efforts to present their positions as unshaken by attacks, whether by other dogmatists or by Skeptics. It also produced a willingness to search for wisdom in writings found outside of the Greek philosophical tradition. Thus, we begin to find in this period an increasing number of references to, for example, Persian, Egyptian, and Hebrew texts. Such texts were, typically, brought in to lend authority to the deliverances of Greek wisdom.

We also find efforts to apply the doctrines found in the writings of the founders of the schools to contemporary problems or questions not explicitly dealt with there. If we embrace a claim made by a certain philosopher, we might be eager to see where that claim leads us, or what it entails. As historians of philosophy, however, we cannot assume that just because a philosopher said A, and *we* think that anyone who says A must also agree to B, that the philosopher himself accepted B. In late ancient philosophy, the systematic treatment of philosophical problems is rooted in reflection on the historical texts and is generally impelled by circumstances to the creation of fresh approaches to old issues or even to issues only vaguely anticipated. In this way, loyal discipleship to the founding masters did not exclude the possibility of original thought.

The last great flowering of ancient Greek philosophy begins with Plotinus and takes us to the end of our period of study. Most of the Greek (or Greek-speaking) philosophers writing in the period 200–600 CE about whom we have any significant information have been since the eighteenth century labeled "Neoplatonists." The term has often been understood in a vaguely reproachful manner, indicating questionable "innovations" in the thinking of these philosophers. It should be noted, however, that they regarded themselves not as innovators, but as faithful followers of the philosophical truths that had been expressed best by Plato, though certainly not by Plato alone.

The appearance of a certain rigidity or homogeneity of thought in this period is owing largely to the fact that these philosophers had a shared commitment to the basic tenets of Platonism, though even at this level, there were significant and subtle variations or disagreements. Indicative of the complex relation between philosophy and the history of philosophy in this period, Neoplatonists formulated two innovations. First, they established the policy in their school of teaching Aristotle as an introduction to Plato rather than the other way around. This they did because they were more interested in philosophical truth than in a linear history of Greek philosophy. Such an approach might occasion surprise if one supposes that Aristotle's philosophy is set in direct opposition to Plato's. Why would one use the philosophy of the opponent of one's champion as an *introduction* to the latter? The simple fact is that Neoplatonists generally held that Aristotle's philosophy represented a version—though in some respects a dissident's version—of Platonism and, accordingly, that the study of his profound exploration of nature paved the way for the "higher mysteries" of Platonism.

Second, and in support of the first innovation, Neoplatonists developed the genre of commentary, both on the works of Aristotle and the dialogues of Plato. To be sure, the first commentaries on these writings antedate the Neoplatonists. Nevertheless, it was they who practiced this way of doing philosophy so assiduously that a good deal of what we know about the entire history of ancient Greek philosophy comes from the extant 15,000 pages or so of Neoplatonic Aristotelian commentary.

The challenge for those who find themselves approaching the ancients with any agenda—religious or otherwise—is to permit them first to speak with their own distinctive voices. That is why the reading of any "secondary" source, however accurate or informed, is no true substitute for a one-on-one encounter with the texts. The art of reading ancient Greek philosophy lies in developing the technique of "noise reduction," that is, learning how to filter out the extraneous issues on *both* sides—ours and theirs. You can judge the progress you are making in grappling with these texts by the number of times you cay say, "I understand that this philosopher is in his own terms addressing the identical human concerns that I would perhaps express in other terms. What he is saying is difficult to believe and perhaps, ultimately, wrong, but not because I have the advantage of living long after he did." If you have just a couple of these moments, you will almost certainly want many more.

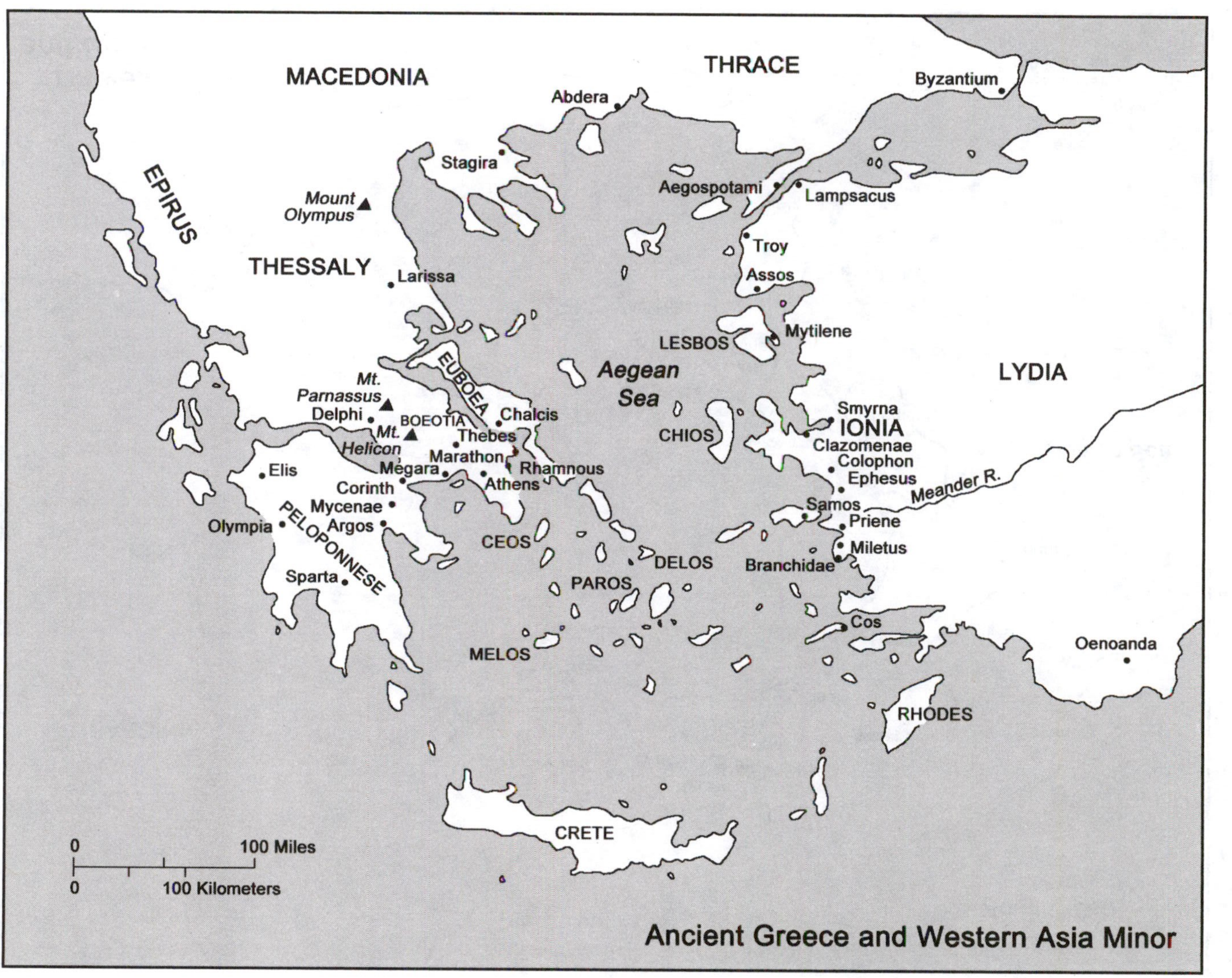

Ancient Greece and Western Asia Minor

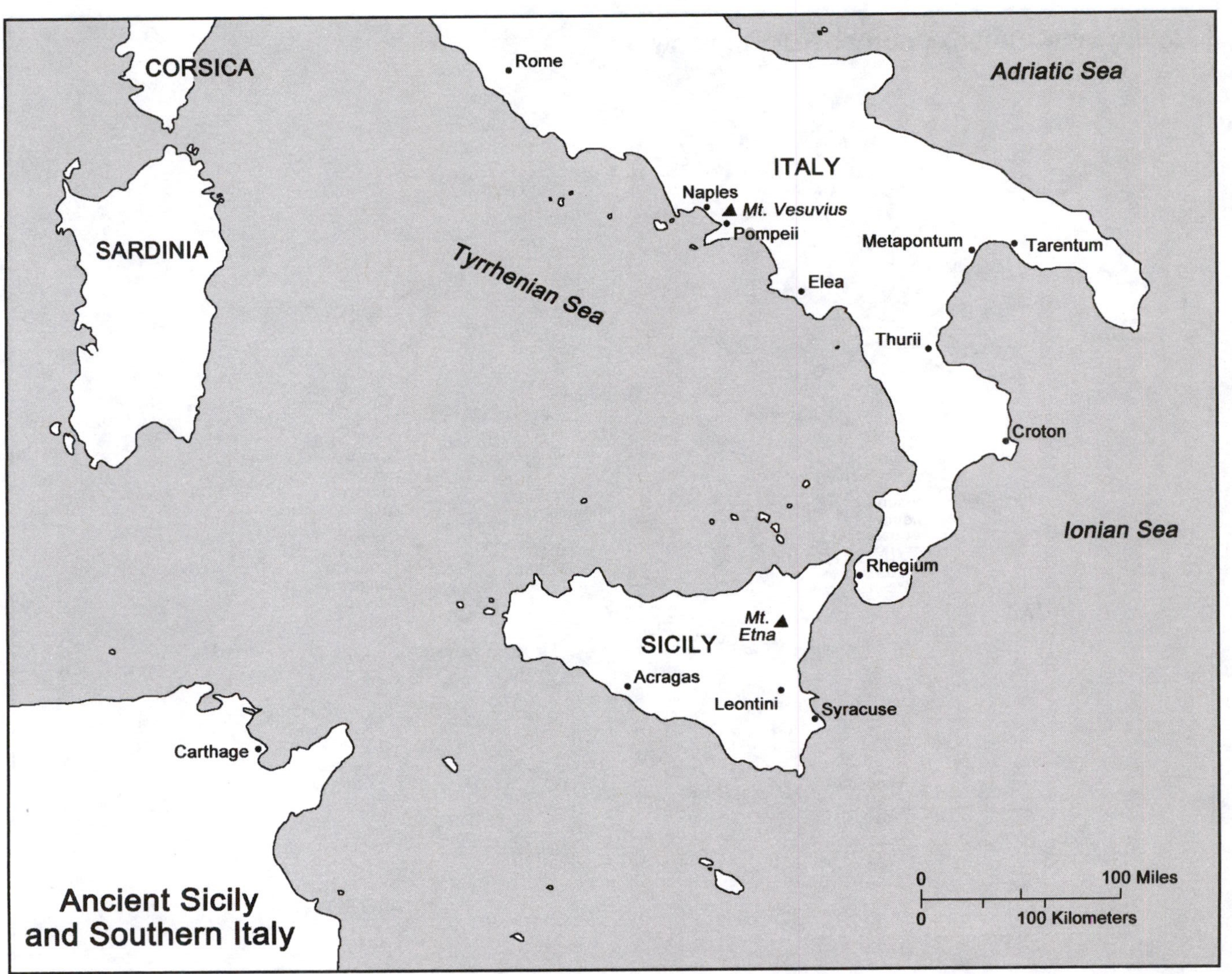
CORSICA
Rome
Adriatic Sea
ITALY
Naples
Mt. Vesuvius
Pompeii
SARDINIA
Metapontum
Tarentum
Tyrrhenian Sea
Elea
Thurii
Croton
Ionian Sea
Rhegium
Mt.
Etna
SICILY
Acragas
Leontini
Syracuse
Carthage
0
100 Miles
0
100 Kilometers
Ancient Sicily
and Southern Italy

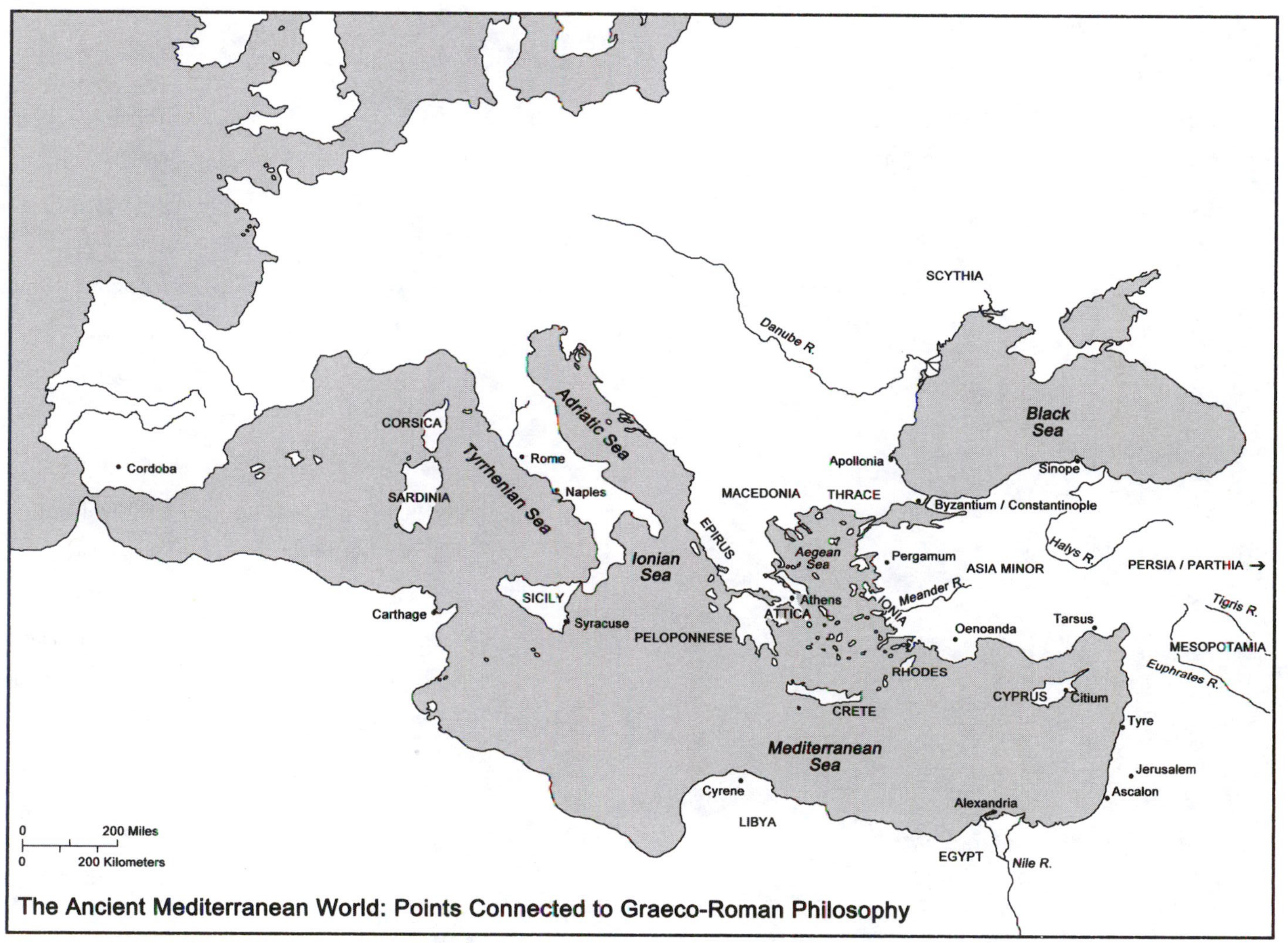

The Ancient Mediterranean World: Points Connected to Graeco-Roman Philosophy

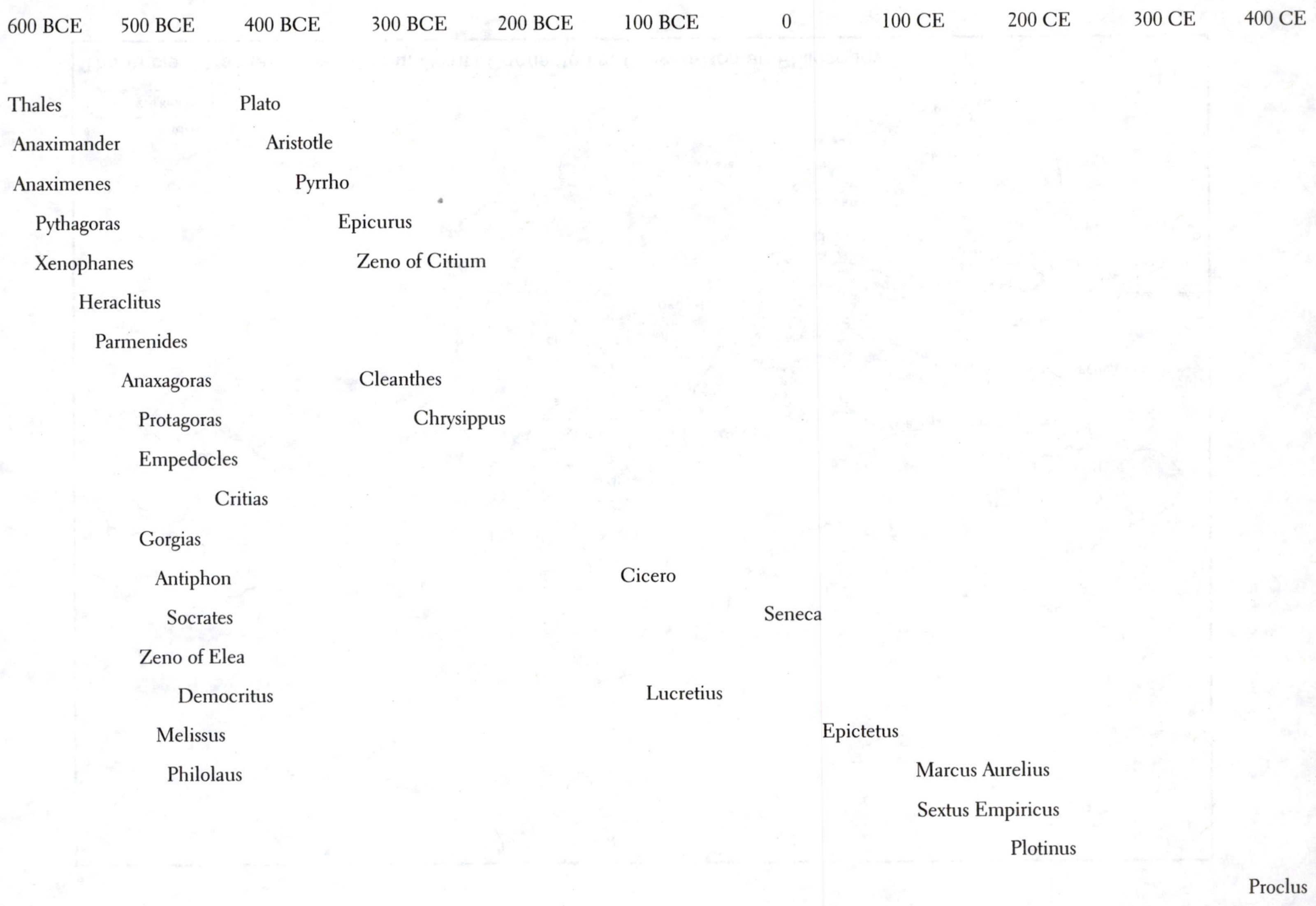

600 BCE 500 BCE 400 BCE 300 BCE 200 BCE 100 BCE 0 100 CE 200 CE 300 CE 400 CE

Thales Plato
Anaximander Aristotle
Anaximenes Pyrrho
Pythagoras Epicurus
Xenophanes Zeno of Citium
Heraclitus
Parmenides
Anaxagoras Cleanthes
Protagoras Chrysippus
Empedocles
Critias
Gorgias
Antiphon Cicero
Socrates Seneca
Zeno of Elea
Democritus Lucretius
Melissus Epictetus
Philolaus Marcus Aurelius
Sextus Empiricus
Plotinus
Proclus

Acknowledgments

The editors wish to thank Lloyd P. Gerson for writing the general introduction to this volume, James Lesher for advice on the Early Greek Philosophy section, Pierre Destrée and John Cooper for comments on the translation of the *Meno*, and especially Rachel E. Kratz for help with the Aristotle introductions and with assembling the manuscript. They are also very grateful to the various translators and editors for allowing use of their work, to Brian Rak for suggesting this project and helping to realize it, to Meera Dash for her heroic work in preparing the volume for the printer, to Deborah Wilkes for aid and comfort, and to all at Hackett Publishing Company for their support.

Note to the Reader

Scholars of ancient Greek and Roman philosophy cite passages in texts using the numbering systems employed in certain standard editions.

Early Greek philosophy: The standard edition is Hermann Diels and Walther Kranz, *Die Fragmente der Vorsokratiker* (fifth edition 1934–1937). A DK or Diels-Kranz number is a numeral + the letter A or B + a second numeral—for example, 11A2. The first numeral identifies the relevant philosopher (Thales in this case); the letter identifies whether the text is a direct quotation from his writings (B) or an indirect report (A); the second numeral identifies where in the series of quotations or reports the text is to be found. Like some other early Greek philosophical texts, Zeno #12 (presented in this volume) is not included in DK. It is referred to as "The Porphyry Argument," because Porphyry, the student and editor of Plotinus, discussed it.

Plato: The numbers printed in the margins derive from the first printed edition, edited by the French scholar Henri Estienne (1531–1598), whose pen name was Stephanus. Since most pages in that edition have five columns of text, a so-called Stephanus number consists of a page number, a column letter (a–e), and (where necessary) a line number.

Aristotle: The standard edition is that of Immanuel Bekker (1785–1871), in which each page has two columns. A Bekker number consists of a page number, a column letter (a–b), and, where necessary, a line number.

Hellenistic, Roman, and Neoplatonic philosophy: The major source for Hellenistic philosophy is Diogenes Laertius, *Lives of the Philosophers* (early third century CE). DL 8.91 refers to Book 8 Paragraph 91 of this ten-book work. The standard edition of the Stoics is H. von Arnim, *Stoicorum Veterum Fragmenta* (1903–1905), abbreviated as SVF.

EARLY GREEK PHILOSOPHY

1
Milesian Monists

The earliest traces of Greek philosophy come from Miletus, a thriving port on the coast of Asia Minor (modern-day Turkey). Its wealthiest citizens could afford to turn their minds from practical affairs to speculative matters, to which they brought the spirit of public debate that characterized their politics. Openness was a feature of their religion, too, since Miletus had neither a priestly class nor sacred texts. Finally, in economics, the Milesians traded with the older civilizations of Egypt and Mesopotamia and became acquainted with their ideas about the gods, the cosmos, and the stars. From such an exciting milieu of rational criticism, intellectual innovation, and foreign influence emerged three great thinkers: Thales, Anaximander, and Anaximenes.

1a
Thales

Thales lived in the late seventh and early sixth centuries BCE. Other founders of great philosophical and religious traditions belong to the same period: Zarathustra in Persia, Gautama Buddha in India, and both Confucius and Lao Tzu in China. Though Thales did not found a religion, later Greeks esteemed him as one of their Seven Sages, since he began a tradition of critical inquiry into many subjects, including geometry, astronomy, and cosmology. One of his most famous achievements was the prediction of a solar eclipse in 585. Like the Babylonians, Thales viewed water as, in some sense, the basic stuff of the cosmos. Even though his Milesian successors rejected this view of his, they very much followed in his footsteps, seeking to explain everything by appeal to some basic principle and offering reasons for their own candidates. If Thales wrote anything, none of it survives. But the following short accounts from Aristotle reveal the new spirit of critical speculation he initiated, as well as his debt to older, animist ideas. "All things," Thales allegedly said, "are full of gods."

1. Of those who first pursued philosophy, the majority believed that the only principles of all things are principles in the form of matter. For that of which all existing things are composed and that out of which they originally come into being and that into which they finally perish, the substance persisting but changing in its attributes, this they state is the element and principle of things that are. . . . For there must be one or more than one nature out of which the rest come to be, while it is preserved.

(Aristotle, *Metaphysics* 1.3.983b6–18 = 11A2)

From A *Presocratics Reader*, edited by Patricia Curd. Translations by Richard D. McKirahan unless otherwise indicated (Indianapolis: Hackett Publishing Company, 1996).

2. However, not all agree about the number and form of such a principle, but Thales, the founder of this kind of philosophy, declares it to be water. (This is why he indicated that the earth rests on water.) Maybe he got this idea from seeing that the nourishment of all things is moist, and that the hot itself comes to be from this and lives on this (the principle of all things is that from which they come to be)—getting this idea from this consideration and also because the seeds of all things have a moist nature; and water is the principle of the nature of moist things.

(Aristotle, *Metaphysics* 1.3.983b18–27 = 11A12)

3. Some people claim that it [the earth] rests on water. Indeed, this account, attributed to Thales of Miletus, is the oldest we have. It rests, allegedly, because it floats, like wood and other such things (for in fact none of these by nature rests on air, but does on water)—as if the same account that applies to the earth didn't also have to apply to the water that supports the earth!

(Aristotle, *On the Heavens* 2.13.294a28–34 = 11A14; tr. Reeve)

4. Some declare that it [the soul] is mixed in the whole [universe], and perhaps this is why Thales thought all things are full of gods.

(Aristotle, *On the Soul* 1.5.411a7–8 = 11A22)

5. From what has been related about him, it seems that Thales, too, supposed that the soul was something that produces motion, if indeed he said that the magnet has soul, because it moves iron.

(Aristotle, *On the Soul* 405a19–21 = 11A22; tr. Curd)

1b
Anaximander

Anaximander was said to have been a student of Thales. Like him, he reduced the complexity of the cosmos to one thing, which he called *the indefinite*. This abstraction introduced into Greek philosophy the notion of a supersensible reality. Treating this reality as divine, Anaximander characterized it as steering all things in a lawlike way and as exacting retribution for their injustice to one another. Though described somewhat poetically, the indefinite addressed a problem that Thales seems not to have recognized—that of explaining how opposite natures could give rise to one another, how something wet (water), for example, could produce something dry (earth).

1. Of those who declared that the first principle is one, moving and indefinite, Anaximander . . . said that the indefinite was the first principle and element of things that are, and he was the first to introduce this name for the first principle [i.e., he was the first to call the first principle indefinite.] He says that the first principle is neither water nor any other of the things called elements, but some other nature which is indefinite, out of which come to be all the heavens and the worlds in them. The things that are perish into the things out of which they come to be, according to necessity, for they pay penalty and retribution to each other for their injustice in accordance with the ordering of time, as he says in rather poetical language.

(Simplicius, *Commentary on Aristotle's Physics* 24.13–21 = 12B1 + A9)

2. This does not have a first principle, but this seems to be the first principle of the rest, and to contain all things and steer all things, as all declare who do not fashion other causes aside from the infinite . . . and this is divine. For it is deathless and indestructible, as Anaximander says and most of the natural philosophers.

(Aristotle, *Physics* 3.4.203b10–5 = 12A15)

3. Some, like Anaximander . . . declare that the earth is at rest on account of its similarity. For it is no more fitting for what is established at the center and equally related to the extremes to move up rather than down or sideways. And it is impossible for it to make a move simultaneously in opposite directions. Therefore, it is at rest of necessity.
(Aristotle, *On the Heavens* 2.13.295b11–6 = 12A26)

4. He also declares that in the beginning humans were born from other kinds of animals, since other animals quickly manage on their own, and humans alone require lengthy nursing. For this reason, in the beginning they would not have been preserved if they had been like this.
(pseudo-Plutarch, *Miscellanies* 179.2 = 12A10)

1c
Anaximenes

Anaximenes made *air* the basic stuff of his cosmos, allegedly noticing that moist air, when condensed, became clouds, and that clouds, when condensed still further, became rainwater. Apparently this led him to speculate that if water were condensed still further, it would become earth, and that more rarefied, it would become fire. Although Anaximenes may seem to have retreated from the bold abstraction of Anaximander's indefinite, he did specify a process by which things might be converted into one another—namely, condensation and rarefaction. This apparently impersonal mechanism marked an important departure from Anaximander's use of divine justice to explain change. But Anaximenes did not eliminate divinity altogether from his thought: "Air," he believed, "is a god."

1. Anaximenes . . . like Anaximander, declares that the underlying nature is one and boundless, but not indeterminate as Anaximander held, but definite, saying that it is air. It differs in rarity and density according to the substances [it becomes]. Becoming finer it comes to be fire; being condensed it comes to be wind, then cloud, and when still further condensed it becomes water, then earth, then stones, and the rest come to be out of these. He too makes motion eternal and says that change also comes to be through it.
(Theophrastus, quoted by Simplicius, *Commentary on Aristotle's Physics* 24.26–25.1 = 13A5)

2. Just as our soul, being air, holds us together and controls us, so do breath and air surround the whole cosmos. (Aetius 1.3.4 = 13B2)

3. Anaximenes . . . said that the principle is unlimited [boundless] air, out of which come to be things that are coming to be, things that have come to be, and things that will be, and gods and divine things. The rest come to be out of the products of this. The form of air is the following: when it is most even, it is invisible, but it is revealed by the cold and the hot and the wet, and movement. It is always moving, for all the things that undergo change would not change unless it were moving. For when it becomes condensed and finer, it appears different. For when it is dissolved into what is finer, it comes to be fire, and on the other hand air comes to be winds when it becomes condensed. Cloud results from air through felting, and water when this happens to a greater degree. When condensed still more it becomes earth and when it reaches the absolutely densest stage it becomes stones.
(Hippolytus, *Refutation* 1.7.1–3 = 13A7)

4. Anaximenes determined that air is a god and that it comes to be and is without measure, infinite and always in motion.
(Cicero, *On the Nature of the Gods* 1.10.26 = 13A10)

2

Three Iconoclasts

2a

Pythagoras and the Pythagoreans

Pythagoras was born c. 570 BCE off the coast of Asia Minor on the island of Samos, which was near Miletus and the steadily encroaching Persian Empire. But he did not remain there his whole life. Dissatisfied with the rule of Polycrates, the tyrant whom Persia supported, he left the eastern Mediterranean in 530, finally settling in Croton, on the coast of southern Italy. Pythagoras' emigration westward had important consequences for Greek philosophy, since it brought Pythagoreanism to the Greek colonies of Italy and Sicily, where it would flourish for over a century. Pythagoras himself helped ensure this longevity, establishing a society of followers that became the first true school of Greek philosophy.

Pythagoreanism also developed quickly into a religion. Devotees employed rituals, dietary restrictions, and contemplation of the divine cosmic order in the hope of purifying their souls and preparing them for future reincarnations. So foreign to the traditional religion of the Greeks, these doctrines and ascetic practices seem to have been influenced by the religions of territories under Persian control. For example, in the Indian province of Gandhara, the doctrine of reincarnation had emerged much earlier. And just as Zoroastrians divided the cosmos between two opposing forces—those of good and light against those of evil darkness—so too did the Pythagoreans, who added such mathematical opposites as odd and even to their own dualistic division of the cosmos.

Mathematics is the inquiry with which Pythagoras is most commonly associated nowadays, thanks largely to the theorem that bears his name (in a right triangle the square of the hypotenuse equals the sum of the squares of the two adjacent sides). Although this theorem had been known already to the Babylonians for a millennium, Pythagoras may have developed the first proof of it. Perhaps more important to the Pythagoreans than such arguments, however, were the unusual properties they associated with numbers. Like other ancient Greeks, they did their arithmetic with pebbles in the sand, forming shapes by arranging them with the help of a carpenter's square, or *gnomon*. Beginning with one pebble, for example, they surrounded it with a *gnomon*, adding either an odd number of pebbles along its edge, making a square, or an even number, making a rectangle. Since the ratio of a square's sides is always limited to one (e.g., 2:2, 3:3, etc.), whereas the ratios of a rectangle's sides are unlimited in their plurality (e.g., 2:3, 3:4, etc.), the Pythagoreans associated "limit" with "odd" and "one," but "unlimited" with "even" and "plurality." Further associating the first set with goodness and light, and the second with evil darkness, they seem to have prescribed the contemplation of the former and proscribed that of the latter.

Such contemplation involved the study not only of arithmetic and geometry, but also of music and astronomy. Taking lyre strings and fretting them according to certain ratios (e.g., 1:2, 2:3, 3:4), they produced musical harmonies (the octave, fifth, and fourth, respectively), and so gained further evidence of the power of mathematics. For harmony was determined not by the material composition of strings but by their order, structure, or form. Abandoning the Milesian quest for the material substrate of the cosmos, then, the Pythagoreans emphasized the cosmic order and structure. In fact, Pythagoras was said to have been the first to use the word *kosmos* (which means "order" in Greek) to refer to the whole world. Discerning *kosmos* also in the movements of the heavenly bodies, his followers even assumed that these movements created harmonies, the so-called music of the spheres. Although they could not hear this music, they believed that the divine Pythagoras could. Similarly, they believed that he alone could remember his past incarnations.

The goal of all Pythagoreans was to imitate their master. By engaging in philosophy, studying the cosmos, assimilating its order, and thereby purifying the soul, they hoped also to achieve a divinity like his. This program of purification and divinization, along with several of its central doctrines, seems to have exercised considerable influence on Plato. As a result, the Pythagorean synthesis of cosmology, psychology, and religion would become important, not just to ancient Greek philosophers from Plato through Plotinus, but also to later philosophers deeply in their debt.

1. Once [Pythagoras] passed by as a puppy was being beaten,
the story goes, and in pity said these words:
"Stop, don't beat him, since it is the soul of a man, a friend of mine,
which I recognized when I heard it crying."

(Diogenes Laertius, *Lives of the Philosophers* 8.36 = Xenophanes 21B7)

2. Thus [Pherecydes] excelled in both manhood and reverence
and even in death has a delightful life for his soul,
if indeed Pythagoras was truly wise about all things,
he who truly knew and had learned thoroughly the opinions of men.

(Diogenes Laertius, *Lives of the Philosophers* 1.120 = Ion 36B4)

3. There was a certain man among them who knew very holy matters
who possessed the greatest wealth of mind,
mastering all sorts of wise deeds.
For when he reached out with all his mind
easily he would survey every one of the things that are,
yea, within ten and even twenty generations of humans.

(Porphyry, *Life of Pythagoras* 30 = Empedocles 31B129)

4. Heraclides of Pontus says that Pythagoras said the following about himself. Once he had been born Aethalides and was believed to be the son of Hermes. When Hermes told him to choose whatever he wanted except immortality, he asked to retain both alive and dead the memory of what happened to him. . . . Afterwards he entered into Euphorbus and was wounded by Menelaus. Euphorbus said that once he had been born as Aethalides and received the gift from Hermes, and told of the migration of his soul and what plants and animals it had belonged to and all it had experienced in Hades. When Euphorbus died his soul entered Hermotimus, who, wishing to provide evidence, went to Branchidae, entered the sanctuary of Apollo, and showed the shield Menelaus had dedicated. (He said that when Menelaus was sailing away from Troy he dedicated the shield to Apollo.) The shield had already rotted away and only the ivory facing was preserved. When Hermotimus died, it [the soul] became Pyrrhus the Delian fisherman, and again remembered everything. . . . When Pyrrhus died it became Pythagoras and remembered all that has been said.

(Diogenes Laertius, *Lives of the Philosophers* 8.4–5 = 14,8)

5. Those called Pythagoreans took hold of mathematics and were the first to advance that study, and being brought up in it, they believed that its principles are the principles of all things that are. Since numbers are naturally first among these, and in numbers they thought they observed many likenesses to things that are and that come to be . . . and since they saw the attributes and ratios of musical scales in numbers, and other things seemed to be made in the likeness of numbers in their entire nature, and numbers seemed to be primary in all nature, they supposed the elements of numbers to be the elements of all things that are.

(Aristotle, *Metaphysics* 1.5.985b23–986a2 = 58B4)

6. The elements of numbers are the even and the odd, and of these the latter is limited and the former unlimited. The One is composed of both of these (for it is both even and odd) and number springs from the One; and numbers, as I have said, constitute the whole universe.

(Aristotle, *Metaphysics* 1.5.986a17–21 = 58B5)

7. The Pythagoreans similarly posited two principles, but added something peculiar to themselves, not that the limited and the unlimited are distinct natures like fire or earth or something similar, but that the unlimited itself and the One itself are the substance of what they are predicated of. This is why they call number the substance of all things.

(Aristotle, *Metaphysics* 1.5.987a13–9 = 58B8)

8. They say that the unlimited is the even. For when this is surrounded and limited by the odd it provides things with the quality of unlimitedness. Evidence of this is what happens with numbers. For when gnomons are placed around the one, and apart, in the one case the shape is always different, and in the other it is always one.

(Aristotle, *Physics* 3.4.203a10–5 = 58B28)

9. The tetractys[1] is a certain number, which being composed of the four first numbers produces the most perfect number, ten. For one and two and three and four come to be ten. This number is the first tetractys, and is called the source of ever flowing nature since according to them the entire cosmos is organized according to *harmonia*, and *harmonia* is a system of three concords—the fourth, the fifth, and the octave—and the proportions of these three concords are found in the aforementioned four numbers.

(Sextus Empiricus, *Against the Professors* 7.94–5; not in DK)

10. Others of the same cast of mind claim that there are ten principles, which they say are coordinate pairs:

limit	unlimited
odd	even
one	plurality
right	left
male	female
at rest	moving
straight	bent
light	darkness
good	evil
square	oblong

This, it seems, is also the view of Alcmaeon of Croton, who either got the account from them or they from him. . . . He says, you see, that most things relating to human beings come in pairs, but the opposites he mentions are not, like the Pythagorean ones, well defined, but arbitrary . . . whereas the Pythagoreans said how many opposites there are and which ones.

(Aristotle, *Metaphysics* 1.5.986a22–b2 = DK 58B5; tr. Reeve)

Philolaus of Croton

Philolaus of Croton was born c. 470 BCE, a quarter century after the death of Pythagoras. He seems to have been both a physician and a philosopher. Although Pythagorean doctrines were usually guarded jealously, Philolaus nonetheless published a book in which he revealed them, adding contributions of his own. The first fragment that follows seems to be his book's opening sentence.

1. The *tetractys* ("fourness") of the decad was an equilateral triangle composed of ten pebbles. With one pebble at the apex, two in the next row, three in the third, and four at the bottom, each side had four pebbles. This symbol thus represented the harmonic ratios they discovered (1:2, 2:3, 3:4), among other things; by it the Pythagoreans swore their oaths. Accordingly, the number four became important to those who fell under the spell of Pythagoreanism—especially Empedocles and Plato.

1. Nature in the cosmos was fitted together out of unlimiteds and limiters; both the cosmos as a whole and everything in it.

(Diogenes Laertius, *Lives of the Philosophers* 8.85 = Philolaus 44B1)

2. It is necessary that the things that are be all either limiters or unlimiteds, or both limiters and unlimiteds; but they could not always be unlimiteds only. Since, then, it appears that they are neither from limiters only nor from unlimiteds only, it is thus clear that both the cosmos and the things in it were fitted together from both limiters and unlimiteds. And things in their activities make this clear. For, some of them, from limiters, limit; some, from both limiters and unlimiteds, both limit and do not limit; and others, from unlimiteds, will be clearly unlimited.

(Stobaeus, *Selections* 1.21.7a = Philolaus 44B2)

3. Concerning nature and harmony it is like this: the being of things which is eternal and nature itself admit of divine and not human knowledge except that it was not possible for any of the things that are and are known by us to come to be, without the existence of the being of the things from which the cosmos was put together, both the limiters and the unlimiteds. And since these principles existed, being neither alike nor of the same kind, it would have been impossible for them to be ordered, if harmony had not come upon them, in whatever way it came to be. Those things that are alike and of the same kind were in no need of harmony, but those that are unlike and not of the same kind, nor of the same speed, it is necessary that these be linked together by harmony, if they are going to be held in an arrangement [*kosmos*].

(Stobaeus, *Selections* 1.21.7d = 44B6)

4. The magnitude of the scale [*harmonia*] is the fourth and the fifth. The fifth is greater than the fourth by a tone. For from the highest [string; the lowest in pitch] to the middle [string] is a fourth; from the middle to the lowest [string; the highest in pitch] is a fifth; from the lowest [string] to the third is a fourth; from the third to the highest [string] is a fifth. That which is in the midst of the middle [string] and the third is a tone. The fourth is the ratio 3:4, the fifth is 3:2, and the octave is 2:1. Thus the scale [*harmonia*] is five tones and two semitones, the fifth is three tones and a semitone, and the fourth is two tones and a semitone.

(Stobaeus, *Selections* 1.21.7d = 44B6a)

5. And indeed all things that are known have number. For without this nothing whatever could possibly be thought of or known.

(Stobaeus, *Selections* 1.21.7b = 44B4)

6. Both the ancient theologians and the prophets also testify that the soul has been yoked together with the body as a punishment and is buried in it as in a tomb.

(Clement, *Miscellanies* 3.17.1 = 44B14; tr. Reeve)

2b
Xenophanes

Xenophanes was born in Colophon, on the coast of Asia Minor, not far from Samos and Miletus. A contemporary of Pythagoras, he too left the region and traveled westward, possibly to escape the Persian conquest of Colophon in 547 BCE. By his own account, he then spent "sixty-seven years tossing my thought throughout the land of Greece." A wandering poet and philosopher, he wrote not only about drink, love, and war but also about nature, the divine, and knowledge. Finding fossils of fish inland, for example, he deduced that water had once covered the earth. Perhaps on the basis of such empirical observation, he projected a cosmic cycle of generation and destruction in which sometimes water, sometimes earth prevailed.

More novel than his natural theories were his theological verses. Written in the traditional meter of epic poetry, these criticized Olympian religion and introduced a new sort of divinity into

Greece. Free from the immorality of the Homeric gods, free from the racial specificity of national gods, free even from human form altogether, his one god was all-seeing, all-thinking, all-powerful, and though entirely immobile himself, "shakes all things by the thought of his mind." Xenophanes' god thus resembles those of Middle Eastern monotheisms. But he neither creates the world nor reveals himself to it; he could be known only through human inquiry.

Xenophanes was nonetheless conscious of human limits. He was the first Greek philosopher to distinguish between knowledge and mere belief, and he seems to have concluded his book with these self-effacing words: "Let these things be believed as resembling the truth." Despite his caution, and despite the shortage of arguments in his extant fragments, Xenophanes' critique of anthropomorphic gods and his vision of an intellectual god was assumed by subsequent Greek philosophers who wrote about the divine.

1. Homer and Hesiod have ascribed to the gods all deeds
which among men are a reproach and a disgrace:
thieving, adultery, and deceiving one another.
(Sextus Empiricus, *Against the Professors* 9.193 = 21B11)

2. Mortals believe that the gods are born
and have human clothing, voice and form.
(Clement, *Miscellanies* 5.109 = 21B14)

3. Ethiopians say that their gods are flat-nosed and dark,
Thracians that theirs are blue-eyed and red-haired.
(Clement, *Miscellanies* 7.22 = 21B16)

4. If oxen and horses and lions had hands
and were able to draw with their hands and do the same things as men,
horses would draw the shapes of gods to look like horses
and oxen to look like oxen, and each would make the
gods' bodies have the same shape as they themselves had.
(Clement, *Miscellanies* 5.110 = 21B15)

5. Xenophanes used to say that those who say that the gods are born are just as impious as those who say that they die, since in both ways it follows that there is a time when the gods do not exist.
(Aristotle, *Rhetoric* 2.23.1399b6–9 = 21A12)

6. God is one, greatest among gods and men,
not at all like mortals in body or thought.
(Clement, *Miscellanies* 5.109 = 21B23)

7. All of him sees, all of him thinks, all of him hears.
(Sextus Empiricus, *Against the Professors* 9.144 = 21B24)

8. But without effort he shakes all things by the thought of his mind.
(Simplicius, *Commentary on Aristotle's Physics* 23.19 = 21B25)

9. He always remains in the same place, moving not at all,
nor is it fitting for him to go to different places at different times.
(Simplicius, *Commentary on Aristotle's Physics* 23.10 = 21B26)

10. By no means did the gods reveal all things to mortals from the beginning,
but in time, by searching, they discover better.
(Stobaeus, *Selections* 1.8.2 = 21B18)

11. No man has seen nor will anyone know
the truth about the gods and all the things I speak of.
For even if a person should in fact say what is absolutely the case,
nevertheless he himself does not know, but belief is fashioned
over all things [or, in the case of all persons].
(Sextus Empiricus, *Against the Professors* 7.49.110 = 21B34)

12. Xenophanes declared that the sea is salty because many mixtures flow together in it. . . . He believes that earth is being mixed into the sea and over time it is being dissolved by the moisture, saying that he has the following kinds of proofs, that sea shells are found in the middle of the earth and in mountains, and the impressions of a fish and seals have been found at Syracuse in the quarries, and the impression of a laurel leaf

in the depth of the stone in Paros, and on Malta flat shapes of all marine life. He says that these things occurred when all things were covered with mud long ago and the impressions were dried in the mud. All humans are destroyed when the earth is carried down into the sea and becomes mud, and then there is another beginning of coming to be, and this change occurs in all the world orders.

(Hippolytus, *Refutation* 1.14.5–6 = 21A33)

13. All things that come into being and grow are earth and water.

(Philoponus, *Commentary on Aristotle's Physics* 1.5.125 = 21B29)

2c
Heraclitus

Heraclitus was born c. 540 BCE in Ephesus, which lay between Colophon and Miletus. The nobility of his birth may help explain the contempt for his fellow men manifest in his writings. Neither poets nor philosophers escaped his withering scorn: Homer should be flogged; Xenophanes had no real insight; and the wisdom of Pythagoras was in fact "evil trickery." Nonetheless, Heraclitus proposed a notion of cosmic harmony rather like Pythagoras', and a notion of intellectual divinity rather like Xenophanes'. He died c. 480, isolated from fellow citizens and philosophers alike.

Known in antiquity as "the riddler," Heraclitus' mysterious aphorisms have vexed interpreters up to the present day. In many of them, everyday objects and events are used to reveal the hidden nature of the cosmos. A river, whose waters must flow if it is to continue in existence, shows how movement or flux can make something both stable and persistent. A bow illustrates how the tension of opposites can make something unified and harmonious. Moving like a river and in tension like a bow, fire exists by striving with its fuel. Making strife or war "the father of all and king of all," Heraclitus appropriates for fire a role traditionally assigned to Zeus, king of the Olympian gods. Thus calling traditional Greek religion into question, Heraclitus imagines the whole cosmos as an eternal fire. Echoing Anaximenes, he says that other elements are exchanged for fire in a cosmic cycle. Echoing Anaximander, he says that fire will "judge and convict all things."

Such a cycle of impersonal judgment may appear unjust to humans. But to God—who is simply fire by another name—all is "beautiful and good and just." The divine law of the cosmos embodied in this cycle is the *logos*. This Greek word means many things: "law," "account," and "reason," to name a few. Because of this important ambiguity, the fragment with which Heraclitus may have opened his book, the first one presented here, is itself ambiguous. By warning that humans are unable to understand the *logos*, Heraclitus seems to mean that they misunderstand both the law of the cosmos and his own efforts to speak about it. Some blame his obscure sayings rather than human nature for this failure. But if the cosmos is as he describes it—with stasis in movement, harmony in opposition, and creation in strife—the most accurate representation of it may positively require a *logos* that is itself elusive and contradictory.

Not surprisingly, subsequent philosophers drew diverse inspiration from Heraclitus. Plato seems to have accepted his observations on flux as an accurate description of the material world—where "all things flow"—but not of the world of transcendent, unchanging forms. The Skeptics later highlighted his aphorisms about the effects of perspective, explaining how the same things appear differently to different observers, especially to members of different species. Their rivals, the Stoics, used his cycle of fire to develop their own doctrine of periodic cosmic conflagration. They also trusted his divine *logos*, resigning themselves to its necessity, no matter how unjust it might appear. One of his recent admirers, Friedrich Nietzsche, wrote that "the world forever needs the truth, so the world forever needs Heraclitus."

1. This *logos* holds always but humans always prove unable to understand it, both before hearing it and when they have first heard it. For though all things come to be [or, happen] in accordance with this *logos*, humans are like the inexperienced when they experience such words and deeds as I set out, distinguishing each in accordance with its nature and saying how it is. But other people fail to notice what they do when awake, just as they forget what they do while asleep.

(Sextus Empiricus, *Against the Professors* 7.132 = 22B1)

2. For this reason it is necessary to follow what is common. But although the *logos* is common, most people live as if they had their own private understanding.

(Sextus Empiricus, *Against the Professors* 7.133 = 22B2)

3. Heraclitus said that Homer deserved to be expelled from the contests and flogged, and Archilochus likewise.

(Diogenes Laertius, *Lives of the Philosophers* 9.1 = 22B42)

4. Eyes and ears are bad witnesses to people if they have barbarian souls.

(Sextus Empiricus, *Against the Professors* 7.126 = 22B107)

5. Human nature has no insight, but divine nature has it.

(Origen, *Against Celsus* 6.12 = 22B78)

6. A man is called infantile by a divinity as a child is by a man.

(Origen, *Against Celsus* 6.12 = 22B79)

7. The wise is one alone; it is unwilling and willing to be called by the name of Zeus.

(Clement, *Miscellanies* 5.115.1 = 22B32)

8. Nature loves to hide.

(Themistius, *Orations* 5.69b = 22B123)

9. The Lord whose oracle is at Delphi neither speaks nor conceals, but gives a sign.

(Plutarch, *On the Pythian Oracle* 404d = 22B93)

10. Right thinking is the greatest excellence, and wisdom is to speak the truth and act in accordance with nature, while paying attention to it.

(Stobaeus, *Selections* 3.1.178 = 22B112)

11. Listening not to me but to the *logos* it is wise to agree that all things are one.

(Hippolytus, *Refutation* 9.9.1 = 22B50)

12. Things taken together are whole and not whole, [something which is] being brought together and brought apart, in tune and out of tune; out of all things there comes a unity, and out of a unity all things.

([Aristotle] *On the World* 5.396b20 = 22B10)

13. They do not understand how, though at variance with itself, it agrees with itself. It is a backwards-turning attunement like that of the bow and lyre.

(Hippolytus, *Refutation* 9.9.2 = 22B51)

14. Those who speak with understanding must rely firmly on what is common to all as a city must rely on law [or, its law] and much more firmly. For all human laws are nourished by one law, the divine law; for it has as much power as it wishes and is sufficient for all and is still left over.

(Stobaeus, *Selections* 3.1.179 = 22B114)

15. What is opposed brings together; the finest harmony (*harmonia*) is composed of things at variance, and everything comes to be in accordance with strife.

(Aristotle, *Nicomachean Ethics* 8.2.1155b4 = 22B8)

16. The sea is the purest and most polluted water: to fishes drinkable and bringing safety, to humans undrinkable and destructive.

(Hippolytus, *Refutation* 9.10.5 = 22B61)

17. Asses would choose rubbish rather than gold.

(Aristotle, *Nicomachean Ethics* 10.5.1176a7 = 22B9)

18. The wisest of humans will appear as an ape in comparison with a god in respect of wisdom, beauty, and all other things.

(Plato, *Hippias Major* 289b4–5 = 22B83)

19. The most beautiful arrangement is a pile of things poured out at random.

(Theophrastus, *Metaphysics* 15 = 22B124)

20. The road up and the road down are one and the same.

(Hippolytus, *Refutation* 9.10.4 = 22B60)

21. Upon those who step into the same rivers, different and again different waters flow.

(Arius Didymus, *fr.* 39.2 [*Dox.gr.* 471.4] = 22B12)

22. The beginning and the end are common on the circumference of a circle.

(Porphyry, *Notes on Homer* [*Iliad* 24.200] = 22B103)

23. The same thing is both living and dead, waking and sleeping, young and old; for these things transformed are those, and those transformed back again are these.

(pseudo-Plutarch, *Consolation to Apollonius* 106e = 22B88; modified by Miller)

24. It is death to souls to become water, death to water to become earth, but from earth comes water and from water soul.

(Clement, *Miscellanies* 6.17.2 = 22B36)

25. The turnings of fire: first, sea; and of sea, half is earth and half fiery waterspout. . . . Earth is poured out as sea, and is measured according to the same ratio [*logos*] it was before it became earth.

(Clement, *Miscellanies* 5.104.3, 5 = 22B31a, b)

26. Fire lives the death of earth and air lives the death of fire, water lives the death of air, earth that of water.

(Maximus of Tyre 41.4 = 22B76a)

27. The cosmos, the same for all, none of the gods nor of humans has made, but it was always and is and shall be: an ever-living fire being kindled in measures and being extinguished in measures.

(Clement, *Miscellanies* 5.103.6 = 22B30)

28. Changing, it rests.

(Plotinus, *Enneads* 4.8.1 = 22B84a; modified by Curd)

29. Even the posset[1] separates if it is not being stirred.

(Theophrastus, *On Vertigo* 9 = 22B125)

30. All things are an exchange for fire and fire for all things, as goods for gold and gold for goods.

(Plutarch, *On the E at Delphi* 338d–e = 22B90)

31. Thunderbolt steers all things.

(Hippolytus, *Refutation* 9.10.7 = 22B64)

32. War is the father of all and king of all, and some he shows as gods, others as humans; some he makes slaves, others free.

(Hippolytus, *Refutation* 9.9.4 = 22B53)

33. It is necessary to know that war is common and justice is strife and that all things happen in accordance with strife and necessity.

(Origen, *Against Celsus* 6.42 = 22B80)

34. For fire will advance and judge and convict all things.

(Hippolytus, *Refutation* 9.10.6 = 22B66)

35. Fire is want and satiety.

(Hippolytus, *Refutation* 9.10.7 = 22B65)

36. God is day and night, winter and summer, war and peace, satiety and hunger, but changes, the way [fire,] when mingled with perfumes, is named according to the scent of each.

(Hippolytus, *Refutation* 9.10.8 = 22B67)

37. To God all things are beautiful and good and just, but humans have supposed some unjust and others just. (Porphyry, *Notes on Homer* [*Iliad* 4.4] = 22B102)

38. Immortal mortals, mortal immortals [or, immortals are mortal, mortals are immortal], living the death of the others and dying their life.

(Hippolytus, *Refutation* 9.10.6 = 22B62)

39. They vainly purify themselves with blood when defiled with it, as if a man who had stepped into mud were to wash if off with mud. He would be thought mad if anyone noticed him acting thus.

(Aristocritus, *Theosophia* 68; Origen, *Against Celsus* 7.62 = 22B5)

40. Corpses are more fit to be thrown out than dung.

(Plutarch, *Table Talk* 669a = 22B96)

41. You would not discover the limits of the soul although you travelled every road: it has so deep a *logos*.

(Diogenes Laertius, *Lives of the Philosophers* 9.7 = 22B45)

42. A person's character is his fate.

(Stobaeus, *Selections* 4.40.23 = 22B119; modified by Reeve)

43. It is difficult to fight against anger, for whatever it wants it buys at the price of soul.

(Plutarch, *Coriolanus* 22.2 = 22B85)

1. The posset, or *kykeon*, was a mixed drink of wine, barley, and grated cheese.

3
Eleatic Monism

Elea was on the western coast of southern Italy, close to the Pythagorean colonies founded there in the late sixth century BCE. Not long afterward, Parmenides developed a breathtaking argument for monism—not a monism of the Milesian variety, which drew its justification from empirical observations, but a severe monism of an entirely new sort. Apparently rejecting the evidence of the senses altogether, Parmenides deduced the unity of all that is, using thought alone. Also from Elea, Zeno studied under him and developed ingenious arguments to refute the growing opposition to his teacher's extreme view. From faraway Samos, Melissus may have traveled to Elea to join the others. Whether or not he did, he earned the title "Eleatic" for his own lucid arguments that all things are one.

3a
Parmenides

Parmenides was born c. 515 BCE. His fellow citizens eventually regarded him so highly that they adopted a legal code he wrote and followed it for 500 years. Such genius for practical affairs is nowhere evident in his poem, which ranks among the most abstract texts in all Greek philosophy. Though Parmenides wrote in the epic meter of Homer and Hesiod and, like them, invokes a goddess, he did not resort to mythological explanations. If anything, his goddess seems to symbolize the divinity of pure thought. For Parmenides expressed philosophical ideas of such power and novelty that they set the agenda for many of his successors.

His argument begins with the premise "that it is, and that it is not possible for it not to be." Thus forbidding the existence of what-is-not as contradictory, and then as unthinkable and unspeakable, he proceeds to criticize everything contaminated with nonbeing, including change, motion, division, difference, and time. Change, for example, involves either something coming into being from not being, or going out of being into not being. Similarly, time presupposes the past and the future, each of which is included in what-is-not (now). Hence what-is must be unchangeable, immovable, indivisible, homogeneous, and eternally present. Once he has deduced this extreme monism, his goddess warns him against the deceptive dualism of mortal opinions.

Ancient biographies report that Parmenides studied under Xenophanes, so that his monism may have been influenced by his teacher's account of the one supreme god. Another possible source may have been his connections with the Pythagoreans, since they were nearby and likewise enjoined purification of thought. His Eleatic successors defended and elaborated his arguments, while the so-called Pluralists—Anaxagoras, Empedocles, and the Atomists—tried to rehabilitate motion and change in the face of his criticisms.

1. The mares which carry me as far as my spirit ever aspired
were escorting me, when they brought me and proceeded along the renowned road
of the goddess, which brings a knowing mortal to all cities one by one.
On this path I was being brought, on it wise mares were bringing me,
straining the chariot, and maidens were guiding the way.
The axle in the center of the wheel was shrilling forth the bright sound of a musical pipe,

ablaze, for it was being driven forward by two rounded
wheels at either end, as the daughters of the Sun
were hastening to escort [me] after leaving the house of Night
for the light, having pushed back the veils from their heads with their hands.
There are the gates of the roads of Night and Day,
and a lintel and a stone threshold contain them.
High in the sky they are filled by huge doors
of which avenging Justice holds the keys that fit them.
The maidens beguiled her with soft words
and skillfully persuaded her to push back the bar for them
quickly from the gates. They made
a gaping gap of the doors when they opened them,
swinging in turn in their sockets the bronze posts
fastened with bolts and rivets. There, straight through them then,
the maidens held the chariot and horses on the broad road.
And the goddess received me kindly, took my
right hand in hers, and addressed me with these words:

Young man, accompanied by immortal charioteers,
who reach my house by the horses which bring you,
welcome—since it was not an evil destiny that sent you forth to travel
this road (for indeed it is far from the beaten path of humans),
but Right and Justice. There is need for you to learn all things—
both the unshaken heart of well-persuasive Truth
and the opinions of mortals, in which there is no true reliance.
But nevertheless you will learn these too—that the things that appear
must genuinely be, being always, indeed, all things.

(lines 1–30: Sextus Empiricus, *Against the Professors* 7.111–4; lines 28–32; Simplicius, *Commentary on Aristotle's On the Heavens*, 557.25–558.2 = 28B1; modified by Curd)

2. Come now, I will tell you—and bring away my story safely
when you have heard it—
the only ways of inquiry there are for thinking:
the one, that it is and that it is not possible for it not to be,
is the path of Persuasion (for it attends upon Truth),
the other, that it is not and that it is necessary for it not to be,
this I point out to you to be a path completely unlearnable,
for neither may you know that which is not (for it is not to be accomplished)
nor may you declare it.

(Proclus, *Commentary on Plato's Timaeus* 1.345.18; lines 3–8. Simplicius, *Commentary on Aristotle's Physics* 116.28 = 28B.2; modified by Curd)

3. Thinking and being are the same.

(Clement, *Miscellanies* 6.23; Plotinus 5.1.8 = 28B.2; modified by Miller)

4. And it is all common to me
From where I am to begin; for to there shall I come back again.

(Proclus, *Commentary on Plato's Parmenides* 1.708 = 28B5; tr. Curd)

5. That which is there to be spoken and thought of must be.
For it is possible for it to be,
but not possible for nothing to be. I bid you consider this.
For [I bar] you from this first way of inquiry,
but next from the way on which mortals, knowing nothing,
two-headed, wander. For helplessness
in their breasts guides their wandering mind. But they are carried on
equally deaf and blind, amazed, hordes without judgement,
for whom both to be and not be are judged the same and
not the same, and the path of all is backward-turning.

(Simplicius, *Commentary on Aristotle's Physics* 86.27–8; 117.4–13 = 28B6; modified by Curd)

6. For in no way may this prevail, that things that are not, are.
But you, bar your thought from this way of inquiry,
and do not let habit born from much experience compel you along this way
to direct your sightless eye and sounding ear and tongue,
but judge by reason the heavily contested testing spoken by me.

(lines 1–2: Plato, *Sophist* 242a; lines 2–6, Sextus Empiricus, *Against the Professors* 7.114 = 28B7)

7. There is still left a single story
of a way, that it is. On this way there are signs
exceedingly many—that being ungenerated it is also imperishable,
whole and of a single kind and unshaken and complete.
Nor was it ever nor will it be, since it is now, all together
one, continuous. For what birth will you seek it?
How and from where did it grow? I will not permit you to say
or to think [that it grew] from what-is-not; for it is not to be said or thought
that it is not. What necessity would have stirred it up
to grow later rather than earlier, beginning from nothing?
Thus it must either fully be or not.
Nor will the force of conviction ever permit anything to come to be
from what is not beside it. For this reason, Justice has permitted it
neither to come to be nor to perish, relaxing her shackles,
but holds fast. But the decision about these matters lies in this:
it is or it is not. But it has been decided, as is necessary,
to let go the one way as unthinkable, and nameless (for it is not a true way) and that the other is and is real.
How could what-is be in the future? How could it come to be?
For if it came into being, it is not, nor if it is ever going to be.
In this way, coming to be has been extinguished and destruction is unheard of.
Nor is it divided, since it all is alike;
nor is it any more in any way, which would keep it from holding together,
or any less, but it is all full of what-is.
Therefore, it is all continuous, for what-is draws near to what-is.
But unchanging in the limits of great bonds,
it is without start or finish, since coming to be and destruction
were banished far away and true conviction drove them off.
Remaining the same in the same and by itself it lies
and so stays there fixed; for mighty Necessity
holds it in the bonds of a limit, which pens it in all round,
since it is right for what-is to be not incomplete;
for it is not lacking; if it were, it would lack everything.
Thinking and the thought that it is are the same.
For not without what-is, in which it is expressed,
will you find thinking; for nothing else either is or will be
except that which is, since Fate shackled it
to be whole and unchanging; wherefore it has been named all things
mortals have established, persuaded that they are true—
to come to be and to perish, to be and not [to be],
and to change place and alter bright color.
But since there is a furthest limit, it is complete,
on all sides like the bulk of a well-rounded ball,
evenly balanced in every way from the middle; for it must be not at all greater
or smaller here than there.
For neither is there what-is-not—which would stop it from reaching
its like—nor is what-is in such a way that there could be more of what-is
here and less there, since it is all inviolate;
for equal to itself on all sides, it meets with its limits uniformly.

At this point I stop for you my reliable account and thought

concerning Truth; from here on, learn mortal opinions,
listening to the deceitful ordering of my words.
For they made up their minds to name two forms,
of which it is not right to name one—in this they have gone astray—
and they distinguished things opposite in body, and established signs
apart from one another—for one, the aetherial fire of flame,
mild, very light, the same as itself in every direction,
but not same as the other; but that other one, in itself
is opposite—dark night, a dense and heavy body.
I declare to you all the ordering as it appears,
so that no mortal opinion may ever overtake you.

(Simplicius, *Commentary on Aristotle's Physics* 145.1–146.25 [lines 1–52]; 39.1–9 [lines 50–61] = 28B8; modified by Curd)

3b
Melissus

Melissus was from the island of Samos. As leader of its navy in 441 BCE, he twice defeated an Athenian fleet under the command of no less a general than Pericles. As a philosopher, however, he was more of a follower—not of Pythagoras, who had long ago abandoned Samos, but of Parmenides, with whom he may have studied. Writing in prose rather than poetry, Melissus produced a remarkably lucid explanation of his teacher's monism. There is only one real thing, he argued, and it is ungenerated, indestructible, indivisible, unchangeable, motionless, and homogeneous. Beyond mere explanation of Eleatic philosophy, the writings of Melissus also offer some innovations. By arguing that the one real thing cannot be rearranged, for example, he may have been criticizing his Pluralist contemporaries. Most importantly, however, Melissus contradicts Parmenides in two ways. Parmenides' One was a spatially limited sphere existing in an eternal present; Melissus makes his One both spatially and temporally infinite.

1. Whatever was, always was and always will be. For if it came to be, it is necessary that before it came to be it was nothing. Now if it was nothing, in no way could anything come to be out of nothing.

(Simplicius, *Commentary on Aristotle's Physics* 162.23–6 = 30B1)

2. Now since it did not come to be, it is and always was and always will be, and does not have a beginning or an end, but is unlimited. For if it had come to be it would have a beginning (for having come to be it would have begun at some time) and an end (for having come to be it would have ended at some time). But since it neither began nor ended, it always was and always will be and does not have a beginning or end. For whatever is not entire cannot always be.

(Simplicius, *Commentary on Aristotle's Physics* 29.22–6, 109.20–5 = 30B2)

3. [Just as he says that what came to be some time is limited in its being, he also wrote clearly that what always is is unlimited in being, saying:] But just as it always is, so also it must always be unlimited in magnitude. [But by "magnitude" he does not mean what is extended in space.]

(Simplicius, *Commentary on Aristotle's Physics* 109.29–32 = 30B3)

4. Nothing that has both a beginning and an end is either eternal or unlimited. And so whatever does not have them is unlimited.

(Simplicius, *Commentary on Aristotle's Physics* 110.2–4 = 30B4)

5. If it is not one, it will come to a limit against something else.

(Simplicius, *Commentary on Aristotle's Physics* 110.5–6 = 30B5)

6. For if it is [unlimited], it will be one. For if there were two, they could not be unlimited, but would have limits against each other.

(Simplicius, *Commentary on Aristotle's On the Heavens* 557.14–7 = 30B6)

7. Thus it is eternal and unlimited and one and all alike.

And it cannot perish, or become greater, or be rearranged, or feel pain or distress. For if it experienced any of these, it would no longer be one. For if it became different, it is necessary that what-is is not alike, but what previously was perishes, and what-is-not comes to be. Now if it should become different by one hair in ten thousand years, it will all perish in all of time.

But it is not possible for it to be rearranged, either. For the arrangement that previously was is not destroyed and an arrangement that is not does not come to be. But when nothing either comes to be in addition or is destroyed or becomes different, how could anything that is be rearranged? For if it became at all different, it would indeed already have been rearranged.

Nor does it feel pain. For it could not be all if it were feeling pain. For a thing feeling pain could not always be. Nor does it have equal power to what is healthy. Nor would it be alike if it were feeling pain. For it would feel pain either because something is being taken away or added, and it would no longer be alike.

Nor would what is healthy be able to feel pain. For what is healthy and what-is would perish, and what-is-not would come to be.

And the same argument applies to feeling distress as to feeling pain.

Nor is any of it empty. For what is empty is nothing, and of course what is nothing would not be. Nor does it move. For it is not able to give way anywhere, but is full. For if it were empty it would give way into the empty. But since it is not empty, it does not have anywhere to give way.

It cannot be dense and rare. For it is impossible for the rare to be equally full as the dense, but the rare immediately proves to be emptier than the dense.

And it is necessary to make this the grounds for deciding whether something is full or not full: if something moves or can move, it is not full. But if it neither moves nor can move, it is full.

Now it is necessary that it is full if it is not empty. Now if it is full, it does not move.

(Simplicius, *Commentary on Aristotle's Physics* 111.18–112.15 = 30B7)

8. Now this argument is the strongest indication that it is only one. But also the following are indications.

For if there were many, they would have to be such as I say the one is.

For if there is earth and water and air and fire and iron and gold, and one thing is alive and another is dead, and black and white, and all the other things that people say are true, if indeed these are, and we see and hear correctly, each must be such as we decided at first, and must not change or come to be different, but each thing must always be just as it is. But as the case stands, we say we see and hear and understand correctly.

We think that what is hot becomes cold and what is cold, hot, and what is hard becomes soft, and what is soft, hard, and what is alive dies and comes to be from what is not alive, and all these things become different, and anything that was and what is now are not at all alike, but iron, which is hard, is worn away by contact with the finger, and also gold and stone and anything else that seems to be strong, and earth and stone come to be from water.

Now these things do not agree with one another. For we say that there are many things that are eternal and have forms and strength, but all of them seem to us to become different and change from what we see at each moment.

Now it is clear that we were not seeing correctly and that that plurality does not correctly seem to be. For they would not change if they were real, but would be as each of them seemed. For nothing is stronger than what is real.

But if it changes, what-is is destroyed, and what-is-not has come to be.

Thus, if there are many, they must be like the one.

(Simplicius, *Commentary on Aristotle's On the Heavens* 558.19–559.12 = 30B8)

9. [That he intends what-is to be bodiless he indicated, saying:] Now if it is, it must be one. But being one, it must not have body. But if it had thickness, it would have parts and no longer would be one.

(Simplicius, *Commentary on Aristotle's Physics* 109.34–110.2 = 30B9)

10. For he himself proves that what-is is indivisible. For if what-is is divided, it moves. But if it moved, it would not be. [But by "magnitude" he means the greatness of its being.]

(Simplicius, *Commentary on Aristotle's Physics* 109.32–4 = 30B10; modified by Curd)

11. Being one it is all alike. For if it were unlike, being plural, it would no longer be one, but many.

(pseudo-Aristotle, *On Melissus, Xenophanes and Gorgias* 1.974a12–4 = 30A5)

3c
Zeno

Zeno was born c. 490 BCE in Elea, where he became Parmenides' student. Rather than defending his teacher's views directly, Zeno attacked instead the assumptions of his opponents, aiming to expose the paradoxes inherent in them. This strategy was later called "dialectic." It is most evident in the techniques of the Sophists and Socrates, but Aristotle acknowledged Zeno as its inventor. Of the forty arguments Zeno developed in his book, fewer than a quarter have survived. Two of them seek to undermine the notion of place and the reliability of the senses (particularly hearing). All the others attack the notions of plurality and motion by exploiting the tricky notion of infinity. The Pluralists naturally strove to address these arguments. Aristotle later developed responses that were long considered decisive. When the early modern philosophers rejected Aristotle's basic metaphysical assumptions, however, Zeno once again became a focus of both philosophical and mathematical attention.

1. [See Plato, *Parmenides* 127b–128d, pages 233–4 of this volume.]

2. For if it should be added to something else that exists, it would not make it any bigger. For if it were of no size and was added, it [the thing it is added to] cannot increase in size. And so it follows immediately that what is added is nothing. But if when it is subtracted, the other thing is no smaller, nor is it increased when it is added, clearly the thing being added or subtracted is nothing.

(Simplicius, *Commentary on Aristotle's Physics* 139.11–5 = 29B2)

3. But if it exists, each thing must have some size and thickness, and part of it must be apart from the rest. And the same reasoning holds concerning the part that is in front. For that too will have size and part of it will be in front. Now it is the same thing to say this once and to keep saying it forever. For no such part of it will be last, nor will there be one part [of any such part] not related to another. Therefore, if there are many things, they must be both small and large; so small as not to have size, but so large as to be unlimited.

(Simplicius, *Commentary on Aristotle's Physics* 141.2–8 = 29B1)

4. If there are many, they must be just as many as they are and neither more nor less than that. But if they are as many as they are, they would be limited. If there are many, things that are are unlimited. For there are always others between the things that are, and again others between those, and so the things that are are unlimited.

(Simplicius, *Commentary on Aristotle's Physics* 140.29–33 = 29B3)

5. Zeno's arguments about motion which present difficulties for those who try to solve them are four. First is the argument which says that there is no motion because that which is moving must reach the midpoint before the end.

(Aristotle, *Physics* 6.9.239b9–13 = 29A25)

6. The second is the one called "Achilles." This is to the effect that the slowest as it runs will never be caught by the quickest. For the pursuer must first reach the point from which the pursued departed, so that the slower must always be some distance in front. This is the same argument as The Dichotomy, but it differs in not dividing the given magnitude in half.

(Aristotle, *Physics* 6.9.239b14–20 = 29A26)

7. The third argument is the one just stated, that the arrow is stopped while it is moving. This follows from assuming that time is composed of "nows."

(Aristotle, *Physics* 6.9.239b30–3 = 29A27)

8. For if, he says, everything is always at rest when it occupies a space equal to itself, and what is moving is always "in the now," the moving arrow is motionless.

(Aristotle, *Physics* 6.9.239b5–7 = 29A27)

9. The fourth argument is about the equal bodies moving in a stadium past equal bodies in the opposite direction, the one group moving from the end of the stadium, the other from the middle, at equal speed. He claims in this argument that it follows that half the time is equal to the double. The mistake is in thinking that an equal magnitude moving with equal speed takes an equal time in passing something moving as it does in passing something at rest. But this is false. Let A's represent the equal stationary bodies, *B*'s represent the bodies beginning from the middle of the A's, equal in number and size to the A's, and C's represent the bodies beginning from the end, equal in number and size to these and having the same speed as the *B*'s. It follows that the first *B* is at the end at the same time as the first C, as they [the *B*'s and C's] move past each other, and the [first] C has passed by all the *B*'s but the *B*'s have passed half the A's. And so the time is half. For each of them is next to each thing for an equal time. It follows simultaneously that the *B*'s have passed by all the C's, for the first C and the first *B* will be at the ends at the same time, because both have been next to the A's for an equal time.

(Aristotle, *Physics* 6.9.239b33–240a17 = 29A28)

10. If place exists, where is it? For everything that exists is in a place. Therefore, place is in a place. This goes on to infinity. Therefore, place does not exist.

(Simplicius, *Commentary on Aristotle's Physics* 562.3–6 = 29B5)

11. ZENO: "Tell me, Protagoras, does a single millet seed make a noise when it falls, or one ten-thousandth of a millet seed?"

PROTAGORAS: "No."

ZENO: "Does a bushel of millet seeds make a noise when it falls, or doesn't it?"

PROTAGORAS: "It does."

ZENO: "But isn't there a ratio between the bushel of millet seeds and one millet seed, or one ten-thousandth of a millet seed?"

PROTAGORAS: "Yes there is."

ZENO: "So won't there be the same ratios of their sounds to one another? For as the things that make the noise [are to one another], so are the noises [to one another]. But since this is so, if the bushel of millet seeds makes a noise, so will a single millet seed and one ten-thousandth of a millet seed."

(Simplicius, *Commentary on Aristotle's Physics* 1108.18–25 = 29A29)

12. For if, he says, it is divisible, let it have been cut in two, and then each of the parts in two, and as this goes on forever, it is clear, he says, that either some last least and uncuttable magnitudes will remain, unlimited in number, and the whole will be made up of an infinite number of these least things; or it will vanish and it will indeed have dissolved into nothing, and it will be made up of nothing; but these [consequences] are absurd. Therefore it will not be divided but it will remain one. Moreover, as it is everywhere alike, if it is indeed divisible, it will be everywhere alike divisible, and not on the one hand here but not there. Let it now have been divided everywhere; it is then clear that again nothing will remain, but it will have vanished, and if indeed it is made up [of parts], it will again be made up of nothing. For if something remains, it will not yet have come to be divided everywhere. So that, he says, it is clear from these considerations that what-is will be undivided and partless and one.

(Simplicius, *Commentary on Aristotle's Physics* 139.27–140.6 = "The Porphyry Argument"; tr. Curd)

4

PLURALISTS

IN RESPONSE TO PARMENIDES, a disparate group of philosophers—Empedocles, Anaxagoras, and the Atomists Leucippus and Democritus—developed three very different views of the cosmos, each attempting to accommodate change while acknowledging the Eleatic argument against generation and destruction. Roughly speaking, they did so by interpreting change as some kind of rearrangement, mixing, or separating of stuff that has always existed. Sharing this project, though little else, they are often categorized together as Pluralists—a fact that testifies to the enormous influence of Parmenides' thought.

4a

EMPEDOCLES

EMPEDOCLES WAS BORN c. 492 BCE in Acragas, a thriving city in Sicily, close to both Elea and the Pythagoreans of southern Italy. Also nearby was Thurii, founded in 444, which counted among its settlers such distinguished intellectuals as Protagoras the Sophist and Herodotus the historian. Himself a physician, poet, prophet, and political leader as well as a philosopher, Empedocles was the first great synthesizer of Greek philosophy.

Rather than explaining the cosmos by one thing, he began with the four offered by his eastern predecessors: water, air, earth, and fire. Aristotle later called these the four "elements," but Empedocles called them "roots," suggesting their inherent power of growth. Each of these roots persisted, undergoing neither generation nor destruction, and thus heeding at least some of the Eleatic prohibitions. Ignoring others, Empedocles credited the senses' reports about the world, and he allowed change to occur within it by a mixture and separation of roots. Two forces, Love and Strife, effected this change, giving rise to a cosmic cycle in which one or the other dominated. With Love supreme, all was mixed together in a cosmic sphere that resembled the Eleatic One. When Strife gained control, however, the roots separated out, as did individual souls.

These souls (*daimones*) were doomed for a certain time to inhabit the bodies of living creatures, higher or lower according to their merits or demerits. Empedocles claimed that he himself had been "a boy and a girl and a bush and a bird." A portion of his poetry called *Katharmoi*, or *Purifications*, taught the practices that would help souls return to their original unity in Love. This required abstinence from meat, since animals were souls that were undergoing punishment. But it also precluded eating any living thing, including plants. Empedocles even enjoined celibacy, since sex helped create another bodily prison for a soul.

By heeding these warnings, souls could secure higher incarnations with each successive life, eventually becoming a physician, poet, prophet, or political leader. From this penultimate stage, all that remained was to achieve the wealth of divine intelligence and become, as Empedocles himself claimed to be, "an immortal god." Consummating his own purification and ascension to the divine, Empedocles was said to have ended his final embodiment (c. 432) by leaping into the volcano of Mount Etna.

1. Friends who dwell in the great city on the yellow Acragas
on the heights of the citadel, you whose care is good deeds,
respectful havens for strangers, untouched by evil,
hail! I go about among you, an immortal god, no longer mortal,
honored among all, as it seems,
wreathed with headbands and blooming garlands.
Wherever I go to their flourishing cities,
I am revered by the men and women. And they follow together
in tens of thousands, inquiring where lies the path to profit,
some in need of prophecy, while others,
pierced for a long time with harsh pains,
asked to hear the voice of healing for all diseases.
(Diogenes Laertius, *Lives of the Philosophers* 8.62 [lines 1–10]; Clement, *Miscellanies* 6.30 [lines 9–11] = 31B112)

2. If you fix them in your strong intelligence
and gaze upon them propitiously with pure attention,
these things will all be very much present to you all your life long
and from them you will obtain many others. For these very things
grow into each kind of character, depending on each person's nature.
But if you reach out for other kinds of things, the millions
of evils that are found among men which blunt their thoughts,
indeed they will leave you immediately as time revolves,
longing to come to their own dear kind.
For know that all things possess thought and a portion of intelligence.
(Hippolytus, *Refutation* 7.29.25 = 31B110)

3. You will learn all the drugs there are for evils and a safeguard against old age,
since for you alone I am bringing all these things to pass.
You will stop the force of tireless winds which rush
over the earth and devastate the plowed fields with their blasts.
And, if you wish, you will arouse their breath again.
You will change black rain to seasonable dryness
for people, and summer drought you will change
into tree-nourishing waters which pour from the sky.
And you will bring the strength of a dead man back from Hades.
(Diogenes Laertius, *Lives of the Philosophers* 8.59 = 31B111)

4. But come, I shall first tell you the beginning . . .
from which all that we now look upon came to be clear,
earth and the sea with many waves and moist air
and the Titan *aither*,[1] squeezing all things round about in a circle.
(Clement, *Miscellanies* 5.48.3 = 31B38)

5. It is not possible to reach and approach [the divine] with the eyes
or grasp [it] with our hands, by which the most powerful
highway of persuasion strikes the minds of men.
(Clement, *Miscellanies* 5.81.2 = 31B133)

6. I will tell a double story. For at one time they grow to be only one
out of many, but at another they grow apart to be many out of one.
Double is the coming to be of mortal things, and double is their failing.
For the coming together of all things produces one birth and destruction,
and the other is nurtured and flies apart when they grow apart again.
And these never cease continually interchanging,
at one time all coming together into one by Love
and at another each being borne apart by the hatred of Strife.
Thus in that they have learned to grow to be one out of many
and in that they again spring apart as many when the one grows apart,
in that way they come to be and their life is not lasting,
but in that they never cease interchanging continually,
in this way they are always unchanging in a cycle.

1. *Aither* was thought to be fiery upper air.

But come, listen to my words, for learning increases wisdom.
For as I previously said, while declaring the bounds of my words,
I will tell a double story. For at one time they grew to be only one
Out of many, but at another they grew apart to be many out of one:
fire and water and earth and the immense height of air,
and deadly Strife apart from them, equal in all directions
and Love among them, equal in length and breadth.
Behold her with your mind, and do not sit with your eyes starting in amazement.
She is also recognized as innate in mortal limbs.
Through her they have kindly thoughts and do peaceful deeds,
Calling her by the appellation Joy and also Aphrodite.
No mortal man has seen her spinning
among them. But listen to the undeceitful course of my account.
For these [the four elements] are all equal and of the same age,
but each rules in its own province and possesses its own individual character,
but they dominate in turn as time revolves.
And nothing is added to them, nor do they leave off,
for if they were perishing continuously, they would no longer be.
But what could increase this totality? And where would it come from?
And how [or, where] could it perish, since nothing is empty of these?
But there are just these very things, and running through one another
at different times they come to be different things and yet are always and continuously the same.
(Simplicius, *Commentary on Aristotle's Physics* 158.1–159.4 = 31B17)

7. Hear first the four roots of all things:
Shining Zeus and life-bringing Hera and Aidoneus
and Nestis who with her tears moistens mortal Springs. (Aetius 1.3.20 = 31B6)

8. But come, behold this witness of my previous discourse,
if anything in the foregoing was feeble in form:
the sun, brilliant to see and hot everywhere,
all the immortal things that are drenched in the heat and shining light,
and rain in all things, dark and cold,
and from earth stream forth things rooted and solid.
In Anger they are all separate and have their own forms,
but they come together in Love and yearn for one another.
For from these come all things that were and are and will be in the future.
Trees have sprouted and men and women,
and beasts and birds and fishes nurtured in water,
and long-lived gods highest in honors.
For there are just these things, and running through one another
they come to have different appearances, for mixture changes them.
(Simplicius, *Commentary on Aristotle's Physics* 159.13–26 = 31B21)

9. Pleasant earth in her well-made crucibles obtained
two parts of bright Nestis out of the eight,
and four of Hephaestus, and white bones came into being,
fitted together divinely by the glues of Harmonia.
(Simplicius, *Commentary on Aristotle's Physics* 300.21–4 = 31B96)

10. Earth came together by chance in about equal quantity to these,
Hephaestus and rain and all-shining *aither*,
anchored in the perfect harbors of Cypris,
either a bit more or a bit less of it among more of them.
From them blood came into being and other forms of flesh.
(Simplicius, *Commentary on Aristotle's Physics* 32.6–10 = 31B98)

11. Fools. For their thoughts are not far-reaching,
who expect that there comes to be what previously was not,
or that anything perishes and is completely destroyed.
(Plutarch, *Against Colotes* 1113c = 31B11)

12. For it is impossible to come to be from what in no way is,
and it is not to be accomplished and is unheard of that what-is perishes absolutely.
For each time it will be where a person thrusts it each time.

([Aristotle] *On Melissus Xenophanes Gorgias* 975b1–4 = 31B12)

13. I will tell you another thing. There is coming to be of not a single one of all
mortal things, nor is there any end of deadly death,
but only mixture, and separation of what is mixed,
and nature is the name given to them by humans.

(Plutarch, *Against Colotes* 1111F = 31B8)

14. Whenever they arrive in the *aither* mixed so as to form a man
or one of the wild beasts or bushes
or birds, that is when [people] speak of coming into being;
and whenever they are separated, that [is what they call] the
ill-starred fate of death.
They do not call it as is right, but I myself too assent to their convention.

(Plutarch, *Against Colotes* 1113D = 31B9)

15. None of the whole is either empty or over-full.

(Aetius 1.18.2 = 31B13)

16. But I shall return to that path of songs
which I recounted before, drawing off from one account this account.
When Strife had reached the lowest depth
of the vortex, and Love comes to be in the middle of the whirl,
at this point all these things come together to be one single thing,
not at once, but willingly banding together, different ones from different places.
As they were mixed, myriads of tribes of mortal things poured forth,
but many contrariwise remained unmixed while they were mingling—
all that strife still held back aloft. For it had not
entirely completed its blameless retreat from them to the furthest limits of the circle,
but it remained in some of the limbs, while from others it had withdrawn.
But as far as it would continually run out ahead,
so far continually would follow in pursuit
the gentle immortal onset of blameless Love.
Immediately things became mortal which formerly had learned to be immortal,
and things previously unmixed became mixed, interchanging their paths.
As they were mixed, myriads of tribes of mortal things poured forth,
fitted with all kinds of forms, a wonder to behold.

(Simplicius, *Commentary on Aristotle's On the Heavens* 529.1–15 [lines 1–15]; *Commentary on Aristotle's Physics* 32.13–33.2 [lines 3–17] = 31B35)

17. When they were coming together, Strife was being displaced to the extremity.

(Stobaeus, *Selections* 1.10.11 = 31B36)

18. They [i.e., the four elements] dominate in turn as the cycle revolves,
and they decrease into one another and grow in their turn, as destined.
For there are just these things, and running through one another
they come to be both humans and the tribes of other beasts
at one time coming together into a single cosmos by Love
and at another each being borne apart by the hatred of Strife,
until they grow together into one, the whole, and become subordinate.

(Simplicius, *Commentary on Aristotle's Physics* 33.19–34.3 = 31B26)

19. But equal to itself on all sides, and wholly without limit,
a rounded sphere, exulting in its circular solitude.

(Stobaeus, *Selections* 1.15.2 = 31B28)

20. For I have already once become a boy and a girl
and a bush and a bird and a fish.

(Diogenes Laertius, *Lives of the Philosophers* 8.7 = 31B117)

21. In the end they are prophets and poets and physicians and political leaders among men on earth, and from there they arise as gods mightiest in honors.

(Aelian, *Nature of Animals* = 31B127; modified by Miller)

22. Sharing the same hearth and table with other immortals relieved of human distress, unwearied.
(Clement, *Stomateis* 5.122.3 = 31B147)

23. For he [Apollo, or god in general] is not furnished in his limbs with a human head.
Two branches do not spring from his back.
He has no feet, no swift limbs, no hairy genitals,
but is only mind, holy and indescribable,
darting through the entire *kosmos* with his swift thoughts.
(Ammonius, *Commentary on Aristotle's On Interpretation* 249.1–5 = 31B134)

24. Blessed is he who possesses wealth of divine intelligence
but wretched whose concern is a dim opinion about the gods.
(Clement, *Miscellanies* 5.140 = 31B132)

25. There is an oracle of Necessity, an ancient decree of the gods,
eternal and sealed with broad oaths,
that whenever anyone pollutes his own dear limbs with the sin of murder,
. . . commits offense and swears a false oath—
divinities [*daimones*] who possess immensely long life—
he wanders away from the blessed ones for thrice ten thousand seasons,
growing to be through time all different kinds of mortals
taking the difficult paths of life one after another.
For the force of *aither* pursues them to the sea
and the sea spits them out onto the surface of the earth, and the earth into the rays
of the shining sun, and he [the sun] casts them into the vortices of *aither.*
One receives them after another, but all hate them.
Of them I am now one, a fugitive from the gods and a wanderer,
putting my reliance on raving Strife.
(Hippolytus, *Refutation of All Heresies* 7.29.14–23 [lines 1–2, 4–14]; Plutarch, *On Exile* 607C [lines 1, 3, 5–16] = 31B115)

26. Will you not cease from harsh-sounding murder? Do you not see
that you are devouring each other in the carelessness of your thought?
(Sextus Empiricus, *Against the Professors* 9.129 = 31B136)

27. A father lifts up his own dear son who has changed form,
and, praying, slaughters him, committing a great folly. And they are at a loss,
sacrificing him as he entreats them. But he, refusing to hear the cries,
slaughters him and attends an evil feast in his halls.
Likewise a son seizes his father and children their mother
and tearing out their life devour the dear flesh.
(Sextus Empiricus, *Against the Professors* 9.129 = 31B137)

4b
Anaxagoras

Anaxagoras was born c. 500 BCE in Clazomenae, on the Ionian coast. Like most of the other philosophers from this region, he investigated natural phenomena. Ancient biographers report that he was conscripted by the Persian army that Xerxes sent to attack Athens. Perhaps for that reason, he became the first philosopher to inhabit the city that was soon to become the capital of Greek philosophy. One of his teachings was that the sun was not a god but a hot stone—like the meteorite that fell on Aegospotami in 467. Because of this belief and also because of his association with the great Athenian statesman Pericles, he was allegedly tried and convicted for impiety c. 450. In any case, he left Athens for Lampsacus in Asia Minor, where he died c. 428.

While accepting Parmenides' arguments against generation and destruction, Anaxagoras proposed to explain change by appeal to one bold idea: "In everything there is a portion of everything."

In a loaf of bread, for example, is mixed a portion of hair. Thus, when we eat this loaf, we extract some of the hair it contains to add to the growth of our own. We are changed, as is the bread, and yet nothing new is generated, nor is anything old destroyed. Portions are merely redistributed. But there is no smallest portion, Anaxagoras insists, and so within the portion of hair is another of bread, and within this portion of bread another of hair, ad infinitum. Indeed, within the loaf are portions of bone and flesh, hot and cold, and many other things. It is a loaf of bread, nonetheless, because of the preponderance of bread portions.

In the beginning, Anaxagoras claims, the cosmos was completely mixed: "All things were together." All things, that is, except Mind (*nous*). Since in everything there is a portion of everything, were Mind mixed with anything, it would also have to be mixed with everything, compromising its power. Instead, it remains pure, even as it causes the cosmos to rotate and the various portions it contains to separate from one another. Knowing all, it orders all. In the *Phaedo*, Socrates says that he was pleased when he heard of the supreme role Anaxagoras assigned to Mind but was later disappointed to find that it did not aim at what was best. Aristotle considered Anaxagoras to be "like a sober man in contrast with the babble of his predecessors."

1. All things were together, unlimited in both amount and smallness. For the small too was unlimited. And when [or, since] all things were together, nothing was manifest on account of smallness. For air and *aither* dominated all things, both being unlimited. For these are the largest ingredients in the totality, both in amount and in size.

   (Simplicius, *Commentary on Aristotle's Physics* 155.26–30 = 59B1)

2. For both air and *aither* are being separated off from the surrounding multitude and what surrounds is unlimited in amount.

   (Simplicius, *Commentary on Aristotle's Physics* 155.31–156.1 = 59B2)

3. For of the small there is no smallest, but always a smaller (for what is cannot not be). But also of the large there is always a larger, and it is equal in amount to the small. But in relation to itself, each is both large and small.

   (Simplicius, *Commentary on Aristotle's Physics* 164.17–20 = 59B3)

4. These things being so, it is necessary to suppose that in all things that are being mixed together there are many things of all kinds, and seeds of all things, having all kinds of shapes and colors and flavors; and that humans too were compounded and all the other animals that possess life; and that there are inhabited cities and cultivated fields for the humans just as with us, and that there are for them a sun and a moon and the rest just as with us, and that the earth grows many things of all kinds for them, of which they gather the most useful into their dwelling and use it. I have said these things about the separating off, because [or, that] it would have occurred not only with us, but elsewhere too.

   (Simplicius, *Commentary on Aristotle's Physics* 34.29–35.9 = 59B4a)

5. But before these things separated off, when [or, since] all things were together, not even any color was manifest, for the mixture of all things prevented it—the wet and the dry, the hot and the cold, the bright and the dark, there being also much earth in the mixture and seeds unlimited in amount, in no way like one another. For none of the other things are alike either, the one to the other. Since this is so, it is necessary to suppose that all things were in the whole.

   (Simplicius, *Commentary on Aristotle's Physics* 34.21–6 = 59B4b)

6. It is necessary to know that although [or, since] these things have been separated apart in this way, all things are not at all less or more (for it is not to be accomplished that they are more than all), but all things are always equal.

   (Simplicius, *Commentary on Aristotle's Physics* 156.10–2 = 59B5)

7. And since the portions of both the large and the small are equal in amount, in this way too all

things would be in everything; nor can they be separate, but all things have a portion of everything. Since there cannot be a smallest, nothing can be separated or come to be by itself, but as in the beginning now too all things are together. But in all things there are many things, equal in amount, both in the larger and the smaller of the things being separated off.

(Simplicius, *Commentary on Aristotle's Physics* 164.26–165.1 = 59B6)

8. As these things are thus rotating and being separated off by both force and speed, the speed causes the force, and their speed is like the speed of nothing now found among humans, but altogether many times as fast.

(Simplicius, *Commentary on Aristotle's Physics* 35.14–8 = 59B9)

9. For how could hair come to be from not hair or flesh from not flesh?

(*Scholium on Gregory of Nazianzus* 36.911 Migne = 59B10)

10. In everything there is a portion of everything except Mind, but Mind is in some things too.

(Simplicius, *Commentary on Aristotle's Physics* 164.23–4 = 59B11)

11. The rest have a portion of everything, but Mind is unlimited and self-ruled and is mixed with no thing, but is alone and by itself. For if it were not by itself but were mixed with something else, it would have a share of all things, if it were mixed with anything. For in everything there is a portion of everything, as I have said before. And the things mixed together with it would hinder it so that it would rule no thing in the same way as it does being alone and by itself. For it is the finest of all things and the purest, and it has all judgement about everything and the greatest power. And Mind rules all things that possess life—both the larger and the smaller. And Mind ruled the entire rotation, so that it rotated in the beginning. And at first it began to rotate from a small area, but it [now] rotates over a greater range and it will rotate over a [still] greater one. And Mind knew all the things that are being mixed together and separated off and separated apart. And Mind set in order all things, whatever kinds of things were to be—whatever were and all that are now and whatever will be—and also this rotation in which are now rotating the stars and the sun and the moon, and the air and *aither* that are being separated off. This rotation caused the separating off. And the dense is being separated off from the rare and the hot from the cold and the bright from the dark and the dry from the wet. But there are many portions of many things. And nothing is being completely separated off or separated apart one from another except Mind. All Mind is alike, both the larger and the smaller. But nothing else is like anything else, but each single thing is and was most plainly those things of which it contains most.

(Simplicius, *Commentary on Aristotle's Physics* 164.24–5; 156.13–157.4 = 59B12)

12. And when Mind began to cause motion, separating off proceeded to occur from all that was moved, and all that Mind moved was separated apart, and as things were being moved and separated apart, the rotation caused much more separating apart to occur.

(Simplicius, *Commentary on Aristotle's Physics* 300.31–301.1 = 59B13)

13. Mind, which is always, is very much even now where all other things are too, in the surrounding multitude and in things that have come together in the process of separating and in things that have separated off.

(Simplicius, *Commentary on Aristotle's Physics* 157.7–9 = 59B14)

14. The Greeks are wrong to accept coming to be and perishing, for no thing comes to be, nor does it perish, but they are mixed together from things that are and they are separated apart. And so they would be correct to call coming to be being mixed together, and perishing being separated apart.

(Simplicius, *Commentary on Aristotle's Physics* 163.20–4 = 59B17)

15. On account of their [the senses'] feebleness we are unable to discern the truth.

(Sextus Empiricus, *Against the Professors* 7.90 = 59B21)

4c

The Atomists: Leucippus and Democritus

Leucippus was the first to propose Atomism, the theory that the cosmos is constituted of many "uncuttables" (*a-tomon* in Greek means "un-cuttable"). These atoms are neither generated nor destroyed, but change can occur when they are rearranged. Leucippus wrote two books—one entitled *The Great World System* and another *On Mind*—that likely appeared in the decade after 440 BCE. All that survives of his writing is one sentence (the first fragment that follows). Little else is known about him except that he taught Democritus.

Born c. 460 in Abdera, a town in Thrace that also produced Protagoras, Democritus refined his teacher's theory throughout a life so long that it made him a contemporary of Socrates, Plato, and even the young Aristotle. Democritus wrote more than sixty books on a range of subjects that included not only natural philosophy and ethics but also mathematics, literary criticism, medicine, military strategy, and painting. Only fragments of these books survive, but there is enough testimony about his atomistic theory to reconstruct its main features.

According to Democritus, there are an infinite number of atoms with different sizes and shapes, each located at a different place in the surrounding void. These strike each other and, either rebounding or becoming entangled, form infinitely many arrangements, thus accounting for the infinite variety of the sensible world. For different arrangements of atoms strike the atoms of our senses in different ways—some directly through touch, and others indirectly by emitting thin atomic films, or effluences. The repercussions of these blows eventually reach our soul, which is itself nothing but a collection of particularly fine atoms.

Democritus also recognized the skeptical problems raised by this picture. Since our contact with the world is always mediated, at the very least by our own idiosyncratic atomic arrangement, what guarantees the accuracy of our perceptions? "By convention [*nomos*] sweet, by convention bitter . . . but in reality [*physis*] atoms and void." The contrast thus introduced between *nomos* and *physis* preoccupied the Sophists and the generation of Athenians they influenced. Democritus himself was no Skeptic, however, since he thought that reason could not doubt perception without undermining its own source of knowledge.

He did not flinch from the paradoxical implications of his theory for human action. What we do in the present has long been determined by a causal chain of collisions stretching back to infinity. Marching according to these atomic orders, then, we must somehow try to be cheerful while alive: there is nothing after death but the dissipation of our soul atoms into the void. Completely ignored by Plato and constantly criticized by Aristotle, Atomism awaited Epicurus to make it one of the three main philosophical schools of the Hellenistic period. After another long hiatus through the Middle Ages, it was resurrected in the early modern period. Anticipating the discoveries of modern science as well as the naturalistic temperament of many modern philosophers, Democritus has since appeared as one of the prophetic thinkers of antiquity.

1. No thing happens at random but all things as a result of a reason and by necessity.
(Aetius 1.25.4 = 67B2)

2. Democritus leaves aside purpose, but refers all things which nature employs to necessity.
(Aristotle, *Generation of Animals* 5.8.789b2–4 = 68A66)

3. [Concerning necessity] Democritus [speaks of] knocking against [each other] and motion and "blow" of matter. (Aetius 1.26.2 = 68A66)

4. Leucippus and his associate Democritus declare the full and the empty [void] to be the elements, calling the former "what-is" and the other "what-is-not." Of these the one, "what-is," is full and

solid, the other, "what-is-not," is empty [void] and rare. (This is why they say that what-is is no more than what-is-not, because the void is no less than body is.) These are the material causes of existing things. . . . They declare that the differences [among these] are the causes of the rest. Moreover, they say that the differences are three: shape, arrangement, and position. For they say that what-is differs only in "rhythm," "touching," and "turning"—and of these "rhythm" is shape, "touching" is arrangement, and "turning" is position. For A differs from N in shape, AN from NA in arrangement, and Z from N in position. Concerning the origin and manner of motion in existing things, these men too, like the rest, lazily neglected to give an account.

(Aristotle, *Metaphysics* 1.4.985b4–20 = 67A6)

5. After making the shapes, Democritus and Leucippus make alteration and coming to be out of them: coming to be and destruction by means of separation and combination, alteration by means of arrangement and position. Since they held that the truth is in the appearance, and appearances are opposite and unlimited, they made the shapes unlimited, so that by reason of changes of the composite, the same thing seems opposite to different people, and it shifts position when a small amount is mixed in, and it appears completely different when one thing shifts position. For tragedy and comedy come to be out of the same letters.

(Aristotle, *On Generation and Corruption* 1.2.315b6–15 = 67A97)

6. Democritus believes that the nature of the eternal things is small beings unlimited in multitude. As a place for these he hypothesizes something else, unlimited in size, and he calls the place by the names "void," "nothing" and "unlimited" [or, "infinite"] and he calls each of the substances "hing"[1] and "compact" and "what-is." He holds that the substances are so small that they escape our senses. They have all kinds of forms and shapes and differences in size. Out of these as elements he generates and combines visible and perceptible bodies. [These substances] contend with one another and move in the void on account of their dissimilarity and the other differences I have mentioned, and as they move they strike against one another and become entangled in a way that makes them be in contact and close to one another, but does not make any thing out of them that is truly one, for it is quite foolish [to think] that two or more things could ever come to be one. The grounds he gives for why the substances stay together up to a point are that the bodies fit together and hold each other fast. For some of them are rough, some are hooked, others concave and others convex, while yet others have innumerable other differences. So he thinks that they cling to each other and stay together until some stronger necessity comes along from the environment and shakes them and scatters them apart. He describes the generation and its contrary, separation, not only for animals but also for plants, *kosmoi*, and altogether for all perceptible bodies.

(Aristotle, *On Democritus*, quoted by Simplicius, *Commentary on Aristotle's On the Heavens* 295.1–22 = 68A37)

7. Leucippus . . . did not follow the same path as Parmenides and Xenophanes concerning things that are, but seemingly the opposite one. For while they made the universe one, immovable, ungenerated, and limited, and did not even permit the investigation of what-is-not, he posited the atoms as unlimited and ever moving elements and an unlimited multitude of shapes among them on the grounds that they are no more like this than like that, since he observed that coming to be and change are unceasing in things that are. Further, he posited that what-is is no more than what-is-not, and both are equally causes of what comes to be. For supposing the substance of the atoms to be compact and full, he said it is "being" and that it moves in the void, which he called "not-being" and which he declares is no less than what-is. His associate, Democritus of Abdera, likewise posited the full and the void as principles, of which he calls the former "being" and the latter "not-being." For positing the atoms as matter for the things that are they generate the rest by means of their differences. These are three:

1. "Hing" is "nothing" without the "not." A similar trick works in Greek: *den* is *ouden* without the *ou*.

rhythm, turning, and touching, i.e., shape, position, and arrangement. For like is by nature moved by like, and things of the same kind move towards one another, and each of the shapes produces a different composition when arranged in a different compound. Thus, since the principles are unlimited, they reasonably promised to account for all attributes and substances—how and through what cause anything comes to be. This is why they say that only those who make the elements unlimited account for everything reasonably. They say that the multitude of the shapes among the atoms is unlimited on the grounds that they are no more like this than like that. For they themselves assign this as a cause of the unlimitedness.

(Simplicius, *Commentary on Aristotle's Physics* 28.4–26 = 67A8 = 68A38)

8. These men [Leucippus, Democritus, and Epicurus] said that the principles are unlimited in multitude, and they believed them to be atoms and indivisible and incapable of being acted upon because they are compact and have no share of void. (For they claimed that division occurs where there is void in bodies.) These atoms, which are separate from one another in the unlimited void and differ in shape and size and position, and arrangement, move in the void, and when they overtake one another the collide, and some rebound in whatever direction they may happen to, but others become entangled in virtue of the relation of their shapes, sizes, positions, and arrangements, and stay together, and this is how compounds are produced.

(Simplicius, *Commentary on Aristotle's On the Heavens* 242.18–26 = 67A14)

9. Those who abandoned division to infinity on the grounds that we cannot divide to infinity and as a result cannot guarantee that the division cannot end, declared that bodies are composed of indivisible things and are divided into indivisibles. Except that Leucippus and Democritus hold that the cause of the primary bodies' indivisibility is not only their inability to be affected but also their minute size and lack of parts.

(Simplicius, *Commentary on Aristotle's Physics* 925.10–5 = 67A13)

10. Democritus would appear to have been persuaded by arguments that are relevant and appropriate to the science of nature. The point will be clear as we proceed. For there is a difficulty in supposing that there is some body, a magnitude, that is everywhere divisible and that this [the complete division] is possible. For what will there be that escapes the division? . . . Now since such a body is everywhere divisible, let it be divided. What, then, will be left? A magnitude? But this cannot be. For there will be something that has not been divided, whereas we supposed that it was everywhere divisible. But if there will be no body or magnitude left and yet the division will take place, either [the original body] will consist of points and its components will be without magnitude, or it will be nothing at all, so that it could come to be out of nothing and be composed of nothing, and the whole thing would then be nothing but an appearance. Likewise, if it is composed of points, it will not be a quantity. For when they were in contact and there was a single magnitude and they coincided, they made the whole thing none the larger. For when it is divided into two or more, the whole is not smaller or larger than before. And so, even if all the points are put together they will not make any magnitude. . . . These problems result from supposing that any body whatever of any size is everywhere divisible. . . . And so, since magnitudes cannot be composed of contacts or points, it is necessary for there to be indivisible bodies and magnitudes.

(Aristotle, *On Generation and Corruption* 1.2.316a13–b16 = 68A48b)

11. When Democritus said that the atoms are in contact with each other, he did not mean contact strictly speaking . . . but the condition in which the atoms are near one another and not far apart is what he called contact. For no matter what, they are separated by the void.

(Philoponus, *Commentary on Aristotle's On Generation and Corruption* 158.27–159.3 = 67A7)

12. Leucippus and Democritus said that their primary bodies, the atoms, are always moving in the unlimited void by compulsion.

(Simplicius, *Commentary on Aristotle's On the Heavens* 583.18–20 = 67A16)

13. Democritus, saying that the atoms are naturally motionless, declares that they move "by a blow."
(Simplicius, *Commentary on Aristotle's Physics* 42.10–1 = 68A47)

14. Democritus says that the primary bodies (these are the compact things) do not possess weight but move by knocking against one another in the unlimited, and there can be an atom the size of the cosmos. (Aetius 1.12.6 = 68A47)

15. What does Democritus say? That substances unlimited in multitude, atomic and not different in kind, and moreover incapable of acting or being acted upon, are in motion, scattered in the void. When they approach one another or collide or become entangled, the compounds appear as water or fire or as a plant or a human, but all things are atoms, which he calls forms; there is nothing else. For from what-is-not there is no coming to be, and nothing could come to be from things that are because on account of their hardness the atoms are not acted upon and do not change.
(Plutarch, *Against Colotes* 8 1110F–1111A = 68A57)

16. He makes sweet that which is round and good-sized; astringent that which is large, rough, polygonal, and not rounded; sharp tasting, as its name indicates, that which is sharp in body, and angular, bent and not rounded; pungent that which is round and small and angular and bent; salty that which is angular and good-sized and crooked and equal sided; bitter that which is round and smooth, crooked and small sized; oily that which is fine and round and small.
(Theophrastus, *Causes of Plants* 6.1.6 = 68A129)

17. Nonetheless he is found condemning them [the senses]. For he says, "We in fact understand nothing exactly [or, exact], but what changes according to the disposition both of the body and of the things that enter it and offer resistance to it."
(Sextus Empiricus, *Against the Professors* 7.136 = 68B9)

18. There are two kinds of judgment, one legitimate and the other bastard. All the following belong to the bastard: sight, hearing, smell, taste, touch. The other is legitimate and is separated from this. When the bastard one is unable to see or hear or smell or taste or grasp by touch any further in the direction of smallness, but [we need to go still further] towards what is fine, [then the legitimate one enables us to carry on].
(Sextus Empiricus, *Against the Professors* 7.138 = 68B11)

19. A person must know by this rule that he is separated from reality.
(Sextus Empiricus, *Against the Professors* 7.136 = 68B6)

20. In fact it will be clear that to know in reality what each thing is like is a matter of perplexity.
(Sextus Empiricus, *Against the Professors* 7.136 = 68B8)

21. By convention [or, custom], sweet; by convention, bitter; by convention, hot; by convention, cold; by convention, color; but in reality, atoms and void.
(Sextus Empiricus, *Against the Professors* 7.135 = 68B9 (= B125))

22. Wretched mind, after taking your evidence from us do you throw us down? Throwing us down is a fall for you!
(Galen, *On Medical Experience* 15.8 = 68B125; B125 also includes a restatement of B9)

23. Best for a person is to live his life being as cheerful and as little distressed as possible. This will occur if he does not make his pleasures in mortal things.
(Stobaeus, *Selections* 3.1.47 = 68B189)

24. All those who make their pleasures from the belly, exceeding the right time for food, drink, or sex, have short-lived pleasures—only for as long as they eat or drink—but many pains.
(Stobaeus, *Selections* 3.18.35 = 68B235)

5
THE SOPHISTS

THE SOPHISTS WERE men of their times, developing techniques and ideas to suit the rapid changes in Greek culture during the second half of the fifth century. After the Greeks, led by the Athenians, had repelled the Persians in the early decades of the same century, Athens became the center of a Greek world united first by a common enemy and then increasingly by Athenian coercion. With power concentrated in this prosperous democracy, which was controlled by an assembly of male citizens, demand soon emerged for teachers of rhetoric to train speakers in effective political oratory. Foreigners such as Protagoras and Gorgias gravitated to the imperial capital to meet this demand, sometimes charging handsome fees for their lessons. Although celebrated by many Athenians, especially those who advanced politically under their instruction, they were never entirely accepted by the aristocracy, who saw their own hereditary influence being usurped by politicians trained in new methods of debate and persuasion. Plato did the most to contribute to the pejorative connotation of their name (*sophistēs* originally just meant "wise man") by portraying them as opportunists who dazzled audiences but lacked any real wisdom. Yet the Sophists were more substantial thinkers than their subsequent reputation suggests. As the following samples of their work reveal, they developed subtle positions in epistemology, metaphysics, ethics, and politics.

5a
PROTAGORAS

PROTAGORAS WAS BORN in Abdera c. 490 BCE, making him about thirty years older than Democritus, the other great philosopher from that city. His visits to Athens made him famous, rich, and a friend of Pericles, putting him at the center of Greek political and intellectual life. For example, Protagoras was invited to draft a political constitution for the Athenian colony of Thurii, which was founded in southern Italy in 444. He died in 420. Later Greek authors offered conflicting accounts of his thought, which makes it difficult to reconstruct a coherent Protagorean philosophy; but it is widely agreed that he wrote several books, including *On Truth* (also called *The Throws*, an allusion to the wrestling moves that resembled his dialectical technique), *Contrary Arguments* (which proposed equally compelling arguments on both sides of a series of questions), and *On the Gods* (which claimed that we could know nothing about them).

1. Man is the measure of all things—of things that are, that they are, and of things that are not, that they are not.

   (Sextus Empiricus, *Against the Professors* 7.60 = 80B1; modified by Miller)

2. Concerning the gods I am unable to know either that they are or that they are not, or what their appearance is like. For many are the things that hinder knowledge: the obscurity of the matter and the shortness of human life.

   (Eusebius, *Preparation of the Gospel* 14.3.7 = 80B4)

3. There are two opposing arguments [*logoi*] concerning everything.

   (Diogenes Laertius, *Lives of the Philosophers* 9.51 = 80B6a; tr. Curd)

4. To make the weaker argument [*logos*] the stronger.
(Aristotle, *Rhetoric* 1402a23 = 80B6b; tr. Curd)

5. Education is not implanted in the soul unless one reaches a greater depth.
(Plutarch, *On Practice* 178.25 = 80B11)

6. [See Plato, *Protagoras* 320d–328c, pages 82–6.]

5b
Gorgias

Gorgias was born at the same time as Protagoras but survived him by many years, reportedly living more than a century. A few of his speeches survive, including the *Encomium of Helen*, which was a showpiece intended to persuade students to enroll in his courses. Although Greek tradition reviled Helen as the cause of the Trojan War, Gorgias defends her. She should not be blamed for leaving her husband, he argues, because she acted under the compulsion of one or more irresistible forces. Foremost among them was the persuasive speech (*logos*) of her seducer, Alexander (Paris). "Persuasion," says Gorgias, "has the force of necessity." He thus advertised his services in the content of his argument as much as with the style of its presentation.

In the second selection, *On Nothing*, Gorgias offers a clever parody of the Eleatics. They argued that nothing (what-is-not) can neither be, be thought of, nor be spoken about. Gorgias argues that the same holds for what-is—that it cannot be, and that even if it could be, it could not be comprehended, and that even if it could be comprehended, it could not be expressed. Coming serially in a speech delivered with Gorgias' oratorical skill, the effect of these difficult arguments must have been impressive. Although often fallacious—in ways that Gorgias probably noticed, and may even have intended—they are most valuable for their novel discussion of speech itself. "It is not the case," wrote Gorgias, "that *Logos* makes manifest the great number of objects." Speech, he seems to imply, is a world unto itself and Gorgias its master.

Encomium of Helen

What is becoming to a city is manpower, to a body beauty, to a soul wisdom, to an action virtue, to a speech truth, and the opposites of these are unbecoming. Man and woman and speech and deed and city and object should be honored with praise if praiseworthy and incur blame if unworthy, for it is an equal error and mistake to blame the praisable and to praise the blamable. It is the duty of one and the same man both to speak the needful rightly and to refute [the unrightfully spoken. Thus it is right to refute] those who rebuke Helen, a woman about whom the testimony of inspired poets has become univocal and unanimous as had the ill omen of her name, which has become a reminder of misfortunes. For my part, by introducing some reasoning into my speech, I wish to free the accused of blame and, having reproved her detractors as prevaricators and proved the truth, to free her from their ignorance.

Now it is not unclear, not even to a few, that in nature and in blood the woman who is the subject of this speech is preeminent among preeminent men and women. For it is clear that her mother was Leda, and her father was in fact a god, Zeus, but allegedly a mortal, Tyndareus, of whom the former was shown to be her father because he was and the latter was disproved because he was said to be, and the one was the most powerful of men and the other the lord of all.

Born from such stock, she had godlike beauty, which taking and not mistaking, she kept. In many did she work much desire for her love, and her one body was the cause of bringing together many bodies of men thinking great thoughts for great goals, of

---

Translated by George Kennedy, from *The Older Sophists*, edited by Rosamond Kent Sprague (Indianapolis: Hackett Publishing Company, 2001).

whom some had greatness of wealth, some the glory of ancient nobility, some the vigor of personal agility, some command of acquired knowledge. And all came because of a passion which loved to conquer and a love of honor which was unconquered. Who it was and why and how he sailed away, taking Helen as his love, I shall not say. To tell the knowing what they know shows it is right but brings no delight. Having now gone beyond the time once set for my speech, I shall go on to the beginning of my future speech, and I shall set forth the causes through which it was likely that Helen's voyage to Troy should take place.

For either by will of Fate and decision of the gods and vote of Necessity did she do what she did, or by force reduced or by words seduced [or by love possessed]. Now if through the first, it is right for the responsible one to be held responsible; for god's predetermination cannot be hindered by human premeditation. For it is the nature of things, not for the strong to be hindered by the weak, but for the weaker to be ruled and drawn by the stronger, and for the stronger to lead and the weaker to follow. God is a stronger force than man in might and in wit and in other ways. If then one must place blame on Fate and on a god, one must free Helen from disgrace.

But if she was raped by violence and illegally assaulted and unjustly insulted, it is clear that the raper, as the insulter, did the wronging, and the raped, as the insulted, did the suffering. It is right then for the barbarian who undertook a barbaric undertaking in word and law and deed to meet with blame in word, exclusion in law, and punishment in deed. And surely it is proper for a woman raped and robbed of her country and deprived of her friends to be pitied rather than pilloried. He did the dread deeds; she suffered them. It is just therefore to pity her but to hate him.

But if it was speech which persuaded her and deceived her heart, not even to this is it difficult to make an answer and to banish blame as follows. Speech is a powerful lord, which by means of the finest and most invisible body effects the divinest works: it can stop fear and banish grief and create joy and nurture pity. I shall show how this is the case, since it is necessary to offer proof to the opinion of my hearers: I both deem and define all poetry as speech with meter. Fearful shuddering and tearful pity and grievous longing come upon its hearers, and at the actions and physical sufferings of others in good fortunes and in evil fortunes, through the agency of words, the soul is wont to experience a suffering of its own. But come, I shall turn from one argument to another. Sacred incantations sung with words are bearers of pleasure and banishers of pain, for, merging with opinion in the soul, the power of the incantation is wont to beguile it and persuade it and alter it by witchcraft. There have been discovered two arts of witchcraft and magic: one consists of errors of soul and the other of deceptions of opinion. All who have and do persuade people of things do so by molding a false argument. For if all men on all subjects had [both] memory of things past and [awareness] of things present and foreknowledge of the future, speech would not be similarly similar, since as things are now it is not easy for them to recall the past nor to consider the present nor to predict the future. So that on most subjects most men take opinion as counselor to their soul, but since opinion is slippery and insecure it casts those employing it into slippery and insecure successes. What cause then prevents the conclusion that Helen similarly, against her will, might have come under the influence of speech, just as if ravished by the force of the mighty? For it was possible to see how the force of persuasion prevails; persuasion has the form of necessity, but it does not have the same power. For speech constrained the soul, persuading it which it persuaded, both to believe the things said and to approve the things done. The persuader, like a constrainer, does the wrong and the persuaded, like the constrained, in speech is wrongly charged. To understand that persuasion, when added to speech, is wont also to impress the soul as it wishes, one must study: first, the words of astronomers who, substituting opinion for opinion, taking away one but creating another, make what is incredible and unclear seem true to the eyes of opinion; then, second, logically necessary debates in which a single speech, written with art but not spoken with truth, bends a great crowd and persuades; [and] third, the verbal disputes of philosophers in which the swiftness of thought is also shown making the belief in an opinion subject to easy change. The effect of speech upon the condition of the soul is comparable to the power of drugs over the nature of bodies. For just as different drugs dispel different secretions from the body, and some bring an end to disease and others to life, so also in the case of speeches, some distress, others delight, some cause fear, others make the hearers bold, and some drug and bewitch the soul with a kind of evil persuasion.

It has been explained that if she was persuaded by speech she did not do wrong but was unfortunate. I shall discuss the fourth cause in a fourth passage. For if it was love which did all these things, there will be no difficulty in escaping the charge of the sin which is alleged to have taken place. For the things we see do not have the nature which we wish them to have, but the nature which each actually has. Through sight the soul receives an impression even in its inner features. When belligerents in war buckle on their warlike accoutrements of bronze and steel, some designed for defense, others for offense, if the sight sees this, immediately it is alarmed and it alarms the soul, so that often men flee, panic-stricken, from future danger [as though it were] present. For strong as is the habit of obedience to the law, it is ejected by fear resulting from sight, which coming to a man causes him to be indifferent both to what is judged honorable because of the law and to the advantage to be derived from victory. It has happened that people, after having seen frightening sights, have also lost presence of mind for the present moment; in this way fear extinguishes and excludes thought. And many have fallen victim to useless labor and dread diseases and hardly curable madnesses. In this way the sight engraves upon the mind images of things which have been seen. And many frightening impressions linger, and what lingers is exactly analogous to [what is] spoken. Moreover, whenever pictures perfectly create a single figure and form from many colors and figures, they delight the sight, while the creation of statues and the production of works of art furnish a pleasant sight to the eyes. Thus it is natural for the sight to grieve for some things and to long for others, and much love and desire for many objects and figures is engraved in many men.

If, therefore, the eye of Helen, pleased by the figure of Alexander, presented to her soul eager desire and contest of love, what wonder? If, [being] a god, [love has] the divine power of the gods, how could a lesser being reject and refuse it? But if it is a disease of human origin and a fault of the soul, it should not be blamed as a sin, but regarded as an affliction. For she came, as she did come, caught in the net of Fate, not by the plans of the mind, and by the constraints of love, not by the devices of art.

How then can one regard blame of Helen as just, since she is utterly acquitted of all charge, whether she did what she did through falling in love or persuaded by speech or ravished by force or constrained by divine constraint?

I have by means of speech removed disgrace from a woman; I have observed the procedure which I set up at the beginning of the speech; I have tried to end the injustice of blame and the ignorance of opinion; I wished to write a speech which would be a praise of Helen and a diversion to myself.

On Nothing

1. He concludes as follows that nothing is: if [something] is, either what-is is or what-is-not [is], or both what-is and what-is-not are. But it is the case neither that what-is is, as he will show, nor that what-is-not is, as he will justify, nor that both what-is and what-is-not are, as he will teach this too. Therefore, it is not the case that anything is. And in fact, what-is-not is not. For if what-is-not is, it will be and not be at the same time. For in that it is considered as not being, it will not be, but in that it *is* not being, on the other hand, it will be. But it is completely absurd that something be and not be at the same time. Therefore, it is not the case that what-is-not is.

   And differently: if what-is-not is, what-is will not be, since they are opposites, and if being is an attribute of what-is-not, not-being will be an attribute of what-is. But it is certainly not the case that what-is is not, and so neither will what-is-not be.

   Further, neither is it the case that what-is is. For if what-is is, it is either eternal or generated or eternal and generated at the same time. But it is neither eternal nor generated nor both, as

---

From *A Presocratics Reader*, edited by Patricia Curd. Translations by Richard D. McKirahan unless otherwise indicated (Indianapolis: Hackett Publishing Company, 1996).

we will show. Therefore it is not the case that what-is is.

For if what-is is eternal (we must begin at this point), it does not have any beginning. For everything that comes to be has some beginning, but what is eternal, being ungenerated, did not have a beginning. But if it does not have a beginning, it is unlimited, and if it is unlimited it is nowhere. For if it is anywhere, that in which it is is different from it, and so what-is will no longer be unlimited, since it is enclosed in something. For what encloses is larger than what is enclosed, but nothing is larger than what is unlimited, and so what is unlimited is not anywhere. Further, it is not enclosed in itself, either. For "that in which" and "that in it" will be the same, and what-is will become two, place and body (for "that in which" is place, and "that in it" is body). But this is absurd, so what-is is not in itself, either. And so, if what-is is eternal, it is unlimited, but if it is unlimited it is nowhere, and if it is nowhere it is not. So if what-is is eternal, it is not at all.

Further, what-is cannot be generated either. For if it has come to be it did so either from a thing that is or from a thing that is not. But it has come to be neither from what-is (for if it is a thing that is, it has not come to be, but already is), nor from what-is-not (for what-is-not cannot generate anything, since what generates anything must of necessity share in existence). Therefore, it is not the case that what-is is generated either.

In the same ways, it is not both eternal and generated at the same time. For these exclude one another, and if what-is is eternal it has not come to be, and if it has come to be it is not eternal. So if what-is is neither eternal nor generated nor both together, what-is would not be.

And differently, if it is, it is either one or many. But it is neither one nor many, as will be shown. Therefore it is not the case that what-is is.

For if it is one, it is either a quantity or continuous or a magnitude or a body. But whichever of these it is, it is not one, but being a quantity, it will be divided, and if it is continuous it will be cut. Similarly if conceived as a magnitude it will not be indivisible. And if it chances to be a body, it will be three-dimensional, for it will have length, width and depth. But it is absurd to say that what-is is none of these. Therefore, it is not the case that what-is is one.

Further, it is not many. For if it is not one, it is not many either. For the many is a compound of individual ones, and so since [the thesis that what-is is] one is refuted, [the thesis that what-is is] many is refuted along with it.

But it is altogether clear from this that neither what-is nor what-is-not is. It is easy to conclude that neither is it the case that both of them are, what-is and what-is-not.

For if what-is-not is and what-is is, then what-is-not will be the same as what-is as regards being. And for this reason neither of them is. For it is agreed that what-is-not is not, and what-is has been shown to be the same as this. So it too will not be. However, if what-is is the same as what-is-not, it is not possible for both to be. For if both [are], then they are not the same, and if [they are] the same, then [it is] not [the case that] both [are].

It follows that nothing is. For if neither what-is is nor what-is-not nor both, and nothing aside from these is conceived of, nothing is.

2. Next in order is to teach that even if something is, it is unknowable and inconceivable by humans.

For if things that are thought of, says Gorgias, are not things-that-are, what-is is not thought of. And reasonably so. For just as if things that are thought of have the attribute of being white, being thought of would be an attribute of white things, so if things that are thought of have the attribute of not being things-that-are, not to be thought of will necessarily be an attribute of things-that-are. This is why the claim is sound and preserves the sequence of argument, that if things that are thought of are not things-that-are, what-is is not thought of. But things that are thought of (for we must assume this) are not things-that-are, as we will show. Therefore it is not the case that what-is is thought of.

Further, it is completely clear that things that are thought of are not things-that-are. For if things that are thought of are things-that-are, all things that are thought of are—indeed, however anyone thinks of them. But this is apparently false. For if someone thinks of a person flying or chariots racing in the sea, it is not the case that forthwith a person is flying or chariots racing in the sea. And so, it is not the case that things that are thought of are things-that-are.

In addition, if things that are thought of are things-that-are, things-that-are-not will not be thought of. For opposites have opposite attributes, and what-is-not is opposite to what-is. For this reason, if being thought of is an attribute of what-is, not being thought of will assuredly be an attribute of what-is-not. But this is absurd. For Scylla and Chimaera and many things-that-are-not are thought of. Therefore it is not the case that what-is is thought of.

And just as things that are seen are called visible because they are seen and things that are heard are called audible because they are heard, and we do not reject visible things because they are not heard or dismiss audible things because they are not seen (for each ought to be judged by its own sense, not by another), so also things that are thought of will be, even if they may not be seen by vision or heard by hearing, because they are grasped by their own criterion. So if someone thinks that chariots race in the sea, even if he does not see them, he ought to believe that there are chariots racing in the sea. But this is absurd. Therefore it is not the case that what-is is thought of and comprehended.

3. But even if it should be comprehended, it cannot be expressed to another.

For if things-that-are are visible and audible and generally perceptible, and in fact are external objects, and of these the visible are comprehended by vision and the audible by hearing, and not vice versa, how can these be communicated to another? For that by which we communicate is *Logos*, but *Logos* is not the objects, the things-that-are. Therefore it is not the case that we communicate things-that-are to our neighbors, but *Logos*, which is different from the objects. So just as the visible could not become audible and vice versa, thus, since what-is is an external object, it could not become our *Logos*. But if it were not *Logos*, it would not have been revealed to another.

In fact, *Logos*, he says, is composed from external things, i.e., perceptible things, falling upon us. For from encountering flavor there arises in us the *Logos*, which is expressed with reference to this quality, and from the incidence on the senses of color arises the *Logos* with reference to color. But if so, it is not the *Logos* that makes manifest the external [object], but the external [object] that comes to be communicative of the *Logos*.

Further, it is not possible to say that *Logos* is an object in the way visible and audible things are, so that objects which are can be communicated by it, which is an object which is. For, he says, even if *Logos* is an object, it anyway differs from all other objects, and visible bodies differ most from *Logos*. For the visible is grasped by one organ, *Logos* by another. Therefore it is not the case that *Logos* makes manifest the great number of objects, just as they do not reveal the nature of one another.

(Sextus Empiricus, *Against the Professors* 7.65–86 = 82B3)

5c
Dissoi Logoi

The date of the short treatise excerpted here is not known, although scholars place its composition c. 400 BCE. It has been attributed to several notable authors, including Socrates. Protagoras famously said that "there are two arguments (*logoi*) concerning everything," and the *Dissoi Logoi*, or "Twofold Arguments," demonstrates this by addressing several questions central to Greek philosophy. Are justice and injustice the same or different? Arguments are presented on both sides. Likewise for truth and falsehood. One of these arguments foreshadows the Liar Paradox ("This sentence is false") that became the subject of philosophical debate in the Hellenistic period and continues to preoccupy modern thinkers. In the final section presented here, the author presents twofold arguments about the teachability of wisdom and virtue. Some of these same arguments appear again in Plato's *Protagoras*.

Concerning Just and Unjust

Twofold arguments are also put forward concerning the just and the unjust. And some say that the just is one thing and the unjust another, and others that the just and the unjust are the same. And I shall try to support this latter view.

And, in the first place, I shall argue that it is just to tell and to deceive. My opponents would declare that it is [right and just] to do these things to one's enemies but disgraceful and wicked to do so [to one's friends]. [But how is it just to do so to one's enemies] and not to one's dearest friends? Take the example of parents: suppose one's father or mother ought to drink or eat a remedy and is unwilling to do so, isn't it just to give the remedy in a gruel or drink and to deny that it is in it? Therefore, from this one example, it is [just] to tell lies and to deceive one's parents.

And, in fact, to steal the belongings of one's friends and to use force against those one loves most is just. For instance, if a member of the household is in some sort of grief or trouble and intends to destroy himself with a sword or a rope or some other thing, it is right, isn't it, to steal these things, if possible, and, if one should come in too late and catch the person with the thing in his hand, to take it away by force?

And how is it not just to enslave one's enemies [and] to sell a whole city into slavery if one is able to capture it?

And to break into the public buildings of one's fellow citizens appears to be just. Because, if one's father has been imprisoned and is under sentence of death as a result of having been overthrown by his political rivals, then isn't it just to dig your way in to remove your father stealthily and save him?

And what about breaking an oath: suppose a man is captured by the enemy and takes a firm oath that, if he is set free, he will betray his city: [would] this man do right if he kept his oath? I don't think so, but rather if he [should] save his city and his friends and the temples of [his] fathers by breaking it. Thus it follows that it is right to break an oath. And it is right to plunder a temple. I'm not talking about the civic temples, but about those common to the whole of Greece, such as the ones at Delphi and Olympia: when the barbarian was on the point of conquering Greece, and the safety of the country lay in the temple funds, wasn't it right to take these and use them for the war?

And to murder one's nearest and dearest is right: in the case of Orestes and of Alcmaeon, even the god answered that they were right to have done as they did.

I shall turn to the arts and to the writings of the poets. In the writing of tragedies and in painting, who[ever] deceives the most in creating things similar to the true, this man is the best. I want also to present the testimony of older poetry, of Cleobulina, for instance:

> I saw a man stealing and deceiving by force,
> And to do this by force was an action most just.

These lines were written a long time ago. The next passages are from Aeschylus:

> God does not stand aloof from just deceit,

[and]

> There are times when god respects an opportunity
> for lies.

But to this, too, an opposite argument is put forward: that the just and the unjust are different things, and that as the name differs, so does the thing named.

For instance, if anyone should ask those who say that unjust and just are the same whether they have yet done anything just for their parents, they will say yes. But then they have done something unjust, because they admit that unjust and just are the same thing.

Just take another case: if you know some man to be just, then you know the same man to be also unjust, and again if you know a man to be large, you also know him to be small, by the same argument. And [if] the sentence is pronounced, "Let him die the death for having done many acts of injustice," then let him die the death for having done [many acts of justice].

Translated by Rosamond Kent Sprague, from *The Older Sophists*, edited by Rosamond Kent Sprague (Indianapolis: Hackett Publishing Company, 2001).

Enough on these topics: I shall go on to what is said by those who claim to prove that just and unjust are the same. To state that to steal the enemy's possessions is just would also show the same action to be unjust if their argument is true, and so in the other cases.

And they bring in the arts, to which just and unjust do not apply. As for the poets, they write their poems to give men pleasure, and not for the sake of truth.

Concerning Truth and Falsehood

Twofold arguments are also put forward concerning the false and the true, concerning which one person says that a false statement is one thing and a true statement another, while others say the true statement is the same as the false.

And I hold the latter view: in the first place, because they are both expressed in the same words, and secondly, because whenever a statement is made, if things [should] turn out to be as stated, then the statement is true, but if they should not turn out to be as stated, the same statement is false.

Suppose the statement accuses a certain man of temple-robbery: if the thing actually happened, the statement is true, but if it did not happen, it is false. And the same argument is used by a man defending himself against such a charge. And the lawcourts judge the same statement to be both true and false.

And, again, suppose we are all sitting in a row and each of us says, "I am an initiate," we all utter the same words, but I would be the only person making a true statement, since I am the only person who is one.

From these remarks it is clear that the same statement is false whenever falsehood is present in it and true whenever truth is present (just the way a man is the same person when he is a child and a young man and an adult and an old man).

But it is also said that a false statement is one thing and a true statement another, and that as the name differs [so does the thing named]. Because, if anyone should ask those who say that the same statement is both false and true whether their own statement is false or true, if they answer "false" then it is clear that the true and false are two different things, and if they answer "true," then this same statement is also false.

And if anyone ever says or bears witness that certain things are true, then these same things are also false. And if he knows some man to be true, he knows the same man to be false.

As a result of the argument they say that if a thing comes to pass, the statement they make is true, but if it does not, then the statement is false. If so, [it isn't the name that differs in these cases but the thing named.

And,] again, [if anyone should ask] jurymen what they are judging because they are not present at the events, even they themselves agree that that in which falsehood is mingled is false, and that in which truth is mingled is true. This constitutes a total difference. . . .

Concerning Wisdom and Virtue, Whether They Are Teachable

A certain statement is put forward which is neither true nor new: it is that wisdom and virtue can neither be taught nor learned. And those who say this use the following proofs: That it is not possible, if you were to hand a thing over to someone else, for you still to have this thing; this is one proof. Another proof is that, if they had been teachable, there would have been acknowledged teachers of them, as in the case of music. A third proof is that the men in Greece who became wise would have taught their art to their friends. A fourth proof is that, before now, some have been to the Sophists and derived no benefit form them. A fifth proof is that many who have *not* associated with the Sophists have become notable.

But I think this statement is very simpleminded: I know that teachers teach letters, these being the things a teacher knows, and that lyre-players teach lyre-playing. In answer to the second proof, that there are in fact no acknowledged teachers, whatever else do the Sophists teach except wisdom and virtue? And what were the followers of Anaxagoras and Pythagoras? With respect to the third point, Polycleitus taught his son to be a sculptor. And even if a particular man did *not* teach, this would not prove anything, but if a single man *did* teach this would be evidence that teaching is possible. With respect to the fourth point, that some do not become wise in spite of associating with the Sophists, many people also do not succeed in learning their letters in spite of studying them.

There does exist also a natural bent by means of which a person who does not study with the Sophists becomes competent, if he is well endowed, to master most things easily after learning a few elements from the very persons from whom we also learn our words. As for our words, one man learns more from his father and fewer from his mother, and another man the other way around. And if someone is not persuaded that we learn our words but thinks we are born knowing them, let him form a judgment from what follows: if someone should send a child away to the Persians as soon as he was born and should bring him up there, hearing nothing of the Greek tongue, he would speak Persian. And if one were to bring a Persian child here, he would speak Greek. We learn our words in this fashion, and we don't know who our teachers are.

Thus my argument is complete, and you have its beginning, middle, and end. And I don't say that wisdom and virtue are teachable, but that these proofs do not satisfy me.

Sophistic Political Thought

In the second half of the fifth century BCE, Athenian intellectuals became preoccupied with the relationship between *nomos* (convention, custom, or law) and *physis* (nature). Herodotus, for example, had presented the customs of many foreign nations in his *Histories*, undermining the Greeks' confidence in the naturalness of their own. Even the Atomists, as we saw earlier in this anthology, drew a distinction between custom and nature. "By *nomos* bitter, by *nomos* sweet," wrote Democritus, but "in *physis* atoms and void." The implication of Atomism was that although we are accustomed to one world, a humane world of tastes and values, the real world is far different. The advent of the Peloponnesian War (431–404 BCE) brought this stark distinction to the forefront of Greek politics. Civil wars like that of Corcyra, and the plague that decimated Athens, highlighted the irrelevance of *nomoi* once the power to enforce them had disintegrated.

5d
Antiphon

The author of the following passages was likely Antiphon of Rhamnous, born c. 480 BCE. Since Rhamnous was a village in Attica, the territory of greater Athens, Antiphon enjoyed the privileges of citizenship. Unlike most Sophists, therefore, he was permitted to participate in Athenian politics, rather than merely teaching others how to do so. This participation led eventually to his execution in 411, when the oligarchic revolt he helped to lead against the long-standing democracy failed.

He was a famously effective orator. One of his books, *Tetralogies* (*Four Speeches*), presented groups of opening and closing speeches for both the prosecution and the defense, showing a dialectical dexterity equal to that of Gorgias. Like him, Antiphon ascribed great power to *logos*—for good as well as ill. He reportedly offered his services as a psychotherapist, promising to "treat the distressed by means of words." In two other books, *On Concord* and *On Truth*, he treated subjects as diverse as astronomy, meteorology, biology, and cosmology. The fragments that follow are from these philosophical works.

In the long fragment for which Antiphon is now best known, he distinguishes the city's laws (*nomoi*) from the decrees of nature (*physis*), arguing in a manner typical of the late fifth-century BCE Sophists that our advantage lies with obedience to the second but not the first. No one, he says, acts justly by nature. We are just only under the social constraints of punishment and reward.

1. Justice is a matter of not transgressing what the laws prescribe in whatever city you are a citizen of. A person would make most advantage of justice for himself if he treated the laws as important in the presence of witnesses, and treated the decrees of nature as important when alone and with no witnesses present. For the decrees of laws are extra additions, those of nature are necessary; those of the laws are the products of agreement, not of natural growth, whereas those of nature are the products of natural growth, not of agreement. If those who made the agreement do not notice a person transgressing the prescriptions of laws, he is free from both disgrace and penalty, but not so if they do notice him. But if, contrary to possibility, anyone violates any of the things which are innate by nature, the evil is no less if no one notices him and no greater if all observe. For he does not suffer harm as a result of opinion, but as a result of truth.

This is the entire purpose of considering these matters—that most of the things that are just according to law are established in a way which is hostile to nature. For laws have been established for the eyes, as to what they must see and what they must not, and for the ears, as to what they must hear and what they must not, and for the tongue, as to what it must say and what it must not, and for the hands, as to what they must do and what they must not, and for the feet, as to where they must go and where they must not, for the mind, as to what it must desire and what it must not. Now the things from which the laws deter humans are no more in accord with or suited to nature than the things which they promote.

Living and dying are matters of nature, and living results for them from what is advantageous, dying from what is not advantageous. But the advantages which are established by the laws are bonds on nature, and those established by nature are free.

And so, things that cause distress, at least when thought of correctly, do not help nature more than things that give joy. Therefore, it will not be painful things rather than pleasant things which are advantageous. For things that are truly advantageous must not cause harm but benefit. Now the things that are advantageous by nature are among these. . . .

[But according to law, those are correct] who defend themselves after suffering and are not first to do wrong, and those who do good to parents who are bad to them, and who permit others to accuse them on oath but do not themselves accuse on oath. You will find most of these cases hostile to nature. They permit people to suffer more pain when less is possible, and to have less pleasure when more is possible, and to receive injury when it is not necessary.

Now if some assistance came from the laws for those who submitted to these conditions and some damage to those who do not submit but resist, obedience to the laws would not be unhelpful. But as things are, it is obvious that the justice that stems from the law is insufficient to rescue those who submit. In the first place, it permits the one who suffers to suffer and the wrongdoer to do wrong, and it was not at the time of the wrongdoing able to prevent either the sufferer from suffering or the wrongdoer from doing wrong. And when the case is brought to trial, there is no special advantage for the one who has suffered over the wrongdoer. For he must persuade the jury that he suffered and that he is able to exact the penalty. And it is open to the wrongdoer to deny it. . . . However convincing the accusation is on behalf of the accuser, the defense can be just as convincing. For victory comes through speech.

(Oxyrhynchus Papyrus XI no. 1364, ed. Hunt, col. 1 line 6–col. 7 line 15 = 87B44)

2. In all human beings the mind leads the body into health or disease or anything else.

(Galen, *Commentary on Hippocrates' "The Doctor's Workshop"* 18B656 = 87B2; tr. Curd, with Reeve and Cohen)

3. Time is a thought or a measure, not a reality.

(Aetius 1.22.6 = 87B9; tr. Curd, with Reeve and Cohen)

From *A Presocratics Reader*, edited by Patricia Curd. Translations by Richard D. McKirahan unless otherwise indicated (Indianapolis: Hackett Publishing Company, 1996).

4. If someone were to bury a bed and the rotting wood came to life, it would become not a bed, but a tree.

(Harpocration, *Lexicon v. embios* = 87B15; tr. Curd, with Reeve and Cohen)

5e
Critias

Critias' first known appearance on the Athenian political scene was in 415 BCE, when he was probably a young man. Like Alcibiades, his friend, he became a suspect in the mutilation of the Herms (phallic statues of Hermes that marked boundaries throughout Athens). Also like Alcibiades, he escaped prosecution for this impiety, although he made his atheism amply clear in later years. The following fragment shows Critias a partisan of the common Sophistic view that *nomoi* are human inventions; so too are the gods. Some scholars attribute this verse fragment to Euripides, which would constitute a striking example (there are others) of the influence of Sophistic political thought on Athenian tragedy. After Spartan victory in the Peloponnesian War, Critias led a pro-Spartan cadre of Athenian aristocrats called the Thirty Tyrants, who wrested political control from democratic hands for a brief period (404–403), and who were notorious for their brutality. He died in the front line of a losing battle to defend their power. Socrates was executed a few years later, in part, it is thought, because he was believed to have been the teacher of Critias.

There was a time when the life of men was uncivilized and bestial and subservient to brute force, a time when neither was there any prize for the good nor for the wicked did any chastisement arise. It seems to me that men next set up laws as chastisers, that Justice might become tyrant [equally of all] and might have Arrogance as a slave. Should anyone commit an error, he was penalized. Next, since laws hindered them from committing obvious crimes by force, yet they acted secretly, it seems to me that at this point some clever and wise man [for the first time] invented fear [of the gods] for mortals, that the wicked might experience fear, even if they act or say or think [something] in secret. As a consequence he introduced the divine: "There is a deity flourishing with indestructible life. Through mind it hears, sees, is extremely thoughtful, and attends to these things, bearing divine nature [in itself]. It will hear all that is said among mortals and will be able to see all that is done. If in silence you plan some evil, this will not escape the notice of the gods. For thought is in it [to too great a degree]." Making these statements, he introduced the most pleasant of doctrines and with false discourse obscured the truth. He claimed that the god inhabited a place where, merely by mentioning it, he could have frightened men extremely. He recognized that from this source there were fears for mortals and benefits for their wretched way of life, coming from heavenly revolution, where he saw that there existed lightning flashes and frightful thunderclaps and the star-spangled frame of heaven, the lovely embroidery of Time, wise craftsman. From here the bright mass of the star proceeds and damp storm moves out toward earth. With such fears did he encircle men, through whom he settled the deity well via discourse and in a suitable location; and through laws he quelled lawlessness.

5f
Anonymus Iamblichi

Anonymus Iamblichi is the name given by scholars to the unknown author whose treatise on *nomos* survives only because it was transcribed seven centuries later by the Neoplatonist Iamblichus. This treatise is especially valuable because it shows the diversity of opinion among Sophists about the value of obedience to *nomos*. The following excerpt begins with a discussion of self-discipline and its role in a judicious love of one's soul. It continues by arguing that life in a community is necessary for humans, and that such a life requires the observance of laws. It concludes with a list of the several benefits of lawfulness (*eunomia*), and another of the costs of lawlessness (*anomia*). All of these benefits, however, are benefits of living in a lawful society, rather than of being lawful oneself. Seeming lawful is usually necessary to participate in a lawful society, but the author does not consider the advantages of a secretly lawless life in a generally lawful society.

Surely it is necessary for every man to be very self-disciplined to a special degree. He would be particularly self-disciplined if he should be superior to the influence of money, for it is in respect to this that all men are corrupted, and if he should be unsparing of his own soul, with an earnest purpose fixed on what is right, and if he should be intent upon the pursuit of virtue. With regard to both of these most men are lacking in self-discipline. Because of some such thing as this they are affected in the following way: they are over-anxious about their souls, because it is the soul that is life; they are oversparing of it; and they are concerned about it because of their love of life and because they are so closely connected with the soul with which they grew up. And they love possessions because of the following things which frighten them. What are these? Sickness, old age, sudden penalties or losses—I do not mean penalties of the laws, for it is possible to take precautions and be on one's guard against incurring these, but such penalties or losses as conflagrations, the deaths of members of one's household, of animals, and other misfortunes, of which some pertain to the body, others to the soul, and others to one's estate. Because of all these misfortunes, in order that he may be in a position to use his money to meet these contingencies, every man desires wealth. But there are some other factors which no less than those already mentioned drive men on to money-making—I mean, ambitious rivalry with one another, jealousy, and the exercise of political power-situations in which they consider money of great importance, because it is helpful for such purposes. The man who is really good does not seek out a reputation clad in the ornaments belonging to another man but by his own virtue.

With regard to love of one's own soul we might believe as follows: if it fell to a man's lot to be ageless and immortal for all future time, provided that he were not killed by another man, there might be a ready pardon granted to the man who is oversparing of his soul. But since it falls to a man's lot, if his life is lengthened, to suffer old age, which is a greater evil, and not to be immortal, it shows great ignorance and the use of bad judgment and goals if a man preserves this soul into dishonor and does not leave an immortal glory to take its place—and everlasting and immortal fame in place of a soul which is only mortal.

Furthermore, we must not rush towards a consideration of our own advantage, nor should we consider either that the power which is based on a consideration of one's advantage is virtue, or that obeying the laws is cowardice. For this attitude is most base, and from it arises everything which is just the reverse of what is good, namely immorality and the inflicting of injury. If men were given such a nature that they were not able to live alone, but formed an association with one another under pressure of necessity, and found out our general way of life and the skills related to it, and cannot associate and live

---

Translated by Margaret E. Reesor, from *The Older Sophists*, edited by Rosamond Kent Sprague (Indianapolis: Hackett Publishing Company, 2001).

with one another without observance of law (for this would be a greater punishment than living alone), we can conclude, then, that because of these necessities Law and Justice are kings among men, and that they could in no way change, for by nature they have been firmly fixed.

If there should be anyone who had from the beginning of his life, a nature such as we shall describe: if he should be invulnerable, not subject to disease, free from emotion, extraordinary, and hard as adamant in body and soul, perhaps someone might believe that the power based on consideration of one's own advantage would be sufficient for such a man, on the grounds that a man of that type is invulnerable even if he does not submit to the law. The man who believes this is wrong. If there should be such a man, as in fact there could not be, such a man would be preserved if he placed himself on the side of the laws and what is just, strengthening these and using his strength to support these and what confirms them, but otherwise he could not endure. For it would appear that all men would be in a state of hostility to a man formed of such a nature, and because of their own observance of law and their numbers, they would surpass such a man in skill or force and they would get the better of him. Accordingly, it appears that power itself, the real power, is preserved by law and justice.

An atmosphere of trust is the first result of the observance of law. It benefits all men greatly and may be classed among those important things which are called good.

Community of property has its origin in this, and accordingly, even if the property is small, it is still sufficient since it is shared, but without mutual trust it is not sufficient even if it is great.

And the changes of fortune which affect wealth and one's life, whether good or bad, are most suitably directed by men if they observe the law. Those who have good fortune enjoy it in safety and with no fear of attack; those who have bad fortune receive help from those who enjoy good fortune because of their common dealings and mutual trust, since both of these have their basis in the observance of law.

Because of the observance of law, time lies fallow with respect to public business, but it is tillable in regard to the activities of life.

Under the observance of law, men are freed from the most unpleasant concern, but they enjoy the most pleasant; for a concern about public business is most unpleasant, but a concern about the activities of life is most pleasant.

If they go to sleep, for this is a rest from trouble for men, they approach it without fear and without painful anxieties; when they rise from it, they enjoy the same state of mind. They are not seized with sudden fright, nor after this most pleasant change do they expect the day to be, nor, after a most pleasant sleep, do they await [anxiously] the outcome of the day.

Pleasantly, forming thoughts which feel no anxiety about the activities of life, they lighten the burden of their search for good things with hopes and expectations which are credible. For all this the observance of law is responsible.

And as for that which brings the greatest trouble to men, war which leads to subjugation and slavery, to face this is more difficult for those who do not observe law and less difficult for those who do observe it.

And there are many other good things in the observance of law which provide assistance in life and a consolation for the hardships which arise from it; but the evils which result from a failure to observe law are as follows:

First, men have no leisure for the activities [of life] and are concerned about what is most unpleasant—public business rather than these activities; they hoard money because of the lack of mutual trust and the lack of common dealings but they do not share it, and in this way money becomes scare, even if it exists in large quantities.

Changes of fortune, both bad and good, serve opposite purposes; for good fortune is not safe when there is no observance of law, but is subject to plots; and ill fortune is not driven away but grows stronger as the result of lack of trust and lack of common dealings.

External war is kindled all the more, and internal strife for the same reason, and if it has not happened earlier, it happens that men are involved in public business continually because of plots arising among themselves, which force them to be on their guard continuously and to plot against one another.

When they are awake their thoughts are not pleasant; and when they have gone to sleep, they do not find a pleasant place of refuge but one that is filled with fear. An awakening which is full of fear and dread leads them to a sudden recollection of their troubles; these and all other evils which I have mentioned previously result from a failure to observe law.

Tyranny, an evil of such proportions and so monstrous, arises from nothing else than the nonobservance of law. Some men think, although they are wrong in their opinion, that a tyrant is established from some other cause, and that men who are deprived of their freedom are not themselves responsible, since they have been overpowered by the tyrant who has been established. In this they are wrong. Whoever thinks that the rise of a king or of a tyrant is due to any other cause than nonobservance of law and consideration of one's own advantage is stupid. For when everybody turns to evil practices, this result follows, for it is not possible for men to live without laws and justice. Whenever these two, law and justice, depart from the people, then the guardianship and protection of these people pass into the hands of one man. For how otherwise could sole authority pass into the hands of one man, unless the law which was in the interests of the people had already been driven out?

This man who is to depose justice and take away the law which is common to all and expedient for all, must be as hard as adamant, if he is going to strip this away from the people, since he is one and they are many. If he were only human and like everybody else he would not be able to do this; but, on the contrary, if he were to reestablish what had already ceased to exist, he could be sole ruler. That is why some men have not observed this happening.

PLATO

PLATO WAS BORN in Athens in 429 BCE and died there in 348–347. His father, Ariston, traced his ancestry to Codrus, who was supposedly king of Athens in the eleventh century BCE; his mother, Perictione, was related to Solon, architect of the Athenian constitution (594–593). While Plato was still a boy, his father died and his mother married Pyrilampes, a friend of the great Athenian statesman Pericles. Hence Plato was familiar with Athenian politics from childhood and was expected to enter it himself. Partly in reaction to the execution of his mentor and teacher Socrates in 399, he turned instead to philosophy, thinking that only it could bring true justice to human beings and put an end to civil war and political upheaval.

Few ancient authors have been as lucky as Plato. His works, which are predominantly dialogues, all seem to have survived. They are customarily divided into four chronological groups, though the precise ordering (especially within groups) is controversial:

EARLY: *Apology, Charmides, Crito, Euthyphro, Hippias Minor, Hippias Major, Ion, Laches, Lysis, Menexenus*

TRANSITIONAL: *Euthydemus, Gorgias, Meno, Protagoras*

MIDDLE: *Cratylus, Phaedo, Symposium, Republic, Phaedrus, Parmenides, Theaetetus*

LATE: *Timaeus, Critias, Sophist, Statesman, Philebus, Laws*

Plato also contributed to philosophy by founding the Academy, arguably the first university. This was a center of research and teaching both in theoretical subjects and also in more practical ones. Eudoxus, who gave a geometrical explanation of the presumed revolutions of the sun, moon, and planets around the earth, brought his own students with him to join Plato, and studied and taught in the Academy; Theaetetus developed solid geometry there. But cities also invited members of the Academy to help them in the practical task of developing new political constitutions.

The Academy lasted for some two and a half centuries after Plato died, ending around 80 BCE. Its early leaders, including his own nephew Speusippus, who succeeded him as head, all modified his teachings in various ways. Later, influenced by the early dialogues, which end in puzzlement (*aporia*), the Academy, under Arcesilaus, Carneades, and other philosophers, practiced Skepticism; later still, influenced by different dialogues, Platonists were more dogmatic. Platonism of one sort or another—Middle or Neo- or something else—remained the dominant philosophy in the pagan world of late antiquity, influencing St. Augustine among others. Much of what passed for Plato's thought until the nineteenth century, when German scholars pioneered a return to Plato's writings themselves, was a mixture of these different "Platonisms."

Given the vast span and diversity of Plato's writings and the fact that they are dialogues, not treatises, it is little wonder that they were read in many different ways even by Plato's ancient followers. In this respect nothing has changed: different schools of philosophy and textual interpretation continue to find profoundly different messages and different methods in Plato. Doctrinal continuities, discontinuities, and outright contradictions of one sort or another are discovered, disputed, rediscovered, and disputed afresh. Neglected dialogues are taken up anew, old favorites reinterpreted. New questions are raised, old ones resurrected and reformulated: Is Plato's Socrates really the great ironist of philosophy, or a largely nonironic figure? Is Plato a systematic philosopher with answers to give, or an explorer of philosophical ideas only? Is he primarily a theorist about universals, a moralist, or a mystic with an otherworldly view about the nature of reality and the place of the human psyche in it? Or is he all of these at once? Does the dramatic structure of the dialogues undermine their apparent philosophical arguments? Should Plato's negative remarks about the efficacy of written philosophy (*Phaedrus* 274b–278b) lead us to look behind his dialogues for what Plato's student Aristotle refers to as the "so-called unwritten doctrines" (*Physics* 209b14–15)?

Besides this continued engagement with Plato's writings, there is, of course, the not entirely separate engagement with the problems Plato brought to philosophy, the methods he invented to address them, and the solutions he suggested and explored. So many and various are these, however, that they constitute not just Plato's philosophy but much of philosophy proper. Part of his legacy, they are also what we inevitably bring to our reading of him.

Socrates

Socrates is the central figure in most of Plato's works. In some dialogues he is thought to be—and probably is—based to some extent on the historical Socrates. As a result, these are often called "Socratic" dialogues. In the so-called transitional, middle, and late dialogues, however, he is thought to be increasingly a mouthpiece for ideas that go well beyond Plato's Socratic heritage.

In the Socratic dialogues, philosophy consists almost exclusively in philosophically pointed questioning of people about conventionally recognized moral virtues. What is piety (*Euthyphro*)? Socrates asks, or courage (*Laches*)? or temperance (*Charmides*)? He seems to take for granted, moreover, that there are correct answers to these questions—that piety, courage, and temperance are each some definite characteristic or form (*eidos*, idea). He does not discuss the nature of these forms, however, or develop any explicit theory of them or our knowledge of them. He does not, for that matter, explain his interest in definitions, or justify his claim that if we do not know what, for example, justice is, we cannot know whether it is a virtue, whether it makes its possessor happy, or anything else of any significance about it (*Republic* 354b–c).

Despite this silence on Socrates' part, however, there is ample evidence that he sought definitions of forms because he thought of forms as epistemic first principles, and that he did so because his model of genuine or expert knowledge was that of craft (*technē*). As a shoemaker, for instance, treats a well-made shoe as a pattern or paradigm in making another, so the moral expert, if he existed, would look to the form of piety (or whatever) in order to decide what actions or people were pious and what it was that made them so (*Euthyphro* 6d–e). It is especially in the *Phaedrus*, with its attempt to say what a properly scientific rhetoric would look like, that we see these ideas being developed.

Socrates' style of questioning is called (by us, not him) an *elenchus*—from the Greek verb *elenchein*, meaning "to examine or refute": he asks what justice is; his interlocutor puts forward a definition he sincerely believes to be correct, at least for the moment; and he refutes this definition by showing that it conflicts with other beliefs the interlocutor sincerely holds and doesn't think he can reasonably abandon. In the ideal situation, which is never actually portrayed in the Socratic dialogues, this process continues until a satisfactory definition emerges—one that is not inconsistent with other sincerely held beliefs, and so can withstand elenctic scrutiny.

The goal of an elenchus is not just to reach adequate definitions of the virtues, however. Its primary aim is *moral reform*. For Socrates believes that, by curing people of the arrogance of thinking they know when they do not, leading the elenctically examined life makes them happier and more virtuous than anything else. Philosophizing is so important for human welfare, indeed, that Socrates is willing to accept execution rather than give it up (*Apology* 29b–d, 30a, 36c–e, 38a, 41b–c).

Platonic Philosophy

In a number of dialogues, Plato connects the relativist doctrines he attributes to some of the Sophists with the metaphysical theory of Heraclitus, according to which the perceptible things or characteristics we see around us are in constant flux or change—always *becoming*, never *being*. In the *Theaetetus*, he argues that Protagoras' claim that "man is the measure of all things" presupposes that the world is in flux; in the *Cratylus*, he suggests that the theory of flux may itself be the result of projecting Protagorean relativism onto the world (411b–c). Nonetheless, Plato seems to accept some version of this theory himself (see Aristotle, *Metaphysics* 987a32–4). In the *Symposium*, for example, Diotima argues that "everything mortal is preserved, not, like the divine, by always being the same in every way, but because what is departing and aging leaves behind something new, something such as it had been" (208a–b).

The theory of flux has clear repercussions for the Socratic elenchus. If perceptible things and characteristics are always in flux, how can justice or love be stable forms? How can there be stable definitions of them to serve as correct answers to Socrates' questions? And if there are no stable definitions, how can there be such a thing as knowledge of them? More generally, if perceptible things and characteristics are always in flux, always *becoming*, how can anything *be* anything? How can one know or say what anything *is*? Aristotle tells us that it was reflection on these fundamental questions that led Plato to "separate" the forms from perceptible things and characteristics (*Metaphysics* 987a29–b1). The famous ladder of love in the *Symposium* seems to reflect this separation (210a–212b).

Conceived in this way, forms seemed to Plato to offer solutions to the metaphysical and epistemological problems to which the elenchus and flux give rise. As intelligible objects, set apart from the perceptible world, they are above the sway of flux, and so are available as stable objects of knowledge, stable meanings or referents for words. As real, stable, and mind-independent entities, they provide the basis for the definitions Socrates seeks.

Like many proposed solutions to philosophical problems, however, Plato's raises new problems of its own. If forms really are separate from the world of flux our senses reveal to us, how can we know them? How can our words connect with them? If items in the perceptible world really are separate from forms, how can they owe what share of being they have to forms? In the *Meno*, *Phaedo*, and *Phaedrus*, Plato answers the first of these questions by appeal to the doctrine of recollection (*anamnēsis*). We have knowledge of forms through our soul's having had direct prenatal contact with them; we forget this knowledge when our souls become embodied at birth; then we "recollect" it in this life when our memories are appropriately jogged. He answers the second question by saying that items in the world of flux "participate" in forms by resembling them. Thus perceptible objects possess the characteristic of beauty because they resemble the form of beauty, which is itself beautiful in a special and basic way (*Symposium* 210b–211e).

The doctrine of recollection presupposes the immortality of the soul—something Plato argues for in the *Phaedrus* (245c ff.) and elsewhere (*Phaedo* 69e ff., *Republic* 10). It also presupposes some method of jogging our memories in a reliable way. This method is dialectic, which is a descendant of the Socratic elenchus. The "method of division," discussed in the *Phaedrus* (265d–266b) is part of dialectic, since it explains how correct definition must proceed.

Once acquired, such correct definitions are available as first principles or starting points for the various sciences. But if these are treated as "absolute," that is, to be accepted without argument, there is a problem: if the starting points are false, the entire system collapses (*Republic* 510c–d). It is here that dialectic comes in again. It defends these starting points—it renders them "unhypothetical"—not by deriving them from something yet more primitive (which is impossible, since they are "starting" points) but by defending them against all objections, by solving all the *aporiai*, or problems, to which they give rise (534b–c, 437a). With the objections solved, our intellectual vision is cleared and we are able then to see the forms these definitions define in something like the way we did before our souls became embodied (540a–b).

In the process of their dialectical defense, the definitions themselves undergo conceptual revamping, so that their consistency with one another—and hence their immunity to dialectical (elenctic) refutation—is revealed and ensured. This enables the philosopher (to whom the craft of dialectic belongs) to knit them all together into a single unified science of everything and so to "see things as a whole" (*Republic* 557c; cf. *Symposium* 210d–e). It is this unified science that provides the philosopher—and him alone—with genuine knowledge (533d–534a).

EUTHYPHRO, APOLOGY, AND CRITO

IN 399 BCE, AT THE AGE OF SEVENTY, Socrates was brought to trial by Meletus on a writ of impiety. In the *Euthyphro*, he is on his way to a preliminary hearing at which he will hear Meletus' formal charges for the first time and at which the official in charge of impiety cases—the King Archon—will determine whether there is a case to answer. Appropriately enough, the topic of the dialogue is the nature of piety. The *Apology* is (or purports to be) the speech of defense given at the trial itself. Under examination by Socrates, Meletus identifies his charges as these: Socrates is an atheist who believes in strange daimonic activities, in the visitations of a *daimonion*, or divine voice; he corrupts the youth by teaching these beliefs to them. A majority of the jurors found Socrates guilty of these charges. Athenian law allowed him to propose a counterpenalty to the death penalty demanded by Meletus and required the jury to choose which of them to impose. A yet larger majority of them voted for the death penalty. In the *Crito*, Socrates is in prison awaiting death by hemlock poisoning. Crito wants him to escape; Socrates explains why he cannot. The topic is legal or political obligation.

EUTHYPHRO

2 EUTHYPHRO:[1] What's new, Socrates, to make you leave the Lyceum,[2] where you usually spend your time, to spend it here today at the court of the King Archon?[3] Surely, *you* don't have some sort of lawsuit before the King, as I do.

SOCRATES: *Athenians* don't call it a lawsuit, Euthyphro, but an indictment.

EUTHYPHRO: What? Someone has indicted you, b
apparently, for I'm not going to accuse *you* of indicting someone else!

From *The Trials of Socrates: Six Classic Texts*, edited by C.D.C. Reeve (Indianapolis: Hackett, 2002).

1. Euthyphro was a *mantis*, or prophet (3b–c, 3e), a self-proclaimed authority on Greek religion (4e–5a), who takes very literally the stories embodied in its myths (5e–6b). If he is the Euthyphro mentioned in Plato's *Cratylus*, he was also interested in language and etymology (396d–397a).

2. The Lyceum was one of three great gymnasia outside the city walls of Athens.

3. The nine archons, chosen annually, were the chief public officials in Athens: one was civilian head of

SOCRATES: No, I certainly haven't.

EUTHYPHRO: But someone else has indicted you?

SOCRATES: Exactly.

EUTHYPHRO: Who is he?

SOCRATES: I hardly know the man myself, Euthyphro. He's young and unknown, it seems. But I believe his name's Meletus. He belongs to the Pitthean deme—if you recall a Meletus from that deme,[4] with straight hair, not much of a beard, and a slightly hooked nose?

EUTHYPHRO: No, I don't recall him, Socrates. But tell me, what indictment has he brought against you?

c SOCRATES: What indictment? Not a trivial one, it seems to me. I mean, it's no small thing for a young man to have come to know such an important matter. You see, according to him, he knows how the young men are being corrupted, and who's corrupting them. He's probably a wise man, who's seen that my own ignorance is corrupting his contemporaries, and is coming to accuse me to their mother the city, so to speak. In fact, he seems to me to be the only one who's starting up in politics correctly. For it is
d correct to take care of the young first, to make them the best possible, just as it's reasonable for a good farmer to take care of the young plants first and all the others afterward. And so Meletus, too, is presum-
3 ably first weeding out those of us who corrupt the young shoots, as he claims. Then, after that, he'll clearly take care of the older people and bring about the greatest goods, both in number and in quality, for the city. That, at any rate, is the likely outcome of such a start.

EUTHYPHRO: I hope it happens, Socrates, but I'm terribly afraid the opposite may result. You see, by attempting to do an injustice to you, it seems to me he's simply starting out by wronging the city at its very hearth.[5] Tell me, what on earth does he say you're doing that corrupts the young?

SOCRATES: Strange things, my excellent friend, at *b*
any rate on first hearing: he says I'm an inventor of gods. And because I invent new gods, and don't acknowledge the old ones, he's indicted me for the latter's sake, so he says.

EUTHYPHRO: I understand, Socrates. That's no doubt because you say your daimonic sign comes to you on each occasion. So he has written this indictment against you for making innovations in religious matters and comes before the court to slander you, knowing that such things are easy to misrepresent to the majority of people.[6] Why, they even mock *me* as if I were crazy, when I speak in the Assembly on religious matters and predict the future for them! And yet not one of my predictions has failed to come true. *c*
But all the same, they envy anyone like ourselves.[7] We mustn't give them a thought, though. Just meet them head on.

SOCRATES: Yes, my dear Euthyphro, but being mocked is presumably nothing to worry about. Athenians, it seems to me, aren't much concerned if they think someone's clever, so long as he doesn't teach his own wisdom. But if they think he's making other people wise like himself, they get angry, whether out of envy, as you say, or for some other reason. *d*

EUTHYPHRO: As to that, I certainly have no desire to test their attitude toward *me*.

SOCRATES: Don't worry. They probably think you rarely put yourself at other people's disposal, and aren't willing to teach your own wisdom. But I'm afraid they think my love of people makes me tell whatever little I know unreservedly to any man,[8] not only without charging a fee,[9] but even glad to lose money, so long as someone cares to listen to

---

state, one was head of the army (*polemarchos*), and six had judicial roles (*thesmothetai*). The King Archon dealt with important religious matters (such as the indictment against Socrates for impiety) and also with homicide (the subject of Euthyphro's indictment). The king's court, or porch (*stoa*), was in the marketplace (*agora*).

4. A deme was a relatively independent administrative unit rather like a village or township. Athens consisted of 139 of them.

5. The reference is to the communal hearth in the Prytaneum (*Apology* 36d note), which was the symbolic center of Athens.

6. Five hundred (or 501) of whom will serve on the jury that will eventually try Socrates.

7. That is, people who have the gift of prophecy. Socrates' sign is mantic, or prophetic (*Apology* 40a).

8. See *Apology* 30a.

9. See *Apology* 19d–20a, 31a–c.

e me. So, as I was just saying, if they were going to mock me, as you say they do you, there'd be nothing unpleasant about their spending time in the law court playing around and laughing. But if they're going to be serious, the outcome's unclear, except to you prophets.

EUTHYPHRO: Well, it will probably come to nothing, Socrates, and you'll fight your case satisfactorily, as I think I'll fight mine.

SOCRATES: But now, Euthyphro, what *is* this case of yours? Are you defending or prosecuting?

EUTHYPHRO: Prosecuting.

SOCRATES: Whom?

4 EUTHYPHRO: Someone I'm again thought to be crazy for prosecuting.

SOCRATES: What's that? Is your prosecution a wild-goose chase?

EUTHYPHRO: The goose is long past chasing: he's quite old.

SOCRATES: Who is he?

EUTHYPHRO: My father.

SOCRATES: My good man! Your own *father?*

EUTHYPHRO: Yes, indeed.

SOCRATES: But what's the charge? What's the lawsuit about?

EUTHYPHRO: Murder, Socrates.

SOCRATES: In the name of Heracles![10] Well,
b Euthyphro, I suppose most people don't know how it can be correct to do this. I mean, I can't imagine any ordinary person taking that action correctly, but only someone who's already far advanced in wisdom.

EUTHYPHRO: Yes, by Zeus, Socrates, far advanced indeed.

SOCRATES: Is the man your father killed one of your relatives then? Of course he must be, mustn't he? You'd hardly be prosecuting him for murder on behalf of a stranger.[11]

EUTHYPHRO: It's ridiculous, Socrates, for you to think it makes any difference whether the dead man's a stranger or a relative. It's ridiculous not to see that the sole consideration should be whether the killer killed justly or not. If he did, let him go, if he didn't, prosecute—if, that is to say, the killer shares your own hearth and table.[12] For the pollution's the same if you knowingly associate with such a person and don't *c*
cleanse yourself and him by bringing him to justice.

In point of fact, though, the victim was a day laborer[13] of mine, and when we were farming on Naxos, he worked the land there for us. Well, he got drunk, became enraged with one of our household slaves, and cut his throat. So my father tied him hand and foot, threw him in a ditch, and sent a man here to find out from the official interpreter what should be done. In the meantime, he ignored and neglected his captive as a murderer, thinking it mattered nothing if he did die. And that's just what happened: *d*
hunger, cold, and being tied up caused his death before the messenger got back from the interpreter.

That's precisely why my father and my other relatives are angry with me: because I'm prosecuting my father for murder on the murderer's behalf, when my father didn't even kill him, so they claim, and when, even if he definitely did kill him, it's wrong—since the dead man was a murderer—to concern yourself with the victim in that case. You see, it's impious, they say, for a son to prosecute his father for murder. *e*
Little do they know, Socrates, about the gods' position on the pious and the impious!

SOCRATES: But, in the name of Zeus, Euthyphro, do you think *you* have such exact knowledge about the positions the gods take, and about the pious and the impious, that in the face of these events, you've no fear of acting impiously yourself in bringing your father to trial?

EUTHYPHRO: I'd be no use at all, Socrates, and Euthyphro would be no different from the majority *5*
of people, if I didn't have exact knowledge of all such things.

---

10. Heracles (Hercules) was a hero of legendary strength. His famous labors—twelve extraordinarily difficult tasks—are alluded to at *Apology* 22a.

11. Normally, the close relatives of the victim took responsibility for prosecuting his murderer.

12. It is because Euthyphro shares hearth and table with his father—and so risks being contaminated by the pollution (*miasma*) thought to adhere to murderers—that he feels especially obliged to prosecute him.

13. A *pelatēs* or *thēs* (15d) was a free man who worked for his daily hire. He was, therefore, less a member of Euthyphro's household than even a slave would have been.

Socrates: So, my excellent Euthyphro, the best thing, it seems, is for me to become your student, and to challenge Meletus on this very point before his case comes to trial, telling him that even in the past I always considered it of great importance to know about religious matters, and that now, when he says I've done wrong through improvising and innovating concerning the gods, I've become your student. Shouldn't I say to him, "Meletus, if you agree that
b Euthyphro is wise about the gods, you should also regard me as correctly acknowledging them and drop the charge. But if you don't agree, prosecute this teacher of mine rather than me, for corrupting the old men—myself and his own father, me by his teaching, and his father by admonishment and punishment." If he isn't convinced by me, and doesn't drop the charge or prosecute you instead of me, shouldn't I say the same things in court as in my challenge to him?

Euthyphro: Yes, by Zeus, Socrates, and if he tried
c bringing an indictment against *me*, I think I'd soon find his weak spots, and the question in court would very quickly be about him rather than about me.

Socrates: I realize that as well as you do, my dear friend, and that's why I'm eager to become your student. I know that this Meletus, as well as others no doubt, pretends not to notice *you* at all, whereas he has seen *me* so sharply and so easily that he has indicted me for impiety.

Now then, in the name of Zeus, tell me what you were just claiming to know so clearly. What sort of thing would you say the holy and the unholy are, whether in cases of murder or of anything else? Or
d isn't the pious itself the same as itself in every action? And conversely, isn't the impious entirely the opposite of the pious? And whatever's going to count as impious, isn't it itself similar to itself—doesn't it, as regards impiety, possess one single characteristic?

Euthyphro: Absolutely, Socrates.

Socrates: Tell me, then, what do you say the pious and the impious are?

Euthyphro: Very well, I say that what's pious is precisely what I'm doing now: prosecuting those who commit an injustice, such as murder or temple robbery, or those who've done some other such wrong,
e regardless of whether they're one's father or one's mother or anyone else whatever. Not prosecuting them, on the other hand, is what's impious.

Why, Socrates, look at the powerful evidence I have that the law requires this—evidence I've already offered to show other people that such actions are right, that one must not let an impious person go, no matter who he may happen to be. You see, those very people acknowledge Zeus as the best and most just 6
of the gods, and yet they agree that he put his own father in fetters because he unjustly swallowed down his children, and that *he*, in his turn, castrated *his* father because of other similar injustices.[14] Yet they're extremely angry with *me*, because I'm prosecuting *my* father for his injustice. And so they contradict themselves in what they say about the gods and about me.

Socrates: Could this be the reason, Euthyphro, I face indictment, that when people say such things about the gods, I find them somehow hard to accept? That, it seems, is why some people will say I'm a wrongdoer. But now if you, who know so much about such matters, share these views, it seems that the rest of us must assent to them too. I mean, what can we b
possibly say in reply, when we admit ourselves that we know nothing about them? But tell me, by the god of friendship, do you really believe those stories are true?

Euthyphro: Yes, and still more amazing things, Socrates, that the majority of people don't know.

Socrates: And do you believe that there really is war among the gods? And terrible hostilities and battles, and other such things of the sort the poets relate, and that the good painters embroider on our sacred objects—I'm thinking particularly of the robe covered c
with embroideries of such scenes that's carried up to the Acropolis at the Great Panathenaean festival?[15] Are we to say that these are true, Euthyphro?

---

14. Cronus mutilated his father, Uranus (Sky), by cutting off his genitals when he was copulating with Gaea (Earth). He ate the children he had with his sister Rhea. Aided by her, however, their son Zeus escaped, overthrew Cronus, and fettered him.

15. The Acropolis, set on the steep rocky hill that dominates Athens, was the central fortress and principal sanctuary of the goddess Athena. It was the site of the Parthenon, as well as of other temples. The Great Panathenaean festival took place every four years and was a more elaborate version of the yearly festival that marked Athena's birthday. At it, her statue in the Parthenon received a new robe embroidered with scenes from the mythical battle of the gods and the giants.

Euthyphro: Not only those, Socrates, but as I mentioned just now, I will, if you like, tell you lots of other things about religious matters that I'm sure you'll be amazed to hear.

Socrates: I wouldn't be surprised. But tell me about them some other time, when we've the leisure. Now, however, try to answer more clearly the very question I asked before. You see, my friend, you didn't
d teach me adequately earlier when I asked what the
pious was, but you told me that what you're now doing is pious, prosecuting your father for murder.

Euthyphro: Yes, and what I said was true, Socrates.

Socrates: Perhaps. But surely, Euthyphro, there are also many other things you call pious.

Euthyphro: Yes, indeed.

Socrates: Do you remember, then, that what I urged you to do wasn't to teach me about one or two of the many pieties, but rather about the form itself, by virtue of which all the pieties are pious? You see, you said, I believe, that it was by virtue of one characteristic that the impieties are impious, and the
e pieties pious. Or don't you remember?

Euthyphro: I do indeed.

Socrates: Then teach me what that characteristic itself is, in order that by concentrating on it and using it as a model, I may call pious any action of yours or anyone else's that is such as it, and may deny to be pious whatever isn't such as it.

Euthyphro: If that's what you want, Socrates, that's what I'll tell you.

Socrates: That *is* what I want.

Euthyphro: In that case: what's loved by the gods
7 is pious, and what's not loved by the gods is impious.

Socrates: Excellent, Euthyphro! You've now given the sort of answer I was looking for. Whether it's true, however, that I don't know. But clearly you'll go on to demonstrate fully that what you say *is* true.

Euthyphro: Yes, indeed.

Socrates: Come on, then, let's examine what it is we're saying. A god-loved thing or a god-loved person is pious, whereas a god-hated thing or a god-hated person is impious. And the pious isn't the same as the impious, but its exact opposite. Isn't that what we're saying?

Euthyphro: It is indeed.

Socrates: And does it seem to be true?

b Euthyphro: It does seem so, Socrates.

Socrates: And haven't we also said that the gods quarrel and differ with one another, and that there's mutual hostility among them?

Euthyphro: Indeed, we did say that.

Socrates: But what are the issues, my good friend, on which differences produce hostility and anger? Let's examine it this way. If you and I differed about which of two groups was more numerous, would our differences on this issue make us hostile and angry toward one another? Or would we turn to calculation
and quickly resolve our differences? c

Euthyphro: Of course.

Socrates: Again, if we differed about which was larger or smaller, we'd turn to measurement and quickly put a stop to our difference.

Euthyphro: That's right.

Socrates: And we'd turn to weighing, I imagine, to settle a dispute about which was heavier or lighter?

Euthyphro: Certainly.

Socrates: Then what sorts of issues *would* make us angry and hostile toward one another if we disagreed about them and were unable to reach a settlement? Perhaps you can't say just offhand. But
examine, while I'm speaking, whether they're issues d
about the just and unjust, fine and shameful, good and bad. Whenever we become enemies, aren't these the issues on which disagreement and an inability to reach a settlement make enemies of us—both you and I and all other human beings?

Euthyphro: That is the difference, Socrates, and those are the things it has to do with.

Socrates: And what about the *gods*, Euthyphro? If indeed they differ, mustn't it be about those same things?

Euthyphro: Absolutely.

Socrates: Then, according to your account, my e
noble Euthyphro, different sets of gods, too, consider different things to be just, or fine or shameful, or good or bad. For if they didn't differ about these, they wouldn't quarrel, would they?

Euthyphro: That's right.

Socrates: Then are the very things that each group of them regards as fine, good, and just also the ones they love, and are the opposites of these the ones they hate?

Euthyphro: Of course.

Socrates: But the very same things, so you say,
that some gods consider to be just and others unjust 8

are also the ones that lead them to quarrel and war with one another when they have disputes about them. Isn't that right?

EUTHYPHRO: It is.

SOCRATES: Then the same things, it seems, are both hated and loved by the gods, and so the same things would be both god-hated and god-loved.

EUTHYPHRO: It seems that way.

SOCRATES: So, on your account, Euthyphro, the same things would be both pious and impious.

EUTHYPHRO: Apparently.

SOCRATES: So, you haven't answered my question, my excellent friend. You see, I wasn't asking you what the selfsame thing is that's both pious and impious. But a thing that's god-loved is, it seems, also god-
b hated. It follows, Euthyphro, that it wouldn't be at all surprising if what you're now doing in prosecuting your father was something pleasing to Zeus but displeasing to Cronus and Uranus, or lovable to Hephaestus and displeasing to Hera,[16] and similarly for any other gods who may differ from one another on the matter.

EUTHYPHRO: But, Socrates, I think that on this point, at least, none of the gods do differ—that anyone
c who has unjustly killed another should be punished.

SOCRATES: Is that so? Well, what about men, Euthyphro? Have you never heard them arguing that someone who has killed unjustly or done anything else unjustly should *not* be punished?

EUTHYPHRO: Why yes, they never stop arguing like that, whether in the law courts or in other places. For people who've committed all sorts of injustices will do or say anything to escape punishment.

SOCRATES: But do they agree, Euthyphro, that they've committed injustice, and, in spite of agreeing, do they still say that they shouldn't be punished?

EUTHYPHRO: No, they certainly don't say that.

SOCRATES: So it isn't just anything that they'll do or say. You see, I don't think they'd dare to say or argue that if they act *unjustly*, they should not be punished.
Instead, I think they deny acting unjustly, don't they? d

EUTHYPHRO: That's true, they do.

SOCRATES: So they don't argue that someone who acts unjustly should not be punished, though they do, perhaps, argue about *who* acted unjustly, *what* his unjust action consisted of, and *when* he did it.

EUTHYPHRO: That's true.

SOCRATES: Then doesn't the very same thing happen to the gods as well—if indeed they do quarrel about just and unjust actions, as on your account they do, and if one lot says that others have done wrong, and another lot denies it? For surely no one, my excellent friend, whether god or human being, dares to say
that one who acts unjustly should not be punished. e

EUTHYPHRO: Yes, what you say is true, Socrates, at least the main point.

SOCRATES: I think that men and gods who argue, Euthyphro, if indeed gods really do argue, argue instead about *actions*. It's about some action that they differ, some of them saying that it was done justly, others unjustly. Isn't that so?

EUTHYPHRO: Of course.

SOCRATES: Come then, my dear Euthyphro, and 9
teach me, too, that I may become wiser. A man committed murder while employed as a day laborer and died as a result of being tied up before the master who tied him up found out from the proper authorities what to do about him. What evidence do you have that all the gods consider this man to have been killed unjustly, and that it's right for a *son* to prosecute and
denounce his *father* for murder on behalf of such a b
man? Come, try to give me a clear proof that all gods undoubtedly consider this action to be right.If you can give me adequate proof of that, I'll never stop praising your wisdom.

EUTHYPHRO: But presumably that's no small task, Socrates, though I could of course prove it to you very clearly.

SOCRATES: I understand. You think I'm a slower learner than the jury, since it's clear that you'll prove to *them* that those actions of your father's were unjust and that the gods all hate them.

EUTHYPHRO: I'll prove it to them very clearly, Socrates, provided they'll listen to what I say.

SOCRATES: They'll listen all right, provided you c
seem to speak well. But a thought occurred to me while you were speaking, and I'm still examining it in

16. Hephaestus, the god of fire and of blacksmithing, was armor maker to the gods. His mother, Hera, the wife and sister of Zeus, threw Hephaestus off Olympus because he was lame and deformed. This act pleased her, not him. In revenge, Hephaestus made her a throne that held her captive when she sat on it. This act pleased him, not her. Similarly, Cronus cannot have been pleased at being fettered by Zeus (see 6a note).

my own mind: "Suppose Euthyphro so taught me that I became thoroughly convinced that all the gods do consider a death like that to be unjust. What more would I have learned from Euthyphro about what the pious and the impious are? *That action* would indeed be god-hated, so it seems. Yet it became evident just now that the pious and the impious aren't defined by that fact, since it became evident that what's god-hated is also god-loved. So I'll let you off on that point, Euthyphro. If you like, let's suppose that all the gods consider the action unjust, and that they all hate it. Is
d that, then, the correction we're now making in the account, that what *all* the gods hate is impious while what they *all* love is pious, and that whatever some love and others hate is neither or both? Is that how you'd now like us to define the pious and the impious?

Euthyphro: What's to prevent it, Socrates?

Socrates: Nothing on my part, Euthyphro. But you examine your own view, and whether by assuming it you'll most easily teach me what you promised.

e Euthyphro: All right, I'd say that the pious is what all the gods love, and its opposite, what all the gods hate, is the impious.

Socrates: Then aren't we going to examine that in turn, Euthyphro, to see whether what we said is true? Or are we going to let it alone and accept it from ourselves and from others just as it stands? And if someone merely asserts that something is so, are we going to concede that it's so? Or are we going to examine what the speaker says?

Euthyphro: We're going to examine it. However, I for my part think that this time what we said *is* true.

10 Socrates: Soon, my good friend, we'll be better able to tell. Consider the following: is the pious loved by the gods because it's pious? Or is it pious because it's loved?

Euthyphro: I don't know what you mean, Socrates.

Socrates: All right, I'll try to put it more clearly. We speak of a thing's being carried or carrying, and of its being led or leading, and of being seen or seeing. And you understand that these things are all different from one another and how they differ?

Euthyphro: I think I understand, at any rate.

Socrates: Then is there also something that's loved, and is it different from something that's loving?

Euthyphro: Certainly.

b Socrates: Then tell me whether the carried thing is a carried thing because it's carried or because of something else.

Euthyphro: No, it's because of that.

Socrates: Again, the led thing is so, then, because it's led and the seen thing because it's seen?

Euthyphro: Of course.

Socrates: So it's not seen because it's a seen thing; on the contrary, it's a seen thing because it's seen; nor is it because it's a led thing that it's led, rather it's because it's led that it's a led thing; nor is something carried because it's a carried thing, rather it's a carried thing because it's carried. So is what I mean completely clear, Euthyphro? I mean this: if
something's changed in some way or affected in c
some way, it's not changed because it's a changed thing; rather, it's a changed thing because it's changed. Nor is it affected because it's an affected thing; rather, it's an affected thing because it's affected. Or don't you agree with that?

Euthyphro: I do.

Socrates: Then isn't a loved thing, too, either a thing changed or a thing affected by something?

Euthyphro: Of course.

Socrates: And so the same holds of it as of our earlier examples: it's not because it's a loved thing that it's loved by those who love it; rather it's because it's loved that it's a loved thing?

Euthyphro: Necessarily.

Socrates: Now what are we saying about the d
pious, Euthyphro? On your account, isn't it loved by all the gods?

Euthyphro: Yes.

Socrates: So is that because it's pious or because of something else?

Euthyphro: No, it's because it's pious.

Socrates: So it's loved because it's pious, not pious because it's loved?

Euthyphro: Apparently.

Socrates: On the other hand, what's god-loved is loved—that is to say, god-loved—because the gods love it?

Euthyphro: Certainly.

Socrates: Then the god-loved is not what's pious, Euthyphro, nor is the pious what's god-loved, as you claim, but one differs from the other.

Euthyphro: How so, Socrates? e

Socrates: Because we agreed that the pious is loved because it's pious, not pious because it's loved. Didn't we?

Euthyphro: Yes.

SOCRATES: The god-loved, on the other hand, is so because it is loved by the gods; it's god-loved by the very fact of being loved. But it's not because it's god-loved that it's being loved.

EUTHYPHRO: That's true.

SOCRATES: But if the god-loved and the pious were really the same thing, my dear Euthyphro, then, if the pious were loved because it's pious, what's god-loved would in turn be loved because it's god-loved;
11 and if what's god-loved were god-loved because it was loved by the gods, the pious would in turn be pious because it was loved by them. But, as it is, you can see that the two are related in the opposite way, as things entirely different from one another. For one of them is lovable because it's loved, whereas the other is loved because it's lovable.

And so, Euthyphro, when you're asked what the pious is, it looks as though you don't want to reveal its being to me, but rather to tell me one of its affections—that this happens to the pious, that it's loved by all the gods. What explains it's being loved, how-
b ever, you still haven't said. So please don't keep it hidden from me, but rather say again from the beginning what it is that explains the pious's being loved by the gods or having some other affection—for we won't disagree about which ones it has. Summon up your enthusiasm, then, and tell me what the pious and the impious are.

EUTHYPHRO: But Socrates, *I* have no way of telling you what I have in mind. For whatever proposals we put forward keep somehow moving around and won't stay put.

c SOCRATES: Your proposals, Euthyphro, seem to be the work of my ancestor, Daedalus! Indeed, if I were to state them and put them forward myself, you might perhaps make a joke of me, and say that it's because of my kinship with him that my works of art in words run away and won't stay put.[17] But, as it is, the proposals are your own. So you need a different joke, since it's for *you* that they won't stay put, as you can see yourself.

EUTHYPHRO: But it seems to me, Socrates, that pretty much the same joke does apply in the case of our definitions. You see, *I'm* not the one who makes them move around and not stay put. Rather, *you* seem to me to be the Daedalus, since as far as I'm d
concerned they would have stayed put.

SOCRATES: Then, my friend, it looks as though I've grown cleverer in my area of expertise than my venerated ancestor, in that he made only his own works not stay put, whereas I do this to my own, it seems, and also to other people's. And the most subtle thing about my area of expertise is that I'm wise in it without wanting to be. You see, I'd prefer to have accounts stay put and be immovably established for me than to acquire the wealth of Tantalus[18] and the wisdom of Daedalus combined. But e
enough of this. Since you seem to me to be getting sated, I'll do my best to help you teach me about the pious—and don't you give up before you do. See whether you don't think that the pious as a whole must be just.

EUTHYPHRO: Yes, I do.

SOCRATES: Then is the just as a whole also pious? 12
Or while the pious as a whole is just, is the just as a whole not pious, but part of it pious and part of it something else?

EUTHYPHRO: I don't follow what you're saying, Socrates.

SOCRATES: And yet you're as much younger as wiser than I. But as I say, your wealth of wisdom has weakened you. Well, pull yourself together, my dear fellow. What I'm saying isn't hard to understand. You see, what I'm saying is just the opposite of what the poet said, who wrote:

> With Zeus the maker, who caused all these things
> to come about,
> You will not quarrel, since where there's dread b
> there's shame too.[19]

---

17. Daedalus was a legendary sculptor of great skill. His statues were so lifelike that they moved around by themselves just like living things. Socrates' father, Sophroniscus, is alleged to have been a sculptor or stone carver, and some of the statues on the Acropolis may have been attributed to Socrates himself.

18. Tantalus, son of Zeus, was a legendary king proverbial for his wealth, who enjoyed the privilege of dining with the gods. He killed and cooked his son, Pelops, and mixed pieces of his flesh in with the gods' food to see whether they could detect it. He was punished in Hades by being "tantalized"—any food or water he reached for always eluded his grasp.

19. Author unknown.

I disagree with this poet. Shall I tell you where?

EUTHYPHRO: Of course.

SOCRATES: It doesn't seem to me that "where there's dread there's shame too." For many people seem to me to dread disease and poverty and many other things of that sort, but though they dread them, they feel no shame at what they dread. Or don't you agree?

EUTHYPHRO: Of course.

SOCRATES: But where there's shame, there is also dread. For if anyone feels shame at a certain action—if he's ashamed of it—doesn't he fear, doesn't he
c dread, a reputation for wickedness at the same time?

EUTHYPHRO: He certainly does dread it.

SOCRATES: Then it isn't right to say that "where there's dread, there's shame too." But where there's shame there's also dread, even though shame isn't found everywhere there's dread. You see, dread is broader than shame, I think. For shame is a part of fear, just as odd is of number. Hence where there's a number, there isn't something odd too, but where there's something odd there is also a number. Do you follow me now at least?

EUTHYPHRO: Of course.

SOCRATES: Well, that's the sort of thing I was asking
d just now: whenever there's something just, is there also something pious? Or is something just whenever it's pious, but not pious whenever it's just, because the pious is part of the just? Is that what we're to say, or do you disagree?

EUTHYPHRO: No, let's say that, since it seems to me you're right.

SOCRATES: Then consider the next point. If the pious is a part of what's just, we must, it seems, find out what part of the just the pious is. Now if you asked me about one of the things we just mentioned, for example, which part of number is the even—that is to say, what sort of number it is—I'd say that it's any number not indivisible by two, but divisible by it. Or don't you agree?

EUTHYPHRO: Yes, I do.

e SOCRATES: Then you try to teach me in the same fashion what part of the just is pious. Then we can tell Meletus not to treat us unjustly any longer or indict us for impiety, since I've now been sufficiently instructed by you about what things are holy or pious and what aren't.

EUTHYPHRO: Well then, it seems to me, Socrates, that the part of the just that's holy or pious is the one concerned with tending to the gods, while the remaining part of the just is concerned with tending to human beings.

SOCRATES: You seem to me to have put that very
well, Euthyphro. But I'm still lacking one small 13
piece of information. You see, I don't yet understand this tending you're talking about. You surely don't mean that in just the way that there's tending to other things, there's tending to the gods too. We do speak this way, don't we? We say, for example, that not everyone knows how to tend to horses, but only horse trainers. Isn't that right?

EUTHYPHRO: Of course.

SOCRATES: Because horse training is expertise in tending to horses?

EUTHYPHRO: Yes. b

SOCRATES: Nor does everyone know how to tend to dogs, but only dog trainers.

EUTHYPHRO: That's right.

SOCRATES: Because dog training is expertise in tending to dogs.

EUTHYPHRO: Yes.

SOCRATES: And cattle breeding is expertise in tending to cattle.

EUTHYPHRO: Of course.

SOCRATES: Well, but piety or holiness is tending to the gods, Euthyphro? That's what you're saying?

EUTHYPHRO: It is.

SOCRATES: But doesn't all tending accomplish the same end? I mean something like some good or benefit for what's being tended to—as you see that horses tended to by horse trainers are benefited and made better. Or don't you agree that they are?

EUTHYPHRO: Yes, I do.

SOCRATES: And so dogs, of course, are benefited by
dog training and cattle by cattle breeding, and simi- c
larly for all the others. Or do you think that tending aims to harm what's being tended?

EUTHYPHRO: No, by Zeus, I don't.

SOCRATES: Rather, it aims to benefit it?

EUTHYPHRO: Certainly.

SOCRATES: Then if piety is tending to the gods, does it benefit the gods and make the gods better? Would you concede that whenever you do something pious, you're making some god better?

EUTHYPHRO: No, by Zeus, I wouldn't.

SOCRATES: No, I didn't think that that was what you meant, Euthyphro—far from it. But it is why I asked what you did mean by tending to the gods, *d* because I didn't think you meant that sort of tending.

EUTHYPHRO: And you were right, Socrates, since that's not the sort I meant.

SOCRATES: All right. But then what sort of tending to the gods would the pious be?

EUTHYPHRO: The very sort of tending, Socrates, that slaves provide to their masters.

SOCRATES: I understand. Then it would seem to be some sort of service to the gods.

EUTHYPHRO: It is indeed.

SOCRATES: Now could you tell me about service to doctors? What result does that service—insofar as it is service—aim to produce? Don't you think it aims at health?

EUTHYPHRO: I do.

SOCRATES: What about service to shipbuilders? What result does the service aim to produce?

EUTHYPHRO: Clearly, Socrates, its aim is a ship.

e SOCRATES: And in the case of service to builders, I suppose, the aim is a house?

EUTHYPHRO: Yes.

SOCRATES: Then tell me, my good friend, at what result does service to the gods aim? Clearly, you know, since you say you've a finer knowledge of religious matters than any other human being.

EUTHYPHRO: Yes, and what I say is true, Socrates.

SOCRATES: Then tell me, in the name of Zeus, what is that supremely fine result that the gods produce by using our services?

EUTHYPHRO: They produce many fine ones, Socrates.

14 SOCRATES: So too do generals, my friend. Nonetheless, you could easily tell me the main one, which is to produce victory in war, is it not?

EUTHYPHRO: Certainly.

SOCRATES: And farmers, too, I think, produce many fine results. Nonetheless, the main one is to produce food from the earth.

EUTHYPHRO: Of course.

SOCRATES: What, then, about the many fine results that the gods produce? Which is the main one they produce?

EUTHYPHRO: I told you a moment ago, Socrates, *b* that it's a pretty difficult task to learn the exact truth about all these matters. But to put it simply: if a person knows how to do and say the things that are pleasing to the gods in prayer and sacrifice—those are the ones that are pious. And actions like them preserve both the private welfare of households and the common welfare of the city, whereas those that are the opposite of pleasing are unholy, and they, of course, overturn and destroy everything.

SOCRATES: If you'd wanted to, Euthyphro, you could have put the main point I asked about much more briefly. But you're not eager to teach me—that's clear. You see, when you were just now on the *c* point of answering you turned away. If you had given the answer, I'd already have been adequately instructed by you about piety. But as it is, the questioner must follow the one being questioned wherever he leads. Once again, then, what are you saying that the pious, or piety, is? Didn't you say that it was some sort of knowledge of sacrificing and praying?

EUTHYPHRO: Yes, I did.

SOCRATES: And sacrificing is giving to the gods, and praying is asking from them?

EUTHYPHRO: Yes, indeed, Socrates.

SOCRATES: So, on that account, piety would be knowing how to ask from the gods and how to give *d* to them.

EUTHYPHRO: You've grasped my meaning perfectly, Socrates.

SOCRATES: Yes, my friend, that's because I really desire your wisdom and apply my mind to it, so that what you say won't fall on barren ground. But tell me, what is this service to the gods? You say it's asking for things from them and giving things to them?

EUTHYPHRO: I do.

SOCRATES: Well then, wouldn't asking in the right way consist of asking for the things we need from them?

EUTHYPHRO: What else could it be?

SOCRATES: And, conversely, giving in the right way would consist of giving them, in turn, the things they *e* need from us? For surely giving someone what he didn't at all need isn't something that an expert in the art of giving would do.

EUTHYPHRO: That's true, Socrates.

SOCRATES: Then piety, Euthyphro, would be a sort of expertise in mutual trading between gods and men.

EUTHYPHRO: Yes, trading, if that's what you prefer to call it.

SOCRATES: I don't prefer anything, if it isn't true. But tell me, what benefit do the gods get from the gifts they receive from us? I mean, what they give is clear to everyone, since we possess nothing good that *15* they don't give us. But how are they benefited by what they receive from us? Or do we get so much the better of them in the trade that we receive all our good things from them while they receive nothing from us?

EUTHYPHRO: But Socrates, do you really think gods are benefited by what they receive from us?

SOCRATES: If not, Euthyphro, what could those gifts of ours to gods possibly be?

EUTHYPHRO: What else do you think but honor and reverence and—as I said just now—what's pleasing to them.

b SOCRATES: So is the pious pleasing to the gods, Euthyphro, but not beneficial to them or loved by them?

EUTHYPHRO: No, I think that it's in fact the most loved of all.

SOCRATES: So, once again, it seems, the pious is what's loved by the gods.

EUTHYPHRO: Absolutely.

SOCRATES: Well, if you say that, can you wonder that your accounts seem not to stay put but to move around? And will you accuse me of being the Daedalus who makes them move, when you yourself are far more expert than Daedalus in the art of making them move in a circle? Or don't you see that our account has circled back again to the same place? For *c* surely you remember that earlier we discovered the pious and the god-loved are not the same, but different from one another. Or don't you remember that?

EUTHYPHRO: Yes, I do.

SOCRATES: Then don't you realize that you're now saying the pious is what the gods love? And that's the same, isn't it, as what's god-loved? Or is that not so?

EUTHYPHRO: Of course, it is.

SOCRATES: Then either we weren't right to agree before, or, if we were right, our present suggestion is wrong.

EUTHYPHRO: So it seems.

SOCRATES: So we must examine again from the beginning what the pious is, since I won't willingly give up until I learn this. Don't scorn me, but apply your mind to the matter in as many ways and as fully *d* as you can, and then tell me the truth—for you must know it, if indeed any human being does, and, like Proteus,[20] you mustn't be let go until you tell it. For if you didn't know with full clarity what the pious and the impious are, you'd never have ventured to prosecute your old father for murder on behalf of a day laborer. On the contrary, you wouldn't have risked acting wrongly because you'd have been afraid before the gods and ashamed before men. As things stand, *e* however, I well know that you think you have fully clear knowledge of what's pious and what isn't. So tell me what you think it is, my excellent Euthyphro, and don't conceal it.

EUTHYPHRO: Some other time, Socrates. You see, I'm in a hurry to get somewhere, and it's time for me to be off.

SOCRATES: What a way to treat me, my friend! Going off like that and dashing the high hopes I had that I'd learn from you what things are pious and what aren't. Then I'd escape Meletus' indictment by showing him that Euthyphro had now made me wise in *16* religious matters, and ignorance would no longer cause me to improvise and innovate about them. What's more, I'd live a better way for the rest of my life.

APOLOGY

17 I don't know, men of Athens, how you were affected by my accusers. As for me, I was almost carried away by them, they spoke so persuasively. And yet almost nothing they said is true. Among their many falsehoods, however, one especially amazed me: that you must be careful not to be deceived by me, since I'm a dangerously clever speaker. That they aren't *b* ashamed at being immediately refuted by the facts, once it becomes apparent that I'm not a clever speaker at all, that seems to me most shameless of them. Unless, of course, the one they call "clever" is

From *The Trials of Socrates: Six Classic Texts,* edited by C.D.C. Reeve (Indianapolis: Hackett Publishing Company, 2002). Translation by C.D.C. Reeve. Copyright © 2002. Reprinted by permission of the publisher.

20. Proteus, the Old Man of the Sea, was a god who could change himself into any shape he wished. In this way, he avoided being captured, until his daughter, Eidothea, revealed this secret: keep tight hold of him, no matter what he changes into.

the one who tells the truth. If that's what they mean,
I'd agree that I'm an orator—although not one of
their sort. No, indeed. Rather, just as I claimed, they
have said little or nothing true, whereas from me
you'll hear the whole truth. But not, by Zeus, men of
Athens, expressed in elegant language like theirs,
c arranged in fine words and phrases. Instead, what you
hear will be spoken extemporaneously in whatever
words come to mind, and let none of you expect me
to do otherwise—for I put my trust in the justice of
what I say. After all, it wouldn't be appropriate at my
age, gentlemen, to come before you speaking in polished, artificial language like a young man.

Indeed, men of Athens, this I positively entreat of
you: if you hear me making my defense using the
same sort of language that I'm accustomed to use
both in the marketplace next to the bankers' tables—
where many of you have heard me—and also in
other places, please don't be surprised or create an
uproar on that account. For the fact is that this is the
d first time I've appeared before a law court, although
I'm seventy years old. So the language of this place is
totally foreign to me. Now, if I were really a foreigner,
you'd certainly forgive me if I spoke in the accents
18 and manner in which I'd been raised. So now, too,
I'm asking you, justly it seems to me, to overlook my
manner of speaking (maybe it will be less good,
maybe it will be better), but consider and apply your
mind to this alone, whether I say what's just or not.
For that's the virtue or excellence of a juror,[1] just as
the orator's lies in telling the truth.

The first thing justice demands, then, men of
Athens, is that I defend myself from the first false
accusations made against me and from my first
accusers, and then from the later accusations and the
later accusers. You see, many people have been
accusing me in front of you for very many years
b now—and nothing they say is true. And I fear them
more than Anytus[2] and the rest, though the latter are
dangerous as well. But the earlier ones, gentlemen,
are more dangerous. They got hold of most of you
from childhood and persuaded you with their accusations against me—accusations no more true than
the current ones. They say there's a man called
Socrates, a "wise" man, a thinker about things in the
heavens, an investigator of all things below the earth,
and someone who makes the weaker argument the c
stronger. Those who've spread this rumor, men of
Athens, are my dangerous accusers, since the people
who hear them believe that those who investigate
such things do not acknowledge the gods either.
Moreover, those accusers are numerous and have
been accusing me for a long time now. Besides, they
also spoke to you at that age when you would most
readily believe them, when some of you were children or young boys. Thus they simply won their case
by default, as there was no defense. But what's most
unreasonable in all this is that I can't discover even
their names and tell them to you—unless one of
them happens to be a comic playwright. In any case, d
the ones who used malicious slander to persuade
you—as well as those who persuaded others after
having been persuaded themselves—all of these are
impossible to deal with. One cannot bring any of
them here to court or cross-examine them. One must
literally fight with shadows to defend oneself and
cross-examine with no one to respond.

So you too, then, should allow, as I claimed, that
there are two groups of accusers: those who accused
me just now and the older ones I've been discussing.
Moreover, you should consider it proper for me to
defend myself against the latter first, since you've e
heard them accusing me earlier, and at much greater
length, than these recent ones here.

All right. I must defend myself, then, men of
Athens, and try to take away in this brief time preju- 19
dices you acquired such a long time ago. Certainly,
that's the outcome I'd wish for—if it's in any way better for you and for me—and I'd like to succeed in my

1. A member of an Athenian jury (a *dikastēs*) combined the responsibilities that are divided between judge and jury in our legal system. Hence *dikastēs* is sometimes translated as "judge" and sometimes (as in the present translation) as "juror."

2. Anytus was a democratic leader who helped restore democracy to Athens in 403 BCE after the overthrow of the Thirty Tyrants (32c note), under whom he had lost most of his wealth. As a general in the Athenian army he faced indictment, but he allegedly "bribed the jury and was acquitted" (Aristotle, *Constitution of Athens* 27.5). There is evidence that he believed Socrates was responsible for the ruin of his son and that he was passionately opposed to the Sophists (Plato, *Meno* 89e–92c).

defense. But I think it's a difficult task, and I am not at all unaware of its nature. Let it turn out, though, in whatever way pleases the god. I have to obey the law and defend myself.

Let's examine, then, from the beginning, what the
b charge is from which the slander against me arose—the very one on which Meletus relied when he wrote the present indictment of me. Well, then, what exactly did the slanderers say to slander me? Just as if they were real accusers their affidavit must be read. It's something like this:

> Socrates commits injustice and is a busybody, in that he investigates the things beneath the earth and in the heavens, makes the weaker argument
> c the stronger, and teaches these things to others.

Indeed, you saw these charges expressed yourselves in Aristophanes' comedy.[3] There, some fellow named Socrates swings around claiming he's walking on air and talking a lot of other nonsense on subjects that I know neither a lot nor a little but nothing at all about. Not that I mean to disparage this knowledge, if anyone's wise in such subjects—I don't want to have to defend myself against more of Meletus' lawsuits!—but I, men of Athens, take no part in them. I call on the majority of you as witnesses to this, and I
d appeal to you to make it perfectly plain to one another—those of you who've heard me conversing (as many of you have). Tell one another, then, whether any of you has ever heard me discussing such subjects, either briefly or at length, and from this you'll realize that the other things commonly said about me are of the same baseless character.

In any case, none of them is true. And if you've heard from anyone that I undertake to educate people and charge fees, that's not true either. Although, it also
e seems to me to be a fine thing if anyone's able to educate people in the way Gorgias of Leontini does, and Prodicus of Ceos, and Hippias of Elis.[4] For each of them, gentlemen, can enter any city and persuade the young—who may associate with any of their own fellow citizens they want to free of charge—to abandon those associations, and associate with them instead, pay them a fee, and be grateful to them besides.

Since we're on that topic, I heard that there's another wise gentleman here at present, from Paros. For I happened to run into a man who has spent more money on Sophists than everyone else put together—Callias, the son of Hipponicus.[5] So I questioned him, since he has two sons himself.

"Callias," I said, "if your two sons had been born colts or calves, we could engage and pay a knowledgeable supervisor—one of those expert horse breeders or farmers—who could turn them into fine and good examples of their proper virtue or excel- b
lence. But now, seeing that they're human beings, whom do you have in mind to engage as a supervisor? Who is it that has the knowledge of *this* virtue, the virtue of human beings and of citizens? I assume you've investigated the matter, because you have two sons. Is there such a person," I asked, "or not?"

"Certainly," he replied.

"Who is he?" I said.

"His name's Evenus, Socrates," he replied, "from Paros. He charges five minas."[6]

---

3. The version of *Clouds* referred to here, which is earlier than the revised version we possess, was first staged in 423 BCE.

4. All three, like Evenus of Paros mentioned below, were Sophists—itinerant professors who charged sometimes substantial fees for popular lectures and specialized instruction in a wide variety of fields, including natural science, rhetoric, grammar, ethics, and politics. Sophists did not constitute a single school or movement, however, and were neither doctrinally nor organizationally united. Gorgias of Leontini in Sicily (c. 480–376) was primarily a teacher of rhetoric who was noted for his distinctive style. He is the author of the *Defense of Palamedes*, parts of which bear a striking resemblance to the *Apology* and may have either influenced or been influenced by it. Plato named a dialogue critical of rhetoric after him. Prodicus of Ceos, about whom little is known, was also a fifth-century teacher of rhetoric, with an interest in fine distinctions of meaning (*Protagoras* 337a–c) and the correctness of names (*Cratylus* 384a–c). Hippias of Elis, like Prodicus a contemporary of Socrates, claimed expertise in astronomy, physics, grammar, poetry, and other subjects. Two Platonic dialogues are named after him; he also appears in *Protagoras* (315b–c, 337c–338b).

5. Callias was one of the richest men in Greece and a patron of the Sophists. Plato's *Protagoras* is set in his house.

6. Evenus is described as a poet (*Phaedo* 60c–e) and as an orator (*Phaedrus* 267a). A few fragments of his

I thought Evenus blessedly happy if he truly did
c possess that expertise and taught it for so modest a fee. I, at any rate, would pride myself and give myself airs if I had knowledge of those things. But in fact, men of Athens, I don't know them.

Now perhaps one of you will interject: "But Socrates, what, then, is *your* occupation? What has given rise to these slanders against you? Surely if you weren't in fact occupied with something out of the ordinary, if you weren't doing something different from most people, all this rumor and talk wouldn't have arisen. Tell us, then, what it is, so that we don't judge
d you hastily." These are fair questions, I think, for the speaker to ask, and I'll try to show you just what it is that has brought me this slanderous reputation. Listen, then. Perhaps, some of you will think I'm joking. But you may be sure that I'll be telling you the whole truth.

You see, men of Athens, I've acquired this reputation because of nothing other than a sort of wisdom. What sort of wisdom, you ask, is that? The very sort, perhaps, that is *human* wisdom. For it may just be that I really do have that sort of wisdom, whereas the people I mentioned just now may, perhaps, be wise because they possess *superhuman* wisdom. I don't know what else to call it, since I myself certainly
e don't possess that knowledge, and whoever says I do is lying and speaking in order to slander me.

Please don't create an uproar, men of Athens, even if you think I'm somehow making grand claims. You see, I'm not the author of the story I'm about to tell, though I'll refer you to a reliable source. In fact, as a witness to the existence of my wisdom—if indeed it is a sort of wisdom—and to its nature, I'll present the god at Delphi to you.[7]

You remember Chaerephon, no doubt.[8] He was a friend of mine from youth and also a friend of your
21 party, who shared your recent exile and restoration.[9] You remember, then, what sort of man Chaerephon was, how intense he was in whatever he set out to do. Well, on one occasion in particular he went to Delphi and dared to ask the oracle[10]—as I said, please don't create an uproar, gentlemen—he asked, exactly as I'm telling you, whether anyone was wiser than myself. The Pythia drew forth the response that no one is wiser. His brother here will testify to you about it, since Chaerephon himself is dead.[11]

Please consider my purpose in telling you this, b
since I'm about to explain to you where the slander against me has come from. You see, when I heard these things, I thought to myself as follows: "What can the god be saying? What does his riddle mean? For I'm only too aware that I've no claim to being

elegies survive. A drachma was a day's pay for someone engaged in public works; a mina was a hundred silver drachmas.

7. Apollo, who was god of, among other things, healing, prophecy, purification, care for young citizens, music, and poetry.

8. A long-time companion of Socrates. He makes brief appearances in *Charmides* and *Gorgias*.

9. Members of the democratic party left Athens when the Thirty Tyrants came to power in 404 BCE. They returned to power when the tyrants were overthrown in 403.

10. The Delphic Oracle was one of the most famous in antiquity. There were two methods of consulting it. One method, involving the sacrifice of sheep and goats, was quite expensive but resulted in a written response. The other—the so-called method of the two beans—was substantially cheaper but resulted only in a response by lot. Since Chaerephon was notoriously poor, it seems probable that he consulted the oracle by the latter method (something also suggested by Socrates' characterization of the priestess as *drawing forth* the response at 21a). The inscriptions on the walls of the temple well convey the spirit the oracle stood for: know thyself; do nothing in excess; observe the limit; hate hubris; bow before the divine; glory not in strength. There is no unambiguous record of the oracle's ever having praised anyone for what we would think of as his significant or noteworthy positive achievements or abilities. On the other hand, there are many stories of the following kind. Someone who is powerful, grand, famous for his wisdom, or in some other way noteworthy for his accomplishments, asks the oracle to say who is wisest, most pious, happiest, or what have you, expecting that he himself will be named. But the oracle names some unknown person living in humble and quiet obscurity. What we know about the oracle, then, makes it very unlikely that it was praising Socrates for his positive contributions to wisdom and very likely that it was using him—as he himself comes to believe that it was (23a–b)—as an example of someone who was wise because he made no hubristic claims to wisdom.

11. The brother is Chaerecrates.

wise in anything either great or small. What can he mean, then, by saying that I'm wisest? Surely he can't be lying: that isn't lawful for him."

For a long time I was perplexed about what he meant. Then, very reluctantly, I proceeded to examine it in the following sort of way. I approached one of the people thought to be wise, assuming that in his
c company, if anywhere, I could refute the pronouncement and say to the oracle, "Here's someone wiser than I, yet you said I was wisest."

Then I examined this person—there's no need for me to mention him by name; he was one of our politicians. And when I examined him and talked with him, men of Athens, my experience was something like this: I thought this man seemed wise to many people, and especially to himself, but wasn't. Then I tried to show him that he thought himself
d wise, but wasn't. As a result, he came to dislike me, and so did many of the people present. For my part, I thought to myself as I left, "I'm wiser than that person. For it's likely that neither of us knows anything fine and good, but he thinks he knows something he doesn't know, whereas I, since I don't in fact know, don't think that I do either. At any rate, it seems that I'm wiser than he in just this one small way: that what I don't know, I don't think I know." Next, I approached another man, one of those thought to be wiser than the first, and it seemed to me that the same thing
e occurred, and so I came to be disliked by that man too, as well as by many others.

After that, then, I kept approaching one person after another. I realized, with distress and alarm, that I was arousing hostility. Nevertheless, I thought I must attach the greatest importance to what pertained to the god. So, in seeking what the oracle meant, I had to go to all those with any reputation
22 for knowledge. And, by the dog, men of Athens—for I'm obliged to tell the truth before you—I really did experience something like this: in my investigation in response to the god, I found that, where wisdom is concerned, those who had the best reputations were practically the most deficient, whereas men who were thought to be their inferiors were much better off. Accordingly, I must present all my wanderings to you as if they were labors of some sort that I undertook in order to prove the oracle utterly irrefutable.

You see, after the politicians, I approached the
poets—tragic, dithyrambic,[12] and the rest—thinking *b*
that in their company I'd catch myself in the very act of being more ignorant than they. So I examined the poems with which they seemed to me to have taken the most trouble and questioned them about what they meant, in order that I might also learn something from them at the same time.

Well, I'm embarrassed to tell you the truth, gentlemen, but nevertheless it must be told. In a word, almost all the people present could have discussed these poems better than their authors themselves. And so, in the case of the poets as well, I soon realized it wasn't wisdom that enabled them to compose their
poems, but some sort of natural inspiration, of just *c*
the sort you find in seers and soothsayers. For these people, too, say many fine things, but know nothing of what they speak about. The poets also seemed to me to be in this sort of situation. At the same time, I realized that, because of their poetry, they thought themselves to be the wisest of people about the other things as well when they weren't. So I left their company, too, thinking that I had gotten the better of them in the very same way as of the politicians.

Finally, I approached the craftsmen. You see, I was conscious of knowing practically nothing myself, but
I knew I'd discover that they, at least, would know *d*
many fine things. And I wasn't wrong about this. On the contrary, they did know things that I didn't know, and in that respect they were wiser than I. But, men of Athens, the good craftsmen also seemed to me to have the very same flaw as the poets: because he performed his own craft well, each of them also thought himself to be wisest about the other things, the most important ones; and this error of theirs seemed to overshadow their wisdom. So I asked myself on behalf
of the oracle whether I'd prefer to be as I am, not in *e*
any way wise with their wisdom nor ignorant with their ignorance, or to have both qualities as they did. And the answer I gave to myself, and to the oracle, was that it profited me more to be just the way I was.

From this examination, men of Athens, much hostility has arisen against me of a sort that is harshest

12. A dithyramb was a choral song in honor of the god Dionysus.

23 and most onerous. This has resulted in many slanders, including that reputation I mentioned of being "wise." You see, the people present on each occasion think that I'm wise about the subjects on which I examine others. But in fact, gentlemen, it's pretty certainly the god who is really wise, and by his oracle he meant that human wisdom is worth little or nothing. And it seems that when he refers to the Socrates here
b before you and uses my name, he makes me an example, as if he were to say, "That one among you is wisest, mortals, who, like Socrates, has recognized that he's truly worthless where wisdom's concerned."

So even now I continue to investigate these things and to examine, in response to the god, any person, citizen, or foreigner I believe to be wise. Whenever he seems not to be so to me, I come to the assistance of the god and show him that he's not wise. Because of this occupation, I've had no leisure worth talking about for either the city's affairs or my own domestic ones; rather, I live in extreme poverty because of my
c service to the god.

In addition to these factors, the young people who follow me around of their own accord, those who have the most leisure, the sons of the very rich, enjoy listening to people being cross-examined. They often imitate me themselves and in turn attempt to cross-examine others. Next, I imagine they find an abundance of people who think they possess some knowledge, but in fact know little or nothing. The result is that those they question are angry not at themselves, but at me, and say that Socrates is a thoroughly
d pestilential fellow who corrupts the young. Then, when they're asked what he's doing or teaching, they've nothing to say, as they don't know. Yet, so as not to appear at a loss, they utter the stock phrases used against all who philosophize: "things in the sky and beneath the earth," and "not acknowledging the gods," and "making the weaker argument the stronger." For they wouldn't be willing to tell the truth, I imagine: that it has become manifest they pretend to know, but know nothing. So, seeing that these people are, I imagine, ambitious, vehement, and numerous, and have
e been speaking earnestly and persuasively about me, they've long been filling your ears with vehement slanders. On the basis of these slanders, Meletus has brought his charges against me, and Anytus and Lycon along with him: Meletus is aggrieved on behalf of the poets, Anytus on behalf of the artisans and politicians, and Lycon on behalf of the orators. So, as I began by 24
saying, I'd be amazed if I could rid your minds of this slander in the brief time available, when there's so much of it in them.

There, men of Athens, is the truth for you. I've spoken it without concealing or glossing over anything, whether great or small. And yet I pretty much know that I make enemies by doing these very things. And that's further evidence that I'm right—that this is the prejudice against me and these its causes. Whether you investigate these matters now or later, you'll find b
it to be so.

Enough, then, for my defense before you against the charges brought by my first accusers. Next, I'll try to defend myself against Meletus—who is, he claims, both good and patriotic—and against my later accusers. Once again, then, just as if they were really a different set of accusers, their affidavit must be examined in turn. It goes something like this:

> Socrates is guilty of corrupting the young, and of not acknowledging the gods the city acknowledges, but new daimonic activities instead.

Such, then, is the charge. Let us examine each point c
in this charge.

Meletus says, then, that I commit injustice by corrupting the young. But I, men of Athens, reply that it's Meletus who is guilty of playing around with serious matters, of lightly bringing people to trial, and of professing to be seriously concerned about things he has never cared about at all—and I'll try to prove this.

Step forward, Meletus, and answer me. You regard it as most important, do you not, that our young peo- d
ple be as good as possible?

I certainly do.

Come, then, and tell these jurors who improves them. Clearly you know, since you care. For having discovered, as you assert, the one who corrupts them—namely, myself—you bring him before these jurors and accuse him. Come, then, speak up, tell the jurors who it is that improves them. Do you see, Meletus, that you remain silent and have nothing to say? Yet don't you think that's shameful and sufficient evidence of exactly what I say, that you care nothing at all? Speak up, my good man. Who improves them?

The laws.

But that's not what I'm asking, my most excellent
e fellow, but rather which *person*, who knows the laws themselves in the first place, does this?

These gentlemen, Socrates, the jurors.

What are you saying, Meletus? Are they able to educate and improve the young?

Most certainly.

All of them, or some but not others?

All of them.

That's good news, by Hera, and a great abundance of benefactors that you speak of! What, then, about
25 the audience present here? Do they improve the young or not?

Yes, they do so too.

And what about the members of the Council?[13]

Yes, the councilors too.

But, if that's so, Meletus, surely those in the Assembly, the assemblymen, won't corrupt the young, will they? Won't they all improve them too?

Yes, they will too.

But then it seems that all the Athenians except for me make young people fine and good, whereas I alone corrupt them. Is that what you're saying?

Most emphatically, that's what I'm saying.

I find myself, if you're right, in a most unfortunate situation. Now answer me this. Do you think that the same holds of horses? Do people in general improve
b them, whereas one particular person corrupts them or makes them worse? Or isn't it wholly the opposite: one particular person—or the very few who are horse trainers—is able to improve them, whereas the majority of people, if they have to do with horses and make use of them, make them worse? Isn't that true, Meletus, both of horses and of all other animals? Of course it is, whether you and Anytus say so or not. Indeed, our young people are surely in a very happy situation if only one person corrupts them, whereas all the rest benefit them.

c Well then, Meletus, it has been adequately established that you've never given any thought to young people—you've plainly revealed your indifference—and that you care nothing about the issues on which you bring me to trial.

Next, Meletus, tell us, in the name of Zeus, whether it's better to live among good citizens or bad ones. Answer me, sir. Surely, I'm not asking you anything difficult. Don't bad people do something bad to whoever's closest to them at the given moment, whereas good people do something good?

Certainly.

Now is there anyone who wishes to be harmed d
rather than benefited by those around him? Keep answering, my good fellow. For the law requires you to answer. Is there anyone who wishes to be harmed?

Of course not.

Well, then, when you summon me here for corrupting the young and making them worse, do you mean that I do so intentionally or unintentionally?

Intentionally, *I* say.

What's that, Meletus? Are you so much wiser at your age than I at mine, that you know bad people do something bad to whoever's closest to them at the given moment, and good people something good? Am I, by contrast, so very ignorant that I don't know e
even this: that if I do something bad to an associate, I risk getting back something bad from him in return? And is the result, as you claim, that I do so very bad a thing intentionally?

I'm not convinced by you of that, Meletus, and neither, I think, is anyone else. No, either I'm not corrupting the young or, if I am corrupting them, it's *un*intentionally, so that in either case what you say is 26
false. But if I'm corrupting them unintentionally, the law doesn't require that I be brought to court for such mistakes—that is, unintentional ones—but that I be taken aside for private instruction and admonishment. For it's clear that if I'm instructed, I'll stop doing what I do unintentionally. You, however, avoided associating with me and were unwilling to instruct me. Instead, you bring me here, where the law requires you to bring those in need of punishment, not instruction.

Well, men of Athens, what I said before is absolutely clear by this point, namely, that Meletus b
has never cared about these matters to any extent, great or small. Nevertheless, please tell us now, Meletus, how is it you say I corrupt the young? Or is it absolutely clear, from the indictment you wrote,

---

13. The Council consisted of 500 male citizens over the age of thirty, elected annually by lot, fifty from each of the ten tribes of Athens (32b note). The Council met daily (except for some holidays and the like) as a steering committee for the Assembly. Its responsibilities included state finance, public buildings, and the equipment of navy and cavalry.

that it's by teaching them not to acknowledge the gods the city acknowledges, but new daimonic activities instead? Isn't that what you say I corrupt them by teaching?

I most emphatically do say that.

Then, in the name of those very gods we're now discussing, Meletus, speak yet more clearly, both for
c my sake and for that of these gentlemen. You see, I'm unable to tell what you mean. Is it that I teach people to acknowledge that some gods exist—so that I, then, acknowledge their existence myself and am not an out-and-out atheist and am not guilty of that—yet not, of course, the very ones acknowledged by the city, but different ones? Is that what you're charging me with, that they're different ones? Or are you saying that I myself don't acknowledge any gods at all, and that that's what I teach to others?

That's what I mean, that you don't acknowledge any gods at all.

d You're a strange fellow, Meletus! What makes you say that? Do I not even acknowledge that the sun and the moon are gods, then, as other men do?

No, by Zeus, gentlemen of the jury, he doesn't, since he says that the sun's a stone and the moon earth.

My dear Meletus, do you think it's Anaxagoras you're accusing?

Are you that contemptuous of the jury? Do you think they're so illiterate that they don't know that the books of Anaxagoras of Clazomenae are full of such arguments? And, in particular, do young people learn these views from me, views they can occasion-
e ally acquire in the Orchestra[14] for a drachma at most and that they'd ridicule Socrates for pretending were his own—especially as they're so strange? In the name of Zeus, is that really how I seem to you? Do I acknowledge the existence of no god at all?

No indeed, by Zeus, none at all.

You aren't at all convincing, Meletus, not even, it seems to me, to yourself. You see, men of Athens, this fellow seems very arrogant and intemperate to me and to have written this indictment simply out of some sort of arrogance, intemperance, and youthful rashness. Indeed, he seems to have composed a
27 sort of riddle in order to test me: "Will the so-called wise Socrates recognize that I'm playing around and contradicting myself? Or will I fool him along with the other listeners?" You see, he seems to me to be contradicting himself in his indictment, as if he were to say, "Socrates is guilty of not acknowledging gods, but of acknowledging gods." And that's just childish playing around, isn't it?

Please examine with me, gentlemen, why it seems to me that this is what he's saying. And you, Meletus, answer us. But you, gentlemen, please remem- b
ber what I asked of you at the beginning: don't create an uproar if I make my arguments in my accustomed manner.

Is there anyone, Meletus, who acknowledges that human activities exist but doesn't acknowledge human beings? Make him answer, gentlemen, and don't let him make one protest after another. Is there anyone who doesn't acknowledge horses but does acknowledge equine activities? Or who doesn't acknowledge that musicians exist but does acknowledge musical activities? There's no one, best of men—if you don't want to answer, I must answer for you and for the others here. But at least answer my next question. Is there anyone who acknowledges the existence of daimonic activities but doesn't c
acknowledge daimons?

No, there isn't.

How good of you to answer, if reluctantly and when compelled to by these gentlemen. Well then, you say that I acknowledge daimonic activities, whether new or familiar, and teach about them. But then, on your account, I do at any rate acknowledge daimonic activities, and to this you've sworn in your indictment against me. However, if I acknowledge daimonic activities, surely it's absolutely necessary that I acknowledge daimons. Isn't that so? Yes, it is—I assume you agree, since you don't answer. But don't we believe that daimons are either gods or, at any rate, children of gods? Yes or no? d

Of course.

Then, if indeed I do believe in daimons, as you're saying, and if daimons are gods of some sort, that's precisely what I meant when I said that you're presenting us with a riddle and playing around: you're saying that I don't believe in gods and, on the contrary, that I do believe in gods, since in fact I do at least believe in daimons. But if, on the other hand, daimons are children of gods, some sort of bastard offspring of a nymph, or of whomever else tradition

14. The Orchestra was part of the marketplace (*agora*) in Athens.

says each one is the child, what man could possibly
believe that children of gods exist, but not gods? That
e would be just as unreasonable as believing in the
children of horses and asses—namely, mules—while
not believing in the existence of horses and asses.

Well then, Meletus, you must have written these
things to test us or because you were at a loss about
what genuine injustice to charge me with. There's no
conceivable way you could persuade any man with
even the slightest intelligence that the same person
believes in both daimonic activities and gods, and,
on the contrary, that this same person believes nei-
28 ther in daimons, nor in gods, nor in heroes.[15]

In fact, then, men of Athens, it doesn't seem to me
to require a long defense to show that I'm not guilty
of the charges in Meletus' indictment, but what I've
said is sufficient. But what I was also saying earlier,
that much hostility has arisen against me and among
many people—you may be sure that's true. And *it's*
what will convict me, if I am convicted: not Meletus
or Anytus, but the slander and malice of many people. It has certainly convicted many other good men
as well, and I imagine it will do so again. There's no
b danger it will stop with me.

But perhaps someone may say, "Aren't you
ashamed, Socrates, to have engaged in the sort of
occupation that has now put you at risk of death?" I,
however, would be right to reply to him, "You're not
thinking straight, sir, if you think that a man who's
any use at all should give any opposing weight to the
risk of living or dying, instead of looking to this alone
whenever he does anything: whether his actions are
just or unjust, the deeds of a good or bad man. You
see, on your account, all those demigods who died
c on the plain of Troy were inferior people, especially
the son of Thetis, who was so contemptuous of danger when the alternative was something shameful.
When he was eager to kill Hector, his mother, since
she was a goddess, spoke to him, I think, in some
such words as these: 'My child, if you avenge the
death of your friend Patroclus and slay Hector, you
will die yourself immediately,' so the poem goes, 'as
your death is fated to follow next after Hector's.' But
though he heard that, he was contemptuous of death
and danger, for he was far more afraid of living as a
bad man and of failing to avenge his friends: 'Let me *d*
die immediately, then,' it continues, 'once I've given
the wrongdoer his just deserts, so that I do not
remain here by the curved ships, a laughingstock
and a burden upon the earth.' Do you really suppose
he gave a thought to death or danger?"

You see, men of Athens, this is the truth of the
matter: Wherever someone has stationed himself
because he thinks it best, or wherever he's been stationed by his commander, there, it seems to me, he
should remain, steadfast in danger, taking no
account at all of death or of anything else, in comparison to what's shameful. I'd therefore have been
acting scandalously, men of Athens, if, when I'd *e*
been stationed in Potidea, Amphipolis, or Delium[16]
by the leaders you had elected to lead me, I had, like
many another, remained where they'd stationed me
and run the risk of death. But if, when the god stationed me here, as I became thoroughly convinced
he did, to live practicing philosophy, examining
myself and others, I had—for fear of death or anything else—abandoned my station. 29

That would have been scandalous, and someone
might have rightly and justly brought me to court for
not acknowledging that gods exist, by disobeying the
oracle, fearing death, and thinking I was wise when I
wasn't. You see, fearing death, gentlemen, is nothing
other than thinking one is wise when one isn't, since
it's thinking one knows what one doesn't know. I
mean, no one knows whether death may not be the
greatest of all goods for people, but they fear it as if
they knew for certain that it's the worst thing of all.
Yet surely this is the most blameworthy ignorance of *b*
thinking one knows what one doesn't know. But I,
gentlemen, may perhaps differ from most people by
just this much in this matter too. And if I really were
to claim to be wiser than anyone in any way, it would
be in this: that as I don't have adequate knowledge
about things in Hades, so too I don't think that I have
knowledge. To act unjustly, on the other hand, to disobey someone better than oneself, whether god or
man, that I do know to be bad and shameful. In any
case, I'll never fear or avoid things that may for all I
know be good more than things I know are bad.

15. Heroes are demigods (28c), children of gods and mortals, whose existence therefore entails the existence of gods.

16. Three battles in the Peloponnesian War between Athens and its allies and Sparta and its allies.

c Suppose, then, you're prepared to let me go now
and to disobey Anytus, who said I shouldn't have
been brought to court at all, but that since I had been
brought to court, you had no alternative but to put
me to death because, as he stated before you, if I
were acquitted, soon your sons would all be entirely
corrupted by following Socrates' teachings. Suppose,
confronted with that claim, you were to say to me,
"Socrates, we will not obey Anytus this time. Instead,
we are prepared to let you go. But on the following
condition: that you spend no more time on this inves-
d tigation and don't practice philosophy, and if you're
caught doing so, you'll die." Well, as I just said, if you
were to let me go on these terms, I'd reply to you,
"I've the utmost respect and affection for you, men of
Athens, but I'll obey the god rather than you, and as
long as I draw breath and am able, I won't give up
practicing philosophy, exhorting you and also showing the way to any of you I ever happen to meet, saying just the sorts of things I'm accustomed to say:

> My excellent man, you're an Athenian, you belong
> to the greatest city, renowned for its wisdom and
> strength; are you not ashamed that you take care to
> acquire as much wealth as possible—and reputa-
> e tion and honor—but that about wisdom and truth,
> about how your soul may be in the best possible
> condition, you take neither care nor thought?

Then, if one of you disagrees and says that he *does*
care, I won't let him go away immediately, but I'll
question, examine, and test him. And if he doesn't
seem to me to possess virtue, though he claims he
does, I'll reproach him, saying that he treats the most
30 important things as having the least value, and inferior ones as having more. This I will do for anyone I
meet, young or old, alien or fellow citizen—but especially for you, my fellow citizens, since you're closer
kin to me. This, you may be sure, is what the god
orders me to do. And I believe that no greater good
for you has ever come about in the city than my service to the god. You see, I do nothing else except go
around trying to persuade you, both young and old
b alike, not to care about your bodies or your money as
intensely as about how your soul may be in the best
possible condition. I say,

> It's not from wealth that virtue comes, but from virtue comes money, and all the other things that are good for human beings, both in private and in public life.

Now if by saying this, I'm corrupting the young, *this* is what you'd have to think to be harmful. But if anyone claims I say something other than this, he's talking nonsense."

"It's in that light," I want to say, "men of Athens,
that you should obey Anytus or not, and let me go or
not—knowing that I wouldn't act in any other way,
not even if I were to die many times over." c

Don't create an uproar, men of Athens. Instead, please abide by my request not to create an uproar at what I say, but to listen. For I think it will profit you to listen. You see, I'm certainly going to say some further things to you at which you may perhaps exclaim—but by no means do so.

You may be sure that if you put me to death—a
man of the sort I said I was just now—you won't
harm me more than you harm yourselves. Certainly,
Meletus or Anytus couldn't harm me in any way:
that's not possible. For I don't think it's lawful for a d
better man to be harmed by a worse. He may, of
course, kill me, or perhaps banish or disenfranchise
me. And these *he* believes to be very bad things, and
others no doubt agree. But *I* don't believe this.
Rather, I believe that doing what he's doing now—
attempting to kill a man unjustly—is far worse.

So, men of Athens, I'm far from pleading in my
own defense now, as might be supposed. Instead, I'm
pleading in yours, so that you don't commit a great
wrong against the god's gift to you by condemning e
me. If you put me to death, you won't easily find
another like me. For, even if it seems ridiculous to say
so, I've literally been attached to the city, as if to a
large thoroughbred horse that was somewhat sluggish
because of its size and needed to be awakened by
some sort of gadfly. It's as just such a gadfly, it seems
to me, that the god has attached me to the city—one
that awakens, cajoles, and reproaches each and every
one of you and never stops alighting everywhere on 31
you the whole day. You won't easily find another like
that, gentlemen. So if you obey me, you'll spare my
life. But perhaps you'll be resentful, like people awakened from a doze, and slap at me. If you obey Anytus,
you might easily kill me. Then you might spend the
rest of your lives asleep, unless the god, in his com-
passion for you, were to send you someone else.

That I am indeed the sort of person to be given as a
b gift to the city by the god, you may recognize from
this: it doesn't seem a merely human matter—does
it?—for me to have neglected all my own affairs and
to have put up with this neglect of my domestic life
for so many years now, but always to have minded
your business, by visiting each of you in private, like a
father or elder brother, to persuade you to care about
virtue. Of course, if I were getting anything out of it or
if I were being paid for giving this advice, my conduct
would be intelligible. But, as it is, you can plainly see
for yourselves that my accusers, who so shamelessly
c accused me of everything else, couldn't bring themselves to be so utterly shameless as to call a witness to
say that I ever once accepted or asked for payment. In
fact, it's *I* who can call what I think is a sufficient witness that I'm telling the truth—my poverty.

But perhaps it may seem strange that I, of all people,
give this advice by going around and minding other
people's business in private, yet do not venture to go
before your Assembly and give advice to the city in
public. The reason for that, however, is one you've
heard me give many times and in many places: A
divine and daimonic thing comes to me—the very
d thing Meletus made mocking allusion to in the
indictment he wrote. It's something that began happening to me in childhood: a sort of voice comes,
which, whenever it does come, always holds me back
from what I'm about to do but never urges me forward. *It* is what opposes my engaging in politics—
and to me, at least, its opposition seems entirely right.
For you may be sure, men of Athens, that if I'd tried
to engage in politics I'd have perished long ago and
have benefited neither you nor myself.

e Please don't resent me if I tell you the truth. The
fact is that no man will be spared by you or by any
other multitude of people if he genuinely opposes a
lot of unjust and unlawful actions and tries to prevent
32 them from happening in the city. On the contrary,
anyone who really fights for what's just, if indeed he's
going to survive for even a short time, must act privately not publicly.

I'll present substantial evidence of that—not
words, but what you value, deeds. Listen, then, to
what happened to me, so you may see that fear of
death wouldn't lead me to submit to a single person
contrary to what's just, not even if I were to perish at
once for not submitting. The things I'll tell you are
of a vulgar sort commonly heard in the law courts,
but they're true nonetheless.

You see, men of Athens, I never held any other pub- b
lic office in the city, but I've served on the Council.
And it happened that my own tribe, Antiochis, was
presiding[17] when you wanted to try the ten generals—
the ones who failed to rescue the survivors of the
naval battle—as a group.[18] That was unlawful, as you
all came to recognize at a later time. On that occasion, I was the only presiding member opposed to
your doing something illegal, and I voted against you.
And though the orators were ready to lay information
against me and have me summarily arrested,[19] and
you were shouting and urging them on, I thought that
I should face danger on the side of law and justice,
rather than go along with you for fear of imprison- c
ment or death when your proposals were unjust.

This happened when the city was still under
democratic rule. But later, when the oligarchy had
come to power, it happened once more. The Thirty[20]

---

17. A *phulē* is not a tribe in our sense, but an administrative division of the citizen body, most probably of military origin. The presiding committee of the Council (25a note) consisted of the fifty members of one of the ten tribes, selected by lot to serve for one-tenth of the year. It arranged meetings of the Council and Assembly, received envoys and letters to the state, and conducted other routine business.

18. After the naval battle at Arginusae on the Ionian coast of Asia Minor (406 BCE), ten Athenian generals were indicted for failing to rescue survivors and to pick up the bodies of the dead. Both Council and Assembly voted to try them as a group, which was against Athenian law.

19. *Endeiknunai . . . kai apagein: Endeixis* (lay information against) and *apagoge* (have summarily arrested) were formal legal actions of a specific sort.

20. After Athens was defeated by Sparta in 404 BCE, its democratic government was replaced by a brutal oligarchy, the so-called Thirty Tyrants, which survived barely eight months. During that time it allegedly executed some 1,500 people, and many more went intoexile to escape. Two members of the Thirty—Critias and Charmides—were relatives of Plato and appear as Socratic interlocutors in the dialogues named after them. Socrates' association with them is often thought to have been one of the things that led to his indictment.

summoned me and four others to the Tholus[21] and
ordered us to arrest Leon of Salamis[22] and bring him
from Salamis to die. They gave many such orders to
many other people too, of course, since they wanted
to implicate as many as possible in their crimes. On
that occasion, however, I showed once again not by
words but by deeds that I couldn't care less about
d death—if that isn't putting it too bluntly—but that all
I care about is not doing anything unjust or impious.
You see, that government, powerful though it was,
didn't frighten me into unjust action: when we came
out of the Tholus, the other four went to Salamis and
arrested Leon, whereas I left and went home. I might
have died for that if the government hadn't fallen
shortly afterward.

There are many witnesses who will testify before
e you about these events.

Do you imagine, then, that I'd have survived all
these years if I'd been regularly active in public
affairs, and had come to the aid of justice like a good
man, and regarded that as most important, as one
should? Far from it, men of Athens, and neither
would any other man. But throughout my entire life,
33 in any public activities I may have engaged in, it was
evident I was the sort of person—and in private life I
was the same—who never agreed to anything with
anyone contrary to justice, whether with others or
with those who my slanderers say are my students. In
fact, I've never been anyone's teacher at any time.
But if anyone, whether young or old, wanted to listen
to me while I was talking and performing my own
task, I never begrudged that to him. Neither do I
b engage in conversation only when I receive a fee and
not when I don't. Rather, I offer myself for questioning to rich and poor alike, or, if someone prefers, he
may listen to me and answer my questions. And if any
one of these turned out well, or did not do so, I can't
justly be held responsible, since I never at any time
promised any of them that they'd learn anything from
me or that I'd teach them. And if anyone says that he
learned something from me or heard something in
private that all the others didn't also hear, you may *c*
be sure he isn't telling the truth.

Why, then, you may ask, do some people enjoy
spending so much time with me? You've heard the
answer, men of Athens. I told you the whole truth:
it's because they enjoy listening to people being
examined who think they're wise but aren't. For it's
not unpleasant. In my case, however, it's something,
you may take it from me, I've been ordered to do by
the god, in both oracles and dreams, and in every
other way that divine providence ever ordered any
man to do anything at all.

All these things, men of Athens, are both true and
easily tested. I mean, if I really do corrupt the young *d*
or have corrupted them in the past, surely if any of
them had recognized when they became older that
I'd given them bad advice at some point in their
youth, they'd now have come forward themselves to
accuse me and seek redress. Or else, if they weren't
willing to come themselves, some of their family
members—fathers, brothers, or other relatives—if
indeed their kinsmen had suffered any harm from
me—would remember it now and seek redress.

In any case, I see many of these people present
here: first of all, there's Crito, my contemporary and *e*
fellow demesman, the father of Critobulus here;[23]
then there's Lysanius of Sphettus, father of Aeschines
here;[24] next, there's Epigenes' father, Antiphon of
Cephisia here.[25] Then there are others whose brothers have spent time in this way: Nicostratus, son of
Theozotides,[26] brother of Theodotus—by the way,
Theodotus is dead, so that Nicostratus is at any rate
not being held back by him; and Paralius here, son
of Demodocus, whose brother was Theages;[27] and

21. The Tholus was a dome-shaped building, also called the Skias ("parasol"). The presiding committee of the Council (32b note 17) took its meals there.

22. Leon is otherwise unknown. The episode, however, is widely reported.

23. Crito was a well-off farm owner (*Euthydemus* 291e), able and willing to help his friends financially (38b, *Crito* 44b–c).

24. Aeschines of Sphettus (fourth century BCE) was a devoted follower of Socrates, present at his death (*Phaedo* 59b). He taught oratory and wrote speeches for the law courts. He also wrote Socratic dialogues, only fragments of which are extant.

25. Epigenes was present at Socrates' death (*Phaedo* 59b) and was a member of his circle.

26. Theozotides introduced two important democratic reforms after the fall of the Thirty Tyrants (32c note 20).

27. Otherwise largely unknown.

34 there's Adeimantus, the son of Ariston, whose brother
is Plato here, and Aeantodorus, whose brother here is
Apollodorus.[28] And there are many others I could
mention, some of whom Meletus most certainly
ought to have called as witnesses in the course of his
own speech. If he forgot to do so, let him call them
now—I yield time to him. Let him tell us if he has
any such witness. No, it's entirely the opposite, gentlemen. You'll find that they're all prepared to come
to my aid, their corruptor, the one who, Meletus
b and Anytus claim, is doing harm to their families.
Of course, the corrupted ones themselves might
indeed have reason to come to my aid. But the
*un*corrupted ones, their relatives, who are older men
now, what reason could they possibly have to support
me, other than the right and just one: that they know
perfectly well that Meletus is lying, whereas I am
telling the truth?

Well then, gentlemen, those, and perhaps other similar things, are pretty much all I have to say in my
defense. But perhaps one of you might be resentful
when he recalls his own behavior. Perhaps when he
c was contesting even a lesser charge than this charge,
he positively entreated the jurors with copious tears,
bringing forward his children and many other relatives and friends as well, in order to arouse as much
pity as possible. And then he finds that I'll do none of
these things, not even when I'm facing what might be
considered the ultimate danger. Perhaps someone
with these thoughts might feel more willful where
I'm concerned and, made angry by these very same
thoughts, cast his vote in anger. Well, if there's some-
d one like that among you—of course, I don't expect
there to be, but *if* there is—I think it appropriate for
me to answer him as follows: "I do indeed have relatives, my excellent man. As Homer puts it,[29] I too
'wasn't born from oak or from rock' but from human
parents. And so I do have relatives, sons too, men of
Athens, three of them, one already a young man
while two are still children. Nonetheless, I won't
bring any of them forward here and then entreat you
to vote for my acquittal."

Why, you may ask, will I do none of these things?
Not because I'm willful, men of Athens, or want to e
dishonor you—whether I'm boldly facing death or
not is a separate story. The point has to do with reputation—yours and mine and that of the entire city:
it doesn't seem noble to me to do these things, especially at my age and with my reputation—for
whether truly or falsely, it's firmly believed in any
case that Socrates is superior to the majority of peo- 35
ple in some way. Therefore, if those of *you* who are
believed to be superior—in either wisdom or
courage or any other virtue whatever—behave like
that, it would be shameful.

I've often seen people of this sort when they're on
trial: they're thought to be someone, yet they do
astonishing things—as if they imagined they'd suffer
something terrible if they died and would be immortal if only you didn't kill them. People like that seem
to me to bring such shame to the city that any foreigner might well suppose that those among the
Athenians who are superior in virtue—the ones they b
select from among themselves for political office and
other positions of honor—are no better than women.
I say this, men of Athens, because none of us who are
in any way whatever thought to be someone should
behave like that, nor, if we attempt to do so, should
you allow it. On the contrary, you should make it
clear you're far more likely to convict someone who
makes the city despicable by staging these pathetic
scenes than someone who minds his behavior.

Reputation aside, gentlemen, it doesn't seem just
to me to entreat the jury—nor to be acquitted by c
entreating it—but rather to inform it and persuade
it. After all, a juror doesn't sit in order to grant justice
as a favor, but to decide where justice lies. And he
has sworn on oath not that he'll favor whomever he
pleases, but that he'll judge according to law. We
shouldn't accustom you to breaking your oath, then,
nor should you become accustomed to doing so—
neither of us would be doing something holy if we
did. Hence don't expect me, men of Athens, to act
toward you in ways I consider to be neither noble, d
nor just, nor pious—most especially, by Zeus, when
I'm being prosecuted for *impiety* by Meletus here.
You see, if I tried to persuade and to force you by
entreaties, after you've sworn an oath, I clearly
would be teaching you not to believe in the existence of gods, and my defense would literally convict

---

28. Apollodorus, an enthusiastic follower of Socrates, given to emotion (*Phaedo* 59a–b, 117c–d), is the narrator in the *Symposium*.

29. Homer, *Odyssey* 19.163.

me of not acknowledging gods. But that's far from being the case: I do acknowledge them, men of Athens, as none of my accusers does. I turn it over to you and to the god to judge me in whatever way will be best for me and for yourselves.

e There are many reasons, men of Athens, why I'm not resentful at this outcome—that you voted to convict me—and this outcome wasn't unexpected by me.
36 I'm much more surprised at the number of votes cast on each side: I didn't think that the decision would be by so few votes but by a great many. Yet now, it seems, that if a mere thirty votes had been cast differently, I'd have been acquitted. Or rather, it seems to me that where Meletus is concerned, I've been acquitted even as things stand. And not merely acquitted. On the contrary, one thing at least is clear to everyone: if Anytus had not come forward with Lycon to accuse me, Meletus would have been fined a thousand drachmas, since he wouldn't have
b received a fifth of the votes.

But be that as it may, the man demands the death penalty for me. Well then, what counterpenalty should I now propose to you, men of Athens? Or is it clear that it's whatever I deserve? What then should it be? What do I deserve to suffer or pay just because I didn't mind my own business throughout my life? Because I didn't care about the things most people care about—making money, managing an estate, or being a general, a popular leader, or holding some other political office, or joining the cabals and factions that come to exist in a city—but thought myself too honest, in truth, to engage in these things and
c survive? Because I didn't engage in things, if engaging in them was going to benefit neither you nor myself, but instead went to each of you privately and tried to perform what I claim is the greatest benefaction? That was what I did. I tried to persuade each of you to care first not about any of his possessions, but about himself and how he'll become best and wisest; and not primarily about the city's possessions, but about the city itself; and to care about all other things in the same way.

d What, then, do I deserve to suffer for being such a man? Something good, men of Athens, if I'm indeed to propose a penalty that I truly deserve. Yes, and the sort of good thing, too, that would be appropriate for me. What, then, is appropriate for a poor man who is a public benefactor and needs to have the leisure to exhort you? Nothing could be more appropriate, men of Athens, than for such a man to be given free meals in the Prytaneum—much more so for him, at any rate, than for any one of you who has won a victory at Olympia, whether with a single horse or with a pair or a team of four.[30] You see, he makes you think you're happy, whereas I make you actually happy. Besides, he doesn't need to be sustained in that way, but I do need it. So if, as justice demands, e
I must propose a penalty I deserve, that's the penalty
I propose: free meals in the Prytaneum. 37

Now perhaps when I say this, you may think I'm speaking in a quite willful manner—just as when I talked about appeals to pity and supplications. That's not so, men of Athens, rather it's something like this: I'm convinced that I never intentionally do injustice to any man—but I can't get you to share my conviction, because we've talked together a short time. I say this, because if you had a law, as other men in fact do, not to try a capital charge in a single day, but over b
several, I think you'd be convinced. But as things stand, it isn't easy to clear myself of huge slanders in a short time.

Since *I'm* convinced that I've done injustice to no one, however, I'm certainly not likely to do myself injustice, to announce that I deserve something bad and to propose a penalty of that sort for myself. Why should I do that? In order not to suffer what Meletus proposes as a penalty for me, when I say that I don't know whether it's a good or a bad thing? As an alternative to that, am I then to choose one of the things I know very well to be bad and propose it? Imprisonment, for example? And why should I live in prison, c
enslaved to the regularly appointed officers, the Eleven?[31] All right, a fine with imprisonment until I pay? But in my case the effect would be precisely the one I just now described, since I haven't the means to pay.

Well then, should I propose exile? Perhaps that's what *you'd* propose for me. But I'd certainly have to have an excessive love of life, men of Athens, to be so

---

30. The Prytaneum, a building on the northeast slope of the Acropolis, was the symbolic center of Athens, where the communal hearth was housed.

31. Officials appointed by lot to be in charge of prisons and executions.

irrational as to do that. I see that you, my fellow citizens, were unable to tolerate my discourses and dis-
d cussions but came to find them so burdensome and
odious that you're now seeking to get rid of them. Is
it likely, then, that I'll infer that others will find them
easy to bear? Far from it, men of Athens. It would be
a fine life for me, indeed, a man of my age, to go into
exile and spend his life exchanging one city for
another, because he's always being expelled. You see,
I well know that wherever I go, the young will come
to hear me speaking, just as they do here. And if I
drive them away, they will themselves persuade their
elders to expel me; whereas if I don't drive them
away, their fathers and relatives will expel me
e because of these same young people.

Now perhaps someone may say, "But by keeping
quiet and minding your own business, Socrates,
wouldn't it be possible for you to live in exile for us?"
This is the very hardest point on which to convince
some of you. You see, if I say that to do *that* would be
to disobey the god, and that this is why I can't mind
my own business, you won't believe me, since you'll
38 suppose I'm being ironical. But again, if I say it's the
greatest good for a man to discuss virtue every day,
and the other things you've heard me discussing and
examining myself and others about, on the grounds
that the unexamined life isn't worth living for a
human being, you'll believe me even less when I say
that. But in fact, things are just as I claim them to be,
men of Athens, though it isn't easy to convince you
of them. At the same time, I'm not accustomed to
thinking that I deserve anything bad. If I had the
b means, I'd have proposed a fine of as much as I could
afford to pay, since that would have done me no
harm at all. But as things stand, I don't have them—
unless you want me to propose as much as I'm in fact
able to pay. Perhaps I could pay you about a mina of
silver. So I propose a fine of that amount.

One moment, men of Athens. Plato here, and
Crito, Critobulus, and Apollodorus as well, are urging me to propose thirty minas and saying that they
themselves will guarantee it.[32] I propose a fine of that
amount, therefore, and these men will be sufficient
guarantors to you of the silver.

For the sake of a little time, men of Athens, you're c
going to earn from those who wish to denigrate our
city both the reputation and the blame for having
killed Socrates—that wise man. For those who wish
to reproach you will, of course, claim that I'm wise,
even if I'm not. In any case, if you'd waited a short
time, this would have happened of its own accord.
You, of course, see my age, you see that I'm already
far along in life and close to death. I'm saying this
not to all of you, but to those who voted for the death
penalty. And to those same people I also say this: Per- d
haps you imagine, gentlemen, that I was convicted
for lack of the sort of arguments I could have used to
convince you, if I'd thought I should do or say anything to escape the penalty. Far from it. I *have* been
convicted for a lack—not of arguments, however,
but of bold-faced shamelessness and for being
unwilling to say the sorts of things to you you'd have
been most pleased to hear, with me weeping and
wailing, and doing and saying many other things I
claim are unworthy of me, but that are the very sorts e
of things you're used to hearing from everyone else.
No, I didn't think then that I should do anything
servile because of the danger I faced, and so I don't
regret now that I defended myself as I did. I'd far
rather die after such a defense than live like that.

You see, whether in a trial or in a war, neither I nor
anyone else should contrive to escape death at all 39
costs. In battle, too, it often becomes clear that one
might escape death by throwing down one's weapons
and turning to supplicate one's pursuers. And in
each sort of danger there are many other ways one
can contrive to escape death, if one is shameless
enough to do or say anything. The difficult thing,
gentlemen, isn't escaping death; escaping villainy is
much more difficult, since it runs faster than death.
And now I, slow and old as I am, have been over- b
taken by the slower runner while my accusers, clever
and sharp-witted as they are, have been overtaken by
the faster one—vice. And now I take my leave, convicted by you of a capital crime, whereas they stand
forever convicted by the truth of wickedness and
injustice. And just as I accept my penalty, so must
they. Perhaps, things *had* to turn out this way, and I
suppose it's good they have.

Next, I want to make a prophecy to those who con- c
victed me. Indeed, I'm now at the point at which

32. Thirty minas (3,000 silver drachmas) was almost ten years' salary for someone engaged in public works.

men prophesy most—when they're about to die. I say
to you men who condemned me to death that as
soon as I'm dead vengeance will come upon you, and
it will be much harsher, by Zeus, than the vengeance
you take in killing me. You did this now in the belief
that you'll escape giving an account of your lives. But
I say that quite the opposite will happen to you.
There will be more people to test you, whom I now
d restrain, though you didn't notice my doing so. And
they'll be all the harsher on you, since they're
younger, and you'll resent it all the more. You see, if
you imagine that by killing people you'll prevent anyone from reproaching you for not living in the right
way, you're not thinking straight. In fact, to escape is
neither possible nor noble. On the contrary, what's
best and easiest isn't to put down other people, but to
prepare oneself to be the best one can. With that
prophecy to those of you who voted to convict me, I
take my leave.

e However, I'd gladly discuss this result with those who
voted for my acquittal while the officers of the court
are busy and I'm not yet on my way to the place
where I must die. Please stay with me, gentlemen,
just for that short time. After all, there's nothing to
prevent us from having a talk with one another while
it's still in our power. To you whom I regard as
40 friends I'm willing to show the meaning of what has
just now happened to me. You see, gentlemen of the
jury—for in calling *you* "jurors" I no doubt use the
term correctly—an amazing thing has happened to
me. In previous times, the usual prophecies of my
daimonic sign were always very frequent, opposing
me even on trivial matters, if I was about do something that wasn't right. Now, however, something has
happened to me, as you can see for yourselves, that
one might think to be, and that's generally regarded
as being, the worst of all bad things. Yet the god's sign
b didn't oppose me when I left home this morning, or
when I came up here to the law court, or anywhere
in my speech when I was about to say something,
even though in other discussions it has often stopped
me in the middle of what I was saying. Now, however, where this affair is concerned, it has opposed
me in nothing I either said or did.

What, then, do I suppose is the explanation for
that? I'll tell you. You see, it's likely that what has happened to me is a good thing and that those of you
who suppose death to be bad make an incorrect supposition. I've strong evidence of this, since there's no c
way my usual sign would have failed to oppose me,
if I weren't about to achieve something good.

But let's bear in mind that the following is also a
strong reason to hope that death may be something
good. Being dead is one of two things: either the
dead are nothing, as it were, and have no awareness
whatsoever of anything at all; or else, as we're told,
it's some sort of change, a migration of the soul from
here to another place. Now, if there's in fact no
awareness, but it's like sleep—the kind in which the d
sleeper has no dream whatsoever—then death would
be an amazing advantage. For I imagine that if someone had to pick a night in which he slept so soundly
that he didn't even dream and had to compare all the
other nights and days of his life with that one, and
then, having considered the matter, had to say how
many days or nights of his life he had spent better or
more pleasantly than that night—I imagine that not
just some private individual, but even the great
king,[33] would find them easy to count compared to e
the other days and nights. Well, if death's like that, *I*
say it's an advantage, since, in that case, the whole of
time would seem no longer than a single night.

On the other hand, if death's a sort of journey from
here to another place, and if what we're told is true,
and all who've died are indeed there, what could be
a greater good than that, gentlemen of the jury? If on
arriving in Hades and leaving behind the people who 41
claim to be jurors here, one's going to find those who
are truly jurors or judges, the very ones who are said
to sit in judgment there too—Minos,[34] Rhadaman-
thys, Aeachus, Triptolemus, and all the other
demigods who were just in their own lifetimes—
would the journey be a wretched one?

Or again, what would any one of you not give to
talk to Orpheus and Museus, Hesiod and Homer?[35]
I'd be willing to die many times over, if that were
true. You see, for myself, at any rate, spending time b
there would be amazing: when I met Palamedes or

---

33. The king of Persia, whose wealth and power made him a popular exemplar of human success and happiness.

34. Minos was a legendary king of Crete.

35. Orpheus was a legendary bard and founder of the mystical religion of Orphism. Museus, usually associated with Orpheus, was also a legendary bard.

Ajax, the son of Telemon, or anyone else of old who died because of an unjust verdict, I could compare my own experience with theirs—as I suppose it wouldn't be unpleasing to do. And in particular, the most important thing: I could spend time examining and searching people there, just as I do here, to find out who among them is wise, and who thinks he is, but isn't.

What wouldn't one give, gentlemen of the jury, to
c be able to examine the leader of the great expedition
against Troy, or Odysseus, or Sisyphus,[36] or countless other men and women one could mention? To talk to them there, to associate with them and examine them, wouldn't that be inconceivable happiness? In any case, the people there certainly don't kill one for doing it. For if what we're told is true, the people there are both happier in all other respects than the people here and also deathless for the remainder of time.

But you too, gentlemen of the jury, should be of good hope in the face of death, and bear in mind this single truth: nothing bad can happen to a good
d man, whether in life or in death, nor are the gods
unconcerned about his troubles. What has happened to me hasn't happened by chance; rather, it's clear to me that to die now and escape my troubles was a better thing for me. It was for this very reason that my sign never opposed me. And so, for my part, I'm not at all angry with those who voted to condemn me or with my accusers. And yet this wasn't what they had in mind when they were condemning and accusing me. No, they thought to harm me—and for that they deserve to be blamed.

This small favor, however, I ask of them. When my e
sons come of age, gentlemen, punish them by harassing them in the very same way that I harassed you, if they seem to you to take care of wealth or anything before virtue, if they think they're someone when they're no one. Reproach them, just as I reproached you: tell them that they don't care for the things they should and think they're someone when they're
worth nothing. If you will do that, I'll have received 42
my own just deserts from you, as will my sons.

But now it's time to leave, I to die and you to live. Which of us goes to the better thing, however, is unclear to everyone except the god.

Crito

43 SOCRATES: Why have you come at this hour, Crito?
Isn't it still early?

CRITO: It is indeed.

SOCRATES: About what time?

CRITO: Just before dawn.

SOCRATES: I'm surprised the prison warden was willing to let you in.

CRITO: He knows me by now, Socrates, I come here so often. And besides I've done him a good turn.

SOCRATES: Have you just arrived or have you been here for a while?

CRITO: For quite a while.

b SOCRATES: Then why didn't you wake me right
away, instead of sitting there in silence?

CRITO: In the name of Zeus, Socrates, I wouldn't do that! I only wish I weren't so sleepless and distressed myself. I've been amazed all this time to see how peacefully you were sleeping, and I deliberately kept from waking you, so that you could pass the time as pleasantly as possible. In the past—indeed, throughout my entire life—I've often counted you happy in your disposition, but never more so than in this present misfortune. You bear it so easily and calmly.

SOCRATES: Well, Crito, it would be an error for someone of my age to complain when the time has come when he must die.

CRITO: Other people get overtaken by such mis- c
fortunes too, Socrates, but their age doesn't prevent them in the least from complaining about their fate.

SOCRATES: That's right. But tell me, why *have* you come so early?

CRITO: I bring bad news, Socrates. Not bad in your view, it seems to me, but bad and hard in mine and

36. Sisyphus is a legendary king and founder of Corinth.

From *The Trials of Socrates: Six Classic Texts,* edited by C.D.C. Reeve (Indianapolis: Hackett Publishing Company, 2002). Translation by C.D.C. Reeve.

that of all your friends—and hardest of all, I think, for me to bear.

SOCRATES: What news is that? Or has the ship
d returned from Delos, at whose return I must die?[1]

CRITO: No, it hasn't returned *yet*, but I think it will arrive today, judging from the reports of people who've come from Sunium,[2] where they left it. It's clear from these reports that it will arrive today. And so tomorrow, Socrates, you must end your life.

SOCRATES: I pray that it may be for the best, Crito. If it pleases the gods, let it be so. All the same, I don't think it will arrive today.

44 CRITO: What evidence have you for that?

SOCRATES: I'll tell you. I must die on the day after the ship arrives.

CRITO: That's what the authorities say, at least.

SOCRATES: Then I don't think it will arrive today, but tomorrow. My evidence for this comes from a dream I had in the night a short while ago. So it looks as though you chose the right time not to wake me.

CRITO: What was your dream?

SOCRATES: I thought a beautiful, graceful woman
b came to me, robed in white. She called me and said,
"Socrates, you will arrive 'in fertile Phthia' on the
third day."[3]

CRITO: What a strange dream, Socrates.

SOCRATES: Yet its meaning is quite clear, Crito—at least, it seems so to me.

CRITO: All too clear, apparently. But look here, Socrates, it's still not too late to take my advice and save yourself. You see, if you die, I won't just suffer a single misfortune. On the contrary, not only will I
lose a friend the like of whom I'll never find again,
but, in addition, many people, who don't know you
or me well, will think that I didn't care about you,
since I could have saved you if I'd been willing to c
spend the money. And indeed what reputation could
be more shameful than being thought to value
money more than friends? For the majority of people
won't believe that it was you yourself who refused to
leave this place, though we were urging you to do so.

SOCRATES: But my dear Crito, why should we care so much about what the majority think? After all, the most decent ones, who are worthier of consideration, will believe that matters were handled in just the way they were in fact handled.

CRITO: But you can surely see, Socrates, that one d
should care about majority opinion too. Your present
situation itself shows clearly that the majority can do
not just minor harms but the very worst things to
someone who's been slandered in front of them.

SOCRATES: I only wish, Crito, that the majority *could* do the very worst things, then they might also be able to do the very best ones—and everything would be fine. But as it is, they can do neither, since they can't make someone either wise or unwise—the effects *they* produce are really the result of chance.

CRITO: Well, if you say so. But tell me this, e
Socrates. You're not worried about me and your
other friends, are you—fearing that if you escaped,
the informers[4] would give us trouble, and that we
might be forced to give up all our property, pay heavy
fines, or even suffer some further penalty? If you're
afraid of anything like that, dismiss it from your 45
mind. After all, we're surely justified in running this
risk to save you or an even greater one if need be.
Now take my advice, and don't refuse me.

SOCRATES: Yes, those things do worry me, Crito, among many others.

CRITO: Then don't fear them: the sum of money that certain people I know will accept in order to

1. Legend had it that Athens was once obliged to send King Minos of Crete an annual tribute of seven young men and seven maidens to be given to the Minotaur—a monster, half man and half bull, that he kept in a labyrinth. With the help of a thread given to him by Minos' daughter Ariadne, Theseus, a legendary king of Athens, made his way through the labyrinth, killed the Minotaur, and escaped, thus ending the tribute. Each year, Athens commemorated these events by sending a mission of thanks to the sanctuary of Apollo on the sacred island of Delos. No executions could take place in Athens until the mission returned from its voyage. See *Phaedo* 58a–c.

2. A headland on the southeast coast of Attica, about thirty miles from Athens.

3. Homer, *Iliad* 9.363.

4. The *sukophantai* were individuals who prosecuted others in order to get the reward offered in Athenian law to successful prosecutors as public benefactors, or as a way of blackmailing someone who would pay to avoid prosecution, or for personal or political gain of some other sort.

save you and get you out of here isn't that large. Next,
don't you see how cheap these informers are and how
little money is needed to deal with them? My own
wealth's available to you, and it, I think, should be
b enough. Next, even if your concern for me makes
you unwilling to spend my money, there are foreign
visitors here who are willing to spend theirs. One of
them, Simmias of Thebes, has even brought enough
money for this very purpose; and Cebes, too, and a
good many others are also willing to contribute. So,
as I say, don't let these fears make you hesitate to save
yourself. And don't let it trouble you, as you were saying in court, that if you went into exile you wouldn't
c know what to do with yourself. You see, wherever else
you may go, there'll be people to welcome you. If
you want to go to Thessaly, I have friends there who'll
make much of you and protect you, so that no one in
Thessaly will give you any trouble.[5]

Besides, Socrates, I think that what you're doing
isn't just: throwing away your life, when you could
save it, and hastening the very sort of fate for yourself
that your enemies would hasten—and indeed have
hastened—in their wish to destroy you. What's more
I think you're also betraying those sons of yours by
going away and deserting them when you could
d bring them up and educate them. So far as you're
concerned, they must take their chances in life; and
the chance they'll get, in all likelihood, is just the
one that orphans usually get when they lose their parents. No. Either one shouldn't have children at all, or
one ought to see their upbringing and education
through to the end. But you seem to me to be choosing the easiest way out, whereas one should choose
whatever a good and brave man would choose—particularly when one claims to have cared about virtue
throughout one's life.

e I feel ashamed on your behalf and on behalf of
myself and your friends. I fear that it's going to seem
that this whole business of yours has been handled
with a certain cowardice on our part. The case was
brought to court when it needn't have been brought.
Then there was the actual conduct of the trial. And
now, to crown it all, this absurd finale to the affair. It's
going to seem that we let the opportunity slip
46 because of some vice, such as cowardice, on our part,
since we didn't save you nor did you save yourself,
although it was quite possible had we been of even the
slightest use.

See to it, then, Socrates, that all this doesn't turn out
badly and a shameful thing both for you and for us.
Come, deliberate—or rather, at this hour it's not a matter of deliberating but of having deliberated already—
and only one decision remains. You see, everything
must be done this coming night; and if we delay, it will
no longer be possible. For all these reasons, Socrates,
please take my advice and don't refuse me.

Socrates: My dear Crito, your enthusiasm's most b
valuable, provided it's of the right sort. But if it isn't,
the greater it is, the more difficult it will be to deal
with. We must therefore examine whether we should
do what you advise or not. You see, I'm not the sort of
person who's just now for the first time persuaded by
nothing within me except the argument that on
rational reflection seems best to me; I've *always* been
like that. I can't now reject the arguments I stated
before just because this misfortune has befallen me.
On the contrary, they seem pretty much the same to
me, and I respect and value the same ones as I did c
before. So if we have no better ones to offer in the present situation, you can be sure I won't agree with you—
not even if the power of the majority to threaten us, as
if we were children, with the bogeymen of imprisonment, execution, and confiscation of property were far
greater than it is now.

What, then, is the most reasonable way to examine
these matters? Suppose we first take up the argument
you stated about people's opinions. Is it true or not that d
one should pay attention to some opinions but not to
others? Or was it true before I had to die, whereas it's
now clear that it was stated idly, for the sake of argument, and is really just childish nonsense? For my part,
I'm eager to join you, Crito, in a joint examination of
whether this argument will appear any differently to
me, now that I'm here, or the same, and of whether we
should dismiss it from our minds or be persuaded by it.

It used to be said, I think, by people who thought
they were talking sense, that, as I said a moment ago,
one should take some people's opinions seriously but
not others. By the gods, Crito, don't you think that was
true? You see, in all human probability, *you* are not
going to die tomorrow, and so the present situation
won't distort your judgment. Consider, then, don't you 47

5. Thessaly is a region in the north of Greece.

think it's a sound argument that one shouldn't value all the opinions people have, but some and not others, and not those of everyone, but those of some people and not of others? What do you say? Isn't that true?

CRITO: It is.

SOCRATES: And we should value good opinions, but not bad ones?

CRITO: Yes.

SOCRATES: And the good ones are those of wise people and the bad ones those of unwise people?

CRITO: Of course.

SOCRATES: Come then, what of such questions as this? When a man's primarily engaged in physical training, does he pay attention to the praise or blame
b or opinion of every man or only to those of the one man who's a doctor or a trainer?

CRITO: Only to those of the one man.

SOCRATES: Then he should fear the blame and welcome the praise of that one man, but not those of the majority of people.

CRITO: Clearly.

SOCRATES: So his actions and exercises, his eating and drinking, should be guided by the opinion of the one man, the knowledgeable and understanding supervisor, rather than on that of all the rest?

CRITO: That's right.

c SOCRATES: Well, then, if he disobeys that one man and sets no value on his opinion or his praises but values those of the majority of people who have no understanding, won't something bad happen to him?

CRITO: Of course.

SOCRATES: And what is this bad effect? Where does it occur? In what part of the one who disobeys?

CRITO: Clearly, it's in his body, since that's what it destroys.

SOCRATES: That's right. And isn't the same true in other cases, Crito? No need to go through them all, but, in particular, in cases of just and unjust things, shameful and fine ones, good and bad ones—in cases of what we're now deliberating about—is it the opinion of the majority we should follow and fear? Or is
d it the opinion of the one man—if there is one who understands these things—we should respect and fear above all others? On the grounds that, if we don't follow it, we shall seriously damage and maim that part of us which, as we used to say, is made better by what's just but is destroyed by what's unjust. Or is there no truth in that?

CRITO: I certainly think there is, Socrates.

SOCRATES: Come then, suppose we destroy the part of us that is made better by what's healthy but is seriously damaged by what causes disease when we don't follow the opinion of people who have understanding. Would our lives be worth living once it has
been seriously damaged? And that part, of course, is e
the body, isn't it?

CRITO: Yes.

SOCRATES: Then are our lives worth living with a wretched, seriously damaged body?

CRITO: Certainly not.

SOCRATES: But our lives *are* worth living when the part of us that's maimed by what's unjust and benefited by what's just is seriously damaged? Or do we consider it—whichever part of us it is to which justice and injustice pertain—to be inferior to the body? 48

CRITO: Certainly not.

SOCRATES: On the contrary, it's more valuable?

CRITO: Far more.

SOCRATES: Then, my very good friend, we should not give so much thought to what the majority of people will say about us, but think instead of what the person who understands just and unjust things will say—the one man and the truth itself. So your first claim—that we should give thought to the opinion of the majority about what's just, fine, good, and their opposites—isn't right.

"But," someone might say, "the majority can put us to death."

CRITO: That's certainly clear too. It would indeed b
be said, Socrates.

SOCRATES: That's right. And yet, my dear friend, the argument we've gone through still seems the same to me, at any rate, as it did before. And now examine this further one to see whether we think it still stands or not: the most important thing isn't living, but living well.

CRITO: Yes, it still stands.

SOCRATES: And the argument that living well, living a fine life, and living justly are the same—does it still stand or not?

CRITO: It still stands.

SOCRATES: Then in the light of these agreements, we should examine whether or not it would be just c for me to try to get out of here when the Athenians haven't acquitted me. And if it does seem just, we should make the attempt, and if it doesn't, we should abandon the effort.

As for those other considerations you raise about loss of money and people's opinions and bringing up children—they, in truth, Crito, are appropriate considerations for people who readily put one to death and would as readily bring one back to life again if they could, without thinking; I mean, the majority of people. For us, however, the argument has made the decision. There's nothing else to be examined besides the very thing we just mentioned: whether we—both the ones who are rescued and also the rescuers themselves—will be acting justly if
d we pay money to those who would get me out of here and do them favors, or whether we will in truth be acting unjustly if we do those things. And if it appears that we will be acting unjustly in doing them, we have no need at all to give any opposing weight to our having to die—or suffer in some other way—if we stay here and mind our behavior when the alternative is doing injustice.

CRITO: What you *say* seems true to me, Socrates. But I wish you'd consider what we're to *do*.

SOCRATES: Let's examine that question together, my dear friend, and if you can oppose anything I say, oppose it, and I'll be persuaded by you. But if you
e can't, be a good fellow and stop telling me the same thing over and over, that I should leave here against the will of the Athenians. You see, I think it very important that I act in this matter having persuaded you, rather than against your will. Consider, then,
49 the starting point of our inquiry, to see if you find it adequately formulated, and try to answer my questions as you really think best.

CRITO: I'll certainly try.

SOCRATES: Do we say that one should never do injustice intentionally? Or may injustice be done in some circumstances but not in others? Is doing injustice never good or fine, as we have often agreed in the past? Or have all these former agreements been discarded during these last few days? Can you and I at our age, Crito, have spent so long in serious dis-
b cussion with one another without realizing that we ourselves were no better than a pair of children? Or is what we used to say true above all else: that whether the majority of people agree or not, and whether we must suffer still worse things than at present or ones that are easier to bear, it's true, all the same, that doing injustice in any circumstances is bad and shameful for the one who does it? Is that what we say or not?

CRITO: It is what we say.

SOCRATES: So one should never do injustice.

CRITO: Certainly not.

SOCRATES: So one shouldn't do injustice in return for injustice, as the majority of people think—seeing that one should *never* do injustice.

CRITO: Apparently not. c

SOCRATES: Well then, should one do wrong or not?

CRITO: Certainly not, Socrates.

SOCRATES: Well, what about when someone does wrong in return for having suffered wrongdoing? Is that just, as the majority of people think, or not just?

CRITO: It's not just at all.

SOCRATES: No, for there's no difference, I take it, between doing wrong and doing injustice?

CRITO: That's right.

SOCRATES: So one must neither do injustice in return nor wrong any man, no matter what one has suffered at his hands. And, Crito, in agreeing to this, watch out that you're not agreeing to anything contrary to what you believe. You see, I know that only a d
few people do believe or will believe it. And between those who believe it and those who don't, there's no common basis for deliberation, but each necessarily regards the other with contempt when they see their deliberations. You too, then, should consider very carefully whether you share that belief with me and whether the following is the starting point of our deliberations: that it's never right to do injustice, or to do injustice in return, or to retaliate with bad treatment when one has been treated badly. Or do you disagree and not share this starting point? You see, I've believed this for a long time myself and still believe it now. But if you've come to some other opinion, say so. Instruct me. If you stand by the for- e
mer one, however, then listen to my next point.

CRITO: Yes, I do stand by it and share it with you, so go on.

SOCRATES: Then I'll state the next point—or rather, ask a question: should one do the things one has agreed with someone to do, provided they are just, or should one cheat?

CRITO: One should do them.

SOCRATES: Then consider what follows. If we leave
50 this place without having persuaded the city, are we treating some people badly—and those whom we should least of all treat in that way—or not? Are we standing by agreements that are just or not?

CRITO: I can't answer your question, Socrates, since I don't understand it.

SOCRATES: Well, look at it this way. Suppose we were about to run away from here—or whatever what we'd be doing should be called. And suppose the Laws and the city community came and confronted us, and said,

"Tell us, Socrates, what do you intend to do? Do you intend anything else by this act you're attempting than to destroy us Laws, and the city as a whole, to the extent that you can? Or do you think that a city
b can continue to exist and not be overthrown if the legal judgments rendered in it have no force, but are deprived of authority and undermined by the actions of private individuals?"

What shall we say in response to that question, Crito, and to others like it? For there's a lot that one might say—particularly, if one were an orator—on behalf of this law we're destroying, the one requiring that legal judgments, once rendered, have authority.
c Or shall we say to them, "Yes, that's what we intend, for the city treated us unjustly and didn't judge our lawsuit correctly." Is that what we're to say—or what?

CRITO: Yes, by Zeus, that's what we're to say, Socrates.

SOCRATES: Then what if the Laws replied, "Was that also part of the agreement between you and us, Socrates? Or did you agree to stand by whatever judgments the city rendered?" Then, if we were surprised at the words, perhaps they might say, "Don't be surprised at what we're saying, Socrates, but answer us—since you're so accustomed to using question and answer. Come now, what charge have you to bring
d against the city and ourselves that you should try to destroy us? In the first place, wasn't it we who gave you birth—wasn't it through us that your father married your mother and produced you? Tell us, do you have some complaint about the correctness of those of us Laws concerned with marriage?"

"No, I have no complaint," I'd reply.

"Well then, what about the Laws dealing with the bringing up and educating of children, under which you were educated yourself? Didn't those of us Laws who regulate that area prescribe correctly when we ordered your father to educate you in the arts and physical training?"

"They prescribed correctly," I'd reply.

"Good. Then since you were born, brought up, e
and educated, can you deny, first, that you're our offspring and slave, both yourself and your ancestors? And if that's so, do you think that what's just is based on an equality between you and us, that whatever we try to do to you it's just for you to do to us in return? As regards you and your father (or you and your master, if you happened to have one), what's just isn't based on equality, and so you don't return whatever treatment you receive—answering back when you're
criticized or striking back when you're struck, or 51
doing many other such things. As regards you and your fatherland and its Laws, then, are these things permitted? If we try to destroy you, believing it to be just, will you try to destroy us Laws and your fatherland, to the extent that you can? And will you claim that you're acting justly in doing so—you the man who really cares about virtue? Or are you so wise that it has escaped your notice that your fatherland is more worthy of honor than your mother and father and all your other ancestors; that it is more to be
revered and more sacred and is held in greater b
esteem both among the gods and among those human beings who have any sense; that you must treat your fatherland with piety, submitting to it and placating it more than you would your own father when it is angry; that you must either persuade it or else do whatever it commands; that you must mind your behavior and undergo whatever treatment it prescribes for you, whether a beating or imprisonment; that if it leads you to war to be wounded or killed, that's what you must do, and that's what is just—not to give way or retreat or leave where you were stationed, but, on the contrary, in war and law courts, and everywhere else, to do whatever your city
or fatherland commands or else persuade it as to c
what is really just; and that while it is impious to violate the will of your mother or father, it is yet less so than to violate that of your fatherland."

What are we to say to that, Crito? Are the Laws telling the truth or not?

CRITO: Yes, I think they are.

SOCRATES: "Consider, then, Socrates," the Laws might perhaps continue, "whether we're also telling the truth in saying this: that you aren't treating us justly in what you're now trying to do. You see, we gave you birth, upbringing, and education, and have provided you, as well as every other citizen, with a
d share of all the fine things we could. Nonetheless, if any Athenian—who has been admitted to adult status and has observed both how affairs are handled in the city and ourselves, the Laws—is dissatisfied with us and wishes to leave, we grant him permission to take his property and go wherever he pleases. Not one of us Laws stands in his way or forbids it. If any one of you is dissatisfied with us and the city and wishes to go to a colony or to live as an alien elsewhere, he may go
e wherever he wishes and hold on to what's his.

"*But* if any of you stays here, after he has observed the way we judge lawsuits and the other ways in which we manage the city, then we say that he has agreed with us by his action to do whatever we command. And we say that whoever does not obey commits a threefold injustice: he disobeys us as his parents; he disobeys us as those who brought him up; and, after having agreed to obey us, he neither obeys nor persuades us, if we're doing something that isn't right. Yet we offer him a choice and do not harshly command him to do what he's told. On the contrary,
52 we offer two alternatives: he must either persuade us or do what we say. And he does neither. These, then, are the charges, Socrates, to which we say you too will become liable, if you do what you have in mind—and you won't be among the least liable of the Athenians, but among the most."

Then, if I were to say, "Why is that?" perhaps they might justifiably reproach me by saying that I am among the Athenians who have made that agreement with them in the strongest terms.

b "Socrates," they would say, "we have the strongest evidence that you were satisfied with us and with the city. After all, you'd never have stayed at home here so much more consistently than all the rest of the Athenians if you weren't also much more consistently satisfied. You never left the city for a festival, except once to go to the Isthmus.[6] You never went anywhere else, except for military service. You never went abroad as other people do. You had no desire to acquaint yourself with other cities or other laws. On the contrary, we and our city sufficed for you. So c
emphatically did you choose us and agree to live as a citizen under us, that you even produced children here. *That's* how satisfied you were with the city.

"Moreover, even at your very trial, you could have proposed exile as a counterpenalty if you'd wished, and what you're now trying to do against the city's will, you could then have done with its consent. On that occasion, you prided yourself on not feeling resentful that you had to die. You'd choose death before exile—so you said. Now, however, you feel no shame at those words and show no regard for us Laws as you try to destroy us. You're acting exactly the way d
the most wretched slave would act by trying to run away, contrary to your commitments and your agreements to live as a citizen under us.

"First, then, answer us on this very point: are we telling the truth when we say that you agreed, by deeds not words, to live as a citizen under us? Or is that untrue?"

What are we to reply to that, Crito? Mustn't we agree?

CRITO: We must, Socrates.

SOCRATES: "Well then," they might say, "surely you're breaking the commitments and agreements e
you made with us. You weren't coerced or tricked into agreeing or forced to decide in a hurry. On the contrary, you had seventy years in which you could have left if you weren't satisfied with us or if you thought those agreements unjust. You, however, preferred neither Sparta nor Crete—places you often say have good law and order—nor any other Greek or 53
foreign city. On the contrary, you went abroad less often than the lame, the blind, or other handicapped people. Hence it's clear that you, more than any other Athenian, have been consistently satisfied with your city and with us Laws—for who would be satisfied by a city but not by its laws? Won't you, then, stand by your agreements now? Yes, you will, if you're

6. The Isthmus is the narrow strip of land connecting the Peloponnese to the rest of Greece, where the Isthmian Games were held.

persuaded by us, Socrates, and at least you won't make yourself a laughingstock by leaving the city.

"For consider now: if you break those agreements, if you commit any of these wrongs, what good will you do yourself or your friends? You see, it's pretty
b clear that your friends will risk being exiled themselves as well as being disenfranchised and having their property confiscated. As for you, if you go to one of the nearest cities, Thebes or Megara—for they both have good laws—you will be arriving there, Socrates, as an enemy of their political systems, and those who care about their own cities will look on you with suspicion, regarding you as one who undermines laws. You will also confirm your jurors in their opinion, so that they will think they judged your law-
c suit correctly. For anyone who undermines laws might very well be considered a corruptor of young and ignorant people.

"Will you, then, avoid cities with good law and order, and men of the most respectable kind? And if so, will your life be worth living? Or will you associate with these people and be shameless enough to converse with them? And what will you say, Socrates? The very things that you said here, about how virtue and justice are man's most valuable possessions, along with law and lawful conduct. Don't you think Socrates and everything about him will look unseemly? Surely, you must.

d "Or will you keep away from those places and go to Crito's friends in Thessaly? After all, there's complete disorder and laxity there, so perhaps they'd enjoy hearing about your absurd escape from prison when you dressed up in disguise, wore a peasant's leather jerkin or some other such escapee's outfit, and altered your appearance. And will no one remark on the fact that you, an old man, with probably only a
e short time left to live, were so greedy for life that you dared to violate the most important laws? Perhaps not, provided you don't annoy anyone. Otherwise, you'll hear many disparaging things said about you. Will you live by currying favor with every man and acting the slave—and do nothing in Thessaly besides eat, as if you'd gone to live in Thessaly for a good din-
54 ner? As for those arguments about justice and the rest of virtue, where, tell us, will they be?

"Is it that you want to live for your children's sake, then, to bring them up and educate them? Really? Will you bring them up and educate them by taking them to Thessaly and making foreigners of them, so they can enjoy that privilege too? If not, will they be better brought up and educated here without you, provided that you're still alive? 'Of course,' you may say, because your friends will take care of them. Then will they take care of them if you go to Thessaly, but not take care of them if you go to Hades? If those who call themselves your friends are worth anything at all, you surely can't believe that. b

"No, Socrates, be persuaded by us who reared you. Don't put a higher value on children, on life, or on anything else than on what's just, so that when you reach Hades you may have all this to offer as your defense before the authorities there. For if you do do that, it doesn't seem that it will be better for you *here*, or for any of your friends, or that it will be more just or more pious. And it won't be better for you when you arrive *there* either. As it is, you'll leave here—if you do leave—as one who has been treated unjustly
not by us Laws, but by men. But suppose you leave, c
suppose you return injustice for injustice and bad treatment for bad treatment in that shameful way, breaking your agreements and commitments with us and doing bad things to those whom you should least of all treat in that way—yourself, your friends, your fatherland, and ourselves. Then we'll be angry with you while you're still alive, and our brothers, the Laws of Hades, won't receive you kindly there, knowing that you tried to destroy us to the extent you could. Come, then, don't let Crito persuade you to
follow his advice rather than ours." d

That, Crito, my dear friend, is what I seem to hear them saying, you may be sure. And, just like those Corybantes who think they are still hearing the flutes, the echo of their arguments reverberates in me and makes me incapable of hearing anything else. No, as far as my present thoughts go, at least, you may be sure that if you argue against them, you will speak in vain. All the same, if you think you can do any more, please tell me.

CRITO: No, Socrates, I've nothing to say.

SOCRATES: Then, let it be, Crito, and let's act in e
that way, since that's the way the god is leading us.

Protagoras

In the following selection, the great Sophist Protagoras (some fragments of whose writings are included in this anthology) explains his view of virtue.

When we had all taken our seats, Protagoras said,
"Now, then, Socrates, since these gentlemen also are
present, would you please say what it was you brought
up to me a little while ago on the young man's behalf."
318 "Well, Protagoras," I said, "as to why we have
come, I'll begin as I did before. Hippocrates here has
gotten to the point where he wants to be your student, and, quite naturally, he would like to know
what he will get out of it if he does study with you.
That's really all we have to say."
Protagoras took it from there and said, "Young man,
this is what you will get if you study with me: The very
b day you start, you will go home a better man, and the
same thing will happen the day after. Every day, day
after day, you will get better and better."
When I heard this I said, "What you're saying, Protagoras, isn't very surprising, but quite likely. Why,
even you, though you are so old and wise, would get
better if someone taught you something you didn't
happen to know already. But what if the situation
were a little different, and Hippocrates here all of a
sudden changed his mind and set his heart on study-
c ing with this young fellow who has just come into
town, Zeuxippus of Heraclea,[1] and came to him, as
he now comes to you, and heard from him the very
same thing as from you—that each day he spent with
him he would become better and make progress. If
Hippocrates asked him in what way he would
become better, and toward what he would be making
progress, Zeuxippus would say at painting. And if he
were studying with Orthagoras of Thebes[2] and he
heard from him the same thing as he hears from you
and asked him in what he would be getting better
every day he studied with him, Orthagoras would say d
at flute-playing. It is in this way that you must tell me
and the young man on whose behalf I am asking the
answer to this question: If Hippocrates studies with
Protagoras, exactly how will he go away a better man
and in what will he make progress each and every
day he spends with you?"
Protagoras heard me out and then said, "You put
your question well, Socrates, and I am only too glad
to answer those who pose questions well. If Hippocrates comes to me he will not experience what he
would if he studied with some other Sophist. The
others abuse young men, steering them back again, e
against their will, into subjects the likes of which
they have escaped from at school, teaching them
arithmetic, astronomy, geometry, music, and
poetry"—at this point he gave Hippias a significant
look—but if he comes to me he will learn only what
he has come for. What I teach is sound deliberation, 319
both in domestic matters—how best to manage one's
household, and in public affairs—how to realize
one's maximum potential for success in political
debate and action."
"Am I following what you are saying?" I asked.
"You appear to be talking about the art of citizenship,
and to be promising to make men good citizens."
"This is exactly what I claim, Socrates."
"Well, this is truly an admirable technique you
have developed, if indeed you have. There is no
point in my saying to you anything other than exactly b
what I think. The truth is, Protagoras, I have never
thought that this could be taught, but when you say
it can be, I can't very well doubt it. It's only right that
I explain where I got the idea that this is not teachable, not something that can be imparted from one
human being to another. I maintain, along with the
rest of the Greek world, that the Athenians are wise.
And I observe that when we convene in the Assembly and the city has to take some action on a building project, we send for builders to advise us; if it has
to do with the construction of ships, we send for shipwrights; and so forth for everything that is considered c

---

1. Zeuxippus (more commonly spelled Zeuxis) was a painter who flourished in the late fifth century BCE.

2. Orthagoras was renowned for his excellent playing on the flute (*aolos*).

learnable and teachable. But if anyone else, a person
not regarded as a craftsman, tries to advise them, no
matter how handsome and rich and well-born he
might be, they just don't accept him. They laugh at
him and shout him down until he either gives up trying to speak and steps down himself, or the archer-
police remove him forcibly by order of the board.
d This is how they proceed in matters which they consider technical. But when it is a matter of deliberating on city management, anyone can stand up and
advise them, carpenter, blacksmith, shoemaker, merchant, ship-captain, rich man, poor man, well-born,
low-born—it doesn't matter—and nobody blasts him
for presuming to give counsel without any prior train-
e ing under a teacher. The reason for this is clear: They
do not think that this can be taught. Public life aside,
the same principle holds also in private life, where
the wisest and best of our citizens are unable to transmit to others the virtues that they possess. Look at
Pericles,[3] the father of these young men here. He
320 gave them a superb education in everything that
teachers can teach, but as for what he himself is
really wise in, he neither teaches them that himself
nor has anyone else teach them either, and his sons
have to browse like stray sacred cattle and pick up
virtue on their own wherever they might find it. Take
a good look at Clinias, the younger brother of Alcibiades here. When Pericles became his guardian he
was afraid that he would be corrupted, no less, by
Alcibiades. So he separated them and placed Clinias
in Ariphron's house and tried to educate him there.
b Six months later he gave him back to Alcibiades
because he couldn't do anything with him. I could
mention a great many more, men who are good
themselves but have never succeeded in making anyone else better, whether family members or total
strangers. Looking at these things, Protagoras, I just
don't think that virtue can be taught. But when I hear
what you have to say, I waver; I think there must be
something in what you are talking about. I consider
you to be a person of enormous experience who has
learned much from others and thought through a
great many things for himself. So if you can clarify
for us how virtue is teachable, please don't begrudge
us your explanation."

"I wouldn't think of begrudging you an explana- c
tion, Socrates," he replied. "But would you rather that
I explain by telling you a story, as an older man to a
younger audience, or by developing an argument?"

The consensus was that he should proceed in
whichever way he wished. "I think it would be more
pleasant," he said, "if I told you a story.

"There once was a time when the gods existed but d
mortal races did not. When the time came for their
appointed genesis, the gods molded them inside the
earth, blending together earth and fire and various
compounds of earth and fire. When they were ready
to bring them to light, the gods put Prometheus and
Epimetheus in charge of decking them out and
assigning to each its appropriate powers and abilities.

"Epimetheus begged Prometheus for the privilege
of assigning the abilities himself. 'When I've completed the distribution,' he said, 'you can inspect it.'
Prometheus agreed, and Epimetheus started distributing abilities.

"To some he assigned strength without quickness; e
the weaker ones he made quick. Some he armed;
others he left unarmed but devised for them some
other means for preserving themselves. He compen- 321
sated for small size by issuing wings for flight or an
underground habitat. Size was itself a safeguard for
those he made large. And so on down the line, balancing his distribution, making adjustments, and taking precautions against the possible extinction of any
of the races.

"After supplying them with defenses against
mutual destruction, he devised for them protection b
against the weather. He clothed them with thick
pelts and tough hides capable of warding off winter
storms, effective against heat, and serving also as
built-in, natural bedding when they went to sleep.
He also shod them, some with hooves, others with
thick pads of bloodless skin. Then he provided them
with various forms of nourishment, plants for some,
fruit from trees for others, roots for still others. And
there were some to whom he gave the consumption
of other animals as their sustenance. To some he
gave the capacity for few births; to others, ravaged by
the former, he gave the capacity for multiple births,
and so ensured the survival of their kind.

"But Epimetheus was not very wise, and he c
absentmindedly used up all the powers and abilities
on the nonreasoning animals; he was left with the

---

3. Pericles (c. 495–429 BCE) was the greatest fifth-century Athenian statesman and general.

human race, completely unequipped. While he was
floundering about at a loss, Prometheus arrived to
inspect the distribution and saw that while the other
animals were well provided with everything, the
human race was naked, unshod, unbedded, and
unarmed, and it was already the day on which all of
them, human beings included, were destined to
d emerge from the earth into the light. It was then that
Prometheus, desperate to find some means of survival for the human race, stole from Hephaestus and
Athena wisdom in the practical arts together with fire
(without which this kind of wisdom is effectively useless) and gave them outright to the human race. The
wisdom it acquired was for staying alive; wisdom for
living together in society, political wisdom, it did not
acquire, because that was in the keeping of Zeus.
Prometheus no longer had free access to the high
citadel that is the house of Zeus, and besides this, the
guards there were terrifying. But he did sneak into
e the building that Athena and Hephaestus shared to
practice their arts, and he stole from Hephaestus the
322 art of fire and from Athena her arts, and he gave them
to the human race. And it is from this origin that the
resources human beings needed to stay alive came
into being. Later, the story goes, Prometheus was
charged with theft, all on account of Epimetheus.

"It is because humans had a share of the divine dispensation that they alone among animals worshipped
the gods, with whom they had a kind of kinship, and
erected altars and sacred images. It wasn't long
before they were articulating speech and words and
b had invented houses, clothes, shoes, and blankets,
and were nourished by food from the earth. Thus
equipped, human beings at first lived in scattered isolation; there were no cities. They were being
destroyed by wild beasts because they were weaker in
every way, and although their technology was adequate to obtain food, it was deficient when it came to
fighting wild animals. This was because they did not
yet possess the art of politics, of which the art of war
is a part. They did indeed try to band together and
survive by founding cities. The outcome when they
did so was that they wronged each other, because
c they did not possess the art of politics, and so they
would scatter and again be destroyed. Zeus was afraid
that our whole race might be wiped out, so he sent
Hermes to bring justice and a sense of shame to
humans, so that there would be order within cities
and bonds of friendship to unite them. Hermes asked
Zeus how he should distribute shame and justice to
humans. 'Should I distribute them as the other arts
were? This is how the others were distributed: one
person practicing the art of medicine suffices for
many ordinary people; and so forth with the other
practitioners. Should I establish justice and shame d
among humans in this way, or distribute it to all?' 'To
all,' said Zeus, 'and let all have a share. For cities
would never come to be if only a few possessed these,
as is the case with the other arts. And establish this
law as coming from me: Death to him who cannot
partake of shame and justice, for he is a pestilence to
the city.'

"And so it is, Socrates, that when the Athenians
(and others as well) are debating architectural excellence, or the virtue proper to any other professional
specialty, they think that only a few individuals have
the right to advise them, and they do not accept e
advice from anyone outside these select few. You've
made this point yourself, and with good reason, I
might add. But when the debate involves political
excellence, which must proceed entirely from justice 323
and temperance, they accept advice from anyone,
and with good reason, for they think that this particular virtue, political or civic virtue, is shared by all, or
there wouldn't be any cities. This must be the explanation for it, Socrates.

"And so you won't think you've been deceived,
consider this as further evidence for the universal
belief that all humans have a share of justice and the
rest of civic virtue. In the other arts, as you have said,
if someone claims to be a good flute-player or whatever, but is not, people laugh at him or get angry b
with him, and his family comes round and remon-
strates with him as if he were mad. But when it
comes to justice or any other social virtue, even if
they know someone is unjust, if that person publicly
confesses the truth about himself, they will call this
truthfulness madness, whereas in the previous case
they would have called it a sense of decency. They
will say that everyone ought to claim to be just, c
whether they are or not, and that it is madness not to
pretend to justice, since one must have some trace of
it or not be human.

"This, then, is my first point: It is reasonable to
admit everyone as an adviser on this virtue, on the
grounds that everyone has some share of it. Next I will

attempt to show that people do not regard this virtue as natural or self-generated, but as something taught and carefully developed in those in whom it is developed.

d "In the case of evils that men universally regard as afflictions due to nature or bad luck, no one ever gets angry with anyone so afflicted or reproves, admonishes, punishes, or tries to correct them. We simply pity them. No one in his right mind would try to do anything like this to someone who is ugly, for example, or scrawny or weak. The reason is, I assume, that they know that these things happen to people as a natural process or by chance, both these ills and their opposites. But in the case of the good things that
e accrue to men through practice and training and teaching, if someone does not possess these goods but rather their corresponding evils, he finds himself the object of anger, punishment, and reproof.
324 Among these evils are injustice, impiety, and in general everything that is opposed to civic virtue. Offenses in this area are always met with anger and reproof, and the reason is clearly that this virtue is regarded as something acquired through practice and teaching. The key, Socrates, to the true significance of punishment lies in the fact that human
b beings consider virtue to be something acquired through training. For no one punishes a wrong-doer in consideration of the simple fact that he has done wrong, unless one is exercising the mindless vindictiveness of a beast. Reasonable punishment is not vengeance for a past wrong—for one cannot undo what has been done—but is undertaken with a view
c to the future, to deter both the wrong-doer and whoever sees him being punished from repeating the crime. This attitude towards punishment as deterrence implies that virtue is learned, and this is the attitude of all those who seek requital in public or in private. All human beings seek requital from and punish those who they think have wronged them, and the Athenians, your fellow citizens, especially do so. Therefore, by my argument, the Athenians are among those who think that virtue is acquired and taught. So it is with good reason that your fellow citizens accept a blacksmith's or a cobbler's advice in
d political affairs. And they do think that virtue is acquired and taught. It appears to me that both these propositions have been sufficiently proved, Socrates.

"Now, on to your remaining difficulty, the problem you raise about good men teaching their sons everything that can be taught and making them wise in these subjects, but not making them better than anyone else in the particular virtue in which they themselves excel. On this subject, Socrates, I will
abandon story for argument. Consider this: Does *e*
there or does there not exist one thing which all citizens must have for there to be a city? Here and nowhere else lies the solution to your problem. For if such a thing exists, and this one thing is not the art of
the carpenter, the blacksmith, or the potter, but jus- *325*
tice, and temperance, and piety—what I may collectively term the virtue of a man, and if this is the thing which everyone should share in and with which every man should act whenever he wants to learn anything or do anything, but should not act without
it, and if we should instruct and punish those who do *b*
not share in it, man, woman, and child, until their punishment makes them better, and should exile from our cities or execute whoever doesn't respond to punishment and instruction; if this is the case, if such is the nature of this thing, and good men give their sons an education in everything but this, then we have to be amazed at how strangely our good men behave. For we have shown that they regard this thing as teachable both in private and public life. Since it is something that can be taught and nurtured, is it possible that they have their sons taught everything in which there is no death penalty for not understanding it, but when their children are faced
with the death penalty or exile if they fail to learn *c*
virtue and be nurtured in it—and not only death but confiscation of property and, practically speaking, complete familial catastrophe—do you think they do not have them taught this or give them all the attention possible? We must think that they do, Socrates.

"Starting when they are little children and continuing as long as they live, they teach them and correct *d*
them. As soon as a child understands what is said to him, the nurse, mother, tutor, and the father himself fight for him to be as good as he possibly can, seizing on every action and word to teach him and show him that this is just, that is unjust, this is noble, that is ugly, this is pious, that is impious, he should do this, he should not do that. If he obeys willingly, fine; if not, they straighten him out with threats and blows as if he were a twisted, bent piece of wood. After this
they send him to school and tell his teachers to pay *e*
more attention to his good conduct than to his

grammar or music lessons. The teachers pay attention to these things, and when the children have
learned their letters and are getting to understand
writing as well as the spoken language, they are given
the works of good poets to read at their desks and
326 have to learn them by heart, works that contain
numerous exhortations, many passages describing in
glowing terms good men of old, so that the child is
inspired to imitate them and become like them. In a
similar vein, the music teachers too foster in their
young pupils a sense of moral decency and restraint,
and when they learn to play the lyre they are taught
b the works of still more good poets, the lyric and
choral poets. The teachers arrange the scores and
drill the rhythms and scales into the children's souls,
so that they become gentler, and their speech and
movements become more rhythmical and harmonious. For all of human life requires a high degree of
rhythm and harmony. On top of all this, they send
their children to an athletic trainer so that they may
have sound bodies in the service of their now fit
c minds and will not be forced to cowardice in war or
other activities through physical deficiencies.

"This is what the most able, i.e., the richest, do.
d Their sons start going to school at the earliest age
and quit at the latest age. And when they quit school,
the city in turn compels them to learn the laws and
to model their lives on them. They are not to act as
they please. An analogy might be drawn from the
practice of writing-teachers, who sketch the letters
faintly with a pen in workbooks for their beginning
students and have them write the letters over the patterns they have drawn. In the same way the city has
drawn up laws invented by the great lawgivers in the
past and compels them to govern and be governed
by them. She punishes anyone who goes beyond
these laws, and the term for this punishment in your
e city and others is, because it is a corrective legal
action, 'correction.'

"When so much care and attention is paid to
virtue, Socrates, both in public and private, are you
still puzzled about virtue being teachable? The wonder would be if it were not teachable.

"Why, then, do many sons of good fathers never
amount to anything? I want you to understand this
too, and in fact it's no great wonder, if what I've just
327 been saying is true about virtue being something in
which no one can be a layman if there is to be a city.
For if what I am saying is true—and nothing could
be more true: Pick any other pursuit or study and
reflect upon it. Suppose, for instance, there could be
no city unless we were all flute-players, each to the
best of his ability, and everybody were teaching
everybody else this art in public and private and rep-
rimanding the poor players and doing all this unstint- *b*
ingly, just as now no one begrudges or conceals his
expertise in what is just and lawful as he does his
other professional expertise. For it is to our collective
advantage that we each possess justice and virtue,
and so we all gladly tell and teach each other what is
just and lawful. Well, if we all had the same eagerness and generosity in teaching each other flute-playing, do you think, Socrates, that the sons of good
flute-players would be more likely to be good flute-
players than the sons of poor flute-players? I don't
think so at all. When a son happened to be naturally *c*
disposed toward flute-playing, he would progress and
become famous; otherwise, he would remain obscure.
In many cases the son of a good player would turn
out to be a poor one, and the son of a poor player
would turn out to be good. But as flute-players, they
would all turn out to be capable when compared
with ordinary people who had never studied the
flute. Likewise you must regard the most unjust person ever reared in a human society under law as a *d*
paragon of justice compared with people lacking
education and lawcourts and the pervasive pressure
to cultivate virtue, savages such as the playwright
Pherecrates[4] brought on stage at last year's Lenaean
festival. There's no doubt that if you found yourself
among such people, as did the misanthropes in that
play's chorus, you would be delighted to meet up *e*
with the likes of Eurybatus and Phrynondas[5] and
would sorely miss the immorality of the people here.
As it is, Socrates, you affect delicate sensibilities,
because everyone here is a teacher of virtue, to the
best of his ability, and you can't see a single one. You
might as well look for a teacher of Greek; you 328
wouldn't find a single one of those either. Nor would

---

4. Pherecrates was an Athenian writer of comic plays and prizewinner at the Lenaion, a dramatic competition in the late fifth century BCE.

5. Eurybatus and Phrynondas were historical individuals whose names in literature had become synonymous with viciousness.

you be any more successful if you asked who could teach the sons of our craftsmen the very arts which they of course learned from their fathers, to the extent that their fathers were competent, and their friends in the trade. It would be difficult to produce someone who could continue their education, whereas it would be easy to find a teacher for the totally unskilled. It is the same with virtue and everything else. If there is someone who is the least bit more advanced in virtue than ourselves, he is to be cherished.

b “I consider myself to be such a person, uniquely qualified to assist others in becoming noble and good, and worth the fee that I charge and even more, so much so that even my students agree. This is why
I charge according to the following system: a student c
pays the full price only if he wishes to; otherwise, he goes into a temple, states under oath how much he thinks my lessons are worth, and pays that amount.

“There you have it, Socrates, my mythic story and my argument that virtue is teachable and that the Athenians consider it to be so, and that it is no wonder that worthless sons are born of good fathers and good sons of worthless fathers, since even the sons of
Polyclitus, of the same age as Paralus and Xanthippus d
here, are nothing compared to their father, and the same is true for the sons of other artisans. But it is not fair to accuse these two yet; there is still hope for them, for they are young.”

MENO, PHAEDO, AND SYMPOSIUM

THESE THREE DIALOGUES are linked by the emergence and development in them of Plato's famous theory of forms. The *Meno* begins with the question of whether virtue can be taught. This leads to an inquiry into virtue: what is the one form shared in common by all the virtues that makes each of them a virtue (72c–d)? Various answers are proposed and rejected. Then Meno introduces a general problem for the inquiry: if neither he nor Socrates knows what virtue is, how will they recognize it if they find it (80d)? Socrates answers with the theory of recollection, which he attempts to underwrite by the examination of the slave boy (82a–86c). The dialogue ends with a return to the original topic of whether virtue can be taught. The theory of recollection presupposes that the soul is immortal. In the *Phaedo*, explicit arguments are given in favor of this presupposition, the theory of recollection is modified and enriched, and we learn more about the nature of forms and about their role not just in ethics but in science and cosmology. The *Phaedo*, which—like the *Crito*—is set in the prison where Socrates spends his last days, ends with an account of his death. In the *Symposium*, Plato gives one of his most vivid accounts of the ascent of the soul from visible, tangible particulars to intelligible, abstract forms, and we learn that it is love (*erōs*) that leads us to make that ascent.

MENO

MENO:[1] Can you tell me, Socrates, is virtue some-
70 thing acquired by teaching? Or is it something acquired not by teaching, but by practice? Or is it something acquired neither by practice nor by learning, but something human beings possess by nature or in some other way?

SOCRATES: In the past, Meno, the inhabitants of Thessaly were well-reputed among the Greeks—admired for their horsemanship and their wealth. But now for their wisdom too, it seems to me—
especially the Larissans, your friend Aristippus' b

1. A young aristocrat from Pharsalus in Thessaly.

fellow-citizens.[2] You have Gorgias to thank for that.[3] When he arrived in Larissa, he acquired as lovers for his wisdom the leading Aleuadae—among them your own lover Aristippus—and the other leading Thessalians as well. And he got you into this habit of answering fearlessly and high-mindedly when anyone asks you anything—as is reasonable enough if
you have the knowledge. After all, he too makes him-
c self available to any Greek to ask him any question
they want, and none of them fail to get an answer. But here in Athens, my friend, we are in the opposite situation. There has been a drought of wisdom, so to
speak, and there is a good chance that wisdom has
71 left these parts to go live with you. At any rate, if you
wanted to question anyone who lives here in that way, there is no one who wouldn't laugh and say: "Stranger, apparently you think I am somehow divinely blessed, that I know whether virtue is something acquired by teaching or whatever the way is that human beings get it. I am so far from knowing whether it is something acquired by teaching, or not by teaching, that in fact I do not know at all what in the world virtue itself is."

Well, I am also that way myself, Meno. I share the
b poverty of my fellow citizens in this matter. I
reproach myself for not knowing anything whatever about virtue. But if I do not know what it is, how could I know what *sort* of thing it is? Or do you think it is possible for someone, who does not know at all who Meno is, to know whether Meno is beautiful or rich or in fact of noble birth, or the opposites of these? Do you think that is possible?

MENO: No, I do not. But, Socrates, do you really
not know what virtue is? Are we to report *this* about
c you to the folks back home?

SOCRATES: Not only that, my friend, but also that I have never met anyone else I thought did know.

MENO: What? Didn't you meet Gorgias[4] when he was here?

SOCRATES: I did.

MENO: And you didn't think he knew?

SOCRATES: I haven't a very good memory, Meno, so I cannot tell you at present what I thought of him then. Maybe he does know. Presumably, you know what he
said. So remind me what it was. Or if you prefer, speak *d*
for yourself. I imagine you think the same as he.

MENO: I do.

SOCRATES: Well in that case, let's leave him out of it, since in fact he is not here. But as for yourself, by the gods, Meno, what do you say virtue is? Tell me, don't be begrudging. The result may be that I spoke a very lucky falsehood when I said that I had never yet met anyone who knew this, if it comes to light that you and Gorgias do know it.

MENO: I will tell you, Socrates; it is not difficult.
First, then, if you want to know a man's virtue, that is *e*
easy. This is a man's virtue: to take part in the city's affairs capably, and by doing so to benefit his friends and harm his enemies,[5] while taking care that he himself does not suffer anything like that. If you want a woman's virtue, that is not difficult to describe. She must manage the household well, look after its contents, and be obedient to the man. There is a different virtue for a child, one for a male and one for a female, and for an older man, one for a free man, if
you want to know that, and one for a slave, if you
want to know that. There are very many other 72
virtues, too, so there is no puzzle about telling you what virtue is. You see, for each of the affairs and stages of life, and in relation to each particular function, there is a virtue for each of us—and it is the same way, I think, Socrates, for vice.

SOCRATES: I seem to be enjoying a great stroke of good luck indeed, Meno, if, while inquiring about one virtue, I have turned up something like a swarm of virtues in your possession. But, Meno, keeping to
this image of swarms, suppose I asked you about
being a bee, what a bee is, and you said that bees are *b*
many and multifarious. What would you reply if I asked you: "Do you mean they are many and multifarious and different from one another in this—in each being bees? Or do they not differ at all in that, but in some other way—for example, in beauty or size or some other such way?" Tell me, how would you answer if questioned like that?

---

2. Aristippus was a member of the Aleuaedae, the ruling family of Larissa, the major city of Thessaly in northern Greece, not to be confused with the philosopher of the same name.

3. See *Apology* 19e note.

4. Gorgias came to Athens in 427 BCE and perhaps on other occasions as well.

5. A common Greek view, which Socrates rejects. See *Crito* 49c–d.

MENO: This is what I'd say: they do not differ at all one from another in being bees.

c SOCRATES: So if I went on and said: "Then tell me about that thing itself, Meno—that in which they do not differ, but are all the same. What do you say *it* is?" No doubt you would have an answer to give me.

MENO: I would.

SOCRATES: It is the same with the virtues, too. Even if they are many and multifarious, surely they all have one identical form, because of which they are all virtues. And it is right, I would suppose, for the one who is answering to look to *that* in order to make clear what virtue actually is to the one who asked. Or d don't you understand what I mean?

MENO: I think I understand. But I don't yet grasp what you are asking as firmly as I would like.

SOCRATES: Is it only about virtue that you think this way, Meno—that there is one for a man, another for a woman's, and so on for the others? Or do you think the same about health and size and strength? Do you think health is one for a man, another for a woman? Or is there the same form everywhere, if it really is health, e whether for a man or for anything else whatever?

MENO: I think health, at any rate, is the same, both for a man and for a woman.

SOCRATES: What about size and strength, then? If in fact a woman is strong, will she be strong by virtue of the same form, by the same strength? By "the same strength" I mean this: strength does not differ at all as regards being strength, whether it is in a man or in a woman. Or do you think there is some difference?

MENO: No, I don't.

73 SOCRATES: Then will virtue differ, as regards being virtue, whether it is in a child or in an old man, in a woman or in a man?

MENO: Well, I somehow think, Socrates, that this is no longer like those other cases.

SOCRATES: What? Weren't you saying that a man's virtue is to manage a city well, and a woman's a household?

MENO: Yes, I was.

SOCRATES: Well then, is it possible to manage a city well or a household or anything else whatever, while not managing it temperately and justly?

MENO: Certainly not.

SOCRATES: And if they really manage it justly and b temperately, isn't it by means of justice and temperance that they will manage it?

MENO: Necessarily.

SOCRATES: So both men and women will need the same things, if they are really going to be good—justice and temperance.

MENO: Apparently.

SOCRATES: What about a child and an old man? If they were intemperate and unjust, could they possibly be good?

MENO: Certainly not.

SOCRATES: But if they were temperate and just?

MENO: Yes.

SOCRATES: So all human beings are good in the c same way, since they are good if they possess the same things.

MENO: So it seems.

SOCRATES: But surely if their virtue were not the same, they would not be good in the same way.

MENO: Certainly not.

SOCRATES: So, since the virtue of them all is the same, try to tell me, try to recollect, what Gorgias says it is—and you say with him.

MENO: Well, what else than to be able to rule people? If you are really inquiring about one thing that covers all of them. d

SOCRATES: Yes indeed, I am inquiring about that. But is that same virtue the virtue of a child, Meno, and of a slave—to be able to rule over their master? Do you think that the one who rules would still be a slave?

MENO: No, I don't think so at all, Socrates.

SOCRATES: No, that wouldn't be reasonable, my very good man. And consider this further point too. Virtue, you say, is "ability to rule." Are we not to add "justly," not "unjustly"?

MENO: Yes, I think that's right. For justice, Socrates, is virtue.

SOCRATES: Virtue, Meno? Or *a* virtue? e

MENO: What do you mean by that?

SOCRATES: The same as with anything else. For example, roundness, if you like. I would say about roundness that it is *a* shape, not that it is just simply shape. My reason for speaking like that is that there are other shapes.

MENO: Yes, and you would be speaking rightly, since I also say that it is not only justice that is virtue, but that there are other virtues too.

SOCRATES: Which ones are? Tell me. I could men- 74 tion other shapes to you, if you asked me to. So you do likewise. Mention some other virtues to me.

MENO: Well, I think courage is a virtue, and temperance and wisdom and high-mindedness, and very many others.

SOCRATES: As before, Meno, the same thing has happened to us. Again, we have found many virtues when we were inquiring about one, though in a different way than in the previous case. But the one that extends through all of them we cannot find.

MENO: No, for I cannot yet grasp, Socrates, what you are inquiring about—one virtue that covers all of
b them, as in the other cases.

SOCRATES: That isn't surprising. But I am eager, if I can, to move us closer to it. For you understand, surely, that this is just how it is in all of them: if someone were to ask you, as I asked previously, "What is shape, Meno?" and you said that it was roundness, and he then asked, as I did, "Is roundness shape or *a* shape?" you would no doubt reply that it is *a* shape.

MENO: Of course.

SOCRATES: The reason being that there are other
c shapes too?

MENO: Yes.

SOCRATES: And if he went on to ask you what sorts of shapes, you would tell him?

MENO: I would.

SOCRATES: Again, if he asked you in the same way what color is, and you said "white," and he went on to ask, "Is white color or *a* color?" you would say that it is *a* color, because there are other colors too?

MENO: I would.

SOCRATES: And if he asked you to mention some other colors, you would mention others that are no
d less colors than white is?

MENO: Yes.

SOCRATES: Then, if he pursued the argument as I did, and said, "We keep arriving at many things. Please don't answer me like that. You call these many things by a single name, and say that none of them is not a shape. And you say that even though they are opposites of one another. So tell me just what is this thing that encompasses the round no less than the straight, the one you call shape, so that you say that
e the round is no more shape than is the straight?" Or don't you say that?

MENO: I do.

SOCRATES: Well then, when you speak like that, do you mean that the round is no more round than straight, or that the straight is no more straight than round?

MENO: Of course not, Socrates.

SOCRATES: Instead, you mean that the round is no more shape than is the straight, or the straight than the round?

MENO: True.

SOCRATES: Well then, what is this thing of which this is the name—"shape"? Try to say. If you said to the questioner who asked you in this way about
shape or color, "I don't understand what you want, 75
my man, nor even what you mean," he would probably be amazed and say, "You don't understand that I am inquiring about what in all these cases is the same?" Even in this case, Meno, would you be unable to answer, if someone were to ask you, "What is it that is the same in all these cases—in the case of the round and the straight and the rest—the thing that you call shape?" Try to say. By doing so you will also get practice for your answer about virtue.

MENO: No, please, Socrates, you answer. b

SOCRATES: You want me to indulge you?

MENO: Yes, indeed.

SOCRATES: And then you will be willing to tell me about virtue?

MENO: I will.

SOCRATES: I must give it a try, since it is worth it.

MENO: It certainly is.

SOCRATES: Come on then, let's try to tell you what shape is. See whether you accept that it is this: shape for us is that thing which, alone among the things that are, always goes along with color. Is that answer enough for you, or are you inquiring after some other sort? You see, I would certainly be satisfied if you told
me about virtue in just that way. c

MENO: But that's silly, Socrates.

SOCRATES: How do you mean?

MENO: I mean that shape, if I am not mistaken, is according to your account what always goes along with color. All right. So if someone were to say that he didn't know color, but had the same puzzle about it as with shape, what sort of answer do you think you would have given him?

SOCRATES: I think a true one. And if my questioner were one of those eristical[6] and contentious wise fellows, I would say to him, "I have given my answer. If
what I say isn't correct, your function is to demand d

6. Someone who aims at scoring points rather than at discovering the truth. See *Republic* 537e–539c.

an account and then refute it." But if people want to engage in discussion with one another as friends, the way you and I are doing now, they must answer more gently, as it were, and in a more dialectical manner.[7] And it is perhaps more dialectical not to answer with the truth alone, but also to do so in terms which the answerer agrees he knows. I too, then, will try to answer you in that way. So tell me, is there something
e you call an end? I mean something like a limit or a boundary—I mean the same thing by all of them. Perhaps, Prodicus would disagree with us,[8] but *you* surely say there is such a thing as having limits or ends. That is the sort of thing I mean—nothing complex.

MENO: Yes I do. I think I understand what you mean, too.

SOCRATES: Well then, is there something you call a surface, and something else again you call a solid—
76 for example, the ones in geometry?

MENO: Yes, there is.

SOCRATES: Then you can already understand from these what I say shape is. You see, in the case of every shape, I say that what a solid meets its limit in is shape.

MENO: And what do you say color is, Socrates?

SOCRATES: You are outrageous, Meno! You cause an old man trouble, commanding him to answer, while you yourself aren't willing to recollect and tell
b us what Gorgias says virtue is.

MENO: You tell me this, Socrates, and I will tell you that.

SOCRATES: A man would know blindfold, Meno, just from the way you engage in discussion, that you are beautiful and still have lovers![9]

MENO: How so?

SOCRATES: Because you do nothing except give commands when you speak, the way spoiled boys do, who act like tyrants while their bloom lasts. At the same time, too, you have probably noticed my
c weakness for beautiful boys. So I will indulge you and answer.

MENO: By all means, indulge me!

SOCRATES: Would you like me to give an answer Gorgias-fashion, the way it would be easiest for you to follow?

MENO: Yes, of course I would.

SOCRATES: Well then, don't you both talk about certain effluences from things, the way Empedocles does?[10]

MENO: Certainly.

SOCRATES: And pores into which and through which the effluences travel?

MENO: Indeed.

SOCRATES: And some of the effluences fit certain pores, whereas others are too small or too large?

MENO: That's right. *d*

SOCRATES: And is there something you call sight?

MENO: There is.

SOCRATES: Well, from this, then, "grasp what I mean," as Pindar says.[11] Color is an effluence from shapes that is commensurate with sight, and so perceptible.

MENO: I think that is an excellent answer, Socrates.

SOCRATES: Probably because it is put in a way you are accustomed to. At the same time, I suppose, you realize that you could use the same things to say what sound is, and smell, and many other things of that sort. *e*

MENO: Of course.

SOCRATES: It is a "deep" answer indeed, Meno, so it pleases you more than the one about shape.

MENO: Yes, it does.

SOCRATES: Yet, I am convinced it is not a *better* one, son of Alexidemus. On the contrary, the other is better. And I don't think you would disagree, if you did not have to leave, as you mentioned yesterday, before the celebration of the Mysteries, but could stay and be initiated.[12]

MENO: But I would stay, Socrates, if you could tell me many things like that. 77

---

7. See *Republic* 454a.

8. See *Apology* 19e and note.

9. Boys had older male lovers from the arrival of puberty (probably quite late in the ancient world) until their beard became full. Meno is presumably a borderline case.

10. See pages 19–23 of this volume.

11. Pindar (518–438 BCE), a lyric poet from Boeotia, was most famous for his poems celebrating the victors in the Olympian, Pythian, and other games. The source of the quotation is *fr.* 121 Turyn = 94 Bowra.

12. Eleusis—one of the major demes in Athens (see *Euthyphro* 2b note)—was the center of a cult that played a prominent role in Athenian civic religion. Some of its rituals were secret mysteries, known only to initiates. Initiation began in February. So the dramatic

SOCRATES: Then I certainly won't be any less than
eager to tell you them—both for your sake and for my
own. But I fear I won't be able to give you many
answers of that sort. Come on, though, you also keep
your promise to me, and try to say what virtue as a
whole is. Stop making many out of one, as the jokers
say each time someone breaks something, but leave
virtue whole and sound and say what it is. You got
b models, at least, from me.

MENO: In that case, Socrates, I think virtue, as the poets say, is "enjoying beautiful things and having power."[13] And so I say this is what virtue is, to desire beautiful things and have the power to get them.

SOCRATES: Do you mean that the one who desires beautiful things desires good ones?

MENO: Yes, of course.

SOCRATES: On the assumption that there are some
people who desire bad things, and others good ones?
Don't you think, my very good man, that everyone
c desires good things?

MENO: No, I don't.

SOCRATES: But some desire bad ones?

MENO: Yes.

SOCRATES: Thinking the bad ones are good, do you mean? Or actually recognizing they are bad and desiring them all the same?

MENO: Both, I think.

SOCRATES: Really? You think someone recognizes that the bad things are bad but desires them all the same?

MENO: Of course.

SOCRATES: What do you mean by that he desires? That he possesses them for himself?

MENO: That he possesses them for himself. What else?

SOCRATES: Thinking that the bad things benefit
d the one who gets them? Or knowing that the bad
things harm the one who possesses them?

MENO: Some thinking that the bad things benefit; others recognizing that they harm.

SOCRATES: Do you also think that those who think that the bad things benefit recognize that the bad things are bad?

MENO: Not at all, I certainly do not think that.

SOCRATES: Then it is clear that *they*—the ones
who do not know about them—don't desire bad
things; rather, they desire things that they think are
good, though in fact they are bad. Hence, those who *e*
don't know about these things and think that they are
good clearly do desire good things. Don't they?

MENO: It looks as though they do, anyway.

SOCRATES: What about those who desire bad things, thinking, so you claim, that bad things harm the one who gets them? They recognize, surely, that they will be harmed by them?

MENO: They must.

SOCRATES: But don't they think that those who are 78
harmed are—to the extent that they are harmed—
wretched?

MENO: They must be aware of that too.

SOCRATES: And that the wretched are unhappy?

MENO: Yes, I think so.

SOCRATES: Is there anyone who wants to be wretched and unhappy?

MENO: I don't think so, Socrates.

SOCRATES: Then no one wants bad things, Meno, if indeed he does not want to be like that. For what is being wretched other than wanting bad things and getting them?

MENO: It looks as though you are right, Socrates—
no one wants bad things. *b*

SOCRATES: Well, weren't you saying just now that virtue is wanting good things and having power?

MENO: Yes, I did say that.

SOCRATES: Well, the wanting part of this statement holds of everyone, and so in this respect at least no one is better than anyone else.

MENO: Apparently.

SOCRATES: But it is clear then that if indeed someone is better than someone else, it must be as regards power that he is better.

MENO: Certainly.

SOCRATES: So this, it seems, is virtue according to your account: the power to get good things.

MENO: I think, Socrates, that the way you are *c*
interpreting me now is entirely correct.

SOCRATES: Let's also see, then, whether you are speaking the truth, since you may prove to have spoken correctly. You say that the power to get good things is virtue?

MENO: I do.

---

date of the conversation is presumably just before that. Plato uses initiation into the Eleusinian mysteries as a metaphor for initiation into philosophy at *Gorgias* 497c, *Symposium* 209e–210a, and *Theaetetus* 155e.

13. Source unknown.

Socrates: And the things you call good are things like wealth and health aren't they?

Meno: Yes, I think getting gold and silver is good and also honors and public offices in the city.

Socrates: But you don't think anything else is good besides things of that sort?

Meno: No, just all things of that sort.

d Socrates: All right. Getting gold and silver is virtue. So says Meno, family friend of the Great King![14] Do you add "justly and piously" to this "getting," Meno? Or does that make no difference? Even if someone gets these things *unjustly*, do you call it virtue all the same?

Meno: Certainly not, Socrates.

Socrates: But vice?

Meno: Certainly.

Socrates: So it seems that justice, temperance, piety, or some other part of virtue must be added to
e this getting. If not, it will not be virtue, even though it is a getting of good things.

Meno: No, for how could it be virtue without them?

Socrates: And *not* getting gold and silver, either for oneself or for someone else, when it is not just to do so, isn't this also virtue, this not-getting?

Meno: Apparently.

Socrates: So getting good things won't be any more virtue than not getting them. Instead, what is done with justice is virtue, while what is done without anything like it, is vice.

79 Meno: I think it must be as you claim.

Socrates: Now, didn't we say a moment ago that each of these is a part of virtue—justice, temperance, and everything of that sort?

Meno: Yes.

Socrates: Really, Meno? Are you teasing me?

Meno: Why, Socrates?

Socrates: Because I begged you just now not to break virtue into pieces or exchange it for smaller coins. I even gave you models of how you should answer. But you pay no attention to that, and tell me
b that virtue is getting good things with justice. And justice, you say, is part of virtue.

Meno: I do.

Socrates: It follows, then, from what you agree to, that doing whatever one does with a part of virtue is virtue. For you say that justice is a part of virtue, as well as each of the others.

Meno: So?

Socrates: What I mean is this. I begged you to say what virtue as a whole is. But you, far from saying what it is, claim that every action is virtue if it is done with a part of virtue—just as if you had said what
virtue as a whole is and I already know it, and would c
continue to do so even if you broke it up into pieces. So it seems to me that you need to start again with the same question, my friend. What is virtue, if every action done with a part of virtue is virtue? For that is what someone is saying when he says that every action done with justice is virtue. Don't you think you need to go back to the same question? Or do you think someone knows what a part of virtue is, when he does not know what virtue itself is?

Meno: No, I don't think that.

Socrates: No. Also if you remember when I was
answering you just now about shape, I think we d
rejected that sort of answer—one that tries to answer in terms of things that are still being inquired about and have not yet been agreed to.

Meno: Yes, and we were right to reject it, Socrates.

Socrates: Then, my good Meno, when virtue as a whole is still being inquired about, you shouldn't suppose you will make it clear to anyone by couching your answer in terms of its parts, or that you will make anything else clear by speaking the same way. Rather, you should accept that the same question
needs to be asked again. What is this virtue about e
which you say the things you say? Or do you think I am talking nonsense?

Meno: No, I think what you say is right.

Socrates: Then answer again from the beginning. What do both you and that friend of yours say virtue is?

Meno: Socrates, I heard before I ever met you that
you are never anything but puzzled yourself and that 80
you make others puzzled too. And now, I see for myself that you are using sorcery on me, drugging me, and simply subduing me with spells, so that I am full of puzzles. Indeed, you seem to me—if I may make a little joke—to be altogether very similar, both in appearance and other respects, to the flat, saltwater

---

14. Xerxes I, king of Persia (486–465 BCE), led the unsuccessful invasion of Greece in the Persian Wars. He was regarded as the richest and most powerful ruler imaginable. Meno may have had some hereditary connection with the Persian royal house.

stingray, since it too always numbs whoever comes
near and touches it. And you, I think, have now done
something like that to me. You see, my soul and my
mouth feel truly numb, and so I do not have an
b answer for you. Yet on countless occasions, I have
talked at length about virtue, in front of lots of people—very well, too, or so *I* thought. But now I cannot
say at all what sort of thing it is. And so I think your
decision not to travel away from here or live abroad
was a good one. For if you did things like this as a foreigner in another city, you might well be arrested as
a sorcerer.

SOCRATES: You are a tricky customer, Meno! You
almost had me fooled!

MENO: How exactly, Socrates?

c SOCRATES: I know why you produced that image
of me.

MENO: Why?

SOCRATES: To get a counterimage of yourself in
return! I know that all beautiful boys enjoy a game of
image-making. After all, it profits them. For the images
of beautiful boys, I suppose, are also beautiful. But I
am not going to give a counterimage of you. As for
me, if the stingray is numb itself, and only for that
reason numbs others too, I am like it—otherwise not.
You see, it is not that *I* am puzzle-free but make others puzzled. On the contrary, I am completely puzzled myself, and that is how I make others puzzled
too. And now, as far as virtue is concerned, I do not
d know what it is. Perhaps, you knew before you came
into contact with me, but now you are like someone
who does not know. All the same, I want to consider
the matter with you and join you in inquiring about
what it is.

MENO: And how are you going to inquire about it,
Socrates, when you do not at all know what it is? For
what sort of thing, from among the ones you do not
know, will you take as the object of your inquiry?
And even if you do happen to bump right into it,
how are you going to know that *it* is the thing you did
not know?

SOCRATES: I understand what you want to say,
e Meno. Do you see how eristical the argument is that
you are spinning? According to it, so it seems, it is
not possible for a person to inquire about what he
knows, or about what he does not know. After all, he
wouldn't inquire about what he knows—since he knows
it, and there is no need to inquire about something
like that—or about what he does not know—since
he does not know what he is to inquire about.

MENO: Well, don't you think it is a beautiful argu- *81*
ment, Socrates?

SOCRATES: No, I do not.

MENO: Can you tell me why?

SOCRATES: Yes, I can. You see, I have heard men
and women who are wise in divine matters. . . .

MENO: Saying what?

SOCRATES: Something true, I think, and beautiful.

MENO: What is it? And who are the ones who say it?

SOCRATES: The ones who say it are those priests
and priestesses who have made it their concern to be
able to give an account of their practices.[15] Pindar
says it, too, as well as many other poets who are god- *b*
like men. And what they say is this. See whether you
think they are telling the truth. They say the human
soul is immortal. At one time it comes to an end—
which is what people call dying—and at another is
born again. But it is never destroyed. Because of this,
they say, one should live one's life as piously as possible. For from whomever

> Persephone accepts requital for her ancient
> grief, in the ninth year, to the sun above
> she returns their souls again,
> and from these, stately kings, *c*
> men swift in strength, in wisdom unsurpassed,
> arise. And for the rest of time, heroes holy
> by men they shall be called.[16]

Since the soul is immortal, then, and has been born
many times, and has seen both the things here and
the ones in Hades—in fact, all things—there is nothing it has not learned. So it is in no way surprising
that it can recollect about virtue and other things,
since it knew them before. For, since all nature is
akin, and the soul has learned all things, nothing *d*
prevents someone who is recollecting one thing—

---

15. Their identity is unknown.

16. Probably a quotation from Pindar. Persephone, daughter of Demeter and Zeus, and wife of Hades, was queen of the underworld. Her grief, in this instance, was probably for her son, Dionysus, who was devoured by the Titans. Zeus blasted them with a thunderbolt, but human beings sprang from their ashes, and so are involved in their guilt and must make atonement to Persephone.

which men call learning it—from discovering all the rest for himself, provided he is courageous and doesn't get tired of inquiry. For the whole of inquiry or learning, in that case, is recollection. So one should not be persuaded by that eristical argument, since it would make us idle. It is pleasant for men who are soft to hear. But the present one makes us
e energetic and eager to inquire. Trusting in its truth, I am willing to inquire with you about what virtue is.

MENO: Yes, Socrates. But what do you mean we do not learn, that what we call learning is in fact recollection? Can you teach me that this is so?

SOCRATES: I said a moment ago, Meno, that you were a tricky customer! And now you ask if I can
82 teach you, when I say there is no teaching but only recollection, so that I shall be immediately revealed to have contradicted myself!

MENO: By Zeus, Socrates, I didn't ask you with that in mind, but from force of habit! But if you can somehow show me that it is as you say, please show me.

SOCRATES: Well, it is not easy. All the same, I am willing to try for your sake. Call over to me one of the many attendants you have here, whichever one you
b like, so that I can demonstrate it for you in his case.

MENO: Certainly. [*Addressing a slave boy*] Come over here.

SOCRATES: Is he a Greek? Does he speak Greek, at least?

MENO: Yes, indeed. He is homegrown.

SOCRATES: Pay attention, then, and see whether he seems to you to be recollecting or learning from me.

MENO: Yes, I will.

SOCRATES: [*Turning to the boy*] Tell me, boy, do you know that a square figure looks like this? [*He draws the square ABCD in Figure 1.*]

BOY: I do.

SOCRATES: A square figure, then, is one that has all these four lines equal [*points to AB, BC, CD,*
c *and DA*].[17]

BOY: Certainly.

SOCRATES: And doesn't it also have these across the middle equal [*points to EF, GH*]?

BOY: Yes.

Figure 1

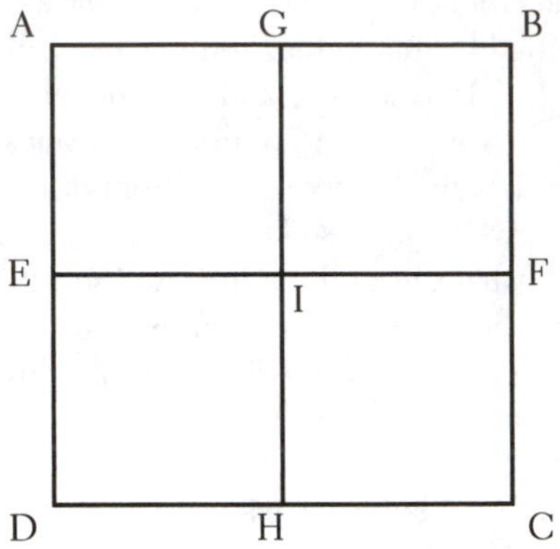

A G B
E I F
D H C

SOCRATES: Now couldn't there be a larger figure of this sort [*points to ABCD*] or a smaller one [*points to AGIE or one of the other inner squares*]?

BOY: Certainly.

SOCRATES: Then, if this side [*AB*] were two feet, and this one [*BC*] were two feet, how many feet would the whole be? Look at it this way. If it were two feet this way [*AB*], but only one this way [*BF*], wouldn't the figure [*ABFE*] be one times two feet?

BOY: Yes.

SOCRATES: But since it is also two feet in this direction [*BC*], isn't it twice two? d

BOY: It is.

SOCRATES: So it is twice two feet?

BOY: Yes.

SOCRATES: How many feet, then, is twice two? Count them and tell me?

BOY: [*Counting the interior squares*] Four, Socrates.

SOCRATES: Now, couldn't there be another figure twice the size of this one [*ABCD*], but similar to it, having all its lines [*AB, BC, CD, DA, GH, EF*] equal just like this one?

BOY: Yes.

SOCRATES: How many feet will it be?

BOY: Eight.

SOCRATES: Come on then, try to tell me how long each side in it will be. In this one [*ABCD*], it is two feet. What is it in the one that is twice the size? e

BOY: Clearly then, Socrates, it will be twice the size.

SOCRATES: Do you see, Meno, that I am not teaching him anything, but that all I am doing is asking questions? And at this point he thinks he knows how long a side will result in a figure of eight feet. Do you not agree?

17. Strictly speaking, a rhombus not a square, since a square must have four equal angles as well. The equality of the sides is the pertinent feature for the demonstration, however.

MENO: I do.

SOCRATES: Well, does he know?

MENO: Certainly not.

SOCRATES: But he thinks, at least, that it results from a side twice as long.

MENO: Yes.

SOCRATES: Now watch him recollect in order, which is the way one should recollect. [*Turning back to the boy*] Now you tell me this. You say that a figure twice the size results from a side twice as long? I
83 mean one like this, not long in this way [*AB*] and short in that [*BF*], but equal in all directions, as this one [*ABCD*] is, but twice its size, or eight feet. See if you still think it will result from a side twice as long.

Figure 2

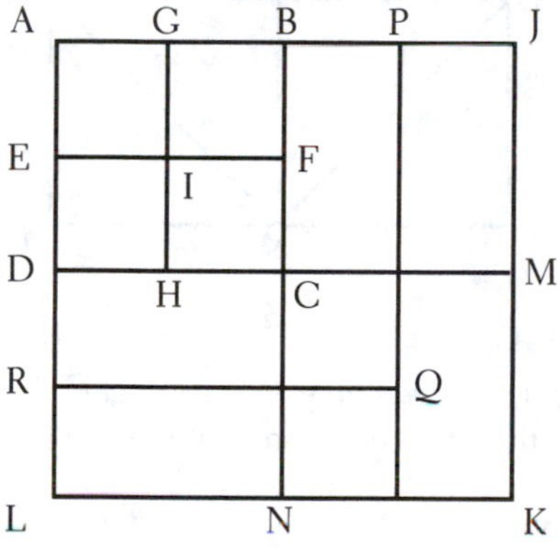

BOY: Yes, I do.

SOCRATES: Well, isn't this line [*AJ*] twice as long as this [*AB*] if we add a second line of the same length [*BJ*] from here [*B*]? [*He draws the line BJ in Figure* 2.]

BOY: Certainly.

SOCRATES: And it [*AJ*], you say, will result in a fig-
b ure of eight feet, if there are four like it?

BOY: Yes.

SOCRATES: Then let's draw four equal sides starting from it. [*Socrates draws JK, KL, LD*] Wouldn't it [*AJKL*] be what you say is eight feet?

BOY: Certainly.

SOCRATES: Now, in it there are these four figures [*ABCD, BJMC, CMKN, DCNL*], each of which is equal to this four-foot one [*ABCD*].

BOY: Yes.

SOCRATES: Then, how big is it? Isn't it four times as big?

BOY: Certainly.

SOCRATES: Then is four times the same size as twice?

BOY: No, by Zeus, it isn't!

SOCRATES: Then how many times is it the same as?

BOY: Four times.

SOCRATES: So from a line twice as long, my boy, a
figure results that is not twice as big, but four times. c

BOY: That's true.

SOCRATES: For a figure of four times four feet is sixteen feet. Isn't it?

BOY: Yes.

SOCRATES: So a figure of eight feet results from what line? Didn't this one [*AJ*] result in a figure four times as big?

BOY: It did.

SOCRATES: And this quarter here [*ABCD*] results from this half here [*AB*]?

BOY: Yes.

SOCRATES: All right. But isn't the eight-foot figure double this one [*ABCD*] and half this one [*AJKL*]?

BOY: Yes.

SOCRATES: Will it result from a line longer than this one [*AB*] but shorter than this one here [*AJ*]? Or won't it?

BOY: Yes, I think so.

SOCRATES: Good. You see, what you think is what d
you should give as your answer. So tell me, isn't this one [*AB*] two feet, and this one [*AJ*] four?

BOY: Yes.

SOCRATES: Then the line from which the eight-foot figure results must be greater than this two-foot one [*AB*], but less than this four-foot one [*AJ*].

BOY: It must.

SOCRATES: Then try to tell me how long you think
it is. e

BOY: Three feet.

SOCRATES: Well, if indeed it is to be three feet, let's take half of this line [*BJ*] as well [*he marks the point P in Figure* 2] and it [*AP*] will be three feet. For there are two here [*AB*] and one here [*BP*]. And over here [*he marks the point R*], similarly, there are two feet here [*AD*] and one here [*DR*]. And the resulting figure [*he completes the square APQR*] is the one you mention.

BOY: Yes.

SOCRATES: Then if this [*AR*] is three and this [*AP*] is three, isn't the whole figure that results three times three feet?

Boy: Apparently so.

Socrates: And three times three is how many feet?

Boy: Nine.

Socrates: But the one that was twice the size had to be how many feet?

Boy: Eight.

Socrates: So the eight-foot figure does not at all result from the three-foot line either.

Boy: No, indeed.

Socrates: But from which one does it result? Try to tell us exactly. If you don't want to calculate its length, point to which one it results from.

84 Boy: But, by Zeus, Socrates, I really don't know.

Socrates: [*Turning to Meno*] Do you see, Meno, what point he has reached as he proceeds on the path of recollection? At first, he did not know what the side of the eight-foot figure is, just as he does not at all know at this point either. But then he at least thought he knew, answered confidently as if he knew, and didn't think he was puzzled. At this point, however, he now does believe he is puzzled, and as he does not
b in fact know, he does not think he does either.

Meno: That's true.

Socrates: Then isn't he now better off as regards the thing he did not know?

Meno: I agree with that too.

Socrates: By making him puzzled, then, and numbing him like a stingray, have we done him any harm?

Meno: No, I don't think so.

Socrates: We have certainly done something useful, it seems, as regards finding out how the matter stands. For now he might actually inquire into it with pleasure, since he does not know, whereas before he thought he could easily speak well in front of lots of people and on lots of occasions about the
c figure that is twice the size, and how it must have a side twice as long.

Meno: So it seems.

Socrates: Well, do you think he would have tried to inquire or learn about what he thought he knew, but did not know, before he fell into puzzlement, came to believe that he did not know, and became anxious to know?

Meno: I don't think so, Socrates.

Socrates: So didn't numbing profit him?

Meno: I think so.

Socrates: Observe, then, what he will discover starting from this puzzlement, as he inquires with me—but I shall only be asking questions, not teaching. You be on your guard to see whether you discover me teaching or expounding something to him d
at any point, instead of questioning him about his own beliefs. [*Socrates turns back to the slave boy, erasing everything from Figure 2 except the square ABCD*] Now you tell me, isn't this our four-foot figure? You understand?

Figure 3

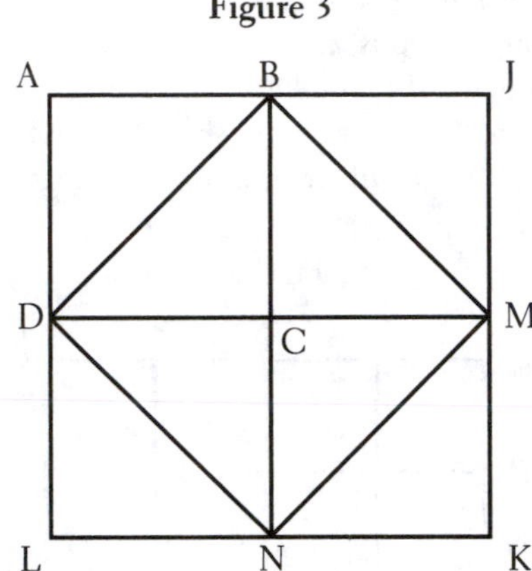

Boy: I do.

Socrates: [*Beginning to draw Figure* 3] And we can add this other one here that is equal to it [*draws BJMC*]?

Boy: Yes.

Socrates: And this third one that is equal to each of them [*draws MKNC*]?

Boy: Yes.

Socrates: Then we could fill in this one in the corner [*draws NLD*]?

Boy: Certainly.

Socrates: Then won't these four equal figures result?

Boy: Yes.

Socrates: Then, this whole resulting one [*AJKL*] is how many times as big as this one [*ABCD*]? e

Boy: Four times.

Socrates: But we needed one that was twice as big. Don't you remember?

Boy: Certainly.

Socrates: Now doesn't this line from corner to corner [*he draws BD as an example of the sort of line he means*] cut each of these figures [*the four interior squares*] in two? 85

Boy: Yes.

Socrates: Then aren't the four resulting lines [*he draws BM, MN, ND*] equal, the ones enclosing this figure [*BMND*]?

Boy: Yes, they are.

Socrates: Now consider. How large is this figure?

Boy: I don't know.

Socrates: Has each of these lines cut off the inner half of these four figures? Or not?

Boy: Yes.

Socrates: Then how many of this size [*BCD*] are there in this one [*BMND*]?

Boy: Four.

Socrates: And how many in this [*ABCD*]?

Boy: Two.

Socrates: And what is four to two?

Boy: It is twice it.

Socrates: How many feet in this [*BMND*] as a result?

Boy: Eight.

b **Socrates:** From what line?

Boy: From this one [*BD*].

Socrates: From the one that stretches from one corner to the other of the four-foot one?

Boy: Yes.

Socrates: Experts call that the diagonal.[18] Hence if "diagonal" is its name, it would be from the diagonal, you say, Meno's slave boy, that the twice-as-big figure results.

Boy: Yes, certainly, Socrates.

Socrates: [*Turning to Meno*] What do you think, Meno? Is there any belief he gave as an answer that is not his own?

c **Meno:** No, they are his own.

Socrates: And yet he did not know the answer, as we said a short while ago.

Meno: That's right.

Socrates: But these beliefs were in him, at least, were they not?

Meno: Yes.

Socrates: So the one who does not have knowledge about whatever things he does not know has true beliefs in him about the things he does not know?

Meno: Apparently.

Socrates: And now, by contrast, these beliefs have been stirred up in him like a dream. But if someone asks him these same questions many times and in many ways, you know that in the end he will have knowledge of them that is no less exact than
anyone else's. *d*

Meno: So it seems.

Socrates: Then he will have knowledge without being taught by anyone but only questioned, since *he* will have recovered the knowledge *from inside himself*.

Meno: Yes.

Socrates: But recovering knowledge himself from within himself is recollection, is it not?

Meno: Of course.

Socrates: So didn't he either get the knowledge he now has at some time or else always have it?

Meno: Yes.

Socrates: Well, if he always had it, he would always have known. And if he got it at some time, at least he did not get it in his present life. Or did someone teach him to do geometry? For if so, he will do
the same in every part of geometry, and in all other *e*
subjects too. Is there anyone, then, who has taught him all that? You certainly ought to know, especially since he was born and brought up in your household.

Meno: No, I know no one has ever taught him.

Socrates: But he has these beliefs, does he not?

Meno: Apparently, he must, Socrates.

Socrates: Well, if he did not get them in his present life, isn't it clear now that he got or learned them
at some other time? *86*

Meno: Apparently.

Socrates: At that time, then, when he was not a human being?[19]

Meno: Yes.

Socrates: Well, if for whatever time he is a human being, and for whatever time he is not one, there are true beliefs in him, which result in knowledge when awakened by questioning, won't his soul be for all time in a state of learnedness? For it is clear that for all time he either is, or is not, a human being.

Meno: Apparently.

Socrates: Then if the truth about the things that
are is always in our soul, the soul is immortal. So *b*
you should confidently try to inquire about and to

---

18. *Diametron:* a word also used for the diameter of a circle, the axis of a sphere, and the hypotenuse of a triangle.

19. Before his soul was embodied in a human body. See *Republic* 619e–620c.

recollect what you do not happen to know at present—that is, what you do not remember.

MENO: I think you are right, Socrates, but I do not know *how*.

SOCRATES: I think I am too, Meno. And while there are other aspects of the argument on which I would not entirely insist, that we shall be better and more courageous and less idle if we think we should inquire about what we do not know than if we think that it is not possible to find what we do not know and that we shouldn't inquire about it—that is something
c I would fight for to the death, if I could, both in word and deed.

MENO: Yes, I think you are right about that, at least, Socrates.

SOCRATES: Since we agree, then, that one should inquire about what one does not know, do you want us to try to inquire together about what virtue is?

MENO: I certainly do. Nevertheless, Socrates, what I would most like to consider and hear about is the very thing I asked at the beginning: should we inquire on the assumption that virtue is something
d present in human beings by teaching, or by nature, or in what way?

SOCRATES: Well, Meno, if I ruled not only myself but you as well, we would not consider whether virtue is acquired by teaching or not before inquiring about what it is. However, since you are not even trying to rule yourself—in order to remain free, I suppose—but are trying to rule me and succeeding in ruling me, I shall agree. What else am I to do? So it seems we must consider what sort of thing something is when we do not yet know what it is. If you won't do anything
e else, though, at least relax your rule a little bit for my sake, and agree to investigate *from a hypothesis* whether it is acquired by teaching or whatever. By "from a hypothesis," I mean, the way geometers often conduct their investigations. When someone asks them, for example, whether this figure [*Socrates points to ABCD in Figures* 2 *and* 3] can be inscribed in this circle [*Figure* 4] as a triangle, one of them
87 might reply, "I don't know yet whether it is the sort that can, but I think I have a hypothesis, so to speak, which is useful in dealing with the question. If this figure [*ABCD*] is such that, when one applies it to the given line here [*points to AJ*], it falls short by a figure similar to the one applied [*BCMJ*], I think one thing follows, and another if it is impossible for this to

Figure 4

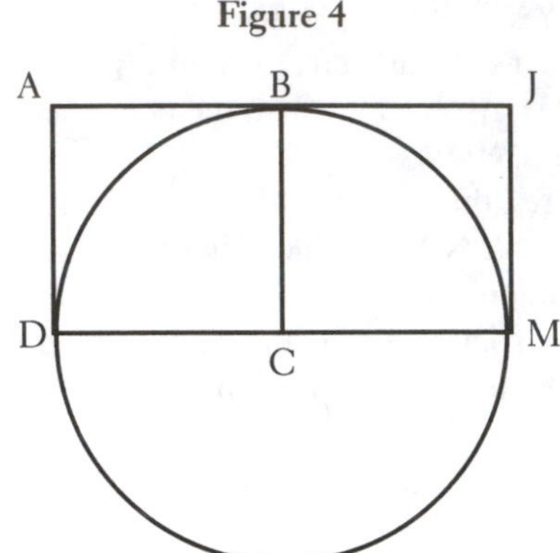

happen. By adopting a hypothesis, then, I am willing
to tell you whether it is possible or not to inscribe it in b
the circle."[20] It is the same for us, too, where virtue is concerned. Since we do not know what it is or what sort of thing it is, let's consider by adopting a hypothesis whether it is something acquired by teaching, or not something acquired by teaching. Let's proceed as follows: Among the things belonging to the soul, what sort would virtue have to be if it is to be something not acquired by teaching, or not something acquired by teaching? First, if it is a different sort of thing than knowledge, or the same sort, is it acquired by teaching or not—or as we said just now, acquired by recollection? It makes no difference to us which name is
used. Let's say, acquired by teaching. Or isn't this, at c
least, clear to everyone, that a person is not taught anything except knowledge?

MENO: I think so.

SOCRATES: But *if* virtue is some sort of knowledge, it clearly would be acquired by teaching.

MENO: Of course.

SOCRATES: So we finished with that quickly: if it is the one sort of thing, it is acquired by teaching; if the other, not.

MENO: Certainly.

SOCRATES: Next, it seems, we should consider whether virtue is knowledge or a different sort of thing than knowledge.

MENO: Yes, I think we should consider that next. d

SOCRATES: Well then, do we say that it—I mean, virtue—is something good? And does this hypothesis stay put for us, that it is a good thing?

20. The interpretation of Figure 4 is conjectural.

MENO: Certainly.

SOCRATES: Then if there is something that is good, other than and separate from knowledge, perhaps virtue might not be some sort of knowledge. But if nothing is good that is not included in knowledge, we may correctly suspect that it is some sort of knowledge.

MENO: That's right.

SOCRATES: And it is by virtue that we are good.

MENO: Yes.

e SOCRATES: And if good, beneficial. For all good
things are beneficial. Aren't they?

MENO: Yes.

SOCRATES: Then virtue is a beneficial thing.

MENO: That necessarily follows from the things we have agreed to.

SOCRATES: Then let's consider one by one the sorts of things that benefit us. Health does, we say, and strength and beauty and wealth. These and things like them are the ones we say are beneficial. Aren't they?

MENO: Yes.

SOCRATES: But these same things, we say, some-
88 times harm. Or do you disagree with that?

MENO: No, I agree.

SOCRATES: Consider, then, what guides each of these when they benefit us, and what when they harm. Doesn't it benefit when there is correct use, and harm when there isn't?

MENO: Certainly.

SOCRATES: In addition, then, let's also consider the ones having to do with the soul. Temperance is one, you say, and justice and courage and ease-in-learning and good memory and high-mindedness and everything of that sort?

MENO: I do.

SOCRATES: Consider, then. Don't the ones among
b them that seem to you to be not knowledge, but
something other than knowledge, sometimes harm and sometimes benefit? Take courage, for example. If courage is not wisdom, but a sort of boldness, then, when a person is bold without understanding, isn't he harmed, when with understanding, benefited?

MENO: Yes.

SOCRATES: Similarly, too, with temperance and ease-in-learning. When things are learned or acquired by training together with understanding, aren't they beneficial, when without understanding, harmful?

MENO: Very much so.

SOCRATES: In a word, then, all of the soul's under- *c*
takings and acts of endurance, when guided by wisdom, end in happiness, when by folly, in the opposite.

MENO: It seems so.

SOCRATES: So if virtue is one of the things in the soul and is necessarily beneficial, it must be wisdom, since in fact all the others having to do with the soul, taken by themselves, are neither beneficial nor harmful, but become harmful or beneficial when wisdom or folly is
added. According to this argument, then, since virtue *d*
is beneficial it must be some sort of wisdom.

MENO: Yes, I think so.

SOCRATES: In fact, in the case of all the others too—wealth and the rest—that we said just now are sometimes good, sometimes harmful, isn't something similar true? When wisdom guides the rest of the soul, it makes all the other things in the soul beneficial, while foolishness makes them harmful. Similarly, with these things too, when the soul uses
and guides them correctly, doesn't it make them ben- *e*
eficial, when not correctly, harmful?

MENO: Certainly.

SOCRATES: And doesn't the wise one guide correctly, the foolish one incorrectly?

MENO: That's right.

SOCRATES: Then, can't we say the same in the case of all of them? In human beings all the rest depend on the soul. Those of the soul itself depend on wisdom, if they are going to be good things. And so, by
this argument, what is beneficial would be wisdom. 89
And we say that virtue is a beneficial thing?

MENO: Certainly.

SOCRATES: So we say that virtue is wisdom, either the whole thing or some part of it?

MENO: I think what we are saying, Socrates, is quite right.

SOCRATES: If that is so, then, good men would not be good by nature.

MENO: No, I don't think they would.

SOCRATES: Indeed, if they were, the following would also be the case. If good men were good by
nature, we would surely have people who recognized *b*
those of the young who were good by nature. And when they had pointed them out to us, we would guard them in our acropolis,[21] sealing them up

21. A fortified high place in a city, where public treasures were kept.

much more carefully than gold, so that no one could corrupt them, but that they, when they reached maturity, might be useful to their cities.

MENO: That seems reasonable enough, Socrates.

SOCRATES: So, since good men are not good by c nature, are they so by learning?

MENO: That now seems necessary to me. And clearly, Socrates, on our hypothesis that virtue is knowledge, it is acquired by teaching.

SOCRATES: Perhaps so, by Zeus! But perhaps we weren't right to agree to that.

MENO: It certainly seemed right a moment ago.

SOCRATES: Yes, but if any of it is going to be sound, it must seem right not just a moment ago, but also now and in the future.

MENO: Well then, what is it? What is it you are d thinking that makes you uneasy about it and makes you fear that virtue is not knowledge?

SOCRATES: I shall tell you, Meno. That it is acquired by teaching, if indeed it is knowledge—*that* I do not retract as incorrect. But consider whether you think it is reasonable to fear that it is not knowledge. Tell me this: if anything whatever is acquired by teaching—not just virtue—mustn't there be teachers and learners of it?

MENO: I think so.

SOCRATES: Then again won't the opposite hold? If e there were neither teachers nor learners of something, wouldn't it be right to conjecture that it is not acquired by teaching?

MENO: That's right. But don't you think there are teachers of virtue?

SOCRATES: I have often inquired, certainly, to see if there are any teachers of it, but try as I may, I can't find any. Yet I carried out my inquiry with many people, especially those I thought most experienced in the matter. And in fact, Meno, Anytus here has sat down beside us at just the right time. Let's share our inquiry with him. It would be reasonable for us to 90 share it. For, first, Anytus is the son of a wealthy and wise father, Anthemion,[22] who has become wealthy not by chance or as a result of a gift—like Ismenias of Thebes, who recently acquired the wealth of Polycrates[23]—but by his own wisdom and carefulness. Next, as regards other things too, he seems not to be a haughty, scornful, or offensive citizen, but a moderate and well-behaved man. Finally, he brought up and educated Anytus well, as the majority of Atheni- b ans think—at any rate, they choose him for their highest offices.[24] It is right, then, to inquire with such people to see whether there are any teachers of virtue or not, and who they are. So Anytus, please inquire with us, with me and your friend Meno here, into this matter of who the teachers of virtue might be. Consider it this way. If we wanted Meno here to become a good doctor, what teachers would we send c him to? Wouldn't we send him to doctors?

ANYTUS: Certainly.

SOCRATES: What if we wanted him to become a good shoemaker? Wouldn't we send him to shoemakers?[25]

ANYTUS: Yes.

SOCRATES: And similarly in all the other cases?

ANYTUS: Certainly.

SOCRATES: Then consider the same cases again and tell me this. We say that we would be right to send him to doctors if we want him to become a doctor. When we say this, are we saying that we would be sensible to send him to those who claim to possess d the art rather than those who don't, and who charge a fee for this very thing, and declare themselves to be teachers of anyone who wants to come to them and learn? Isn't it with these considerations in mind that we would be right to send him there?

ANYTUS: Yes.

SOCRATES: And doesn't the same apply to flute-playing and the rest? It would be the height of ignorance, if we wanted to make someone a flute-player, e to be unwilling to send him to those who undertake to teach the art, but to trouble other people, when they neither claim to be teachers nor have a single learner in the thing we want the one we send to learn

22. On Anytus, see *Apology* 18b note. About Anthemion we know pretty much only what we are told here.

23. Polycrates, a leading Athenian democrat, wrote (a lost) *Accusation of Socrates*. Xenophon's *Socrates' Defense to the Jury* is thought to be a response to it. Ismenias may have accepted money from Polycrates to help overthrow the Thirty Tyrants and restore the democracy. See *Apology* 32c and note 20. Ismenias is mentioned at *Republic* 336a in a context that suggests Platonic disapproval.

24. Anytus was chosen as *stratēgos*—general—in 409 BCE and may have held other offices as well.

25. Anytus and his father may have been tanners.

from them. Don't you think that would be the height
of irrationality?

ANYTUS: Yes, I do, by Zeus, and of lack of education besides!

SOCRATES: That's right. So now you and I can
deliberate together about your guest Meno here. You
91 see, he has been telling me for a long time, Anytus,
that he wants the wisdom and virtue by which people
manage their households and cities well, look after
their parents, and know how to welcome fellow citizens and foreigners and send them off, in a way worthy of a good man. Consider then, to whom it would
b be right for us to send him to learn this virtue. Or, is
it absolutely clear, according to our discussion just
now, that we should send him to those who undertake to be teachers of virtue, declare themselves available to any Greek who wants to learn, and charge a
set fee for it?

ANYTUS: And who do you say these people are,
Socrates?

SOCRATES: You surely know as well as I do that they
are the ones people call Sophists.

ANYTUS: In the name of Heracles,[26] be quiet,
c Socrates! May no one belonging to me, whether family members or friends, citizens or foreigners, be
seized by such madness as to go to those people, and
be ruined. For they plainly pervert and corrupt those
who associate with them.

SOCRATES: What are you saying, Anytus? Do they
alone differ so much from others who claim to know
how to do some good, that they not only don't benefit what one entrusts to them, like the others, but do
the opposite and actually corrupt it? And they openly
d claim to deserve payment for doing *that*? I don't
know, frankly, how I am to believe you. Indeed, I
know that one man, Protagoras, earned more money
from this sort of wisdom than Phidias—who produced such conspicuously beautiful work—and ten
other sculptors combined. Anyway, what you say is
incredible. Those who repair old shoes and mend
cloaks couldn't escape detection for thirty days if they
e gave back the cloaks and shoes in worse condition
than they got them. On the contrary, if they did that,
they would soon starve to death. So how could Protagoras escape detection by the whole of Greece, if,
for more than forty years, he corrupted those who
associated with him and sent them off worse than
when they came? He was almost seventy years old, I
think, when he died and had practiced his art for
forty years. And in all that time, right up to the present day, his good reputation hasn't diminished. And
Protagoras is not the only one. On the contrary, there
are many others as well, some earlier than he, some 92
still alive. On your account, are we to say that they
led the young astray and ruined them knowingly, or
in a way that escaped detection even by themselves?
Are we to claim they are as mad as that, those who
some say are the wisest people there are?

ANYTUS: They are far from mad, Socrates. The
young people who give them money are much more
so, and their relatives who allow them do it are even
madder than they. But by far the maddest of all are b
the cities that allow these men in when they arrive
and don't expel any citizen or foreigner who attempts
to do anything like that.

SOCRATES: Has one of these Sophists wronged you,
Anytus? Why are you so hard on them?

ANYTUS: No, by Zeus, I have never associated with
any of them or allowed anyone of mine to do so.

SOCRATES: So you have absolutely no experience
of these men?

ANYTUS: No, and hope to remain that way.

SOCRATES: You are a strange fellow! How do you
know whether there is anything good or bad in this c
undertaking of theirs, if you have absolutely no experience of it?

ANYTUS: It's easy! I *know* who these people are.
Whether I lack or don't lack experience of them has
nothing to do with it.

SOCRATES: Perhaps you are a prophet, Anytus! For
I wonder how else you could know about them, given
the things you yourself say. Really though, we weren't
inquiring about who the people are that will make
Meno wicked if he goes to them. Let *these* be the d
Sophists, if you like. But tell us, and do some good for
this family friend of yours by telling him, to whom
should he go in so large a city in order to become
worthy of mention for the virtue I described just now.

ANYTUS: Why don't you tell him yourself?

SOCRATES: But I did say who I thought the teachers
of these things are. But you said I was talking nonsense. And perhaps there is something in what you
say. But now it is your turn to tell him to which of the e
Athenians he should go. Name whomever you like.

26. See *Euthyphro* 4a and note.

Anytus: Why should he be told one person's name? Without exception, any fine and good Athenian he happens to meet will make him better than the Sophists, provided he is willing to believe them.

Socrates: Did these men become fine and good by chance? Without having learned from anyone, are they nevertheless able to teach others what they
93 themselves didn't learn?

Anytus: I think they learned from their predecessors, who were fine and good men too. Or don't you think there have been many good men in this city?

Socrates: I think, Anytus, both that there are men here who are good in political affairs, and that there have been just as many in the past. But were they also good teachers of their own virtue? You see, that is what our discussion is about, not whether there are good men here or not, or whether there have been in the past, but whether virtue really is acquired by teaching—that is what we have been considering for a long
b time. But to consider that is to consider this: do good men, whether now or in the past, also know how to pass on to someone else this virtue that makes them good, or is it something a person cannot pass on or receive from someone else? That is what Meno and I have been inquiring about for a long time. On the basis of your own account, consider it this way:
c Wouldn't you say that Themistocles[27] was a good man?

Anytus: Yes, among the best of them all.

Socrates: Then wouldn't you also say that he was a good teacher of his own virtue if anyone was?

Anytus: I suppose so—if he *wanted* to be.

Socrates: Do you think he wouldn't have wanted others to become fine and good men, not even his own son? Do you think he begrudged it to him and deliberately did not pass on the virtue that made him
d good himself? Haven't you heard that Themistocles had his son Cleophantus taught to be a good horseman? Why, he could stay standing upright on horseback, throw the javelin from horseback while standing upright, and do many other amazing things, which Themistocles had had him educated in and made clever at, and which depend on having good teachers. Haven't you heard that from older people?

Anytus: I have.

Socrates: So no one could claim that his son's *nature* was bad.

Anytus: No, they probably couldn't. e

Socrates: What about this? Have you ever heard anyone young or old say that Themistocles' son Cleophantus was a good and wise man in the way his father was?

Anytus: Certainly not.

Socrates: So are we to think that he wanted to educate his son in those other things, but not to make him any better than his neighbors when it came to the wisdom he himself possessed—*if*, of course, virtue really is acquired by teaching.

Anytus: By Zeus, probably not!

Socrates: That is your sort of teacher of virtue for you, then—the one even you agree was among the best in the past. But let's consider another, Aristides son of Lysimachus.[28] Don't you agree that he 94
was good?

Anytus: I certainly do, absolutely.

Socrates: Well, didn't he too do the best job of any Athenian of educating his son Lysimachus in anything that depended on teachers? But do you think he made him a better man than anyone else? You have associated with him, I assume, and see what he is like. Or take Pericles,[29] if you prefer—since he was a man of such high-minded wisdom. You know he brought up two sons, Paralus and Xanthippus? b

Anytus: I do.

Socrates: You also know, then, that he taught them to be horsemen second to none in Athens, and that he had them educated in musical and physical training and all the other things that depend on expertise, so as to be second to none. Didn't he want

---

27. Themistocles (c. 524–459 BCE) was an Athenian statesman and chief architect of the Greek victory in the war against the Persians. He was ostracized by Athens at the end of the 470s and was later condemned to death in his absence, on suspicion of Medism—intriguing with the Persians against Greece.

28. Lysimachus was a prominent fifth-century Athenian statesman, noted for his justice. In the *Gorgias* (526a–b), he is included in a small group of "men who are fine and good in this virtue of justly managing whatever is entrusted to them." Like his near contemporary, Themistocles, he was ostracized by Athens in 483–482 BCE on suspicion of being a Persian sympathizer.

29. Pericles (c. 495–429 BCE) was the most important democratic leader in Athens, from the 440s until his death. He was involved in the building program of the

to make them good men, then? I think he did want to, but that it may be something that can't be acquired by teaching. And lest you think it was only a few utterly useless Athenians who were incapable of this undertaking, consider that Thucydides also
c brought up two sons, Melesias and Stephanus.[30] He educated them well in other things, and made them the finest wrestlers in Athens. For he gave one to Xanthias to train, and the other to Eudorus—and they were thought to be the finest wrestlers of their time. Don't you remember?

ANYTUS: Yes, I have heard that.

SOCRATES: Well, isn't it clear that he would never
d have taught his sons expensive things, but failed to teach them at no expense what would make them good men—*if* this were acquired by teaching? Was Thucydides a useless man, perhaps, who didn't have many friends among the Athenians and their allies? No, he belonged to a prominent family and had great power in the city and in the rest of Greece. So if it were acquired by teaching, he would have found
e someone to make his sons good men, whether a fellow countryman or a foreigner, if he himself didn't have the leisure to do it because he was taking care of the city. But I suspect, Anytus my friend, that virtue is not something acquired by teaching.

ANYTUS: It seems to me, Socrates, that you readily speak ill of people. I would advise you—if you are willing to trust me—to be careful. Perhaps, in other cities too, it is easier to do evil to people than good. It certainly is in this one. But then, I think you know
95 that as well as I.[31]

SOCRATES: I think Anytus is angry, Meno, and I am not surprised. You see, in the first place, he thinks I am disparaging these men. Second, he thinks he is one of them. But if he ever comes to know what speaking ill is really like, he will stop being angry. At present, however, he doesn't know. Tell me, though, are there also fine and good men in your country?

MENO: Certainly.

SOCRATES: Then are they willing to offer themselves as teachers to the young men? b

MENO: No, by Zeus, they aren't, Socrates! But sometimes you hear them say it is acquired by teaching, sometimes that it isn't.

SOCRATES: Are we to say they are teachers of this thing, then, when they do not even agree about *that*?

MENO: It seems not, Socrates.

SOCRATES: What about these Sophists, then, who alone profess to be so, do you think they are teachers of virtue?

MENO: In fact, that's what I particularly admire about Gorgias, Socrates, that you never hear him c
promise to teach it. He even ridicules the others when he hears them promise. It is *speaking* he thinks he should make people clever at.

SOCRATES: So you don't think the Sophists are teachers of virtue, either?

MENO: I can't tell, Socrates. Like most people, sometimes I think so, sometimes not.

SOCRATES: Do you know it isn't just you or the other politicians who sometimes think that it is acquired by teaching, sometimes that it isn't? Do you know even the poet Theognis says the same thing?[32] d

MENO: In which verses?

SOCRATES: In his elegiacs where he says—

> Drink and eat with them, and with them
> Sit, be pleasing to those with great power.
> You will learn noble things, you see, from noble men.
> But if with bad ones you mix,
> You will lose even what understanding you already
> have. e

Do you see that in these lines he speaks as if virtue is acquired by teaching?

MENO: Yes, apparently so.

SOCRATES: In others, though, he makes a little change:

440s and 430s that resulted in the Parthenon and much else. In the *Gorgias* (515b–516d), he is included among a group of political figures who failed to make the Athenians into fine and good men.

30. Thucydides (born c. 500 BCE) was the leading conservative opponent of Pericles. He was ostracized c. 443. The great historian of the same name may have been his grandson.

31. A reference, perhaps, to the events described at *Apology* 31e–32e.

32. Theognis was a sixth-century BCE elegiac poet from Megara. Not all of the 1,400 verses attributed to him are in all likelihood his. Socrates quotes lines 33–6 (with one inconsequential variation) and 434–8, in the order 435, 434, 436–8 (which doesn't greatly affect the sense).

> If understanding could be produced and put into a man,

he says roughly that

> Many and great would be the fees earned

by those able to do it, and that

> Never from a good father would a bad son be born,
> 96 If words of wisdom are trusted. But teaching
> Will never make a bad man good.

Do you see that he makes opposite claims about one and the same thing?

Meno: Apparently so.

Socrates: Well, can you name any other thing that those who say they are teachers of it are not only not generally agreed to be teachers of it to others, but are not even agreed to know it themselves, but instead to be useless at the very thing they claim to
b teach? Or that those who are generally agreed to be fine and good men themselves sometimes say that it is acquired by teaching, sometimes that it isn't? Would you say that those who are that confused about anything are teachers of it in the proper sense?

Meno: No, by Zeus, I cannot.

Socrates: Then if neither the Sophists nor the fine and good men themselves are teachers of the thing, is it not clear that no other people are?

Meno: No, I don't think they are.

Socrates: But if there are no *teachers,* there are
c no learners either?

Meno: I think that's right.

Socrates: But didn't we agree that a thing of which there are neither teachers nor learners is not acquired by teaching?

Meno: We did agree.

Socrates: Now, isn't it the case that there are no teachers of virtue to be seen anywhere?

Meno: That's right.

Socrates: And if there are no teachers, there are no learners either?

Meno: Apparently so.

Socrates: So virtue isn't something acquired by teaching?

Meno: It seems not, if our way of considering it is
d in fact correct. So I really wonder, Socrates, whether there aren't ever any good men at all—or else what could be the way those who come to be good do so?

Socrates: It looks, Meno, as though you and I are pretty useless men, and Gorgias has not adequately educated you or Prodicus or me. Above all, then, we ought to pay attention to ourselves and search out someone who will make us better *one way or another.*
I say this in view of our recent inquiry, because we e
ridiculously failed to see that it is not only under the guidance of knowledge that people conduct their affairs correctly and well. And that may be why the knowledge is also escaping us of the way in which men who are good become so.

Meno: What do you mean, Socrates?

Socrates: I mean this. That good men must be beneficial is something we correctly agreed couldn't
be otherwise. Didn't we? 97

Meno: Yes.

Socrates: And that they will be beneficial if they guide us correctly in our affairs is also something we agreed to correctly, I suppose?

Meno: Yes.

Socrates: But that it is not possible to guide correctly if one is not wise is something, it looks like, we agreed to *incorrectly*.

Meno: How do you mean?

Socrates: I shall tell you. If someone who knew the road to Larissa,[33] or anywhere else you like, were to walk there and guide others, wouldn't he guide them correctly and well?

Meno: Certainly.

Socrates: But what if someone had a correct
belief as to which road it was, though he had never b
gone on it and had no knowledge of it, wouldn't he also guide them correctly?

Meno: Certainly.

Socrates: And as long as he has correct belief, I suppose, about what the other one has knowledge of, he will be no worse a guide than the one who is wise about it, even though he has only true belief, not wisdom.

Meno: No, no worse.

Socrates: So true belief is no worse a guide to the correctness of action than wisdom. And that is what we left out just now in considering what sort of thing

33. The city of Larissa in Thessaly was close to Meno's hometown, Pharsalus.

virtue was. We said that wisdom alone is a guide to
c acting correctly, whereas there was, it seems, true
belief as well.

MENO: Yes, it seems so.

SOCRATES: So correct belief is no less beneficial than knowledge.

MENO: Except by this much, Socrates—the one with knowledge will always hit the mark, while the one with correct belief will sometimes hit it, sometimes not.

SOCRATES: What do you mean? Won't the one who always has correct opinion always hit it, as long as his belief is correct?

MENO: That does seem necessary to me. So, I wonder, Socrates, if that's right, why knowledge is much
d more highly valued than correct belief, and what it is
that makes one different from the other.

SOCRATES: Do you know, then, why you wonder about this, or shall I tell you?

MENO: By all means tell me.

SOCRATES: It is because you haven't paid attention to the statues of Daedalus.[34] But perhaps there aren't any in your country.

MENO: In reference to what do you say that?

SOCRATES: That they, too, if they aren't tied down, run away and flee, but if they are tied down, stay put.

e MENO: So what?

SOCRATES: It is not of much value to acquire one
of his works that is untied, since, like a runaway slave,
it won't stay put. But a tied-down one is worth a lot,
since his works are very beautiful. In reference to
what do I say that? In reference to true beliefs. For
true beliefs—as long as they stay put—are a beautiful
thing, too, and everything they bring about is good.
98 They aren't willing to stay put for long, however, but
flee from a person's soul. So they aren't of much
value until someone ties them down by reasoning out
the explanation. And that, Meno my friend, is recollection—as we agreed before. When they are tied
down, they first become bits of knowledge, then they
stay put. That is why knowledge is more valuable
than true belief, and it is being tied down that makes
knowledge different from true belief.

MENO: Yes, by Zeus, Socrates, it does seem to be something like that!

SOCRATES: And yet I, too, speak as someone who
doesn't know, but conjectures. However, in saying b
that correct belief is a different thing than knowledge—there, I think, I am not at all conjecturing.
On the contrary, if there were anything else that I
would say I know—and there are few things I would
say it about—at any rate, I would put down this, too,
as one of the things I know.

MENO: And you would be right, Socrates.

SOCRATES: Well then, is it not correct to say that when correct belief guides, the outcome of each action is no worse than when knowledge does?

MENO: I think that's right too.

SOCRATES: So correct belief is not worse than c
knowledge or any less beneficial when it comes to
actions, nor the man who has correct belief than the
one who has knowledge.

MENO: That's true.

SOCRATES: And we agreed that the good man is beneficial.

MENO: Yes.

SOCRATES: Then, since it is not only through
knowledge that good men—if they exist—are good
and beneficial to their cities, but also through correct
belief, and since neither of these is something people
possess by nature, neither knowledge nor true d
belief . . . or do you think either of them is possessed
by nature?

MENO: No, I do not.

SOCRATES: Then, since neither is possessed by nature, good men will not have goodness by nature, either.

MENO: Certainly not.

SOCRATES: Then, since they do not have it by nature, we next set out to consider whether it is something acquired by teaching.

MENO: Yes.

SOCRATES: And didn't it seem that it would be acquired by teaching, if virtue were wisdom?

MENO: Yes.

SOCRATES: And that if it were acquired by teaching, it would be wisdom?

MENO: Certainly.

SOCRATES: And that if there were teachers, it
would be acquired by teaching, but if there weren't, e
it wouldn't be acquired by teaching?

MENO: Yes.

---

34. See *Euthyphro* 11b–e and note.

SOCRATES: But we agreed there aren't any teachers of it?

MENO: That's right.

SOCRATES: So we agreed that it is not acquired by teaching and is not wisdom?

MENO: Certainly.

SOCRATES: But we do agree that it *is* good?

MENO: Yes.

SOCRATES: And that what guides correctly is beneficial and good?

MENO: Certainly.

SOCRATES: And that what alone guides correctly is
99 two things, true belief and knowledge, and only if he
has these does a person guide correctly. For the
things that come about correctly by chance do not
come about through human guidance, and in those
where a man does guide toward the right thing, you
find one of these two, true belief or knowledge.

MENO: I think that's right.

SOCRATES: Then, since it is not acquired by teaching, virtue is no longer knowledge, either.

MENO: Apparently not.

SOCRATES: So, of the two good and beneficial
b things, one has been ruled out, and so it cannot be
knowledge that is a guide in political affairs.

MENO: It seems not.

SOCRATES: Then it is not by some sort of wisdom, or by being wise, that men such as Themistocles and his associates, or those whom Anytus here just mentioned, guided their cities. For this very reason, they can't make others like themselves, seeing that they aren't what they are on account of knowledge.

MENO: It seems to be as you say, Socrates.

SOCRATES: Then, if it is not by knowledge, the
remaining possibility is that it is by true belief, that it
c is by using *it* that political men guide their cities correctly, since they are no different as regards wisdom
from soothsayers and prophets. For the latter, too,
while divinely inspired, say many true things, but have
no knowledge whatsoever about the things they say.

MENO: It looks that way.

SOCRATES: Then isn't it right, Meno, to call these men godlike—the ones who without understanding achieve many great successes in the things they do and say?

MENO: Certainly.

SOCRATES: So wouldn't we be right to call the
soothsayers and prophets we mentioned just now
godlike, as well as all the poets? And to say that the d
politicians are by no means the least godlike of them,
since they are inspired and possessed by the god, when
they achieve success in saying many great things,
while knowing nothing about the things they say?

MENO: Certainly.

SOCRATES: Women too, I suppose, Meno, call good men godlike; and when the Spartans praise a good man, they say "He is a godlike man."

MENO: And apparently, Socrates, they are right in
doing it. But perhaps Anytus here will be annoyed at e
you for saying so.

SOCRATES: I am not concerned about that. We
shall talk with him again, Meno, some other time.
For the present, if we have inquired and spoken correctly throughout this entire discussion, virtue is not
acquired by nature or by teaching, but comes to be
present by divine dispensation, without understanding, in those in whom it does come to be present—
provided, of course, there is not some political man 100
who is able to make someone else a politician. If
there were, he could pretty much be said to be
among the living what Homer said Tiresias was
among the dead. Among those in Hades, he said,
"He alone is wise, the others flit around as shadows."[35] In the same way here, such a man would be
like a truly real thing in comparison to shadows as
regards virtue.

MENO: I think what you said is absolutely right,
Socrates. b

SOCRATES: On the basis of this reasoning, then, Meno, it appears to us that it is by divine dispensation that virtue comes to be present in those in whom it comes to be present. But we will know that with certainty when, before inquiring about the way virtue comes to be present in people, we first try to inquire about what virtue itself is by itself. Now, however, it is time for me to go be somewhere. Try to persuade your friend Anytus here, too, of the things you yourself have been persuaded of, so that he will be more gentle. You see, if you do persuade him, you will also profit the Athenians.[36]

---

35. Homer, *Odyssey* 10.495.

36. A prophetic allusion, presumably, to Anytus' role in having Socrates executed, thereby depriving Athens of his beneficial services.

PHAEDO

57 ECHECRATES: Were you with Socrates yourself, Phaedo, on the day when he drank the poison in prison, or did someone else tell you about it?

PHAEDO: I was there myself, Echecrates.

ECHECRATES: What are the things he said before
he died? And how did he die? I should be glad to hear
this. Hardly anyone from Phlius visits Athens nowa-
b days, nor has any stranger come from Athens for
some time who could give us a clear account of what
happened, except that he drank the poison and died,
but nothing more.

58 PHAEDO: Did you not even hear how the trial went?

ECHECRATES: Yes, someone did tell us about that, and we wondered that he seems to have died a long time after the trial took place. Why was that, Phaedo?

PHAEDO: That was by chance, Echecrates. The day before the trial, as it happened, the prow of the ship that the Athenians send to Delos had been crowned with garlands.

ECHECRATES: What ship is that?

PHAEDO: It is the ship in which, the Athenians say,
Theseus once sailed to Crete, taking with him the two
lots of seven victims.[1] He saved them and was himself
b saved. The Athenians vowed then to Apollo, so the
story goes, that if they were saved they would send a
mission to Delos every year. And from that time to this
they send such an annual mission to the god. They
have a law to keep the city pure while it lasts, and no
execution may take place once the mission has begun
until the ship has made its journey to Delos and
returned to Athens, and this can sometimes take a
c long time if the winds delay it. The mission begins
when the priest of Apollo crowns the prow of the ship,
and this happened, as I say, the day before Socrates'
trial. That is why Socrates was in prison a long time
between his trial and his execution.

ECHECRATES: What about his actual death, Phaedo? What did he say? What did he do? Who of his friends were with him? Or did the authorities not allow them to be present and he died with no friends present?

PHAEDO: By no means. Some were present, in fact, d
a good many.

ECHECRATES: Please be good enough to tell us all that occurred as fully as possible, unless you have some pressing business.

PHAEDO: I have the time and I will try to tell you the whole story, for nothing gives me more pleasure than to call Socrates to mind, whether talking about him myself, or listening to someone else do so.

ECHECRATES: Your hearers will surely be like you in this, Phaedo. So do try to tell us every detail as exactly as you can.

PHAEDO: I certainly found being there an astonishing experience. Although I was witnessing the death e
of one who was my friend, I had no feeling of pity, for
the man appeared happy in both manner and words
as he died nobly and without fear, Echecrates, so that
it struck me that even in going down to the under- 59
world he was going with the gods' blessing and that
he would fare well when he got there, if anyone ever
does. That is why I had no feeling of pity, such as
would seem natural in my sorrow, nor indeed of
pleasure, as we engaged in philosophical discussion
as we were accustomed to do—for our arguments
were of that sort—but I had a strange feeling, an
unaccustomed mixture of pleasure and pain at the
same time as I reflected that he was just about to die.
All of us present were affected in much the same way,
sometimes laughing, then weeping; especially one of
us, Apollodorus—you know the man and his ways.

ECHECRATES: Of course I do. b

PHAEDO: He was quite overcome; but I was myself disturbed, and so were the others.

ECHECRATES: Who, Phaedo, were those present?

PHAEDO: Among the local people there was Apollodorus, whom I mentioned, Critobulus and his father,[2] also Hermogenes, Epigenes, Aeschines, and

---

1. Legend says that Minos, king of Crete, compelled the Athenians to send seven youths and seven maidens every year to be sacrificed to the Minotaur until Theseus saved them and killed the monster.

2. The father of Critobulus is Crito, after whom the dialogue *Crito* is named.

Antisthenes. Ctesippus of Paeania was there, Menexenus and some others. Plato, I believe, was ill.

ECHECRATES: Were there some foreigners present?

c PHAEDO: Yes, Simmias from Thebes with Cebes
and Phaedondes, and from Megara, Euclides and Terpsion.

ECHECRATES: What about Aristippus and Cleombrotus? Were they there?

PHAEDO: No. They were said to be in Aegina.

ECHECRATES: Was there anyone else?

PHAEDO: I think these were about all.

ECHECRATES: Well then, what do you say the conversation was about?

PHAEDO: I will try to tell you everything from the
d beginning. On the previous days also both the others
and I used to visit Socrates. We forgathered at daybreak at the court where the trial took place, for it was close to the prison, and each day we used to wait around talking until the prison should open, for it did not open early. When it opened we used to go in to Socrates and spend most of the day with him. On this
e day we gathered rather early, because when we left
the prison on the previous evening we were informed that the ship from Delos had arrived, and so we told each other to come to the usual place as early as possible. When we arrived the gatekeeper who used to answer our knock came out and told us to wait and not go in until he told us to. "The Eleven,"[3] he said, "are freeing Socrates from his bonds and telling him how his death will take place today." After a short
60 time he came and told us to go in. We found Socrates
recently released from his chains, and Xanthippe—you know her—sitting by him, holding their baby. When she saw us, she cried out and said the sort of thing that women usually say: "Socrates, this is the last time your friends will talk to you and you to them." Socrates looked at Crito. "Crito," he said, "let someone take her home." And some of Crito's people
b led her away lamenting and beating her breast.

Socrates sat up on the bed, bent his leg, and rubbed it with his hand, and as he rubbed he said: "What a strange thing that which men call pleasure seems to be, and how astonishing the relation it has with what is thought to be its opposite, namely pain! A man cannot have both at the same time. Yet if he pursues and catches the one, he is almost always bound to catch the other also, like two creatures with
one head. I think that if Aesop had noted this he c
would have composed a fable that a god wished to reconcile their opposition but could not do so, so he joined their two heads together, and therefore when a man has the one, the other follows later. This seems to be happening to me. My bonds caused pain in my leg, and now pleasure seems to be following."

Cebes intervened and said: "By Zeus, yes, Socrates, you did well to remind me. Evenus[4] asked me the day before yesterday, as others had done before, what
induced you to write poetry after you came to prison, d
you who had never composed any poetry before, putting the fables of Aesop into verse and composing the hymn to Apollo. If it is of any concern to you that I should have an answer to give to Evenus when he repeats his question, as I know he will, tell me what to say to him."

Tell him the truth, Cebes, he said, that I did not do this with the idea of rivaling him or his poems, for I knew that would not be easy, but I tried to find out
the meaning of certain dreams and to satisfy my con- e
science in case it was this kind of art they were frequently bidding me to practice. The dreams were something like this: the same dream often came to me in the past, now in one shape now in another, but saying the same thing: "Socrates," it said, "practice and cultivate the arts." In the past I imagined that it was instructing and advising me to do what I was
doing, such as those who encourage runners in a 61
race, that the dream was thus bidding me do the very thing I was doing, namely, to practice the art of philosophy, this being the highest kind of art, and I was doing that.

But now, after my trial took place, and the festival of the god was preventing my execution, I thought that, in case my dream was bidding me to practice this popular art, I should not disobey it but compose
poetry. I thought it safer not to leave here until I had b
satisfied my conscience by writing poems in obedience to the dream. So I first wrote in honor of the god of the present festival. After that I realized that a poet, if he is to be a poet, must compose fables, not arguments. Being no teller of fables myself, I took the stories I knew and had at hand, the fables of Aesop, and I versified the first ones I came across. Tell this to

3. The Eleven were the police commissioners of Athens.

4. See *Apology* 20b and note.

Evenus, Cebes, wish him well and bid him farewell, and tell him, if he is wise, to follow me as soon as *c* possible. I am leaving today, it seems, as the Athenians so order it.

Said Simmias: "What kind of advice is this you are giving to Evenus, Socrates? I have met him many times, and from my observation he is not at all likely to follow it willingly."

How so, said he, is Evenus not a philosopher?

I think so, Simmias said.

Then Evenus will be willing, like every man who partakes worthily of philosophy. Yet perhaps he will not take his own life, for that, they say, is not right. As he said this, Socrates put his feet on the ground *d* and remained in this position during the rest of the conversation.

Then Cebes asked: "How do you mean Socrates, that it is not right to do oneself violence, and yet that the philosopher will be willing to follow one who is dying?"

Come now, Cebes, have you and Simmias, who keep company with Philolaus,[5] not heard about such things?

Nothing definite, Socrates.

Indeed, I too speak about this from hearsay, but I do not mind telling you what I have heard, for it is perhaps most appropriate for one who is about to *e* depart yonder to tell and examine tales about what we believe that journey to be like. What else could one do in the time we have until sunset?

But whatever is the reason, Socrates, for people to say that it is not right to kill oneself? As to your question just now, I have heard Philolaus say this when staying in Thebes, and I have also heard it from others, but I have never heard anyone give a clear account of the matter.

62 Well, he said, we must do our best, and you may yet hear one. And it may well astonish you if this subject, alone of all things, is simple, and it is never, as with everything else, better at certain times and for certain people to die than to live. And if this is so, you may well find it astonishing that those for whom it is better to die are wrong to help themselves, and that they must wait for someone else to benefit them.

And Cebes, lapsing into his own dialect, laughed quietly and said: "Zeus knows it is."

Indeed, said Socrates, it does seem unreasonable *b* when put like that, but perhaps there is reason to it. There is the explanation that is put in the language of the mysteries, that we men are in a kind of prison, and that one must not free oneself or run away. That seems to me an impressive doctrine and one not easy to understand fully. However, Cebes, this seems to me well expressed, that the gods are our guardians and that men are one of their possessions. Or do you not think so?

I do, said Cebes.

And would you not be angry if one of your possessions killed itself when you had not given any sign *c* that you wished it to die, and if you had any punishment you could inflict, you would inflict it?

Certainly, he said.

Perhaps then, put in this way, it is not unreasonable that one should not kill oneself before a god had indicated some necessity to do so, like the necessity now put upon us.

That seems likely, said Cebes. As for what you *d* were saying, that philosophers should be willing and ready to die, that seems strange, Socrates, if what we said just now is reasonable, namely, that a god is our protector and that we are his possessions. It is not logical that the wisest of men should not resent leaving this service in which they are governed by the best of masters, the gods, for a wise man cannot believe that he will look after himself better when he is free. A foolish man might easily think so, that he must escape from his master; he would not reflect that one *e* must not escape from a good master but stay with him as long as possible, because it would be foolish to escape. But the sensible man would want always to remain with one better than himself. So, Socrates, the opposite of what was said before is likely to be true; the wise would resent dying, whereas the foolish would rejoice at it.

I thought that when Socrates heard this he was pleased by Cebes' argumentation. Glancing at us, he *63* said: "Cebes is always on the track of some arguments; he is certainly not willing to be at once convinced by what one says."

Said Simmias: "But actually, Socrates, I think myself that Cebes has a point now. Why should truly wise men want to avoid the service of masters better than themselves, and leave them easily? And I think Cebes is aiming his argument at you, because you

---

5. See pages 6–7 of this volume.

are bearing leaving us so lightly, and leaving those
good masters, as you say yourself, the gods."

b You are both justified in what you say, and I think
you mean that I must make a defense against this, as
if I were in court.

You certainly must, said Simmias.

Come then, he said, let me try to make my defense
to you more convincing than it was to the jury. For,
Simmias and Cebes, I should be wrong not to resent
dying if I did not believe that I should go first to other
wise and good gods, and then to men who have died
and are better than men are here. Be assured that, as
c it is, I expect to join the company of good men. This
last I would not altogether insist on, but if I insist on
anything at all in these matters, it is that I shall come
to gods who are very good masters. That is why I am
not so resentful, because I have good hope that some
future awaits men after death, as we have been told
for years, a much better future for the good than for
the wicked.

Well now, Socrates, said Simmias, do you intend to
d keep this belief to yourself as you leave us, or would
you share it with us? I certainly think it would be a
blessing for us too, and at the same time it would be
your defense if you convince us of what you say.

I will try, he said, but first let us see what it is that
Crito here has, I think, been wanting to say for quite
a while.

What else, Socrates, said Crito, but what the man
who is to give you the poison has been telling me for
some time, that I should warn you to talk as little as
possible. People get heated when they talk, he says,
e and one should not be heated when taking the poison, as those who do must sometimes drink it two or
three times.

Socrates replied: "Take no notice of him; only let
him be prepared to administer it twice or, if necessary, three times."

I was rather sure you would say that, Crito said, but
he has been bothering me for some time.

Let him be, he said. I want to make my argument
before you, my judges, as to why I think that a man
who has truly spent his life in philosophy is probably right to be of good cheer in the face of death and
64 to be very hopeful that after death he will attain the
greatest blessings yonder. I will try to tell you, Simmias and Cebes, how this may be so. I am afraid
that other people do not realize that the one aim of
those who practice philosophy in the proper manner is to practice for dying and death. Now if this is
true, it would be strange indeed if they were eager
for this all their lives and then resent it when what
they have wanted and practiced for a long time
comes upon them.

Simmias laughed and said: "By Zeus, Socrates,
you made me laugh, though I was in no laughing b
mood just now. I think that the majority, on hearing
this, will think that it describes the philosophers very
well, and our people in Thebes would thoroughly
agree that philosophers are nearly dead and that the
majority of men is well aware that they deserve to be.

And they would be telling the truth, Simmias,
except for their being aware. They are not aware of
the way true philosophers are nearly dead, nor of
the way they deserve to be, nor of the sort of death c
they deserve.

But never mind them, he said, let us talk among
ourselves. Do we believe that there is such a thing as
death?

Certainly, said Simmias.

Is it anything else than the separation of the soul
from the body? Do we believe that death is this,
namely, that the body comes to be separated by itself
apart from the soul, and the soul comes to be separated by itself apart from the body? Is death anything
else than that?

No, that is what it is, he said.

Consider then, my good sir, whether you share my
opinion, for this will lead us to a better knowledge of d
what we are investigating. Do you think it is the part
of a philosopher to be concerned with such so-called
pleasures as those of food and drink?

By no means.

What about the pleasures of sex?

Not at all.

What of the other pleasures concerned with the
service of the body? Do you think such a man prizes
them greatly, the acquisition of distinguished clothes
and shoes and the other bodily ornaments? Do you
think he values these or despises them, except insofar e
as one cannot do without them?

I think the true philosopher despises them.

Do you not think, he said, that in general such a
man's concern is not with the body but that, as far as
he can, he turns away from the body toward the soul?

I do.

65 So in the first place, such things show clearly that
the philosopher more than other men frees the soul
from association with the body as much as possible?

Apparently.

A man who finds no pleasure in such things and
has no part in them is thought by the majority not to
deserve to live and to be close to death; the man, that
is, who does not care for the pleasures of the body.

What you say is certainly true.

Then what about the actual acquiring of knowledge? Is the body an obstacle when one associates
with it in the search for knowledge? I mean, for
b example, do men find any truth in sight or hearing,
or are not even the poets forever telling us that we do
not see or hear anything accurately, and surely if
those two physical senses are not clear or precise, our
other senses can hardly be accurate, as they are all
inferior to these. Do you not think so?

I certainly do, he said.

When then, he asked, does the soul grasp the
truth? For whenever it attempts to examine anything
with the body, it is clearly deceived by it.

c True.

Is it not in reasoning if anywhere that any reality
becomes clear to the soul?

Yes.

And indeed the soul reasons best when none of
these senses troubles it, neither hearing nor sight, nor
pain nor pleasure, but when it is most by itself, taking leave of the body and as far as possible having no
contact or association with it in its search for reality.

That is so.

d And it is then that the soul of the philosopher
most disdains the body, flees from it, and seeks to be
by itself?

It appears so.

What about the following, Simmias? Do we say
that there is such a thing as the Just itself, or not?

We do say so, by Zeus.

And the Beautiful, and the Good?

Of course.

And have you ever seen any of these things with
your eyes?

In no way, he said.

Or have you ever grasped them with any of your
bodily senses? I am speaking of all things such as Bigness, Health, Strength and, in a word, the reality of
e all other things, that which each of them essentially
is. Is what is most true in them contemplated through
the body, or is this the position: whoever of us pre-
pares himself best and most accurately to grasp that
thing itself which he is investigating will come closest to the knowledge of it?

Obviously.

Then he will do this most perfectly who
approaches the object with thought alone, without
associating any sight with his thought, or dragging 66
in any sense perception with his reasoning, but who,
using pure thought alone, tries to track down each
reality pure and by itself, freeing himself as far as possible from eyes and ears, and in a word, from the
whole body, because the body confuses the soul and
does not allow it to acquire truth and wisdom whenever it is associated with it. Will not that man reach
reality, Simmias, if anyone does?

What you say, said Simmias, is indeed true.

All these things will necessarily make the true *b*
philosophers believe and say to each other something
like this: "There is likely to be something such as a
path to guide us out of our confusion, because as
long as we have a body and our soul is fused with
such an evil we shall never adequately attain what we
desire, which we affirm to be the truth. The body
keeps us busy in a thousand ways because of its need
for nurture. Moreover, if certain diseases befall it, *c*
they impede our search for the truth. It fills us with
wants, desires, fears, all sorts of illusions, and much
nonsense, so that, as it is said, in truth and in fact no
thought of any kind ever comes to us from the body.
Only the body and its desires cause war, civil discord,
and battles, for all wars are due to the desire to
acquire wealth, and it is the body and the care of it, *d*
to which we are enslaved, which compel us to
acquire wealth, and all this makes us too busy to
practice philosophy.

Worst of all, if we do get some respite from it and
turn to some investigation, everywhere in our
investigations the body is present and makes for
confusion and fear, so that it prevents us from seeing the truth.

"It really has been shown to us that, if we are ever to
have pure knowledge, we must escape from the body *e*
and observe things in themselves with the soul by
itself. It seems likely that we shall, only then, when we
are dead, attain that which we desire and of which we
claim to be lovers, namely, wisdom, as our argument

shows, not while we live; for if it is impossible to attain any pure knowledge with the body, then one of two things is true: either we can never attain knowledge or we can do so after death. Then and not before, the
67 soul is by itself apart from the body. While we live, we shall be closest to knowledge if we refrain as much as possible from association with the body and do not join with it more than we must, if we are not infected with its nature but purify ourselves from it until the god himself frees us. In this way we shall escape the contamination of the body's folly; we shall be likely to be in the company of people of the same kind, and by our own efforts we shall know all that is pure, which is
b presumably the truth, for it is not permitted to the impure to attain the pure."

Such are the things, Simmias, that all those who love learning in the proper manner must say to one another and believe. Or do you not think so?

I certainly do, Socrates.

And if this is true, my friend, said Socrates, there is good hope that on arriving where I am going, if anywhere, I shall acquire what has been our chief pre-
c occupation in our past life, so that the journey that is now ordered for me is full of good hope, as it is also for any other man who believes that his mind has been prepared and, as it were, purified.

It certainly is, said Simmias.

And does purification not turn out to be what we mentioned in our argument some time ago, namely, to separate the soul as far as possible from the body and accustom it to gather itself and collect itself out
d of every part of the body and to dwell by itself as far as it can both now and in the future, freed, as it were, from the bonds of the body?

Certainly, he said.

And that freedom and separation of the soul from the body is called death?

That is altogether so.

It is only those who practice philosophy in the right way, we say, who always most want to free the soul; and this release and separation of the soul from the body is the preoccupation of the philosophers?

So it appears.

Therefore, as I said at the beginning, it would be ridiculous for a man to train himself in life to live in a state as close to death as possible, and then to resent
e it when it comes?

Ridiculous, of course.

In fact, Simmias, he said, those who practice philosophy in the right way are in training for dying, and they fear death least of all men. Consider it from this point of view: if they are altogether estranged from the body and desire to have their soul by itself, would it not be quite absurd for them to be afraid and resentful when this happens? If they did not gladly set out for a place, where, on arrival, they may hope to attain that for which they had yearned during their lifetime, that 68
is, wisdom, and where they would be rid of the presence of that from which they are estranged?

Many men, at the death of their lovers, wives, or sons, were willing to go to the underworld, driven by the hope of seeing there those for whose company they longed, and being with them. Will then a true lover of wisdom, who has a similar hope and knows that he will never find it to any extent except in Hades, be resentful of dying and not gladly undertake the journey thither? One must surely think so, my friend, if he is a true philosopher, for he is firmly b
convinced that he will not find pure knowledge anywhere except there. And if this is so, then, as I said just now, would it not be highly unreasonable for such a man to fear death?

It certainly would, by Zeus, he said.

Then you have sufficient indication, he said, that any man whom you see resenting death was not a lover c
of wisdom but a lover of the body, and also a lover of wealth or of honors, either or both.

It is certainly as you say.

And, Simmias, he said, does not what is called courage belong especially to men of this disposition?

Most certainly.

And the quality of moderation which even the majority call by that name, that is, not to get swept off one's feet by one's passions, but to treat them with disdain and orderliness, is this not suited only to those d
who most of all despise the body and live the life of philosophy?

Necessarily so, he said.

If you are willing to reflect on the courage and moderation of other people, you will find them strange.

In what way, Socrates?

You know that they all consider death a great evil?

Definitely, he said.

And the brave among them face death, when they do, for fear of greater evils?

That is so.

Therefore, it is fear and terror that make all men brave, except the philosophers. Yet it is illogical to be brave through fear and cowardice.

e It certainly is.

What of the moderate among them? Is their experience not similar? Is it license of a kind that makes them
moderate? We say this is impossible, yet their experience of this unsophisticated moderation turns out to be
similar: they fear to be deprived of other pleasures
which they desire, so they keep away from some pleasures because they are overcome by others. Now to be
mastered by pleasure is what they call license, but what
69 happens to them is that they master certain pleasures
because they are mastered by others. This is like what
we mentioned just now, that in some way it is a kind of
license that has made them moderate.

That seems likely.

My good Simmias, I fear this is not the right
exchange to attain virtue, to exchange pleasures for
pleasures, pains for pains, and fears for fears, the
b greater for the less like coins, but that the only valid
currency for which all these things should be
exchanged is wisdom. With this we have real courage
and moderation and justice and, in a word, true virtue,
with wisdom, whether pleasures and fears and all such
things be present or absent. When these things are
exchanged for one another in separation from wisdom, such virtue is only an illusory appearance of
virtue; it is in fact fit for slaves, without soundness or
truth, whereas, in truth, moderation and courage and
justice are a purging away of all such things, and wis-
c dom itself is a kind of cleansing or purification. It is
likely that those who established the mystic rites for us
were not inferior persons but were speaking in riddles
long ago when they said that whoever arrives in the
underworld uninitiated and unsanctified will wallow
in the mire, whereas he who arrives there purified and
initiated will dwell with the gods. There are indeed, as
those concerned with the mysteries say, many who
d carry the thyrsus, but the Bacchants are few.[6] These
latter are, in my opinion, no other than those who
have practiced philosophy in the right way. I have in
my life left nothing undone in order to be counted
among these as far as possible, as I have been eager to
be in every way. Whether my eagerness was right and
we accomplished anything, we shall, I think, know for
certain in a short time, god willing, on arriving yonder.

This is my defense, Simmias and Cebes, that I am
likely to be right to leave you and my masters here e
without resentment or complaint, believing that
there, as here, I shall find good masters and good
friends. If my defense is more convincing to you than
to the Athenian jury, it will be well.

When Socrates finished, Cebes intervened:
Socrates, he said, everything else you said is excel- 70
lent, I think, but men find it very hard to believe
what you said about the soul. They think that after it
has left the body it no longer exists anywhere, but
that it is destroyed and dissolved on the day the man
dies, as soon as it leaves the body; and that, on leaving it, it is dispersed like breath or smoke, has flown
away and gone, and is no longer anything anywhere.
If indeed it gathered itself together and existed by
itself and escaped those evils you were recently enu-
merating, there would then be much good hope, b
Socrates, that what you say is true; but to believe this
requires a good deal of faith and persuasive argument, to believe that the soul still exists after a man
has died and that it still possesses some capability and
intelligence.

What you say is true, Cebes, Socrates said, but what shall we do? Do you want to discuss whether this is likely to be true or not?

Personally, said Cebes, I should like to hear your opinion on the subject.

I do not think, said Socrates, that anyone who
heard me now, not even a comic poet, could say that c
I am babbling and discussing things that do not concern me, so we must examine the question thoroughly, if you think we should do so. Let us examine
it in some such a manner as this: whether the souls
of men who have died exist in the underworld or not.
We recall an ancient theory that souls arriving there
come from here, and then again that they arrive here
and are born here from the dead. If that is true, that
the living come back from the dead, then surely our
souls must exist there, for they could not come back d
if they did not exist, and this is a sufficient proof that
these things are so if it truly appears that the living
never come from any other source than from the
dead. If this is not the case we should need another
argument.

6. That is, the true worshippers of Dionysus, as opposed to those who only carry the external symbols of his worship.

Quite so, said Cebes.

Do not, he said, confine yourself to humanity if you want to understand this more readily, but take all animals and all plants into account, and, in short, for
e all things which come to be, let us see whether they come to be in this way, that is, from their opposites if they have such, as the beautiful is the opposite of the ugly and the just of the unjust, and a thousand other things of the kind. Let us examine whether those that have an opposite must necessarily come to be from their opposite and from nowhere else, as for example when something comes to be larger it must necessarily become larger from having been smaller before.

Yes.

Then if something smaller comes to be, it will
71 come from something larger before, which became smaller?

That is so, he said.

And the weaker comes to be from the stronger, and the swifter from the slower?

Certainly.

Further, if something worse comes to be, does it not come from the better, and the juster from the more unjust?

Of course.

So we have sufficiently established that all things come to be in this way, opposites from opposites?

Certainly.

There is a further point, something such as this,
b about these opposites: between each of those pairs of opposites there are two processes: from the one to the other and then again from the other to the first; between the larger and the smaller there is increase and decrease, and we call the one increasing and the other decreasing?

Yes, he said.

And so too there is separation and combination, cooling and heating, and all such things, even if sometimes we do not have a name for the process, but in fact it must be everywhere that they come to be from one another, and that there is a process of becoming from each into the other?

Assuredly, he said.

c Well then, is there an opposite to living, as sleeping is the opposite of being awake?

Quite so, he said.

What is it?

Being dead, he said.

Therefore, if these are opposites, they come to be from one another, and there are two processes of generation between the two?

Of course.

I will tell you, said Socrates, one of the two pairs I was just talking about, the pair itself and the two processes, and you will tell me the other. I mean, to
sleep and to be awake; to be awake comes from sleep- d
ing, and to sleep comes from being awake. Of the two processes, one is going to sleep, the other is waking up. Do you accept that, or not?

Certainly.

You tell me in the same way about life and death. Do you not say that to be dead is the opposite of being alive?

I do.

And they come to be from one another?

Yes.

What comes to be from being alive?

Being dead.

And what comes to be from being dead?

One must agree that it is being alive.

Then, Cebes, living creatures and things come to be from the dead?

So it appears, he said. e

Then our souls exist in the underworld.

That seems likely.

Then in this case one of the two processes of becoming is clear, for dying is clear enough, is it not?

It certainly is.

What shall we do then? Shall we not supply the opposite process of becoming? Is nature to be lame in this case? Or must we provide a process of becoming opposite to dying?

We surely must.

And what is that?

Coming to life again.

Therefore, he said, if there is such a thing as com- 72
ing to life again, it would be a process of coming from the dead to the living?

Quite so.

It is agreed between us then that the living come from the dead in this way no less than the dead from the living and, if that is so, it seems to be a sufficient proof that the souls of the dead must be somewhere whence they can come back again.

I think, Socrates, he said, that this follows from what we have agreed on.

Consider in this way, Cebes, he said, that, as I
b think, we were not wrong to agree. If the two processes of becoming did not always balance each other as if they were going round in a circle, but generation proceeded from one point to its opposite in a straight line and it did not turn back again to the other opposite or take any turning, do you realize that all things would ultimately be in the same state, be affected in the same way, and cease to become?

How do you mean? he said.

It is not hard to understand what I mean. If, for example, there was such a process as going to sleep, but no corresponding process of waking up, you realize that in the end everything would show the story of
c Endymion[7] to have no meaning. There would be no point to it because everything would have the same experience as he had and be asleep. And if everything were combined and nothing separated, the saying of Anaxagoras[8] would soon be true, "that all things were mixed together." In the same way, my dear Cebes, if everything that partakes of life were to
d die and remain in that state and not come to life again, would not everything ultimately have to be dead and nothing alive? Even if the living came from some other source, and all that lived died, how could all things avoid being absorbed in death?

It could not be, Socrates, said Cebes, and I think what you say is altogether true.

I think, Cebes, said he, that this is very definitely the case and that we were not deceived when we agreed on this: coming to life again in truth exists,
e the living come to be from the dead, and the souls of the dead exist.

Furthermore, Socrates, Cebes rejoined, such is also the case if that theory is true that you are accustomed to mention frequently, that for us learning is no other than recollection. According to this, we
73 must at some previous time have learned what we now recollect. This is possible only if our soul existed somewhere before it took on this human shape. So according to this theory too, the soul is likely to be something immortal.

Cebes, Simmias interrupted, what are the proofs of this? Remind me, for I do not quite recall them at the moment.

There is one excellent argument, said Cebes, namely that when men are interrogated in the right manner, they always give the right answer of their own accord, and they could not do this if they did not possess the knowledge and the right explanation inside them. Then if one shows them a diagram or something else of that kind, this will show most
clearly that such is the case.[9] b

If this does not convince you, Simmias, said Socrates, see whether you agree if we examine it in some such way as this, for do you doubt that what we call learning is recollection?

It is not that I doubt, said Simmias, but I want to experience the very thing we are discussing, recollection, and from what Cebes undertook to say, I am now remembering and am pretty nearly convinced. Nevertheless, I should like to hear now the way you were intending to explain it.

This way, he said. We surely agree that if anyone c
recollects anything, he must have known it before.

Quite so, he said.

Do we not also agree that when knowledge comes to mind in this way, it is recollection? What way do I mean? Like this: when a man sees or hears or in some other way perceives one thing and not only knows that thing but also thinks of another thing of which the knowledge is not the same but different, are we not right to say that he recollects the second thing that comes into his mind?

How do you mean? d

Things such as this: to know a man is surely a different knowledge from knowing a lyre.

Of course.

Well, you know what happens to lovers: whenever they see a lyre, a garment, or anything else that their beloved is accustomed to use, they know the lyre, and the image of the boy to whom it belongs comes into their mind. This is recollection, just as someone, on seeing Simmias, often recollects Cebes, and there are thousands of other such occurrences.

Thousands indeed, said Simmias.

Is this kind of thing not recollection of a kind? he
said, especially so when one experiences it about e
things that one had forgotten, because one had not seen them for some time?—Quite so.

7. Endymion was granted eternal sleep by Zeus.

8. See pages 23–5 of this volume.

9. Cf. *Meno* 81e ff.

Further, he said, can a man seeing the picture of a horse or a lyre recollect a man, or seeing a picture of Simmias recollect Cebes?—Certainly.

Or seeing a picture of Simmias, recollect Simmias himself?—He certainly can.

74 In all these cases the recollection can be occasioned by things that are similar, but it can also be occasioned by things that are dissimilar?—It can.

When the recollection is caused by similar things, must one not of necessity also experience this: to consider whether the similarity to that which one recollects is deficient in any respect or complete?—One must.

Consider, he said, whether this is the case: we say that there is something that is equal. I do not mean a stick equal to a stick or a stone to a stone, or anything of that kind, but something else beyond all these, the Equal itself. Shall we say that this exists or not?

b Indeed we shall, by Zeus, said Simmias, most definitely.

And do we know what this is?—Certainly.

Whence have we acquired the knowledge of it? Is it not from the things we mentioned just now, from seeing sticks or stones or some other things that are equal we come to think of that other which is different from them? Or doesn't it seem to you to be different? Look at it also this way: do not equal stones and sticks sometimes, while remaining the same, appear to one to be equal and to another to be unequal?—Certainly they do.

c But what of the equals themselves? Have they ever appeared unequal to you, or Equality to be Inequality?

Never, Socrates.

These equal things and the Equal itself are therefore not the same?

I do not think they are the same at all, Socrates.

But it is definitely from the equal things, though they are different from that Equal, that you have derived and grasped the knowledge of equality?

Very true, Socrates.

Whether it be like them or unlike them?

Certainly.

It makes no difference. As long as the sight of one thing makes you think of another, whether it be simi-
d lar or dissimilar, this must of necessity be recollection?

Quite so.

Well then, he said, do we experience something like this in the case of equal sticks and the other equal objects we just mentioned? Do they seem to us to be equal in the same sense as what is Equal itself? Is there some deficiency in their being such as the Equal, or is there not?

A considerable deficiency, he said.

Whenever someone, on seeing something, realizes that that which he now sees wants to be like some e
other reality but falls short and cannot be like that other since it is inferior, do we agree that the one who thinks this must have prior knowledge of that to which he says it is like, but deficiently so?

Necessarily.

Well, do we also experience this about the equal objects and the Equal itself, or do we not?

Very definitely.

We must then possess knowledge of the Equal before that time when we first saw the equal objects 75
and realized that all these objects strive to be like the Equal but are deficient in this.

That is so.

Then surely we also agree that this conception of ours derives from seeing or touching or some other sense perception, and cannot come into our mind in any other way, for all these senses, I say, are the same.

They are the same, Socrates, at any rate in respect to that which our argument wishes to make plain.

Our sense perceptions must surely make us realize b
that all that we perceive through them is striving to reach that which is Equal but falls short of it; or how do we express it?

Like that.

Then before we began to see or hear or otherwise perceive, we must have possessed knowledge of the Equal itself if we were about to refer our sense perceptions of equal objects to it, and realized that all of them were eager to be like it, but were inferior.

That follows from what has been said, Socrates.

But we began to see and hear and otherwise perceive right after birth?

Certainly.

We must then have acquired the knowledge of the c
Equal before this.

Yes.

It seems then that we must have possessed it before birth.

It seems so.

Therefore, if we had this knowledge, we knew before birth and immediately after not only the

Equal, but the Greater and the Smaller and all such
things, for our present argument is no more about
d the Equal than about the Beautiful itself, the Good
itself, the Just, the Pious and, as I say, about all those
things which we mark with the seal of "what it is,"
both when we are putting questions and answering
them. So we must have acquired knowledge of them
all before we were born.

That is so.

If, having acquired this knowledge in each case, we have not forgotten it, we remain knowing and have knowledge throughout our life, for to know is to acquire knowledge, keep it, and not lose it. Do we not call the losing of knowledge forgetting?

e Most certainly, Socrates, he said.

But, I think, if we acquired this knowledge before birth, then lost it at birth, and then later by the use of our senses in connection with those objects we mentioned, we recovered the knowledge we had before, would not what we call learning be the recovery of our own knowledge, and we are right to call this recollection?

Certainly.

76 It was seen to be possible for someone to see or
hear or otherwise perceive something, and by this to
be put in mind of something else which he had forgotten and which is related to it by similarity or difference. One of two things follows, as I say: either we
were born with the knowledge of it, and all of us
know it throughout life, or those who later, we say,
are learning, are only recollecting, and learning
would be recollection.

That is certainly the case, Socrates.

Which alternative do you choose, Simmias? That we
b are born with this knowledge or that we recollect later
the things of which we had knowledge previously?

I have no means of choosing at the moment, Socrates.

Well, can you make this choice? What is your opinion about it? A man who has knowledge would be able to give an account of what he knows, or would he not?

He must certainly be able to do so, Socrates, he said.

And do you think everybody can give an account of the things we were mentioning just now?

I wish they could, said Simmias, but I'm afraid it is much more likely that by this time tomorrow there will be no one left who can do so adequately.

So you do not think that everybody has knowledge c
of those things?

No indeed.

So they recollect what they once learned?

They must.

When did our souls acquire the knowledge of them? Certainly not since we were born as men.

Indeed no.

Before that then?

Yes.

So then, Simmias, our souls also existed apart from the body before they took on human form, and they had intelligence.

Unless we acquire the knowledge at the moment of birth, Socrates, for that time is still left to us.

Quite so, my friend, but at what other time do we d
lose it? We just now agreed that we are not born with
that knowledge. Do we then lose it at the very time
we acquire it, or can you mention any other time?

I cannot, Socrates. I did not realize that I was talking nonsense.

So this is our position, Simmias? he said. If those
realities we are always talking about exist, the Beautiful and the Good and all that kind of reality, and we
refer all the things we perceive to that reality, discovering that it existed before and is ours, and we com- e
pare these things with it, then, just as they exist, so
our soul must exist before we are born. If these realities do not exist, then this argument is altogether
futile. Is this the position, that there is an equal
necessity for those realities to exist, and for our souls
to exist before we were born? If the former do not
exist, neither do the latter?

I do not think, Socrates, said Simmias, that there is
any possible doubt that it is equally necessary for both
to exist, and it is opportune that our argument comes
to the conclusion that our soul exists before we are 77
born, and equally so that reality of which you are now
speaking. Nothing is so evident to me personally as
that all such things must certainly exist, the Beautiful,
the Good, and all those you mentioned just now. I
also think that sufficient proof of this has been given.

Then what about Cebes? said Socrates, for we must persuade Cebes also.

He is sufficiently convinced I think, said Simmias,
though he is the most difficult of men to persuade by
argument, but I believe him to be fully convinced
that our soul existed before we were born. I do not b

think myself, however, that it has been proved that the soul continues to exist after death; the opinion of the majority which Cebes mentioned still stands, that when a man dies his soul is dispersed and this is the end of its existence. What is to prevent the soul coming to be and being constituted from some other source, existing before it enters a human body and then, having done so and departed from it, itself dying and being destroyed?

c You are right, Simmias, said Cebes. Half of what
needed proof has been proved, namely, that our soul existed before we were born, but further proof is needed that it exists no less after we have died, if the proof is to be complete.

It has been proved even now, Simmias and Cebes,
said Socrates, if you are ready to combine this argument with the one we agreed on before, that every
living thing must come from the dead. If the soul
d exists before, it must, as it comes to life and birth,
come from nowhere else than death and being dead,
so how could it avoid existing after death since it
must be born again? What you speak of has, then,
even now been proved. However, I think you and
Simmias would like to discuss the argument more
fully. You seem to have this childish fear that the
e wind would really dissolve and scatter the soul, as it
leaves the body, especially if one happens to die in a
high wind and not in calm weather.

Cebes laughed and said: Assuming that we were afraid, Socrates, try to change our minds, or rather do not assume that we are afraid, but perhaps there is a child in us who has these fears; try to persuade him not to fear death like a bogey.

You should, said Socrates, sing a charm over him every day until you have charmed away his fears.

78 Where shall we find a good charmer for these
fears, Socrates, he said, now that you are leaving us?

Greece is a large country, Cebes, he said, and there are good men in it; the tribes of foreigners are also numerous. You should search for such a charmer among them all, sparing neither trouble nor expense, for there is nothing on which you could spend your money to greater advantage. You must also search among yourselves, for you might not easily find people who could do this better than yourselves.

b That shall be done, said Cebes, but let us, if it
pleases you, go back to the argument where we left it.

Of course it pleases me.

Splendid, he said.

We must then ask ourselves something like this: what kind of thing is likely to be scattered? On behalf of what kind of thing should one fear this, and for what kind of thing should one not fear it? We should then examine to which class the soul belongs, and as a result either fear for the soul or be of good cheer.

What you say is true.

Is not anything that is composite and a compound c
by nature liable to be split up into its component parts, and only that which is noncomposite, if anything, is not likely to be split up?

I think that is the case, said Cebes.

Are not the things that always remain the same and in the same state most likely not to be composite, whereas those that vary from one time to another and are never the same are composite?

I think that is so.

Let us then return to those same things with which
we were dealing earlier, to that reality of whose exis- d
tence we are giving an account in our questions and
answers; are they ever the same and in the same state,
or do they vary from one time to another; can the
Equal itself, the Beautiful itself, each thing in itself,
the real, ever be affected by any change whatever? Or
does each of them that really is, being uniform by
itself, remain the same and never in any way tolerate
any change whatever?

It must remain the same, said Cebes, and in the same state, Socrates.

What of the many beautiful particulars, be they
men, horses, clothes, or other such things, or the many e
equal particulars, and all those which bear the same
name as those others? Do they remain the same or, in
total contrast to those other realities, one might say,
never in any way remain the same as themselves or in
relation to each other?

The latter is the case, they are never in the same state.

These latter you could touch and see and perceive 79
with the other senses, but those that always remain the same can be grasped only by the reasoning power of the mind? They are not seen but are invisible?

That is altogether true, he said.

Do you then want us to assume two kinds of existences, the visible and the invisible?

Let us assume this.

And the invisible always remains the same, whereas the visible never does?

Let us assume that too.

b Now one part of ourselves is the body, another part is the soul?

Quite so.

To which class of existence do we say the body is more alike and akin?

To the visible, as anyone can see.

What about the soul? Is it visible or invisible?

It is not visible to men, Socrates, he said.

Well, we meant visible and invisible to human eyes; or to any others, do you think?

To human eyes.

Then what do we say about the soul? Is it visible or not visible?

Not visible.

So it is invisible?—Yes.

c So the soul is more like the invisible than the body, and the body more like the visible?—Without any doubt, Socrates.

Haven't we also said some time ago that when the soul makes use of the body to investigate something, be it through hearing or seeing or some other sense—for to investigate something through the body is to do it through the senses—it is dragged by the body to the things that are never the same, and the soul itself strays and is confused and dizzy, as if it were drunk, insofar as it is in contact with that kind of thing?

Certainly.

d But when the soul investigates by itself it passes into the realm of what is pure, ever existing, immortal, and unchanging, and being akin to this, it always stays with it whenever it is by itself and can do so; it ceases to stray and remains in the same state as it is in touch with things of the same kind, and its experience then is what is called wisdom?

Altogether well said and very true, Socrates, he said.

e Judging from what we have said before and what we are saying now, to which of these two kinds do you think that the soul is more alike and more akin?

I think, Socrates, he said, that on this line of argument any man, even the dullest, would agree that the soul is altogether more like that which always exists in the same state rather than like that which does not.

What of the body?

That is like the other.

Look at it also this way: when the soul and the 80
body are together, nature orders the one to be subject and to be ruled, and the other to rule and be master. Then again, which do you think is like the divine and which like the mortal? Do you not think that the nature of the divine is to rule and to lead, whereas it is that of the mortal to be ruled and be subject?

I do.

Which does the soul resemble?

Obviously, Socrates, the soul resembles the divine, and the body resembles the mortal.

Consider then, Cebes, whether it follows from all
that has been said that the soul is most like the b
divine, deathless, intelligible, uniform, indissoluble, always the same as itself, whereas the body is most like that which is human, mortal, multiform, unintelligible, soluble, and never consistently the same. Have we anything else to say to show, my dear Cebes, that this is not the case?

We have not.

Well then, that being so, is it not natural for the body to dissolve easily, and for the soul to be altogether indissoluble, or nearly so?

Of course. c

You realize, he said, that when a man dies, the visible part, the body, which exists in the visible world and which we call the corpse, whose natural lot it would be to dissolve, fall apart, and be blown away, does not immediately suffer any of these things but remains for a fair time, in fact, quite a long time if the man dies with his body in a suitable condition and at a favorable season? If the body is emaciated or embalmed, as in Egypt, it remains almost whole for a remarkable length of time, and even if the body
decays, some parts of it, namely bones and sinews d
and the like, are nevertheless, one might say, deathless. Is that not so?—Yes.

Will the soul, the invisible part which makes its way to a region of the same kind, noble and pure and invisible, to Hades in fact, to the good and wise god whither, god willing, my soul must soon be going—will the soul, being of this kind and nature, be scattered and destroyed on leaving the body, as the
majority of men say? Far from it, my dear Cebes and e
Simmias, but what happens is much more like this: if it is pure when it leaves the body and drags nothing bodily with it, as it had no willing association with the body in life, but avoided it and gathered itself

81 together by itself and always practiced this, which is
no other than practicing philosophy in the right way,
in fact, training to die easily. Or is this not training
for death?

It surely is.

A soul in this state makes its way to the invisible,
which is like itself, the divine and immortal and wise,
and arriving there it can be happy, having rid itself of
confusion, ignorance, fear, violent desires, and the
other human ills and, as is said of the initiates, truly
spend the rest of time with the gods. Shall we say this,
Cebes, or something different?

This, by Zeus, said Cebes.

b But I think that if the soul is polluted and impure
when it leaves the body, having always been associated with it and served it, bewitched by physical
desires and pleasures to the point at which nothing
seems to exist for it but the physical, which one can
touch and see or eat and drink or make use of for sexual enjoyment, and if that soul is accustomed to hate
and fear and avoid that which is dim and invisible to
the eyes but intelligible and to be grasped by philosophy—do you think such a soul will escape pure and
by itself?

c Impossible, he said.

It is no doubt permeated by the physical, which
constant intercourse and association with the body, as
well as considerable practice, has caused to become
ingrained in it?

Quite so.

We must believe, my friend, that this bodily element is heavy, ponderous, earthy, and visible.
Through it, such a soul has become heavy and is
dragged back to the visible region in fear of the
d unseen and of Hades. It wanders, as we are told,
around graves and monuments, where shadowy
phantoms, images that such souls produce, have
been seen, souls that have not been freed and purified but share in the visible, and are therefore seen.

That is likely, Socrates.

It is indeed, Cebes. Moreover, these are not the
souls of good but of inferior men, which are forced to
wander there, paying the penalty for their previous
e bad upbringing. They wander until their longing for
that which accompanies them, the physical, again
imprisons them in a body, and they are then, as is
likely, bound to such characters as they have practiced in their life.

What kind of characters do you say these are,
Socrates?

Those, for example, who have carelessly practiced
gluttony, violence, and drunkenness are likely to join
a company of donkeys or of similar animals. Do you 82
not think so?

Very likely.

Those who have esteemed injustice highly, and
tyranny and plunder, will join the tribes of wolves
and hawks and kites, or where else shall we say that
they go?

Certainly to those, said Cebes.

And clearly, the destination of the others will conform to the way in which they have behaved?

Clearly, of course.

The happiest of these, who will also have the best
destination, are those who have practiced popular b
and social virtue, which they call moderation and
justice and which was developed by habit and practice, without philosophy or understanding?

How are they the happiest?

Because it is likely that they will again join a social
and gentle group, either of bees or wasps or ants, and
then again the same kind of human group, and so be
moderate men.

That is likely.

No one may join the company of the gods who has
not practiced philosophy and is not completely pure c
when he departs from life, no one but the lover of
learning. It is for this reason, my friends Simmias and
Cebes, that those who practice philosophy in the
right way keep away from all bodily passions, master
them, and do not surrender themselves to them; it is
not at all for fear of wasting their substance and of
poverty, which the majority and the money-lovers
fear, nor for fear of dishonor and ill repute, like the
ambitious and lovers of honors, that they keep away
from them.

That would not be natural for them, Socrates, said
Cebes.

By Zeus, no, he said. Those who care for their own d
soul and do not live for the service of their body dismiss all these things. They do not travel the same road
as those who do not know where they are going but,
believing that nothing should be done contrary to philosophy and their deliverance and purification, they
turn to this and follow wherever philosophy leads.

How so, Socrates?

I will tell you, he said. The lovers of learning know
e that when philosophy gets hold of their soul, it is
imprisoned in and clinging to the body, and that it is
forced to examine other things through it as through
a cage and not by itself, and that it wallows in every
kind of ignorance. Philosophy sees that the worst feature of this imprisonment is that it is due to desires, so
that the prisoner himself is contributing to his own
83 incarceration most of all. As I say, the lovers of learning know that philosophy gets hold of their soul when
it is in that state, then gently encourages it and tries to
free it by showing them that investigation through the
eyes is full of deceit, as is that through the ears and the
other senses. Philosophy then persuades the soul to
withdraw from the senses insofar as it is not compelled to use them and bids the soul to gather itself
together by itself, to trust only itself and whatever real-
b ity, existing by itself, the soul by itself understands,
and not to consider as true whatever it examines by
other means, for this is different in different circumstances and is sensible and visible, whereas what the
soul itself sees is intelligible and invisible. The soul of
the true philosopher thinks that this deliverance must
not be opposed and so keeps away from pleasures and
desires and pains as far as he can; he reflects that violent pleasure or pain or passion does not cause merely
c such evils as one might expect, such as one suffers
when one has been sick or extravagant through desire,
but the greatest and most extreme evil, though one
does not reflect on this.

What is that, Socrates? asked Cebes.

That the soul of every man, when it feels violent
pleasure or pain in connection with some object,
inevitably believes at the same time that what causes
such feelings must be very clear and very true, which
it is not. Such objects are mostly visible, are they not?

Certainly.

d And doesn't such an experience tie the soul to the
body most completely?

How so?

Because every pleasure or pain provides, as it
were, another nail to rivet the soul to the body and to
weld them together. It makes the soul corporeal, so
that it believes that truth is what the body says it is.
As it shares the beliefs and delights of the body, I
think it inevitably comes to share its ways and manner of life and is unable ever to reach Hades in a
pure state; it is always full of body when it departs, so
that it soon falls back into another body and grows
with it as if it had been sewn into it. Because of this, e
it can have no part in the company of the divine, the
pure and uniform.

What you say is very true, Socrates, said Cebes.

This is why genuine lovers of learning are moderate and brave, or do you think it is for the reasons the
majority says they are?

I certainly do not. 84

Indeed no. This is how the soul of a philosopher
would reason: it would not think that while philosophy must free it, it should while being freed surrender itself to pleasures and pains and imprison itself
again, thus laboring in vain like Penelope at her web.
The soul of the philosopher achieves a calm from
such emotions; it follows reason and ever stays with it
contemplating the true, the divine, which is not the
object of opinion. Nurtured by this, it believes that b
one should live in this manner as long as one is alive
and, after death, arrive at what is akin and of the
same kind, and escape from human evils. After such
nurture there is no danger, Simmias and Cebes, that
one should fear that, on parting from the body, the
soul would be scattered and dissipated by the winds
and no longer be anything anywhere.

When Socrates finished speaking there was a long c
silence. He appeared to be concentrating on what
had been said, and so were most of us. But Cebes and
Simmias were whispering to each other. Socrates
observed them and questioned them. Come, he said,
do you think there is something lacking in my argument? There are still many doubtful points and many
objections for anyone who wants a thorough discussion of these matters. If you are discussing some other
subject, I have nothing to say, but if you have some
difficulty about this one, do not hesitate to speak for
yourselves and expound it if you think the argument
could be improved, and if you think you will do bet- d
ter, take me along with you in the discussion.

I will tell you the truth, Socrates, said Simmias.
Both of us have been in difficulty for some time, and
each of us has been urging the other to question you
because we wanted to hear what you would say, but
we hesitated to bother you, lest it be displeasing to
you in your present misfortune.

When Socrates heard this he laughed quietly and
said: "Really, Simmias, it would be hard for me to per- e
suade other people that I do not consider my present

fate a misfortune if I cannot persuade even you, and you are afraid that it is more difficult to deal with me than before. You seem to think me inferior to the swans in prophecy. They sing before too, but when they realize that they must die they sing most and 85 most beautifully, as they rejoice that they are about to depart to join the god whose servants they are. But men, because of their own fear of death, tell lies about the swans and say that they lament their death and sing in sorrow. They do not reflect that no bird sings when it is hungry or cold or suffers in any other way, neither the nightingale nor the swallow nor the hoopoe, though they do say that these sing laments b when in pain. Nor do the swans, but I believe that as they belong to Apollo, they are prophetic, have knowledge of the future, and sing of the blessings of the underworld, sing and rejoice on that day beyond what they did before. As I believe myself to be a fellow servant with the swans and dedicated to the same god, and have received from my master a gift of prophecy not inferior to theirs, I am no more despondent than they on leaving life. Therefore, you must speak and ask whatever you want as long as the authorities allow it."

Well spoken, said Simmias. I will tell you my difficulty, c and then Cebes will say why he does not accept what was said. I believe, as perhaps you do, that precise knowledge on that subject is impossible or extremely difficult in our present life, but that it surely shows a very poor spirit not to examine thoroughly what is said about it, and to desist before one is exhausted by an all-around investigation. One should achieve one of these things: learn the truth about these things or find it for oneself, or, if that is d impossible, adopt the best and most irrefutable of men's theories, and, borne upon this, sail through the dangers of life as upon a raft, unless someone should make that journey safer and less risky upon a firmer vessel of some divine doctrine. So even now, since you have said what you did, I will feel no shame at asking questions, and I will not blame myself in the future because I did not say what I think. As I examine what we said, both by myself and with Cebes, it does not seem to be adequate.

e Said Socrates: "You may well be right, my friend, but tell me how it is inadequate."

In this way, as it seems to me, he said: "One might make the same argument about harmony, lyre, and strings, that a harmony is something invisible, without body, beautiful and divine in the attuned lyre, whereas 86 the lyre itself and its strings are physical, bodily, composite, earthy, and akin to what is mortal. Then if someone breaks the lyre, cuts or breaks the strings, and then insists, using the same argument as you, that the harmony must still exist and is not destroyed because it would be impossible for the lyre and the strings, which are mortal, still to exist when the strings are broken, and for the harmony, which is akin and of the same nature as the divine and immortal, to be b destroyed before that which is mortal; he would say that the harmony itself still must exist and that the wood and the strings must rot before the harmony can suffer. And indeed Socrates, I think you must have this in mind, that we really do suppose the soul to be something of this kind; as the body is stretched and held together by the hot and the cold, the dry and the moist, and other such things, and our soul is a mixture and c harmony of those things when they are mixed with each other rightly and in due measure. If then the soul is a kind of harmony or attunement, clearly, when our body is relaxed or stretched without due measure by diseases and other evils, the soul must immediately be destroyed, even if it be most divine, as are the other harmonies found in music and all the works of artists, and the remains of each body last for a long time until they rot or are burned. Consider what we shall say in answer to one who deems the soul to be a mixture of d bodily elements and to be the first to perish in the process we call death."

Socrates looked at us keenly, as was his habit, smiled, and said: "What Simmias says is quite fair. If one of you is more resourceful than I am, why did he not answer him, for he seems to have handled the e argument competently. However, I think that before we answer him, we should hear Cebes' objection, in order that we may have time to deliberate on an answer. When we have heard him we should either agree with them, if we think them in tune with us or, if not, defend our own argument. Come then, Cebes. What is troubling you?"

I tell you, said Cebes, the argument seems to me to 87 be at the same point as before and open to the same objection. I do not deny that it has been very elegantly and, if it is not offensive to say so, sufficiently proved that our soul existed before it took on this present form, but I do not believe the same applies to

its existing somewhere after our death. Not that I agree with Simmias' objection that the soul is not stronger and much more lasting than the body, for I think it is superior in all these respects. "Why then," the argument might say, "are you still unconvinced? Since you see that when the man dies, the weaker part continues to exist, do you not think that the more
b lasting part must be preserved during that time?" On this point consider whether what I say makes sense.

Like Simmias, I too need an image, for I think this argument is much as if one said at the death of an old weaver that the man had not perished but was safe and sound somewhere, and offered as proof the fact
c that the cloak the old man had woven himself and was wearing was still sound and had not perished. If one was not convinced, he would be asked whether a man lasts longer than a cloak which is in use and being worn, and if the answer was that a man lasts much longer, this would be taken as proof that the man was definitely safe and sound, since the more temporary thing had not perished. But Simmias, I do not think that is so, for consider what I say. Anybody could see that the man who said this was talking nonsense. That weaver had woven and worn out many such cloaks. He perished after many of them, but
d before the last. That does not mean that a man is inferior and weaker than a cloak. The image illustrates, I think, the relationship of the soul to the body, and anyone who says the same thing about them would appear to me to be talking sense, that the soul lasts a long time while the body is weaker and more short-lived. He might say that each soul wears out many bodies, especially if it lives many years.

If the body were in a state of flux and perished
e while the man was still alive, and the soul wove afresh the body that is worn out, yet it would be inevitable that whenever the soul perished it would be wearing the last body it wove and perish only before this last. Then when the soul perished, the body would show the weakness of its nature by soon decaying and disappearing. So we cannot trust this
88 argument and be confident that our soul continues to exist somewhere after our death. For, if one were to concede, even more than you do, to a man using that argument, if one were to grant him not only that the soul exists in the time before we are born, but that there is no reason why the soul of some should not exist and continue to exist after our death, and thus frequently be born and die in turn; if one were to grant him that the soul's nature is so strong that it can survive many bodies, but if, having granted all this, one does not further agree that the soul is not damaged by its many births and is not, in the end, altogether destroyed in one of those deaths, he might say that no one knows which death and dissolution of the *b*
body brings about the destruction of the soul, since not one of us can be aware of this. And in that case, any man who faces death with confidence is foolish, unless he can prove that the soul is altogether immortal. If he cannot, a man about to die must of necessity always fear for his soul, lest the present separation of the soul from the body bring about the complete destruction of the soul.

When we heard what they said we were all *c*
depressed, as we told each other afterward. We had been quite convinced by the previous argument, and they seemed to confuse us again, and to drive us to doubt not only what had already been said but also what was going to be said, lest we be worthless as critics or the subject itself admitted of no certainty.

ECHECRATES: By the gods, Phaedo, you have my sympathy, for as I listen to you now I find myself saying to myself: "What argument shall we trust, now *d*
that that of Socrates, which was extremely convincing, has fallen into discredit?" The statement that the soul is some kind of harmony has a remarkable hold on me, now and always, and when it was mentioned, it reminded me that I had myself previously thought so. And now I am again quite in need, as if from the beginning, of some other argument to convince me that the soul does not die along with the man. Tell me then, by Zeus, how Socrates tackled the argument. Was he obviously distressed, as you say you people *e*
were, or was he not, but quietly came to the rescue of his argument, and did he do so satisfactorily or inadequately? Tell us everything as precisely as you can.

PHAEDO: I have certainly often admired Socrates, Echecrates, but never more than on this occasion. 89
That he had a reply was perhaps not strange. What I wondered at most in him was the pleasant, kind, and admiring way he received the young men's argument, and how sharply he was aware of the effect the discussion had on us, and then how well he healed our distress and, as it were, recalled us from our flight and defeat and turned us around to join him in the examination of their argument.

ECHECRATES: How did he do this?

PHAEDO: I will tell you. I happened to be sitting on *b* his right by the couch on a low stool, so that he was sitting well above me. He stroked my head and pressed the hair on the back of my neck, for he was in the habit of playing with my hair at times. "Tomorrow, Phaedo," he said, "you will probably cut this beautiful hair."

Likely enough, Socrates, I said.

Not if you take my advice, he said.

Why not? said I.

It is today, he said, that I shall cut my hair and you *c* yours, if our argument dies on us, and we cannot revive it. If I were you, and the argument escaped me, I would take an oath, as the Argives did, not to let my hair grow before I fought again and defeated the argument of Simmias and Cebes.

But, I said, they say that not even Heracles could fight two people.

Then call on me as your Iolaus, as long as the daylight lasts.

I shall call on you, but in this case as Iolaus calling on Heracles.

It makes no difference, he said, but first there is a certain experience we must be careful to avoid.

What is that? I asked.

d That we should not become misologues, as people become misanthropes.

There is no greater evil one can suffer than to hate reasonable discourse.

Misology and misanthropy arise in the same way. Misanthropy comes when a man without knowledge or skill has placed great trust in someone and believes him to be altogether truthful, sound, and trustworthy; then, a short time afterward he finds him to be wicked and unreliable, and then this happens in another case; when one has frequently had that experience, especially with *e* those whom one believed to be one's closest friends, then, in the end, after many such blows, one comes to hate all men and to believe that no one is sound in any way at all. Have you not seen this happen?

I surely have, I said.

This is a shameful state of affairs, he said, and obviously due to an attempt to have human relations without any skill in human affairs, for such skill would lead one to believe, what is in fact true, that the very good and the very wicked are both quite rare, 90
and that most men are between those extremes.

How do you mean? said I.

The same as with the very tall and the very short, he said. Do you think anything is rarer than to find an extremely tall man or an extremely short one? Or a dog or anything else whatever? Or again, one extremely swift or extremely slow, ugly or beautiful, white or black? Are you not aware that in all those cases the most extreme at either end are rare and few, but those in between are many and plentiful?

Certainly, I said.

Therefore, he said, if a contest of wickedness were *b* established, there too the winners, you think, would be very few?

That is likely, said I.

Likely indeed, he said, but arguments are not like men in this particular.

I was merely following your lead just now. The similarity lies rather in this: it is as when one who lacks skill in arguments puts his trust in an argument as being true, then shortly afterward believes it to be false—as sometimes it is and sometimes it is not—and so with another argument and then another. You know how those in particular who spend their time studying contradiction in the end believe themselves *c* to have become very wise and that they alone have understood that there is no soundness or reliability in any object or in any argument, but that all that exists simply fluctuates up and down as if it were in the Euripus[10] and does not remain in the same place for any time at all.

What you say, I said, is certainly true.

It would be pitiable, Phaedo, he said, when there is a true and reliable argument and one that can be understood, if a man who has dealt with such arguments as appear at one time true, at another time *d* untrue, should not blame himself or his own lack of skill but, because of his distress, in the end gladly shift the blame away from himself to the arguments, and spend the rest of his life hating and reviling reasonable discussion and so be deprived of truth and knowledge of reality.

Yes, by Zeus, I said, that would be pitiable indeed.

---

10. The Euripus is the straits between the island of Euboea and Boeotia on the Greek mainland; its currents were both violent and variable.

e This then is the first thing we should guard against, he said. We should not allow into our minds the conviction that argumentation has nothing sound about it; much rather we should believe that it is we who are not yet sound and that we must take courage and be eager
91 to attain soundness, you and the others for the sake of your whole life still to come, and I for the sake of death itself. I am in danger at this moment of not having a philosophical attitude about this, but like those who are quite uneducated, I am eager to get the better of you in argument, for the uneducated, when they engage in argument about anything, give no thought to the truth about the subject of discussion but are only eager that those present will accept the position they have set forth. I differ from them only to this extent: I shall not be eager to get the agreement of those present that what I say is true, except incidentally, but I shall be very eager that I should myself be thoroughly convinced that things are so. For I am thinking—see in how contentious a spirit—that if what I say is true, it is
b a fine thing to be convinced; if, on the other hand, nothing exists after death, at least for this time before I die I shall distress those present less with lamentations and my folly will not continue to exist along with me—that would be a bad thing—but will come to an end in a short time. Thus prepared, Simmias and Cebes, he said, I come to deal with your argument. If you will
c take my advice, you will give but little thought to Socrates but much more to the truth. If you think that what I say is true, agree with me; if not, oppose it with every argument and take care that in my eagerness I do not deceive myself and you and, like a bee, leave my sting in you when I go.

We must proceed, he said, and first remind me of what you said if I do not appear to remember it. Simmias, as I believe, is in doubt and fear that the soul,
d though it is more divine and beautiful than the body, yet predeceases it, being a kind of harmony. Cebes, I thought, agrees with me that the soul lasts much longer than the body, but that no one knows whether the soul often wears out many bodies and then, on leaving its last body, is now itself destroyed. This then is death, the destruction of the soul, since the body is always being destroyed. Are these the questions, Simmias and Cebes, which we must investigate?

e They both agreed that they were.

Do you then, he asked, reject all our previous statements, or some but not others?

Some, they both said, but not others.

What, he said, about the statements we made that learning is recollection and that, if this was so, our 92
soul must of necessity exist elsewhere before us, before it was imprisoned in the body?

For myself, said Cebes, I was wonderfully convinced by it at the time, and I stand by it now also, more than by any other statement.

That, said Simmias, is also my position, and I should be very surprised if I ever changed my opinion about this.

But you must change your opinion, my Theban friend, said Socrates, if you still believe that a harmony is a composite thing and that the soul is a kind of harmony of the elements of the body in a state of tension, for surely you will not allow yourself to maintain that b
a composite harmony existed before those elements from which it had to be composed, or would you?

Never, Socrates, he said.

Do you realize, he said, that this is what you are in fact saying when you state that the soul exists before it takes on the form and body of a man and that it is composed of elements which do not yet exist? A harmony is not like that to which you compare it; the lyre and the strings and the notes, though still unharmonized, exist; the harmony is composed last of all, c
and is the first to be destroyed. How will you harmonize this statement with your former one?

In no way, said Simmias.

And surely, he said, a statement about harmony should do so more than any other.

It should, said Simmias.

So your statement is inconsistent? Consider which of your statements you prefer, that learning is recollection or that the soul is a harmony.

I much prefer the former, Socrates. I adopted the d
latter without proof, because of a certain probability and plausibility, which is why it appeals to most men. I know that arguments of which the proof is based on probability are pretentious and, if one does not guard against them, they certainly deceive one, in geometry and everything else. The theory of recollection and learning, however, was based on an assumption worthy of acceptance, for our soul was said to exist also before it came into the body, just as the reality does that is of the kind that we qualify by the words "what it is," and I convinced myself that I was quite e
correct to accept it. Therefore, I cannot accept the

theory that the soul is a harmony either from myself or anyone else.

What of this, Simmias? Do you think it natural for
93 a harmony, or any other composite, to be in a different state from that of the elements of which it is composed?

Not at all, said Simmias.

Nor, as I think, can it act or be acted upon in a different way than its elements?

He agreed.

One must therefore suppose that a harmony does not direct its components, but is directed by them.

He accepted this.

A harmony is therefore far from making a movement, or uttering a sound, or doing anything else, in a manner contrary to that of its parts.

Far from it indeed, he said.

Does not the nature of each harmony depend on the way it has been harmonized?

I do not understand, he said.

b Will it not, if it is more and more fully harmonized, be more and more fully a harmony, and if it is less and less fully harmonized, it will be less and less fully a harmony?

Certainly.

Can this be true about the soul, that one soul is more and more fully a soul than another, or is less and less fully a soul, even to the smallest extent?

Not in any way.

Come now, by Zeus, he said. One soul is said to
c have intelligence and virtue and to be good, another to have folly and wickedness and to be bad. Are those things truly said?

They certainly are.

What will someone who holds the theory that the soul is a harmony say that those things are which reside in the soul, that is, virtue and wickedness? Are these some other harmony and disharmony? That the good soul is harmonized and, being a harmony, has within itself another harmony, whereas the evil soul is both itself a lack of harmony and has no other within itself?

I don't know what to say, said Simmias, but one who holds that assumption must obviously say something of that kind.

d We have previously agreed, he said, that one soul is not more and not less a soul than another, and this means that one harmony is not more and more fully, or less and less fully, a harmony than another. Is that not so?

Certainly.

Now that which is no more and no less a harmony is not more or less harmonized. Is that so?

It is.

Can that which is neither more nor less harmonized partake more or less of harmony, or does it do so equally?

Equally.

Then if a soul is neither more nor less a soul than e
another, it has been harmonized to the same extent?

This is so.

If that is so, it would have no greater share of disharmony or of harmony?

It would not.

That being the case, could one soul have more wickedness or virtue than another, if wickedness is disharmony and virtue harmony?

It could not.

But rather, Simmias, according to correct reason- 94
ing, no soul, if it is a harmony, will have any share of wickedness, for harmony is surely altogether this very thing, harmony, and would never share in disharmony.

It certainly would not.

Nor would a soul, being altogether this very thing, a soul, share in wickedness?

How could it, in view of what has been said?

So it follows from this argument that all the souls of all living creatures will be equally good, if souls are by nature equally this very thing, souls.

I think so, Socrates.

Does our argument seem right, he said, and does it b
seem that it should have come to this, if the hypothesis that the soul is a harmony was correct?

Not in any way, he said.

Further, of all the parts of a man, can you mention any other part that rules him than his soul, especially if it is a wise soul?

I cannot.

Does it do so by following the affections of the body or by opposing them? I mean, for example, that when the body is hot and thirsty the soul draws him to the opposite, to not drinking; when the body is
hungry, to not eating, and we see a thousand other c
examples of the soul opposing the affections of the body. Is that not so?

It certainly is.

On the other hand, we previously agreed that if the soul were a harmony, it would never be out of tune with the stress and relaxation and the striking of the strings or anything else done to its composing elements, but that it would follow and never direct them?

We did so agree, of course.

Well, does it now appear to do quite the opposite,
d ruling over all the elements of which one says it is
composed, opposing nearly all of them throughout
life, directing all their ways, inflicting harsh and
painful punishment on them, at times in physical
culture and medicine, at other times more gently by
threats and exhortations, holding converse with
desires and passions and fears as if it were one thing
talking to a different one, as Homer wrote somewhere in the *Odyssey* where he says that Odysseus
"struck his breast and rebuked his heart saying,
'Endure, my heart, you have endured worse than
this.'"[11]

e Do you think that when he composed this the poet thought that his soul was a harmony, a thing to be directed by the affections of the body? Did he not rather regard it as ruling over them and mastering them, itself a much more divine thing than a harmony?

Yes, by Zeus, I think so, Socrates.

95 Therefore, my good friend, it is quite wrong for us to say that the soul is a harmony, and in saying so we would disagree both with the divine poet Homer and with ourselves.

That is so, he said.

Very well, said Socrates. Harmonia of Thebes seems somehow reasonably propitious to us. How and by what argument, my dear Cebes, can we propitiate Cadmus?[12]

I think, Cebes said, that you will find a way. You
dealt with the argument about harmony in a manner
that was quite astonishing to me. When Simmias was
b speaking of his difficulties I was very much wondering whether anyone would be able to deal with his
argument, and I was quite dumbfounded when right
away he could not resist your argument's first
onslaught. I should not wonder therefore if that of
Cadmus suffered the same fate.

My good sir, said Socrates, do not boast, lest some
malign influence upset the argument we are about to
make. However, we leave that to the care of the god, but
let us come to grips with it in the Homeric fashion, to see
if there is anything in what you say. The sum of your
problem is this: you consider that the soul must be proved *c*
to be immortal and indestructible before a philosopher
on the point of death, who is confident that he will fare
much better in the underworld than if he had led any
other kind of life, can avoid being foolish and simpleminded in this confidence. To prove that the soul is
strong, that it is divine, that it existed before we were born
as men, all this, you say, does not show the soul to be
immortal but only longlasting. That it existed for a very
long time before, that it knew much and acted much,
makes it no more immortal because of that; indeed, its *d*
very entering into a human body was the beginning of its
destruction, like a disease; it would live that life in distress
and would in the end be destroyed in what we call death.
You say it makes no difference whether it enters a body
once or many times as far as the fear of each of us is concerned, for it is natural for a man who is no fool to be
afraid, if he does not know and cannot prove that the soul
is immortal. This, I think, is what you maintain, Cebes; I
deliberately repeat it often, in order that no point may
escape us, and that you may add or subtract something if *e*
you wish.

And Cebes said: "There is nothing that I want to add or subtract at the moment. That is what I say."

Socrates paused for a long time, deep in thought.
He then said: "This is no unimportant problem that 96
you raise, Cebes, for it requires a thorough investigation of the cause of generation and destruction. I
will, if you wish, give you an account of my experience in these matters. Then if something I say seems
useful to you, make use of it to persuade us of your
position."

I surely do wish that, said Cebes.

Listen then, and I will, Cebes, he said. When I was
a young man I was wonderfully keen on that wisdom
which they call natural science, for I thought it splendid to know the causes of everything, why it comes to
be, why it perishes, and why it exists. I was often *b*
changing my mind in the investigation, in the first

11. Homer, *Odyssey* 20.17–8.

12. Harmonia was in legend the wife of Cadmus, the founder of Thebes. Socrates' punning joke is simply that, having dealt with Harmonia (harmony), we must now deal with Cadmus (i.e., Cebes, the other Theban).

instance, of questions such as these: Are living creatures nurtured when heat and cold produce a kind of
putrefaction, as some say? Do we think with our blood,
or air, or fire, or none of these, and does the brain provide our senses of hearing and sight and smell, from
which come memory and opinion, and from memory
and opinion which has become stable, comes knowledge? Then again, as I investigated how these things
perish and what happens to things in the sky and on
c the earth, finally I became convinced that I have no
natural aptitude at all for that kind of investigation,
and of this I will give you sufficient proof. This investigation made me quite blind even to those things
which I and others thought that I clearly knew before,
so that I unlearned what I thought I knew before,
about many other things and specifically about how
men grew. I thought before that it was obvious to any-
d body that men grew through eating and drinking, for
food adds flesh to flesh and bones to bones, and in the
same way appropriate parts were added to all other
parts of the body, so that the man grew from an earlier
small bulk to a large bulk later, and so a small man
became big. That is what I thought then. Do you not
think it was reasonable?

I do, said Cebes.

Then further consider this: I thought my opinion
e was satisfactory, that when a large man stood by a
small one he was taller by a head, and so a horse was
taller than a horse. Even clearer than this, I thought
that ten was more than eight because two had been
added, and that a two-cubit length is larger than a
cubit because it surpasses it by half its length.

And what do you think now about those things?

That I am far, by Zeus, from believing that I know
the cause of any of those things. I will not even allow
myself to say that where one is added to one, either
the one to which it is added or the one that is added
97 becomes two, or that the one added and the one to
which it is added become two because of the addition of the one to the other. I wonder that, when each
of them is separate from the other, each of them is
one, nor are they then two, but that, when they come
near to one another, this is the cause of their becoming two, the coming together and being placed closer
to one another. Nor can I any longer be persuaded
that when one thing is divided, this division is the
b cause of its becoming two, for just now the cause of
becoming two was the opposite. At that time it was
their coming close together and one was added to the
other, but now it is because one is taken and separated from the other.

I do not any longer persuade myself that I know
why a unit or anything else comes to be, or perishes
or exists by the old method of investigation, and I do
not accept it, but I have a confused method of my
own. One day I heard someone reading, as he said, *c*
from a book of Anaxagoras, and saying that it is Mind
that directs and is the cause of everything. I was
delighted with this cause, and it seemed to me good,
in a way, that Mind should be the cause of all. I
thought that if this were so, the directing Mind would
direct everything and arrange each thing in the way
that was best. If then one wished to know the cause
of each thing, why it comes to be or perishes or exists,
one had to find what was the best way for it to be, or *d*
to be acted upon, or to act. On these premises, then,
it befitted a man to investigate only, about this and
other things, what is best. The same man must
inevitably also know what is worse, for that is part of
the same knowledge. As I reflected on this subject I
was glad to think that I had found in Anaxagoras a
teacher about the cause of things after my own heart,
and that he would tell me, first, whether the earth is *e*
flat or round, and then would explain why it is so of
necessity, saying which is better, and that it was better to be so. If he said it was in the middle of the universe, he would go on to show that it was better for it
to be in the middle, and if he showed me those things
I should be prepared never to desire any other kind 98
of cause. I was ready to find out in the same way
about the sun and the moon and the other heavenly
bodies, about their relative speed, their turnings and
whatever else happened to them, how it is best that
each should act or be acted upon. I never thought
that Anaxagoras, who said that those things were
directed by Mind, would bring in any other cause for
them than that it was best for them to be as they are.
Once he had given the best for each as the cause for *b*
each and the general cause of all, I thought he would
go on to explain the common good for all, and I
would not have exchanged my hopes for a fortune. I
eagerly acquired his books and read them as quickly
as I could in order to know the best and the worst as
soon as possible.

This wonderful hope was dashed as I went on reading and saw that the man made no use of Mind, nor

gave it any responsibility for the management of
c things, but mentioned as causes air and ether and
water and many other strange things. That seemed to
me much like saying that Socrates' actions are all due
to his mind, and then in trying to tell the causes of
everything I do, to say that the reason that I am sitting
here is because my body consists of bones and
sinews, because the bones are hard and are separated
by joints, that the sinews are such as to contract and
d relax, that they surround the bones along with flesh
and skin which hold them together, then as the
bones are hanging in their sockets, the relaxation and
contraction of the sinews enable me to bend my
limbs, and that is the cause of my sitting here with
my limbs bent.

Again, he would mention other such causes for my
talking to you: sounds and air and hearing, and a
thousand other such things, but he would neglect to
mention the true causes, that, after the Athenians
e decided it was better to condemn me, for this reason
it seemed best to me to sit here and more right to
remain and to endure whatever penalty they ordered.
For by the dog, I think these sinews and bones could
99 long ago have been in Megara or among the Boeo-
tians, taken there by my belief as to the best course,
if I had not thought it more right and honorable to
endure whatever penalty the city ordered rather than
escape and run away. To call those things causes is
too absurd. If someone said that without bones and
sinews and all such things, I should not be able to do
what I decided, he would be right, but surely to say
that they are the cause of what I do, and not that I
have chosen the best course, even though I act with
b my mind, is to speak very lazily and carelessly. Imagine not being able to distinguish the real cause from
that without which the cause would not be able to act
as a cause. It is what the majority appear to do, like
people groping in the dark; they call it a cause, thus
giving it a name that does not belong to it. That is
why one man surrounds the earth with a vortex to
c make the heavens keep it in place, another makes the
air support it like a wide lid. As for their capacity of
being in the best place they could possibly be put,
this they do not look for, nor do they believe it to
have any divine force, but they believe that they will
sometime discover a stronger and more immortal
Atlas to hold everything together more, and they do
not believe that the truly good and "binding" binds
and holds them together. I would gladly become the
disciple of any man who taught the workings of that
kind of cause. However, since I was deprived and d
could neither discover it myself nor learn it from
another, do you wish me to give you an explanation
of how, as a second-best, I busied myself with the
search for the cause, Cebes?

I would wish it above all else, he said.

After this, he said, when I had wearied of investigating things, I thought that I must be careful to
avoid the experience of those who watch an eclipse
of the sun, for some of them ruin their eyes unless
they watch its reflection in water or some such mate- e
rial. A similar thought crossed my mind, and I feared
that my soul would be altogether blinded if I looked
at things with my eyes and tried to grasp them with
each of my senses.

So I thought I must take refuge in discussions and
investigate the truth of things by means of words.
However, perhaps this analogy is inadequate, for I
certainly do not admit that one who investigates 100
things by means of words is dealing with images any
more than one who looks at facts. However, I started
in this manner: taking as my hypothesis in each case
the theory that seemed to me the most compelling, I
would consider as true, about cause and everything
else, whatever agreed with this, and as untrue whatever did not so agree. But I want to put my meaning
more clearly for I do not think that you understand
me now.

No, by Zeus, said Cebes, not very well.

This, he said, is what I mean. It is nothing new, but b
what I have never stopped talking about, both elsewhere and in the earlier part of our conversation. I
am going to try to show you the kind of cause with
which I have concerned myself. I turn back to those
oft-mentioned things and proceed from them. I
assume the existence of a Beautiful, itself by itself, of
a Good and a Great and all the rest. If you grant me
these and agree that they exist, I hope to show you
the cause as a result, and to find the soul to be
immortal.

Take it that I grant you this, said Cebes, and hasten c
to your conclusion.

Consider then, he said, whether you share my
opinion as to what follows, for I think that, if there is
anything beautiful besides the Beautiful itself, it is
beautiful for no other reason than that it shares in

that Beautiful, and I say so with everything. Do you agree to this sort of cause?—I do.

d I no longer understand or recognize those other sophisticated causes, and if someone tells me that a thing is beautiful because it has a bright color or shape or any such thing, I ignore these other reasons—for all these confuse me—but I simply, naively, and perhaps foolishly cling to this, that nothing else makes it beautiful other than the presence of, or the sharing in, or however you may describe its relationship to that Beautiful we mentioned, for I will not insist on the precise nature of the relationship, but that all beautiful things are beautiful by the Beautiful. That, I think, is the safest answer I can give
e myself or anyone else. And if I stick to this I think I shall never fall into error. This is the safe answer for me or anyone else to give, namely, that it is through Beauty that beautiful things are made beautiful. Or do you not think so too?—I do.

And that it is through Bigness that big things are big and the bigger are bigger, and that smaller things are made small by Smallness?—Yes.

And you would not accept the statement that one
101 man is taller than another by a head and the shorter man shorter by the same, but you would bear witness that you mean nothing else than that everything that is bigger is made bigger by nothing else than by Bigness, and that is the cause of its being bigger, and the smaller is made smaller only by Smallness and this is why it is smaller. I think you would be afraid that some opposite argument would confront you if you said that someone is bigger or smaller by a head, first, because the bigger is bigger and the smaller smaller
b by the same, then because the bigger is bigger by a head which is small, and this would be strange, namely, that someone is made bigger by something small. Would you not be afraid of this?

I certainly would, said Cebes, laughing.

Then you would be afraid to say that ten is more than eight by two, and that this is the cause of the excess, and not magnitude and because of magnitude, or that two cubits is bigger than one cubit by half and not by Bigness, for this is the same fear. —Certainly.

Then would you not avoid saying that when one is
c added to one it is the addition and when it is divided it is the division that is the cause of two? And you would loudly exclaim that you do not know how else each thing can come to be except by sharing in the particular reality in which it shares, and in these cases you do not know of any other cause of becoming two except by sharing in Twoness, and that the things that are to be two must share in this, as that which is to be one must share in Oneness, and you would dismiss these additions and divisions and other such subtleties, and leave them to those wiser than yourself to
answer. But you, afraid, as they say, of your own d
shadow and your inexperience, would cling to the safety of your own hypothesis and give that answer. If someone then attacked your hypothesis itself, you would ignore him and would not answer until you had examined whether the consequences that follow from it agree with one another or contradict one another. And when you must give an account of your hypothesis itself you will proceed in the same way: you will assume another hypothesis, the one which seems
to you best of the higher ones until you come to some- e
thing acceptable, but you will not jumble the two as the debaters do by discussing the hypothesis and its consequences at the same time, if you wish to discover any truth. This they do not discuss at all nor give any thought to, but their wisdom enables them to mix
everything up and yet to be pleased with themselves, 102
but if you are a philosopher I think you will do as I say.

What you say is very true, said Simmias and Cebes together.

ECHECRATES: Yes, by Zeus, Phaedo, and they were right, I think he made these things wonderfully clear to anyone of even small intelligence.

PHAEDO: Yes indeed, Echecrates, and all those present thought so too.

ECHECRATES: And so do we who were not present but hear of it now. What was said after that?

PHAEDO: As I recall it, when the above had been accepted, and it was agreed that each of the Forms
existed, and that other things acquired their name by b
having a share in them, he followed this up by asking: if you say these things are so, when you then say that Simmias is taller than Socrates but shorter than Phaedo, do you not mean that there is in Simmias both tallness and shortness?—I do.

But, he said, do you agree that the words of the
statement "Simmias is taller than Socrates" do not c
express the truth of the matter? It is not, surely, the nature of Simmias to be taller than Socrates because he is Simmias but because of the tallness he happens

to have? Nor is he taller than Socrates because Socrates is Socrates, but because Socrates has smallness compared with the tallness of the other?—True.

Nor is he shorter than Phaedo because Phaedo is Phaedo, but because Phaedo has tallness compared with the shortness of Simmias?—That is so.

d So then Simmias is called both short and tall, being between the two, presenting his shortness to be overcome by the tallness of one, and his tallness to overcome the shortness of the other. He smilingly added, I seem to be going to talk like a book, but it is as I say. The other agreed.

My purpose is that you may agree with me. Now it seems to me that not only Tallness itself is never willing to be tall and short at the same time, but also that the tallness in us will never admit the short or be
e overcome, but one of two things happens: either it flees and retreats whenever its opposite, the short, approaches, or it is destroyed by its approach. It is not willing to endure and admit shortness and be other than it was, whereas I admit and endure shortness and still remain the same person and am this short man. But Tallness, being tall, cannot venture to be
103 small. In the same way, the short in us is unwilling to become or to be tall ever, nor does any other of the opposites become or be its opposite while still being what it was; either it goes away or is destroyed when that happens.—I altogether agree, said Cebes.

When he heard this, someone of those present—I have no clear memory of who it was—said: "By the gods, did we not agree earlier in our discussion[13] to the very opposite of what is now being said, namely, that the larger came from the smaller and the smaller from the larger, and that this simply was how opposites came to be, from their opposites, but now I think we are saying that this would never happen?"

On hearing this, Socrates inclined his head toward the speaker and said: "You have bravely reminded us, but you do not understand the difference between
b what is said now and what was said then, which was that an opposite thing came from an opposite thing; now we say that the opposite itself could never become opposite to itself, neither that in us nor that in nature. Then, my friend, we were talking of things that have opposite qualities and naming these after them, but now we say that these opposites themselves, from the presence of which in them things get their name, never can tolerate the coming to be from one *c*
another." At the same time he looked to Cebes and said: "Does anything of what this man says also disturb you?"

Not at the moment, said Cebes, but I do not deny that many things do disturb me.

We are altogether agreed then, he said, that an opposite will never be opposite to itself.—Entirely agreed.

Consider then whether you will agree to this further point. There is something you call hot and something you call cold.—There is.

Are they the same as what you call snow and *d*
fire?—By Zeus, no.

So the hot is something other than fire, and the cold is something other than snow?—Yes.

You think, I believe, that being snow it will not admit the hot, as we said before, and remain what it was and be both snow and hot, but when the hot approaches it will either retreat before it or be destroyed.—Quite so.

So fire, as the cold approaches, will either go away or be destroyed; it will never venture to admit coldness and remain what it was, fire and cold.—What you say is true. *e*

It is true then about some of these things that not only the Form itself deserves its own name for all time, but there is something else that is not the Form but has its character whenever it exists. Perhaps I can make my meaning clearer: the Odd must always be given this name we now mention. Is that not so? —Certainly.

Is it the only one of existing things to be called *104*
odd?—this is my question—or is there something else than the Odd which one must nevertheless also always call odd, as well as by its own name, because it is such by nature as never to be separated from the Odd? I mean, for example, the number three and many others. Consider three: do you not think that it must always be called both by its own name and by that of the Odd, which is not the same as three? That is the nature of three, and of five, and of half of all the numbers; each of them is odd, but it is not the Odd. *b*
Then again, two and four and the whole other column of numbers; each of them, while not being the same as the Even, is always even. Do you not agree?—Of course.

13. 70d–71a above.

Look now. What I want to make clear is this: not only do those opposites not admit each other, but this is also true of those things which, while not being opposite to each other yet always contain the opposites, and it seems that these do not admit that Form which is opposite to that which is in them; when it
c approaches them, they either perish or give way. Shall we not say that three will perish or undergo anything before, while remaining three, becoming even?—Certainly, said Cebes.

Yet surely two is not the opposite of three? —Indeed it is not.

It is then not only opposite Forms that do not admit each other's approach, but also some other things that do not admit the onset of opposites.—Very true.

Do you then want us, if we can, to define what these are?—I surely do.

d Would they be the things that compel whatever they occupy not only to contain their form but also always that of some opposite?—How do you mean?

As we were saying just now, you surely know that what the Form of three occupies must be not only three but also odd.—Certainly.

And we say that the opposite Form to the Form that achieves this result could never come to it.—It could not.

Now it is Oddness that has done this?—Yes.

And opposite to this is the Form of the Even?—Yes.

e So then the Form of the Even will never come to three?—Never.

Then three has no share in the Even?—Never.

So three is uneven?—Yes.

As for what I said we must define, that is, what kind of things, while not being opposites to something, yet do not admit the opposite, as for example the triad, though it is not the opposite of the Even, yet does not
105 admit it because it always brings along the opposite of the Even, and so the dyad in relation to the Odd, fire to the Cold, and very many other things, see whether you would define it thus: not only does the opposite not admit its opposite, but that which brings along some opposite into that which it occupies, that which brings this along will not admit the opposite to that which it brings along. Refresh your memory, it is no worse for being heard often. Five does not admit the form of the Even, nor will ten, its double, admit the form of the Odd. The double itself is an opposite of something else, yet it will not admit the form of the Odd. Nor do one-and-a-half and other such fractions b
admit the form of the Whole, nor will one-third, and so on, if you follow me and agree to this.

I certainly agree, he said, and I follow you.

Tell me again from the beginning, he said, and do not answer in the words of the question, but do as I do. I say that beyond that safe answer, which I spoke of first, I see another safe answer. If you should ask me what, coming into a body, makes it hot, my reply c
would not be that safe and ignorant one, that it is heat, but our present argument provides a more sophisticated answer, namely, fire, and if you ask me what, on coming into a body, makes it sick, I will not say sickness but fever. Nor, if asked the presence of what in a number makes it odd, I will not say oddness but oneness, and so with other things. See if you now sufficiently understand what I want.—Quite sufficiently.

Answer me then, he said, what is it that, present in a body, makes it living?—A soul.

And is that always so?—Of course. d

Whatever the soul occupies, it always brings life to it?—It does.

Is there, or is there not, an opposite to life? —There is.

What is it?—Death.

So the soul will never admit the opposite of that which it brings along, as we agree from what has been said?

Most certainly, said Cebes.

Well, and what do we call that which does not admit the form of the even?—The uneven.

What do we call that which will not admit the just and that which will not admit the musical?

The unmusical, and the other the unjust. e

Very well, what do we call that which does not admit death?

The deathless, he said.

Now the soul does not admit death?—No.

So the soul is deathless?—It is.

Very well, he said. Shall we say that this has been proved, do you think?

Quite adequately proved, Socrates.

Well now, Cebes, he said, if the uneven were of necessity indestructible, surely three would be inde- 106
structible?—Of course.

And if the nonhot were of necessity indestructible, then whenever anyone brought heat to snow, the

snow would retreat safe and unthawed, for it could
not be destroyed, nor again could it stand its ground
and admit the heat?—What you say is true.

In the same way, if the noncold were indestructible, then when some cold attacked the fire, it would
neither be quenched nor be destroyed, but retreat
safely.—Necessarily.

b Must then the same not be said of the deathless? If
the deathless is also indestructible, it is impossible for
the soul to be destroyed when death comes upon it.
For it follows from what has been said that it will not
admit death or be dead, just as three, we said, will not
be even nor will the odd; nor will fire be cold, nor the
heat that is in the fire. But, someone might say, what
c prevents the odd, while not becoming even as has
been agreed, from being destroyed, and the even to
come to be instead? We could not maintain against
the man who said this that it is not destroyed, for the
uneven is not indestructible. If we had agreed that it
was indestructible we could easily have maintained
that at the coming of the even, the odd and the three
have gone away and the same would hold for fire and
the hot and the other things.—Surely.

d And so now, if we are agreed that the deathless is
indestructible, the soul, besides being deathless, is
indestructible. If not, we need another argument.

—There is no need for one as far as that goes, for
hardly anything could resist destruction if the deathless, which lasts forever, would admit destruction.

All would agree, said Socrates, that the god, and
the Form of life itself, and anything that is deathless,
are never destroyed.—All men would agree, by Zeus,
to that, and the gods, I imagine, even more so.

e If the deathless is indestructible, then the soul,
if it is deathless, would also be indestructible?
—Necessarily.

Then when death comes to man, the mortal part
of him dies, it seems, but his deathless part goes away
safe and indestructible, yielding the place to death.
—So it appears.

107 Therefore the soul, Cebes, he said, is most certainly deathless and indestructible and our souls will
really dwell in the underworld.

I have nothing more to say against that, Socrates,
said Cebes, nor can I doubt your arguments. If Simmias here or someone else has something to say, he
should not remain silent, for I do not know to what
further occasion other than the present he could put
it off if he wants to say or to hear anything on these
subjects.

Certainly, said Simmias, I myself have no remaining grounds for doubt after what has been said; nevertheless, in view of the importance of our subject
and my low opinion of human weakness, I am bound *b*
still to have some private misgivings about what we
have said.

You are not only right to say this, Simmias,
Socrates said, but our first hypotheses require clearer
examination, even though we find them convincing.
And if you analyze them adequately, you will, I think,
follow the argument as far as a man can, and if the
conclusion is clear, you will look no further.—That
is true.

It is right to think then, gentlemen, that if the *c*
soul is immortal, it requires our care not only for
the time we call our life, but for the sake of all time,
and that one is in terrible danger if one does not
give it that care. If death were escape from everything, it would be a great boon to the wicked to get
rid of the body and of their wickedness together
with their soul. But now that the soul appears to be *d*
immortal, there is no escape from evil or salvation
for it except by becoming as good and wise as possible, for the soul goes to the underworld possessing
nothing but its education and upbringing, which
are said to bring the greatest benefit or harm to the
dead right at the beginning of the journey yonder.

We are told that when each person dies, the
guardian spirit who was allotted to him in life proceeds to lead him to a certain place, whence those
who have been gathered together there must, after *e*
being judged, proceed to the underworld with the
guide who has been appointed to lead them thither
from here. Having there undergone what they must
and stayed there the appointed time, they are led
back here by another guide after long periods of time.
The journey is not as Aeschylus' Telephus[14] describes *108*
it. He says that only one single path leads to Hades,
but I think it is neither one nor simple, for then there
would be no need of guides; one could not make any
mistake if there were but one path. As it is, it is likely
to have many forks and crossroads; and I base this
judgment on the sacred rites and customs here.

14. Not extant.

The well-ordered and wise soul follows the guide
and is not without familiarity with its surroundings,
but the soul that is passionately attached to the body,
b as I said before, hovers around it and the visible
world for a long time, struggling and suffering much
until it is led away by force and with difficulty by its
appointed spirit. When the impure soul which has
performed some impure deed joins the others after
being involved in unjust killings, or committed other
crimes which are akin to these and are actions of
souls of this kind, everybody shuns it and turns away,
c unwilling to be its fellow traveler or its guide; such a
soul wanders alone completely at a loss until a certain time arrives and it is forcibly led to its proper
dwelling place. On the other hand, the soul that has
led a pure and moderate life finds fellow travelers
and gods to guide it, and each of them dwells in a
place suited to it.

There are many strange places upon the earth, and
the earth itself is not such as those who are used to
discourse upon it believe it to be in nature or size, as
someone has convinced me.

d Simmias said: "What do you mean, Socrates? I
have myself heard many things said about the earth,
but certainly not the things that convince you. I
should be glad to hear them."

Indeed, Simmias, I do not think it requires the skill
of Glaucus[15] to tell you what they are, but to prove
them true requires more than that skill, and I should
perhaps not be able to do so. Also, even if I had the
e knowledge, my remaining time would not be long
enough to tell the tale. However, nothing prevents
my telling you what I am convinced is the shape of
the earth and what its regions are.

Even that is sufficient, said Simmias.

109 Well then, he said, the first thing of which I am
convinced is that if the earth is a sphere in the middle of the heavens, it has no need of air or any other
force to prevent it from falling. The homogeneous
nature of the heavens on all sides and the earth's own
equipoise are sufficient to hold it, for an object balanced in the middle of something homogeneous will
have no tendency to incline more in any direction
than any other but will remain unmoved. This, he
said, is the first point of which I am persuaded.

And rightly so, said Simmias.

Further, the earth is very large, and we live around
the sea in a small portion of it between Phasis and the b
pillars of Heracles, like ants or frogs around a swamp;
many other peoples live in many such parts of it.
Everywhere about the earth there are numerous hollows of many kinds and shapes and sizes into which
the water and the mist and the air have gathered. The
earth itself is pure and lies in the pure sky where the
stars are situated, which the majority of those who c
discourse on these subjects call the ether. The water
and mist and air are the sediment of the ether, and
they always flow into the hollows of the earth. We,
who dwell in the hollows of it, are unaware of this,
and we think that we live above, on the surface of the
earth. It is as if someone who lived deep down in the
middle of the ocean thought he was living on its surface. Seeing the sun and the other heavenly bodies d
through the water, he would think the sea to be the
sky; because he is slow and weak, he has never
reached the surface of the sea or risen with his head
above the water or come out of the sea to our region
here, nor seen how much purer and more beautiful
it is than his own region, nor has he ever heard of it
from anyone who has seen it.

Our experience is the same: living in a certain
hollow of the earth, we believe that we live upon its
surface; the air we call the heavens, as if the stars
made their way through it; this too is the same:
because of our weakness and slowness we are not e
able to make our way to the upper limit of the air; if
anyone got to this upper limit, if anyone came to it
or reached it on wings and his head rose above it,
then just as fish on rising from the sea see things in
our region, he would see things there and, if his
nature could endure to contemplate them, he would
know that there is the true heaven, the true light,
and the true earth, for the earth here, these stones 110
and the whole region, are spoiled and eaten away,
just as things in the sea are by the salt water.

Nothing worth mentioning grows in the sea, nothing, one might say, is fully developed; there are caves
and sand and endless slime and mud wherever there
is earth—not comparable in any way with the beauties of our region. So those things above are in their
turn far superior to the things we know. Indeed, if this
is the moment to tell a tale, Simmias, it is worth hear- b
ing about the nature of things on the surface of the
earth under the heavens.

15. A proverbial expression whose origin is obscure.

At any rate, Socrates, said Simmias, we should be
glad to hear this story.

Well then, my friend, in the first place it is said that
the earth, looked at from above, looks like those
spherical balls made up of twelve pieces of leather; it
is multicolored, and of these colors those used by our
c painters give us an indication; up there the whole
earth has these colors, but much brighter and purer
than these; one part is sea-green and of marvelous
beauty, another is golden, another is white, whiter
than chalk or snow; the earth is composed also of the
other colors, more numerous and beautiful than any
we have seen. The very hollows of the earth, full of
d water and air, gleaming among the variety of other
colors, present a color of their own so that the whole
is seen as a continuum of variegated colors. On the
surface of the earth the plants grow with corresponding beauty, the trees and the flowers and the fruits,
and so with the hills and the stones, more beautiful
in their smoothness and transparency and color. Our
e precious stones here are but fragments, our cor-
nelians, jaspers, emeralds, and the rest. All stones
there are of that kind, and even more beautiful. The
reason is that there they are pure, not eaten away or
spoiled by decay and brine, or corroded by the water
and air which have flowed into the hollows here and
bring ugliness and disease upon earth, stones, the
111 other animals, and plants. The earth itself is adorned
with all these things, and also with gold and silver
and other metals. These stand out, being numerous
and massive and occurring everywhere, so that the
earth is a sight for the blessed. There are many other
living creatures upon the earth, and also men, some
living inland, others at the edge of the air, as we live
on the edge of the sea, others again live on islands
surrounded by air close to the mainland. In a word,
b what water and the sea are to us, the air is to them,
and the ether is to them what the air is to us. The climate is such that they are without disease, and they
live much longer than people do here; their eyesight,
hearing, and intelligence and all such are as superior
to ours as air is superior to water and ether to air in
purity; they have groves and temples dedicated to the
gods, in which the gods really dwell, and they com-
c municate with them by speech and prophecy and by
the sight of them; they see the sun and moon and
stars as they are, and in other ways their happiness is
in accord with this.

This then is the nature of the earth as a whole and
of its surroundings; around the whole of it there are
many regions in the hollows; some are deeper and
more open than that in which we live; others are
deeper and have a narrower opening than ours, and d
there are some that have less depth and more width.
All these are connected with each other below the
surface of the earth in many places by narrow and
broader channels, and thus have outlets through
which much water flows from one to another as into
mixing bowls; huge rivers of both hot and cold water
thus flow beneath the earth eternally, much fire and
large rivers of fire, and many of wet mud, both more e
pure and more muddy, such as those flowing in
advance of the lava and the stream of lava itself in
Sicily. These streams then fill up every and all regions
as the flow reaches each, and all these places move up
and down with the oscillating movement of the earth.
The natural cause of the oscillation is as follows: one
of the hollows of the earth, which is also the biggest,
pierces through the whole earth; it is that which 112
Homer mentioned when he said: "Far down where is
the deepest pit below the earth . . . ,"[16] and which he
elsewhere, and many other poets, call Tartarus; into
this chasm all the rivers flow together, and again flow
out of it, and each river is affected by the nature of the b
land through which it flows. The reason for their flowing into and out of Tartarus is that this water has no
bottom or solid base, but it oscillates up and down in
waves, and the air and wind about it do the same, for
they follow it when it flows to this or that part of the
earth. Just as when people breathe, the flow of air goes
in and out, so here the air oscillates with the water
and creates terrible winds as it goes in and out.
Whenever the water retreats to what we call the c
lower part of the earth, it flows into those parts and
fills them up as if the water were pumped in; when it
leaves that part for this, it fills these parts again, and
the parts filled flow through the channels and
through the earth and in each case arrive at the
places to which the channels lead and create seas
and marshes and rivers and springs. From there the
waters flow under the earth again, some flowing d
around larger and more numerous regions, some
around smaller and shallower ones, then flow back
into Tartarus, some at a point much lower than

16. Homer, *Iliad* 8.14; cf. 8.481.

where they issued forth, others only a little way, but
all of them at a lower point, some of them at the
opposite side of the chasm, some on the same side;
some flow in a wide circle around the earth once or
many times like snakes, then go as far down as possible, then go back into the chasm of Tartarus. From
e each side it is possible to flow down as far as the center, but not beyond, for this part that faces the river
flow from either side is steep.

There are many other large rivers of all kinds, and
among these there are four of note; the biggest which
flows on the outside (of the earth) in a circle is called
Oceanus; opposite it and flowing in the opposite
113 direction is the Acheron; it flows through many other
deserted regions and further underground makes its
way to the Acherusian lake to which the souls of the
majority come after death and, after remaining there
for a certain appointed time, longer for some, shorter
for others, they are sent back to birth as living creatures. The third river issues between the first two, and
close to its source it falls into a region burning with
b much fire and makes a lake larger than our sea, boiling with water and mud. From there it goes in a circle, foul and muddy, and winding on its way it
comes, among other places, to the edge of the
Acherusian lake but does not mingle with its waters;
then, coiling many times underground it flows lower
down into Tartarus; this is called the Pyriphlegethon,
and its lava streams throw off fragments of it in vari-
c ous parts of the earth. Opposite this the fourth river
issues forth, which is called Stygion, and it is said to
flow first into a terrible and wild region, all of it blue-
gray in color, and the lake that this river forms by
flowing into it is called the Styx. As its waters fall into
the lake they acquire dread powers; then diving
below and winding around it flows in the opposite
direction from the Pyriphlegethon and into the opposite side of the Acherusian lake; its waters do not mingle with any other; it too flows in a circle and into
Tartarus opposite the Pyriphlegethon. The name of
that fourth river, the poets tell us, is Cocytus.

d Such is the nature of these things. When the dead
arrive at the place to which each has been led by his
guardian spirit, they are first judged as to whether they
have led a good and pious life. Those who have
lived an average life make their way to the Acheron
and embark upon such vessels as there are for them
and proceed to the lake. There they dwell and are
purified by penalties for any wrongdoing they may *e*
have committed; they are also suitably rewarded for
their good deeds as each deserves. Those who are
deemed incurable because of the enormity of their
crimes, having committed many great sacrileges or
wicked and unlawful murders and other such
wrongs—their fitting fate is to be hurled into Tartarus
never to emerge from it. Those who are deemed to
have committed great but curable crimes, such as
doing violence to their father or mother in a fit of tem- *114*
per, but who have felt remorse for the rest of their lives,
or who have killed someone in a similar manner, these
must of necessity be thrown into Tartarus, but a year
later the current throws them out, those who are guilty
of murder by way of Cocytus, and those who have done
violence to their parents by way of the Pyriphlegethon.
After they have been carried along to the Acherusian
lake, they cry out and shout, some for those they have
killed, others for those they have maltreated, and call- *b*
ing them they then pray to them and beg them to allow
them to step out into the lake and to receive them. If
they persuade them, they do step out and their punishment comes to an end; if they do not, they are taken
back into Tartarus and from there into the rivers, and
this does not stop until they have persuaded those they
have wronged, for this is the punishment which the
judges imposed on them.

Those who are deemed to have lived an extremely *c*
pious life are freed and released from the regions of
the earth as from a prison; they make their way up to
a pure dwelling place and live on the surface of the
earth. Those who have purified themselves sufficiently by philosophy live in the future altogether
without a body; they make their way to even more
beautiful dwelling places which it is hard to describe
clearly, nor do we now have the time to do so.
Because of the things we have enunciated, Simmias,
one must make every effort to share in virtue and wisdom in one's life, for the reward is beautiful and the
hope is great.

No sensible man would insist that these things are *d*
as I have described them, but I think it is fitting for a
man to risk the belief—for the risk is a noble one—
that this, or something like this, is true about our
souls and their dwelling places, since the soul is evidently immortal, and a man should repeat this to
himself as if it were an incantation, which is why I
have been prolonging my tale. That is the reason

e why a man should be of good cheer about his own soul, if during life he has ignored the pleasures of the body and its ornamentation as of no concern to him and doing him more harm than good, but has seriously concerned himself with the pleasures of learning, and adorned his soul not with alien but with its 115 own ornaments, namely, moderation, righteousness, courage, freedom, and truth, and in that state awaits his journey to the underworld.

Now you, Simmias, Cebes, and the rest of you, Socrates continued, will each take that journey at some other time, but my fated day calls me now, as a tragic character might say, and it is about time for me to have my bath, for I think it better to have it before I drink the poison and save the women the trouble of washing the corpse.

b When Socrates had said this Crito spoke. Very well, Socrates, what are your instructions to me and the others about your children or anything else? What can we do that would please you most?—Nothing new, Crito, said Socrates, but what I am always saying, that you will please me and mine and yourselves by taking good care of your own selves in whatever you do, even if you do not agree with me now, c but if you neglect your own selves, and are unwilling to live following the tracks, as it were, of what we have said now and on previous occasions, you will achieve nothing even if you strongly agree with me at this moment.

We shall be eager to follow your advice, said Crito, but how shall we bury you?

In any way you like, said Socrates, if you can catch me and I do not escape you. And laughing quietly, looking at us, he said: I do not convince Crito that I am d this Socrates talking to you here and ordering all I say, but he thinks that I am the thing which he will soon be looking at as a corpse, and so he asks how he shall bury me. I have been saying for some time and at some length that after I have drunk the poison I shall no longer be with you but will leave you to go and enjoy some good fortunes of the blessed, but it seems that I have said all this to him in vain in an attempt to reassure you and myself too. Give a pledge to Crito on my e behalf, he said, the opposite pledge to that he gave the jury. He pledged that I would stay; you must pledge that I will not stay after I die, but that I shall go away, so that Crito will bear it more easily when he sees my body being burned or buried and will not be angry on my behalf, as if I were suffering terribly, and so that he should not say at the funeral that he is laying out, or carrying out, or burying Socrates. For know you well, my dear Crito, that to express oneself badly is not only faulty as far as the language goes, but does some harm to the soul. You must be of good cheer, and say you are 116 burying my body, and bury it in any way you like and think most customary.

After saying this he got up and went to another room to take his bath, and Crito followed him and he told us to wait for him. So we stayed, talking among ourselves, questioning what had been said, and then again talking of the great misfortune that had b befallen us. We all felt as if we had lost a father and would be orphaned for the rest of our lives. When he had washed, his children were brought to him—two of his sons were small and one was older—and the women of his household came to him.

He spoke to them before Crito and gave them what instructions he wanted.

Then he sent the women and children away, and he himself joined us. It was now close to sunset, for he had stayed inside for some time. He came and sat down after his bath and conversed for a short while, when the officer of the Eleven came and stood by c him and said: "I shall not reproach you as I do the others, Socrates. They are angry with me and curse me when, obeying the orders of my superiors, I tell them to drink the poison.

"During the time you have been here I have come to know you in other ways as the noblest, the gentlest, and the best man who has ever come here. So now too I know that you will not make trouble for me; you know who is responsible, and you will direct your anger against them. You know what message I bring. Fare you well, and try to endure what you must as easily as possible." The officer was weeping as he turned d away and went out. Socrates looked up at him and said: "Fare you well also; we shall do as you bid us." And turning to us he said: "How pleasant the man is! During the whole time I have been here he has come in and conversed with me from time to time, a most agreeable man. And how genuinely he now weeps for me. Come, Crito, let us obey him. Let someone bring the poison if it is ready; if not, let the man prepare it."

But Socrates, said Crito, I think the sun still shines e upon the hills and has not yet set. I know that others drink the poison quite a long time after they have received the order, eating and drinking quite a bit, and some of them enjoy intimacy with their loved ones. Do not hurry; there is still some time.

It is natural, Crito, for them to do so, said Socrates, 117 for they think they derive some benefit from doing this, but it is not fitting for me. I do not expect any benefit from drinking the poison a little later, except to become ridiculous in my own eyes for clinging to life, and be sparing of it when there is none left. So do as I ask and do not refuse me.

Hearing this, Crito nodded to the slave who was standing near him; the slave went out and after a time came back with the man who was to administer the poison, carrying it made ready in a cup. When Socrates saw him he said: "Well, my good man, you are an *b* expert in this; what must one do?"—"Just drink it and walk around until your legs feel heavy, and then lie down and it will act of itself." And he offered the cup to Socrates, who took it quite cheerfully, Echecrates, without a tremor or any change of feature or color, but looking at the man from under his eyebrows as was his wont, asked: "What do you say about pouring a libation from this drink? It is allowed?"—"We only mix as much as we believe will suffice," said the man.

c I understand, Socrates said, but one is allowed, indeed one must, utter a prayer to the gods that the journey from here to yonder may be fortunate. This is my prayer and may it be so.

And while he was saying this, he was holding the cup, and then drained it calmly and easily. Most of us had been able to hold back our tears reasonably well up until then, but when we saw him drinking it and after he drank it, we could hold them back no longer; my own tears came in floods against my will. So I covered my face. I was weeping for myself, not for him—for my misfortune in being deprived of such a comrade. Even before me, Crito was unable to *d* restrain his tears and got up. Apollodorus had not ceased from weeping before, and at this moment his noisy tears and anger made everybody present break down, except Socrates. "What is this," he said, "you strange fellows. It is mainly for this reason that I sent the women away, to avoid such unseemliness, for I *e* am told one should die in good-omened silence. So keep quiet and control yourselves."

His words made us ashamed, and we checked our tears. He walked around, and when he said his legs were heavy he lay on his back as he had been told to do, and the man who had given him the poison touched his body, and after a while tested his feet and legs, pressed hard upon his foot and asked him if he felt this, and Socrates said no. Then he pressed his 118 calves, and made his way up his body and showed us that it was cold and stiff. He felt it himself and said that when the cold reached his heart he would be gone. As his belly was getting cold Socrates uncovered his head—he had covered it—and said—these were his last words—"Crito, we owe a cock to Asclepius;[17] make this offering to him and do not forget."—"It shall be done," said Crito, "tell us if there is anything else." But there was no answer. Shortly afterward Socrates made a movement; the man uncovered him, and his eyes were fixed. Seeing this Crito closed his mouth and his eyes.

Such was the end of our comrade, Echecrates, a man who, we would say, was of all those we have known the best, and also the wisest and the most upright.

SYMPOSIUM

WE ENTER THE conversation just as Aristophanes, the great comic dramatist, is about to make his speech in praise of love.

From Plato, *Symposium*, translated by Alexander Nehamas and Paul Woodruff (Indianapolis: Hackett Publishing Company, 1989). Copyright (c) 1989. Reprinted by permission of the publisher.

"Eryximachus," Aristophanes said, "indeed I do have 189c in mind a different approach to speaking than the one the two of you used, you and Pausanias. You see, I think people have entirely missed the power of Love, because, if they had grasped it, they'd have built the greatest temples and altars to him and made the

17. A cock was sacrificed to Asclepius by the sick people who slept in his temples, hoping for a cure.

greatest sacrifices. But as it is, none of this is done for him, though it should be, more than anything else!
d For he loves the human race more than any other god, he stands by us in our troubles, and he cures those ills we humans are most happy to have mended. I shall, therefore, try to explain his power to you; and you, please pass my teaching on to everyone else."

First you must learn what Human Nature was in the beginning and what has happened to it since, because long ago our nature was not what it is now, but very different. There were three kinds of human beings,
e that's my first point—not two as there are now, male and female. In addition to these, there was a third, a combination of those two; its name survives, though the kind itself has vanished. At that time, you see, the word "androgynous" really meant something: a form made up of male and female elements, though now there's nothing but the word, and that's used as an insult. My second point is that the shape of each human being was completely round, with back and sides in a circle; they had four hands each, as many
190 legs as hands, and two faces, exactly alike, on a rounded neck. Between the two faces, which were on opposite sides, was one head with four ears. There were two sets of sexual organs, and everything else was the way you'd imagine it from what I've told you. They walked upright, as we do now, whatever direction they wanted. And whenever they set out to run fast, they thrust out all their eight limbs, the ones they had then, and spun rapidly, the way gymnasts do cartwheels, by bringing their legs around straight.

b Now here is why there were three kinds, and why they were as I described them: The male kind was originally an offspring of the sun, the female of the earth, and the one that combined both genders was an offspring of the moon, because the moon shares in both. They were spherical, and so was their motion, because they were like their parents in the sky.

In strength and power, therefore, they were terrible, and they had great ambitions. They made an attempt on the gods, and Homer's story about Ephialtes and Otus was originally about them: how they tried to
c make an ascent to heaven so as to attack the gods.[1] Then Zeus and the other gods met in council to discuss what to do, and they were sore perplexed. They couldn't wipe out the human race with thunderbolts and kill them all off, as they had the giants, because that would wipe out the worship they receive, along with the sacrifices we humans give them. On the other hand, they couldn't let them run riot. At last, after great effort, Zeus had an idea.

"I think I have a plan," he said, "that would allow
human beings to exist and stop their misbehaving: d
they will give up being wicked when they lose their strength. So I shall now cut each of them in two. At one stroke they will lose their strength and also become more profitable to us, owing to the increase in their number. They shall walk upright on two legs. But if I find they still run riot and do not keep the peace," he said, "I will cut them in two again, and they'll have to make their way on one leg, hopping."

So saying, he cut those human beings in two, the e
way people cut sorbapples before they dry them or the way they cut eggs with hairs. As he cut each one, he commanded Apollo to turn its face and half its neck toward the wound, so that each person would see that he'd been cut and keep better order. Then Zeus commanded Apollo to heal the rest of the wound, and Apollo did turn the face around, and he drew skin from all sides over what is now called the stomach, and there he made one mouth, as in a pouch with a drawstring, and fastened it at the center
of the stomach. This is now called the navel. Then 191
he smoothed out the other wrinkles, of which there were many, and he shaped the breasts, using some such tool as shoemakers have for smoothing wrinkles out of leather on the form. But he left a few wrinkles around the stomach and the navel, to be a reminder of what happened long ago.

Now, since their natural form had been cut in two, each one longed for its own other half, and so they would throw their arms about each other, weaving themselves together, wanting to grow together. In
that condition they would die from hunger and gen- b
eral idleness, because they would not do anything apart from each other. Whenever one of the halves died and one was left, the one that was left still sought another and wove itself together with that. Sometimes the half he met came from a woman, as we'd call her now, sometimes it came from a man; either way, they kept on dying.

Then, however, Zeus took pity on them, and came up with another plan: he moved their genitals

1. Homer, *Iliad* 5.385; *Odyssey* 11.305 ff.

around to the front! Before then, you see, they used
c to have their genitals outside, like their faces, and
they cast seed and made children, not in one
another, but in the ground, like cicadas. So Zeus
brought about this relocation of genitals, and in
doing so he invented interior reproduction, *by* the
man *in* the woman. The purpose of this was so that,
when a man embraced a woman, he would cast his
seed and they would have children; but when male
embraced male, they would at least have the satisfaction of intercourse, after which they could stop
d embracing, return to their jobs, and look after their
other needs in life. This, then, is the source of our
desire to love each other. Love is born into every
human being; it calls back the halves of our original
nature together; it tries to make one out of two and
heal the wound of human nature.

Each of us, then, is a "matching half" of a human
whole, because each was sliced like a flatfish, two out
of one, and each of us is always seeking the half that
matches him. That's why a man who is split from the
double sort (which used to be called "androgynous")
e runs after women. Many lecherous men have come
from this class, and so do the lecherous women who
run after men. Women who are split from a woman,
however, pay no attention at all to men; they are oriented more toward women, and lesbians come from
this class. People who are split from a male are male-
oriented. While they are boys, because they are chips
192 off the male block, they love men and enjoy lying
with men and being embraced by men; those are the
best of boys and lads, because they are the most manly
in their nature. Of course, some say such boys are
shameless, but they're lying. It's not because they have
no shame that such boys do this, you see, but because
they are bold and brave and masculine, and they tend
to cherish what is like themselves. Do you want me to
b prove it? Look, these are the only kind of boys who
grow up to be real men in politics. When they're
grown men, they are lovers of young men, and they
naturally pay no attention to marriage or to making
babies, except insofar as they are required by local
custom. They, however, are quite satisfied to live their
lives with one another unmarried. In every way, then,
this sort of man grows up as a lover of young men and
a lover of Love, always rejoicing in his own kind.

And so, when a person meets the half that is his
very own, whatever his orientation, whether it's to
young men or not, then something wonderful happens: the two are struck from their senses by love, by c
a sense of belonging to one another, and by desire,
and they don't want to be separated from one
another, not even for a moment.

These are the people who finish out their lives
together and still cannot say what it is they want from
one another. No one would think it is the intimacy of
sex—that mere sex is the reason each lover takes so
great and deep a joy in being with the other. It's obvi- d
ous that the soul of every lover longs for something
else; his soul cannot say what it is, but like an oracle it
has a sense of what it wants, and like an oracle it hides
behind a riddle. Suppose two lovers are lying together
and Hephaestus stands over them with his mending
tools, asking, "What is it you human beings really
want from each other?" And suppose they're perplexed, and he asks them again: "Is this your heart's
desire, then—for the two of you to become parts of the
same whole, as near as can be, and never to separate,
day or night? Because if that's your desire, I'd like to
weld you together and join you into something that is
naturally whole, so that the two of you are made into e
one. Then the two of you would share one life, as long
as you lived, because you would be one being, and by
the same token, when you died, you would be one and
not two in Hades, having died a single death. Look at
your love, and see if this is what you desire: wouldn't
this be all the good fortune you could want?"

Surely you can see that no one who received such
an offer would turn it down; no one would find anything else that he wanted. Instead, everyone would
think he'd found out at last what he had always
wanted: to come together and melt together with the
one he loves, so that one person emerged from two.
Why should this be so? It's because, as I said, we used
to be complete wholes in our original nature, and
now "Love" is the name for our pursuit of wholeness, 193
for our desire to be complete.

Long ago we were united, as I said; but now the
god has divided us as punishment for the wrong we
did him, just as the Spartans divided the Arcadians.[2]

---

2. Arcadia included the city of Mantinea, which opposed Sparta and was rewarded by having its population divided and dispersed in 385 BCE. Aristophanes seems to be referring anachronistically to those events; such anachronisms are not uncommon in Plato.

So there's a danger that if we don't keep order before
the gods, we'll be split in two again, and then we'll
be walking around in the condition of people carved
on gravestones in bas-relief, sawn apart between the
nostrils, like half dice. We should encourage all
b men, therefore, to treat the gods with all due reverence, so that we may escape this fate and find wholeness instead. And we will, if Love is our guide and
our commander. Let no one work against him.
Whoever opposes Love is hateful to the gods, but if
we become friends of the god and cease to quarrel
with him, then we shall find the young men that are
meant for us and win their love, as very few men do
nowadays.

c Now don't get ideas, Eryximachus, and turn this
speech into a comedy.

Don't think I'm pointing this at Pausanias and Agathon. Probably, they both do belong to the group that are entirely masculine in nature. But I am speaking about everyone, men and women alike, and I say there's just one way for the human race to flourish: we must bring love to its perfect conclusion, and each of us must win the favors of his very own young man, so that he can recover his original nature. If that is the ideal, then, of course, the nearest approach to it is best in present circumstances, and that is to win the favor of young men who are naturally sympathetic to us.

d If we are to give due praise to the god who can give
us this blessing, then, we must praise Love. Love does
the best that can be done for the time being: he draws
us toward what belongs to us. But for the future, Love
promises the greatest hope of all: if we treat the gods
with due reverence, he will restore to us our original
nature, and by healing us, he will make us blessed
and happy.

"That," he said, "is my speech about Love, Eryximachus. It is rather different from yours. As I begged
you earlier, don't make a comedy of it. I'd prefer to
e hear what all the others will say—or, rather, what
each of them will say, since Agathon and Socrates are
the only ones left."

WE TAKE UP the conversation with Socrates' report of what Diotima taught him about love.

201d Now I'll let you go. I shall try to go through for you
the speech about Love I once heard from a woman
of Mantinea, Diotima—a woman who was wise about many things besides this: once she even put off the plague for ten years by telling the Athenians what sacrifices to make. She is the one who taught me the art of love, and I shall go through her speech as best I can on my own, using what Agathon and I have agreed to as a basis.

Following your lead, Agathon, one should first
describe who Love is and what he is like, and after- *e*
ward describe his works—I think it will be easiest for
me to proceed the way Diotima did and tell you how
she questioned me.

You see, I had told her almost the same things Agathon told me just now: that Love is a great god and that he belongs to beautiful things. And she used the very same arguments against me that I used against Agathon; she showed how, according to my very own speech, Love is neither beautiful nor good.

So I said, "What do you mean, Diotima? Is Love ugly, then, and bad?"

But she said, "Watch your tongue! Do you really *202*
think that, if a thing is not beautiful, it has to be ugly?"

"I certainly do."

"And if a thing's not wise, it's ignorant? Or haven't you found out yet that there's something in between wisdom and ignorance?"

"What's that?"

"It's judging things correctly without being able to give a reason. Surely you see that this is not the same as knowing—for how could knowledge be unreasoning? And it's not ignorance either—for how could what hits the truth be ignorance? Correct judgment, of course, has this character: it is *in between* understanding and ignorance."

"True," said I, "as you say." *b*

"Then don't force whatever is not beautiful to be ugly, or whatever is not good to be bad. It's the same with Love: when you agree he is neither good nor beautiful, you need not think he is ugly and bad; he could be something in between," she said.

"Yet everyone agrees he's a great god," I said.

"Only those who don't know?" she said. "Is that how you mean 'everyone'? Or do you include those who do know?"

"Oh, everyone together."

And she laughed. "Socrates, how could those who *c*
say that he's not a god at all agree that he's a great
god?"

"Who says that?" I asked.

"You, for one," she said, "and I for another."

"How can you say this!" I exclaimed.

"That's easy," said she. "Tell me, wouldn't you say that all gods are beautiful and happy? Surely you'd never say a god is not beautiful or happy?"

"Zeus! Not I," I said.

"Well, by calling anyone 'happy,' don't you mean they possess good and beautiful things?"

d "Certainly."

"What about Love? You agreed he needs good and beautiful things, and that's why he desires them—because he needs them."

"I certainly did."

"Then how could he be a god if he has no share in good and beautiful things?"

"There's no way he could, apparently."

"Now do you see? You don't believe Love is a god either!"

"Then, what could Love be?" I asked. "A mortal?"

"Certainly not."

"Then, what is he?"

"He's like what we mentioned before," she said. "He is in between mortal and immortal."

"What do you mean, Diotima?"

e "He's a great spirit, Socrates. Everything spiritual, you see, is in between god and mortal."

"What is their function?" I asked.

"They are messengers who shuttle back and forth between the two, conveying prayer and sacrifice from men to gods, while to men they bring commands from the gods and gifts in return for sacrifices. Being in the middle of the two, they round out the whole
203 and bind fast the all to all. Through them all divination passes, through them the art of priests in sacrifice and ritual, in enchantment, prophecy, and sorcery. Gods do not mix with men; they mingle and converse with us through spirits instead, whether we are awake or asleep. He who is wise in any of these ways is a man of the spirit, but he who is wise in any other way, in a profession or any manual work, is merely a mechanic. These spirits are many and various, then, and one of them is Love."

b "Who are his father and mother?" I asked.

"That's rather a long story," she said. "I'll tell it to you, all the same."

"When Aphrodite was born, the gods held a celebration. Poros, the son of Metis, was there among them.[3] When they had feasted, Penia came begging, as poverty does when there's a party, and stayed by the gates. Now Poros got drunk on nectar (there was no wine yet, you see) and, feeling drowsy, went into the garden of Zeus, where he fell asleep. Then Penia
schemed up a plan to relieve her lack of resources: c
she would get a child from Poros. So she lay beside him and got pregnant with Love. That is why Love was born to follow Aphrodite and serve her: because he was conceived on the day of her birth. And that's why he is also by nature a lover of beauty, because Aphrodite herself is especially beautiful.

"As the son of Poros and Penia, his lot in life is set to be like theirs. In the first place, he is always poor, and he's far from being delicate and beautiful (as
ordinary people think he is); instead, he is tough and d
shriveled and shoeless and homeless, always lying on the dirt without a bed, sleeping at people's doorsteps and in roadsides under the sky, having his mother's nature, always living with Need. But on his father's side he is a schemer after the beautiful and the good; he is brave, impetuous, and intense, an awesome hunter, always weaving snares, resourceful in his pursuit of intelligence, a lover of wisdom[4] through all his life, a genius with enchantments, potions, and clever pleadings.

"He is by nature neither immortal nor mortal. But e
now he springs to life when he gets his way; now he dies—all in the very same day. Because he is his father's son, however, he keeps coming back to life, but then anything he finds his way to always slips away, and for this reason Love is never completely without resources, nor is he ever rich.

"He is in between wisdom and ignorance as well. 204
In fact, you see, none of the gods loves wisdom or wants to become wise—for they are wise—and no one else who is wise already loves wisdom; on the other hand, no one who is ignorant will love wisdom either or want to become wise. For what's especially difficult about being ignorant is that you are content with yourself, even though you're neither beautiful

---

3. *Poros* means "way" or "resource." His mother's name, *Mētis*, means "cunning." *Penia* means "poverty."

4. I.e., a philosopher.

and good nor intelligent. If you don't think you need anything, of course you won't want what you don't think you need."

b "In that case, Diotima, who *are* the people who
love wisdom, if they are neither wise nor ignorant?"

"That's obvious," she said. "A child could tell you. Those who love wisdom fall in between those two extremes. And Love is one of them, because he is in love with what is beautiful, and wisdom is extremely beautiful. It follows that Love *must* be a lover of wisdom and, as such, is in between being wise and being ignorant. This, too, comes to him from his parentage, from a father who is wise and resourceful and a mother who is not wise and lacks resource.

c "My dear Socrates, that, then, is the nature of the
Spirit called Love. Considering what you thought
about Love, it's no surprise that you were led into
thinking of Love as you did. On the basis of what you
say, I conclude that you thought Love was *being loved*,
rather than *being a lover*. I think that's why Love struck
you as beautiful in every way: because it is what is
really beautiful and graceful that deserves to be loved,
and this is perfect and highly blessed; but being a lover
takes a different form, which I have just described."

So I said, "All right then, my friend. What you say
d about Love is beautiful, but if you're right, what use
is Love to human beings?"

"I'll try to teach you that, Socrates, after I finish this. So far I've been explaining the character and the parentage of Love. Now, according to you, he is love for beautiful things. But suppose someone asks us, 'Socrates and Diotima, what is the point of loving beautiful things?'

"It's clearer this way: 'The lover of beautiful things has a desire; what does he desire?'"

"That they become his own," I said.

"But that answer calls for still another question, that is, 'What will this man have, when the beautiful things he wants have become his own?'"

e I said there was no way I could give a ready answer
to that question.

Then she said, "Suppose someone changes the question, putting 'good' in place of 'beautiful,' and asks you this: 'Tell me, Socrates, a lover of good things has a desire; what does he desire?'"

"That they become his own," I said.

"And what will he have, when the good things he wants have become his own?"

"This time it's easier to come up with the answer," 205
I said. "He'll have happiness."

"That's what makes happy people happy, isn't it—possessing good things. There's no need to ask further, 'What's the point of wanting happiness?' The answer you gave seems to be final."

"True," I said.

"Now this desire for happiness, this kind of love—do you think it is common to all human beings and that everyone wants to have good things forever and ever? What would you say?"

"Just that," I said. "It is common to all."

"Then, Socrates, why don't we say that everyone is b
in love," she asked, "since everyone always loves the
same things? Instead, we say some people are in love
and others not; why is that?"

"I wonder about that myself," I said.

"It's nothing to wonder about," she said. "It's because we divide out a special kind of love, and we refer to it by the word that means the whole—'love'; and for the other kinds of love we use other words."

"What do you mean?" I asked.

"Well, you know, for example, that 'poetry' has a
very wide range. After all, everything that is responsible for creating something out of nothing is a kind of c
poetry; and so all the creations of every craft and profession are themselves a kind of poetry, and everyone
who practices a craft is a poet."

"True."

"Nevertheless," she said, "as you also know, these craftsmen are not called poets. We have other words for them, and out of the whole of poetry we have marked off one part, the part the Muses give us with melody and rhythm, and we refer to this by the word that means the whole. For this alone is called 'poetry,' and those who practice this part of poetry are called poets."

"True." d

"That's also how it is with love. The main point is this: every desire for good things or for happiness is 'the supreme and treacherous love' in everyone. But those who pursue this along any of its many other ways—through making money, or through the love of sports, or through philosophy—we don't say that *these* people are in love, and we don't call them lovers. It's only when people are devoted exclusively to one special kind of love that we use these words that really belong to the whole of it: 'love' and 'in love' and 'lovers.'"

"I am beginning to see your point," I said.

e "Now there is a certain story," she said, "according to which lovers are those people who seek their other halves. But according to my story, a lover does not seek the half or the whole, unless, my friend, it turns out to be good as well. I say this because people are even willing to cut off their own arms and legs if they think they are diseased. I don't think an individual takes joy in what belongs to him personally unless by 'belonging to me' he means 'good' and by 'belonging to another' he means 'bad.' That's because what
206 everyone loves is really nothing other than the good. Do you disagree?"

"Zeus! Not I," I said.

"Now, then," she said. "Can we simply say that people love the good?"

"Yes," I said.

"But shouldn't we add that, in loving it, they want the good to be theirs?"

"We should."

"And not only that," she said. "They want the good to be theirs forever, don't they?"

"We should add that too."

"In a word, then, love is wanting to possess the good forever."

b "That's very true," I said.

"This, then, is the object of love," she said. "Now, how do lovers pursue it? We'd rightly say that when they are in love they do something with eagerness and zeal. But what is it precisely that they do? Can you say?"

"If I could," I said, "I wouldn't be your student, filled with admiration for your wisdom, and trying to learn these very things."

"Well, I'll tell you," she said. "It is giving birth in beauty, whether in body or in soul."

c "It would take divination to figure out what you mean. I can't."

"Well, I'll tell you more clearly," she said. "All of us are pregnant, Socrates, both in body and in soul, and, as soon as we come to a certain age, we naturally desire to give birth. Now no one can possibly give birth in anything ugly; only in something beautiful. That's because when a man and a woman come together in order to give birth, this is a godly affair. Pregnancy, reproduction—this is an immortal thing for a mortal animal to do, and it cannot occur d
in anything that is out of harmony, but ugliness is out of harmony with all that is godly. Beauty, however, is in harmony with the divine. Therefore the goddess who presides at childbirth—she's called Moira or Eilithuia—is really Beauty.[5] That's why, whenever pregnant animals or persons draw near to beauty, they become gentle and joyfully disposed and give birth and reproduce; but near ugliness they are foulfaced and draw back in pain; they turn away and shrink back and do not reproduce, and because they hold on to what they carry inside them, the labor is painful. This is the source of the great excitement about beauty that comes to anyone who is pregnant and already teeming with life: e
beauty releases them from their great pain. You see, Socrates," she said, "what Love wants is not beauty, as you think it is."

"Well, what is it, then?"

"Reproduction and birth in beauty."

"Maybe," I said.

"Certainly," she said. "Now, why reproduction? It's because reproduction goes on forever; it is what mor- 207
tals have in place of immortality. A lover must desire immortality along with the good, if what we agreed earlier was right, that Love wants to possess the good forever. It follows from our argument that Love must desire immortality."

All this she taught me, on those occasions when she spoke on the art of love. And once she asked, "What do you think causes love and desire, Socrates? Don't you see what an awful state a wild animal is in when it wants to reproduce? Footed and winged ani- b
mals alike, all are plagued by the disease of Love. First they are sick for intercourse with each other, then for nurturing their young—for their sake the weakest animals stand ready to do battle against the strongest and even to die for them, and they may be racked with famine in order to feed their young. They would do anything for their sake. Human beings, you'd think, would do this because they understand the reason for it; but what causes wild c
animals to be in such a state of love? Can you say?"

And I said again that I didn't know.

---

5. Moira is known mainly as a Fate, but she was also a birth goddess and was identified with the birth goddess Eilithuia.

So she said, "How do you think you'll ever master the art of love, if you don't know that?"

"But that's why I came to you, Diotima, as I just said. I knew I needed a teacher. So tell me what causes this, and everything else that belongs to the art of love."

"If you really believe that Love by its nature aims at what we have often agreed it does, then don't be
d surprised at the answer," she said. "For among animals the principle is the same as with us, and mortal nature seeks so far as possible to live forever and be immortal. And this is possible in one way only: by reproduction, because it always leaves behind a new young one in place of the old. Even while each living thing is said to be alive and to be the same—as a person is said to be the same from childhood until he turns into an old man—even then he never consists of the same things, though he is called the same, but
e he is always being renewed and in other respects passing away, in his hair and flesh and bones and blood and his entire body. And it's not just in his body, but in his soul, too, for none of his manners, customs, opinions, desires, pleasures, pains, or fears ever remains the same, but some are coming to be in him while others are passing away. And what is still far stranger than that is that not only does one branch
208 of knowledge come to be in us while another passes away and that we are never the same even in respect of our knowledge, but that each single piece of knowledge has the same fate. For what we call *studying* exists because knowledge is leaving us, because forgetting is the departure of knowledge, while studying puts back a fresh memory in place of what went away, thereby preserving a piece of knowledge, so that it seems to be the same. And in that way every-
b thing mortal is preserved, not, like the divine, by always being the same in every way, but because what is departing and aging leaves behind something new, something such as it had been. By this device, Socrates," she said, "what is mortal shares in immortality, whether it is a body or anything else, while the immortal has another way. So don't be surprised if everything naturally values its own offspring, because it is for the sake of immortality that everything shows this zeal, which is Love."

c Yet when I heard her speech I was amazed, and spoke: "Well," said I, "Most wise Diotima, is this really the way it is?"

And in the manner of a perfect Sophist she said, "Be sure of it, Socrates. Look, if you will, at how human beings seek honor. You'd be amazed at their irrationality, if you didn't have in mind what I spoke about and if you hadn't pondered the awful state of love they're in, wanting to become famous and 'to lay up glory immortal forever,' and how they're ready to brave any danger for the sake of this, much more than they are for their children; and they are prepared to spend money, suffer through all sorts of ordeals, and
even die for the sake of glory. Do you really think that *d*
Alcestis would have died for Admetus," she asked, "or that Achilles would have died after Patroclus, or that your Codrus would have died so as to preserve the throne for his sons,[6] if they hadn't expected the memory of their virtue—which we still hold in honor—to be immortal? Far from it," she said. "I believe that anyone will do anything for the sake of immortal
virtue and the glorious fame that follows; and the *e*
better the people, the more they will do, for they are all in love with immortality.

"Now, some people are pregnant in body, and for this reason turn more to women and pursue love in that way, providing themselves through childbirth with immortality and remembrance and happiness,
as they think, for all time to come; while others are 209
pregnant in soul—because there surely *are* those who are even more pregnant in their souls than in their bodies, and these are pregnant with what is fitting for a soul to bear and bring to birth. And what is fitting? Wisdom and the rest of virtue, which all poets beget, as well as all the craftsmen who are said to be creative. But by far the greatest and most beautiful part of wisdom deals with the proper ordering of cities and households, and that is called moderation
and justice. When someone has been pregnant with *b*
these in his soul from early youth, while he is still a virgin, and, having arrived at the proper age, desires to beget and give birth, he too will certainly go about seeking the beauty in which he would beget; for he will never beget in anything ugly. Since he is pregnant, then, he is much more drawn to bodies that are beautiful than to those that are ugly; and if he also

6. Codrus was the legendary last king of Athens. He gave his life to satisfy a prophecy that promised victory to Athens and salvation from the invading Dorians if their king was killed by the enemy.

has the luck to find a soul that is beautiful and noble
c and well-formed, he is even more drawn to this com-
bination; such a man makes him instantly teem with ideas and arguments about virtue—the qualities a virtuous man should have and the customary activities in which he should engage; and so he tries to educate him. In my view, you see, when he makes contact with someone beautiful and keeps company with him, he conceives and gives birth to what he has been carrying inside him for ages. And whether they are together or apart, he remembers that beauty. And in common with him he nurtures the newborn; such people, therefore, have much more to share than do the parents of human children, and have a firmer bond of friendship, because the children in whom they have a share are more beautiful and more
d immortal. Everyone would rather have such children
than human ones, and would look up to Homer, Hesiod, and the other good poets with envy and admiration for the offspring they have left behind—offspring, which, because they are immortal themselves, provide their parents with immortal glory and remembrance. For example," she said, "those are the sort of children Lycurgus[7] left behind in Sparta as the saviors of Sparta and virtually all of Greece. Among
e you the honor goes to Solon for his creation of your
laws. Other men in other places everywhere, Greek or barbarian, have brought a host of beautiful deeds into the light and begotten every kind of virtue. Already many shrines have sprung up to honor them for their immortal children, which hasn't happened yet to anyone for human offspring.

210 "Even you, Socrates, could probably come to be
initiated into these rites of love. But as for the purpose of these rites when they are done correctly—that is the final and highest mystery, and I don't know if you are capable of it. I myself will tell you," she said, "and I won't stint any effort. And you must try to follow if you can.

"A lover who goes about this matter correctly must begin in his youth to devote himself to beautiful bodies. First, if the leader[8] leads aright, he should love one body and beget beautiful ideas there; then he
b should realize that the beauty of any one body is
brother to the beauty of any other and that if he is to pursue beauty of form he'd be very foolish not to think that the beauty of all bodies is one and the same. When he grasps this, he must become a lover of all beautiful bodies, and he must think that this wild gaping after just one body is a small thing and despise it.

"After this he must think that the beauty of people's souls is more valuable than the beauty of their bodies, so that if someone is decent in his soul, even
though he is scarcely blooming in his body, our lover c
must be content to love and care for him and to seek to give birth to such ideas as will make young men better. The result is that our lover will be forced to gaze at the beauty of activities and laws and to see that all this is akin to itself, with the result that he will think that the beauty of bodies is a thing of no importance. After customs he must move on to various
kinds of knowledge. The result is that he will see the d
beauty of knowledge and be looking mainly not at beauty in a single example—as a servant would who favored the beauty of a little boy or a man or a single custom (being a slave, of course, he's low and small-minded)—but the lover is turned to the great sea of beauty, and, gazing upon this, he gives birth to many gloriously beautiful ideas and theories, in unstinting love of wisdom,[9] until, having grown and been
strengthened there, he catches sight of such knowl- e
edge, and it is the knowledge of such beauty. . . .

"Try to pay attention to me," she said, "as best you can. You see, the man who has been thus far guided in matters of Love, who has beheld beautiful things in the right order and correctly, is coming now to the goal of Loving: all of a sudden he will catch sight of
something wonderfully beautiful in its nature; that, 211
Socrates, is the reason for all his earlier labors:

"First, it always *is* and neither comes to be nor passes away, neither waxes nor wanes. Second, it is not beautiful this way and ugly that way, nor beautiful at one time and ugly at another, nor beautiful in relation to one thing and ugly in relation to another; nor is it beautiful here but ugly there, as it would be if it were beautiful for some people and ugly for others. Nor will the beautiful appear to him in the guise of a face or hands or anything else that belongs to the body. It will not appear to him as one idea or one kind of

7. Lycurgus was supposed to have been the founder of the oligarchic laws and stern customs of Sparta.

8. I.e., Love.

9. I.e., philosophy.

b knowledge. It is not anywhere in another thing, as in
an animal, or in earth, or in heaven, or in anything
else, but itself by itself with itself, it is always one in
form; and all the other beautiful things share in that,
in such a way that when those others come to be or
pass away, this does not become the least bit smaller
or greater nor suffer any change. So when someone
rises by these stages, through loving boys correctly,
c and begins to see this beauty, he has almost grasped
his goal. This is what it is to go aright, or be led by
another, into the mystery of Love: one goes always
upward for the sake of this Beauty, starting out from
beautiful things and using them like rising stairs: from
one body to two and from two to all beautiful bodies,
then from beautiful bodies to beautiful customs, and
from customs to learning beautiful things, and from
these lessons he arrives in the end at this lesson,
d which is learning of this very Beauty, so that in the
end he comes to know just what it is to be beautiful.

"And there in life, Socrates, my friend," said the woman from Mantinea, "there if anywhere should a person live his life, beholding that Beauty. If you once see that, it won't occur to you to measure beauty by gold or clothing or beautiful boys and youths—who, if you see them now, strike you out of your senses, and make you, you and many others, eager to be with the boys you love and look at them forever, if there were any way to do that, forgetting food and drink, everything but looking at them and
being with them. But how would it be, in our view," *e*
she said, "if someone got to see the Beautiful itself,
absolute, pure, unmixed, not polluted by human
flesh or colors or any other great nonsense of mortality, but if he could see the divine Beauty itself in its *212*
one form? Do you think it would be a poor life for a
human being to look there and to behold it by that
which he ought, and to be with it? Or haven't you
remembered," she said, "that in that life alone, when
he looks at Beauty in the only way that Beauty can be
seen—only then will it become possible for him to
give birth not to images of virtue (because he's in
touch with no images), but to true virtue (because he
is in touch with the true Beauty). The love of the
gods belongs to anyone who has given birth to true
virtue and nourished it, and if any human being
could become immortal, it would be he." *b*

This, Phaedrus and the rest of you, was what Diotima told me. I was persuaded. And once persuaded, I try to persuade others too that human nature can find no better workmate for acquiring this than Love. That's why I say that every man must honor Love, why I honor the rites of Love myself and practice them with special diligence, and why I commend them to others. Now and always I praise the power and courage of Love so far as I am able. Consider this
speech, then, Phaedrus, if you wish, a speech in *c*
praise of Love. Or if not, call it whatever and however you please to call it.

Republic

Book 1

Synopsis

On his way home from a religious festival, Socrates meets Polemarchus and accompanies him to the house of his aged father, Cephalus. Socrates and Cephalus discuss the burdens of old age. Cephalus claims that, while these burdens are eased by wealth, it is people's characters and habits, not their ages, that determine what their lives are like. Wealth is mostly important, he claims, because it reduces the likelihood of being tempted into injustice by poverty, and so lessens the fear of what will happen after death. This leads to a discussion of justice, which will itself culminate—many books later—in a myth about the afterlife (Book 10). Cephalus claims that justice consists of speaking the truth and paying one's debts. Before he can respond to Socrates' criticism of his definition, Polemarchus interrupts. Cephalus hands over the argument to him and goes off to attend to a sacrifice to the gods. An examination of Polemarchus follows, in the course of which he is forced to abandon a number of different views about justice he has adopted along the way. Thrasymachus demands that Socrates give his own positive account of justice, but is persuaded to give an account himself instead. Justice, he claims, is what is advantageous for the stronger. Thrasymachus defends it with two separate arguments (338d–341a, 343a–344c), which Socrates then attempts to refute. We take up Socrates' narrative at the moment when Thrasymachus enters the discussion.

Now, while we were speaking, Thrasymachus had
336b *tried many times to take over the discussion but was restrained by those sitting near him, who wanted to hear our argument to the end. When we paused after what I had just said, however, he could not keep quiet any longer: crouched up like a wild beast about to spring, he hurled himself at us as if to tear us to pieces. Polemarchus and I were frightened and flustered as he roared into our midst:*

What nonsense you two have been talking all this
c time, Socrates! Why do you act like naïve people, giving way to one another? If you really want to know what justice is, don't just ask questions and then indulge your love of honor by refuting the answers. You know very well it is easier to ask questions than to answer them. Give an answer yourself and tell us what *you* say the just is. And don't tell me it is the right,
d the beneficial, the profitable, the gainful, or the advantageous, but tell me clearly and exactly what you mean. For I won't accept such nonsense from you.

His words startled me and, looking at him, I was afraid. And I think if I had not seen him before he looked at me, I would have been dumbstruck.[1] *But as it was, I happened to look at him just as he began to be exasperated by our argument, so I was able to*
e *answer; and trembling a little, I said:*

Do not be too hard on us, Thrasymachus. If Polemarchus and I made an error in our investigation of the accounts, you may be sure we did so involuntarily. If we were searching for gold, we would never voluntarily give way to each other, if by doing so we would destroy our chance of finding it. So do not think that in searching for justice, a thing more honorable than a large quantity of gold, we would foolishly give way to one another or be less than completely serious about finding it. You surely must not think that, my friend, but rather—as I do—that we are incapable of finding it. Hence it is surely far more appropriate for us to be pitied by you clever people than to be given rough treatment. 337

When he heard that, he gave a loud sarcastic laugh:

By Heracles! That is Socrates' usual irony for you! I knew this would happen. I even told these others earlier that you would be unwilling to answer, that you would be ironic and do anything rather than give an answer, if someone questioned *you*.

SOCRATES: That is because you are a wise fellow, Thrasymachus. You knew very well if you ask someone how much twelve is, and in putting the question you warn him, "Don't tell me, man, that twelve is b
twice six, or three times four, or six times two, or four times three; for I won't accept such nonsense from you"—it was obvious to you, I imagine, that no one could respond to a person who inquired in that way. But suppose he said to you: "What do you mean, Thrasymachus; am I not to give any of the answers you mention, not even if twelve happens to be one of those things? You are amazing. Do you want me to say something other than the truth? Or do you mean something else?" What answer would you give him? c

THRASYMACHUS: Well, so you think the two cases are alike?

SOCRATES: Why shouldn't I? But even if they are not alike, yet seem so to the person you asked, do you think he is any less likely to give the answer that seems right to him, whether we forbid him to do so or not?

THRASYMACHUS: Is that what you are going to do, give one of the forbidden answers?

SOCRATES: I would not be surprised—provided it is the one that seems right to me after I have investigated the matter.

---

1. In Greek superstition, anyone seen by a wolf before he sees it is struck dumb.

Thrasymachus: What if I show you another answer about justice, one that is different from all
d these and better than any of them? What penalty would you deserve then?

Socrates: The very one that is appropriate for someone who does not know—what else? And what is appropriate is to learn from the one who does know. That, therefore, is what I deserve to suffer.

Thrasymachus: What a pleasant fellow you are! But in addition to learning, you must pay money.

Socrates: I will if I ever have any.

Glaucon: He has it already. If it is a matter of money, speak, Thrasymachus. We will all contribute for Socrates.

Thrasymachus: Oh yes, sure, so that Socrates can
e carry on as usual: he gives no answer himself, and if someone else does, he takes up his account and refutes it.

Socrates: How can someone give an answer, my excellent man, when, first of all, he does not know and does not claim to know, and then, even if he does have some opinion about the matter, is forbidden by no ordinary man to express any of the things he thinks? No, it is much more appropriate for you to
338 answer, since you say you do know and can tell us. Don't be obstinate. Give your answer as a favor to me and do not begrudge your teaching to Glaucon and the others.

While I was saying this, Glaucon and the others begged him to do as I asked. Thrasymachus clearly wanted to speak in order to win a good reputation, since he thought he had a very good answer. But he pretended to want to win a victory at my expense by having me do the answering. However, he agreed in the end, and then said:

b That is Socrates' wisdom for you: he himself isn't willing to teach but goes around learning from others and isn't even grateful to them.

Socrates: When you say I learn from others, you are right, Thrasymachus; but when you say I do not give thanks, you are wrong. I give as much as I can. But I can give only praise, since I have no money. And just how enthusiastically I give it, when someone seems to me to speak well, you will know as soon as you have answered, since I think you will speak well.

Thrasymachus: Listen, then. I say justice is nothing other than what is advantageous for the stronger. c
Well, why don't you praise me? No, you are unwilling.

Socrates: First, I must understand what you mean. For, as things stand, I do not. What is advantageous for the stronger, you say, is just. What on earth do you mean, Thrasymachus? Surely you do not mean something like this: Polydamas, the pancratist, is stronger than we are. Beef is advantageous for his body. So, this food is also both advantageous and just for us who are weaker than he? d

Thrasymachus: You disgust me, Socrates. You interpret my account in the way that does it the most evil.

Socrates: That's not it at all, my very good man; I only want you to make your meaning clearer.

Thrasymachus: Don't you know, then, that some cities are ruled by a tyranny, some by a democracy, and some by an aristocracy?

Socrates: Of course I do.

Thrasymachus: And that what is stronger in each city is the ruling element?

Socrates: Certainly.

Thrasymachus: And each type of rule makes laws that are advantageous for itself: democracy makes e
democratic ones, tyranny tyrannical ones, and so on with the others. And by so legislating, each declares that what is just for its subjects is what is advantageous for itself—the ruler—and it punishes anyone who deviates from this as lawless and unjust. That, Socrates, is what I say justice is, the same in all cities: what is advantageous for the established rule. Since the established rule is surely stronger, anyone who 339
does the rational calculation correctly will conclude that the just is the same everywhere—what is advantageous for the stronger.

Socrates: Now I see what you mean. Whether it is true or not, I will try to find out. But you yourself have answered that what is just is what is advantageous, Thrasymachus, whereas you forbade me to answer that. True, you have added *for the stronger* to it.

Thrasymachus: And I suppose you think that is an insignificant addition. b

Socrates: It isn't clear yet whether it is significant. What *is* clear is that we must investigate whether or not it is true. I agree that what is just is something advantageous. But you add *for the stronger*. I do not know about that. We will have to look into it.

Thrasymachus: Go ahead and look.

Socrates: That is just what I am going to do. Tell me, then, you also claim, don't you, that it is just to obey the rulers?

Thrasymachus: I do.

Socrates: And are the rulers in each city infalli-
c ble, or are they liable to error?

Thrasymachus: No doubt, they are liable to error.

Socrates: So, when they attempt to make laws, they make some correctly, others incorrectly?

Thrasymachus: I suppose so.

Socrates: And a law is correct if it prescribes what is advantageous for the rulers themselves, and incorrect if it prescribes what is disadvantageous for them? Is that what you mean?

Thrasymachus: It is.

Socrates: And whatever laws the rulers make must be obeyed by their subjects, and that is what is just?

Thrasymachus: Of course.

Socrates: According to your account, then, it isn't
d only just to do what is advantageous for the stronger, but also the opposite: what is not advantageous.

Thrasymachus: What is that you are saying?

Socrates: The same as you, I think. But let's examine it more closely. Haven't we agreed that the rulers are sometimes in error as to what is best for themselves when they give orders to their subjects, and yet that it is just for their subjects to do whatever their rulers order? Wasn't that agreed?

Thrasymachus: I suppose so.

Socrates: You will also have to suppose, then,
e that you have agreed that it is just to do what is disadvantageous for the rulers and those who are stronger, whenever they unintentionally order what is bad for themselves. But you say, too, that it is just for the others to obey the orders the rulers gave. You are very wise, Thrasymachus, but doesn't it necessarily follow that it is just to do the opposite of what you said, since the weaker are then ordered to do what is disadvantageous for the stronger?

340 Polemarchus: By Zeus, Socrates, that's absolutely clear.

And Clitophon interrupted:

Of course it is, if you are to be his witness, at any rate.

Polemarchus: Who needs a witness? Thrasymachus himself agrees that the rulers sometimes issue orders that are bad for them, and that it is just for the others to obey them.

Clitophon: That, Polemarchus, is because Thrasymachus maintained that it is just to obey the orders of the rulers.

Polemarchus: Yes, Clitophon, and he also maintained that what is advantageous for the stronger is
just. And having maintained both principles, he b
went on to agree that the stronger sometimes order the weaker, who are subject to them, to do things that are disadvantageous for the stronger themselves. From these agreements it follows that what is advantageous for the stronger is no more just than what is not advantageous.

Clitophon: But what he meant by what is advantageous for the stronger is what the stronger *believes* to be advantageous for him. That is what he maintained the weaker must do, and that is what he maintained is what is just.

Polemarchus: But it is not what he said.

Socrates: It makes no difference, Polemarchus. If
Thrasymachus wants to put it that way now, let's c
accept it. But tell me, Thrasymachus, is that what you intended to say, that what is just is what the stronger believes to be advantageous for him, whether it is in fact advantageous for him or not? Is that what we are to say you mean?

Thrasymachus: Not at all. Do you think I would call someone who is in error stronger at the very moment he errs?

Socrates: I did think you meant that, when you agreed that the rulers are not infallible but sometimes make errors.

Thrasymachus: That is because you are a quib-
bler in arguments, Socrates. I mean, when someone d
makes an error in the treatment of patients, do you call him a doctor in virtue of the fact that he made that very error? Or, when someone makes an error in calculating, do you call him an accountant in virtue of the fact that he made that very error in calculation? I think we express ourselves in words that, taken literally, do say that a doctor is in error, or an accountant, or a grammarian. But each of these, to the extent that he is what we call him, never makes
errors, so that, according to the precise account (and e
you are a stickler for precise accounts), no craftsman ever makes errors. It is when his knowledge fails him that he makes an error, and, in virtue of the fact that

he made that error, he is no craftsman. No craftsman, wise man, or ruler makes an error at the moment when he is ruling, even though everyone will say that a physician or a ruler makes errors. It is in this loose way that you must also take the answer I gave just now. But the most precise answer is this: a ruler, to the extent that he is a ruler, never makes
341 errors and unerringly decrees what is best for himself, and that is what his subject must do. Thus, as I said from the first, it is just to do what is advantageous for the stronger.

SOCRATES: Well, Thrasymachus, so you think I quibble, do you?

THRASYMACHUS: Yes, I do.

SOCRATES: And you think that I asked the questions I did in a premeditated attempt to do you evil in the argument?

THRASYMACHUS: I am certain of it. But it won't do you any good. You will never be able to do me evil by
b covert means, and without them, you will never be able to overpower me by argument.

SOCRATES: Bless you, Thrasymachus; I would not so much as try! But to prevent this sort of confusion from happening to us again, would you define whether you mean the ruler and stronger in the ordinary sense or in what you were just now calling the precise sense, when you say that it is just for the weaker to do what is advantageous for him, since he is the stronger?

THRASYMACHUS: I mean the ruler in the most precise sense. Now do *that* evil, if you can, and practice your quibbling on it—I ask no favors. But you will find there is nothing you can do.

SOCRATES: Do you think that I am crazy enough to
c try to shave a lion[2] and quibble with Thrasymachus?

THRASYMACHUS: Well, you certainly tried just now, although you were a good-for-nothing at it, too!

SOCRATES: That's enough of that! Tell me: is a doctor—in the precise sense, the one you mentioned before—a moneymaker or someone who treats the sick? Tell me about the one who is really a doctor.

THRASYMACHUS: Someone who treats the sick.

SOCRATES: What about a ship's captain? Is the true captain a ruler of sailors, or a sailor?

THRASYMACHUS: A ruler of sailors.

SOCRATES: In other words, we should not take any account of the fact that he sails in a ship, and he should not be called a sailor for that reason. For it is d
not because he is sailing that he is called a ship's captain, but because of the craft he practices and his rule over sailors?

THRASYMACHUS: True.

SOCRATES: And is there something that is advantageous for each of these?

THRASYMACHUS: Certainly.

SOCRATES: And isn't it also the case that the natural aim of the craft is to consider and provide what is advantageous for each?

THRASYMACHUS: Yes, that is its aim.

SOCRATES: And is anything advantageous for each of the crafts themselves besides being as perfect as possible?

THRASYMACHUS: How do you mean? e

SOCRATES: It is like this: suppose you asked me whether it is satisfactory for a body to be a body, or whether it needs something else. I would answer, "Of course it needs something. In fact, that is why the craft of medicine has been discovered—because a body is deficient and it is not satisfactory for it to be like that. To provide what is advantageous, that is what the craft was developed for." Do you think I am speaking correctly in saying this, or not?

THRASYMACHUS: Correctly.

SOCRATES: What about medicine itself? Is it deficient? Does a craft need some further virtue, as the 342
eyes are in need of sight and the ears of hearing, so that another craft is needed to consider and provide what is advantageous for them? Does a craft have some similar deficiency itself, so that each craft needs another to consider what is advantageous for it? And does the craft that does the considering need still another, and so on without end? Or does each consider by itself what is advantageous for it? Does it need neither itself nor another craft to consider b
what—in light of its own deficiency—is advantageous for it? Indeed, is there no deficiency or error in any craft? And is it inappropriate for any craft to consider what is advantageous for anything besides that with which it deals? And since it is itself correct, is it without fault or impurity so long as it is wholly and precisely the craft it is? Consider this with that precision of language you mentioned. Is it so or not?

THRASYMACHUS: It appears to be so.

2. Proverbial characterization of an almost impossible task.

Socrates: Doesn't it follow that medicine does not consider what is advantageous for medicine, but
c for the body?

Thrasymachus: Yes.

Socrates: And horse breeding does not consider what is advantageous for horse breeding, but for horses? Indeed, no other craft considers what is advantageous for itself—since it has no further needs—but what is advantageous for that with which it deals?

Thrasymachus: Apparently so.

Socrates: Now surely, Thrasymachus, the various crafts rule over and are stronger than that with which they deal?

He gave in at this point as well, very reluctantly.

Socrates: So no kind of knowledge considers or enjoins what is advantageous for itself, but what is
d advantageous for the weaker, which is subject to it.

He finally agreed to this too, although he tried to fight it. When he had agreed, however, I said:

Surely then, no doctor, to the extent that he is a doctor, considers or enjoins what is advantageous for himself, but what is advantageous for his patient? For we agreed that a doctor, in the precise sense, is a ruler of bodies, not a moneymaker. Isn't that what we agreed?

Thrasymachus: Yes.

Socrates: So a ship's captain, in the precise sense, is a ruler of sailors, not a sailor?

e Thrasymachus: That is what we agreed.

Socrates: Doesn't it follow that a ship's captain and ruler won't consider and enjoin what is advantageous for a captain, but what is advantageous for a sailor and his subject?

He reluctantly agreed.

Socrates: So then, Thrasymachus, no one in any position of rule, to the extent that he is a ruler, considers or enjoins what is advantageous for himself, but what is advantageous for his subject—that on which he practices his craft. It is to his subject and what is advantageous and proper for it that he looks, and everything he says and does, he says and does for it.

When we reached this point in the argument and it
was clear to all that his account of justice had 343
turned into its opposite, instead of answering, Thrasymachus said:

Tell me, Socrates, do you still have a wet nurse?

Socrates: What is that? Shouldn't you be giving answers rather than asking such things?

Thrasymachus: Because she is letting you run around sniveling and doesn't wipe your nose when you need it, since it is her fault that you do not know the difference between sheep and shepherds.

Socrates: What exactly is it I do not know?

Thrasymachus: You think that shepherds and cowherds consider what is good for their sheep and cat- b
tle, and fatten them and take care of them with some aim in mind other than what is good for their master and themselves. Moreover, you believe that rulers in cities—true rulers, that is—think about their subjects in a different way than one does about sheep, and that what they consider night and day is something other than what is advantageous for themselves. You
are so far from understanding justice and what is just, c
and injustice and what is unjust, that you do not realize that justice is really the good of another, what is advantageous for the stronger and the ruler, and harmful to the one who obeys and serves. Injustice is the opposite, it rules those simpleminded—for that is what they really are—just people, and the ones it rules do what is advantageous for the other who is stronger; and they make the one they serve happy, but they do not make themselves the least bit happy.

You must consider it as follows, Socrates, or you d
will be the most naïve of all: a just man must always get less than does an unjust one. First, in their contracts with one another, when a just man is partner to an unjust, you will never find, when the partnership ends, that the just one gets more than the unjust, but less. Second, in matters relating to the city, when taxes are to be paid, a just man pays more on an equal amount of property, an unjust one less; but when the city is giving out refunds, a just man gets nothing while an unjust one makes a large profit. Finally, when each of them holds political
office, a just person—even if he is not penalized in e
other ways—finds that his private affairs deteriorate more because he has to neglect them, that he gains no advantage from the public purse because of his

justice, and that he is hated by his relatives and
acquaintances because he is unwilling to do them an
unjust favor. The opposite is true of an unjust man in
every respect. I mean, of course, the person I
described before: the man of great power who does
better than everyone else. He is the one you should
344 consider if you want to figure out how much more
advantageous it is for the individual to be unjust than
just. You will understand this most easily if you turn
your thoughts to injustice of the most complete sort,
the sort that makes those who do injustice happiest,
and those who suffer it—those who are unwilling to
do injustice—most wretched. The sort I mean is
tyranny, because it uses both covert means and force
to appropriate the property of others—whether it is
sacred or secular, public or private—not little by little, but all at once. If someone commits a part of this
b sort of injustice and gets caught, he is punished and
greatly reproached—temple robbers, kidnappers,
housebreakers, robbers, and thieves are what these
partly unjust people are called when they commit
those harms. When someone appropriates the possessions of the citizens, on the other hand, and then
kidnaps and enslaves the possessors as well, instead of
these shameful names he is called happy and blessed:
c not only by the citizens themselves, but even by all who
learn that he has committed the whole of injustice. For
it is not the fear of doing injustice, but of suffering it,
that elicits the reproaches of those who revile injustice.
So you see, Socrates, injustice, if it is on a large
enough scale, is stronger, freer, and more masterful
than justice. And, as I said from the beginning, justice is what is advantageous for the stronger, while
injustice is profitable and advantageous for oneself.

Having, like a bath attendant, emptied this great
d *flood of words into our ears all at once, Thrasy-*
machus was thinking of leaving. But those present
wouldn't let him. They made him stay and give an
account of what he had said. And I myself was par-
ticularly insistent:

You are marvelous, Thrasymachus; after hurling
such a speech at us, you surely cannot be thinking of
leaving before you have adequately instructed us—or
learned yourself—whether you are right or not. Or
do you think it is a trivial matter you are trying to
e determine, and not rather a way of life—the one that
would make living life that way most profitable for
each of us?

THRASYMACHUS: Do you mean that I do not think it is a serious matter?

SOCRATES: Either that, or you care nothing for us
and so are not worried about whether we will live better or worse lives because of our ignorance of what
you claim to know. No, be a good fellow and show
some willingness to teach us—you won't do badly for
yourself if you help a group as large as ours. For my 345
own part, I will tell you that I am not persuaded. I do
not believe that injustice is more profitable than justice, not even if you should give it full scope to do
what it wants. Suppose, my good fellow, that there *is*
an unjust person, and suppose he *does* have the
power to do injustice, whether by covert means or
open warfare; nonetheless, he does not persuade me
that injustice is more profitable than justice. Perhaps
someone here besides myself feels the same as I do.
So, blessed though you are, you are going to have to b
fully persuade us that we are wrong to value justice
more highly than injustice in deliberating.

WE RETURN TO the debate for its closing round.

. . . we must now examine the question, as we proposed to do before, of whether just people also live better and are happier than unjust ones. I think it is clear even now from what we have said that this is so, but we must consider it further. After all, the argument concerns no ordinary topic, but the way we ought to live.

THRASYMACHUS: Go ahead and consider.

SOCRATES: I will. Tell me, do you think there is such a thing as the function of a horse?

THRASYMACHUS: I do. 352e

SOCRATES: And would you take the function of a horse or of anything else to be that which one can do only with it, or best with it?

THRASYMACHUS: I don't understand.

SOCRATES: Let me put it this way: is it possible for you to see with anything except eyes?

THRASYMACHUS: Certainly not.

SOCRATES: Or for you to hear with anything except ears?

THRASYMACHUS: No.

Socrates: Would it be right, then, for us to say that these things are their functions?

Thrasymachus: Of course.

Socrates: Again, couldn't you use a dagger, a carv-
353 ing knife, or lots of other things in pruning a vine?

Thrasymachus: Certainly.

Socrates: But nothing would do a better job than a pruning knife designed for the purpose?

Thrasymachus: That's true.

Socrates: Shall we take pruning to be its function, then?

Thrasymachus: Yes.

Socrates: Now I think you will understand better what I was asking earlier when I asked whether the function of each thing is what it alone can do or what it can do better than anything else.

Thrasymachus: I do understand, and I think that
b that is the function of anything.

Socrates: All right. Does there seem to you also to be a virtue for each thing to which some function is assigned? Let's go over the same ground again. We say that eyes have some function?

Thrasymachus: They do.

Socrates: So eyes also have a virtue?

Thrasymachus: They do.

Socrates: And ears have a function?

Thrasymachus: Yes.

Socrates: So they also have a virtue?

Thrasymachus: They have a virtue too.

Socrates: What about everything else? Doesn't the same hold?

Thrasymachus: It does.

Socrates: Well, then. Could eyes perform their
c function well if they lacked their proper virtue but had the vice instead?

Thrasymachus: How could they? For don't you mean if they had blindness instead of sight?

Socrates: Whatever their virtue is. You see, I am not now asking about that, but about whether it is by means of their own proper virtue that their function performs the things it performs well, and by means of vice badly?

Thrasymachus: What you say is true.

Socrates: So, if ears are deprived of their own virtue, they too perform their function badly?

Thrasymachus: Of course.

Socrates: And the same argument applies to
d everything else?

Thrasymachus: So it seems to me, at least.

Socrates: Come on, then, and let's next consider this: does the soul have some function that you could not perform with anything else—for example, taking care of things, ruling, deliberating, and all other such things? Is there anything else besides a soul to which you could rightly assign these and say that they are special to it?

Thrasymachus: No, there is nothing else.

Socrates: Then what about living? Don't we say that it is a function of a soul?

Thrasymachus: Absolutely.

Socrates: And don't we also say that a soul has a virtue?

Thrasymachus: We do.

Socrates: Will a soul ever perform its functions
well, then, Thrasymachus, if it is deprived of its own e
proper virtue, or is that impossible?

Thrasymachus: It is impossible.

Socrates: It is necessary, then, that a bad soul rules and takes care of things badly, and that a good soul does all these things well?

Thrasymachus: It is necessary.

Socrates: Now, didn't we agree that justice is a soul's virtue and injustice its vice?

Thrasymachus: Yes, we did agree.

Socrates: So a just soul and a just man will live well and an unjust one badly.

Thrasymachus: Apparently so, according to your argument.

Socrates: And surely anyone who lives well is
blessed and happy, and anyone who does not is the 354
opposite.

Thrasymachus: Of course.

Socrates: Therefore, a just person is happy and an unjust one wretched.

Thrasymachus: Let's say so.

Socrates: But surely it is profitable, not to be wretched, but to be happy.

Thrasymachus: Of course.

Socrates: So then, blessed Thrasymachus, injustice is never more profitable than justice.

Thrasymachus: Let that be your banquet, Socrates, at the feast of Bendis.

Socrates: Given by you, Thrasymachus, after you became gentle with me and ceased to be difficult. Yet I have not had a good banquet. But that is my
fault, not yours. I seem to have behaved like those b

gluttons who snatch at every dish that passes and taste it before having properly savored the preceding one. Before finding the first thing we inquired about—namely, what justice is—I let that go, and turned to investigate whether it is a kind of vice and ignorance or a kind of wisdom and virtue. Then an argument came up about injustice being more profitable than justice, and I could not refrain from abandoning the previous one and following up on it. Hence the result of the discussion, so far as I am concerned, is that I know nothing. For when I do not
know what justice is, I will hardly know whether it is c
a kind of virtue or not, or whether a person who has it is happy or unhappy.

Books 2 and 3

Synopsis

Unsatisfied with the outcome of Book 1, Glaucon and Adeimantus renew Thrasymachus' views. In response, Socrates must show that justice is choiceworthy (a) because of itself and (b) because of its consequences (357a–358a). Socrates does not complete his argument for (a) until the end of Book 9. Socrates shifts the debate from individual justice to political justice. He will describe an ideal or completely good city—a *kallipolis.* Having located justice in it, he will then look for it in the soul. The first city he describes is dismissed by Glaucon as fit only for pigs, not for sophisticated Athenians. The second city is more luxurious. But the presence in it of appetites for more than the necessities provided in its simpler predecessor leads to civil faction and war. To prevent these from destroying the city, soldier-police are needed. They are the guardians. The natural assets they need and the education they must have are described next. Since musical training begins before physical training, its content—more specifically the sorts of stories that the future guardians should hear about gods and heroes—is the first item of business (377e). The discussion of these stories continues in Book 3. The appropriate style for these stories and the appropriate harmonies and rhythms for lyric odes and songs are characterized. Physical training is next. The final topic is the selection of rulers (including the "myth of the metals") and the housing and lifestyles of the guardians (412b–417b).

Book 2

Socrates' narration continues: *When I had said this, I thought I had done with the discussion.
But it all turned out to be only a prelude, as it were.* 357
You see, Glaucon, who is always very courageous in everything, refused on this occasion, too, to accept Thrasymachus' capitulation. Instead, he said:

Do you want to *seem* to have persuaded us, Socrates, that it is better in every way to be just rather than
unjust, or do you want to *really* persuade us of this? b

Socrates: I want to really persuade you, if I can.

Glaucon: Well, then, you certainly are not doing what you want. Tell me, do you think there is a sort of good we welcome, not because we desire its consequences, but because we welcome it for its own sake—enjoying, for example, and all the harmless pleasures from which nothing results afterward beyond enjoying having them?

Socrates: Certainly, I think there is such a thing.

Glaucon: And is there a sort of good we love for its own sake, and also for the sake of its consequences—knowing, for example, and seeing, and c
being healthy? For we welcome such things, I imagine, on both counts.

Socrates: Yes.

Glaucon: And do you also recognize a third kind of good, such as physical training, medical treatment when sick, medicine itself, or ways of making money generally? We would say that these are burdensome but beneficial to us, and we would not choose them for their own sake, but for the sake of their rewards
and other consequences. d

Socrates: Yes, certainly, there is also this third kind. But what of it?

Glaucon: In which of them do you place justice?

Socrates: I myself put it in the finest one—the 358
one that anyone who is going to be blessed with

happiness must love both because of itself and because of its consequences.

Glaucon: That is not what the masses think. On the contrary, they think it is of the burdensome kind: the one that must be practiced for the sake of the rewards and the popularity that are the consequences of a good reputation, but that is to be avoided as intrinsically burdensome.

Socrates: I know that is the general view. Thrasymachus has been faulting justice and praising injustice on these grounds for some time. But it seems that I am a slow learner.

Glaucon: Come on, then, listen to what I have to
b say as well, and see whether you still have that problem. You see, I think Thrasymachus gave up before he had to, as if he were a snake you had charmed. Yet, to my way of thinking, there was still no demonstration on either side. For I want to hear what justice and injustice are, and what power each has when it is just by itself in the soul. I want to leave out of account the rewards and the consequences of each of them.

So, if you agree, I will renew the argument of Thrasymachus. First, I will state what sort of thing
c people consider justice to be, and what its origins are. Second, I will argue that all who practice it do so unwillingly, as something necessary, not as something good. Third, I will argue that they have good reason to act as they do. For the life of the unjust person is, they say, much better than that of the just one.

It isn't, Socrates, that I believe any of that myself. I am perplexed, indeed, and my ears are deafened listening to Thrasymachus and countless others. But I have yet to hear anyone defend justice in the way
d I want, as being better than injustice. I want to hear it praised *on its own*, and I think that I am most likely to learn this from you. That is why I am going to speak at length in praise of the unjust life: by doing so, I will be showing you the way I want to hear you praising justice and denouncing injustice. But see whether you want me to do what I am saying or not.

Socrates: I want it most of all. Indeed, what subject could a person with any sense enjoy talking and hearing about more often?

Glaucon: Excellent sentiments. Now, listen to
e what I said I was going to discuss first—what justice is like and what its origins are. People say, you see, that to do injustice is naturally good and to suffer injustice bad. But the badness of suffering it far exceeds the goodness of doing it. Hence, those who have done and suffered injustice and who have tasted both—the ones who lack the power to do it and avoid suffering it—decide that it is profitable to come to an
agreement with each other neither to do injustice 359
nor to suffer it. As a result, they begin to make laws and covenants; and what the law commands, they call lawful and just. That, they say, is the origin and very being of justice. It is in between the best and the worst. The best is to do injustice without paying the penalty; the worst is to suffer it without being able to take revenge. Justice is in the middle between these two extremes. People love it, not because it is a good thing, but because they are too weak to do
injustice with impunity. Someone who has the power *b*
to do it, however—someone who is a real man—would not make an agreement with anyone, neither to do injustice nor to suffer it. For him, that would be insanity. That is the nature of justice, according to the argument, Socrates, and those are its natural origins.

We can see most clearly that those who practice it do so unwillingly, because they lack the power to do injustice, if we imagine the following thought-experiment. Suppose we grant to the just and the unjust
person the freedom to do whatever they like. We can *c*
then follow both of them and see where their appetites would lead. And we will catch the just person redhanded, traveling the same road as the unjust one. The reason for this is the desire to do better than others. This is what every natural being naturally pursues as good. But by law and force, it is made to deviate from this path and honor equality.

They would especially have the freedom I am talking about if they had the power that the ancestor of
Gyges of Lydia is said to have possessed. The story *d*
goes that he was a shepherd in the service of the ruler of Lydia. There was a violent thunderstorm, and an earthquake broke open the ground and created a chasm at the place where he was tending his sheep. Seeing this, he was filled with amazement and went down into it. And there, in addition to many other amazing things of which we are told stories, he saw a hollow, bronze horse. There were windowlike openings in it and, peeping in, he saw a corpse, which seemed to be of more than human size, wearing
nothing but a gold ring on its finger. He took off the *e*
ring and came out of the chasm. He wore the ring at the usual monthly meeting of shepherds that

reported to the king on the state of the flocks. And as
he was sitting among the others, he happened to turn
the setting of the ring toward himself, toward the
inside of his hand. When he did this, he became
360 invisible to those sitting near him, and they went on
talking as if he had gone. He was amazed at this and,
fingering the ring, he turned the setting outward
again and became visible. So, he experimented with
the ring to test whether it indeed had this power—
and it did. If he turned the setting inward, he became
invisible; if he turned it outward, he became visible
again. As soon as he realized this, he arranged to
become one of the messengers sent to report to the
king. On arriving there, he seduced the king's wife,
b attacked the king with her help, killed him, and in
this way took over the kingdom.

Let's suppose, then, that there were two such rings,
one worn by the just person, the other by the unjust.
Now no one, it seems, would be so incorruptible that
he would stay on the path of justice, or bring himself
to keep away from other people's possessions and not
touch them, when he could take whatever he wanted
from the marketplace with impunity, go into people's
houses and have sex with anyone he wished, kill or
c release from prison anyone he wished, and do all the
other things that would make him like a god among
humans. And in so behaving, he would do no differently than the unjust person, but both would pursue
the same course.

This, some would say, is strong evidence that no
one is just willingly, but only when compelled. No
one believes justice to be a good thing when it is kept
private, since whenever either person thinks he can
do injustice with impunity, he does it. Indeed, all
men believe that injustice is far more profitable to
themselves than is justice. And what they believe is
d true, so the exponent of this argument will say. For
someone who did not want to do injustice, given this
sort of opportunity, and who did not touch other people's property, would be thought most wretched and
most foolish by everyone aware of the situation.
Though, of course, they would praise him in public,
deceiving each other for fear of suffering injustice. So
much for my second topic.

As for decision itself about the life of the two we
e are discussing, if we contrast the extremes of justice
and injustice, we shall be able to make the decision
correctly; but if we don't, we won't. What, then, is
the contrast I have in mind? It is this: we will subtract
nothing from the injustice of the unjust person, and
nothing from the justice of the just one. On the contrary, we will take each to be perfect in his own pursuit. First, then, let the unjust person act like a clever
craftsman. An eminent ship's captain or doctor, for
example, knows the difference between what his
craft can and cannot do. He attempts the first but lets
the second go by. And if he happens to slip, he can 361
put things right. In the same way, if he is to be completely unjust, let the unjust person correctly attempt
unjust acts and remain undetected. The one who is
caught should be thought inept. For the extreme of
injustice is to be believed to be just without actually
being so. And our completely unjust person must be
given complete injustice—nothing must be subtracted from it. We must allow that, while doing the
greatest injustice, he has nonetheless provided himself with the greatest reputation for justice. If he does
happen to slip up, he must be able to put it right, b
either through his ability to speak persuasively if any
of his unjust activities are discovered, or to use force if
force is needed, because he is courageous and strong
and has provided himself with wealth and friends.

Having hypothesized such a person, let's now put
the just man next to him in our argument—someone
who is simple and noble and who, as Aeschylus says,
does not want to be believed to be good, but to be
so.[1] We must take away his reputation. For a reputation for justice would bring him honor and rewards,
so that it would not be clear whether he is being just c
for the sake of justice, or for the sake of those honors
and rewards. We must strip him of everything except
justice, and make his situation the opposite of the
unjust person's. Though he does no injustice, he
must have the greatest reputation for it, so that he may
be tested with regard to justice by seeing whether or
not he can withstand a bad reputation and its consequences. Let him stay like that, unchanged, until he
is dead—just, but all his life believed to be unjust. In d
this way, both will reach the extremes, the one of justice and the other of injustice, and we will be able to
judge which of them is happier.

---

1. In *Seven against Thebes* 592–4, it is said of Amphiaraus that "he did not wish to be believed to be the best but to be it." The passage continues with the words Glaucon quotes below at 362a–b.

Socrates: Whew! My dear Glaucon, how vigorously you have scoured each of the men in our competition, just as you would a pair of statues for an art competition.

Glaucon: I am doing the best I can. Since the two are as I have described, in any case, it should not be difficult to complete the account of the sort of life that awaits each of them, but it must be done. And if
e what I say sounds crude, Socrates, remember that it is not I who speak, but those who praise injustice at the expense of justice. They will say that the just person in such circumstances will be whipped, stretched on a rack, chained, blinded with a red-hot iron, and, at the end, when he has suffered every sort
362 of bad thing, he will be impaled, and will realize then that one should not want to be just, but to be believed to be just. Indeed, Aeschylus' words are far more correctly applied to the unjust man. For people will say that it is really the unjust person who does not want to be believed to be unjust, but actually to be so, because he bases his practice on the truth about things and does not allow reputation to regulate his life. He is the one who "harvests a deep furrow in his mind, where wise counsels propagate."
b First, he rules his city because of his reputation for justice. Next, he marries into any family he wishes, gives his children in marriage to anyone he wishes, has contracts and partnerships with anyone he wants, and, besides benefiting himself in all these ways, he profits because he has no scruples about doing injustice. In any contest, public or private, he is the winner and does better than his enemies. And by doing better than them, he becomes wealthy, benefits his
c friends, and harms his enemies. He makes adequate sacrifices to the gods and sets up magnificent offerings to them, and takes much better care of the gods—and, indeed, of the human beings he favors—than the just person. So he may reasonably expect that the gods, in turn, will love him more than the just person. That is why they say, Socrates, that gods and humans provide a better life for the unjust person than for the just one.

We omit Adeimantus' long account of how justice should not be defended and take up the discussion with Socrates' response to it and to Glaucon.

Now, I had always admired the natural characters of Glaucon and Adeimantus, but I was especially pleased when I heard what they had to say on this occasion, and I replied:

Sons of that man, Glaucon's lover was not wrong to 368
begin the elegy he wrote, when you distinguished yourselves at the battle of Megara, by addressing you as "Sons of Ariston, godlike family of a famous man."[2] That, my dear friends, was well said, in my view. For something altogether godlike must have affected you if you are not convinced that injustice is better than justice and yet can speak like that on its behalf. And I do believe that you really are unconvinced by your own words. I infer this from your gen- b
eral character, since if I had only your arguments to go on, I would not trust you. The more I trust you, however, the more I am at a loss as to what to do. I do not see how I can be of help. Indeed, I believe I am incapable of it. And here is my evidence: I thought that what I said to Thrasymachus showed that justice is better than injustice, but you won't accept that from me as a proof. On the other hand, I do not see how I can refuse my help. For I fear that it may even be impious to have breath in one's body and the ability to speak, and yet stand idly by and not defend justice when it is being prosecuted. The best c
thing, then, is to give justice any assistance I can.

Glaucon and the others begged me not to abandon the argument but to help in every way to track down what justice and injustice each is, and the truth about their respective benefits. So I told them what I had in mind:

The investigation we are undertaking is not an easy one, in my view, but requires keen eyesight. So, since we are not clever people, I think we should adopt the method of investigation that we would use d
if, lacking keen eyesight, we were told to identify small letters from a distance, and then noticed that the same letters existed elsewhere in a larger size and on a larger surface. We would consider it a godsend,

---

2. Sexual relations between older men and late-adolescent boys were an acceptable part of Athenian social life, especially among the upper classes.

I think, to be allowed to identify the larger ones first, and then to examine the smaller ones to see whether they are really the same.

Adeimantus: Of course we would. But how is this
e case similar to our investigation of justice in your view?

Socrates: I will tell you. We say, don't we, that there is a justice that belongs to a single man, and also one that belongs to a whole city?

Adeimantus: Certainly.

Socrates: And a city is larger than a single man?

Adeimantus: Yes, it is larger.

Socrates: Perhaps, then, there will be more justice in the larger thing, and it will be easier to discern. So, if you are willing, let's first find out what
369 sort of thing justice is in cities, and afterward look for
it in the individual, to see if the larger entity is similar in form to the smaller one.

Adeimantus: I think that is a fine idea.

Socrates: If, in our discussion, we could look at a city coming to be, wouldn't we also see its justice coming to be, and its injustice as well?

Adeimantus: We probably would.

Socrates: And once that process is completed, could we expect to find what we are looking for more easily?

b Adeimantus: Yes, much more easily.

Socrates: Do you think we should try to carry it out then? It is no small task, in my view. So, think it over.

Adeimantus: It has been thought over. Don't do anything besides try.

Socrates: Well, then, a city comes to exist, I believe, because none of us is individually self-sufficient, but each has many needs he cannot satisfy. Or do you think that a city is founded on some other principle?

Adeimantus: No, none.

Socrates: Then because we have many needs,
c and because one of us calls on another out of one
need, and on a third out of a different need, we gather many into a single settlement as partners and helpers. And we call such a shared settlement a city. Isn't that so?

Adeimantus: Yes, indeed.

Socrates: And if they share things with one another—if they give something to one another, or take something from one another—don't they do so because each believes that this is better for himself?

Adeimantus: Of course.

Socrates: Come on, then, let's, in our discussion, create a city from the beginning. But its real creator, it seems, will be our need.

Adeimantus: Certainly.

Socrates: Now, the first and greatest of our needs is
to provide food in order to sustain existence and life. d

Adeimantus: Yes, absolutely.

Socrates: The second is for shelter, and the third is for clothes and things of that sort.

Adeimantus: That's right.

Socrates: Tell me, then, how will a city be able to provide all this? Won't one person have to be a farmer, another a builder, and another a weaver? And shouldn't we add a shoemaker to them, or someone else to take care of our bodily needs?

Adeimantus: Of course.

Socrates: A city with the barest necessities, then, would consist of four or five men?

Adeimantus: Apparently. e

Socrates: Well, then, should each of them contribute his own work for the common use of all? I mean, should a farmer, although he is only one person, provide food for four people, and spend quadruple the time and labor to provide food to be shared by them all? Or should he not be concerned about everyone else? Should he produce one quarter the food in one quarter the time for himself alone?
Should he spend the other three quarters providing a 370
house, a cloak, and shoes? Should he save himself the bother of sharing with other people and mind his own business on his own?

Adeimantus: The first alternative, Socrates, is perhaps easier.

Socrates: There is nothing strange in that, by Zeus. You see, it occurred to me while you were speaking that, in the first place, we are not all born alike. On the contrary, each of us differs somewhat in nature from the others, one being suited to one job,
another to another. Or don't you think so? b

Adeimantus: I do.

Socrates: Well, then, would one person do better work if he practiced many crafts or if he practiced one?

Adeimantus: If he practiced one.

Socrates: And it is also clear, I take it, that if one misses the opportune moment in any job, the work is spoiled.

Adeimantus: It is clear.

SOCRATES: That, I take it, is because the thing that has to be done won't wait until the doer has the leisure to do it. No, instead the doer must, of necessity, pay close attention to what has to be done and
c not leave it for his idle moments.

ADEIMANTUS: Yes, he must.

SOCRATES: The result, then, is that more plentiful and better-quality goods are more easily produced, if each person does one thing for which he is naturally suited and does it at the opportune moment, because his time is freed from all the others.

ADEIMANTUS: Absolutely.

SOCRATES: Then, Adeimantus, we are going to need more than four citizens to provide the things we have mentioned. For a farmer won't make his own plow, it seems, if it is going to be a good one, nor his
d hoe, nor any of his other farm implements. Nor will a carpenter—and he, too, needs lots of tools. And the same is true of a weaver and a shoemaker, isn't it?

ADEIMANTUS: It is.

SOCRATES: So carpenters, metalworkers, and many other craftsmen of that sort will share our little city and make it bigger.

ADEIMANTUS: Yes, indeed.

SOCRATES: Yet it still would not be a very large settlement, even if we added cowherds, shepherds, and other herdsmen, so that the farmers would have cows
e to do their plowing, the builders oxen to share with the farmers in hauling their materials, and the weavers and shoemakers hides and fleeces to use.

ADEIMANTUS: It would not be a small city either, if it had to hold all that.

SOCRATES: Moreover, it is almost impossible, at any rate, to establish the city itself in the sort of place where it will need no imports.

ADEIMANTUS: Yes, that is impossible.

SOCRATES: Then we will need still other people who will import whatever is needed from another city.

ADEIMANTUS: We will.

SOCRATES: And if our servant goes empty-handed to another city, without any of the things needed by those from whom he is trying to get what his own
371 people need, he will come away empty-handed, won't he?

ADEIMANTUS: I should think so.

SOCRATES: Our citizens, then, must produce not only enough for themselves at home, but also goods of the right quality and quantity to satisfy the needs of others.

ADEIMANTUS: Yes, they must.

SOCRATES: So we will need more farmers and other craftsmen in our city.

ADEIMANTUS: Yes.

SOCRATES: And also other servants, I imagine, who are to take care of imports and exports. These are merchants, aren't they?

ADEIMANTUS: Yes.

SOCRATES: We will need merchants too, then.

ADEIMANTUS: Of course.

SOCRATES: And if the trade is carried on by sea, we will need a great many others who have expert knowledge of the business of the sea. b

ADEIMANTUS: A great many, indeed.

SOCRATES: Again, within the city itself, how will people share with one another the things they each produce? It was in order to *share*, after all, that we associated with one another and founded a city.

ADEIMANTUS: Clearly, they must do it by buying and selling.

SOCRATES: Then we will need a marketplace and a currency for such exchange.

ADEIMANTUS: Yes, indeed.

SOCRATES: So if a farmer or any other craftsman brings some of his products to the marketplace, and c
he does not arrive at the same time as those who want to exchange things with him, is he to sit idly in the marketplace, neglecting his own craft?

ADEIMANTUS: Not at all. On the contrary, there will be people who notice this situation and provide the requisite service—in well-organized cities, they are generally those whose bodies are weakest and who are not fit to do any other sort of work. Their job is to wait there in the marketplace and exchange money for the goods of those who have something to d
sell, and then to exchange goods for the money of those who want to buy them.

SOCRATES: This need, then, causes retailers to be present in our city. Those who wait in the marketplace, and provide this service of buying and selling, are called retailers, aren't they, whereas those who travel between cities are merchants?

ADEIMANTUS: Yes, that's right.

SOCRATES: There are also other servants, I think, whose minds would not altogether qualify them for membership in our community, but whose bodies e are strong enough for hard labor. So they sell the use of their strength for a price called a wage, and that is why they are called wage-earners. Isn't that so?

Adeimantus: Yes.

Socrates: So the wage-earners too, it seems, serve to complete our city?

Adeimantus: I think so.

Socrates: Well, then, Adeimantus, has our city now grown to completeness?

Adeimantus: Maybe it has.

Socrates: Then where are justice and injustice to be found in it? With which of the people we considered did they come in?

Adeimantus: I have no idea, Socrates, unless it is
372 somewhere in some need that these people have of one another.

Socrates: Perhaps what you say is right. We must look into it and not back off. First, then, let's see what sort of life people will lead who have been provided for in this way. They will make food, wine, clothes, and shoes, won't they? And they will build themselves houses. In the summer, they will mostly work naked and barefoot, but in the winter they will wear
b adequate clothing and shoes. For nourishment, they will provide themselves with barley meal and wheat flour, which they will knead and bake into noble cakes and loaves and serve up on a reed or on clean leaves. They will recline on couches strewn with yew and myrtles and feast with their children, drink their wine, and, crowned with wreaths, hymn the gods. They will enjoy having sex with one another, but they will produce no more children than their resources
c allow, lest they fall into either poverty or war.

At this point Glaucon interrupted and said:

It seems that you make your people feast without any relishes.

Socrates: True enough, I was forgetting that they will also have relishes—salt, of course, and olives and cheese, and they will boil roots and vegetables the way they boil them in the country. We will give them desserts too, I imagine, consisting of figs, chickpeas, and beans. And they will roast myrtles and acorns before the fire and drink in moderation. And so they
d will live in peace and good health, it seems, and when they die at a ripe old age, they will pass on a similar sort of life to their children.

Glaucon: If you were founding a city of pigs, Socrates, isn't that just what you would provide to fatten *them?*

Socrates: What, then, would you have me do, Glaucon?

Glaucon: Just what is conventional. If they are not to suffer hardship, they should recline on proper couches, I suppose, dine at tables, and have the relishes and desserts that people have nowadays. e

Socrates: All right, I understand. It isn't merely the origins of a city that we are considering, it seems, but those of a city that is *luxurious*, too. And that may not be a bad idea. For by examining such a city, we might perhaps see how justice and injustice grow up in cities. Yet the true city, in my view, is the one we have described: the healthy one, as it were. But if you also want to look at a feverish city, so be it. There is nothing to stop us. You see, the things I mentioned 373
earlier, and the way of life I described, won't satisfy some people, it seems; but couches, tables, and other furniture will have to be added to it, and relishes, of course, and incense, perfumes, prostitutes, pastries—and the multifariousness of each of them. In particular, we cannot just provide them with the necessities we mentioned at first, such as houses, clothes, and shoes; no, instead we will have to get painting and embroidery going, and procure gold and ivory and all sorts of everything of that sort. Isn't that so?

Glaucon: Yes. b

Socrates: Then we will have to enlarge our city again: the healthy one is no longer adequate. On the contrary, we must now increase it in size and population and fill it with a multitude of things that go beyond what is necessary for a city—hunters, for example, and all those imitators. Many of the latter work with shapes and colors; many with music—poets and their assistants, rhapsodes, actors, choral dancers, theatrical producers. And there will have to be craftsmen of multifarious devices, including, among other things, those needed for the adornment of women. In particular, then, we will need more servants—don't you think—such as tutors, wet nurses, c
nannies, beauticians, barbers, and relish cooks and meat cooks, too? Moreover, we will also need people to farm pigs. This animal did not exist in our earlier city, since there was no need for it, but we will need it in this one. And we will also need large numbers of

other meat-producing animals, won't we, if someone is going to eat them?

GLAUCON: We certainly will.

SOCRATES: And if we live like that, won't we have
d a far greater need for doctors than we did before?

GLAUCON: Yes, far greater.

SOCRATES: And the land, I take it, that used to be adequate to feed the population we had then will now be small and inadequate. Or don't you agree?

GLAUCON: I do.

SOCRATES: Won't we have to seize some of our neighbors' land, then, if we are to have enough for pasture and plowing? And won't our neighbors want to seize part of ours in turn, if they too have abandoned themselves to the endless acquisition of money and overstepped the limit of their necessary desires?

e GLAUCON: Yes, that is quite inevitable, Socrates.

SOCRATES: And the next step will be war, Glaucon, don't you agree?

GLAUCON: I do.

SOCRATES: Now, let's not say yet whether the effects of war are good or bad, but only that we have now found the origin of war: it comes from those same factors, the occurrence of which is the source of the greatest evils for cities and the individuals in them.

GLAUCON: Indeed, it does.

SOCRATES: The city must be further enlarged, then, my dear Glaucon, and not just a little, but by the size of a whole army. It will do battle with the invaders
374 in defense of the city's wealth, and of all the other
things we just described.

GLAUCON: Why so? Aren't the inhabitants themselves adequate for that purpose?

SOCRATES: No, not, at any rate, if the agreement that you and the rest of us made when we were founding the city was a good one. I think we agreed, if you remember, that it is impossible for a single person to practice many crafts well.

GLAUCON: True, we did say that.

SOCRATES: Well, then, don't you think that warfare
b is a craft?

GLAUCON: It is, indeed.

SOCRATES: So, should we be more concerned about the craft of shoemaking than the craft of warfare?

GLAUCON: Not at all.

SOCRATES: Well, now, we prevented a shoemaker from trying to be a farmer, weaver, or builder at the same time, instead of just a shoemaker, in order to ensure that the shoemaker's job was done well. Similarly, we also assigned just the one job for which he had a natural aptitude to each of the other people, and said that he was to work at it his whole life, free from having to do any of the other jobs, so as not to
miss the opportune moments for performing it well. c
But isn't it of the greatest importance that warfare be carried out well? Or is fighting a war so easy that a farmer, a shoemaker, or any other artisan can be a soldier at the same time, even though no one can become so much as a good checkers player or dice player if he considers it only as a sideline and does not practice it from childhood? Can someone just pick up a shield, or any other weapon or instrument
of war and immediately become a competent fighter d
in an infantry battle or whatever other sort of battle it may be, even though no other tool makes someone who picks it up a craftsman or an athlete, or is even of any service to him unless he has acquired knowledge of it and has had sufficient practice?

GLAUCON: If tools could do that, they would be valuable indeed.

SOCRATES: Then to the degree that the guardians'
job is most important, it requires the most free- e
dom from other things, as well as the greatest craft and practice.

GLAUCON: I should think so.

SOCRATES: And doesn't it also require a person whose nature is suited to that very practice?

GLAUCON: Certainly.

SOCRATES: Then our task, it seems, is to select, if we can, which natures, which sorts of natures, suit people to guard the city.

WE OMIT THE LENGTHY ACCOUNT of the sort of nature and education guardians should have. We take up the discussion toward the end of Book 3, with the description of the selection of rulers and the housing and lifestyles of them and the other guardians:

Book 3

SOCRATES: All right. Now, what is the next question we have to settle? Isn't it which of these same people will rule and which be ruled?

GLAUCON: Of course. 412c

Socrates: Well, isn't it clear that the older ones must rule, whereas the younger ones must be ruled?

Glaucon: Yes, it is clear.

Socrates: And that the rulers must be the best among them?

Glaucon: Yes, that's clear, too.

Socrates: And aren't the best farmers the ones who are best at farming?

Glaucon: Yes.

Socrates: In the present case, then, since the rulers must be the best of the guardians, mustn't they be the ones who are best at guarding the city?

Glaucon: Yes.

Socrates: Then mustn't they be knowledgeable and capable in this matter, and, in addition, mustn't they care for the city?

d Glaucon: Yes, they must.

Socrates: But a person would care most for what he loved.

Glaucon: Necessarily.

Socrates: And he would love something most if he thought that the same things were advantageous both for it and for himself, and if he thought that when it did well, he would do well, too; and that if it didn't, the opposite would happen.

Glaucon: That's right.

Socrates: Then we must choose from among our guardians the sort of men who seem on the basis of our observation to be most inclined, throughout their entire lives, to do what they believe to be
e advantageous for the city, and most unwilling to do the opposite.

Glaucon: Yes, they would be suitable for the job.

Socrates: I think, then, that we will have to observe them at every stage of their lives to make sure that they are good guardians of this conviction, and that neither compulsion nor sorcery will cause them to discard or forget their belief that they must do what is best for the city.

Glaucon: What do you mean by discarding?

Socrates: I will tell you. It seems to me that the departure of a belief from someone's mind is either voluntary or involuntary—voluntary when he learns that the belief is false; involuntary in the case of all
413 true beliefs.

Glaucon: I understand the voluntary sort, but I still need instruction about the involuntary.

Socrates: What? Don't you know that people are involuntarily deprived of good things, but voluntarily deprived of bad ones? And isn't being deceived about the truth a bad thing, whereas possessing the truth is a good one? Or don't you think that to believe things that are is to possess the truth?

Glaucon: No, you are right. And I do think that people are involuntarily deprived of true beliefs.

Socrates: Then isn't it through theft, sorcery, and compulsion that this happens? *b*

Glaucon: Now I do not understand again.

Socrates: I suppose I am making myself as clear as a tragic poet! By those who have their beliefs stolen from them, I mean those who are overpersuaded, or those who forget; because argument, in the one case, and time, in the other, takes away their beliefs without their noticing. You understand now, don't you?

Glaucon: Yes.

Socrates: Well then, by those who are compelled, I mean those who are made to change their beliefs by some suffering or pain.

Glaucon: I understand that, too, and you are right.

Socrates: And the victims of sorcery, I think you would agree, are those who change their beliefs *c*
because they are charmed by pleasure or terrified by some fear.

Glaucon: It seems to me that all deception is a form of sorcery.

Socrates: Well then, as I was just saying, we must discover which of them are best at safeguarding within themselves the conviction that they must always do what they believe to be best for the city. We must watch them right from childhood, and set them tasks in which a person would be most likely to forget such a conviction or be deceived out of it. And we must select the ones who remember and are difficult *d*
to deceive, and reject the others. Do you agree?

Glaucon: Yes.

Socrates: And we must also subject them to labors, pains, and contests, and watch for the same things there.

Glaucon: That's right.

Socrates: Then we must also set up a third kind of competition for sorcery. Like those who lead colts into noise and tumult to see if they are afraid, we must subject our young people to fears and then plunge them once again into pleasures, so as to test them much more thoroughly than people test gold in *e*

a fire. And if any of them seems to be immune to sorcery, preserves his composure throughout, is a good guardian of himself and of the musical training he has received, and proves himself to be rhythmical and harmonious in all these trials—he is the sort of person who would be most useful, both to himself and to the city. And anyone who is tested as a child,
youth, and adult, and always emerges as being with-
414 out impurities, should be established as a ruler of the
city as well as a guardian, and should be honored in life and receive the most prized tombs and memorials after his death. But those who do not should be rejected. That is the sort of way, Glaucon, that I think rulers and guardians should be selected and established. Though I have provided only a pattern, not the precise details.

GLAUCON: I also think much the same.

SOCRATES: Then wouldn't it really be most correct
b to call these people complete guardians—the ones
who guard against external enemies and internal friends, so that the former will lack the power, and the latter the desire, to do any evil; but to call the young people to whom we were referring as guardians just now, *auxiliaries* and supporters of the guardians' convictions?

GLAUCON: Yes, I think it would.

SOCRATES: How, then, could we devise one of
those useful lies we were talking about a while ago,
c a single noble lie that would, preferably, persuade
even the rulers themselves; but, failing that, the rest of the city?

GLAUCON: What sort of lie?

SOCRATES: Nothing new, but a sort of Phoenician story about something that happened in lots of places prior to this—at least, that is what the poets say and have persuaded people to believe. It has not happened in our day, and I do not know if it could happen. It would take a lot of persuasion to get people to believe it.

GLAUCON: You seem hesitant to tell the story.

SOCRATES: You will realize that I have every reason to hesitate, when I do tell it.

GLAUCON: Out with it. Do not be afraid.

SOCRATES: All right, I will—though I do not know
d where I will get the audacity or the words to tell it.
I will first be trying to persuade the rulers and the soldiers, and then the rest of the city, that the upbringing and the education we gave them were like dreams; that they only imagined they were undergoing all the things that were happening to them, while in fact they themselves were at that time down inside the earth being formed and nurtured, and that their weapons and the rest of their equipment were also manufactured there. When they e
were entirely completed, the earth, their mother, sent them up, so that now, just as if the land in which they live were their mother and nurse, they must deliberate on its behalf, defend it if anyone attacks it, and regard the other citizens as their earthborn brothers.

GLAUCON: It is not for nothing that you were ashamed to tell your lie earlier.

SOCRATES: No, it was only to be expected. But all
the same, you should listen to the rest of the story.
"Although all of you in the city are brothers," we will 415
say to them in telling our story, "when the god was forming you, he mixed gold into those of you who are capable of ruling, which is why they are the most honorable; silver into the auxiliaries; and iron and bronze into the farmers and other craftsmen. For the most part, you will produce children like yourselves;
but, because you are all related, a silver child will
occasionally be born to a golden parent, a golden b
child to a silver parent, and so on. Therefore, the first and most important command from the god to the rulers is that there is nothing they must guard better or watch more carefully than the mixture of metals in the souls of their offspring. If an offspring of theirs is born with a mixture of iron or bronze, they must not
pity him in any way, but assign him an honor appro-
priate to his nature and drive him out to join the c
craftsmen or the farmers. On the other hand, if an offspring of the latter is found to have a mixture of gold or silver, they will honor him and take him up to join the guardians or the auxiliaries. For there is an oracle that the city will be ruined if it ever has an iron or a bronze guardian." So, have you a device that will make them believe this story?

GLAUCON: No, none that would make this group
believe it themselves. But I do have one for their d
sons, for later generations, and for all other people who come after them.

SOCRATES: Well, even that would have a good effect, by making them care more for the city and for

each other. For I think I understand what you mean—namely, that all this will go where *tradition* leads. What *we* can do, however, when we have armed our earthborn people, is lead them forth with their rulers at their head. They must go and look for the best place in the city for a military encampment, a site from which they can most easily control any-
e one in the city who is unwilling to obey the laws, or repel any outside enemy who, like a wolf, attacks the fold. And when they have established their camp and sacrificed to the appropriate gods, they must make their sleeping quarters, mustn't they?

Glaucon: Yes.

Socrates: And mustn't these provide adequate shelter against the storms of winter and the heat of summer?

Glaucon: Yes, of course. After all, I assume you are talking about their living quarters.

Socrates: Yes, but ones for *soldiers*, not moneymakers.

Glaucon: What difference do you think there is
416 between the two, again?

Socrates: I will try to tell you. You see, it is surely the most terrible and most shameful thing in the world for shepherds to rear dogs as auxiliaries to help them with their flocks in such a way that those dogs themselves—because of intemperance, hunger, or some other bad condition—try to do evil to the sheep, acting not like sheepdogs but like wolves.

Glaucon: Of course, that is terrible.

Socrates: So, mustn't we use every safeguard to
b prevent our auxiliaries from treating the citizens like that—because they are stronger—and becoming savage masters rather than gentle allies?

Glaucon: Yes, we must.

Socrates: And wouldn't they have been provided with the greatest safeguard possible if they have been really well educated?

Glaucon: But surely they have been.

Socrates: That is not something that deserves to be asserted so confidently, my dear Glaucon. But what does deserve it is what we were saying just now, that they must have the right education, what-
c ever it is, if they are going to have what will do most to make them gentle to one another and to the ones they are guarding.

Glaucon: That's right.

Socrates: But anyone with any sense will tell us that, besides this education, they must be provided with living quarters and other property of the sort that will neither prevent them from being the best guardians nor encourage them to do evil to the
other citizens. d

Glaucon: And he would be right.

Socrates: Consider, then, whether or not they should live and be housed in some such way as this, if they are going to be the sort of men we described. First, none of them should possess any private property that is not wholly necessary. Second, none should have living quarters or storerooms that are not open for all to enter at will. Such provisions as are required by temperate and courageous men, who are warrior-athletes, they should receive from the other
citizens as wages for their guardianship, the amount e
being fixed so that there is neither a shortfall nor a surplus at the end of the year. They should have common messes to go to, and should live together like soldiers in a camp. We will tell them that they have gold and silver of a divine sort in their souls as a permanent gift from the gods, and have no need of human gold in addition. And we will add that it is impious for them to defile this divine possession by possessing an admixture of mortal gold, because many impious deeds have been done for the sake of the currency of the masses, whereas their sort is pure.
No, they alone among the city's population are for- 417
bidden by divine law to handle or even touch gold and silver. They must not be under the same roof as these metals, wear them as jewelry, or drink from gold or silver goblets. And by behaving in that way, they would save both themselves and the city. But if they acquire private land, houses, and money themselves, they will be household managers and farmers instead of guardians—hostile masters of the other citizens, instead of their allies. They will spend their b
whole lives hating and being hated, plotting and being plotted against, much more afraid of internal than of external enemies—already rushing, in fact, to the brink of their own destruction and that of the rest of the city as well. For all these reasons, let's declare that *that* is how the guardians must be provided with housing and the rest, and establish it as a law. Or don't you agree?

Glaucon: Of course I do.

Book 4

Synopsis

A QUESTION FROM ADEIMANTUS about the happiness of the guardians leads Socrates to clarify the goal of the *kallipolis,* which is not to make any one group of citizens outstandingly happy at the expense of others, but to make everyone as happy as his nature allows (421c). This goal will be achieved, he argues, if the guardians protect the system of elementary education described in Books 2 and 3. For it is what provides the training in political virtue without which no system of laws or constitution can hope to achieve anything worthwhile (423c–427a). The place of religion in the *kallipolis* is then very briefly discussed (427b–c). The *kallipolis* is pronounced complete (427d). Since it is completely good (427e), it must have all the virtues of a city (see 352d–354a): wisdom, courage, temperance, and justice. By the time that search for them is concluded (434d), they have all been identified with distinct structural features of the *kallipolis*. This leads to the argument for the division of the soul into three elements—appetitive, spirited, and rational—that correspond to the three major classes in the *kallipolis*—producers, guardians, and rulers (435c–441c). Once this argument is in place, it remains to find the virtues in the soul and to show that they are the same structural features of it as of the *kallipolis* (441c–444e). Glaucon is ready at this point to pronounce justice more choiceworthy than injustice, but Socrates is not (445a–b). In his view, the question cannot be answered until much more work has been done on virtue and vice. We take up Socrates' narration as he returns to the topic of virtue in the *kallipolis* and in the soul.

SOCRATES: So then, son of Ariston, your city would
427d now seem to be founded. As the next step, look inside it, having got hold of an adequate light somewhere. Look yourself and invite your brother and Polemarchus and the rest of us to help you, to see where justice and injustice might be in it, how they differ from one another, and which of the two must be possessed by the person who is going to be happy, whether that fact is hidden from all gods and humans or not.

And Glaucon said:

That's nonsense! You promised you would look for
them yourself, because you said it was impious for e
you not to defend justice in every way you could.

SOCRATES: You are right to remind me, and I must do what I promised. But you will have to help.

GLAUCON: We will.

SOCRATES: I expect, then, to find justice in the following way. I think our city, if indeed it has been correctly founded, is completely good.

GLAUCON: Yes, it must be.

SOCRATES: Clearly, then, it is wise, courageous, temperate, and just.

GLAUCON: Clearly.

SOCRATES: Then if we find any of these in it, what remains will be what we have not found?

GLAUCON: Of course. 428

SOCRATES: Therefore, as in the case of any other four things, if we were looking for one of them in something and recognized it first, that would be enough to satisfy us. But if we recognized the other three first, that itself would enable us to recognize what we were looking for, since clearly it could not be anything other than the one that remains.

GLAUCON: That's right.

SOCRATES: So, since there also happen to be four things we are interested in, mustn't we look for them in the same way?

GLAUCON: Clearly.

SOCRATES: Now, the first thing I think I can see
clearly in the city is wisdom. And there seems to be b
something odd about it.

GLAUCON: What?

SOCRATES: I think that the city we described is really wise. And that is because it is prudent, isn't it?

GLAUCON: Yes.

SOCRATES: And surely it is clear that this very thing, prudence, is some sort of knowledge. I mean, it certainly is not through *ignorance* that people do the prudent thing, but through knowledge.

GLAUCON: Clearly.

SOCRATES: But there are, of course, many multifarious sorts of knowledge in the city.

GLAUCON: Certainly.

SOCRATES: So, is it because of the knowledge possessed by the carpenters that the city deserves to be described as wise and prudent?

GLAUCON: Not at all. It is called skilled in carpen-
c try because of that.

SOCRATES: So a city shouldn't be called wise because it has the knowledge that deliberates about how wooden things can be best.

GLAUCON: Certainly not.

SOCRATES: What about this, then? What about the knowledge of things made of bronze, or anything else of that sort?

GLAUCON: Not anything of that sort either.

SOCRATES: And not the knowledge of how to produce crops from the soil. On the contrary, it is skilled in farming because of that.

GLAUCON: That's my view.

SOCRATES: Then is there some knowledge in the
city we have just founded, which some of its citizens
have, that does not deliberate about some particular
d thing in the city, but about the city as a whole, and
about how its internal relations and its relations with
other cities will be the best possible.

GLAUCON: There is indeed.

SOCRATES: What is it and who has it?

GLAUCON: It is the craft of guardianship. And the ones who possess it are those rulers we just now called complete guardians.

SOCRATES: Because it has this knowledge, then, how do you describe the city?

GLAUCON: As prudent and really wise.

SOCRATES: Now, do you think that there will be
e more metalworkers in the city, or more of these true
guardians?

GLAUCON: There will be far more metalworkers.

SOCRATES: Of all those who are called by a certain name because they have some sort of knowledge, wouldn't the true guardians be the fewest in number?

GLAUCON: By far.

SOCRATES: So, it is because of the smallest group
or part of itself, and the knowledge that is in it—the
part that governs and rules—that a city founded
according to nature would be wise as a whole. And
this class—which seems to be, by nature, the smallest—is the one that inherently possesses a share of
429 the knowledge that alone among all the other sorts of
knowledge should be called wisdom.

GLAUCON: That's absolutely true.

SOCRATES: So we have found—though I do not know how—this one of the four and its place in the city, too.

GLAUCON: It seems to me, at least, that it has been well and truly found.

SOCRATES: But surely courage and the part of the city it is in, and because of which the city is described as courageous, is not very difficult to spot.

GLAUCON: How so?

SOCRATES: Who would describe a city as cowardly b
or courageous by looking at anything other than that
part which defends it and wages war on its behalf?

GLAUCON: No one would look at anything else.

SOCRATES: Because, I take it, whether the others are courageous or cowardly doesn't make it one or the other.

GLAUCON: No, it doesn't.

SOCRATES: So courage, too, belongs to a city
because of a part of itself—because it has in that part
the power to preserve through everything its belief
that the things, and the sorts of things, that should
inspire terror are the very things, and sorts of things, c
that the lawgiver declared to be such in the course of
educating it. Or don't you call that courage?

GLAUCON: I do not completely understand what you said. Would you mind repeating it?

SOCRATES: I mean that courage is a sort of preservation.

GLAUCON: What sort of preservation?

SOCRATES: The preservation of the belief, inculcated by the law through education, about what
things, and what sorts of things, inspire terror. And by
its preservation "through everything," I mean preserving it though pains, pleasures, appetites, and fears
and not abandoning it. I will compare it to something d
I think it resembles, if you like.

GLAUCON: I would like that.

SOCRATES: You know, then, that when dyers want
to dye wool purple, they first select from wools of
many different colors the ones that are naturally
white. Then they give them an elaborate preparatory
treatment, so that they will accept the color as well as
possible. And only at that point do they dip them in
the purple dye. When something is dyed in this way,
it holds the dye fast, and no amount of washing, e
whether with or without detergent, can remove the
color. But you also know what happens when things
are not dyed in this way, when one dyes wools of

other colors, or even these white ones, without preparatory treatment.

GLAUCON: I know they look washed out and ridiculous.

SOCRATES: You should take it, then, that we too were trying as hard as we could to do something similar when we selected our soldiers and educated them in musical and physical training. It was contrived, you should suppose, for no purpose
430 other than to ensure that—persuaded by us—they would absorb the laws in the best possible way, just like wool does a dye; that as a result, their beliefs about what things should inspire terror, and about everything else, would hold fast because they had the proper nature and rearing; so fast that the dye could not be washed out even by those detergents that are so terribly effective at scouring—pleasure, which is much more terribly effective at this than any chalestrian[1] or alkali, and pain and fear and
b appetite, which are worse than any detergent. This power, then, to preserve through everything the correct and law-inculcated belief about what should inspire terror and what should not is what I, at any rate, call courage. And I will assume it is this, unless you object.

GLAUCON: No, I have no objection. For I presume that the sort of correct belief about these same matters that you find in animals and slaves, which is not the result of education and has nothing at all to do with law, is called something other than courage.

c SOCRATES: You are absolutely right.

GLAUCON: Well, then, I accept your account of courage.

SOCRATES: Yes, do accept it, at any rate, as my account of *political* courage, and you will be right to accept it. If you like, we will discuss that more fully some other time. You see, at the moment, our inquiry is not about courage but about justice. And for the purpose of that inquiry, I think that what we have said is sufficient.

GLAUCON: You are right.

SOCRATES: Two things, then, remain for us to find
d in the city: temperance and—the goal of our entire inquiry—justice.

GLAUCON: Yes, indeed.

SOCRATES: How could we find justice, then, so we won't have to bother with temperance any further?

GLAUCON: Well I, for my part, do not know of any, nor would I want justice to appear first if that means that we are not going to investigate temperance any further. So if you want to please me, look for it before the other.

SOCRATES: Of course I want to. It would be wrong
not to. e

GLAUCON: Go ahead and look, then.

SOCRATES: I will. And seen from here, it is more like a sort of concord and harmony than the previous ones.

GLAUCON: How so?

SOCRATES: Temperance is surely a sort of order, the mastery of certain sorts of pleasures and appetites. People indicate as much when they use the term "self-mastery"—though I do not know in what way. This and other similar things are like tracks that temperance has left. Isn't that so?

GLAUCON: Absolutely.

SOCRATES: Isn't the term "self-mastery" ridiculous, though? For, of course, the one who is master of himself is also the one who is weaker, and the one who is weaker is also the one who masters. After all, the
same person is referred to in all these descriptions. 431

GLAUCON: Of course.

SOCRATES: It seems to me, however, that what this term is trying to indicate is that within the same person's soul, there is a better thing and a worse one. Whenever the naturally better one masters the worse, this is called being master of oneself. At any rate, it is praised. But whenever, as a result of bad upbringing or associating with bad people, the smaller and better one is mastered by the inferior majority, this is blamed as a disgraceful thing and is
called being weaker than oneself, or being intemperate. b

GLAUCON: Yes, that seems plausible.

SOCRATES: Now, then, take a look at our new city and you will find one of these conditions present in it. For you will say that it is rightly described as master of itself, if indeed anything in which the better rules the worse is to be described as temperate and master of itself.

GLAUCON: I am looking, and what you say is true.

SOCRATES: Furthermore, pleasures, pains, and appetites that are numerous and multifarious are
things one would especially find in children, c

1. Carbonate of soda from Chalestra, a town and lake in Macedonia.

women, household slaves, and in the so-called free
d members of the masses—that is, the inferior people.

GLAUCON: Yes.

SOCRATES: But the pleasures, pains, and appetites that are simple and moderate, the ones that are led by rational calculation with the aid of understanding and correct belief, you would find in those few people who are born with the best natures and receive the best education.

GLAUCON: That's true.

SOCRATES: Don't you see, then, that this too is present in your city, and that the appetites of the masses—the inferior people—are mastered there by the wisdom and appetites of the few—the best people?

GLAUCON: I do.

SOCRATES: So, if any city is said to be master of its pleasures and appetites and of itself, it is this one.

GLAUCON: Absolutely.

SOCRATES: So isn't it also temperate because of all this?

GLAUCON: Yes, indeed.

SOCRATES: And moreover, if there is any city in which rulers and subjects share the same belief about
e who should rule, it is this one. Or don't you agree?

GLAUCON: Yes, I certainly do.

SOCRATES: And in which of them do you say temperance is located when they are in this condition? In the rulers or the subjects?

GLAUCON: In both, I suppose.

SOCRATES: Do you see, then, that the hunch we had just now—that temperance is like a sort of harmony—was quite plausible?

GLAUCON: Why is that?

SOCRATES: Because its operation is unlike that of courage and wisdom, each of which resides in one part and makes the city either courageous or wise.
432 Temperance does not work like that, but has literally been stretched throughout the whole, making the weakest, the strongest, and those in between all sing the same song in unison—whether in wisdom, if you like, or in physical strength, if you prefer; or, for that matter, in numbers, wealth, or anything else. Hence we would be absolutely right to say that this unanimity is temperance—this concord between the naturally worse and the naturally better, about which of the two should rule both in the city and in each individual.

b GLAUCON: I agree completely.

SOCRATES: All right. We have now spotted three kinds of virtue in our city. What kind remains, then, that would give the city yet another share of virtue? For it is clear that what remains is justice.

GLAUCON: It is clear.

SOCRATES: So then, Glaucon, we must now station ourselves like hunters surrounding a wood and concentrate our minds, so that justice does not escape us and vanish into obscurity. For it is clear that it is
around here somewhere. Keep your eyes peeled and c
do your best to catch sight of it, and if you happen to see it before I do, show it to me.

GLAUCON: I wish I could help. But it is rather the case that if you use me as a follower who can see only what you point out to him, you will be using me in a more reasonable way.

SOCRATES: Pray for success, then, and follow me.

GLAUCON: I will. You have only to lead.

SOCRATES: And it truly seems to be an impenetrable place and full of shadows. It is dark, at any rate, and difficult to search through. But all the same, we must go on.

GLAUCON: Yes, we must. d

And then I caught sight of something and shouted:

SOCRATES: Ah ha![2] Glaucon, it looks as though there is a track here, and I do not think our quarry will altogether escape us.

GLAUCON: That's good news.

SOCRATES: Oh dear, what a stupid condition in which to find ourselves!

GLAUCON: How so?

SOCRATES: It seems, blessed though you are, that the thing has been rolling around at our feet from the very beginning, and yet, like ridiculous fools, we could not see it. For just as people who are holding something in their hands sometimes search for the very thing they are holding, we did not look in
the right direction but gazed off into the distance, e
and perhaps that is the very reason we did not notice it.

GLAUCON: What do you mean?

SOCRATES: This: I think we have been talking and hearing about it all this time without understanding

---

2. *Iou iou:* usually a cry of woe in tragedy, not (like *iô iô*) a cry of joy.

ourselves, or realizing that we were, in a way, talking about it.

Glaucon: That was a long prelude! Now I want to hear what you mean!

Socrates: Listen, then, and see whether there is anything in what I say. You see, what we laid down at
433 the beginning when we were founding our city, about what should be done throughout it—that, I think, or some form of that, is justice. And surely what we laid down and often repeated, if you remember, is that each person must practice one of the pursuits in the city, the one for which he is naturally best suited.

Glaucon: Yes, we did say that.

Socrates: Moreover, we have heard many people say, and have often said ourselves, that justice is doing one's own work and not meddling with what
b is not one's own.

Glaucon: Yes, we have.

Socrates: This, then, my friend, provided it is taken in a certain way, would seem to be justice—this doing one's own work. And do you know what I take as evidence of that?

Glaucon: No, tell me.

Socrates: After our consideration of temperance, courage, and wisdom, I think that what remains in the city is the power that makes it possible for all of these to arise in it, and that preserves them when they have arisen for as long as it remains there itself.
c And we did say that justice would be what remained when we had found the other three.

Glaucon: Yes, that must be so.

Socrates: Yet, surely, if we had to decide which of these will most contribute to making our city good by being present in it, it would be difficult to decide. Is it the agreement in belief between the rulers and the subjects? The preservation among the soldiers of the law-inculcated belief about what should inspire terror and what should not? The wisdom and
d guardianship of the rulers? Or is what most contributes to making it good the fact that every child, woman, slave, free person, craftsman, ruler, and subject each does his own work and does not meddle with what is not?

Glaucon: Of course it's a difficult decision.

Socrates: It seems, then, that this power—which consists in everyone's doing his own work—rivals wisdom, temperance, and courage in its contribution to the city's virtue.

Glaucon: It certainly does.

Socrates: And wouldn't you say that justice is certainly what rivals them in contributing to the
city's virtue? e

Glaucon: Absolutely.

Socrates: Look at it this way, too, if you want to be convinced. Won't you assign to the rulers the job of judging lawsuits in the city?

Glaucon: Of course.

Socrates: And will they have any aim in judging other than this: that no citizen should have what is another's or be deprived of what is his own?

Glaucon: No, they will have none but that.

Socrates: Because that is just?

Glaucon: Yes.

Socrates: So from that point of view, too, having and doing of one's own, of what belongs to one,
would be agreed to be justice. 434

Glaucon: That's right.

Socrates: Now, see whether you agree with me about this: if a carpenter attempts to do the work of a shoemaker, or a shoemaker that of a carpenter, or they exchange their tools or honors with one another, or if the same person tries to do both jobs, and all other such exchanges are made, do you think that does any great harm to the city?

Glaucon: Not really.

Socrates: But I imagine that when someone who is, by nature, a craftsman or some other sort of moneymaker is puffed up by wealth, or by having a majority of votes, or by his own strength, or by some other b
such thing, and attempts to enter the class of soldiers; or when one of the soldiers who is unworthy to do so tries to enter that of judge and guardian, and these exchange their tools and honors; or when the same person tries to do all these things at once, then I imagine you will agree that these exchanges and this meddling destroy the city.

Glaucon: Absolutely.

Socrates: So, meddling and exchange among these three classes is the greatest harm that can happen to the city and would rightly be called the worst c
evil one could do to it.

Glaucon: Exactly.

Socrates: And wouldn't you say that the worst evil one could do to one's own city is injustice?

Glaucon: Of course.

Socrates: That, then, is what injustice is. But let's
put it in reverse: the opposite of this—when the moneymaking, auxiliary, and guardian class each do their
own work in the city—is justice, isn't it, and makes
the city just?

d Glaucon: That's exactly what I think too.

Socrates: Let's not state it as fixedly established
just yet. But if this kind of thing is agreed by us to
be justice in the case of individual human beings as
well, then we can assent to it. For what else will there
be for us to say? But if it is not, we will have to look
for something else. For the moment, however, let's
complete the inquiry in which we supposed that if
we first tried to observe justice in some larger thing
that possessed it, that would make it easier to see
what it is like in an individual human being. We
e agreed that this larger thing is a city, and so we
founded the best city we could, knowing well that
justice would of course be present in one that was
good. So, let's apply what has come to light for us
there to an individual, and if it is confirmed, all will
be well. But if something different is found in the
case of the individual, we will go back to the city and
test it there. And perhaps by examining them side by
side and rubbing them together like fire-sticks, we
435 can make justice blaze forth and, once it has come to
light, confirm it in our own case.

Glaucon: Well, the road you describe is the right
one, and we should follow it.

Socrates: Well, then, if you call a bigger thing
and a smaller thing by the same name, are they
unalike in the respect in which they are called the
same, or alike?

Glaucon: Alike.

Socrates: So a just man won't differ at all from a
just city with respect to the form of justice but will be
b like it.

Glaucon: Yes, he will be like it.

Socrates: But now, the city, at any rate, was
thought to be just because each of the three natural
classes within it did its own job; and to be temperate,
courageous, and wise, in addition, because of certain
other conditions or states of these same classes.

Glaucon: That's true.

Socrates: Then, my friend, we would expect an
individual to have these same kinds of things in his
soul, and to be correctly called by the same names
as the city because the same conditions are present in
them both. c

Glaucon: Inevitably.

Socrates: Well, you amazing fellow, here is
another trivial investigation we have stumbled into:
does the soul have these three kinds of things in it
or not?

Glaucon: It does not look at all trivial to me. Perhaps, Socrates, there is some truth in the old saying
that everything beautiful is difficult.

Socrates: Apparently so. In fact, you should be
well aware, Glaucon, that it is my belief we will never
ever grasp this matter precisely by methods of the sort
we are now using in our discussions. However, there d
is in fact another longer and more time-consuming
road that does lead there. But perhaps we can manage to come up to the standard of our previous statements and inquiries.

Glaucon: Shouldn't we be content with that? It
would be enough for me, at least for now.

Socrates: Well, then, it will be quite satisfactory
for me, too.

Glaucon: Then do not weary, but go on with
the inquiry.

Socrates: Well, isn't it absolutely necessary for us
to agree to this much: that the very same kinds of e
things and conditions exist in each one of us as exist
in the city? After all, where else would they come
from? You see, it would be ridiculous for anyone
to think that spiritedness did not come to be in cities
from the private individuals who are reputed to have
this quality, such as the Thracians, Scythians, and
others who live to the north of us; or that the same is
not true of the love of learning, which is mostly associated with our part of the world; or of the love of 436
money, which is said to be found not least among the
Phoenicians and Egyptians.

Glaucon: It certainly would.

Socrates: We may take that as being so, then, and
it was not at all difficult to discover.

Glaucon: No, it certainly was not.

Socrates: But this, now, *is* difficult. Do we do
each of them with the same thing or, since there are
three, do we do one with one and another with
another: that is to say, do we learn with one, feel anger
with another, and with yet a third have an appetite
for the pleasures of food, sex, and those closely akin
to them? Or do we do each of them with the whole

b of our soul, once we feel the impulse? *That* is what is difficult to determine in a way that is up to the standards of our argument.

GLAUCON: I think so, too.

SOCRATES: Well, then, let's try in this way to determine whether they are the same as one another or different.

GLAUCON: What way?

SOCRATES: It is clear that the same thing cannot do or undergo opposite things; not, at any rate, in the same respect, in relation to the same thing, at the same time. So, if we ever find that happening here, we will know that we are not dealing with one and the same
c thing, but with many.

GLAUCON: All right.

SOCRATES: Consider, then, what I am about to say.

GLAUCON: Say it.

SOCRATES: Is it possible for the same thing, at the same time, and in the same respect, to be standing still and moving?

GLAUCON: Not at all.

SOCRATES: Let's come to a more precise agreement, in order to avoid disputes later on. You see, if anyone said of a person who is standing still but moving his hands and head, that the same thing is moving and standing still at the same time, we would not consider, I imagine, that he should say that; but rather that in one respect the person is standing still,
d while in another he is moving. Isn't that so?

GLAUCON: It is.

SOCRATES: Then, if the one who said this became still more charming and made the sophisticated point that spinning tops, at any rate, stand still as a whole at the same time as they are also in motion, when, with the peg fixed in the same place, they revolve, or that the same holds of anything else that moves in a circle on the same spot—we would not agree, on the grounds that in such situations it is not in the same respects that these objects are both moving and standing still. On the contrary, we would say that
e these objects have both a straight axis and a circumference in them, and that with respect to the straight axis they stand still—since they do not wobble to either side—whereas with respect to the circumference they move in a circle. But if their straight axis wobbles to the left or right or front or back at the same time as they are spinning, we will say that they are not standing still in any way.

GLAUCON: And we would be right.

SOCRATES: No such objection will disturb us, then, or make us any more likely to believe that the same thing can—at the same time, in the same respect, and in relation to the same thing—undergo, be, or
do opposite things. 437

GLAUCON: They won't have that effect on me at least.

SOCRATES: All the same, in order to avoid going through all these objections one by one and taking a long time to prove them all untrue, let's hypothesize that what we have said is correct and carry on—with the understanding that if it should ever be shown to be incorrect, all the consequences we have drawn from it will be invalidated.

GLAUCON: Yes, that's what we should do.

SOCRATES: Now, wouldn't you consider assent and b
dissent, wanting to have something and rejecting it, taking something and pushing it away, as all being pairs of mutual opposites—whether of opposite doings or of opposite undergoings does not matter?

GLAUCON: Yes, they are pairs of opposites.

SOCRATES: What about thirst, hunger, and the appetites as a whole, and also wishing and willing? Would you include all of them somewhere among the
kinds of things we just mentioned? For example, c
wouldn't you say that the soul of someone who has an appetite wants the thing for which it has an appetite, and draws toward itself what it wishes to have; and, in addition, that insofar as his soul wishes something to be given to it, it nods assent to itself as if in answer to a question, and strives toward its attainment?

GLAUCON: I would.

SOCRATES: What about not-willing, not-wishing, and not-having an appetite? Wouldn't we include them among the very opposites, cases in which the soul pushes and drives things away from itself?

GLAUCON: Of course. d

SOCRATES: Since that is so, won't we say that there is a kind consisting of appetites, and that the most conspicuous examples of them are what we call hunger and thirst?

GLAUCON: We will.

SOCRATES: Isn't the one for food, the other for drink?

GLAUCON: Yes.

SOCRATES: Now, insofar as it is thirst, is it an appetite in the soul for more than what we say it is for? I mean, is thirst a thirst for hot drink or cold, or much drink or little, or—in a word—for drink of a

certain sort? Or isn't it rather that if heat is present in addition to thirst, it causes the appetite to be for
e something cold as well, whereas the addition of cold makes it an appetite for something hot? And if there is much thirst, because of the presence of muchness, won't it cause the desire to be for much drink, and where little for little? But thirst itself will never be for anything other than the very thing that it is in its nature to be an appetite for: namely, drink itself; and, similarly, hunger is for food.

GLAUCON: That's the way it is. By itself, at any rate, each appetite is for its natural object only, while an appetite for an object of this or that sort depends on additions.

SOCRATES: No one should catch us unprepared, then, or disturb us by claiming that no one has an
438 appetite for drink but rather for good drink, nor for food but rather for good food, since everyone's appetite is for good things. And so, if thirst is an appetite, it will be an appetite for good drink or good whatever, and similarly for the other appetites.

GLAUCON: Yes, there might seem to be something in that objection.

SOCRATES: But surely, whenever things are related to something, those that are of a particular sort are related to a particular sort of thing, as it seems to me,
b whereas those that are just themselves are related only to a thing that is just itself.

GLAUCON: I do not understand.

SOCRATES: Don't you understand that the greater is such as to be greater than something?

GLAUCON: Of course.

SOCRATES: Than the less?

GLAUCON: Yes.

SOCRATES: And the much greater than the much less. Isn't that so?

GLAUCON: Yes.

SOCRATES: And the once greater than the once less? And the going-to-be greater than the going-to-be less?

GLAUCON: Certainly.

SOCRATES: And doesn't the same hold of the more in relation to the fewer, the double to the half, and
c everything of that sort; and also of heavier to lighter and faster to slower; and, in addition, of hot to cold, and all other similar things?

GLAUCON: Yes, indeed.

SOCRATES: What about the various kinds of knowledge? Aren't they the same way? Knowledge itself is of what can be learned itself (or of whatever we should take the object of knowledge to be), whereas a particular knowledge of a particular sort is of a particular thing of a particular sort. I mean something like this: when knowledge of building houses was developed, it differed from the other kinds of knowl- d
edge, and so was called knowledge of building. Isn't that so?

GLAUCON: Of course.

SOCRATES: And wasn't that because it was a different sort of knowledge from all the others?

GLAUCON: Yes.

SOCRATES: And wasn't it because it was of a particular sort of thing that it itself became a particular sort of knowledge? And isn't this true of all the crafts and sciences?

GLAUCON: It is.

SOCRATES: Well, then, you should think of that as what I wanted to get across before—if you understand it now—when I said that whenever things are related to something, those that are just themselves are related to things that are just themselves, whereas those of a particular sort are related to things of a particular sort. And I do not at all mean that the sorts in question have to be the same for them both—that e
the knowledge of health and disease is healthy and diseased, or that that of good and bad things is good and bad. On the contrary, I mean that when knowledge occurred that was not just knowledge of the thing itself that knowledge is of, but of something of a particular sort, which in this case was health and disease, the result was that it itself became a particular sort of knowledge; and this caused it to be no longer called simply knowledge but, with the addition of the particular sort, medical knowledge.

GLAUCON: I understand and I think you are right.

SOCRATES: Returning to thirst, then, wouldn't you include it among the things that are related to some- 439
thing just by being what they are? Surely thirst is related to. . . .

GLAUCON: I would. It is related to drink.

SOCRATES: So a particular sort of thirst is for a particular sort of drink. Thirst itself, however, is not for much or little, good or bad, or, in a word, for drink of a particular sort; rather, thirst itself is, by nature, just for drink itself. Right?

GLAUCON: Absolutely.

Socrates: Hence the soul of the thirsty person, insofar as it is simply thirsty, does not want anything else except to drink, and this is what it longs for and b is impelled to do.

Glaucon: Clearly.

Socrates: Then if anything in it draws it back when it is thirsty, wouldn't it be something different from what thirsts and, like a beast, drives it to drink? For surely, we say, the same thing, in the same respect of itself, in relation to the same thing, and at the same time, cannot do opposite things.

Glaucon: No, it cannot.

Socrates: In the same way, I imagine, it is not right to say of the archer that his hands at the same time push the bow away and draw it toward him. On the contrary, we should say that one hand pushes it away, while the other draws it toward him.

c Glaucon: Absolutely.

Socrates: Now, we would say, wouldn't we, that some people are thirsty sometimes, yet unwilling to drink?

Glaucon: Many people often are.

Socrates: What, then, should one say about them? Isn't it that there is an element in their soul urging them to drink, and also one stopping them—something different that masters the one doing the urging?

Glaucon: I certainly think so.

Socrates: Doesn't the element doing the stopping in such cases arise— when it does arise—from rational calculation, while the things that drive and d drag are present because of feelings and diseases?

Glaucon: Apparently so.

Socrates: It would not be unreasonable for us to claim, then, that there are two elements, different from one another; and to call the element in the soul with which it calculates, the rationally calculating element; and the one with which it feels passion, hungers, thirsts, and is stirred by other appetites, the irrational and appetitive element, friend to certain ways of being filled and certain pleasures.

Glaucon: No, it would not. Indeed, it would be a e very natural thing for us to do.

Socrates: Let's assume, then, that we have distinguished these two kinds of elements in the soul. Now, is the spirited element—the one with which we feel anger—a third kind of thing, or is it the same in nature as one of these others?

Glaucon: As the appetitive element, perhaps.

Socrates: But I once heard a story and I believe it. Leontius, the son of Aglaeon, was going up from the Piraeus along the outside of the North Wall when he saw some corpses with the public executioner nearby. He had an appetitive desire to look at them, but at the same time he was disgusted and turned himself away. For a while he struggled and put his hand over his eyes, but finally, mastered by his appetite, he opened his eyes wide and rushed toward 440 the corpses, saying: "Look for yourselves, you evil wretches; take your fill of the beautiful sight."[3]

Glaucon: I have also heard that story myself.

Socrates: Yet, surely, the story suggests that anger sometimes makes war against the appetites as one thing against another.

Glaucon: Yes, it does suggest that.

Socrates: And don't we often notice on other occasions that when appetite forces someone contrary to his rational calculation, he reproaches him- b self and feels anger at the thing in him that is doing the forcing; and just as if there were two warring factions, such a person's spirit becomes the ally of his reason? But spirit partnering the appetites to do what reason has decided should not be done—I do not imagine you would say that you had ever seen that, either in yourself or in anyone else.

Glaucon: No, by Zeus, I would not.

Socrates: And what about when a person thinks he is doing some injustice? Isn't it true that the nobler he is, the less capable he is of feeling angry if c he suffers hunger, cold, or the like at the hands of someone whom he believes to be inflicting this on him justly; and won't his spirit, as I say, refuse to be aroused?

Glaucon: It is true.

Socrates: But what about when a person believes he is being unjustly treated? Doesn't his spirit boil then, and grow harsh and fight as an ally of what he holds to be just? And even if it suffers hunger, cold,

---

3. A fragment of the comedy *Kapēlides* by Theopompus (410–370 BCE) tells us that a certain Leontinus (emended to Leontius because of Plato's reference here) was known for his love of boys as pale as corpses. So Leontinus' desire is probably sexual in origin,and for that reason appetitive. The North and South Walls enclosed an area connecting Athens to Piraeus.

and every imposition of that sort, doesn't it stand firm and win out over them, not ceasing its noble
d efforts until it achieves its purpose, or dies, or, like a dog being called to heel by a shepherd, is called back by the reason alongside it and becomes gentle?

GLAUCON: Your simile is perfect. And, in fact, we did put the auxiliaries in our city to be like obedient sheepdogs for the city's shepherdlike rulers.

SOCRATES: You have understood what I was trying to say very well. But have you also noticed something else about it?

e GLAUCON: What?

SOCRATES: That it is the opposite of what we recently thought about the kind of thing spirit is. You see, then we thought of it as something appetitive. But now, far from saying that, we say that in the faction that takes place in the soul, it is far more likely to take arms on the side of the rationally calculating element.

GLAUCON: Absolutely.

SOCRATES: Is it also different from this, then, or is it some kind of rationally calculating element, so that there are not three kinds of things in the soul, but two—the rationally calculating element and the appetitive one? Or rather, just as there were three classes in the city that held it together— the money-
441 making, the auxiliary, and the deliberative—is there also this third element in the soul, the spirited kind, which is the natural auxiliary of the rationally calculating element, if it has not been corrupted by bad upbringing?

GLAUCON: There must be a third.

SOCRATES: Yes, provided, at any rate, that it can be shown to be as distinct from the rationally calculating element as it was shown to be from the appetitive one.

GLAUCON: But it is not difficult to show that. After all, one can see it even in small children: they are full of spirit right from birth, but as for rational calculation, some of them seem to me never to possess
b it, while the masses do so quite late.

SOCRATES: Yes, by Zeus, you put that really well. Besides, one can see in animals that what you say is true. But, in addition to that, our earlier quotation from Homer also bears it out: "He struck his chest and spoke to his heart."[4] You see, in it Homer clearly presents what has calculated about better and worse,
rebuking what is irrationally angry as though it were c
something different.

GLAUCON: That's exactly right.

SOCRATES: Well, we have had a difficult swim through all that, and we are pretty much agreed that the same classes as are in the city are in the soul of each individual, and an equal number of them too.

GLAUCON: That's true.

SOCRATES: Then doesn't it already necessarily follow that the private individual is wise in the same way and because of the same element as is the city?

GLAUCON: Of course.

SOCRATES: And that the city is courageous in the
same way and because of the same element as is d
the private individual? And that in everything else that pertains to virtue, both are alike?

GLAUCON: Necessarily.

SOCRATES: And so, Glaucon, I take it we will also say that a man is just in exactly the same way as is a city.

GLAUCON: That too follows with absolute necessity.

SOCRATES: But we surely have not forgotten that the city was just because each of the three classes in it does its own work.

GLAUCON: I do not think we have.

SOCRATES: We should also bear in mind, then, that in the case of each one of us as well, the one in whom each of the elements does its own job will be
just and do his own job. e

GLAUCON: Certainly.

SOCRATES: Then isn't it appropriate for the rationally calculating element to rule, since it is really wise and exercises foresight on behalf of the whole soul; and for the spirited kind to obey it and be its ally?

GLAUCON: Of course.

SOCRATES: Now, as we were saying, isn't it a mixture of musical and physical training that makes these elements concordant, tightening and nurturing the
first with fine words and learning, while relaxing, 442
soothing, and making gentle the second by means of harmony and rhythm?

GLAUCON: Yes, exactly.

SOCRATES: And these two elements, having been trained in this way and having truly learned their own jobs and been educated, will be put in charge of the appetitive element—the largest one in each person's soul and, by nature, the most insatiable for money. They will watch over it to see that it does not

4. Homer, *Odyssey* 20.17.

get so filled with the so-called pleasures of the body that it becomes big and strong, and no longer does its
b own job but attempts to enslave and rule over the classes it is not fitted to rule, thereby overturning the whole life of anyone in whom it occurs.

Glaucon: Yes, indeed.

Socrates: And wouldn't these two elements also do the finest job of guarding the whole soul and body against external enemies—the one by deliberating, the other by fighting, following the ruler, and using its courage to carry out the things on which the former had decided?

Glaucon: Yes, they would.

Socrates: I imagine, then, that we call each individual courageous because of the latter part—that is, when the part of him that is spirited in kind preserves
c through pains and pleasures the pronouncements of reason about what should inspire terror and what should not.

Glaucon: That's right.

Socrates: But we call him wise, surely, because of the small part that rules in him, makes those pronouncements, and has within it the knowledge of what is advantageous—both for each part and for the whole, the community composed of all three.

Glaucon: Yes, indeed.

Socrates: What about temperance? Isn't he temperate because of the friendly and concordant relations between these same things: namely, when both the ruler and its two subjects share the belief that the rationally calculating element should rule, and do
d not engage in faction against it?

Glaucon: Temperance in a city and in a private individual is certainly nothing other than that.

Socrates: But surely, now, a person will be just because of what we have so often described and in the way we have so often described.

Glaucon: Necessarily.

Socrates: Well, then, has our justice become in any way blurred? Does it look like anything other than the very thing we found in the city?

Glaucon: It doesn't seem so to me, at least.

Socrates: We could make perfectly sure, if there is still anything in our souls that disputes this, by
e applying everyday tests to it.

Glaucon: Which ones?

Socrates: For example, if we had to come to an agreement about whether a man similar in nature and training to this city of ours had embezzled gold or silver he had accepted for deposit, who do you think would consider him more likely to have done so rather than men of a different sort? *443*

Glaucon: No one.

Socrates: And would he have anything to do with temple robberies, thefts, or betrayals of friends in private life or of cities in public life?

Glaucon: No, nothing.

Socrates: And he would be in no way untrustworthy when it came to promises or other agreements.

Glaucon: How could he be?

Socrates: And surely adultery, disrespect for parents, and neglect of the gods would be more characteristic of any other sort of person than of this one.

Glaucon: Of any other sort, indeed.

Socrates: And isn't the reason for all this the fact that each element within him does its own job where ruling and being ruled are concerned? *b*

Glaucon: Yes, that and nothing else.

Socrates: Are you still looking for justice to be something besides this power that produces men and cities of the sort we have described?

Glaucon: No, by Zeus, I am not.

Socrates: The dream we had has been completely fulfilled, then—I mean the suspicion we expressed that right from the beginning, when we were founding the city, we had, with the help of some god, chanced to hit upon the origin and pattern of justice. *c*

Glaucon: Absolutely.

Socrates: So, Glaucon, it really was—which is why it was so helpful—a sort of image of justice, this principle that it is right for someone who is, by nature, a shoemaker to practice shoemaking and nothing else, for a carpenter to practice carpentry, and the same for all the others.

Glaucon: Apparently so.

Socrates: And in truth, justice is, it seems, something of this sort. Yet it is not concerned with someone's doing his own job on the outside. On the contrary, it is concerned with what is inside; with himself, really, and the things that are his own. It means that he does not allow the elements in him *d*
each to do the job of some other, or the three sorts of elements in his soul to meddle with one another. Instead, he regulates well what is really his own, rules himself, puts himself in order, becomes his own friend, and harmonizes the three elements together,

just as if they were literally the three defining notes of an octave—lowest, highest, and middle—as well as any others that may be in between. He binds together all of these and, from having been many,
e becomes entirely one, temperate and harmonious. Then and only then should he turn to action, whether it is to do something concerning the acquisition of wealth or concerning the care of his body, or even something political, or concerning private contracts. In all these areas, he considers and calls just and fine the action that preserves this inner harmony and helps achieve it, and wisdom the *knowledge* that oversees such action; and he considers and calls unjust any action that destroys this har-
444 mony, and ignorance the *belief* that oversees it.

GLAUCON: That's absolutely true, Socrates.

SOCRATES: Well, then, if we claim to have found the just man, the just city, and what justice really is in them, we won't, I imagine, be thought to be telling a complete lie.

GLAUCON: No, by Zeus, we certainly won't.

SOCRATES: Shall we claim it, then?

GLAUCON: Yes, let's.

SOCRATES: So be it, then. I take it we must look for injustice next.

GLAUCON: Clearly.

SOCRATES: Mustn't it, in turn, be a kind of faction
b among those three—their meddling and interfering with one another's jobs; the rebellion of a part of the soul against the whole in order to rule in it inappropriately, since its nature suits it to be a slave of the ruling class. We will say something like that, I imagine, and that their disorder and wandering is injustice, licentiousness, cowardice, ignorance, and, in a word, the whole of vice.

GLAUCON: That is precisely what they are.

c SOCRATES: Doing unjust actions, then, and being unjust; and, the opposite, doing just ones—they all surely become clear at once, don't they, provided that both injustice and justice are also clear?

GLAUCON: What do you mean?

SOCRATES: That they do not differ in any way from healthy actions and unhealthy ones, that what the latter are in the body, they are in the soul.

GLAUCON: In what respect?

SOCRATES: Surely, healthy actions engender health, unhealthy ones disease.

GLAUCON: Yes.

SOCRATES: Well, doesn't doing just actions also
engender justice, unjust ones injustice? d

GLAUCON: Necessarily.

SOCRATES: But to produce health is to put the elements that are in the body in their natural relations of mastering and being mastered by one another; while to produce disease is to establish a relation of ruling and being ruled by one another that is contrary to nature.

GLAUCON: That's right.

SOCRATES: Doesn't it follow, then, that to produce justice is to establish the elements in the soul in a natural relation of mastering and being mastered by one another, while to produce injustice is to establish a relation of ruling and being ruled by one another that is contrary to nature?

GLAUCON: Absolutely.

SOCRATES: Virtue, then, so it seems, is a sort of health, a fine and good state of the soul; whereas vice
seems to be a shameful disease and weakness. e

GLAUCON: That's right.

SOCRATES: And don't fine practices lead to the possession of virtue, shameful ones to vice?

GLAUCON: Necessarily.

SOCRATES: So it now remains, it seems, for us to
consider whether it is more profitable to do just 445
actions, engage in fine practices, and be just, whether one is known to be so or not; or to do injustice and be unjust, provided that one does not have to pay the penalty and become a better person as a result of being punished.

GLAUCON: But, Socrates, that question seems to me, at least, to have become ridiculous, now that the two have been shown to be as we described. Life does not seem worth living when the body's natural constitution is ruined, not even if one has food and drink of every sort, all the money in the world, and every political office imaginable. So how—even if one
could do whatever one wished, except what would b
liberate one from vice and injustice and make one acquire justice and virtue—could it be worth living when the natural constitution of the very thing by which we live is ruined and in turmoil?

SOCRATES: Yes, it is ridiculous. All the same, since in fact we have reached a point from which we can see with the utmost clarity, as it were, that these things are so, we must not give up.

GLAUCON: That's absolutely the last thing we should do.

SOCRATES: Come up here, then, so that you can see how many kinds of vice there are—the ones, at
c any rate, that are worth seeing.

GLAUCON: I am following. Just tell me.

SOCRATES: Well, from the vantage point, so to speak, that we have reached in our argument, it seems to me that there is one kind of virtue and an unlimited number of kinds of vice, four of which are worth mentioning.

GLAUCON: What do you mean?

SOCRATES: It seems likely that there are as many types of soul as there are types of political constitution of a specific kind.

GLAUCON: How many is that?

SOCRATES: Five types of constitution, and five of soul. d

GLAUCON: Tell me what they are.

SOCRATES: I will tell you that one type would be the constitution we have been describing. However, there are two ways of referring to it: if one outstanding man emerges among the rulers, it is called a kingship; if more than one, it is called an aristocracy.

GLAUCON: That's true.

SOCRATES: Well, then, that is one of the kinds I had in mind. You see, whether many arise or just one, they won't change any of the laws of the city that are
worth mentioning, since they will have been brought e
up and educated in the way we described.

GLAUCON: No, they probably won't.

BOOK 5

Synopsis

THE DISCUSSION OF VIRTUE AND VICE that concluded Book 4 is interrupted by Polemarchus and the other interlocutors, all of whom want Socrates to explain a remark he made (423e–424a) about the guardians sharing their women and children. Socrates' lengthy response occupies the majority of the book. In it, he makes the revolutionary proposal that children should be brought up by the city rather than by their biological parents, and that men and women with the same natural abilities should receive the same education and training and do the same kind of work, including guarding and ruling. The smallest change that would transform an already existing city into the *kallipolis*, Socrates now argues, is for its kings or rulers to become philosophers or vice versa. The remainder of Book 5 is the beginning of Socrates' portrait of philosophers, which continues till the end of Book 7. It consists of a complex argument intended to show that only they can have access to forms, and that without such access knowledge is impossible (474c–480a).

SOCRATES: That, then, is the sort of city and constitu-
449 tion—and the sort of man—I call good and correct.
And if indeed this one is correct, all the others are bad and mistaken, both as city governments and as ways of organizing the souls of private individuals. The deficient ones fall into four kinds.

GLAUCON: What are they?

I was going to describe them in the order in which I thought they developed out of one another. But Pole-
marchus, who was sitting not far from Adeimantus, b
extended his hand, gripped the latter's cloak by the shoulder from above, drew Adeimantus toward him, and, leaning forward himself, said some things in his ear. We overheard nothing of what he said, other than this:

Shall we let it go, then, or what?

ADEIMANTUS: *(Now speaking aloud.)* Certainly not.

SOCRATES: What is it exactly you won't let go?

ADEIMANTUS: You!

SOCRATES: Why exactly? c

ADEIMANTUS: We think you are being lazy, that you are robbing us of a whole important section of the argument in order to avoid having to explain it. You thought we would not notice when you said—as though it were something inconsequential—that, as regards women and children, anyone could see that it will be a case of friends sharing everything in common.

SOCRATES: But isn't that correct, Adeimantus?

ADEIMANTUS: Yes, it is. But it is just like all the rest we have discussed; its correctness requires an explanation of how the sharing will be arranged, since there are many ways to bring it about. So, do not omit
d to tell us about the particular one you have in mind. We have all been waiting for a long time in the expectation that you would surely discuss how procreation will be handled, how the children that are born will be reared, and the whole subject of what you mean by sharing women and children. You see, we think that this makes a considerable difference—indeed, all the difference—to whether a constitution is correct or incorrect. So now that you are beginning to describe another constitution without having analyzed this matter adequately, we are resolved, as you overheard, not to let you go until you explain all this
450 just as you did the rest.

GLAUCON: Include me, too, as having a share in this vote.

And Thrasymachus said:

In fact, you can take it as the resolution of *all* of us, Socrates.

SOCRATES: What a thing to do, attacking me like that. You have started up a huge discussion about the constitution—it will be like starting from the beginning. I was delighted to think I had already completed its description by this time and was satisfied to have what I had said earlier be accepted as is. You do not realize what a swarm of arguments you are now stirring up by making this demand. It was because I
b could see it that I left the topic aside, to avoid all the trouble it would cause us.

THRASYMACHUS: What of it? Don't you think these people have come here now to listen to arguments, not to smelt ore?[1]

SOCRATES: Yes—within moderation, at least.

GLAUCON: But surely it is within moderation, Socrates, for people with any sense to listen to such arguments their whole life long. So never mind about us. Don't you get tired of explaining your views on what we asked about: namely, what the sharing of children and women will amount to for our c
guardians, and how the children will be brought up while they are still small. After all, the time between birth and the beginning of formal education seems to be the most troublesome period of all. So, try to tell us in what way it should be handled.

SOCRATES: It is not easy to explain, my happy fellow. It raises even more doubts than the topics we have discussed so far. One might, in fact, doubt whether what we proposed is possible, and, even if one granted that it is entirely so, one might still have doubts about whether it would be for the best. That, then, is why I was somewhat hesitant to bring it up: I was afraid, my dear comrade, that our argument might seem to be no more than wishful thinking. d

GLAUCON: Do not hesitate at all. You see, your audience won't be inconsiderate, or incredulous, or hostile.

SOCRATES: My very good fellow, are you saying that because you want to encourage me?

GLAUCON: I am.

SOCRATES: Well, you are having precisely the opposite effect. If I were confident that I was speaking with knowledge, your encouragement would be all very well. When one is among knowledgeable and beloved friends, and one is speaking what one knows to be the truth about the most important and most beloved things, one can feel both secure and confident. But to produce arguments when one is e
uncertain and searching, as I am doing, is a frightening thing and makes one feel insecure. I am not 451
afraid of being ridiculed—that would be childish, indeed—but I am afraid that if I fail to secure the truth, just where it is most important to do so, I will not only fall myself but drag my friends down as well. So I bow to Adrasteia, Glaucon, for what I am about to say. You see, I suspect that involuntary homicide is a lesser crime than misleading people about beautiful, good, and just conventions. That is a risk it would be better to run among enemies than among friends. So you have well and truly encouraged me. b

Glaucon laughed and said:

Well, Socrates, if we suffer from any false note you strike in the argument, we will release you, as we would in a homicide case, as guiltless and no deceiver of us. So you may speak with confidence.

---

1. A proverbial expression applied to those who neglect the task at hand for an uncertain profit.

SOCRATES: Well, it is true; the one who is acquitted in that situation is guiltless, so the law says. And if it is true there, it is probably true here, too.

GLAUCON: On these grounds, then, tell us.

SOCRATES: I will have to go back again, then, and say now what perhaps I should have said then in the
c proper place. But maybe it is all right, after having completed a male drama, to perform a female one next—especially when you demand it in this way. For people born and educated as we have described, then, there is, I believe, no correct way to acquire and employ children and women other than to follow the path on which we first set them. Surely, in our argument, we tried to establish the men as guard-dogs of their flock.

GLAUCON: Yes.

SOCRATES: Then let's proceed by giving correspon-
d ding rules for birth and rearing, and see whether they suit us or not.

GLAUCON: How?

SOCRATES: As follows. Do we think that the females of our guard-dogs should join in guarding precisely what the males guard, hunt with them, and share everything with them? Or do we think that they should stay indoors and look after the house,[2] on the grounds that they are incapable of doing this because they must bear and rear the puppies, while the males should work and have the entire care of the flock?

GLAUCON: They should share everything—except that we employ the females as we would weaker ani-
e mals, and the males as we would stronger ones.

SOCRATES: Is it possible, then, to employ an animal for the same tasks as another if you do not give it the same upbringing and education?

GLAUCON: No, it is not.

SOCRATES: Then if we employ women for the same tasks as men, they must also be taught the same things.

452 GLAUCON: Yes.

SOCRATES: Now, we gave the latter musical and physical training.

GLAUCON: Yes.

SOCRATES: So, we must also give these two crafts, as well as military training, to the women, and employ them in the same way.

GLAUCON: That seems reasonable, given what you say.

SOCRATES: But perhaps many of the things we are now saying, because they are contrary to custom, would seem ridiculous if they were put into practice.

GLAUCON: Indeed, they would.

SOCRATES: What do you see as the most ridiculous aspect of them? Isn't it obvious that it is the idea of the women exercising stripped in the palestras alongside the men?[3] And not just the young women, but the older ones too—like the old men we see in b
gymnasiums who, even though their bodies are wrinkled and not pleasant to look at, still love physical training.

GLAUCON: Yes, by Zeus, that *would* look really ridiculous, at least under present conditions.

SOCRATES: Yet, since we have started to discuss the matter, we must not be afraid of the various jokes that the wits will make both about this sort of change in musical and physical training and—even more so—about the change in the bearing of arms and the c
mounting of cavalry horses.

GLAUCON: You are right.

SOCRATES: But since we have started, we must move on to the rougher part of the law, and ask these wits not to do their own job, but to be serious. And we will remind them that it is not long since the *Greeks* thought it shameful and ridiculous (as many barbarians still do) for *men* to be seen stripped, and that when first the Cretans and then the Lacedaemonians began the gymnasiums, the wits of the time had the opportunity to make a comedy of it all. Or don't you think so? d

GLAUCON: I certainly do.

SOCRATES: But when it became clear, I take it, to those who employed these practices, that it was better to strip than to cover up all such parts, the laughter in the eyes faded away because of what the arguments had proved to be best. And this showed that it is a fool who finds anything ridiculous except what is bad, or tries to raise a laugh at the sight of anything except what is stupid or bad, or—putting it the other

2. Respectable, well-to-do women lived secluded lives in most Greek states: they were confined to the household and to domestic work and were largely excluded from the public spheres of culture, politics, and warfare.

3. A palestra was a wrestling school and training ground.

e way around—who takes seriously any standard of what is beautiful other than what is good.

GLAUCON: Absolutely.

SOCRATES: Well, then, shouldn't we first agree about whether our proposals are viable or not? And mustn't we give anyone who wishes to do so—whether it is someone who loves a joke or someone serious—the opportunity to dispute whether the fe-
453 male human does have the natural ability to share in *all* the tasks of the male sex, or in none at all, or in some but not others; and, in particular, whether this holds in the case of warfare? By making the best beginning in this way, wouldn't one also be likely to reach the best conclusion?

GLAUCON: Of course.

SOCRATES: So, would you like us to dispute with one another on their behalf, so that their side of the argument won't be attacked without defenders?

b GLAUCON: Why not?

SOCRATES: Then let's say this on their behalf: "Socrates and Glaucon, you do not need *other people* to dispute you. After all, you yourselves, when you were beginning to found your city, agreed that each one had to do the one job for which he was naturally suited."

GLAUCON: We did agree to that, I think. Of course we did.

SOCRATES: "Can it be, then, that a woman is not by nature very different from a man?"

GLAUCON: Of course she is different.

SOCRATES: "Then isn't it also appropriate to assign a different job to each of them, the one for which they are naturally suited?"

c GLAUCON: Certainly.

SOCRATES: "How is it, then, that you are not making a mistake now and contradicting yourselves, when you say that men and women must do the same jobs, seeing that they have natures that are most distinct?" Do you have any defense, you amazing fellow, against that attack?

GLAUCON: It is not easy to think of one on the spur of the moment. On the contrary, I shall ask—indeed, I am asking—you to explain the argument on our side as well, whatever it is.

SOCRATES: That, Glaucon, and many other problems of the same sort, which I foresaw long ago, was
d what I was afraid of when I hesitated to tackle the law concerning the possession and upbringing of women and children.

GLAUCON: No, by Zeus, it certainly does not seem to be a simple matter.

SOCRATES: No, it is not. But the fact is that whether one falls into a small diving pool or into the middle of the largest sea, one has to swim all the same.

GLAUCON: Of course.

SOCRATES: Then we must swim, too, and try to save ourselves from the sea of argument, hoping for a dolphin to pick us up, or for some other unlikely rescue.[4]

GLAUCON: It seems so. e

SOCRATES: Come on, then, let's see if we can find a way out. We have agreed, of course, that different natures must have different pursuits, and that the natures of a woman and a man are different. But we now say that those different natures must have the same pursuits. Isn't that the charge against us?

GLAUCON: Yes, exactly.

SOCRATES: What a noble power, Glaucon, the
craft of disputation possesses! 454

GLAUCON: Why is that?

SOCRATES: Because many people seem to me to fall into it even against their wills, and think they are engaging not in eristic, but in discussion. This happens because they are unable to examine what has been said by dividing it up into kinds. Instead, it is on the purely verbal level that they look for the contradiction in what has been said, and employ eristic, not dialectic, on one another.

GLAUCON: Yes, that certainly does happen to many people. But surely it is not pertinent to us at the moment, is it?

SOCRATES: It most certainly is. At any rate, we are
in danger of unconsciously dealing in disputation. b

GLAUCON: How?

SOCRATES: We are trying to establish the principle that different natures should not be assigned the same pursuits in a bold and eristic manner, *on the verbal level*. But we did not at all investigate what kind of natural difference or sameness we had in mind, or in what regard the distinction was pertinent, when we assigned different pursuits to different natures and the same ones to the same.

---

4. The story of Arion's rescue by the dolphin is told in Herodotus, *Histories* 1.23–4.

GLAUCON: No, we did not investigate that.

SOCRATES: And because we did not, it is open to
c us, apparently, to ask ourselves whether the natures of bald and long-haired men are the same or opposite. And, once we agree that they are opposite, it is open to us to forbid the long-haired ones to be shoemakers, if that is what the bald ones are to be, or vice versa.

GLAUCON: But that would be ridiculous.

SOCRATES: And is it ridiculous for any other reason than that we did not have in mind *every* kind of difference and sameness in nature, but were keeping our eyes only on the kind of difference and sameness that was pertinent to the pursuits themselves? We meant,
d for example, that a male and female whose souls are suited for medicine have the same nature. Or don't you think so?

GLAUCON: I do.

SOCRATES: But a male doctor and a male carpenter have different ones?

GLAUCON: Of course, completely different.

SOCRATES: In the case of both the male and the female sex, then, if one of them is shown to be different from the other with regard to a particular craft or pursuit, we will say that is the one who should be assigned to it. But if it is apparent that they differ in this respect alone, that the female bears the offspring while the male mounts the female, we will say it has not yet been demonstrated that a woman is different
e from a man with regard to what we are talking about, and we will continue to believe our guardians and their women should have the same pursuits.

GLAUCON: And rightly so.

SOCRATES: Next, won't we urge our opponent to
455 tell us the precise craft or pursuit, relevant to the organization of the city, for which a woman's nature and a man's are not the same but different?

GLAUCON: That would be a fair question, at least.

SOCRATES: Perhaps, then, this other person might say, just as you did a moment ago, that it is not easy to give an adequate answer on the spur of the moment, but that after reflection it would not be at all difficult.

GLAUCON: Yes, he might say that.

SOCRATES: Do you want us to ask the one who disputes things in this way, then, to follow us to see whether we can somehow show him that there is no
b pursuit relevant to the management of the city that is peculiar to women?

GLAUCON: Of course.

SOCRATES: Come on, then, we will say to him, give us an answer: "Is this what you meant by one person being naturally well suited for something and another naturally unsuited: that the one learns it easily, the other with difficulty; that the one, after a little instruction, can discover a lot for himself in the subject being studied, whereas the other, even if he gets a lot of instruction and attention, does not even retain what he was taught; that the bodily capacities of the one adequately serve his mind, while those of the other obstruct his? Are there any other factors than these, by which you distinguish a person who is c
naturally well suited for each pursuit from one who is not?"

GLAUCON: No one will be able to mention any others.

SOCRATES: Do you know of anything practiced by human beings, then, at which the male sex is not superior to the female in all those ways? Or must we make a long story of it by discussing weaving and the preparation of baked and boiled food—the very pursuits in which the female sex is thought to excel, and in which its defeat would expose it to the greatest ridicule of all? d

GLAUCON: It is true that the one sex shows greater mastery than the other in pretty much every area. Yet there are many women who are better than many men at many things. But on the whole, it is as you say.

SOCRATES: Then, my friend, there is no pursuit relevant to the management of the city that belongs to a woman because she is a woman, or to a man because he is a man; but the various natural capacities are distributed in a similar way between both creatures, and women can share by nature in every pursuit, and men in every one, though for the purposes of all of them women are weaker than men.[5] e

GLAUCON: Of course.

SOCRATES: So shall we assign all of them to men and none to women?

GLAUCON: How could we?

---

5. *Epi pasi:* The claim is not that no woman is stronger or better than any man in any such pursuit (which would contradict 455d), but that the physical weakness of women is a relevant factor in all of them.

SOCRATES: We could not. For we will say, I imagine, that one woman is suited for medicine, another not, and that one is naturally musical, another not.

GLAUCON: Of course.

SOCRATES: Won't one be suited for physical train-
456 ing or war, then, while another is unwarlike and not
a lover of physical training?

GLAUCON: I suppose so.

SOCRATES: And one a philosopher (lover of wisdom), another a "misosopher" (hater of wisdom)? And one spirited, another spiritless?

GLAUCON: That too.

SOCRATES: So there is also a woman who is suited to be a guardian, and one who is not. Or wasn't that the sort of nature we selected for our male guardians, too?

GLAUCON: It certainly was.

SOCRATES: A woman and a man can have the same nature, then, relevant to guarding the city—except to the extent that she is weaker and he is stronger.

GLAUCON: Apparently so.

SOCRATES: Women of that sort, then, must be
selected to live and guard with men of the same sort,
b since they are competent to do so and are akin to the
men by nature.

GLAUCON: Of course.

SOCRATES: And mustn't we assign the same pursuits to the same natures?

GLAUCON: Yes, the same ones.

SOCRATES: We have come around, then, to what we said before, and we are agreed that it is not against nature to assign musical and physical training to the female guardians.

GLAUCON: Absolutely.

SOCRATES: So, we are not legislating impossibilities or mere fantasies, at any rate, since the law we
were proposing is in accord with nature. Rather, it is
c the contrary laws that we have now that turn out to be
more contrary to nature, it seems.

GLAUCON: It does seem that way.

SOCRATES: Now, wasn't our inquiry about whether our proposals were both viable and best?

GLAUCON: Yes, it was.

SOCRATES: And that they are in fact viable has been agreed, hasn't it?

GLAUCON: Yes.

SOCRATES: So, we must next come to an agreement about whether they are for the best?

GLAUCON: Clearly.

SOCRATES: Now, as regards producing a woman
who is equipped for guardianship, we won't have one
sort of education that will produce our guardian
men, will we, and another our women—especially
not when it will have the same nature to work on in
both cases? d

GLAUCON: No, we won't.

SOCRATES: What is your belief about this, then?

GLAUCON: What?

SOCRATES: The notion that one man is better or worse than another—or do you think they are all alike?

GLAUCON: Not at all.

SOCRATES: In the city we are founding, who do you think will turn out to be better men: our guardians, who get the education we have described, or the shoemakers, who are educated in shoemaking?

GLAUCON: What a ridiculous question!

SOCRATES: I realize that. Aren't the guardians the
best of the citizens? e

GLAUCON: By far.

SOCRATES: And what about the female guardians? Won't they be the best of the women?

GLAUCON: Yes, they are by far the best, too.

SOCRATES: Is there anything better for a city than that the best possible men and women should come to exist in it?

GLAUCON: No, there is not.

SOCRATES: And that is what musical and physical
training, employed as we have described, will
achieve? 457

GLAUCON: Of course.

SOCRATES: Then the law we were proposing was not only possible, but also best for a city?

GLAUCON: Yes.

SOCRATES: Then the female guardians must strip,
clothing themselves in virtue instead of cloaks. They
must share in warfare, and whatever else guarding the city involves, and do nothing else. But within
these areas, the women must be assigned lighter
tasks than the men, because of the weakness of their
sex. And the man who laughs at the sight of women
stripped for physical training, when their stripping is
for the best, is "plucking the unripe fruit of laughter's b
wisdom," and knows nothing, it seems, about what
he is laughing at or what he is doing. For it is, and

always will be, the finest saying that what is beneficial is beautiful; what is harmful ugly.

Glaucon: Absolutely.

Socrates: May we claim, then, that we are avoiding one wave, as it were, in our discussion of the law about women, so that we are not altogether swept away when we declare that our male and female guardians must share all their pursuits, and that our
c argument is somehow self-consistent when it states that this is both viable and beneficial?

Glaucon: It is certainly no small wave that you are avoiding.

Socrates: You won't think it is so big when you see the next one.

Glaucon: I won't see it unless you tell me about it.

Socrates: The law that is consistent with that one, and with the others that preceded it, is this, I take it.

Glaucon: What?

Socrates: That all these women should be shared among all the men, that no individual woman and
d man should live together, and that the children, too, should be shared, with no parent knowing its own offspring, and no child its parent.

Glaucon: That wave *is* far bigger and more dubitable than the other, both as regards its viability and its benefit.

Socrates: As far as its benefit is concerned, at least, I do not think anyone would argue that the sharing of women and children is not the greatest good, if indeed it is viable. But I imagine there would be a lot of dispute about whether or not it is viable.

e Glaucon: No, *both* could very well be disputed.

Socrates: You mean I will have to face a coalition of arguments. I thought I had at least escaped one of them—namely, whether you thought the proposal was beneficial—and that I would just be left with the argument about whether it is viable or not.

Glaucon: Well, you did not escape unnoticed. So you will have to give an argument for both.

Socrates: I must pay the penalty. But do me this favor: let me take a holiday and act like those lazy
458 people who make a banquet for themselves of their own thoughts when they are walking alone. People like that, as you know, do not bother to find out how any of their appetites might actually be fulfilled, so as to avoid the trouble of deliberating about what is possible and what is not. They assume that what they want is available, and then proceed to arrange all the rest, taking pleasure in going through everything they will do when they get it—thus making their already lazy souls even lazier. Well, I, too, am succumbing to
this weakness at the moment and want to postpone b
consideration of the viability of our proposals until later. I will assume now that they are viable, if you will permit me to do so, and examine how the rulers will arrange them when they come to pass. And I will try to show that, if they were put into practice, they would be the most beneficial arrangements of all, both for the city and for its guardians. These are the things I will try to examine with you first, leaving the others for later—if indeed you will permit this.

Glaucon: You have my permission; so proceed with the examination.

Socrates: Well, then, I imagine that if indeed our rulers, and likewise their auxiliaries, are worthy of
their names, the latter will be prepared to carry out c
orders, and the former to give orders, obeying our laws in some cases and imitating them in the others that we leave to their discretion.

Glaucon: Probably so.

Socrates: Now, you are their lawgiver, and in just the way you selected these men, you will select as the women to hand over to them those who have natures as similar to theirs as possible. And because they have shared dwellings and meals, and none of them has any private property of that sort, they will live
together; and through mixing together in the gymna- d
sia and in the rest of their daily life, they will be driven by innate necessity, I take it, to have sex with one another. Or don't you think I am talking about necessities here?

Glaucon: Not *geometric* necessities, certainly, but *erotic* ones; and they probably have a sharper capacity to persuade and attract most people.

Socrates: They do, indeed. But the next point, Glaucon, is that for them to have unregulated sexual intercourse with one another, or to do anything else of that sort, would not be a pious thing in a city of
happy people, and the rulers won't allow it. e

Glaucon: No, it would not be just.

Socrates: It is clear, then, that we will next have to make marriages as sacred as possible. And sacred marriages will be those that are most beneficial.

Glaucon: Absolutely.

Socrates: How, then, will the most beneficial
ones come about? Tell me this, Glaucon. I see you 459

have hunting dogs and quite a flock of noble birds at home.[6] Have you, by Zeus, noticed anything in particular about their "marriages" and breeding?

GLAUCON: Like what?

SOCRATES: In the first place, though they are all noble animals, aren't there some that are, or turn out to be, the very best?

GLAUCON: There are.

SOCRATES: Do you breed from them all to the same extent, then, or do you try hard to breed as far as possible from the best ones?

GLAUCON: From the best ones.

SOCRATES: And do you breed from the youngest, the
b oldest, or as far as possible from those in their prime?

GLAUCON: From those in their prime.

SOCRATES: And if they were not bred in this way, do you think that your race of birds and dogs would get much worse?

GLAUCON: I do.

SOCRATES: And what do you think about horses and other animals? Is the situation any different with them?

GLAUCON: It would be strange if it were.

SOCRATES: Good heavens, my dear comrade! Then our need for eminent rulers is quite desperate, if indeed the same also holds for the human race.

c GLAUCON: Well, it does hold of them. But so what?

SOCRATES: It follows that our rulers will then have to employ a great many drugs. You know that when people do not need drugs for their bodies, and they are prepared to follow a regimen, we regard even an inferior doctor as adequate. But when drugs are needed, we know that a much bolder doctor is required.

GLAUCON: That's true. But what is your point?

SOCRATES: This: it looks as though our rulers will have to employ a great many lies and deceptions for the benefit of those they rule. And you remember, I
d suppose, we said all such things were useful as a kind of drug.

GLAUCON: And we were correct.

SOCRATES: Well, in the case of marriages and procreation, its correctness is particularly evident.

GLAUCON: How so?

SOCRATES: It follows from our previous agreement that the best men should mate with the best women in as many cases as possible, while the opposite should hold of the worst men and women, and that the offspring of the former should be reared, but not that of the latter, if our flock is going to be an eminent one. And all this must occur without anyone e
knowing except the rulers—if, again, our herd of guardians is to remain as free from faction as possible.

GLAUCON: That's absolutely right.

SOCRATES: So then, we will have to establish by law certain festivals and sacrifices at which we will bring together brides and bridegrooms, and our poets must compose suitable hymns for the marriages that take place. We will leave the number of marriages for 460
the rulers to decide. That will enable them to keep the number of males as constant as possible, taking into account war, disease, and everything of that sort; so that the city will, as far as possible, become neither too big nor too small.

GLAUCON: That's right.

SOCRATES: I imagine that some sophisticated lotteries will have to be created, then, so that an inferior person of that sort will blame chance rather than the rulers at each mating time.

GLAUCON: Yes, indeed.

SOCRATES: And presumably, the young men who are good at war or at other things must—among b
other prizes and awards—be given a greater opportunity to have sex with the women, in order that a pretext may also be created at the same time for having as many children as possible fathered by such men.

GLAUCON: That's right.

SOCRATES: And then, as offspring are born, won't they be taken by the officials appointed for this purpose, whether these are men or women or both—for surely our offices are also open to both women and men.

GLAUCON: Yes.

SOCRATES: And I suppose they will take the offspring of good parents to the rearing pen and hand c
them over to special nurses who live in a separate part of the city. But those of inferior parents, or any deformed offspring of the others, they will hide in a secret and unknown place, as is fitting.[7]

GLAUCON: Yes, if indeed the race of guardians is going to remain pure.

---

6. Both hunting dogs and aviaries were common in rich Greek households.

7. Infanticide by exposure was commonly used in ancient Greece as a method of birth control.

SOCRATES: And won't these nurses also take care of the children's feeding by bringing the mothers to the rearing pen when their breasts are full, while devising every device to ensure that no mother will recognize her offspring? And won't they provide other women
d as wet nurses if the mothers themselves have insufficient milk—taking care, however, that the mothers breast-feed the children for only a moderate period of time, and assigning sleepless nights and similar burdens to the nurses and wet nurses?

GLAUCON: You are making childbearing a soft job for the guardians' women.

SOCRATES: Yes, properly so. But let's take up the next thing we proposed. We said, as you know, that offspring should be bred from parents who are in their prime.

GLAUCON: True.

SOCRATES: Do you agree that a woman's prime
e lasts, on average, for a period of twenty years and a man's for thirty?

GLAUCON: Which years are those?

SOCRATES: A woman should bear children for the city from the age of twenty to that of forty; whereas a man should beget them for the city from the time that he passes his peak as a runner until he reaches fifty-five.

GLAUCON: At any rate, that is the physical and
461 mental prime for both.

SOCRATES: Then if any male who is younger or older than that engages in reproduction for the community, we will say that his offense is neither pious nor just. For the child he fathers for the city, if it escapes discovery, will be begotten and born without the benefit of sacrifices, or of the prayers that priestesses, priests, and the entire city will offer at every marriage festival, asking that from good and beneficial parents ever better and more beneficial offspring
b should be produced. On the contrary, it will be born in darkness through a terrible act of lack of self-control.

GLAUCON: That's right.

SOCRATES: The same law will apply if a man who is still of breeding age has sex with a woman in her prime when the rulers have not mated them.

We will say that he is imposing an illegitimate, unauthorized, and unholy child on the city.

GLAUCON: That's absolutely right.

SOCRATES: But when women and men have passed breeding age, I imagine we will leave them free to have sex with whomever they wish—except that a man may not have sex with his daughter, mother, daughters' daughters, or mother's female ancestors, c
or a woman with her son and his descendants or her father and his ancestors. And we will permit all that only after telling them to be very careful not to let even a single fetus see the light of day, if one should happen to be conceived; but if one does force its way out, they must dispose of it on the understanding that no nurture is available for such a child.

GLAUCON: All that sounds reasonable. But how will they recognize one another's fathers, daughters, and the others you mentioned? d

SOCRATES: They won't. Instead, from the day a man becomes a bridegroom, he will call all offspring born in the tenth month afterward (and in the seventh, of course) his sons, if they are male, and his daughters, if they are female; and they will call him father. Similarly, he will call their children his grandchildren, and they, in turn, will call the group to which he belongs grandfathers and grandmothers. And those who were born at the same time as their mothers and fathers were breeding, they will call their brothers and sisters. Thus, as we were saying just now, they will avoid sexual relations with each e
other. However, the law *will* allow brothers and sisters to have sex with one another, if the lottery works out that way and the Pythia approves.

OMITTING SOCRATES' DESCRIPTION of some aspects of the *kallipolis*, we take up the discussion at the point where Glaucon again raises the question of how such a city can come to exist.

GLAUCON: But, Socrates, I think that if you are allowed to go on talking about this sort of thing, you will never remember the topic you set aside in order to say all this—namely, whether it is possible for this constitution to come into existence, and how it could ever do so. I agree that *if* it came into existence, everything would be lovely for the city that had it. I will even add some advantages that you have left out: they would fight excellently against their enemies because they would be least likely to desert each other. After all, they recognize each other as 471d
brothers, fathers, and sons, and call each other by those names. And if the women, too, joined in their

campaigns, either stationed in the same ranks or in the rear, either to strike terror in the enemy or to provide support should the need ever arise, I know that this would make them quite unbeatable. And I also see all the good things they would have at home that you have omitted. Take it for granted that I agree that
e all these benefits, as well as innumerable others,
would result, *if* this constitution came into existence, and say no more about it. Instead, let's now try to convince ourselves of just this: that it is possible and how it is possible, and let's leave the rest aside.

SOCRATES: All of a sudden, you have practically
472 assaulted my argument and lost all sympathy for my
holding back. Perhaps you do not realize that just as I have barely escaped from the first two waves of objections, you are now bringing the biggest and most difficult of the three down upon me. When you see and hear it, you will have complete sympathy and recognize that I had good reason after all for hesitating and for being afraid to state and try to examine so paradoxical an argument.

GLAUCON: The more you talk like that, the less we will let you get away without explaining how this con-
b stitution could come into existence. So explain it,
and do not delay any further.

SOCRATES: The first thing to recall, then, is that it was our inquiry into the nature of justice and injustice that brought us to this point.

GLAUCON: True. But what of it?

SOCRATES: Oh, nothing. However, if we discover the nature of justice, should we also expect the just man not to differ from justice itself in any way, but, on the contrary, to have entirely the same nature it does? Or will we be satisfied if he approximates as
c closely as possible to it and partakes in it far more
than anyone else?

GLAUCON: Yes, we will be satisfied with that.

SOCRATES: So, it was in order to have a model that we were inquiring into the nature of justice itself and of the completely just man, supposing he could exist, and what he would be like if he did; and similarly with injustice and the most unjust man. We thought that by seeing how they seemed to us to stand with regard to happiness and its opposite, we would also be compelled to agree about ourselves as well: that the one who was most like them would have a fate
d most like theirs. But we were not doing this in order
to demonstrate that it is possible for these men to exist.

GLAUCON: That's true.

SOCRATES: Do you think, then, that someone would be any less good a painter if he painted a model of what the most beautiful human being would be like, and rendered everything in the picture perfectly well, but could not demonstrate that such a man could actually exist?

GLAUCON: No, by Zeus, I do not.

SOCRATES: What about our own case, then? Weren't we trying, as we put it, to produce a model
in our discussion of a good city? e

GLAUCON: Certainly.

SOCRATES: So, do you think that our discussion will be any less satisfactory if we cannot demonstrate that it is possible to found a city that is the same as the one we described in speech?

GLAUCON: Not at all.

SOCRATES: Then that is the truth of the matter. But if, in order to please you, we must do our best to demonstrate how, and under what condition, this would be most possible, you must again grant me the same points for the purposes of that demonstration.

GLAUCON: Which ones?

SOCRATES: Is it possible for anything to be carried
out exactly as described in speech, or is it natural for 473
practice to have less of a grasp of truth than speech does, even if some people do not think so? Do you agree with this or not?

GLAUCON: I do.

SOCRATES: Then do not compel me to demonstrate it as coming about in practice exactly as we have described it in speech. Rather, if we are able to discover how a city that most closely approximates to what we have described could be founded, you must admit that we have discovered how all you have
prescribed could come about. Or wouldn't you be b
satisfied with that? *I* certainly would.

GLAUCON: Me, too.

SOCRATES: Then next, it seems, we should try to discover and show what is badly done in cities nowadays that prevents them from being managed our way, and what the smallest change would be that would enable a city to arrive at our sort of constitution—preferably one change; otherwise, two; otherwise, the fewest in number and the least extensive in effect.

GLAUCON: Absolutely. c

SOCRATES: Well, there is one change we could point to that I think would accomplish this. It certainly is not small or easy, but it *is* possible.

GLAUCON: What is it?

SOCRATES: I am now about to confront what we likened to the greatest wave. Yet, it must be stated, even if it is going to drown me in a wave of outright ridicule and contempt, as it were. So listen to what I am about to say.

GLAUCON: Say it.

SOCRATES: Until philosophers rule as kings in their cities, or those who are nowadays called kings and leading men become genuine and adequate philoso-
d phers so that political power and philosophy become thoroughly blended together, while the numerous natures that now pursue either one exclusively are forcibly prevented from doing so, cities will have no rest from evils, my dear Glaucon, nor, I think, will the human race. And until that happens, the same constitution we have now described in our discussion
e will never be born to the extent that it can, or see the light of the sun. It is this claim that has made me hesitate to speak for so long. I saw how very unbelievable it would sound, since it is difficult to accept that there can be no happiness, either public or private, in any other way.

GLAUCON: Socrates, what a speech, what an argument you have let burst with! But now that you have uttered it, you must expect that a great many people—and not undistinguished ones either—will immediately throw off their cloaks and, stripped for
474 action, snatch any available weapon and make a headlong rush at you, determined to do terrible things to you. So, if you do not defend yourself by argument and escape, you really will pay the penalty of general derision.

SOCRATES: But aren't *you* the one who is responsible for this happening to me?

GLAUCON: And I was right to do it. Still, I won't desert you. On the contrary, I will defend you in any way I can. And what I can do is provide good will and encouragement, and maybe give you more careful answers to your questions than someone else. So, with the promise of this sort of assistance,
b try to demonstrate to the unbelievers that things are as you claim.

SOCRATES: I will have to, especially when you agree to be so great an ally!

If we are going to escape from the people you mention, I think we need to define for them who the philosophers are that we dare to say should rule; so that once that is clear, one can defend oneself by showing that some people are fitted by nature to engage in philosophy *and* to take the lead in a city, *c*
while there are others who should not engage in it, but should follow a leader.

GLAUCON: This would be a good time to define them.

SOCRATES: Come on, then, follow me on the path I am about to take, to see if it somehow leads to an adequate explanation.

GLAUCON: Lead on.

SOCRATES: Do I have to remind you, or do you recall, that when we say someone loves something, if the description is correct, it must be clear not just that he loves some part of it but not another; but, on the contrary, that he cherishes the whole of it?

GLAUCON: You will have to remind me, it seems. I do not recall the point at all. *d*

SOCRATES: I did not expect you to give that response, Glaucon. A passionate man should not forget that *all* boys in the bloom of youth somehow manage to sting and arouse a passionate lover of boys, and seem to merit his attention and passionate devotion. Isn't that the way you people behave to beautiful boys? One, because he is snub-nosed, you will praise as "cute"; another who is hook-nosed you will say is "regal"; while the one in the middle you say is "well proportioned." Dark ones look "manly," and *e*
pale ones are "children of the gods." As for the "honey-colored," do you think that this very term is anything but the euphemistic coinage of a lover who found it easy to tolerate a sallow complexion, provided it was accompanied by the bloom of youth? In a word, you people find any excuse, and use any expression, to avoid rejecting anyone whose flower is *475*
in full bloom.

GLAUCON: If you insist on taking *me* as your example of what passionate men do, I will go along with you . . . for the sake of argument!

SOCRATES: What about lovers of wine? Don't you observe them behaving in just the same way? Don't they find any excuse to indulge their passionate devotion to wine of any sort?

GLAUCON: They do, indeed.

SOCRATES: And you also observe, I imagine, that if honor-lovers cannot become generals, they serve as lieutenants, and if they cannot be honored by important people and dignitaries, they are satisfied with being honored by insignificant and inferior ones, *b* since it is honor as a whole of which they are desirers.

GLAUCON: Exactly.

SOCRATES: Then do you affirm this or not? When we say that someone has an appetite for something, are we to say that he has an appetite for everything of that kind, or for one part of it but not another?

GLAUCON: Everything.

SOCRATES: Then in the case of the philosopher, too, won't we say that he has an appetite for *wisdom*—not for one part and not another, but for all of it?

GLAUCON: True.

SOCRATES: So, if someone is choosy about what he learns, especially if he is young and does not have a *c* rational grasp of what is useful and what is not, we won't say that he is a lover of learning or a philosopher—any more than we would say that someone who is choosy about his food is famished, or has an appetite for food, or is a lover of food rather than a picky eater.

GLAUCON: And we would be right not to say it.

SOCRATES: But someone who is ready and willing to taste every kind of learning, who turns gladly to learning and is insatiable for it, *he* is the one we would be justified in calling a philosopher. Isn't that so?

GLAUCON: In that case, many strange people will *d* be philosophers! I mean, all the lovers of seeing are what they are, I imagine, because they take pleasure in learning things. And the lovers of listening are very strange people to include as philosophers: they would never willingly attend a serious discussion or spend their time that way; yet, just as if their ears were under contract to listen to every chorus, they run around to all the Dionysiac festivals, whether in cities or villages, and never miss one. Are we to say that these people—and others who are students of similar *e* things or of petty crafts—are philosophers?

SOCRATES: Not at all, but they are *like* philosophers.

GLAUCON: Who do you think, then, are the true ones?

SOCRATES: The lovers of seeing the truth.

GLAUCON: That, too, is no doubt correct, but what exactly do you mean by it?

SOCRATES: It would not be easy to explain to someone else. But you, I imagine, will agree to the following.

GLAUCON: What?

SOCRATES: That since beautiful is the opposite of ugly, they are two things.

GLAUCON: Of course. *476*

SOCRATES: And since they are two things, each of them is also one?

GLAUCON: That's true too.

SOCRATES: And the same argument applies, then, to just and unjust, good and bad, and all the forms: each of them is itself one thing, but because they appear all over the place in partnership with actions and bodies, and with one another, each of them appears to be many things.

GLAUCON: That's right.

SOCRATES: Well, then, that is the basis of the distinction I draw: on one side are the lovers of seeing, the lovers of crafts, and the practical people you mentioned a moment ago; on the other, those we are arguing about, the only ones it is correct to *b* call philosophers.

GLAUCON: How do you mean?

SOCRATES: The lovers of listening and seeing are passionately devoted to beautiful sounds, colors, shapes, and everything fashioned out of such things. But their thought is unable to see the nature of the beautiful itself or to be passionately devoted to it.

GLAUCON: That's certainly true.

SOCRATES: On the other hand, won't those who *are* able to approach the beautiful itself, and see it by itself, be rare?

GLAUCON: Very. *c*

SOCRATES: What about someone who believes in beautiful things but does not believe in the beautiful itself, and would not be able to follow anyone who tried to lead him to the knowledge of it? Do you think he is living in a dream, or is he awake? Just consider. Isn't it dreaming to think—whether asleep or awake—that a likeness is not a likeness, but rather the thing itself that it is like?

GLAUCON: I certainly think that someone who does that is dreaming.

SOCRATES: But what about someone who, to take the opposite case, does believe in the beautiful itself, is able to observe both it and the things that participate in it, and does not think that the participants are *d* it, or that it is the participants—do you think he is living in a dream or is awake?

GLAUCON: He is very much awake.

Socrates: So, because this person knows these things, we would be right to describe his thought as knowledge; but the other's we would be right to describe as belief, because he believes what he does?

Glaucon: Certainly.

Socrates: What if the person we describe as believing but not knowing is angry with us and disputes the truth of what we say? Will we have any way
e of soothing and gently persuading him, while disguising the fact that he is not in a healthy state of mind?

Glaucon: We certainly need one, at any rate.

Socrates: Come on, then, consider what we will say to him. Or—once we have told him that nobody envies him any knowledge he may have— that, on the contrary, we would be delighted to discover that he knows something—do you want us to question him as follows? "Tell us this: does someone who knows know something or nothing?" You answer for him.

Glaucon: I will answer that he knows something.

Socrates: Something that is or something that is not?

Glaucon: That is. How could something that is
477 not be known?

Socrates: We are adequately assured of this, then, and would remain so, no matter how many ways we examined it: what completely is, is completely an object of knowledge; and what in no way is, is not an object of knowledge at all?

Glaucon: Most adequately.

Socrates: Good. In that case, then, if anything is such as to be and also not to be, wouldn't it lie in between what purely is and what in no way is?

Glaucon: Yes, in between them.

Socrates: Then, since knowledge deals with what is, ignorance must deal with what is not, while we must look in between knowledge and ignorance for what deals with what lies in between, if there *is* any-
b thing of that sort.

Glaucon: Yes.

Socrates: So, then, do we think there is such a thing as belief?

Glaucon: Of course.

Socrates: Is it a different power from knowledge, or the same?

Glaucon: A different one.

Socrates: So, belief has been assigned to deal with one thing, then, and knowledge with another, depending on what power each has.

Glaucon: Right.

Socrates: Now, doesn't knowledge naturally deal with what is, to know how what is is? But first I think we had better go through the following.

Glaucon: What?

Socrates: We think powers are a type of thing that c
enables us—or anything else that has an ability—to do whatever we are able to do. Sight and hearing are examples of what I mean by powers, if you understand the kind of thing I am trying to describe.

Glaucon: Yes, I do.

Socrates: Listen, then, to what I think about them. A power has no color for me to see, nor a shape, nor any feature of the sort that many other things have, and that I can consider in order to distinguish them for myself as different from one another. In the case of a power, I can consider only
what it deals with and what it does, and it is on that d
basis that I come to call each the power it is: those assigned to deal with the same things and do the same, I call the same; those that deal with different things and do different things, I call different. What about you? What do you do?

Glaucon: The same.

Socrates: Going back, then, to where we left off, my very good fellow: do you think knowledge is itself a power? Or to what type would you assign it?

Glaucon: To that one. It is the most effective power of all.

Socrates: What about belief? Shall we include it
as a power or assign it to a different kind? e

Glaucon: Not at all. Belief is nothing other than the power that enables us to believe.

Socrates: But a moment ago you agreed that knowledge and belief are not the same.

Glaucon: How could anyone with any sense think a fallible thing is the same as an infallible one?

Socrates: Fine. Then clearly we agree that belief
is different from knowledge. 478

Glaucon: Yes, it is different.

Socrates: Each of them, then, since it has a different power, deals by nature with something different?

Glaucon: Necessarily.

Socrates: Surely knowledge deals with what is, to know what is as it is?

Glaucon: Yes.

Socrates: Whereas belief, we say, believes?

Glaucon: Yes.

Socrates: The very same thing that knowledge knows? Can the object of knowledge and the object of belief be the same? Or is that impossible?

Glaucon: It is impossible, given what we have agreed. If different powers by nature deal with different things, and both opinion and knowledge are powers but, as we claim, different ones, it follows
b from these that the object of knowledge and the object of belief cannot be the same.

Socrates: Then if what is is the object of knowledge, mustn't the object of belief be something other than what is?

Glaucon: Yes, it must be something different.

Socrates: Does belief, then, believe what is not? Or is it impossible even to believe what is not? Consider this: doesn't a believer take his belief to deal with something? Or is it possible to believe, yet to believe nothing?

Glaucon: No, it is impossible.

Socrates: In fact, there is some single thing that a believer believes?

Glaucon: Yes.

Socrates: But surely what is not is most correctly
c characterized not as a single thing, but as nothing?

Glaucon: Of course.

Socrates: But we had to assign ignorance to what is not and knowledge to what is?

Glaucon: Correct.

Socrates: So belief neither believes what is nor what is not?

Glaucon: No, it does not.

Socrates: Then belief cannot be either ignorance or knowledge?

Glaucon: Apparently not.

Socrates: Well, then, does it lie beyond these two, surpassing knowledge in clarity or ignorance in opacity?

Glaucon: No, it does neither.

Socrates: Then does belief seem to you to be more opaque than knowledge but clearer than ignorance?

Glaucon: Very much so.

Socrates: It lies within the boundaries deter-
d mined by them?

Glaucon: Yes.

Socrates: So belief will lie in between the two?

Glaucon: Absolutely.

Socrates: Now, didn't we say earlier that if something turned out both to be and not to be at the same time, it would lie in between what purely is and what in every way is not, and that neither knowledge nor ignorance would deal with it; but whatever it was again that turned out to lie in between ignorance and knowledge would?

Glaucon: Correct.

Socrates: And now, what we are calling belief has turned out to lie in between them?

Glaucon: It has.

Socrates: Apparently, then, it remains for us to
find what partakes in both being and not being, and e
cannot correctly be called purely one or the other, so that if we find it, we can justifiably call it the object of belief, thereby assigning extremes to extremes and in-betweens to in-betweens. Isn't that so?

Glaucon: It is.

Socrates: Now that all that has been established, I want him to tell me this—the excellent fellow who believes that there is no beautiful itself, no form of
beauty itself that remains always the same in all 479
respects, but who does believe that there are many beautiful things—I mean, that lover of seeing who cannot bear to hear anyone say that the beautiful is one thing, or the just, or any of the rest—I want him to answer this question: "My very good fellow," we will say, "of all the many beautiful things, is there one that won't also seem ugly? Or any just one that won't seem unjust? Or any pious one that won't seem impious?"

Glaucon: There is not. On the contrary, it is inevitable that they would somehow seem both beautiful and ugly; and the same with the other things you b
asked about.

Socrates: What about the many things that are doubles? Do they seem to be any the less halves than doubles?

Glaucon: No.

Socrates: And again, will things that we say are big, small, light, or heavy be any more what we say they are than they will be the opposite?

Glaucon: No, each of them is always both.

Socrates: Then is each of the many things any more what one says it is than it is not what one says it is?

Glaucon: No, they are like those puzzles one hears at parties, or the children's riddle about the *c* eunuch who threw something at a bat—the one about what he threw at it and what it was in.[8] For these things, too, are ambiguous, and one cannot understand them as fixedly being or fixedly not being, or as both, or as neither.

SOCRATES: Do you know what to do with them, then, or anywhere better to put them than in between being and not being? Surely they cannot be more opaque than what is not, by not-being more than
d it; nor clearer than what is, by *being* more than it.

GLAUCON: That's absolutely true.

SOCRATES: So, we have now discovered, it seems, that the majority of people's many conventional views about beauty and the rest are somehow rolling around between what is not and what purely is.

GLAUCON: We have.

SOCRATES: And we agreed earlier that if anything turned out to be of that sort, it would have to be called an object of belief, not an object of knowledge—a wandering, in-between object grasped by the in-between power.

GLAUCON: We did.

SOCRATES: As for those, then, who look at many beautiful things but do not see the beautiful itself,
e and are incapable of following another who would lead them to it; or many just things but not the just itself, and similarly with all the rest—these people, we will say, have beliefs about all these things, but have no knowledge of what their beliefs are about.

GLAUCON: That is what we would have to say.

SOCRATES: On the other hand, what about those who in each case look at the things themselves that are always the same in every respect? Won't we say that they have knowledge, not mere belief?

GLAUCON: Once again, we would have to.

SOCRATES: Shall we say, then, that these people are passionately devoted to and love the things with which knowledge deals, as the others are devoted to
and love the things with which belief deals? We have *480*
not forgotten, have we, that the latter love and look at beautiful sounds, colors, and things of that sort, but cannot even bear the idea that the beautiful itself is a thing that is?

GLAUCON: No, we have not.

SOCRATES: Will we be striking a false note, then, if we call such people "philodoxers" (lovers of belief) rather than "philosophers" (lovers of wisdom or knowledge)? Will they be very angry with us if we call them that?

GLAUCON: Not if they take my advice. It is not in accord with divine law to be angry with the truth.

SOCRATES: So, those who in each case are passionately devoted to the thing itself are the ones we must call, not "philodoxers," but "philosophers"?

GLAUCON: Absolutely.

BOOK 6

Synopsis

REAL PHILOSOPHERS ARE contrasted with those popularly so called. The former must master the most important subjects (503e), the ones that lead to knowledge of the form of the good (504e–505b). Socrates cannot explain directly what this is, but in the sun and line analogies he tries to give an indirect account of it (507a–511e). We take up the narration as Socrates begins to describe the philosopher-kings that the *kallipolis* will educate and establish as its rulers.

SOCRATES: There is not one city today with a consti- *497b*
tution worthy of the philosophic nature. That is precisely why it is perverted and altered. It is like foreign seed sown in alien ground: it tends to be overpowered

8. The riddle seems to have been this: a man who is not a man saw and did not see a bird that was not a bird in a tree (*xulon*) that was not a tree; he hit (*ballein*) and did not hit it with a stone that was not a stone. The answer is that a eunuch with bad eyesight saw a bat on a rafter, threw a pumice stone at it, and missed. For "he saw a bird" is ambiguous between "he saw what was actually a bird" and "he saw what he took to be a bird," *xulon* means both "tree" and "rafter" or "roof tree," and *ballein* means both "to throw" and "to hit." The rest is obvious.

and to fade away into the native species. Similarly, the philosophic species does not maintain its own power at present, but declines into a different character. But if it were to find the best constitution, as it is itself the best, it would be clear that it is really
c divine and that other natures and pursuits are merely human. Obviously, you are going to ask next what that constitution is.

ADEIMANTUS: You are wrong there. You see, I was not going to ask that, but whether it was the constitution we described when we were founding our city or a different one.

SOCRATES: In all other respects, it is that one. But we said even then that there must always be some people in the city who have a rational account of the constitution, the same one that guided you, the law-
d giver, when you made the laws.

ADEIMANTUS: Yes, we did say that.

SOCRATES: But we did not explain it clearly enough, for fear of what our own objections have made clear: namely, that the demonstration of it would be long and difficult. Indeed, even what remains is not the easiest of all things to discuss.

ADEIMANTUS: What is that?

SOCRATES: How a city can engage in philosophy without being destroyed. You see, all great things are prone to fall and, as the saying goes, beautiful things are really difficult.

ADEIMANTUS: All the same, the demonstration
e won't be complete until this has been cleared up.

SOCRATES: If anything prevents that, it won't be lack of willingness, but lack of ability. At any rate, you will see how passionate *I* am. Look now, in fact, at how passionately and recklessly I am going to argue that a city should practice philosophy in the opposite way to the present one.

ADEIMANTUS: How?

SOCRATES: At present, those who take it up at all do so as young men, just out of childhood, who have yet to take up household management and moneymak-
498 ing. Then, just when they reach the most difficult part they abandon it and are regarded as the most fully trained philosophers. By the most difficult part, I mean the one concerned with arguments. In later life, if others are engaged in it and they are invited and deign to listen to them, they think they have done a lot, since they think this should only be a sideline. And, with a few exceptions, by the time they reach old age they are more thoroughly extinguished than the sun of Heraclitus, since they are never rekindled.[1] *b*

ADEIMANTUS: What should they do instead?

SOCRATES: Entirely the opposite. As young men and children, they should occupy themselves with an education and philosophy suitable to the young. Their bodies are blooming and growing into manhood at this time, and they should take very good care of them, so as to acquire a helper for philosophy. But as they grow older and their soul begins to reach maturity, they should make its exercises more rigorous. Then, when their strength begins to fail and they have retired from politics and military service, they should graze freely in the pastures of philosophy and do nothing else, except as a sideline—I *c*
mean those who are going to live happily and, when the end comes, crown the life they have lived with a fitting providence in that other place.

ADEIMANTUS: You seem to be arguing with real passion, Socrates. But I am sure that most of your hearers will oppose you with even greater passion and won't be convinced in the least—beginning with Thrasymachus.

SOCRATES: Please do not try to raise a quarrel between me and Thrasymachus just as we have become friends—not that we were enemies before. You see, we won't relax our efforts until we convince *d*
him and the others—or at least do something that may benefit them in a later incarnation when, reborn, they happen upon these arguments again.

ADEIMANTUS: You are talking about the short term, I see!

SOCRATES: It is certainly nothing compared to the whole of time! However, it is no wonder that the masses are not convinced by our arguments. I mean, they have never seen a *man* that matched our *plan*—though they have more often seen words purposely chosen to rhyme with one another than just happen- *e*
ing to do so as in the present case. But a man who, as far as possible, matched and rhymed with virtue in word and deed, and wielded dynastic power in a city of the same type—that is something they have never seen even once. Or do you think they have? 499

ADEIMANTUS: No, definitely not.

---

1. Heraclitus' sun was extinguished at night but rekindled the next morning.

Socrates: Nor, bless you, have they spent enough
time listening to fine and free arguments that vigorously seek the truth in every way, so as to acquire
knowledge and keep their distance from all the
sophistries and eristic quibbles that—whether in
public trials or private gatherings—strive for nothing
except reputation and disputation.

Adeimantus: No, they have not.

Socrates: It was for these reasons, and because we
foresaw these difficulties, that we were afraid. All the
b same, we were compelled by the truth to say that no
city, no constitution, and no individual man will ever
become perfect until some chance event compels
those few philosophers who are not vicious (the ones
who are now called useless) to take care of a city,
whether they are willing to or not, and compels the
city to obey them—or until a true passion for true
philosophy flows by some divine inspiration into the
sons of the men now wielding dynastic power or sov-
c ereignty, or into the men themselves. Now, it cannot
be reasonably maintained, in my view, that either or
both of these things is impossible. But if they were,
we would be justly ridiculed for indulging in wishful
thinking. Isn't that so?

Adeimantus: It is.

Socrates: Then if, in the limitless past, some
necessity forced those who were foremost in philosophy to take charge of a city, or is doing so now in
some barbaric place far beyond our ken, or will do so
d in the future, this is something we are prepared to
fight about—our argument that the constitution we
have described has existed, does exist, and will exist,
at any rate, whenever it is that the muse of philosophy gains mastery of a city. It is not impossible for this
to happen, so we are not speaking of impossibilities—
that it is *difficult*, we agree ourselves.

Adeimantus: *I* certainly think so.

Socrates: But the masses do not—is that what
you are going to say?

Adeimantus: They probably don't.

Socrates: Bless you, you should not make such a
wholesale charge against the masses! They will surely
come to hold a different belief if, instead of wanting
e to win a victory at their expense, you soothe them
and try to remove their slanderous prejudice against
the love of learning. You must show them what you
mean by philosophers and define their nature and
500 pursuit the way we did just now. Then they will realize you do not mean the same people they do. And if
they once see it that way, even you will say that they
will have a different opinion from the one you just
attributed to them and will answer differently. Or do
you think that anyone who is gentle and without malice is harsh to one who is not harsh, or malicious to
one who is not malicious? I will anticipate you and
say that I think a few people may have such a harsh
character, but not the majority.

Adeimantus: And I agree, of course.

Socrates: Then don't you also agree that the
harshness of the masses toward philosophy is caused b
by those outsiders who do not belong and who have
burst in like a band of revelers, abusing one another,
indulging their love of quarreling, and always
arguing about human beings—something that is
least appropriate in philosophy?

Adeimantus: I do, indeed.

Socrates: For surely, Adeimantus, someone
whose mind is truly directed toward the things that
are has not the leisure to look down at human affairs
and be filled with malice and hatred as a result of
entering into their disputes. Instead, as he looks at c
and contemplates things that are orderly and always
the same, that neither do injustice to one another nor
suffer it, being all in a rational order, he imitates
them and tries to become as like them as he can. Or
do you think there is any way to prevent someone
from associating with something he admires without
imitating it?

Adeimantus: He can't possibly.

Socrates: Then the philosopher, by associating
with what is orderly and divine, becomes as divine
and orderly as a human being can. Though, mind
you, there are always plenty of slanders around. d

Adeimantus: Absolutely.

Socrates: And if he should come to be compelled
to make a practice—in private and in public—of
stamping what he sees there into the people's characters, instead of shaping only his own, do you think
he will be a poor craftsman of temperance, justice,
and the whole of popular virtue?

Adeimantus: Not at all.

Socrates: And when the masses realize that what
we are saying about him is true, will they be harsh with
philosophers or mistrust us when we say that there is e
no way a city can ever find happiness unless its plan is
drawn by painters who use the divine model?

Adeimantus: They won't be harsh, if they do real-
501 ize this. But what sort of drawing do you mean?

Socrates: They would take the city and people's characters as their sketching slate, but first they would wipe it clean—which is not at all an easy thing to do. And you should be aware that this is an immediate difference between them and others—that they refuse to take either a private individual or a city in hand, or to write laws, unless they receive a clean slate or are allowed to clean it themselves.

Adeimantus: And rightly so.

Socrates: And after that, don't you think they would draw the plan of the constitution?

Adeimantus: Of course.

Socrates: And I suppose that, as they work, they
b would look often in each direction: on the one hand, toward what is in its nature just, beautiful, temperate, and all the rest; and, on the other, toward what they are trying to put into human beings, mixing and blending pursuits to produce a human likeness, based on the one that Homer too called divine and godly when it appeared among human beings.

Adeimantus: Right.

Socrates: They would erase one thing, I suppose, and draw in another, until they had made people's
c characters as dear to the gods as possible.

Adeimantus: At any rate, the drawing would be most beautiful that way.

Socrates: Are we at all persuading the people you said were rushing to attack us, then, that the philosopher we were praising to them is really this sort of painter of constitutions? They were angry because we were entrusting cities to him; are they any calmer at hearing it now?

Adeimantus: They will be much calmer, if they have any sense.

Socrates: After all, how could they possibly dis-
d pute it? Will they deny that philosophers are lovers both of what is and of the truth?

Adeimantus: That would be silly.

Socrates: Or that their nature, as we have described it, is akin to the best?

Adeimantus: They cannot deny that either.

Socrates: Or that such a nature, when it happens to find appropriate pursuits, will not be as completely good and philosophic as any other? Or are they going to claim that the people we excluded are more so?

e Adeimantus: Certainly not.

Socrates: Will they still be angry, then, when we say that until the philosopher class gains mastery of a city, there will be no respite from evils for either city or citizens, and the constitution we have been describing in our discussion will never be completed in practice?

Adeimantus: They will probably be less so.

Socrates: If it is all right with you, then, let's not say that they will simply be less angry, but that they will become altogether gentle and persuaded; so that
out of shame, if nothing else, they will agree. 502

Adeimantus: All right.

Socrates: So let's assume that they have been convinced of this. Will anyone contend, then, that there is no chance that the offspring of kings or men in power could be natural-born philosophers?

Adeimantus: No one could.

Socrates: Could anyone claim that if such offspring are born, they must inevitably be corrupted? We agree ourselves that it is difficult for them to be saved. But that in the whole of time not one of them
could be saved—could anyone contend that? b

Adeimantus: Of course not.

Socrates: But surely the occurrence of one such individual is enough, provided his city obeys him, to bring to completion all the things that now seem so incredible.

Adeimantus: Yes, one is enough.

Socrates: For I suppose that if a ruler established the laws and practices we have described, it is hardly impossible that the citizens would be willing to carry them out.

Adeimantus: Not at all.

Socrates: Would it be either surprising or impossible, then, that others should think as we do?

Adeimantus: I don't suppose so. c

Socrates: But I think our earlier discussion was sufficient to show that these arrangements are best, provided they are possible.

Adeimantus: Indeed, it was.

Socrates: It seems, then, that the conclusion we have now reached about legislation is that the one we are describing is best, provided it is possible; and that while it is difficult for it to come about, it certainly is not impossible.

Adeimantus: Yes, that is the conclusion we have reached.

Socrates: Now that this conclusion has, with
much effort, been reached, we must next deal with
the remaining issues—in what way, by means of what
subjects and pursuits, the saviors of our constitution
d will come to exist, and at what ages they will take up
each of them.

Adeimantus: Yes, we must deal with that.

Socrates: I gained nothing by my cleverness,
then, in omitting from our earlier discussion the troublesome topic of acquiring women, begetting children, and establishing rulers, because I knew the
whole truth would provoke resentment and would be
difficult to bring about. As it turned out, the need to
discuss them arose anyway. Now, the subject of
e women and children has already been discussed. But
that of the rulers has to be taken up again from the
beginning. We said, if you remember, that they must
503 show themselves to be lovers of the city, when tested
by pleasures and pains, by not abandoning this conviction through labors, fears, and all other adversities.
Anyone who was incapable of doing so was to be
rejected, while anyone who always came through
pure—like gold tested in a fire—was to be made
ruler and receive gifts and prizes, both while he lived
and after his death. These were the sorts of things we
were saying while our argument veiled its face and
slipped by, for fear of stirring up the very problems
b that now confront us.

Adeimantus: That's absolutely true. I do remember.

Socrates: I was reluctant, my friend, to say the things we have now dared to say anyway. But now, let's also dare to say that we must establish philosophers as guardians in the most exact sense.

Adeimantus: Let's do so.

Socrates: Bear in mind, then, that there will probably be only a few of them. You see, they have to have the nature we described, and its parts rarely consent to grow together in one person; rather, its many parts grow split off from one another.

c Adeimantus: How do you mean?

Socrates: Ease of learning, good memory, astuteness, and smartness, as you know, and all the other things that go along with them, such as youthful passion and high-mindedness, are rarely willing to grow together simultaneously with a disposition to live an orderly, quiet, and completely stable life. On the contrary, those who possess the former traits are carried by their quick wits wherever chance leads them, and have no stability at all.

Adeimantus: That's true.

Socrates: Those with stable characters, on the
other hand, who do not change easily, whom one
would employ because of their greater reliability, and
who in battle are not easily moved by fears, act in the d
same way when it comes to their studies. They are
hard to get moving and learn with difficulty, as if
they are anesthetized, and are constantly falling
asleep and yawning whenever they have to work
hard at such things.

Adeimantus: They are.

Socrates: Yet we say that someone must have a good and fine share of both characters, or he won't receive the truest education or honor, or be allowed to rule.

Adeimantus: That's right.

Socrates: Then don't you think this will rarely occur?

Adeimantus: Of course.

Socrates: He must be tested, then, in the labors, e
fears, and pleasures we mentioned before. He must
also be exercised in many other subjects, however,
which we did not mention but are adding now, to see
whether his nature can endure the most important
subjects or will shrink from them like the cowards
who shrink from the other tests. 504

Adeimantus: It is certainly important to find that out. But what do you mean by the most important subjects?

Socrates: Do you remember when we distinguished three kinds of things in the soul in order to help bring out what justice, temperance, courage, and wisdom each is?

Adeimantus: If I didn't, I would not deserve to hear the rest.

Socrates: Do you also remember what preceded it?

Adeimantus: No, what?

Socrates: We said, I believe, that in order to get
the finest view of these matters, we would need to take b
a longer road, which would make them plain to anyone who took it, but that it was possible to give
demonstrations that would be up to the standard of
the previous discussion. Heraclitus' sun was extinguished at night but rekindled the next morning. All
of you said that was enough. The result was that our

subsequent discussion, as it seemed to me, was less than exact. But whether or not it satisfied all of you is for you to say.

Adeimantus: I, at any rate, thought you gave us good measure. And so, apparently, did the others.

Socrates: No, my friend, any measure of such
c things that falls short in any way of what is, is not good measure at all, since nothing incomplete is a measure of anything. Some people, however, are occasionally of the opinion that an incomplete treatment is already adequate and that there is no need for further inquiry.

Adeimantus: Yes, a lot of people feel like that. Laziness is the cause.

Socrates: Well, that is a feeling that is least appropriate in a guardian of a city and its laws.

Adeimantus: No doubt.

Socrates: He will have to take the longer road then, comrade, and put no less effort into learning
d than into physical training. For otherwise, as we were just saying, he will never pursue the most important and most appropriate subject to the end.

Adeimantus: Why, aren't these virtues the most important things? Is there something yet more important than justice and the other virtues we discussed?

Socrates: Not only is it more important, but, even in the case of the virtues themselves, it is not enough to look at a mere sketch as we are doing now, while neglecting the most finished portrait. I mean, it is ridiculous, isn't it, to strain every nerve to attain the utmost exactness and clarity about other things of lit-
e tle value, while not treating the most important things as meriting the most exactness?

Adeimantus: It certainly is. But do you think that anyone is going to let you off without asking you what you mean by this most important subject, and what it is concerned with?

Socrates: No, I do not. And you may ask it, too. You have certainly heard the answer often, but now either you are not thinking or you intend to make trouble for me again by interrupting. And I suspect
505 it is more the latter. You see, you have often heard it said that the form of the good is the most important thing to learn about, and that it is by their relation to it that just things and the others become useful and beneficial. And now you must be pretty certain that that is what I am going to say, and, in addition, that we have no adequate knowledge of it. And if we do not know it, you know that even the fullest possible knowledge of other things is of no benefit to us, any more than if we acquire any possession without the good. Or do you think there is any benefit in possessing everything but the good? Or to know b
everything without knowing the good, thereby knowing nothing fine or good?

Adeimantus: No, by Zeus, I do not.

Socrates: Furthermore, you also know that the masses believe pleasure to be the good, while the more refined believe it to be knowledge.

Adeimantus: Of course.

Socrates: And, my friend, that those who believe this cannot show us what sort of knowledge it is, but in the end are forced to say that it is knowledge of the good.

Adeimantus: Which is completely ridiculous.

Socrates: How could it not be, when they blame us for not knowing the good and then turn around c
and talk to us as if we did know it? I mean, they say it is knowledge of the good—as if we understood what they mean when they utter the word "good."

Adeimantus: That's absolutely true.

Socrates: What about those who define the good as pleasure? Are they any less full of confusion than the others? Or aren't even they forced to admit that there are bad pleasures?

Adeimantus: Most definitely.

Socrates: I suppose it follows, doesn't it, that they have to admit that the same things are both good and bad?

Adeimantus: It certainly does. d

Socrates: Isn't it clear, then, that there are lots of serious disagreements about the good?

Adeimantus: Of course.

Socrates: Well, isn't it also clear that many people would choose things that are believed to be just or beautiful, even if they are not, and would act, acquire things, and form beliefs accordingly? Yet no one is satisfied to acquire things that are *believed* to be good. On the contrary, everyone seeks the things that *are* good. In this area, everyone disdains mere reputation.

Adeimantus: Right.

Socrates: That, then, is what every soul pursues, and for its sake does everything. The soul has a hunch that the good is something, but it is puzzled and cannot adequately grasp just what it is or acquire e

the sort of stable belief about it that it has about other things, and so it misses the benefit, if any, that even those other things may give. Are we to accept that
506 even the best people in the city, to whom we entrust everything, must remain thus in the dark about something of this kind and importance?

ADEIMANTUS: That's the last thing we would do.

SOCRATES: Anyway, I imagine that just and fine things won't have acquired much of a guardian in someone who does not even know why they are good. And I have a hunch that no one will have adequate knowledge of them until he knows this.

ADEIMANTUS: That's a good hunch.

SOCRATES: But won't our constitution be perfectly ordered if such a guardian, one who knows these
b things, oversees it?

ADEIMANTUS: It is bound to be. But you yourself, Socrates, do you say the good is knowledge or pleasure, or is it something else altogether?

SOCRATES: What a man! You made it good and clear long ago that other people's opinions about these matters would not satisfy you.

ADEIMANTUS: Well, Socrates, it does not seem right to me for you to be willing to state other people's convictions but not your own, when you have spent
c so much time occupied with these matters.

SOCRATES: What? Do you think it is right to speak about things you do not know as if you do know them?

ADEIMANTUS: Not as if you know them, but you ought to be willing to state what you believe as what you believe.

SOCRATES: What? Haven't you noticed that beliefs without knowledge are all shameful and ugly things, since the best of them are blind? Do you think that those who have a true belief without understanding are any different from blind people who happen to travel the right road?

ADEIMANTUS: They are no different.

SOCRATES: Do you want to look at shameful, blind, and crooked things, then, when you might hear fine,
d illuminating ones from other people?

And Glaucon said:

By Zeus, Socrates, do not stop now, with the end in sight, so to speak! We will be satisfied if you discuss the good the way you discussed justice, temperance, and the rest.

SOCRATES: That, comrade, would well satisfy me too, but I am afraid that I won't be up to it and that I will disgrace myself and look ridiculous by trying. No, bless you, let's set aside what the good itself is for the time being. You see, even to arrive at my current beliefs
about it seems beyond the range of our present discus- e
sion. But I am willing to tell you about what seems to be an offspring of the good and most like it, if that is agreeable to you; or otherwise to let the matter drop.

GLAUCON: Tell us, then. The story about the father remains a debt you will pay another time.

SOCRATES: I wish I could repay it, and you recover 507
the debt, instead of just the interest. So here, then, is this child and offspring of the good itself. But take care I do not somehow deceive you unintentionally by giving you an illegitimate account of the child.[2]

GLAUCON: We will take as much care as possible. So speak on.

SOCRATES: I will once I have come to an agreement with you and reminded you of things we have already said here as well as on many other occasions.

GLAUCON: Which things? b

SOCRATES: We say that there are many beautiful, many good, and many other such things, thereby distinguishing them in words.

GLAUCON: We do.

SOCRATES: We also say there is a beautiful itself and a good itself. And so, in the case of all the things that we then posited as many, we reverse ourselves and posit a single form belonging to each, since we suppose there is a single one, and call it what each is.

GLAUCON: That's true.

SOCRATES: And we say that the one class of things is visible but not intelligible, while the forms are intelligible but not visible.

GLAUCON: Absolutely.

SOCRATES: With what of ours do we see visible things? c

GLAUCON: With our sight.

SOCRATES: And don't we hear audible things with hearing and perceive all other perceptible things with our other senses?

GLAUCON: Of course.

SOCRATES: Have you ever thought about how lavish the craftsman of our senses was in making the power to see and be seen?

---

2. Throughout, Socrates is punning on the word *tokos*, which means either a child or the interest on capital.

Glaucon: No, not really.

Socrates: Well, think of it this way. Do hearing and sound need another kind of thing in order for the former to hear and the latter to be heard—a third
d thing in whose absence the one won't hear or the other be heard?

Glaucon: No.

Socrates: And I think there cannot be many—not to say any—others that need such a thing. Or can you think of one?

Glaucon: No, I cannot.

Socrates: Aren't you aware that sight and the visible realm have such a need?

Glaucon: In what way?

Socrates: Surely sight may be present in the eyes and its possessor may try to use it, and colors may be present in things; but unless a third kind of thing is present, which is naturally adapted for this specific
e purpose, you know that sight will see nothing and the colors will remain unseen.

Glaucon: What kind of thing do you mean?

Socrates: The kind you call light.

Glaucon: You are right.

Socrates: So it is no insignificant form of yoke,
508 then, that yokes the sense of sight and the power to be seen. In fact, it is more honorable than any that yokes other yoked teams. Provided, of course, that light is not something without honor.

Glaucon: And it is surely far from being without honor.

Socrates: Which of the gods in the heavens would you say is the controller of this—the one whose light makes our sight see best and visible things best seen?

Glaucon: The very one you and others would name. I mean, it is clear that what you are asking about is the sun.[3]

Socrates: And isn't sight naturally related to that god in the following way?

Glaucon: Which one?

Socrates: Neither sight itself nor that in which it
b comes to be—namely, the eye—is the sun.

Glaucon: No, it is not.

Socrates: But it is, I think, the most sunlike of the sense organs.

Glaucon: By far the most.

Socrates: And doesn't it receive the power it has from the sun, just like an influx from an overflowing treasury?

Glaucon: Certainly.

Socrates: The sun is not sight either; yet as its cause, isn't it seen by sight itself?

Glaucon: It is.

Socrates: Let's say, then, that this is what I called the offspring of the good, which the good begot as its analogue. What the latter is in the intelligible realm in relation to understanding and intelligible things, the former is in the visible realm in relation to sight c
and visible things.

Glaucon: How? Tell me more.

Socrates: You know that when our eyes no longer turn to things whose colors are illuminated by the light of day, but by the lights of night, they are dimmed and seem nearly blind, as if clear sight were no longer in them.

Glaucon: Of course.

Socrates: Yet I suppose that whenever they are turned to things illuminated by the sun, they see clearly and sight is manifest in those very same eyes? d

Glaucon: Indeed.

Socrates: Well, think about the soul in the same way. When it focuses on something that is illuminated both by truth and what is, it understands, knows, and manifestly possesses understanding. But when it focuses on what is mixed with obscurity, on what comes to be and passes away, it believes and is dimmed, changes its beliefs this way and that, and seems bereft of understanding.

Glaucon: Yes, it does seem like that.

Socrates: You must say, then, that what gives truth to the things known and the power to know to e
the knower is the form of the good. And as the cause of knowledge and truth, you must think of it as an object of knowledge. Both knowledge and truth are beautiful things. But if you are to think correctly, you must think of the good as other and more beautiful than they. In the visible realm, light and sight are rightly thought to be sunlike, but wrongly thought to 509
be the sun. So, here it is right to think of knowledge and truth as goodlike, but wrong to think that either of them is the good—for the state of the good is yet more honored.

Glaucon: It is an incredibly beautiful thing you are talking about, if it provides both knowledge and

3. Helios—the sun—was considered a god.

truth but is itself superior to them in beauty. I mean, you surely do not think that *it* could be pleasure.

SOCRATES: No words of ill omen, please! Instead, examine our analogy in more detail.

b GLAUCON: How?

SOCRATES: The sun, I think you would say, not only gives visible things the power to be seen but also provides for their coming-to-be, growth, and nourishment—although it is not itself coming to be.

GLAUCON: I would.

SOCRATES: Therefore, you should also say that not only do the objects of knowledge owe their being known to the good, but their existence and being are also due to it; although the good is not being, but something yet beyond being, superior to it in rank and power.

And Glaucon quite ridiculously replied:

c By Apollo, what daimonic hyperbole!

SOCRATES: It is your own fault, you forced me to tell my beliefs about it.

GLAUCON: And don't you stop, either—at least, not until you have finished discussing the good's similarity to the sun, if you are omitting anything.

SOCRATES: I am certainly omitting a lot.

GLAUCON: Well don't, not even the smallest detail.

SOCRATES: I think I will have to omit a fair amount. All the same, as far as is now possible, I won't purposely omit anything.

GLAUCON: Please don't.

SOCRATES: Then you should think, as we said, that
d there are these two things, one sovereign of the intelligible kind and place, the other of the visible—I do not say "of the heavens," so as not to seem to you to be playing the Sophist with the name. In any case, do you understand these two kinds, visible and intelligible?

GLAUCON: I do.

SOCRATES: Represent them, then, by a line divided into two unequal sections. Then divide each section—that of the visible kind and that of the intelligible—in the same proportion as the line.[4] In terms now of relative clarity and opacity, you will have as one subsection of the visible, images. By images I mean, first, shadows, then reflections in bodies of *e*
water and in all close-packed, smooth, and shiny *510*
materials, and everything of that sort. Do you understand?

GLAUCON: I do understand.

SOCRATES: Then, in the other subsection of the visible, put the originals of these images—that is, the animals around us, every plant, and the whole class of manufactured things.

GLAUCON: I will.

SOCRATES: Would you also be willing to say, then, that, as regards truth and untruth, the division is in this ratio: as what is believed is to what is known, so the likeness is to the thing it is like?

GLAUCON: Certainly. *b*

SOCRATES: Next, consider how the section of the intelligible is to be divided.

GLAUCON: How?

SOCRATES: As follows: in one subsection, the soul, using as images the things that were imitated before, is forced to base its inquiry on hypotheses, proceeding not to a first principle, but to a conclusion. In the other subsection, by contrast, it makes its way to an unhypothetical first principle, proceeding from a hypothesis, but without the images used in the previous subsection, using forms themselves and making its investigation through them.

GLAUCON: I do not fully understand what you are saying.

SOCRATES: Let's try again. You see, you will understand it more easily after this explanation. I think you *c*
know that students of geometry, calculation, and the like hypothesize the odd and the even, the various figures, the three kinds of angles, and other things akin to these in each of their investigations, regarding them as known. These they treat as hypotheses and do not think it necessary to give any argument for them, either to themselves or to others, as if they were evident to everyone. And going from these first principles through the remaining steps, they arrive in *d*
full agreement at the point they set out to reach in their investigation.

GLAUCON: I certainly know that much.

SOCRATES: Then don't you also know that they use visible forms and make their arguments about them, although they are not thinking about them, but

4. A D C E B
4 2 2 1
VISIBLE INTELLIGIBLE

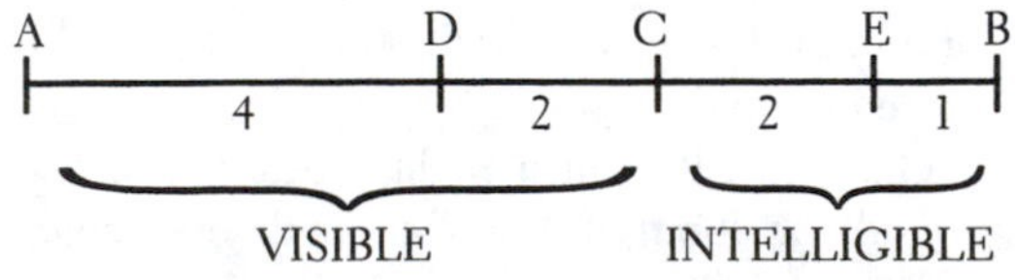

about those other things that they are like? They
make their arguments with a view to the square itself
and the diagonal itself, not the diagonal they draw, and
e similarly with the others. The very things they make
and draw, of which shadows and reflections in water
are images, they now in turn use as images in seeking
to see those other things themselves that one cannot
511 see except by means of thought.

GLAUCON: That's true.

SOCRATES: This, then, is the kind of thing that I said was intelligible. The soul is forced to use hypotheses in the investigation of it, not traveling up to a first principle, since it cannot escape or get above its hypotheses, but using as images those very things of which images were made by the things below them, and which, by comparison to their images, were thought to be clear and to be honored as such.

GLAUCON: I understand that you mean what is
b dealt with in geometry and related crafts.

SOCRATES: Also understand, then, that by the other
subsection of the intelligible I mean what reason
itself grasps by the power of dialectical discussion,
treating its hypotheses, not as first principles, but as
genuine hypotheses (that is, stepping stones and links
in a chain), in order to arrive at what is unhypothetical and the first principle of everything. Having
grasped this principle, it reverses itself and, keeping
hold of what follows from it, comes down to a con-
c clusion, making no use of anything visible at all, but
only of forms themselves, moving on through forms
to forms, and ending in forms.

GLAUCON: I understand, though not adequately—
you see, in my opinion you are speaking of an enormous task. You want to distinguish the part of what is
and is intelligible, the part looked at by the science of
dialectical discussion, as clearer than the part looked
at by the so-called sciences—those for which
hypotheses are first principles. And although those
who look at the latter part are forced to do so by
means of thought rather than sense perception, still,
because they do not go back to a genuine first principle in considering it, but proceed from hypotheses,
you do not think that they have true understanding of d
them, even though—given such a first principle—
they are intelligible. And you seem to me to call the
state of mind of the geometers—and the others of that
sort—thought but not understanding; thought being
intermediate between belief and understanding.

SOCRATES: You have grasped my meaning most
adequately. Join me, then, in taking these four conditions in the soul as corresponding to the four sub-
sections of the line: understanding dealing with the
highest, thought dealing with the second; assign
belief to the third, and imagination to the last. e
Arrange them in a proportion and consider that each
shares in clarity to the degree that the subsection it
deals with shares in truth.

GLAUCON: I understand, agree, and arrange them as you say.

BOOK 7

Synopsis

BOOK 7 BEGINS with the famous Allegory of the Cave, which is intended to fit together with the sun and line analogies (517b) by illustrating the effects of education on the soul (514a). The discussion of the education of philosophers continues. Primary education in musical and physical training and elementary mathematics (535a–537b) is followed by two or three years of compulsory physical training (537b–c), ten years of education in the mathematical sciences (537c–d, 522c–531d), five years of training in dialectic (537d–540a, 531e–535a), and fifteen years of practical political training (539e–540a). After such education, its recipients are ready to see the good itself and to be philosopher-kings (540a).

SOCRATES: Next, then, compare the effect of education and that of the lack of it on our nature to an 514
experience like this. Imagine human beings living in
an underground, cavelike dwelling, with an entrance
a long way up that is open to the light and as wide as
the cave itself. They have been there since childhood, with their necks and legs fettered, so that they

are fixed in the same place, able to see only in front of them, because their fetter prevents them from turn-
b ing their heads around. Light is provided by a fire burning far above and behind them. Between the prisoners and the fire, there is an elevated road stretching. Imagine that along this road a low wall has been built—like the screen in front of people that is provided by puppeteers, and above which they show their puppets.

Glaucon: I am imagining it.

Socrates: Also imagine, then, that there are people alongside the wall carrying multifarious artifacts
c that project above it—statues of people and other animals, made of stone, wood, and every material.
515 And as you would expect, some of the carriers are talking and some are silent.

Glaucon: It is a strange image you are describing, and strange prisoners.

Socrates: They are like us. I mean, in the first place, do you think these prisoners have ever seen anything of themselves and one another besides the shadows that the fire casts on the wall of the cave in front of them?

Glaucon: How could they, if they have to keep
b their heads motionless throughout life?

Socrates: What about the things carried along the wall? Isn't the same true where they are concerned?

Glaucon: Of course.

Socrates: And if they could engage in discussion with one another, don't you think they would assume that the words they used applied to the things they see passing in front of them?

Glaucon: They would have to.

Socrates: What if their prison also had an echo from the wall facing them? When one of the carriers passing along the wall spoke, do you think they would believe that anything other than the shadow passing in front of them was speaking?

Glaucon: I do not, by Zeus.

Socrates: All in all, then, what the prisoners
c would take for true reality is nothing other than the shadows of those artifacts.

Glaucon: That's entirely inevitable.

Socrates: Consider, then, what being released from their bonds and cured of their foolishness would naturally be like, if something like this should happen to them. When one was freed and suddenly compelled to stand up, turn his neck around, walk, and look up toward the light, he would be pained by doing all these things and be unable to see the things whose shadows he had seen before, because of the
flashing lights. What do you think he would say if we d
told him that what he had seen before was silly nonsense, but that now—because he is a bit closer to what is, and is turned toward things that *are* more—he sees more correctly? And in particular, if we pointed to each of the things passing by and compelled him to answer what each of them is, don't you think he would be puzzled and believe that the things he saw earlier were more truly real than the ones he was being shown?

Glaucon: Much more so.

Socrates: And if he were compelled to look at the
light itself, wouldn't his eyes be pained and wouldn't e
he turn around and flee toward the things he is able to see, and believe that they are really clearer than the ones he is being shown?

Glaucon: He would.

Socrates: And if someone dragged him by force away from there, along the rough, steep, upward path, and did not let him go until he had dragged him into the light of the sun, wouldn't he be pained and angry at being treated that way? And when he
came into the light, wouldn't he have his eyes filled 516
with sunlight and be unable to see a single one of the things now said to be truly real?

Glaucon: No, he would not be able to—at least not right away.

Socrates: He would need time to get adjusted, I suppose, if he is going to see the things in the world above. At first, he would see shadows most easily, then images of men and other things in water, then the things themselves. From these, it would be easier for him to go on to look at the things in the sky and the sky itself at night, gazing at the light of the stars and the moon, than during the day, gazing at
the sun and the light of the sun. b

Glaucon: Of course.

Socrates: Finally, I suppose, he would be able to see the sun—not reflections of it in water or some alien place, but the sun just by itself in its own place—and be able to look at it and see what it is like.

Glaucon: He would have to.

Socrates: After that, he would already be able to conclude about it that it provides the seasons and the years, governs everything in the visible world, and is c in some way the cause of all the things that he and his fellows used to see.

GLAUCON: That would clearly be his next step.

SOCRATES: What about when he reminds himself of his first dwelling place, what passed for wisdom there, and his fellow prisoners? Don't you think he would count himself happy for the change and pity the others?

GLAUCON: Certainly.

SOCRATES: And if there had been honors, praises, or prizes among them for the one who was sharpest at identifying the shadows as they passed by; and was best able to remember which usually came earlier, which later, and which simultaneously; and who
d was thus best able to prophesize the future, do you think that our man would desire these rewards or envy those among the prisoners who were honored and held power? Or do you think he would feel with Homer that he would much prefer to "work the earth as a serf for another man, a man without possessions of his own,"[1] and go through any sufferings, rather than share their beliefs and live as they do?

GLAUCON: Yes, I think he would rather suffer any-
e thing than live like that.

SOCRATES: Consider this too, then. If this man went back down into the cave and sat down in his same seat, wouldn't his eyes be filled with darkness, coming suddenly out of the sun like that?

GLAUCON: Certainly.

SOCRATES: Now, if he had to compete once again with the perpetual prisoners in recognizing the shadows, while his sight was still dim and before his eyes
517 had recovered, and if the time required for readjustment was not short, wouldn't he provoke ridicule? Wouldn't it be said of him that he had returned from his upward journey with his eyes ruined, and that it is not worthwhile even to try to travel upward? And as for anyone who tried to free the prisoners and lead them upward, if they could somehow get their hands on him, wouldn't they kill him?

GLAUCON: They certainly would.

SOCRATES: This image, my dear Glaucon, must be
b fitted together as a whole with what we said before. The realm revealed through sight should be likened to the prison dwelling, and the light of the fire inside it to the sun's power. And if you think of the upward journey and the seeing of things above as the upward journey of the soul to the intelligible realm, you won't mistake my intention—since it is what you wanted to hear about. Only the god knows whether it is true. But this is how these phenomena seem to me: in the knowable realm, the last thing to be seen is the form of the good, and it is seen only with toil and trouble. Once one has seen it, however, one
must infer that it is the cause of all that is correct and c
beautiful in anything, that in the visible realm it produces both light and its source, and that in the intelligible realm it controls and provides truth and understanding; and that anyone who is to act sensibly in private or public must see it.

GLAUCON: I agree, so far as I am able.

SOCRATES: Come on, then, and join me in this further thought: you should not be surprised that the ones who get to this point are not willing to occupy themselves with human affairs, but that, on the contrary, their souls are always eager to spend their time above. I mean, that is surely what we would expect, if indeed the image I described before is
also accurate here. d

GLAUCON: It is what we would expect.

SOCRATES: What about when someone, coming from looking at divine things, looks to the evils of human life? Do you think it is surprising that he behaves awkwardly and appears completely ridiculous, if—while his sight is still dim and he has not yet become accustomed to the darkness around him—he is compelled, either in the courts or elsewhere, to compete about the shadows of justice, or about the statues of which they are the shadows; and to dispute the way these things are understood by people who
have never seen justice itself? e

GLAUCON: It is not surprising at all.

SOCRATES: On the contrary, anyone with any
sense, at any rate, would remember that eyes may be 518
confused in two ways and from two causes: when they change from the light into the darkness, or from the darkness into the light. If he kept in mind that the same applies to the soul, then when he saw a soul disturbed and unable to see something, he would not laugh absurdly. Instead, he would see whether it had come from a brighter life and was dimmed through not having yet become accustomed to the dark, or from greater ignorance into

1. Homer, *Odyssey* 11.489–90. The shade of Achilles speaks these words to Odysseus, who is visiting Hades. Plato is likening the cave dwellers to the dead.

greater light and was dazzled by the increased bril-
b liance. Then he would consider the first soul happy
in its experience and life, and pity the latter. But even
if he wanted to ridicule it, at least his ridiculing it
would make him less ridiculous than ridiculing a
soul that had come from the light above.

Glaucon: That's an entirely reasonable claim.

Socrates: Then here is how we must think about
these matters, if that is true: education is not what
some people boastfully declare it to be. They presumably say they can put knowledge into souls that
c lack it, as if they could put sight into blind eyes.

Glaucon: Yes, they do say that.

Socrates: But here is what our present account
shows about this power to learn that is present in
everyone's soul, and the instrument with which each
of us learns: just as an eye cannot be turned around
from darkness to light except by turning the whole
body, so this instrument must be turned around
from what-comes-to-be together with the whole
soul, until it is able to bear to look at what is and at
the brightest thing that is—the one we call the
d good. Isn't that right?

Glaucon: Yes.

Socrates: Of this very thing, then, there would be a craft—namely, of this turning around—concerned with how this instrument can be most easily and effectively turned around, not of putting sight into it. On the contrary, it takes for granted that sight is there, though not turned in the right way or looking where it should look, and contrives to redirect it appropriately.

Glaucon: That's probably right.

Socrates: Then the other so-called virtues of the
soul do seem to be closely akin to those of the body:
they really are not present in it initially, but are added
e later by habit and practice. The virtue of wisdom, on
the other hand, belongs above all, so it seems, to
something more divine, which never loses its power,
but is either useful and beneficial or useless and
harmful, depending on the way it is turned. Or
519 haven't you ever noticed in people who are said to be
bad, but clever, how keen the vision of their little
soul is and how sharply it distinguishes the things it is
turned toward? This shows that its sight is not inferior, but is forced to serve vice, so that the sharper it
sees, the more evils it accomplishes.

Glaucon: I certainly have.

Socrates: However, if this element of this sort of
nature had been hammered at right from childhood,
and struck free of the leaden weights, as it were,
of kinship with becoming, which have been fastened
to it by eating and other such pleasures and indul- b
gences, which pull its soul's vision downward—if, I
say, it got rid of these and turned toward truly real
things, then the same element of the same people
would see them most sharply, just as it now does the
things it is now turned toward.

Glaucon: That's probably right.

Socrates: Isn't it also probable, then—indeed,
doesn't it follow necessarily from what was said
before—that uneducated people who have no
experience of true reality will never adequately govern a city, and neither will people who have been c
allowed to spend their whole lives in education. The
former fail because they do not have a single goal in
life at which all their actions, public and private,
inevitably aim; the latter because they would refuse
to act, thinking they had emigrated, while still alive,
to the Isles of the Blessed.

Glaucon: True.

Socrates: It is our task as founders, then, to compel the best natures to learn what was said before to
be the most important thing: namely, to see the good;
to ascend that ascent. And when they have ascended
and looked sufficiently, we must not allow them to do d
what they are allowed to do now.

Glaucon: What's that, then?

Socrates: To stay there and refuse to go down again to the prisoners in the cave and share their labors and honors, whether the inferior ones or the more excellent ones.

Glaucon: You mean we are to treat them unjustly, making them live a worse life when they could live a better one?

Socrates: You have forgotten again, my friend,
that the law is not concerned with making any one e
class in the city do outstandingly well, but is contriv-
ing to produce this condition in the city as a whole,
harmonizing the citizens together through persuasion or compulsion, and making them share with
each other the benefit they can confer on the community. It produces such men in the city, not in order 520
to allow them to turn in whatever direction each one
wants, but to make use of them to bind the city
together.

Glaucon: That's true. Yes, I had forgotten.

Socrates: Observe, then, Glaucon, that we won't
be unjustly treating those who have become philosophers in our city, but that what we will say to them,
when we compel them to take care of the others and
guard them, will be just. We will say: "When people
like you come to be in other cities, they are justified
b in not sharing in the others' labors. After all, they
have grown there spontaneously, against the will of
the constitution in each of them. And when something grows of its own accord and owes no debt for its
upbringing, it has justice on its side when it is not
keen to pay anyone for its upbringing. But both for
your own sakes and for that of the rest of the city, we
have bred you to be leaders and kings in the hive, so
to speak. You are better and more completely educated than the others, and better able to share in
both types of life.[2] So each of you in turn must go
c down to live in the common dwelling place of the
other citizens and grow accustomed to seeing in the
dark. For when you are used to it, you will see infinitely better than the people there and know precisely what each image is, and also what it is an
image of, because you have seen the truth about fine,
just, and good things. So the city will be awake, governed by us and by you; not dreaming like the majority of cities nowadays, governed by men who fight
against one another over shadows and form factions
d in order to rule—as if that were a great good. No, the
truth of the matter is surely this: a city in which
those who are going to rule are least eager to rule is
necessarily best and freest from faction, whereas a
city with the opposite kind of rulers is governed in
the opposite way."

Glaucon: Yes, indeed.

Socrates: Then do you think the people we have nurtured will disobey us when they hear these things, and be unwilling to share the labors of the city, each in turn, while living the greater part of their time with one another in the pure realm?

Glaucon: No, they couldn't possibly. After all, we
e will be giving just orders to just people. However,
each of them will certainly go to rule as to something
necessary, which is exactly the opposite of what is
done by those who now rule in each city.

Socrates: That's right, comrade. If you can find a
way of life that is better than ruling for those who are
going to rule, your well-governed city will become a 521
possibility. You see, in it alone the truly rich will
rule—those who are rich not in gold, but in the
wealth the happy must have: namely, a good and
rational life. But if beggars—people hungry for private goods of their own—go into public life, thinking
that the good is there for the seizing, then such a city
is impossible. For when ruling is something fought
over, such civil and domestic war destroys these men
and the rest of the city as well.

Glaucon: That's absolutely true.

Socrates: Do you know of any other sort of life
that looks down on political offices besides that of b
true philosophy?

Glaucon: No, by Zeus, I do not.

Socrates: But surely it is those who are not lovers of ruling who must go do it. Otherwise, the rivaling lovers will fight over it.

Glaucon: Of course.

Socrates: Who else, then, will you compel to go be guardians of the city if not those who know best what results in good government, and have different honors and a better life than the political?

Glaucon: No one else.

We take up the subsequent discussion of the education of the philosopher-kings with Socrates' views about their training in dialectic.

Socrates: Moreover, I take it that if the investigation of all the subjects we have mentioned arrives at
what they share in common with one another and 531d
what their affinities are, and draws conclusions about
their kinship, it does contribute something to our
goal and is not labor in vain; but that otherwise it is
in vain.

Glaucon: I have the same hunch myself. But you are still talking about a very big task, Socrates.

Socrates: Do you mean the prelude, or what? Or
don't you know that all these subjects are merely
preludes to the theme itself that must be learned? I
mean, you surely do not think that people who are
clever in these matters are dialecticians. e

Glaucon: No, by Zeus, I do not. Although, I have met a few exceptions.

2. I.e., the practical life of ruling and the theoretical life of doing philosophy.

Socrates: But did it ever seem to you that those who can neither give an account nor approve one know what any of the things are that we say they must know?

Glaucon: Again, the answer is no.

Socrates: Then isn't this at last, Glaucon, the
532 theme itself that dialectical discussion sings? It itself
is intelligible. But the power of sight imitates it. We
said that sight tries at last to look at the animals themselves, the stars themselves, and, in the end, at the
sun itself. In the same way, whenever someone tries,
by means of dialectical discussion and without the
aid of any sense-perceptions, to arrive through reason
at the being of each thing itself, and does not give up
until he grasps what good itself is with understanding
itself, he reaches the end of the intelligible realm,
b just as the other reached the end of the visible one.

Glaucon: Absolutely.

Socrates: Well, then, don't you call this journey dialectic?

Glaucon: I do.

Socrates: Then the release from bonds and the
turning around from shadows to statues and the light;
and then the ascent out of the cave to the sun; and
there the continuing inability to look directly at the
animals, the plants, and the light of the sun, but
instead at divine reflections in water and shadows of
the things that are, and not, as before, merely at shad-
c ows of statues thrown by another source of light that,
when judged in relation to the sun, is as shadowy as
they—all this practice of the crafts we mentioned
has the power to lead the best part of the soul upward
until it sees the best among the things that are, just as
before the clearest thing in the body was led to the
d brightest thing in the bodily and visible world.

Glaucon: I accept that this is so. And yet, I think
it is very difficult to accept; although—in another
way—difficult not to accept! All the same, since the
present occasion is not our only opportunity to hear
these things, but we will get to return to them often
in the future, let's assume that what you said about
them just now is true and turn to the theme itself,
and discuss it in the same way as we did the prelude.
So, tell us then, in what way the power of dialectical
discussion works, into what kinds it is divided, and
what roads it follows. I mean, it is these, it seems, that
e would lead us at last to that place which is a rest from
the road, so to speak, for the one who reaches it, and
an end of his journey.

Socrates: You won't be able to follow me any farther, my dear Glaucon—though not because of any 533
lack of eagerness on my part. You would no longer
see an image of what we are describing, but the truth
itself as it seems to me, at least. Whether it is really so
or not—that's not something on which it is any
longer worth insisting. But that there is some such
thing to be seen, *that* is something on which we must
insist. Isn't that so?

Glaucon: Of course.

Socrates: And mustn't we also insist that the power of dialectical discussion could reveal it only to someone experienced in the subjects we described, and cannot do so in any other way?

Glaucon: Yes, that is worth insisting on, too.

Socrates: At the very least, no one will dispute
our claim by arguing that there is another road of b
inquiry that tries to acquire a systematic and wholly
general grasp of what each thing itself is. By contrast,
all the other crafts are concerned with human beliefs
and appetites, with growing or construction, or with
the care of growing or constructed things. As for the
rest, we described them as to some extent grasping
what is—I mean, geometry and the subjects that follow it. For we saw that while they do dream about
what is, they cannot see it while wide awake as long
as they make use of hypotheses that they leave undis- c
turbed, and for which they cannot give any argument. After all, when the first principle is unknown,
and the conclusion and the steps in between are put
together out of what is unknown, what mechanism
could possibly turn any agreement reached in such
cases into knowledge?

Glaucon: None.

Socrates: Therefore, dialectic is the only investigation that, doing away with hypotheses, journeys to
the first principle itself in order to be made secure. d
And when the eye of the soul is really buried in a sort
of barbaric bog, dialectic gently pulls it out and leads
it upward, using the crafts we described to help it and
cooperate with it in turning the soul around. From
force of habit, we have often called these branches of
knowledge. But they need another name, since they
are clearer than belief and darker than knowledge.
We distinguished them by the term "thought" somewhere before. But I don't suppose we will dispute
about names, with matters as important as those
before us to investigate. e

GLAUCON: Of course not, just as long as they express the state of clarity the soul possesses.

SOCRATES: It will be satisfactory, then, to do what we did before and call the first section knowledge, the second thought, the third opinion, and the fourth 534 imagination. The last two together we call belief, the other two, understanding.[3] Belief is concerned with becoming; understanding with being. And as being is to becoming, so understanding is to belief; and as understanding is to belief, so knowledge is to belief and thought to imagination. But as for the ratios between the things these deal with, and the division of either the believable or the intelligible section into two, let's pass them by, Glaucon, in case they involve us in discussions many times longer than the ones we have already gone through.

GLAUCON: I agree with you about the rest of them, b anyway, insofar as I am able to follow.

SOCRATES: So don't you, too, call someone a dialectician when he is able to grasp an account of the being of each thing? And when he cannot do so, won't you, too, say that to the extent that he cannot give an account of something either to himself or to another, to that extent he does not understand it?

GLAUCON: How could I not?

SOCRATES: Then the same applies to the good. Unless someone can give an account of the form of the good, distinguishing it from everything else, and c can survive all examination as if in a battle, striving to examine things not in accordance with belief, but in accordance with being; and can journey through all that with his account still intact, you will say that he does not know the good itself or any other good whatsoever. And if he does manage to grasp some image of it, you will say that it is through belief, not knowledge, that he grasps it; that he is dreaming and asleep throughout his present life; and that, before he wakes up here, he will arrive in Hades and go to d sleep forever.

GLAUCON: Yes, by Zeus, I will certainly say all that.

SOCRATES: Then as for those children of yours, the ones you are rearing and educating in your discussion, if you ever reared them in fact, I don't suppose that, while they are still as irrational as the proverbial lines,[4] you would allow them to rule in your city or control the most important things.

GLAUCON: No, of course not.

SOCRATES: Won't you prescribe in your legislation, then, that they are to give the most attention to the education that will enable them to ask and answer questions most knowledgeably?

GLAUCON: I will prescribe it—together with you. e

SOCRATES: Doesn't it seem to you, then, that dialectic is just like a capstone we have placed on top of the subjects, and that no other subject can rightly be placed above it, but that our account of the subjects has now come to an end? 535

GLAUCON: It does.

SOCRATES: Then it remains for you to deal with the distribution of these subjects: to whom we will assign them and in what way.

GLAUCON: Clearly.

SOCRATES: Do you remember what sort of people we chose in our earlier selection of rulers?

GLAUCON: How could I not?

SOCRATES: Well then, as regards the other requirements too, you must suppose that these same natures are to be chosen, since we have to select the most stable, the most courageous, and—as far as possible—the best-looking. In addition, we must look not only for people who have a noble and valiant character, b but for those who also have natural qualities conducive to this education of ours.

GLAUCON: Which ones in particular?

SOCRATES: They must be keen on the subjects, bless you, and learn them without difficulty. For people's souls are much more likely to give up during strenuous studies than during physical training. The pain is more their own, you see, since it is peculiar to them and not shared with the body.

GLAUCON: That's true.

SOCRATES: We must also look for someone who has a good memory, is persistent, and is wholeheartedly

---

3. The reference is to 511d–e, where the first section is called understanding (*noēsis*), not knowledge (*epistēmē*). Since thought (*dianoia*) is not now a kind of knowledge, *noēsis* and *epistēmē* have in effect become one and the same. *Epistēmē* and *dianoia* are now jointly referred to as *noēsis*, because that whole section of the line onwhich they appear consists of intelligible objects (*noēton*).

4. A pun made possible by the fact that *alogon* can mean "irrational" (as applied to people) and "incommensurable" (as applied to lines in geometry).

c in love with hard work. How else do you suppose he
would be willing to carry out such hard physical
labors and also complete so much learning and
training?

GLAUCON: He would not, not unless his nature were an entirely good one.

SOCRATES: In any case, the mistake made at present—which, as we said before, explains why philosophy has fallen into dishonor—is that unworthy people take it up. For illegitimate people should not have taken it up, but genuine ones.

GLAUCON: How do you mean?

SOCRATES: In the first place, the one who takes it
up must not be halfhearted in his love of hard work,
with one half of him loving hard work and the other
d shirking it. That is what happens when someone is a
lover of physical training and a lover of hunting and
a lover of all kinds of hard bodily labor; yet is not a
lover of learning, a lover of listening, or a keen investigator, but hates the work involved in all such things. And someone whose love of hard work tends in the opposite direction is also defective.

GLAUCON: That's absolutely true.

SOCRATES: Similarly with regard to truth, won't we
e say that a soul is maimed if it hates a voluntary lie,
cannot endure to have one in itself, and is greatly angered when others lie; but is nonetheless content to accept an involuntary lie, does not get irritated when it is caught being ignorant, and bears its ignorance easily, wallowing in it like a pig?

536 GLAUCON: Absolutely.

SOCRATES: And with regard to temperance, courage, high-mindedness, and all the other parts of virtue, too, we must be especially on our guard to distinguish the illegitimate from the genuine. You see, when private individuals or cities do not know how to investigate all these things fully, they unwittingly employ defectives and illegitimates as their friends or rulers for whatever services they happen to need.

GLAUCON: Yes, that's just what happens.

SOCRATES: So we must take good care in all these
matters, since, if we bring people who are sound of
b limb and mind to so important a subject, and train
and educate them in it, justice itself will not find fault with us, and we will save both the city and its constitution. But if we bring people of a different sort to it, we will achieve precisely the opposite and let loose an even greater flood of ridicule upon philosophy as well.

GLAUCON: That would be a shame.

SOCRATES: It certainly would. But I seem to have made myself a little ridiculous just now.

GLAUCON: In what way?

SOCRATES: I forgot we were playing and spoke too c
vehemently. You see, while I was speaking I looked upon philosophy, and when I saw it undeservedly showered with abuse, I suppose I got irritated and, as if I were angry with those responsible, I said what I had to say in too serious a manner.

GLAUCON: Not too serious for me, by Zeus, as a member of the audience.

SOCRATES: But too serious for me as the speaker. In
any case, let's not forget that in our earlier selection
we chose older people, but here that is not permitted.
You see, we must not believe Solon when he says that d
as someone grows older, he is able to learn a lot. On the contrary, he is even less able to learn than to run. It is to young people that all large and frequent labors properly belong.

GLAUCON: Necessarily so.

SOCRATES: Well, then, calculation, geometry, and all the preparatory education that serves as preparation for dialectic must be offered to them in childhood—and not in the shape of compulsory instruction, either.

GLAUCON: Why's that?

SOCRATES: Because a free person should learn
nothing slavishly. For while compulsory physical e
labors do no harm to the body, no compulsory instruction remains in the soul.

GLAUCON: That's true.

SOCRATES: Well, then, do not use compulsion, my
very good man, to train the children in these subjects; use play instead. That way you will also be able
to see better what each of them is naturally suited for. 537

GLAUCON: What you say makes sense.

SOCRATES: Don't you remember that we also said that the children were to be led into war on horseback as observers, and that, wherever it is safe, they should be brought to the front and given a taste of blood, just like young dogs?

GLAUCON: I do remember.

SOCRATES: Those who always show the greatest facility in dealing with all these labors, studies, and fears must be enrolled in a unit.

b Glaucon: At what age?

Socrates: After they are released from compulsory physical training. For during that period, whether it is two or three years, they are incapable of doing anything else, since weariness and sleep are enemies of learning. At the same time, one of the important tests of each of them is how he fares in physical training.

Glaucon: It certainly is.

Socrates: Then, after that period, those selected
from among the twenty-year-olds will receive greater
honors than the others. Moreover, the subjects they
learned in no particular order in their education as
c children, they must now bring together into a unified
vision of their kinship with one another and with the
nature of what is.

Glaucon: That, at any rate, is the only instruction that remains secure in those who receive it.

Socrates: It is also the greatest test of which nature is dialectical and which is not. For the person who can achieve a unified vision is dialectical, and the one who cannot isn't.

Glaucon: I agree.

Socrates: Well, then, you will have to look out for
those among them who most possess that quality;
d who are resolute in their studies and also resolute in
war and the other things conventionally expected of
them. And when they have passed their thirtieth year,
you will have to select them in turn from among
those selected earlier and assign them yet greater
honors, and test them by means of the power of
dialectical discussion to see which of them can relinquish his eyes and other senses, and travel on in the
company of truth to what itself is. And here, comrade, you have a task that needs a lot of safeguarding.

Glaucon: How so?

Socrates: Don't you realize the harm caused by
e dialectical discussion as it is currently practiced?

Glaucon: What harm?

Socrates: Its practitioners are filled with lawlessness.

Glaucon: They certainly are.

Socrates: Do you think it is at all surprising that this happens to them? Aren't you sympathetic?

Glaucon: Why should I be?

Socrates: It is like the case of a supposititious
child brought up amid great wealth, a large and pow-
538 erful family, and many flatterers, who finds out, when
he has become a man, that he is not the child of his
professed parents and that he cannot discover his real
ones. Do you have any hunch as to what his attitude
would be to the flatterers, and to his supposed parents, during the time when he did not know about
the exchange, and, on the other hand, when he did
know? Or would you rather hear my hunch?

Glaucon: I would.

Socrates: Well, then, my hunch is that he would
be more likely to honor his father, his mother, and
the rest of his supposed family than the flatterers, less b
likely to overlook any of their needs, less likely to treat
them lawlessly in word or deed, and less likely to disobey them than the flatterers in any matters of importance, in the time when he did not know the truth.

Glaucon: Probably so.

Socrates: But when he became aware of the
truth, on the other hand, my hunch is that he would
withdraw his honor and devotion from his family
and increase them for the flatterers, whom he
would obey far more than before, and he would
begin to live the way they did, spend time with them
openly, and—unless he was thoroughly good by c
nature—care nothing for that father of his or any of
the rest of his supposed family.

Glaucon: All that would probably happen as you say. But how is it like the case of those who take up argument?

Socrates: As follows. I take it we hold from childhood convictions about what things are just and fine; we are brought up with them as with our parents; we obey and honor them.

Glaucon: Yes, we do.

Socrates: And there are also other practices,
opposite to those, which possess pleasures that flat- d
ter our soul and attract it to themselves, but which
do not persuade people who are at all moderate—
who continue to honor and obey the convictions of
their fathers.

Glaucon: That's right.

Socrates: What happens, then, when someone of
that sort is met by the question, "What is the fine?"
and, when he answers what he has heard from the
traditional lawgiver, the argument refutes him; and
by refuting him often and in many ways, reduces him
to the belief that the fine is no more fine than shameful, and the same with the just, the good, and the e
things he honored most—what do you think he will
do after that about honoring and obeying his earlier convictions?

Glaucon: It is inevitable that he won't honor or obey them in the same way.

Socrates: Then when he no longer regards them as honorable or as his own kin the way he did before, and cannot discover the true ones, will he be likely to adopt any other sort of life than the one
539 that flatters him?

Glaucon: No, he won't.

Socrates: And so he will be taken, I suppose, to have changed from being law-abiding to being lawless.

Glaucon: Inevitably.

Socrates: Isn't it likely, then, that this is what will happen to people who take up argument in that way, and, as I said just now, don't they deserve a lot of sympathy?

Glaucon: Yes, and pity too.

Socrates: Then if you do not want your thirty-year-olds to be objects of such pity, won't you have to employ every sort of precaution when they take up argument?

Glaucon: Yes, indeed.

Socrates: And isn't one very effective precaution
b not to let them taste argument while they are young? I mean, I don't suppose it has escaped your notice that when young people get their first taste of argument, they misuse it as if it were playing a game, always using it for disputation. They imitate those who have refuted them by refuting others themselves, and, like puppies, enjoy dragging and tearing with argument anyone within reach.

Glaucon: Excessively so.

Socrates: Then, when they have refuted many themselves and been refuted by many, they quickly
c fall into violently disbelieving everything they believed before. And as a result of this, they themselves and the whole of philosophy as well are discredited in the eyes of others.

Glaucon: That's absolutely true.

Socrates: But an older person would not be willing to take part in such madness. He will imitate someone who is willing to engage in dialectical discussion and look for the truth, rather than someone who plays at disputation as a game. He will be more moderate himself and will bring honor, rather than
d discredit, to the practice.

Glaucon: That's right.

Socrates: And wasn't everything we said before this also said as a precaution—that those with whom one takes part in arguments are to be orderly and steady by nature, and not, as now, those, however unsuitable, who chance to come along?

Glaucon: Yes, it was.

Socrates: Is it enough, then, if someone devotes himself continuously and strenuously to taking part in argument, doing nothing else, but training in it just as he did in the physical training that is its counterpart, but for twice as many years?

Glaucon: Do you mean six years or four? e

Socrates: It does not matter. Make it five. You see, after that, you must make them go down into the cave again, and compel them to take command in matters of war and the other offices suitable for young people, so that they won't be inferior to the others in experience. And in these offices, too, they must be tested to see whether they will remain steadfast when they are pulled in different directions, or
give way. 540

Glaucon: How much time do you assign to that?

Socrates: Fifteen years. Then, at the age of fifty, those who have survived the tests and are entirely best in every practical task and every science must be led at last to the end and compelled to lift up the radiant light of their souls, and to look toward what itself provides light for everything. And once they have seen the good itself, they must use it as their model and put the city, its citizens, and themselves in order throughout the remainder of their lives, each in turn. They b
will spend the greater part of their time doing philosophy, but, when his turn comes, each must labor in politics and rule for the city's sake, not as something fine, but rather as something that must be done. In that way, always having educated others like themselves to take their place as guardians of the city, they will depart for the Isles of the Blessed and dwell there. And the city will publicly establish memorials and sacrifices to them as daimons, if the Pythia agrees; but
if not, as happy and divine people. c

Glaucon: Like a sculptor, Socrates, you have produced thoroughly beautiful ruling men!

Socrates: And ruling women, too, Glaucon. You see, you must not think that what I have said applies any more to men than it does to those women of theirs who are born with the appropriate natures.

Glaucon: That's right, if indeed they are to share everything equally with the men, as we said.

Socrates: Well, then, do you agree that the things
d we have said about the city and its constitution are not altogether wishful thinking; that it is difficult for them to come about, but possible in a way, and in no way except the one we described: namely, when one or more true philosophers come to power in a city—people who think little of present honors, regarding them as illiberal and worthless, who prize what is right and the honors that come from it above every-
e thing, and who consider justice as the most important and most essential thing, serving it and fostering it as they set their city in order?

Glaucon: How will they do that?

Socrates: Everyone in the city who is over ten
541 years old they will send into the country. They will take over the children, and far removed from current habits, which their parents possess, they will bring them up in their own ways and laws, which are the ones we described before. And with the city and constitution we were discussing thus established in the quickest and easiest way, it will itself be happy and bring the greatest benefit to the people among whom it comes to be.

Glaucon: That's by far the quickest and easiest way. And in my opinion, Socrates, you have well described how it would come into existence, if it ever
did. b

Socrates: Haven't we said enough, then, about this city and the man who is like it? For surely it is clear what sort of person we will say he has to be.

Glaucon: Yes, it is clear. And as for your question, I think we have reached the end of this topic.

Book 8

Synopsis

The description of the *kallipolis* and the person whose character resembles it—the philosopher-king—is now complete. So Socrates returns to the argument interrupted at the beginning of Book 5. He describes four types of people and four types of constitutions that result when people of these types rule a city. He presents these as four stages in the increasing corruption or decline of the *kallipolis*, explaining why the *kallipolis* will decline by appeal to the Muses' story of the "geometrical number" (546a–547a). The first of the defective cities Socrates describes is a timocracy, which is ruled by people who are themselves ruled by the spirited element in their souls. The second is an oligarchy, which is ruled by people ruled by their necessary appetites. The third is a democracy, which is ruled by people ruled by their unnecessary appetites. The worst city of all is a tyranny, which is ruled by someone ruled by his lawless unnecessary appetites. After a brief excerpt from the opening of the book, we take up Socrates' discussion with his account of democracy and the democratic man.

Socrates: All right. We are agreed, then, Glaucon, 543
that if a city is going to be eminently well governed, women must be shared; children and their entire education must be shared; in both peace and war, pursuits must be shared; and their kings must be those among them who have proved best both in philosophy and where war is concerned.

Glaucon: We are agreed.

Socrates: Moreover, we also granted this: once b
the rulers are established, they will lead the soldiers and settle them in the kind of dwellings we described earlier, which are in no way private, but wholly shared. And surely we also came to an agreement, if you remember, about what sort of possessions they should have.

Glaucon: Yes, I do remember. We thought that none of them should acquire any of the things that others now do; but that, as athletes of war and
guardians, they should receive their minimum yearly c
upkeep from the other citizens as a wage for their guardianship, and take care of themselves and the rest of the city.

Socrates: That's right. But since we have completed that discussion, let's recall the point at which we began the digression that brought us here, so that we can continue on the same path again.

GLAUCON: That is not difficult. You see, much the
same as now, you were talking as if you had completed the description of the city. You were saying
that you would class both the city you described and
the man who is like it as good, even though, as it
d seems, you had a still finer city and man to tell us
about. But in any case, you were saying that the oth-
544 ers were defective, if it was correct. And you said, if I
remember, that of the remaining kinds of constitution four were worth discussing, each with defects we
should observe; and that we should do the same for
the people like them in order to observe them all,
come to an agreement about which man is best and
which worst, and then determine whether the best is
happiest and the worst most wretched, or whether it
is otherwise. I was asking you which four constitu-
b tions you had in mind, when Polemarchus and
Adeimantus interrupted. And that is when you took
up the discussion that led here.

SOCRATES: That's absolutely right.

GLAUCON: Like a wrestler, then, give me the same hold again, and when I ask the same question, try to tell me what you were about to say before.

SOCRATES: If I can.

GLAUCON: In any case, I really want to hear for myself what four constitutions you meant.

SOCRATES: It won't be difficult for you to hear
them. You see, the ones I mean are the very ones that
c already have names: the one that is praised by "the
many," your Cretan or Laconian[1] constitution. The
second—and second in the praise it receives—is
called oligarchy, a constitution filled with a host of
evils. Antagonistic to it, and next in order, is democracy. And "noble" tyranny, surpassing all of them, is
the fourth and most extreme disease of cities. Can
you think of another form of constitution—I mean,
another distinct in form from these? For, no doubt,
d there are dynasties and purchased kingships and
other similar constitutions in between these, which
one finds no less among barbarians than among
Greeks.

GLAUCON: Many strange ones are certainly mentioned, at least.

SOCRATES: Are you aware, then, that there must be
as many forms of human character as there are of
constitutions? Or do you think constitutions arise
from oak or rock[2] and not from the characters of the
people in the cities, which tip the scales, so to speak, e
and drag the rest along with them?

GLAUCON: No, they could not possibly arise from anything other than that.

SOCRATES: So, if there are five of cities, there must also be five ways of arranging private individual souls.

GLAUCON: Of course.

SOCRATES: Now, we have already described the one who is like aristocracy, the one we rightly describe as good and just.

GLAUCON: Yes, we have described him. 545

SOCRATES: Mustn't we next describe the inferior
ones—the victory-loving and honor-loving, which
correspond to the Laconian constitution, followed by
the oligarchic, democratic, and tyrannical—so that,
having discovered the most unjust of all, we can
oppose him to the most just and complete our investigation into how pure justice and pure injustice
stand with regard to the happiness or wretchedness
of the one who possesses them; and be persuaded
either by Thrasymachus to practice injustice or by
the argument that is now coming to light to practice
justice. b

GLAUCON: That's exactly what we must do.

SOCRATES: Then just as we began by looking for
the virtues of character in constitutions before looking for them in private individuals, thinking they
would be clearer in the former, shouldn't we first
examine the honor-loving constitution? I do not
know another name that is commonly applied to it;
it should be called either timocracy or timarchy.
Then shouldn't we examine that sort of man by comparing him to it, and, after that, oligarchy and the oligarchic man, and democracy and the democratic c
man? Fourth, having come to a city that is under a
tyrant and having examined it, shouldn't we look
into a tyrannical soul, and so try to become adequate
judges of the topic we proposed for ourselves?

GLAUCON: That, at any rate, would be a reasonable way for us to go about observing and judging.

SOCRATES: Come on, then, let's try to describe
how timocracy emerges from aristocracy. Or is it simply the case that, in all constitutions, change originates in the ruling element itself when faction breaks d

1. I.e., Spartan.

2. Homer, *Odyssey* 19.163.

out within it; but that if this group remains of one mind, then—however small it is—change is impossible?

GLAUCON: Yes, that's right.

SOCRATES: How, then, Glaucon, will our city be changed? How will faction arise, either between the auxiliaries and the rulers or within either group? Or
e do you want us to be like Homer and pray to the Muses to tell us "how faction first broke out,"[3] and have them speak in tragic tones, playing and jesting with us, as if we were children and they were speaking in earnest?

GLAUCON: How do you mean?

SOCRATES: Something like this: "It is difficult for a city constituted in this way to change. However,
546 since everything that comes-to-be must decay, not even one so constituted will last forever. On the contrary, it, too, must face dissolution. And this is how it will be dissolved: not only plants that grow in the earth, but also animals that grow upon it, have periods of fertility and infertility of both soul and bodies each time their cycles complete a revolution. These cycles are short for what is short-lived and the opposite for what is the opposite. However, even though they are wise, the people you have educated to be leaders in
b your city will, by using rational calculation combined with sense-perception, nonetheless fail to ascertain the periods of good fertility and of infertility for your species. Instead, these will escape them, and so they will sometimes beget children when they should not.

"Now, for the birth of a divine creature there is a cycle comprehended by a perfect number;[4] while for a human being, it is the first number in which are found increases involving both roots and powers, comprehending three intervals and four terms, of factors that cause likeness and unlikeness, cause increase and decrease, and make all things mutually agreeable and rational in their relations to one another. Of these factors, the base ones—four in
c relation to three, together with five—give two harmonies when thrice increased. One is a square, so many times a hundred. The other is of equal length one way, but oblong. One of its sides are 100 squares of the rational diameter of five each diminished by one, or alternatively 100 squares of the irrational diameter each diminished by two. The other side are 100 cubes of three. This whole geometrical number controls better and worse births.[5]

"And when, through ignorance of these, your *d*
guardians join brides and grooms at the wrong time, the children will be neither good-natured nor fortunate. The older generation will choose the best of these children, even though they do not deserve them. And when they in turn acquire their fathers' powers, the first thing they will begin to neglect as guardians will be us, by paying less attention to musical training than they should; and the second is physical training. Hence your young people will become more unmusical. And rulers chosen from among them won't be able to guard well the testing of Hesiod's and your own races—gold, silver, bronze, and *e*
iron. The intermixing of iron with silver and bronze 547
with gold will engender lack of likeness and unharmonious inequality, and these always breed war and hostility wherever they arise. We must declare faction to be 'of this lineage,' wherever and whenever it arises."

GLAUCON: And we will declare that they have answered correctly.

SOCRATES: They must. They are Muses, after all!

GLAUCON: What do the Muses say next? *b*

---

3. Apparently an adaptation of Homer, *Iliad* 16.112–3.

4. The divine creature seems to be the world or universe. See *Timaeus* 30b–d, 32d, 34a–b. Plato does not specify what its number is.

5. The human geometrical number is the product of 3, 4, and 5 "thrice increased": if $(3 \times 4 \times 5) \times (3 \times 4 \times 5) = (3 \times 4 \times 5)^2$ is one increase, $(3 \times 4 \times 5) \times (3 \times 4 \times 5) \times (3 \times 4 \times 5) \times (3 \times 4 \times 5) = (3 \times 4 \times 5)^4$ is three. This formula included "increases involving both roots and powers": $(3 \times 4 \times 5)$ is a root; its indices are powers. It "comprehends" three "intervals," symbolized by $\times$, and four "terms"—namely, the roots. The resulting number, 12,960,000, can be represented geometrically as: (1) a square whose sides are 3,600, or (2) an "oblong" or rectangle whose sides are 4,800 and 2,700. (1) is "so many times 100": 36 times. (2) is obtained as follows. The "rational diameter" of 5 is the nearest rational number to the real diameter of a square whose sides are 5. This diameter = $\sqrt{5^2 + 5^2} = \sqrt{50} = 7$. Since the square of 7 is 49, we get the longer side of the rectangle by diminishing 49 by 1 and multiplying the result by 100. This gives 4,800. The "irrational diameter" of 5 is $\sqrt{50}$. When squared (= 50), diminished by 2 (= 48), and multiplied by 100, this, too, is 4,800. The short side, "100 cubes of

SOCRATES: When faction arose, each of these two races, the iron and the bronze, pulled the constitution toward moneymaking and the acquisition of land, houses, gold, and silver. The other two, by contrast, the gold and silver races—since they are not poor, but naturally rich in their souls—led toward virtue and the old political system. Striving and struggling with one another, they compromised on a middle way: they distributed the land and houses among themselves as private property; enslaved and held as
c serfs and servants those whom they had previously guarded as free friends and providers of upkeep; and took responsibility themselves for making war and for guarding against the ones they had enslaved.

GLAUCON: I think that is how the transformation begins.

SOCRATES: Wouldn't this constitution, then, be somehow in the middle between aristocracy and oligarchy?

GLAUCON: Of course.

WE TURN NOW TO SOCRATES' ACCOUNT of democracy and the democratic man.

555b SOCRATES: Then democracy, it seems, must be considered next—both the way it comes to exist and what it is like when it does—so that when we know the character of this sort of man, we can present him for judgment in turn.

ADEIMANTUS: At any rate, that would be consistent with what we have been doing.

SOCRATES: Well, then, isn't the change from an oligarchy to a democracy due in some way or other to the insatiable desire for the good set before it—the need to become as rich as possible?

ADEIMANTUS: How so?

SOCRATES: Since the rulers rule in it because they c
own a lot, I suppose they are not willing to enact laws to prevent young people who have become intemperate from spending and wasting their wealth, so that by buying and making loans on the property of such people, the rulers themselves can become even richer and more honored.

ADEIMANTUS: That's their primary goal, at any rate.

SOCRATES: So, isn't it clear by now that you cannot honor wealth in a city and maintain temperance in the citizens at the same time, but must inevitably neglect one or the other? d

ADEIMANTUS: That is pretty clear.

SOCRATES: The negligent encouragement of intemperance in oligarchies, then, sometimes reduces people who are not ill born to poverty.

ADEIMANTUS: Indeed, it does.

SOCRATES: And these people sit around in the city, I suppose, armed with stings or weapons—some of them in debt, some disenfranchised, some both—hating and plotting against those who have acquired their property, and all the others as well; passionately longing for revolution. e

ADEIMANTUS: That's right.

SOCRATES: These moneymakers, with their heads down, pretending not to see them, inject the poison of their money into any of the rest who do not resist, and, carrying away a multitude of offspring in interest from their principal, greatly increase the size of the drone and beggar class in the city. 556

ADEIMANTUS: They certainly do increase it greatly.

SOCRATES: In any case, they are not willing to quench evil of this sort as it flares up, either by preventing a person from doing whatever he likes with his own property, or alternatively by passing this other law to do away with such abuses.

ADEIMANTUS: What law?

SOCRATES: The one that is next best and that compels the citizens to care about virtue. You see, if

---

three," = 2,700. The significance of the number is more controversial. The factors "that cause likeness and unlikeness, cause increase and decrease, and make all things mutually agreeable and rational in their relations to one another" are probably the numbers, since odd numbers were thought to cause likeness and even ones unlikeness (Aristotle, *Physics* 203a13–5). Of the numbers significant in human life, one is surely the 100 years of its maximum span (615a–b). Another might be the number of days in the year (roughly 360), and a third might be the divisions of those days into smaller units determined by the sun's place in the sky, since it is the sun that provides for "the coming-to-be, growth, and nourishment" of all visible things (509b). Assuming that those units are the 360 degrees of the sun's path around the earth (a suggestion due to Robin Waterfield), the number of moments in a human life that have a potential effect on its coming-to-be, growth, and nourishment would be 100 × 360 × 360, or 12,960,000—Plato's human geometrical number.

someone prescribed that most voluntary contracts be
b entered into at the lender's own risk, money would be less shamelessly pursued in the city and fewer of those evils we were mentioning just now would develop in it.

Adeimantus: Far fewer.

Socrates: But as it is, and for all these reasons, the rulers in the city treat their subjects in the way we described. And as for themselves and those belonging to them, don't they bring up the young to be fond of luxury, incapable of effort either mental or physical,
c too soft to endure pleasures or pains, and lazy?

Adeimantus: Of course.

Socrates: And haven't they themselves neglected everything except making money and been no more concerned about virtue than poor people are?

Adeimantus: Yes, they have.

Socrates: And when rulers and subjects, socialized in this way, meet on journeys or some other shared undertakings, whether in an embassy or a military campaign; or as shipmates or fellow soldiers; or when they watch one another in dangerous situa-
d tions—in these circumstances, don't you think the poor are in no way despised by the rich? On the contrary, don't you think it is often the case that a poor man, lean and suntanned, is stationed in battle next to a rich one, reared in the shade and carrying a lot of excess flesh, and sees him panting and completely at a loss? And don't you think he believes that it is because of the cowardice of the poor that such people are rich and that one poor man says to another when they meet in private: "These men are ours for
e the taking; they are good for nothing"?

Adeimantus: I know very well they do.

Socrates: Well, just as a sick body needs only a slight shock from outside to become ill and sometimes, even without external influence, becomes divided into factions, itself against itself, doesn't a city in the same condition need only a small pretext—such as one side bringing in allies from an oligarchy or the other from a democracy—to become ill and fight with itself? And doesn't it sometimes become divided into factions even without any external influence?

557 Adeimantus: Yes, violently so.

Socrates: Then democracy comes about, I suppose, when the poor are victorious, kill or expel the others, and give the rest an equal share in the constitution and the ruling offices, and the majority of offices in it are assigned by lot.

Adeimantus: Yes, that is how a democratic political system gets established, whether it comes to exist by force of arms or because intimidation drives its opponents into exile.

Socrates: In what way, then, do these people live? What sort of constitution do they have? For clearly the sort of man who is like it will turn out to be democratic. *b*

Adeimantus: Clearly.

Socrates: Well, in the first place, aren't they free? And isn't the city full of freedom and freedom of speech? And isn't there license in it to do whatever one wants?

Adeimantus: That's what they say, anyway.

Socrates: And where there is license, clearly each person would arrange his own life in whatever way pleases him.

Adeimantus: Clearly.

Socrates: I imagine it is in this constitution, then, *c*
that multifarious people come to exist.

Adeimantus: Of course.

Socrates: It looks, then, as though it is the most beautiful of all the constitutions. For just like an embroidered cloak embroidered with every kind of ornament, it is embroidered with every sort of character, and so would appear to be the most beautiful. And presumably, many people would behave like women and children looking at embroidered objects and actually judge it to be the most beautiful.

Adeimantus: They certainly would.

Socrates: What is more, bless you, it is also a handy place in which to look for a constitution! *d*

Adeimantus: Why is that?

Socrates: Because it contains all kinds of constitutions, as a result of its license. So whoever wants to organize a city, as we were doing just now, probably has to go to a democracy and, as if he were in a supermarket of constitutions, pick out whatever pleases him and establish it.

Adeimantus: He probably wouldn't be at a loss for *e*
examples, anyway!

Socrates: There is no compulsion to rule in this city, even if you are qualified to rule, or to be ruled if you do not want to be; or to be at war when the others are at war, or to keep the peace when the others are keeping it, if you do not want peace; or, even if there happens to be a law preventing you from ruling

or from serving on a jury, to be any the less free to
558 rule or serve on a jury—isn't that a heavenly and
pleasant way to pass the time, while it lasts?

Adeimantus: It probably is—while it lasts.

Socrates: And what about the calm of some of their condemned criminals? Isn't that a sophisticated quality? Or have you never seen people who have been condemned to death or exile in a constitution of this sort staying on all the same and living right in the middle of things, without anyone giving them a thought or staring at them, while they stroll around like a hero?[6]

Adeimantus: Yes, I have seen it a lot.

Socrates: And what about the city's tolerance, its
b complete lack of petty-mindedness, and its utter dis-
regard for the things we took so seriously when we
were founding the city—that unless someone had
transcendent natural gifts, he would never become a
good man if he did not play fine games right from
early childhood and engage in practices that are all
of that same sort? Isn't it magnificent how it tramples
all that underfoot, gives no thought to what sort of
practices someone went in for before he entered politics, and honors him if only he tells them he wishes
c the majority well?

Adeimantus: That's true nobility!

Socrates: These, then, and others akin to them are the characteristics a democracy would possess. And it would, it seems, be a pleasant constitution—lacking rulers but not complexity, and assigning a sort of equality to equals and unequals alike.

Adeimantus: Yes, that's well known!

Socrates: Look and see, then, what sort of private individual resembles it. Or should we first consider, as we did in the case of the constitution, how he comes to exist?

Adeimantus: Yes.

Socrates: Well, doesn't it happen this way?
Mightn't we suppose that our thrifty oligarchic man
d had a son brought up by his father with his father's
traits of character?

Adeimantus: Of course.

Socrates: Then he too would rule by force the pleasures that exist in him—the spendthrift ones that do not make money; the ones that are called unnecessary.

Adeimantus: Clearly.

Socrates: In order not to have a discussion in the dark, would you like us first to define which appetites are necessary and which are not?

Adeimantus: I would.

Socrates: Well, then, wouldn't those we cannot
deny rightly be called necessary? And also those
whose satisfaction benefits us? For we are by nature e
compelled to try to satisfy them both. Isn't that so?

Adeimantus: Of course.

Socrates: So, we would be right to apply the term 559
"necessary" to them?

Adeimantus: We would be right.

Socrates: What about those someone could get rid of if he started practicing from childhood, those whose presence does no good but may even do the opposite? If we said that all of them were unnecessary, would we be right?

Adeimantus: We would be right.

Socrates: Let's pick an example of each, so that we have a pattern to follow.

Adeimantus: Yes, let's.

Socrates: Wouldn't the desire to eat to the point
of health and wellbeing, and the desire for bread and
relishes be necessary ones? b

Adeimantus: I suppose so.

Socrates: The desire for bread is surely necessary on both counts, in that it is beneficial and that unless it is satisfied, we die.

Adeimantus: Yes.

Socrates: And so is the one for relishes, insofar as it is beneficial and conduces to well-being.

Adeimantus: Indeed.

Socrates: What about an appetite that goes
beyond these and seeks other sorts of foods; that, if it
is restrained from childhood and educated, most people can get rid of; and that is harmful to the body and
harmful to the soul's capacity for wisdom and temperance? Wouldn't it be correct to call it unnecessary? c

Adeimantus: Entirely correct.

Socrates: Wouldn't we also say that the latter desires are spendthrift, then, whereas the former are moneymaking because they are useful where work is concerned?

Adeimantus: Certainly.

6. Dead heroes were worshipped as minor deities in Greek religion, particularly in their birthplaces, where their spirits were thought to linger.

Socrates: And won't we say the same about sexual appetites and the rest?

Adeimantus: Yes.

Socrates: And didn't we say that the person we just now called a drone is full of such pleasures and appetites and is ruled by the unnecessary ones, while the one who is ruled by his necessary appetites is a
d thrifty oligarch?

Adeimantus: Of course we did.

Socrates: Let's go back, then, and say how the democrat develops from the oligarch. It seems to me as if it mostly happens this way.

Adeimantus: What way?

Socrates: When a young man who is reared in the uneducated and thrifty manner we described just now tastes the honey of the drones and associates with wild and terrible creatures who can provide multifarious pleasures of every degree of complexity and sort, that probably marks the beginning of his
e transformation from having an oligarchic constitution within him to having a democratic one.

Adeimantus: It most certainly does.

Socrates: So, just as the city changed when one party received help from like-minded alliance outside, doesn't the young man change in turn when external appetites of the same type and quality as it come to the aid of one of the parties within him?

Adeimantus: Absolutely.

Socrates: And I suppose if a counter-alliance comes to the aid of the oligarchic party within him—whether from his father or from the rest of his family,
560 who exhort and reproach him—then there is a faction and an opposing faction within him, and he battles against himself.

Adeimantus: Of course.

Socrates: And sometimes, I suppose, the democratic party yields to the oligarchic, some of its appetites are overcome while others are expelled, and kind of shame rises in the young man's soul and order is restored.

Adeimantus: That does sometimes happen.

Socrates: Moreover, I suppose, as some appetites are expelled, others akin to them are being nurtured undetected because of the father's ignorance of up-
b bringing, and become numerous and strong.

Adeimantus: At any rate, that's what usually happens.

Socrates: Then these desires draw him back to his old associates and, in secret intercourse, breed a multitude of others.

Adeimantus: Of course.

Socrates: Finally, I suppose, they seize the citadel of the young man's soul, since they realize that it is empty of the fine studies and practices and the true arguments that are the best watchmen and guardians in the minds of men loved by the gods.

Adeimantus: By far the best. *c*

Socrates: Then, I suppose, beliefs and arguments that are lying imposters rush up and occupy this same part of him in place of the others.

Adeimantus: They do, indeed.

Socrates: Won't he then return to those Lotus-eaters and live with them openly? And if any help should come to the thrifty part of his soul from his relatives, don't those imposter arguments, having barred the gates of the royal wall within him, prevent the allied force itself from entering and even refusing to admit arguments of older, private individuals as
ambassadors? Proving stronger in the battle, won't they *d*
call reverence foolishness and drive it out as a dishonored fugitive? And calling temperance cowardliness, won't they shower it with abuse and banish it? As for moderate and orderly expenditure, won't they persuade him that it is boorish and illiberal, and join with a multitude of useless appetites to drive it over the border?

Adeimantus: They will indeed.

Socrates: And when they have somehow emptied and purged these from the soul of the one they are
seizing hold of and initiating with solemn rites, they *e*
then immediately proceed to return arrogance, anarchy, extravagance, and shamelessness from exile in a blaze of torchlight, accompanied with a vast chorus of followers and crowned with garlands. They praise them and give them fine names, calling arrogance "good breeding," anarchy "freedom," extravagance "magnificence," and shamelessness "courage." Isn't it
in some such way as this that a young person *561*
exchanges an upbringing among necessary appetites for the freeing and release of useless and unnecessary pleasures?

Adeimantus: Yes, that's clearly the way it happens.

Socrates: Then in his subsequent life, I suppose, someone like that spends no less money, effort, and time on the necessary pleasures than on the unnecessary

pleasures. But if he is lucky and does not go beyond the limits in his bacchic frenzy, and if, as a result of his growing somewhat older, the great tumult within him
passes, he welcomes back some of the exiles and
b ceases to surrender himself completely to the new-
comers. Then, putting all his pleasures on an equal footing, he lives, always surrendering rule over himself to whichever desire comes along, as if it were chosen by lot,[7] until it is satisfied; and after that to another, dishonoring none but satisfying all equally.

ADEIMANTUS: He does, indeed.

SOCRATES: And he does not accept or admit true argument into the guardhouse if someone tells him
that some pleasures belong to fine and good
c appetites and others to bad ones, and that he must
practice and honor the former and restrain and enslave the latter. On the contrary, he denies all this and declares that they are all alike and must be honored on an equal basis.

ADEIMANTUS: That's exactly what he feels and does.

SOCRATES: And so he lives from day to day, gratifying the appetite of the moment. Sometimes he drinks heavily while listening to the flute, while at others he drinks only water and is on a diet. Sometimes he goes in for physical training, while there are others when he is idle and neglects everything. Sometimes he
spends his time engaged in what he takes to be phi- d
losophy. Often, though, he takes part in politics, leaping to his feet and saying and doing whatever happens to come into his mind. If he admires some military men, that is the direction in which he is carried; if some moneymakers, then in that different one. There is neither order nor necessity in his life, yet he calls it pleasant, free, and blessedly happy, and follows it throughout his entire life.

ADEIMANTUS: You have perfectly described the life
of a man devoted to legal equality.[8] e

SOCRATES: I certainly think he is a multifarious man and full of all sorts of characters, beautiful and complex, like the democratic city. Many men and women would envy his life because of the great number of examples of constitutions and characters it contains within it.

ADEIMANTUS: Yes, that's right.

SOCRATES: Well, then, will we set this man alongside democracy as the one who would rightly be 562
called democratic?

ADEIMANTUS: We will.

Book 9

Synopsis

A LENGTHY DESCRIPTION of the tyrant begins the book. Socrates is then ready to respond to the challenge Glaucon raised in Book 2. His response consists of three complex arguments. The first (580a–c) appeals to the description of the five cities and the five corresponding character types. It concludes that a philosopher-king is the happiest and most just of people, a timocrat second, an oligarch third, a democrat fourth, and a tyrant least happy and least just. The second argument (580d–583b) appeals to the triadic division of the soul. Socrates argues that a philosopher's assessment of the relative pleasantness of his life and those of money-lovers and honor-lovers is more reliable than their assessments of the relative pleasantness of his life and theirs. The third argument (583b–588a) uses the metaphysical theory developed in Books 5–7, together with the psychological theory of Book 4, to develop a complex theory of pleasure. It concludes that a philosopher's pleasures are truer and purer than those of a money-lover or honor-lover. Our selection begins with the description of the tyrannical man:

SOCRATES: The tyrannical man himself remains to be 571
investigated: how he evolves from a democratic one, what he is like once he has come to exist, and whether the way he lives is wretched or blessedly happy.

ADEIMANTUS: Yes, he still remains.

7. Many public officials in democratic Athens were elected by lot.

8. *Isonomia:* an important democratic value.

Socrates: Do you know what else I still miss?
Adeimantus: What?
Socrates: I do not think we have adequately distinguished the nature and number of our appetites.
And if that subject is not adequately dealt with, our
b investigation will lack clarity.
Adeimantus: Well, isn't now as fine a time as any?
Socrates: It certainly is. So, consider what I want
to look at in them. It is this: among unnecessary
pleasures and appetites, there are some that seem to
me to be lawless. These are probably present in all of
us, but they are held in check by the laws and by our
better appetites allied with reason. In a few people
they have been eliminated entirely or only a few
weak ones remain, while in others they are stronger
c and more numerous.
Adeimantus: Which ones do you mean?
Socrates: The ones that wake up when we are
asleep, whenever the rest of the soul—the rational,
gentle, and ruling element—slumbers. Then the bestial and savage part, full of food or drink, comes alive,
casts off sleep, and seeks to go and gratify its own
characteristic instincts. You know it will dare to do
anything in such a state, released and freed from all
shame and wisdom. In fantasy, it does not shrink
from trying to have sex with a mother or with anyone
d else—man, god, or beast. It will commit any foul
murder, and there is no food it refuses to eat. In a
word, it does not refrain from anything, no matter
how foolish or shameful.
Adeimantus: That's absolutely true.
Socrates: On the other hand, I suppose someone
who keeps himself healthy and temperate will
awaken his rational element before going to sleep
and feast it on fine arguments and investigations,
which he has brought to an agreed conclusion within
himself. As for the appetitive element, he neither
e starves nor overfeeds it, so it will slumber and not disturb the best element with its pleasure or pain but
572 will leave it alone, just by itself and pure, to investigate and reach out for the perception of something
—whether past, present, or future—that it does not
know. He soothes the spirited element in a similar
way and does not get angry and fall asleep with his
spirit still aroused. And when he has calmed these
two elements and stimulated the third, in which
wisdom resides, he takes his rest. You know this is
the state in which he most readily grasps the truth
and in which the visions appearing in his dreams
are least lawless. b
Adeimantus: I completely agree.
Socrates: Well, we have been led a bit astray and
said a bit too much. What we want to pay attention to
is this: there are appetites of a terrible, savage, and
lawless kind in everyone—even in those of us who
seem to be entirely moderate. This surely becomes
clear in sleep. Do you think I am talking sense? Do
you agree with me?
Adeimantus: Yes, I do agree.
Socrates: Now, recall what we said the democratic man is like. He was the result, we presumed, of
a childhood upbringing by a thrifty father who hon- c
ored only appetites that made money and despised
the unnecessary ones whose objects are amusement
and showing off. Isn't that right?
Adeimantus: Yes.
Socrates: And by associating with more sophisticated men who are full of the appetites we just
described, he starts to indulge in every kind of arrogance and adopt their kind of behavior, because of
his hatred of his father's thrift. But, since he has a better nature than his corrupters, he is pulled in both
directions and settles in the middle between their two
ways of life. And enjoying each in what he takes to be
moderation, he lives a life that is neither illiberal nor d
lawless, transformed now from an oligarch to a democrat.
Adeimantus: Yes, that was—and still is—our
belief about someone like that.
Socrates: Suppose, then, that this man has now
in turn become older and has a son who is also
brought up in his father's way of life.
Adeimantus: I will.
Socrates: Suppose, too, that the same things happen to him as happened to his father: he is led into
all the kinds of lawlessness that those leading him call
total freedom. His father and the rest of his family e
come to the aid of the appetites that are in the middle, while the others help the opposite ones. And
when these terrible enchanters and tyrant-makers
have no hope of keeping hold of the young man in
any other way, they contrive to implant a powerful
passion in him as the popular leader of those idle and
profligate appetites—a sort of great, winged drone. 573
Or do you think passion is ever anything else in such
people?

Adeimantus: I certainly do not think it is.

Socrates: And when the other appetites come buzzing around—filled with incense, perfumes, wreaths, wine, and all the other pleasures found in such company, they feed the drone, make it grow as large as possible, and plant the sting of longing in it. Then this popular leader of the soul adopts madness
b as its bodyguard and is stung to frenzy. If it finds any beliefs or appetites in the man that are regarded as good or are still moved by shame, it destroys them and throws them out, until it has purged him of temperance and filled him with imported madness.

Adeimantus: You have perfectly described how a tyrannical man comes to exist.

Socrates: Is that, then, why Passion has long been called a tyrant?

Adeimantus: Probably so.

Socrates: And hasn't a drunken man, my friend,
c something of a tyrannical cast of mind, too?

Adeimantus: He has.

Socrates: And of course someone who is mad and deranged attempts to rule not only human beings, but gods as well, and expects to be able to rule them.

Adeimantus: Of course.

Socrates: A man becomes tyrannical in the precise sense, then, you marvelous fellow, when his nature or his practices or both together lead him to drunkenness, passion, and melancholia.

Adeimantus: Absolutely.

We take up the discussion with the comparison between the various sorts of people—democratic, tyrannical, and so on—and the relative justice and happiness of their lives.

Socrates: Come on, then, and tell me now at last, like the judge who makes the final decision,[1] who
580b you believe is first in happiness and who second, and judge the others similarly, making five altogether—kingly, timocratic, oligarchic, democratic, tyrannical.

Glaucon: That's an easy judgment. You see, I rank them in the order of their appearance, just as if they were choruses, both in virtue and vice and in happiness and its opposite.

Socrates: Shall we, then, hire a herald, or shall I myself announce that the son of Ariston has given as his verdict that the best and most just is the most happy, and that he is the one who is most kingly and c
rules like a king over himself; whereas the worst and most unjust is the most wretched, and he, again, is the one who, because he is most tyrannical, is the greatest tyrant over himself and his city?

Glaucon: You have announced it!

Socrates: And shall I add that it holds whether or not their characters remain hidden from all human beings and gods?

Glaucon: Do add it.

Socrates: Well, then, that is one of our demonstrations. But look at this second one and see if you think there is anything in it. d

Glaucon: What is it?

Socrates: In just the way a city is divided into three classes, the soul of each person is also divided in three. That is the reason I think there is another demonstration.

Glaucon: What is it?

Socrates: The following. It seems to me that the three also have three kinds of pleasure, one peculiar to each. The same holds of appetites and kinds of rule.

Glaucon: How do you mean?

Socrates: One element, we say, is that with which a person learns; another, that with which he feels anger. As for the third, because it is multiform, we had no one special name for it but named it after the biggest and strongest thing it has in it. I mean we e
called it the appetitive element because of the intensity of its appetites for food, drink, sex, and all the things that go along with them. We also called it the money-loving element, because such appetites are most easily satisfied by means of money. 581

Glaucon: And we were right.

Socrates: So, if we said its pleasure and love are for profit, wouldn't that best bring it together under one heading for the purposes of our argument and make clear to us what we mean when we speak of this part of the soul? And would we be right in calling it money-loving and profit-loving?

Glaucon: I think so, anyway.

1. The reference is to the way plays were judged at dramatic festivals in Athens. A herald announced the results.

Socrates: What about the spirited element? Don't we say that its whole aim is always mastery, victory, and high repute?

b Glaucon: Certainly.

Socrates: Then wouldn't it strike the right note for us to call it victory-loving and honor-loving?

Glaucon: The absolutely right one.

Socrates: But surely it is clear to everyone that the element we learn with is always wholly straining to know where the truth lies, and that of the three it cares least for money and reputation.

Glaucon: By far the least.

Socrates: Wouldn't it be appropriate, then, for us to call it learning-loving and philosophic?

Glaucon: Of course.

Socrates: And doesn't it rule in some people's souls, while one of the others—whichever it happens
c to be—rules in other people's?

Glaucon: Yes.

Socrates: And isn't that why we say there are three primary types of people, philosophic, victory-loving, and profit-loving?

Glaucon: Absolutely.

Socrates: And also three kinds of pleasure, one assigned to each of them?

Glaucon: Exactly.

Socrates: You realize, then, that if you chose to ask each of these three types of people in turn to tell you which of their lives is most pleasant, each would give the highest praise to his own? Won't the money-maker say that, compared to that of making a profit, the pleasures of being honored or of learning are
d worthless unless there is something in them that makes money?

Glaucon: True.

Socrates: What about the honor-lover? Doesn't he think the pleasure of making money is vulgar, while the pleasure of learning—except to the extent that learning brings honor—is smoke and nonsense?

Glaucon: He does.

Socrates: As for the philosopher, what do you suppose he thinks of the other pleasures in compari-
e son to that of knowing where the truth lies and always enjoying some variety of it while he is learning? Won't he think they are far behind? And won't he call them really necessary, since he would have no need for them if they were not necessary for life?

Glaucon: He will. We can be sure of that.

Socrates: Since the pleasures of each kind and the lives themselves dispute with one another—not about which life is finer or more shameful or better or worse—but about which is more pleasant and less painful, how are we to know which of them is speaking the absolute truth? 582

Glaucon: I have no idea how to answer that.

Socrates: Consider the matter this way: how should we judge things if we want to judge them well? Isn't it by experience, knowledge, and argument? Or could someone have better criteria than these?

Glaucon: No, of course not.

Socrates: Consider, then. Of the three types of men, which has most experience of the pleasures we mentioned? Do you think the profit-lover learns what the truth itself is like, or has more experience of the pleasure of knowing, than the philosopher does of making a profit? b

Glaucon: There is a big difference between them. You see, the latter has to have tasted the other kinds of pleasure beginning from childhood. But it is not necessary for the profit-lover to taste or experience how sweet is the pleasure of learning the nature of the things that are—and even if he were eager to, he could not easily do so.

Socrates: So, the philosopher is far superior to the profit-lover in his experience of both kinds of pleasures.

Glaucon: Very far superior. c

Socrates: What about compared to the honor-lover? Is he more inexperienced in the pleasure of being honored than the latter is in the pleasure of knowing?

Glaucon: No. Honor comes to all of them, provided they accomplish their several aims. For the rich man, too, is honored by many people, as well as are the courageous and the wise ones. So, all have experienced what the pleasure of being honored is like. But the pleasure pertaining to the sight of what is cannot be tasted by anyone except the philosopher.

Socrates: So, as far as experience goes, then, he is the finest judge among the three types of men. d

Glaucon: By far.

Socrates: And he alone will have gained his experience with the help of knowledge.

Glaucon: Of course.

Socrates: Moreover, the tool that should be used to judge is not the tool of the profit-lover or the honor-lover, but of the philosopher.

Glaucon: What one is that?

Socrates: Surely we said that judgment should be made by means of arguments. Didn't we?

Glaucon: Yes.

Socrates: And arguments are, above all, his tool.

Glaucon: Absolutely.

Socrates: If the things being judged were best judged by means of wealth and profit, the praise and
e criticism of the profit-lover would necessarily be closest to the truth.

Glaucon: It would indeed.

Socrates: And if by means of honor, victory, and courage, wouldn't it be those of the honor-lover and victory-lover?

Glaucon: Clearly.

Socrates: But since it is by means of experience, knowledge, and argument?

Glaucon: The praise of the philosopher and argument-lover must be closest to the truth.

Socrates: So, of the three pleasures, then, the
583 most pleasant would be that of the part of the soul with which we learn, and the one of us in whom it rules has the most pleasant life.

Glaucon: How could it be otherwise? The knowledgeable person at least praises with authority when he praises his own life.

Socrates: What life and pleasure does the judge say are in second place?

Glaucon: Clearly, those of the warrior and honor-lover, since they are closer to his own than those of the moneymaker.

Socrates: Then those of the profit-lover come last, apparently.

Glaucon: Of course.

Socrates: Well, then, that makes two in a row.
b And twice the just person has defeated the unjust one. Now comes the third, which is dedicated in Olympic fashion to our savior, Olympian Zeus. Observe, then, that the other pleasures—apart from that of the knowledgeable person—are neither entirely true nor pure. On the contrary, they are like some sort of illusionist painting, as I think I have heard some wise person say. Yet, if that were true, it would be the greatest and most decisive of the overthrows.

We omit the final demonstration, which hinges on a rather technical account of pleasure, and take up the discussion as it returns to Glaucon's challenge from Book 2.

Socrates: All right, then. Since we have reached
this point in the argument, let's return to the first 588b
things we mentioned that led us here. I think someone said that doing injustice profits a completely unjust person who is believed to be just. Wasn't that the claim?

Glaucon: Yes, it was.

Socrates: Let's discuss it with its proponent, then, since we have now agreed on the respective effects of doing unjust and doing just things.

Glaucon: How?

Socrates: By fashioning an image of the soul in words, so that the one who said that will know what he was saying.

Glaucon: What sort of image? c

Socrates: One of those creatures that ancient legends say used to exist. The Chimera, Scylla, Cerberus, and the numerous other cases where many different kinds are said to have grown together into one.

Glaucon: Yes, they do describe such things.

Socrates: Well, then, fashion a single species of complex, many-headed beast, with a ring of tame and savage animal heads that it can grow and change at will.

Glaucon: That's a task for a clever fashioner of
images! Still, since language is easier to fashion than d
wax and the like, consider the fashioning done.

Socrates: Now, fashion another single species—of lion—and a single one of human being. But make the first much the largest and the second, second in size.

Glaucon: That's easier—the fashioning is done.

Socrates: Now, join the three in one, so that that they somehow grow together naturally.

Glaucon: They are joined.

Socrates: Then fashion around the outside the image of one of them, that of the human being, so that to anyone who cannot see what is inside, but sees only the outer shell, it will look like a single creature,
a human being. e

Glaucon: The surrounding shell has been fashioned.

Socrates: When someone claims, then, that it profits this human being to do injustice, but that doing what is just brings no advantage, let's tell him that he is saying nothing other than that it profits him to feed well and strengthen the multifarious

beast, as well as the lion and everything that pertains
to the lion; to starve and weaken the human being,
589 so that he is dragged along wherever either of the
other two leads; and not to accustom the two to one
another or make them friends, but leave them to
bite and fight and devour one another.

GLAUCON: Yes, that's exactly what someone who praises doing injustice is saying.

SOCRATES: On the other hand, wouldn't someone
who claims that what is just is profitable be saying we
should do and say what will give the inner human
b being the greatest mastery over the human being, to
get him to take care of the many-headed beast like a
farmer, feeding and domesticating the gentle heads
and preventing the savage ones from growing; to
make the lion's nature his ally; and to care for all in
common, bringing them up in such a way that they
will be friends with each other and with himself?

GLAUCON: Yes, that's exactly what someone who praises justice is saying.

SOCRATES: From every point of view, then, the one
who praises what is just speaks truly while the one who
praises what is unjust speaks falsely. For whether
c we consider pleasure or good reputation or advantage, the one who praises the just tells the truth
while the one who condemns it has nothing sound
to say and condemns with no knowledge of what
he is condemning.

GLAUCON: None at all, in my opinion.

SOCRATES: Then let's persuade him gently—after
all, he is not getting it wrong intentionally—by questioning him as follows: "Bless you, but shouldn't we
claim that this is also the basis of the conventional
views about what is fine and what is shameful: what
is fine is what subordinates the beastlike elements
in our nature to the human one—or better, per-
d haps, to the divine, whereas what is shameful is
what enslaves the tame element to the savage?" Will
he agree, or what?

GLAUCON: He will if he takes my advice.

SOCRATES: Is there anyone, then, in light of this
argument, who profits by acquiring gold unjustly, if
the result is something like this: in taking the gold,
he simultaneously enslaves the best element in himself to the most wicked? If he got the gold by enslav-
e ing his son or daughter to savage and evil men, it
would not profit him, no matter how much he got for
doing it. So, if he ruthlessly enslaves the most divine
element in himself to the most godless and polluted,
how could he fail to be wretched, when he accepts
golden gifts in return for a far more terrible destruction than that of Eriphyle, who took the necklace in 590
return for her husband's soul?[2]

GLAUCON: A much more terrible one. I will answer for him.

SOCRATES: And don't you think intemperance has long been condemned for reasons of this sort; that it is because of vices like it that that terrible creature, the large and multiform beast, is given more freedom than it should be?

GLAUCON: Clearly.

SOCRATES: And aren't stubbornness and peevishness condemned because they inharmoniously increase and stretch the lionlike and snakelike[3]
element? b

GLAUCON: Certainly.

SOCRATES: And aren't luxury and softness condemned for slackening and loosening this same part, because that produces cowardice in it?

GLAUCON: Of course.

SOCRATES: And aren't flattery and illiberality condemned because they subject this same spirited element to the moblike beast, allow it to be showered with abuse for the sake of money and the latter's insatiability, and habituate it from youth to be an ape instead of a lion?

GLAUCON: Yes, indeed. c

SOCRATES: Why do you think someone is reproached for menial work or handicraft? Or shall we say that it is for no other reason than because the best element is naturally weak in him, so that it cannot rule the beasts within him, but can only serve them and learn what flatters them?

---

2. Eriphyle was bribed by Polynices to persuade her husband, Amphiaraus, to take part in an attack on Thebes. He was killed, and she was murdered by her son in revenge.

3. The snakelike element hasn't been previously mentioned, although it may be included in "all that pertains to" the lion (588e). It symbolizes some of the meaner components of the spirited part, such as peevishness, which it would be unnatural to attribute to the noble lion. Snakes were thought to guard shrines and other sacred places. Including a snakelike element in the part of the soul dominant in guardians is, therefore, somewhat natural.

Glaucon: Apparently.

Socrates: In order to ensure, then, that someone
like that is also ruled by something similar to what
rules the best person, we say that he should be the slave
of that best person who has the divine ruler within him-
d self. It is not to harm the slave that we say he should be
ruled, as Thrasymachus supposed was true of all subjects, but because it is better for everyone to be ruled by
a divine and wise ruler—preferably one that is his
own and that he has inside himself; otherwise one
imposed on him from outside, so that we may all be
as alike and as friendly as possible, because we are all
captained by the same thing.

Glaucon: Yes, that's right.

Socrates: This is clearly the aim of the law as
e well, which is the ally of everyone in the city. It is also
our aim in ruling our children. We do not allow
them to be free until we establish a constitution in
them as in a city. That is to say, we take care of their
best part with the similar one in ourselves and equip
591 them with a guardian and ruler similar to our own to
take our place. Only then do we set them free.

Glaucon: Yes, that's clearly so.

Socrates: How, then, will we claim, Glaucon, and on the basis of what argument, that it profits someone to do injustice, or what is intemperate, or some shameful thing that will make him worse, even if it brings more money or power of some other sort?

Glaucon: There's no way we can.

Socrates: Or how can we claim that it profits him
to be undetected in his injustice and not pay the
penalty? I mean, doesn't the one who remains unde-
b tected become even worse, while in the one who
is discovered and punished, the bestial element is
calmed and tamed and the gentle one freed? Doesn't
his entire soul, when it returns to its best nature and
acquires temperance and justice along with wisdom,
achieve a condition that is as more honorable than
that of a body when it acquires strength and beauty
along with health, as a soul is more honorable than a
body?

Glaucon: Absolutely.

Socrates: Won't anyone with any sense, then,
give everything he has to achieve it as long as he
c lives? First, won't he honor the studies that produce
it and not honor the others?

Glaucon: Clearly.

Socrates: Second, as regards the condition and
nurture of his body, not only will he not give himself
over to bestial and irrational pleasure, and live
turned in that direction; but he won't make health
his aim nor give precedence to the ways of becoming
strong or healthy or beautiful, unless he is also going to
become temperate as a result of them. On the contrary,
it is clear that he will always be tuning the harmony of d
his body for the sake of the concord of his soul.

Glaucon: He certainly will, if indeed he is going to be truly musical.

Socrates: Won't he also keep order and concord in his acquisition of money? He won't be dazzled, will he, by what the masses regard as blessed happiness, and—by increasing the size of his wealth without limit—acquire an unlimited number of evils?

Glaucon: Not in my view.

Socrates: On the contrary, he will keep his eye
fixed on the constitution within him and guard e
against disturbing anything there either with too
much money or with too little. Captaining himself
in that way, he will increase and spend his wealth, as
far as possible by reference to it.

Glaucon: That's exactly what he will do.

Socrates: Where honors are concerned, too, he
will keep his eye on the same thing. He will willingly 592
share in and taste those he believes will make him better. But those that might overthrow the established
condition of his soul, he will avoid, both in private
and in public.

Glaucon: So, he won't be willing to take part in politics, then, if that is what he cares about.

Socrates: Yes, by the dog, in his own city, he certainly will. But he may not be willing to do so in his fatherland, unless some divine good luck chances to be his.

Glaucon: I understand. You mean in the city we
have just been founding and describing; the one that
exists in words, since I do not think it exists anywhere
on earth. b

Socrates: But there may perhaps be a model of it in the heavens for anyone who wishes to look at it and to found himself on the basis of what he sees. It makes no difference at all whether it exists anywhere or ever will. You see, he would take part in the politics of it alone, and of no other.

Glaucon: That's probably right.

Book 10

Synopsis

The kind of poetry about human beings permitted in the *kallipolis*—postponed in Book 3 (392a–c)—is returned to. This is the moment at which Socrates' new philosophy-based education confronts the traditional poetry-based one. Central to the discussion is a new account of *mimēsis*—imitation—based on the metaphysical theories of Books 5–7. The next topic is the immortality of the soul. Finally, by appeal to the Myth of Er, Socrates argues that the good consequences of justice both in this life and the next far outweigh those of injustice. This completes the argument that justice is choiceworthy both for its own sake and for its consequences, and so belongs in the best of the three classes of goods that Glaucon distinguished. Our selection is confined to the discussion of the immortality of the soul and the concluding Myth of Er.

608c Socrates: And yet the greatest rewards of virtue, and
the prizes proposed for it, have not been discussed.

Glaucon: You must have something incredibly great in mind, if it is greater than those already mentioned!

Socrates: In a short period of time, could anything really great come to pass? I mean, the entire period from childhood to old age is surely short when compared to the whole of time.

Glaucon: It's a mere nothing.

Socrates: Well, then, do you think an immortal
thing should be seriously concerned with that period
d rather than the whole of time?

Glaucon: I suppose not, but what exactly do you have in mind by that?

Socrates: Haven't you realized that our souls are immortal and never destroyed?

He looked at me and said in amazement:

No, by Zeus, I have not. But are you really in a position to assert that?

Socrates: I certainly ought to be, and I think you are, too. There is nothing difficult about it.

Glaucon: There is for me. So I would be glad to hear from you about this non-difficult topic!

Socrates: Listen then.

Glaucon: All you have to do is speak!

Socrates: Do you think there is a good and a bad?

Glaucon: I do.

Socrates: And do you think about them the same e
way I do?

Glaucon: What way?

Socrates: What destroys and corrupts coincides entirely with the bad, while what preserves and benefits coincides entirely with the good.

Glaucon: I do.

Socrates: And do you think there is a good and a
bad for each thing, such as ophthalmia for the eyes,
sickness for the whole body, blight for grain, rot for
wood, rust for iron and bronze, and, as I say, a natu- 609
ral badness and sickness for nearly everything?

Glaucon: I certainly do.

Socrates: And when one of them attaches itself to something, doesn't it make the thing to which it attaches itself deficient? And in the end, doesn't it break it down completely and destroy it?

Glaucon: Of course.

Socrates: So the badness natural to each thing—
the deficiency peculiar to each—destroys it, but if
that does not destroy it, there is nothing else left to
destroy it. For obviously the good will never destroy b
anything, and again what is neither good nor bad
won't either.

Glaucon: How could it?

Socrates: So if we discover something, the badness of which causes it to deteriorate but cannot break it down and destroy it, won't we immediately know that something with such a nature cannot be destroyed after all?

Glaucon: That seems reasonable.

Socrates: Well, then, what about the soul? Isn't there something that makes it bad?

Glaucon: Certainly. All the things we were discussing earlier: injustice, intemperance, cowardice,
and ignorance. c

Socrates: Do any of these break it down and destroy it? Think about it, so we are not deceived into believing that when an unjust and foolish person is

caught, he is destroyed by injustice, which is a deficiency in a soul. Instead, let's proceed this way: just as the body's deficiency, which is disease, wastes and destroys a body, and brings it to the point of not being a body at all, so all the things we mentioned just now reach the point of not being when their own peculiar
d badness attaches itself to them, is present in them, and destroys them. Isn't that so?

GLAUCON: Yes.

SOCRATES: Come on, then, and look at the soul in the same way. When injustice and the rest of vices are present in it, does their presence in it and attachment to it corrupt and wither it until they bring it to the point of death and separate it from the body?

GLAUCON: No, they never do that.

SOCRATES: But surely it is unreasonable to suppose that a thing is destroyed by something else's deficiency and not by its own?

GLAUCON: It is unreasonable.

SOCRATES: Think about it, Glaucon. We do not
e even believe that a body would be destroyed by the deficiency belonging to foods, whether it is staleness, rottenness, or anything else. But if the foods' own deficiency induces bodily deterioration, we will say the body was destroyed *through* them *by* its own badness, which is disease. But we will never admit that the body is destroyed *by* the deficiency belonging to foods—since they and the body are different
610 things—except when external badness induces the natural badness.

GLAUCON: That's absolutely right.

SOCRATES: By the same argument, then, if the body's deficiency does not induce a soul's own deficiency in a soul, we will never admit that a soul is destroyed by external badness in the absence of its own peculiar deficiency—one thing by another's badness.

GLAUCON: Yes, that's reasonable.

SOCRATES: Well, then, let's refute these arguments and show that what we said was not right. Or, so long as they remain unrefuted, let's never say that the soul
b even comes close to being destroyed by a fever or any other disease, or by killing for that matter—not even if one were to cut the entire body up into the very smallest pieces—until someone demonstrates to us that these conditions of the body make the soul itself more unjust and more impious. But when an external badness is present, while its own particular badness is absent, let's not allow anyone to say that a
soul or anything else whatever is destroyed. c

GLAUCON: But you may be sure no one will ever prove that the souls of the dying are made more unjust by death!

SOCRATES: But suppose someone dares to come to grips with our argument and—simply in order to avoid having to agree that our souls are immortal—dares to say that a dying man does become worse and more unjust. We are sure to reply that if what he says is true, injustice must be as deadly as a disease to those who have it, and that those who catch it must die
because of its own deadly nature—with the worst d
cases dying quickly and the less serious ones more slowly—and not as now in fact happens, where the unjust are put to death because of their injustice by others who inflict the penalty.

GLAUCON: By Zeus, injustice won't seem so altogether terrible if it will be deadly to the person who contracts it, since then it would be an *escape* from evils! But I am more inclined to think that it will be shown to be entirely the opposite—something that
kills others if it can, but makes its possessor very lively e
indeed—and not just lively, but positively sleepless! That's how far it is, in my view, from being deadly.

SOCRATES: You are right. After all, if its own deficiency—its own badness—is not enough to kill and destroy the soul, an evil designed for the destruction of something else will hardly destroy the soul, or anything else except what it is designed to destroy.

GLAUCON: "Hardly" is right, it seems.

SOCRATES: Then when something is not destroyed by a single bad thing—whether its own or an external
one—clearly it must always exist. And if it always 611
exists, it is immortal.

GLAUCON: It must be.

SOCRATES: Well, then, let's assume it to be so. And if it is so, you realize that the same ones will always exist. I mean, they surely could not become fewer in number if none is destroyed, or more numerous either. For if anything immortal is increased, you know that the increase would have to come from the mortal, and then everything would end up being immortal.

GLAUCON: True.

SOCRATES: Then we must not think such a thing—for our argument does not allow it. And we must not think, either, that the soul in its truest nature is full of

multicolored variety and dissimilarity and conflict
b with itself.

GLAUCON: How do you mean?

SOCRATES: It is not easy for something to be immortal when it is composed of many elements and is not composed in the most beautiful way—which is how the soul now seemed to us.

GLAUCON: It probably isn't.

SOCRATES: Yet both our recent argument and others as well require us to accept that the soul *is* immortal. But what it is like in truth, seen as it should be, not maimed by its partnership with the body and
c other bad things, which is how we see it now, what it is like when it has become pure—*that* we can adequately see only by means of rational calculation. And you will find it to be a much more beautiful thing than we thought and get a much clearer view of all the cases of justice and injustice and of all the other things that we have so far discussed. So far, what we have said about the soul is true of it as it appears at present. But the condition we have seen
d it in is like that of all the sea god Glaucus, whose original nature cannot easily be made out by those who catch glimpses of him, because some of the original parts of his body have been broken off, others have been worn away and altogether mutilated by the waves, and other things—shells, seaweeds, and rocks—have grown into him, so that he looks more like any wild beast than what he naturally was. Such, too, is the condition of the soul when we see it beset by myriad bad things. But, Glaucon, we should be looking in another direction.

GLAUCON: Where?

SOCRATES: To its love of wisdom. We must keep in mind what it grasps and the kinds of things with
e which it longs to associate, because it is akin to what is divine and immortal and what always exists, and what it would become if it followed this longing with its whole being and if that impulse lifted it out of the
612 sea in which it now is, and struck off the rocks and shells that, because it now feasts on earth, have grown around it in a wild, earthy, and stony profusion as a result of those so-called happy feastings. And then you would see its true nature, whether multiform or uniform, or somehow some other way. But we have given a pretty good account now, I think, of what its condition is and what form it takes in human life.

GLAUCON: We certainly have.

SOCRATES: In the course of our discussion, then, did we respond to the other points, without having to invoke the rewards and reputations of justice, as you
all said Homer and Hesiod did?[1] Instead, haven't we b
found that justice itself is the best thing for the soul itself, and that the soul should do what is just, whether it has Gyges' ring or not, or even the cap of Hades as well.[2]

GLAUCON: That's absolutely true. We have.

SOCRATES: So, Glaucon, isn't it now at last unobjectionable, in addition, also to give back to justice and the rest of virtue both the kind and quantity of
wages they bring to the soul, both from human beings c
and from gods, both during life and after death?

GLAUCON: Certainly.

SOCRATES: Then will you give *me* back what you borrowed from me in the course of the discussion?

GLAUCON: What in particular?

SOCRATES: I granted you that the just man should seem unjust and the unjust one just. For you thought that even if it would be impossible for these things to remain hidden from both gods and human beings, all the same, it had to be granted for the sake of argument, so that justice itself could be judged in
relation to injustice itself. Don't you remember? d

GLAUCON: *I* would be unjust if I didn't!

SOCRATES: Well, then, since they have now been judged, I ask on behalf of justice for a return of the reputation it in fact has among gods and human beings; and that we agree that it does indeed have such a reputation, and so may carry off the prizes it gains for someone by making him seem just; since we have already seen that it does give the good things that come from being just, and does not deceive those who really possess it.

GLAUCON: That's a just request. e

SOCRATES: Then won't you first give this back, that it certainly does not remain hidden from the gods what each of the two is like?

GLAUCON: We will.

---

1. The reference is to the challenge posed by Glaucon and Adeimantus at 357a–367e. But they, of course, are renewing the challenge posed by Thrasymachus in Book 1 (see 358b–c).

2. The ring of Gyges is discussed at 359c–360c. The cap of Hades also made its wearer invisible.

Socrates: But if it does not remain hidden, one would be loved by the gods and one hated, as we agreed at the beginning.

Glaucon: That's right.

Socrates: And won't we also agree that everything that comes to the one who is loved by gods—insofar as it comes from the gods themselves—is the best
613 possible, unless it is some unavoidable bad thing due to him for an earlier mistake?

Glaucon: Certainly.

Socrates: Similarly, we must suppose that if a just man falls into poverty or disease or some of the other things that seem bad, it will end well for him during his lifetime or even in death. For surely the gods at least will never neglect anyone who eagerly wishes to become just and, by practicing virtue, to make him-
b self as much like a god as a human being can.

Glaucon: It is certainly reasonable to think that a man of that sort won't be neglected by one who is like him.

Socrates: And mustn't we think the opposite of the unjust one?

Glaucon: Definitely.

Socrates: Those, then, are the sorts of prizes that come from the gods to the just man.

Glaucon: That's certainly what I believe.

Socrates: What about from human beings? What does a just man get from them? If we are to assert what is really the case, isn't it this? Aren't clever but unjust men precisely like runners who run well on the first leg but not on the return one? They leap away sharply at first, but in the end they become ridiculous and, heads drooping, run off the field
c uncrowned. True runners, on the other hand, make it to the end, collect the prizes, and are crowned as victors. And isn't it also generally what happens to just people? Toward the end of each course of action and association and of life as a whole, don't they enjoy a good reputation and collect the prizes that come from human beings?

Glaucon: Of course.

Socrates: Will you then allow me to say about
d them what *you* said about the unjust? For I will claim that it is the just who, when they are old enough, hold the ruling offices in their city if they choose, marry from whatever family they choose, and give their children in marriage to whomever they please. Indeed, all the things that you said about the others, I now say about these. As for the unjust, the majority of them, even if they remain hidden when they are young, are caught by the end of the race and ridiculed, and, by the time they get old, have become wretched and are showered with abuse by foreigners and citizens, beaten with whips, and made to suffer those punishments you rightly described as e
crude, such as racking and burning. Imagine I have claimed that they suffer all such things. Well, as I say, see if you will stand for it.

Glaucon: Of course I will. What you say is right.

Socrates: Well, then, while the just man is alive, these are the sorts of prizes, wages, and gifts he receives from gods and human beings, in addition to 614
those good things that justice itself provides.

Glaucon: Fine and secure ones they are, too!

Socrates: Well, they are nothing in number or size compared to those that await each man after death. We must hear about them, too, so that, by hearing them, each of these men may get back in full what he is owed by the argument.

Glaucon: Please describe them, then, since there are not many things it would be more pleasant to hear. b

Socrates: Well, it is not an Alcinous-story I am going to tell you, but that of a brave man called Er, the son of Armenias, by race a Pamphylian.[3] Once upon a time, he was killed in battle. On the tenth day, when the rest of the dead were picked up, they were already putrefying, but he was picked up still quite sound. When he had been taken home and was lying on the pyre before his funeral on the twelfth day, he revived and, after reviving, told what he had seen in the other world.

He said that when his soul had departed, it traveled together with many others and came to a dai- c
monic place, where there were two adjacent openings in the earth and two in the heavens above and opposite them. Judges were seated between these. And, when they had made their judgments, they told the just to go to the right up through the heavens, with signs of the judgments attached to their fronts. But the unjust they told to travel to the left and down. And they too had on their backs signs

3. Books 9–11 of the *Odyssey* were traditionally referred to as *Alkinou apologoi*, the tales of Alcinous. Included among them is the story in Book 11 of Odysseus' descent into Hades.

d of all their deeds. When he himself came forward,
they said that he was to be a messenger to human beings to tell them about the things happening there, and they told him to listen to and look at everything in the place.

Through one of the openings in the heavens and one in the earth, he saw souls departing after judgment had been passed on them. Through the other two, they were arriving. From the one in the earth they came up parched and dusty, while from the one in the heavens they came down pure. And the ones
e that had just arrived seemed to have come from a
long journey, and went off gladly to the meadow, like a crowd going to a festival, and set up camp there. Those that knew one another exchanged greetings and those coming up from the earth asked the others about the things up there, while those from the heavens asked about the others' experiences. They told
615 their stories to one another, the former weeping and
lamenting as they recollected all they had suffered and seen on their journey below the earth—which lasted a thousand years—and the ones from the heavens telling, in turn, about their happy experiences and the inconceivably beautiful sights they had seen.

To tell it all, Glaucon, would take a long time. But the gist, he said, was this: for all the unjust things they had done and for all the people they had wronged, they had paid the penalty for every one in turn, ten times over for each. That is to say, they paid for each injustice once in every hundred years of their journey, so that, on the assumption that a hundred years
b is roughly the length of a human life, they paid a ten-
fold penalty for each injustice. For example, if some of them had caused many deaths or had betrayed cities or armies and reduced them to slavery, or had taken part in other evildoing, they would receive ten times the pain for each of them. On the other hand, if they had done good deeds and become just and pious, they received commensurate awards.

He said some other things about the stillborn and
c those who lived for only a short time, but they are not
worth recounting. And he told of even greater wages for impiety or piety toward gods or parents, and for murder. He said he was there, you see, when someone asked where the great Ardiaius was. This Ardiaius had been a tyrant in a city in Pamphylia just a thousand years before that, and was said to have killed his
d aged father and older brother and committed many
other impious deeds as well. He said the one who was asked responded: "He has not come here and never will. For in fact this, too, was one of the terrible sights we saw. When we were near the mouth, about to come up after all our sufferings were over, we suddenly saw Ardiaius together with some others, almost all of whom were tyrants—although there were also some private individuals among them who
had committed great crimes. They thought that they e
were about to go up, but the mouth would not let them through. Instead, it roared whenever one of these incurably bad people, or anyone else who had not paid a sufficient penalty, tried to go up. At that location, there were savage men, all fiery to look at, standing by, paying attention to the sound, who grabbed some of these people and led them away. But in the case of Ardiaius and others, they bound
their feet, hands, and neck and threw them down 616
and flayed them. They dragged them along the road outside, lacerating them on thorn bushes. They explained to those who were passing by at the time why they were being dragged away, and said that they were to be thrown into Tartarus. He said that of the many and multifarious fears they experienced there, the greatest each of them had was that the sound would be heard as he came up, and that each was very pleased when it was silent as he went up. Such then were the penalties and punishments, and the
rewards that were their counterparts. b

When each group had spent seven days in the meadow, on the eighth they had to move on from there and continue their journey. In four days, they came to a place where they could see stretching from above, through the whole heavens and earth, a straight beam of light, like a column, very closely resembling a rainbow, but brighter and more pure. They reached the beam after traveling another day's journey. And there, in the middle of the light, they
saw stretching from the heavens the ends of its c
bonds—for this light is what binds the heavens, like the cables underneath a trireme, thus holding the entire revolving thing together. From those ends hangs the spindle of Necessity, by means of which all the revolving things are turned. Its shaft and hook were adamant, while its whorl[4] was adamant mixed

---

4. *Sphondulon:* the circular weight that twirls a spindle in weaving.

with materials of other kinds. The nature of the whorl was as follows. Its shape was like the ones here
d on Earth, but from Er's description, we must think of it as being like this: in one large whorl, hollow and scooped out, lay another just like it, only smaller, that fitted into it exactly, the way nested bowls fit together; and similarly a third and a fourth, and four others. For there were eight whorls altogether, lying inside one another, with their rims appearing as circles from above, while from the back they formed one contin-
e uous whorl around the shaft, which is driven right through the center of the eighth.

Now, the first or outermost whorl had the broadest circular rim, that of the sixth was second, third was that of the fourth, fourth that of the eighth, fifth that of the seventh, sixth that of the fifth, seventh that of the third, and eighth that of the second. That of the largest was spangled; that of the seventh was brightest; that of the eighth took its color from the seventh's
617 shining on it; that of the second and fifth were very similar to one another, being yellower than the rest; the third was the whitest in color; the fourth was reddish; and the sixth was second in whiteness.

The spindle as a whole revolved at the same speed, but within the revolving whole the seven inner circles gently revolved in the opposite direction to the whole. Of these, the eighth moved fastest; second,
b and at the same speed as one another, were the seventh, sixth, and fifth; third, it seemed to them, in the speed of its counter-revolution, was the fourth; fourth was the third; and fifth the second.[5]

The spindle revolved on the lap of Necessity. On top of each of its circles stood a Siren, who was carried around by its rotation, emitting a single sound, one single note. And from all eight in concord, a single harmony was produced. And there were three other women seated around it equidistant from one
another, each on a throne. They were the daughters *c*
of Necessity, the Fates, dressed in white with garlands on their heads—Lachesis, Clotho, and Atropos—and they sang to the accompaniment of the Sirens' harmony, Lachesis singing of the past, Clotho of the present, and Atropos of the future. Clotho, using her right hand, touched the outer circumference of the spindle and helped it turn, pausing from time to time; Atropos, with her left, did the same to the inner ones; and Lachesis used each hand in turn
to touch both. *d*

When the souls arrived, they had to go straight to Lachesis. A sort of spokesman first arranged them in ranks; then, taking lots and models of lives from the lap of Lachesis, he mounted a high platform, and said:

"The word of Lachesis, maiden daughter of Necessity! Ephemeral souls. The beginning of another death-bringing cycle for mortal-kind! Your
daimon will not be assigned to you by lot; you will *e*
choose him. The one who has the first lot will be the first to choose a life to which he will be bound by necessity. Virtue has no master: as he honors or dishonors it, so shall each of you have more or less of it. Responsibility lies with the chooser; the god is blameless."

After saying that, the spokesman threw the lots out among them all, and each picked up the one that fell next to him—except for Er, who was not allowed. And to the one who picked it up, it was clear what number he had drawn. After that again
the spokesman placed the models of lives on the *618*
ground before them—many more of them than

5. Plato's description of the beam of light and the spindle is difficult. He compares the light to *hypozomata*, or the ropes that bind a trireme together. These ropes seem to have girded the trireme from stem to stern and to have entered it at both places. Within the trireme, they were connected to some sort of twisting device that allowed them to be tightened when the water caused them to stretch and become slack. The spindle of Necessity seems to be just such a twisting device. Hence, the extremities of the light's bonds must enter into the universe just as the *hypozomata* enter the trireme, and the spindle must be attached to these extremities, so that its spinning tightens the light and holds the universe together. The light is thus like two rainbows around the universe (or the whorl of the spindle), whose ends enter the universe and are attached to the spindle. The upper half of the whorl of the spindle consists of concentric hemispheres that fit into one another, with their lips or rims fitting together in a single plane. The outer hemisphere is that of the fixed stars; the second is the orbit of Saturn; the third of Jupiter; the fourth of Mars; the fifth of Mercury; the sixth of Venus; the seventh of the sun; and the eighth of the moon. The earth is in the center. The hemispheres are transparent and the width of their rims is the distance of the heavenly bodies from one another.

those who were present. They were multifarious: all animal lives were there, as well as all human lives. There were tyrannies among them, some life-long, others ending halfway through in poverty, exile, and beggary. There were lives of famous men—some famous for the beauty of their appearance or for their other strengths or athletic prowess, others for their nobility and the virtues of their ancestors, and also
b some infamous in these respects—and similarly for women. But the structure of the soul was not included, because with the choice of a different life it would inevitably become different. But all the other qualities were mixed with each other and with wealth or poverty, sickness or health, or the states in between.

Here, it seems, my dear Glaucon, a human being faces the greatest danger of all, and because of that each must, to the neglect of all other subjects, take
c care above all else to be a seeker and student of that subject which will enable him to learn and discover who will give him the ability and the knowledge to distinguish a good life from a bad, so that he will always and in any circumstances choose the better one from among those that are possible. He must calculate the effect of all the things we have mentioned just now, both jointly and severally, on the virtue of a life, so as to know what the good and bad effects of beauty are when it is mixed with wealth or poverty
d and this or that state of the soul; what the effects are of high and low birth, private lives and ruling offices, physical strength and weaknesses, ease and difficulties in learning, and all the things that are either naturally part of the soul or can be acquired by it, when they are mixed with one another. On the basis of all that he will be able, by considering the nature of the soul, to reason out which life is better and which
e worse and choose accordingly, calling worse the one that will lead the soul to become more unjust, and better the one that leads it to become more just. Everything else he will ignore. For we have seen that this is the best way to choose, whether in life or death.

Holding this belief with adamantine determination, he must go down to Hades, so that even there he
619 won't be dazzled by wealth and other such evils, and won't rush into tyrannies or other similar practices and so commit irreparable evils, and suffer even greater ones; but instead will know to choose the middle life in such circumstances, and avoid either of the extremes, both in this life, so far as is possible, and in the whole of the life to come. For this is how a human being becomes happiest. *b*

At that point our messenger from the other world also reported that the spokesman said this: "Even for the one who comes last, if he chooses wisely and lives earnestly, there is a satisfactory life available, not a bad one. Let not the first to choose be careless, nor the last discouraged."

When the spokesman had told them that, Er said, the one who drew the first lot came up and immediately chose the greatest tyranny. In his foolishness and greed, you see, he chose it without adequately examining everything, and did not notice that it involved being fated to eat his own children, among other evils. When he examined the life at leisure, *c*
however, he beat his breast and bemoaned his choice, ignoring the warning of the spokesman. For he did not blame himself for these evils, but chance, daimons, and everything except himself. He was one of those who had come down from the heavens, having lived his previous life in an orderly constitution, sharing in virtue through habit but without philosophy.

Generally speaking, not the least number of the *d*
people caught out in this way were souls who came from the heavens, and so were untrained in sufferings. The majority of those from the earth, on the other hand, because they had suffered themselves and had seen others doing so, were in no rush to make their choices. Because of that, and also because of the chance of the lottery, there was an exchange of evils and goods for most of the souls. Yet, if a person, whenever he came to the life that is here, always practiced philosophy in a sound manner, and if the fall of the lot did not put his choice of life among the last, it is likely, from what was *e*
reported by Er about the next world, that not only will he be happy here, but also that his journey from here to there and back again will not be underground and rough, but smooth and through the heavens.

He said it was a sight worth seeing how the various souls chose their lives, since seeing it caused pity, ridicule, and surprise. For the most part, their choice 620
reflected the character of their former life. He saw the soul that had once belonged to Orpheus, he said,

choosing a swan's life: he hated the female sex because of his death at their hands, and so was unwilling to be conceived in a woman and born.[6] He saw the soul of Thamyris choosing a nightingale's life, a swan changing to the choice of a human life, and other musical animals doing the same. The
b twentieth soul chose the life of a lion. It was that of Ajax, son of Telamon, who avoided human life because he remembered the judgment about the armor.[7] The next was that of Agamemnon, which also hated the human race on account of what it suffered, and so changed to the life of an eagle. Allotted a place in the middle, the soul of Atalanta, when it saw the great honors of a male athlete, unable to pass them by, chose his life. After her, he saw the soul of Epeius, son of Panopeus, taking on the nature of a
c craftswoman. Further on, among the last, he saw the soul of the ridiculous Thersites clothing itself as an ape.

Now it chanced that Odysseus' soul drew the last lot of all, and came to make its choice. Remembering its former sufferings, it rejected love of honor, and went around for a long time looking for the life of a private individual who did his own work, and with difficulty it found one lying off somewhere neglected by the others. When it saw it, it said that it would have done the same even if it had drawn the
d first-place lot, and chose it gladly. Similarly, souls went from the other animals into human beings, or into one another; the unjust changing into savage animals, the just into tame ones; and every sort of mixture occurred.

When all the souls had chosen lives, in the same allotted order they went forward to Lachesis. She assigned to each the daimon it had chosen, as
e guardian of its life and fulfiller of its choices. This daimon first led the soul under the hand of Clotho as it turned the revolving spindle, thus ratifying the allotted fate it had chosen. After receiving her touch, he led the soul to the spinning of Atropos, to make the spun fate irreversible. Then, without turning around, it went under the throne of Necessity. When
it had passed through that, and when the others had *621*
also passed through, they all traveled to the plain of Lethe, through burning and choking and terrible heat, for it was empty of trees and earthly vegetation. They camped, since evening was coming on, beside the river of forgetfulness, whose water no vessel can hold. All of them had to drink a certain measure of this water. But those not saved by wisdom drank more than the measure. And as each of them drank, he forgot everything. When they were asleep and
midnight came, there was a clap of thunder and an *b*
earthquake, and they were suddenly carried away from there, this way and that, up to their births, like shooting stars. But Er himself was prevented from drinking the water. Yet how or where he had come back to his body, he did not know, but suddenly recovering his sight he now saw himself lying on the pyre at dawn.

And so, Glaucon, his story was saved and not lost; and it would save us, too, if we were persuaded by it,
since we would safely cross the river Lethe with our *c*
souls undefiled. But if we are persuaded by me, we will believe that the soul is immortal and able to endure every evil and also every good, and always hold to the upward path, practicing justice with wisdom every way we can, so that we will be friends to ourselves and to the gods, both while we remain here on Earth and when we receive the rewards of justice, and go around like victors in the games collecting prizes; and so both in this life and on the thousand-year journey we have described, we will fare well.

---

6. According to one myth, Orpheus was killed and dismembered by Thracian women, or Maenads.

7. Ajax thought that he deserved to be awarded the armor of the dead Achilles, but instead it was awarded to Odysseus. Ajax was maddened by this injustice and later killed himself because of the terrible things he had done while mad.

Parmenides

The following brief selection shows the young Socrates in the company of Parmenides and Zeno, talking not about ethics but about profound and very abstract metaphysical issues: Are things many or—as Plato takes Parmenides to have argued in his poem—only one? Socrates introduces the theory of forms (128e–130a) as a response to Zeno. Parmenides counters with a series of powerful criticisms of that theory. Since Plato wrote Parmenides' lines, this dialogue is a good example of Plato's willingness to submit even his own cherished views to critical scrutiny.

Antiphon said that Pythodorus said that Zeno and Parmenides once came to the Great Panathenaea.
127b Parmenides was already quite venerable, very gray but of distinguished appearance, about sixty-five years old. Zeno was at that time close to forty, a tall, handsome man who had been, as rumor had it, the object of Parmenides' affections when he was a boy.
c Antiphon said that the two of them were staying with Pythodorus, outside the city wall in the Potters' Quarter, and that Socrates had come there, along with a number of others, because they were eager to hear Zeno read his book, which he and Parmenides had just brought to Athens for the first time. Socrates was then quite young.

Zeno was reading to them in person; Parmenides happened to be out. Very little remained to be read
d when Pythodorus, as he related it, came in, and with him Parmenides and Aristotle—the man who later became one of the Thirty. They listened to a little of the book at the very end. But not Pythodorus himself; he had heard Zeno read it before.

Then Socrates, after he had heard it, asked Zeno to
e read the first hypothesis of the first argument again; and when he had read it, Socrates said, "Zeno, what do you mean by this: if things are many, they must then be both like and unlike, but that is impossible, because unlike things can't be like or like things unlike? That's what you say, isn't it?"

"It is," said Zeno.

"If it's impossible for unlike things to be like and like things unlike, isn't it then also impossible for them to be many? Because, if they were many, they would have incompatible properties. Is this the point of your arguments—simply to maintain, in opposition to everything that is commonly said, that things are not many? And do you suppose that each of your arguments is proof for this position, so that you think you give as many proofs that things are not many as your book has arguments? Is that what you're saying—or do I misunderstand?" *128*

"No," Zeno replied. "On the contrary, you grasp the general point of the book splendidly."

"Parmenides," Socrates said, "I understand that Zeno wants to be on intimate terms with you not only in friendship but also in his book. He has, in a way, written the same thing as you, but by changing it round he tries to fool us into thinking he is saying something different. You say in your poem that the all is one, and you give splendid and excellent proofs *b*
for that; he, for his part, says that it is not many and gives a vast array of very grand proofs of his own. So, with one of you saying 'one,' and the other 'not many,' and with each of you speaking in a way that suggests that you've said nothing the same—although you mean practically the same thing—what you've said you appear to have said over the heads of the rest of us."

"Yes, Socrates," said Zeno. "Still, you haven't completely discerned the truth about my book, even though you chase down its arguments and follow their spoor as keenly as a young Spartan hound. First *c*
of all, you have missed this point: the book doesn't at all preen itself on having been written with the intent you described, while disguising it from people, as if that were some great accomplishment. You have mentioned something that happened accidentally. The truth is that the book comes to the defense of Parmenides' argument against those who try to make fun of it by claiming that, if it is one, many *d*
absurdities and self-contradictions result from that

---

argument. Accordingly, my book speaks against those
who assert the many and pays them back in kind with
something for good measure, since it aims to make
clear that their hypothesis, if it is many, would, if
someone examined the matter thoroughly, suffer
consequences even more absurd than those suffered
by the hypothesis of its being one. In that competitive
spirit, then, I wrote the book when I was a young man.
Someone made an unauthorized copy, so I didn't
even have a chance to decide for myself whether or
e not it should see the light. So in this respect you
missed the point, Socrates: you think it was written
not out of a young man's competitiveness, but out of
a mature man's vainglory. Still, as I said, your por-
trayal was not bad."

"I take your point," Socrates said, "and I believe it
129 was as you say. But tell me this: don't you acknowledge that there is a form, itself by itself, of likeness,
and another form, opposite to this, which is what
unlike is? Don't you and I and the other things we
call 'many' get a share of those two entities? And
don't things that get a share of likeness come to be
like in that way and to the extent that they get a share,
whereas things that get a share of unlikeness come to
be unlike, and things that get a share of both come to
be both? And even if all things get a share of both,
though they are opposites, and by partaking of them
are both like and unlike themselves, what's astonishing about that?

b "If someone showed that the likes themselves
come to be unlike or the unlikes like—that, I think,
would be a marvel; but if he shows that things that
partake of both of these have both properties, there
seems to me nothing strange about that, Zeno—not
even if someone shows that all things are one by partaking of oneness, and that these same things are
many by partaking also of multitude.[1] But if he
should demonstrate this thing itself, what one is, to
be many, or, conversely, the many to be one—at this
I'll be astonished.

"And it's the same with all the others: if he could c
show that the kinds and forms[2] themselves have in
themselves these opposite properties, that would call
for astonishment. But if someone should demonstrate that I am one thing and many, what's astonishing about that? He will say, when he wants to show
that I'm many, that my right side is different from my
left, and my front from my back, and likewise with
my upper and lower parts—since I take it I do partake of multitude. But when he wants to show that
I'm one, he will say I'm one person among the seven d
of us, because I also partake of oneness. Thus he
shows that both are true.

"So if—in the case of stones and sticks and such
things—someone tries to show that the same thing is
many and one, we'll say that he is demonstrating
something to be many and one, not the one to be
many or the many one—and we'll say that he is saying nothing astonishing, but just what all of us would
agree to. But if someone first distinguishes as separate the forms, themselves by themselves, of the
things I was talking about a moment ago—for example, likeness and unlikeness, multitude and oneness,
rest and motion, and everything of that sort—and e
then shows that in themselves they can mix together
and separate, I for my part," he said, "would be
utterly amazed, Zeno. I think these issues have been
handled with great vigor in your book; but I would,
as I say, be much more impressed if someone were
able to display this same difficulty, which you and
Parmenides went through in the case of visible
things, also similarly entwined in multifarious ways 130
in the forms themselves—in things that are grasped
by reasoning."

Pythodorus said that, while Socrates was saying all
this, he himself kept from moment to moment
expecting Parmenides and Zeno to get annoyed; but
they both paid close attention to Socrates and often
glanced at each other and smiled, as though they
admired him. In fact, what Parmenides said when

---

1. Like *to hen* ("the one," "oneness"), the expression *plēthos* ("multitude") is also ambiguous. It can refer to a form, to any group of many things (whether concrete particulars or forms), or the character things have if they are many. Corresponding to the ambiguity in the meaning of *one*, between "single" and "unified," there is an ambiguity in the meaning of *multitude*. It can specify a plurality of definite individuals or some mass that lacks unity and definiteness.

2. In this dialogue Plato uses three different abstract expressions to specify forms, two of which occur here: *genos*, which we render as "kind," and *eidos*, which we render as "form." Later he will use a third term *idea*, which we render as "character."

Socrates had finished confirmed this impression.
b “Socrates,” he said, “you are much to be admired for
your keenness for argument! Tell me. Have you yourself distinguished as separate, in the way you mention,
certain forms themselves, and also as separate the
things that partake of them? And do you think that
likeness itself is something, separate from the likeness
we have? And one and many and all the things you
heard Zeno read about a while ago?”

“I do indeed,” Socrates answered.

“And what about these?” asked Parmenides. “Is
there a form, itself by itself, of just, and beautiful, and
good, and everything of that sort?”

“Yes,” he said.

c “What about a form of human being, separate
from us and all those like us? Is there a form itself of
human being, or fire, or water?”

Socrates said, “Parmenides, I’ve often found myself
in doubt whether I should talk about those in the
same way as the others or differently.”

“And what about these, Socrates? Things that
might seem absurd, like hair and mud and dirt, or
anything else totally undignified and worthless? Are
d you doubtful whether or not you should say that a
form is separate for each of these, too, which in turn
is other than anything we touch with our hands?”

“Not at all,” Socrates answered. “On the contrary,
these things are in fact just what we see. Surely it’s
too outlandish to think there is a form for them. Not
that the thought that the same thing might hold in all
cases hasn’t troubled me from time to time. Then,
when I get bogged down in that, I hurry away, afraid
that I may fall into some pit of nonsense and come to
harm; but when I arrive back in the vicinity of the
things we agreed a moment ago have forms, I linger
there and occupy myself with them.”

e “That’s because you are still young, Socrates,” said
Parmenides, “and philosophy has not yet gripped you
as, in my opinion, it will in the future, once you
begin to consider none of the cases beneath your
notice. Now, though, you still care about what people think, because of your youth.

“But tell me this: is it your view that, as you say,
there are certain forms from which these other
things, by getting a share of them, derive their
131 names—as, for instance, they come to be like by getting a share of likeness, large by getting a share of
largeness, and just and beautiful by getting a share of
justice and beauty?”

“It certainly is,” Socrates replied.

“So does each thing that gets a share get as its share
the form as a whole or a part of it? Or could there be
some other means of getting a share apart from these
two?”

“How could there be?” he said.

“Do you think, then, that the form as a whole—
one thing—is in each of the many? Or what do you
think?”

“What’s to prevent its being one, Parmenides?”
said Socrates.

“So, being one and the same, it will be at the same b
time, as a whole, in things that are many and separate; and thus it would be separate from itself.”

“No it wouldn’t,” Socrates said. “Not if it’s like one
and the same day. That is in many places at the same
time and is nonetheless not separate from itself. If it’s
like that, each of the forms might be, at the same
time, one and the same in all.”

“Socrates,” he said, “how neatly you make one and
the same thing be in many places at the same time!
It’s as if you were to cover many people with a sail,
and then say that one thing as a whole is over many.
Or isn’t that the sort of thing you mean to say?”

“Perhaps,” he replied. c

“In that case would the sail be, as a whole, over
each person, or would a part of it be over one person
and another part over another?”

“A part.”

“So the forms themselves are divisible, Socrates,”
he said, “and things that partake of them would partake of a part; no longer would a whole form, but
only a part of it, be in each thing.”

“It does appear that way.”

“Then are you willing to say, Socrates, that our one
form is really divided? Will it still be one?”

“Not at all,” he replied.

“No,” said Parmenides. “For suppose you are going
to divide largeness itself. If each of the many large d
things is to be large by a part of largeness smaller than
largeness itself, won’t that appear unreasonable?”

“It certainly will,” he replied.

“What about this? Will each thing that has
received a small part of the equal have something by
which to be equal to anything, when its portion is less
than the equal itself?”

"That's impossible."

"Well, suppose one of us is going to have a part of the small. The small will be larger than that part of it, since the part is a part of it: so the small itself will be
e larger! And that to which the part subtracted is added will be smaller, not larger, than it was before."

"That surely couldn't happen," he said.

"Socrates, in what way, then, will the other things get a share of your forms, if they can do so neither by getting parts nor by getting wholes?"

"By Zeus!" Socrates exclaimed. "It strikes me that's not at all easy to determine!"

"And what do you think about the following?"

"What's that?"

132 "I suppose you think each form is one on the following ground: whenever some number of things seem to you to be large, perhaps there seems to be some one character, the same as you look at them all, and from that you conclude that the large is one."

"That's true," he said.

"What about the large itself and the other large things? If you look at them all in the same way with the mind's eye, again won't some one thing appear large, by which all these appear large?"

"It seems so."

"So another form of largeness will make its appearance, which has emerged alongside largeness itself and the things that partake of it, and in turn another
b over all these, by which all of them will be large. Each of your forms will no longer be one, but unlimited in multitude."

"But, Parmenides, maybe each of these forms is a thought," Socrates said, "and properly occurs only in minds. In this way each of them might be one and no longer face the difficulties mentioned just now."

"What do you mean?" he asked. "Is each of the thoughts one, but a thought of nothing?"

"No, that's impossible," he said.

"Of something, rather?"

"Yes."

c "Of something that is, or of something that is not?"

"Of something that is."

"Isn't it of some one thing, which that thought thinks is over all the instances, being some one character?"

"Yes."

"Then won't this thing that is thought to be one, being always the same over all the instances, be a form?"

"That, too, appears necessary."

"And what about this?" said Parmenides. "Given your claim that other things partake of forms, won't you necessarily think either that each thing is composed of thoughts and all things think, or that, although they are thoughts, they are unthinking?"

"That isn't reasonable either, Parmenides," he said. "No, what appears most likely to me is this: these forms are like patterns set in nature, and other things d
resemble them and are likenesses; and this partaking of the forms is, for the other things, simply being modeled on them."

"If something resembles the form," he said, "can that form not be like what has been modeled on it, to the extent that the thing has been made like it? Or is there any way for something like to be like what is not like it?"

"There is not."

"And isn't there a compelling necessity for that which is like to partake of the same one form as what is like it? e

"There is."

"But if like things are like by partaking of something, won't that be the form itself?"

"Undoubtedly."

"Therefore nothing can be like the form, nor can the form be like anything else. Otherwise, alongside the form another form will always make its appearance, and if that form is like anything, yet another; 133
and if the form proves to be like what partakes of it, a fresh form will never cease emerging."

"That's very true."

"So other things don't get a share of the forms by likeness; we must seek some other means by which they get a share."

"So it seems."

"Then do you see, Socrates," he said, "how great the difficulty is if one marks things off as forms, themselves by themselves?"

"Quite clearly."

"I assure you," he said, "that you do not yet, if I may put it so, have an inkling of how great the difficulty is if you are going to posit one form in each case b
every time you make a distinction among things."

"How so?" he asked.

"There are many other reasons," Parmenides said, "but the main one is this: suppose someone were to say that if the forms are such as we claim they must

be, they cannot even be known. If anyone should raise that objection, you wouldn't be able to show him that he is wrong, unless the objector happened to be widely experienced and not ungifted, and consented to pay attention while in your effort to show him you dealt with many distant considerations. Otherwise, the person who insists that they are necessar-
c ily unknowable would remain unconvinced."

"Why is that, Parmenides?" Socrates asked.

"Because I think that you, Socrates, and anyone else who posits that there is for each thing some being, itself by itself, would agree, to begin with, that none of those beings is in us."

"Yes—how could it still be itself by itself?" replied Socrates.

"Very good," said Parmenides. "And so all the characters that are what they are in relation to each other have their being in relation to themselves but not in
d relation to things that belong to us. And whether one posits the latter as likenesses or in some other way, it is by partaking of them that we come to be called by their various names. These things that belong to us, although they have the same names as the forms, are in their turn what they are in relation to themselves but not in relation to the forms; and all the things named in this way are *of* themselves but not *of* the forms."

"What do you mean?" Socrates asked.

"Take an example," said Parmenides. "If one of us is somebody's master or somebody's slave, he is surely not a slave of master itself—of what a master is—nor
e is the master a master of slave itself—of what a slave is. On the contrary, being a human being, he is a master or slave of a human being. Mastery itself, on the other hand, is what it is of slavery itself; and, in the same way, slavery itself is slavery of mastery itself. Things in us do not have their power in relation to forms, nor do they have theirs in relation to us; but, I repeat, forms are what they are *of* themselves and in
134 relation to themselves, and things that belong to us are, in the same way, what they are in relation to themselves. You do understand what I mean?"

"Certainly," Socrates said, "I understand."

"So too," he said, "knowledge itself, what knowledge is, would be knowledge of that truth itself, which is what truth is?"

"Certainly."

"Furthermore, each particular knowledge, what it is, would be knowledge of some particular thing, of what that thing is. Isn't that so?"

"Yes."

"But wouldn't knowledge that belongs to us be of the truth that belongs to our world? And wouldn't it follow that each particular knowledge that belongs to
us is in turn knowledge of some particular thing in b
our world?"

"Necessarily."

"But, as you agree, we neither have the forms themselves nor can they belong to us."

"Yes, you're quite right."

"And surely the kinds themselves, what each of them is, are known by the form of knowledge itself?"

"Yes."

"The very thing that we don't have."

"No, we don't."

"So none of the forms is known by us, because we don't partake of knowledge itself."

"It seems not."

"Then the beautiful itself, what it is, cannot be known by us, nor can the good, nor, indeed, can any
of the things we take to be characters themselves." c

"It looks that way."

"Here's something even more shocking than that."

"What's that?"

"Surely you would say that if in fact there is knowledge—a kind itself—it is much more precise than is knowledge that belongs to us. And the same goes for beauty and all the others."

"Yes."

"Well, whatever else partakes of knowledge itself, wouldn't you say that god more than anyone else has this most precise knowledge?"

"Necessarily."

"Tell me, will god, having knowledge itself, then d
be able to know things that belong to our world?"

"Yes, why not?"

"Because we have agreed, Socrates," Parmenides said, "that those forms do not have their power in relation to things in our world, and things in our world do not have theirs in relation to forms, but that things in each group have their power in relation to themselves."

"Yes, we did agree on that."

"Well then, if this most precise mastery and this most precise knowledge belong to the divine, the

gods' mastery could never master us, nor could their
e knowledge know us or anything that belongs to us. No, just as we do not govern them by our governance and know nothing of the divine by our knowledge, so they in their turn are, for the same reason, neither our masters nor, being gods, do they know human affairs."

"If god is to be stripped of knowing," he said, "our argument may be getting too bizarre."

"And yet, Socrates," said Parmenides, "the forms inevitably involve these objections and a host of oth-
135 ers besides—if there are those characters for things, and a person is to mark off each form as 'something itself.' As a result, whoever hears about them is doubtful and objects that they do not exist, and that, even if they *do*, they must by strict necessity be unknowable to human nature; and in saying this he seems to have a point; and, as we said, he is extraordinarily hard to win over. Only a very gifted man can come to
b know that for each thing there is some kind, a being itself by itself; but only a prodigy more remarkable still will discover that and be able to teach someone else who has sifted all these difficulties thoroughly and critically for himself."

"I agree with you, Parmenides," Socrates said. "That's very much what I think too."

"Yet on the other hand, Socrates," said Parmenides, "if someone, having an eye on all the difficulties we have just brought up and others of the same sort, won't allow that there are forms for things and won't mark off a form for each one, he won't have anywhere to turn his thought, since he doesn't allow that for each thing there is a character that is *c*
always the same. In this way he will destroy the power of dialectic entirely. But I think you are only too well aware of that."

"What you say is true," Socrates said.

"What then will you do about philosophy? Where will you turn, while these difficulties remain unresolved?"

"I don't think I have anything clearly in view, at least not at present."

"Socrates, that's because you are trying to mark off something beautiful, and just, and good, and each one of the forms, too soon," he said, "before you have been properly trained. I noticed that the other day *d*
too, as I listened to you conversing with Aristotle here. The impulse you bring to argument is noble and divine, make no mistake about it. But while you are still young, put your back into it and get more training through something people think useless—what the crowd call idle talk. Otherwise, the truth will escape you."

TIMAEUS

THE FOLLOWING SELECTION deals with the creation of the universe. It makes use of the theory of forms, not now in an ethical or metaphysical context, but to deal with the kind of cosmological and scientific issues familiar from the writings of the Presocratics.

TIMAEUS: As I see it, then, we must begin by making the following distinction: What is *that which always is* and has no becoming, and what is *that which becomes*
28 but never is? The former is grasped by understanding, which involves a reasoned account. It is unchanging. The latter is grasped by opinion, which involves unreasoning sense perception. It comes to be and passes away, but never really is. Now everything that comes to be must of necessity come to be by the agency of some cause, for it is impossible for anything to come to be without a cause. So whenever the craftsman looks at what is always changeless and, using a thing of that kind as his model, reproduces its form and character, then, of necessity, all that he so *b*
completes is beautiful. But were he to look at a thing that has come to be and use as his model something that has been begotten, his work will lack beauty.

Now as to the whole universe or world order [*kosmos*]—let's just call it by whatever name is most

---

From Plato, *Timaeus*, translated by Donald J. Zeyl (Indianapolis: Hackett Publishing Company, 2000). Copyright © 2000. Reprinted by permission of the publisher.

acceptable in a given context—there is a question we
need to consider first. This is the sort of question one
should begin with in inquiring into any subject. Has
it always existed? Was there no origin from which it
came to be? Or did it come to be and take its start
from some origin? It has come to be. For it is both vis-
c ible and tangible and it has a body—and all things of
that kind are perceptible. And, as we have shown,
perceptible things are grasped by opinion, which
involves sense perception. As such, they are things
that come to be, things that are begotten. Further, we
maintain that, necessarily, that which comes to be
must come to be by the agency of some cause. Now
to find the maker and father of this universe [*to pan*]
is hard enough, and even if I succeeded, to declare
him to everyone is impossible. And so we must go
back and raise this question about the universe:
Which of the two models did the maker use when he
29 fashioned it? Was it the one that does not change and
stays the same, or the one that has come to be? Well,
if this world of ours is beautiful and its craftsman
good, then clearly he looked at the eternal model.
But if what it it's blasphemous to even say is the case,
then he looked at one that has come to be. Now
surely it it's clear to all that it was the eternal model
he looked at, for, of all the things that have come to
be, our universe is the most beautiful, and of causes
the craftsman is the most excellent. This, then, is
how it has come to be: it is a work of craft, modeled
after that which is changeless and is grasped by a
rational account, that is, by wisdom.

b Since these things are so, it follows by unquestion-
able necessity that this world is an image of something. Now in every subject it is of utmost
importance to begin at the natural beginning, and so,
on the subject of an image and its model, we must
make the following specification: the accounts we
give of things have the same character as the subjects
they set forth. So accounts of what is stable and fixed
and transparent to understanding are themselves stable and unshifting. We must do our very best to make
these accounts as irrefutable and invincible as any
account may be. On the other hand, accounts we
c give of that which has been formed to be like that
reality, since they are accounts of what is a likeness,
are themselves likely, and stand in proportion to the
previous accounts, i.e., what being is to becoming,
truth is to convincingness. Don't be surprised then,
Socrates, if it turns out repeatedly that we won't be
able to produce accounts on a great many subjects—
on gods or the coming to be of the universe—that are
completely and perfectly consistent and accurate.
Instead, if we can come up with accounts no less
likely than any, we ought to be content, keeping in
mind that both I, the speaker, and you, the judges,
are only human. So we should accept the likely tale
on these matters. It behooves us not to look for any- d
thing beyond this.

SOCRATES: Bravo, Timaeus! By all means! We
must accept it as you say we should. This overture of
yours was marvellous. Go on now and let us have the
work itself.

TIMAEUS: Very well then. Now why did he who
framed this whole universe of becoming frame it? Let e
us state the reason why. He was good, and one who
is good can never become jealous of anything. And
so, being free of jealousy, he wanted everything to
become as much like himself as was possible. In fact,
men of wisdom will tell you (and you couldn't do
better than to accept their claim) that this, more than 30
anything else, was the most preeminent reason for
the origin of the world's coming to be. The god
wanted everything to be good and nothing to be bad
so far as that was possible, and so he took over all that
was visible—not at rest but in discordant and disorderly motion—and brought it from a state of disorder
to one of order, because he believed that order was in
every way better than disorder. Now it wasn't permitted (nor is it now) that one who is supremely good
should do anything but what is best. Accordingly, the b
god reasoned and concluded that in the realm of
things naturally visible no unintelligent thing could
as a whole be better than anything which does possess intelligence as a whole, and he further concluded that it is impossible for anything to come to
possess intelligence apart from soul. Guided by this
reasoning, he put intelligence in soul, and soul in
body, and so he constructed the universe. He wanted
to produce a piece of work that would be as excellent and supreme as its nature would allow. This,
then, in keeping with our likely account, is how we
must say divine providence brought our world into c
being as a truly living thing, endowed with soul and
intelligence.

This being so, we have to go on to speak about
what comes next. When the maker made our world,

what living thing did he make it resemble? Let us not stoop to think that it was any of those that have the natural character of a part, for nothing that is a likeness of anything incomplete could ever turn out beautiful. Rather, let us lay it down that the universe resembles more closely than anything else that Living Thing of which all other living things are parts, both individually and by kinds. For that Living Thing comprehends within itself all intelligible living
d things, just as our world is made up of us and all the other visible creatures. Since the god wanted nothing more than to make the world like the best of the intelligible things, complete in every way, he made it a single visible living thing, which contains within
31 itself all the living things whose nature it is to share its kind.

Have we been correct in speaking of *one* universe, or would it have been more correct to say that there are many, in fact infinitely many universes? There is but one universe, if it is to have been crafted after its model. For that which contains all of the intelligible living things couldn't ever be one of a pair, since that would require there to be yet another Living Thing, the one that contained those two, of which they then would be parts, and then it would be more correct to speak of our universe as made in the likeness, now not of those two, but of that other, the one that contains them. So, in order that this living thing should
b be like the complete Living Thing in respect of uniqueness, the Maker made neither two, nor yet an infinite number of worlds. On the contrary, our universe came to be as the one and only thing of its kind, is so now and will continue to be so in the future.

Now that which comes to be must have bodily form, and be both visible and tangible, but nothing could ever become visible apart from fire, nor tangible without something solid, nor solid without earth. That is why, as he began to put the body of the universe together, the god came to make it out of fire and earth. But it isn't possible to combine two things
c well all by themselves, without a third; there has to be some bond between the two that unites them. Now the best bond is one that really and truly makes a unity of itself together with the things bonded by it, and this in the nature of things is best accomplished by proportion. For whenever of three numbers which
32 are either solids or squares the middle term between any two of them is such that what the first term is to it, it is to the last, and, conversely, what the last term is to the middle, it is to the first, then, since the middle term turns out to be both first and last, and the last and the first likewise both turn out to be middle terms, they will all of necessity turn out to have the same relationship to each other, and, given this, will all be unified.

So if the body of the universe were to have come
to be as a two dimensional plane, a single middle b
term would have sufficed to bind together its conjoining terms with itself. As it was, however, the universe was to be a solid, and solids are never joined together by just one middle term but always by two. Hence the god set water and air between fire and earth, and made them as proportionate to one another as was possible, so that what fire is to air, air is to water, and what air is to water, water is to earth. He then bound them together and thus he constructed the visible and tangible universe. This is the c
reason why these four particular constituents were used to beget the body of the world, making it a symphony of proportion.[1] They bestowed friendship upon it, so that, having come together into a unity with itself, it could not be undone by anyone but the one who had bound it together.

Now each one of the four constituents was entirely used up in the process of building the world. The builder built it from all the fire, water, air and earth there was, and left no part or power of any of them
out. His intentions in so doing were these: First, that d
as a living thing it should be as whole and complete
as possible and made up of complete parts. Second, 33
that it should be just one universe, in that nothing would be left over from which another one just like it could be made. Third, that it should not get old and diseased. He realized that when heat or cold or

---

1. A simple example of a proportionate progression that satisfies Plato's requirements in 32a might be that of 2, 4, 8. So: 2:4::4:8 (the first term is to the middle what the middle is to the last, the last term is to the middle what the middle is to the first); 4:2::8:4 or 4:8::2:4 (the middle term turns out to be first and last and the first and last terms turn out to be middles). Since, however, the body of the world is three-dimensional, its components must be represented by "solid" numbers, i.e., numbers that are the products of three numbers. This will require two middle terms.

anything else that possesses strong powers surrounds
a composite body from outside and attacks it, it
destroys that body prematurely, brings disease and
old age upon it and so causes it to waste away. That is
why he concluded that he should fashion the world
as a single whole, composed of all wholes, complete
and free of old age and disease, and why he fashioned
b it that way. And he gave it a shape appropriate to the
kind of thing it was. The appropriate shape for that
living thing that is to contain within itself all the living things would be the one which embraces within
itself all the shapes there are. Hence he gave it a
round shape, the form of a sphere, with its center
equidistant from its extremes in all directions. This of
all shapes is the most complete and most like itself,
which he gave to it because he believed that likeness
is incalculably more excellent than unlikeness. And
c he gave it a smooth round finish all over on the outside, for many reasons. It needed no eyes, since there
was nothing visible left outside it; nor did it need
ears, since there was nothing audible there, either.
There was no air enveloping it that it might need for
breathing, nor did it need any organ by which to take
in food or, again, expel it when it had been digested.
For since there wasn't anything else, there would be
nothing to leave it or come to it from anywhere. It
supplied its own waste for its food. Anything that it
did or experienced it was designed to do or experi-
d ence within itself and by itself. For the builder
thought that if it were self-sufficient, it would be a
better thing than if it required other things.

And since it had no need to catch hold of or fend
off anything, the god thought that it would be pointless to attach hands to it. Nor would it need feet or
34 any support to stand on. In fact, he awarded it the
movement suited to its body—that one of the seven
motions which is especially associated with understanding and intelligence. And so he set it turning
continuously in the same place, spinning around
upon itself. All the other six motions he took away,
and made its movement free of their wanderings.
And since it didn't need feet to follow this circular
path, he begat it without legs or feet.

b Applying this entire train of reasoning to the god
that was yet to be, the eternal god made it smooth
and even all over, equal from the center, a whole and
complete body itself, but also made up of complete
bodies. In its center he set a soul, which he extended
throughout the whole body, and with which he then
covered the body outside. And he set it to turn in a
circle, a single solitary universe, whose very excellence enables it to keep its own company without
requiring anything else. For its knowledge of and
friendship with itself is enough. All this, then,
explains why this world which he begat for himself is
a blessed god.

As for the world's soul, even though we are now
embarking on an account of it *after* we we've already
given an account of its body, it isn't the case that the
god devised it to be younger than the body. For the *c*
god would not have united them and then allow the
elder to be ruled by the younger. We have a tendency
to be casual and random in our speech, reflecting, no
doubt, the whole realm of the casual and random of
which we are a part. The god, however, gave priority
and seniority to the soul, both in its coming to be and
in the degree of its excellence, to be the body's mistress and to rule over it as her subject.

The components from which he made the soul 35
and the way in which he made it were as follows: In
between the *Being* that is indivisible and always
changeless, and the one that is divisible and comes to
be in the corporeal realm, he mixed a third, intermediate form of being, derived from the other two.
Similarly, he made a mixture of the *Same*, and then
one of the *Different*, in between their indivisible and
their corporeal, divisible counterparts. And he took
the three mixtures and mixed them together to make
a uniform mixture, forcing the Different, which was
hard to mix, into conformity with the Same. Now *b*
when he had mixed these two together with Being,
and from the three had made a single mixture, he
redivided the whole mixture into as many parts as his
task required, each part remaining a mixture of the
Same, the Different, and of Being. This is how he
began the division: first he took one portion away
from the whole, and then he took another, twice as
large, followed by a third, one and a half times as
large as the second and three times as large as the
first. The fourth portion he took was twice as large as
the second, the fifth three times as large as the third,
the sixth eight times that of the first, and the seventh
twenty-seven times that of the first.

After this he went on to fill the double and triple 36
intervals by cutting off still more portions from the
mixture and placing these between them, in such a

way that in each interval there were two middle
terms, one exceeding the first extreme by the same
fraction of the extremes by which it was exceeded by
the second, and the other exceeding the first extreme
by a number equal to that by which it was exceeded
by the second. These connections produced intervals
of 3/2, 4/3, and 9/8 within the previous intervals. He
b then proceeded to fill all the 4/3 intervals with the
9/8 interval, leaving a small portion over every time.
The terms of this interval of the portion left over
made a numerical ratio of 256/243. And so it was that
the mixture, from which he had cut off these portions, was eventually completely used up.[2]

Next, he sliced this entire compound in two along
c its length, joined the two halves together center to
center like an X, and bent them back in a circle,
attaching each half to itself end to end and to the
ends of the other half at the point opposite to the one
where they had been joined together. He then
included them in that motion which revolves in the
same place without variation, and began to make the
one the outer, and the other the inner circle. And he
decreed that the outer movement should be the
movement of *the Same,* while the inner one should
be that of *the Different.* He made the movement of
the Same revolve toward the right by way of the side,
and that of the Different toward the left by way of the
diagonal, and he made the revolution of the Same, d
i.e., the uniform, the dominant one in that he left
this one alone undivided, while he divided the inner
one six times, to make seven unequal circles. His
divisions corresponded to the several double and

2. The construction of the world's soul follows three stages:

(1) *The creation of the mixture:* Three preliminary mixtures are created. The first is a mixture of indivisible, changeless Being with divisible Being. The second and third are likewise mixtures of indivisible with divisible Sameness and Difference, respectively. These three preliminary mixtures are themselves mixed to create the final mixture.

(2) *The division of the mixture:* Seven "portions" of the mixture are now marked off, possessing the following numerical values:

First portion:	1
Second portion:	2
Third portion:	3
Fourth portion:	4
Fifth portion:	9
Sixth portion:	8
Seventh portion:	27

(3) *The filling of the intervals:* The values of the first, second, fourth and sixth portions form a series such that each successive portion is twice that of its predecessor. The values of the first, third, fifth and seventh portions form a series such that each successive portion is three times that of its predecessor. Thus intervals between successive portions of the first series are called "double intervals," and those between successive portions of the second series are called "triple intervals." Within each interval there are two "middle terms." The first of these is such that its value is that of the first extreme plus $1/x$ of the first extreme, which is equal to the value of the second extreme minus $1/x$ of the second extreme. This is the "harmonic middle." The second middle term is such that its value is the median between the extremes. This is the "arithmetical middle." Inserting the two middle terms within the original intervals in the first series, we get:

1 – 4/3 – 3/2 – **2** – 8/3 – 3 – **4** – 16/3 – 6 – **8**;

and doing the same with the second series produces:

1 – 3/2 – **2** – 3 – 9/2 – 6 – **9** – 27/2 – 18 – **27**.

Combining the two series in ascending order and omitting duplication we get:

1 – 4/3 – 3/2 – **2** – 8/3 – **3** – **4** – 9/2 – 16/3 – 6 – **8** – **9** – 27/2 – 18 – **27**.

In this series the value of each term but the first is either 4/3 or 3/2 or 9/8 the value of its predecessor. Finally, the intervals of 4/3 (e.g., between 1 and 4/3, or between 3/2 and 2, or 3 and 4) are now themselves "filled" by intervals of 9/8. In the interval between 1 and 4/3, for example, we can insert new intervals each of which multiplies its predecessor by 9/8, but we can do so no more than twice (1 – 9/8 – 81/64) . . . **4/3**), since a third attempt (729/512) would exceed 4/3. The interval between 81/64 can only be filled up with a "leftover," a number by which 81/64 can be multiplied to equal 4/3. The number turns out to be 256/243.

triple intervals, of which there were three each. He
set the circles to go in contrary directions: three to go
at the same speed, and the other four to go at speeds
different from both each other's and that of the other
three. Their speeds, however, were all proportionate
to each other.[3]

Once the whole soul had acquired a form that
e pleased him, he who formed it went on to fashion
inside it all that is corporeal, and, joining center to
center, he fitted the two together. The soul was
woven together with the body from the center on out
in every direction to the outermost limit of the universe, and covered it all around on the outside. And,
revolving within itself, it initiated a divine beginning
of unceasing, intelligent life for all time. Now while
the body of the universe had come to be as a visible
thing, the soul was invisible. But even so, because it
37 shares in reason and harmony, the soul came to be as
the most excellent of all the things begotten by him
who is himself most excellent of all that is intelligible
and eternal.

Because the soul is a mixture of the Same, the Different and Being (the three components we we've
described), because it was divided up and bound
together in various proportions, and because it circles round upon itself, then, whenever it comes into
contact with something whose being is scatterable or
else with something whose being is indivisible, it is
stirred throughout its whole self. It then declares
what exactly that thing is the same as, or what it is different from, and in what respect and in what man- b
ner, as well as when, it turns out that they are the
same or different and are characterized as such. This
applies both to the things that come to be, and to
those that are always changeless. And when this contact gives rise to an account that is equally true
whether it is about what is different or about what is
the same, and is borne along without utterance or
sound within the self-moved thing, then, whenever
the account concerns anything that is perceptible,
the circle of the Different goes straight and proclaims it throughout its whole soul. This is how firm
and true opinions and convictions come about.
Whenever, on the other hand, the account concerns c
any object of reasoning, and the circle of the Same
runs well and reveals it, the necessary result is understanding and knowledge. And if anyone should ever
call that in which these two arise, not soul but something else, what he says will be anything but true.

Now when the Father who had begotten the universe observed it set in motion and alive, a thing that
had come to be as a shrine for the everlasting gods,

3. By speaking of "circles" instead of spheres, Plato seems to have in mind the model of an armillary sphere, a skeleton structure which, by representing whole spheres as rings, enables a viewer to examine the axial positions of spheres within the outer sphere. The circle of *the Same* is a ring of one half of the just described soul compound which in its motion represents the entire sphere, from the center of the earth to the outer limit, the realm of the fixed stars. This sphere moves "toward the right," i.e., from east to west along its axis between the poles along the plane of the equator. The observation point is presumably that of an observer in a northern latitude looking toward the south. The circle of *the Different* is a ring of the remaining half of the soul compound, which is subsequently subdivided into seven smaller rings (spheres), the orbits of the moon, the sun, and the five plantes. Their movements are "toward the left," i.e., in the opposite direction of the movement of the sphere that embraces them, that of *the Same*. The planes these seven rings are parallel to "the diagonal," i.e., the plane of the ecliptic, and presumably all seven rings move within the limits of the Zodiac, that band of constellations which parallels, and is bisected along its length by, the ecliptic. The relation of the plane of the equator to that of the ecliptic, following Plato's sugges-tion that the latter is "diagonal" to the former, may be illustrated as follows:

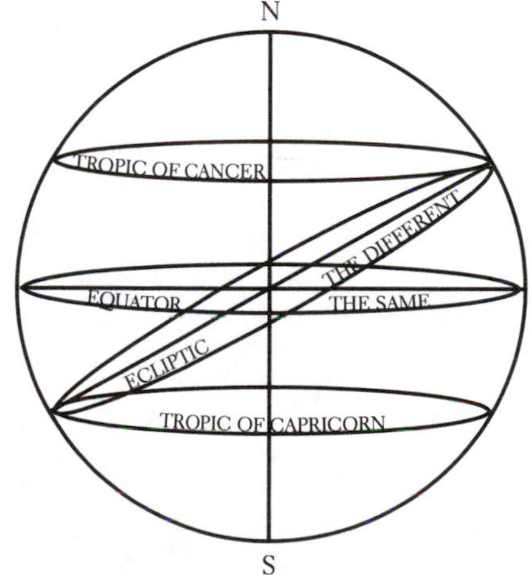

he was well pleased, and in his delight he thought of
d making it more like its model still. So, as the model was itself an everlasting Living Thing, he set himself to bringing this universe to completion in such a way that it, too, would have that character to the extent that was possible. Now it was the Living Thing Thing's nature to be eternal, but it isn't possible to bestow eternity fully upon anything that is begotten. And so he began to think of making a moving image of eternity: at the same time as he brought order to the universe, he would make an eternal image, moving according to number, of eternity remaining in unity. This number, of course, is what we now call "time."

ARISTOTLE

ARISTOTLE WAS BORN in 384 BCE to a well-off family living in the small Macedonian town of Stagira in northern Greece. His father, Nicomachus, who died while Aristotle was still quite young, was doctor to King Amyntas of Macedon; his mother, Phaestis, was wealthy in her own right. When Aristotle was seventeen, his uncle Proxenus sent him to study at Plato's Academy in Athens. He remained there for twenty years, initially as a student, eventually as researcher and teacher.

Plato died in 347, leaving the Academy in the hands of his nephew Speusippus. Aristotle then left Athens for Assos in Asia Minor, where the ruler, Hermeias (a former slave), was a patron of philosophy. He married Hermeias' niece Pythias, with whom he had a daughter, also named Pythias. Three years later, in 345, after Hermeias had been killed by the Persians, Aristotle moved to Mytilene on the island of Lesbos, where he met Theophrastus, who was to become his best student and closest colleague.

In 343, Aristotle was invited by Philip of Macedon to tutor his thirteen-year-old son Alexander (later "the Great"). In 335, he returned to Athens and founded his own school, the Lyceum. While he was there, his wife died and he formed a relationship with Herpyllis, also a native of Stagira. Their son, Nicomachus, was named for Aristotle's father. After Alexander the Great died in 323, anti-Macedonian feeling in Athens grew in strength. Aristotle left for Chalcis in Euboea, where he died twelve months later in 322 at the age of sixty-two.

A list of Aristotle's papers, probably made in the third century BCE, seems to describe most of his extant writings, as well as a number of works (including some dialogues) that are now lost. When Athens was captured by Rome in 87 BCE, these papers were among the spoils of war. About 30 BCE, they were edited, organized into different treatises, and arranged in logical sequence by Andronicus of Rhodes. Most of the writings he thought to be genuinely Aristotelian have been transmitted to us via manuscript copies produced between the ninth and sixteenth centuries CE. The most credible view of these writings is that they are lecture notes written or dictated by Aristotle, not intended for publication. No doubt this accounts for some of their legendary and manifest difficulty.

The Aristotelian World

Of the various things that exist in the world as Aristotle describes it, "some existing things are natural, while others are due to other causes" (*Physics* 192b8–9). Those that exist (or come into existence) by nature have a nature of their own—an internal source of "motion and stability in place, in growth and decay, or in alteration" (192b13–5). Thus, for example, a feline embryo has within it a source that explains why it grows into a cat, why that cat moves and changes in the ways it does, and why it eventually decays and dies. A house or any other artifact, by contrast, has no such source; instead, the source "comes from outside," namely, from the soul of the craftsman who manufactures it (192b30–1; *Metaphysics* 1032a32–b10).

A thing's nature (*physis*), function (*ergon*), and end (*telos*)—or that for the sake of which it exists (*hou heneka*)—are systematically related, since its end is to actualize its nature by performing its function (*Nicomachean Ethics* 1168a6–9). If it cannot perform its function, it ceases to be what it is except in name (*Politics* 1253a23–5). Aristotle's view of natural beings is thus teleological: it sees them as defined by an end for which they are striving, and as needing to have their behavior explained by reference to it. It is this end, essence, or function that determines what the virtues or excellences of such a being are and what its good consists of.

Many of the things characterized as existing by nature or as products of some craft are hylomorphic compounds—compounds of matter (*hylē*) and form (*morphē*). The matter of a statue is the stone or metal from which it is made, while its form is its shape. The matter of human beings is (roughly speaking) their body, and the form, their soul. Even a city is such a compound: its matter is its inhabitants; its form, its *politeia* or constitution. Though the natures of hylomorphic compounds owe something to their matter, "the form is the nature more than the matter is" (*Physics* 193b6–7): change in matter is consistent with their continued existence; change in form isn't. Human beings can survive through material change (they are constantly metabolizing, as we say), but if their form is changed, they cease to exist (*Politics* 1276b1–13). That is why the sort of investigation we find in *De Anima* and in the ethical and political treatises focuses on human souls not bodies.

According to Aristotle, such souls consist of distinct, hierarchically organized elements (*Nicomachean Ethics* 1.13). The lowest rung in the hierarchy is vegetative soul (*to threptikon*), which is responsible for nutrition and growth, and is found in plants and other animals. At the next rung up, we find appetitive soul (*to orektikon*), which is responsible for perception, imagination, and movement, and so is found in other animals but not in plants. This is the nonrational (*alogon*) part of the soul, which though it lacks reason can be influenced by it (1103a1–3, 1151a15–28). The third part of the soul is the rational part (1097b33–1098a8), which is further divided into the scientific part which enables us to study or engage in theoretical activity (*theōria*), and the deliberative part, which enables us to engage in practical or political activity (1139a3–b5).

Because the human soul includes these different elements, the human function, and so the human good, might be defined in terms of all of them or of only some. In the famous function argument (*Nicomachean Ethics* 1.7), Aristotle argues for the latter alternative: the human function is "some sort of life of action of [the part of the soul] that has reason," and so the human good (happiness) turns out to be "the soul's activity that expresses . . . the best and most complete virtue" (1098a4–18). The trouble is that both the scientific part and the deliberative part fit this characterization. Hence human happiness might consist in practical ethical or political activity, in contemplative scientific theorizing, or in a mixture of both. The discussion in *Nicomachean Ethics* 10.6–8 shows how difficult it is to decide which of these Aristotle had in mind.

Science

Each theoretical science Aristotle recognizes deals with a genus—a natural class of beings that have forms or essences (*Posterior Analytics* 87a38–9, *Metaphysics* 1003b19–21). When properly regimented, it may be set out as a structure of demonstrations—syllogistic deductions—from first principles, which are definitions of those essences. Since these definitions are necessary truths, and deductions are necessity preserving, scientific theorems are also necessary.

Though we cannot grasp a *first* principle by demonstrating it from yet more primitive principles, it must—if we are to have scientific knowledge at all—be "better known" than any theorem derived from it (*Nicomachean Ethics* 1139b33–4). This superior knowledge is provided by understanding (*nous*). The process by which it comes within understanding's purview is induction (1139b28–9, 1141a7–8).

As characterized in *Posterior Analytics* 2.19, induction begins with perception of particular things, which, in turn, gives rise to the retention of the perceptual contents in memory. When, from a unified set of such memories, "one universal judgment about similar things" is produced (*Metaphysics* 981a1–7), the result is an experience. Getting from particulars to universals, then, is a largely noninferential process. If we simply attend to particulars, and have understanding, we will get there (*Prior Analytics* 68b15–29; *Posterior Analytics* 88a12–7, 89b10–3). When these universals are analyzed into their elements, and thereby defined, they become scientifically known (*Physics* 184a16–21).

The inductive path to first principles, and so to scientific knowledge generally, begins with perception of particulars and of perceptually accessible, undefined, or unanalyzed universals, and leads to analyzed universals and definitions of them. Then induction gives way to deduction, as we descend via demonstrations to scientific theorems. Perception, unaided by understanding, cannot reach the end of this journey. But without perception the journey cannot so much as begin. Perception, elaborated in theory, is thus the soul's window on the Aristotelian world (*Prior Analytics* 46a17–8; *De Anima* 432a7–9).

Philosophy

It is often and rightly said that Aristotle's philosophical method is *dialectical*. Here is his own description:

> As in all the other cases, we must set out the appearances and first of all go through the puzzles. In this way we must prove the common beliefs [*endoxa*] . . . ideally all the common beliefs, but if not all, then most of them and the most important. For if the problems are solved and the common beliefs are left, it will be an adequate proof. (*Nicomachean Ethics* 1145b2–7)

Appearances are things that appear to someone to be the case. They include, in the first instance, empirical observations or perceptual evidence (*Prior Analytics* 46a17–27; *De Caelo* 297a2–6, 297b23–5). But they also include items that we might not comfortably call observations, such as propositions that strike people as true or that are commonly said or believed. The following is an appearance, for example: "The incontinent person knows that his actions are base, but does them because of his feelings, while the continent person knows that his appetites are base, but because of reason does not follow them" (*Nicomachean Ethics* 1145b12–4). Appearances are typically neither proved nor supported by something else, and are often contrasted with things that are (*Eudemian Ethics* 1216b26–8).

The common beliefs, or *endoxa*, are defined in the *Topics* as "the things believed by everyone or by most people or by the wise (and among the wise by all or most or by those most known and commonly recognized)" (100b22–4). But to count as *endoxa* there must be no disagreement about them (104b31–6). If there is such disagreement, what we have is a puzzle. Indeed, just one notable philosopher rejecting a proposition everyone else accepts is sufficient to create a puzzle (104b19–28). *Endoxa*, in other words, are *deeply* unproblematic beliefs—beliefs based on experience or perception to which there is simply no worthwhile opposition of any sort (104b22–4, 170b6–9).

Dialectic is useful to philosophy, Aristotle says, "because the ability to survey the puzzles on each side of a question makes it easier to notice what is true and false" (*Topics* 101a31–3). Later, he provides another important clue to what he has in mind: "Where knowledge and philosophical wisdom are concerned, the ability to discern and hold in one view the consequences of either hypothesis is no insignificant tool, since then it only remains to make a correct choice of one of them" (163b9–12). The picture emerging from these passages is something like this. The puzzle a philosopher faces is, let's say, to determine whether rule by one person is better than rule by many (*Politics* 3.16). If he is a competent dialectician, he will be able to follow out the consequences of supposing that it is, as well as those of supposing that it is not. He will be able to see what puzzles these consequences in turn face, and he will be able to go through these and determine which can be solved and which cannot. In the end, he will have concluded, we may suppose, that one-person rule is better, provided that the person is outstandingly virtuous (1288a15–29). But in the process of reaching that conclusion some of the *endoxa* on both sides will almost certainly have been modified or clarified, partly accepted and partly rejected (*Topics* 164b6–7). Others will have been decisively rejected as false. But these the philosopher will need to explain away: "For when we have a clear and good account of why a false view appears true, that makes us more confident of the true view" (*Nicomachean Ethics* 1154a24–5). Some beliefs that seemed to be *endoxa*, that seemed to be deeply unproblematic, will thus have fallen from grace. If most of them and the most compelling are still in place, however, that will be an adequate proof of the philosopher's conclusion, because there will be every reason to accept it and no reason not to.

It is because Aristotle employs this method that he almost always begins by looking at what his predecessors have thought about a topic: the views of wise people are likely to contain some truth. It also explains why he often seems to adopt a position in between those of a pair of conflicting parties: if both contain some truth, the best position *should* contain elements of each. There is a joke to the effect that Aristotle died of an excess of moderation, an excessive love of the middle ground. We can now see why he thought this love was just the love of wisdom.

Aristotle's method is dialectic but his goal is scientific; it is to develop a science, to acquire scientific knowledge. The contribution of dialectic to this goal is described as follows:

> [Dialectic] is useful for finding the primary things in each science. For from the principles proper to the science proposed for discussion nothing can be derived about the principles themselves, since the principles are primary among all [the truths contained in the science]; instead they must be discussed through the common beliefs [*endoxa*] in a given area. . . . This is distinctive of dialectic, or more proper to it than to anything else; for since it cross-examines, it provides a way towards the principles of all lines of inquiry. (*Topics* 101a26–b4)

The philosopher knows on the authority of the scientist that the first principles in question are true and their negations false. Yet when he uses his dialectical skill to draw out the consequences of these principles, and of their negations, he sees puzzles and supporting arguments, based on *endoxa*, on both sides. Since he knows that the principles are empirically true, his goal will be to solve the puzzles they face, while undoing the arguments that seem to support their negations. If he is successful, the principle will have been shown to be in accord with most of the most compelling *endoxa*, with the preponderance of deeply unproblematic beliefs.

But so what? The principles were already true, already known to the scientist. How are we epistemically any better off now that they have also been shown to be in accord with the most compelling *endoxa*? Presumably, the answer is just this: we are no longer pulled apart by our epistemic commitments; we see how all the things we believe can be true simultaneously, how each science can be knit into the larger fabric of our deeply unproblematic beliefs. In many texts, indeed, Aristotle characterizes puzzles as knots in our understanding, which dialectical philosophy enables us to untie (*Physics* 253a31–3, 263a15–8; *Metaphysics* 995a27–33, 1032a6–11; *Nicomachean Ethics* 1146a24–7). In others, he characterizes dialectic as enabling us to make beliefs, including first principles, clear (*Prior Analytics* 46a17–30; *De Anima*

413a11–3, *Nicomachean Ethics* 1097b22–4). What dialectical philosophy offers us in regard to the first principles of the sciences, then, is clarity of understanding: no knots.

Aristotle's God

The very best scientific activity—the one that expresses theoretical virtue or excellence of the highest sort—consists in the study of God (*Nicomachean Ethics* 11412a16–20). This is so for the following reason. God is the eternal first mover, or first cause of motion in the universe—which is itself a series of concentric spheres with the earth at its center. But God does not act on the universe to cause it to move. He is not an efficient cause. He moves it in the way that an object of love causes motion in the things that love or desire it (*De Anima* 415a26–b7). In other words, God is a teleological cause, an unmoved mover (*Metaphysics* 1072a25–7). Things express their love for God by trying to be as godlike as possible, something they accomplish by trying to realize their own natures or forms as completely or perfectly as God realizes his. (Compare Diotima's views in Plato's *Symposium*, pages 141–7 in this volume.) This is a struggle for life or existence, since the loss of form, as we saw, is the loss of life or existence. God, however, realizes his form completely and eternally. But since most other living things are both generated and perishable, the best they can do is to give birth to offspring with the same form, and so belonging to the same species, as themselves:

> The most natural of all functions for a living thing . . . is to produce another thing of the same sort as itself (an animal, if it is an animal, and a plant, if it is a plant), in order to share as far as it can in the everlasting and divine. For this is the end they all strive for, and for its sake they do every action that accords with nature. (*De Anima* 415a28–b2)

But because this is an essential fact about their nature, we cannot understand them fully unless we are aware of it and understand what God is. Theology is more intelligible, and hence better to study, than the other sciences for just this reason: they contain an area of darkness that needs to be illuminated by another science, whereas theology can fully illuminate itself (*Posterior Analytics* 87a31–7; *Metaphysics* 1074b34, 1075a11–2; *Nicomachean Ethics* 1141a16–20, 1141b2–8).

Like other animals, human beings can participate in the divine by giving birth to offspring. But they can participate in it yet more fully because they, unlike other animals, have understanding. For God, in Aristotle's view, is pure understanding (*Metaphysics* 983a6–7). That is what is meant by the famous definition of God as *noēsis noēseōs noēsis*—"an understanding [that] is an understanding of understanding" (1074b35). Hence when human beings are actually studying God they are participating in the very activity that is God himself. They thus become much more like God than they do by having children and, in the process, achieve the greatest happiness possible for them (*Nicomachean Ethics* 1177b26–1179a32).

Categories, De Interpretatione, Topics, and Posterior Analytics

The *Categories* gives an account of predication and introduces the notion of a substance. Aristotle proceeds, in *De Interpretatione,* to present an analysis of the structure of statement-making sentences utilizing these ideas. This is followed by the *Topics,* which is concerned with argumentation employing statement-making sentences. In the excerpts from Book 1 presented here, Aristotle discusses the role of dialectic in obtaining first principles (Chapters 1 and 2) as well as some concepts central to his own thought (Chapter 5).

The final building block of the program is provided by the *Posterior Analytics,* which contains Aristotle's theory of knowledge, explanation, and the structure of science. Some of what we know can be justified by being derived from other things we know, which do not themselves need to be so justified, and may be taken as scientific first principles. Aristotle provides a brief account of the acquisition of these in Book 2.

Categories

1

1a If things have only a name in common, and the account of the essence$_{o}$ corresponding to the name is different for each, they are called homonymous. Both a man and a painted animal, for instance, are animals homonymously; for these have only a name in common and the account (corresponding to the name) of the essence is different. For if one says what being an animal is for each of them, one will give a different account in each case.

If things have both the name in common and the same account (corresponding to the name) of the essence, they are called synonymous. Both a man and an ox, for instance, are animals [synonymously], since each is called animal by a common name, and the account of the essence is the same. For if one gives an account of each, saying what being an animal is for each of them, one will give the same account.

If things are called what they are by having a name that is derived from something else, but with a different inflection, they are called paronymous; for example, the grammarian is so called from grammar, and the brave person from bravery.

2

Among things said, some involve combination, while others are without combination. Things involving combination are, for instance, man runs, man wins; things without combination are, for instance, man, ox, run, wins.

Among beings some are said of a subject but are not in any subject; man, for instance, is said of[1] a subject, an individual man, but is not in any subject. Some are in a subject but are not said of any subject.[2] (By 'in a subject' I mean what belongs in something, not as a part, and cannot exist separately from what it is in.) For example, an individual [instance of] grammatical knowledge[3] is in a subject, the soul,

1. **said of:** In "G is said of F," G and F are things, not words. Aristotle is not describing a connection between the words "the individual man" and "man," but a connection between individual men and the species man.

2. **not said . . . subject:** If G is said of F, we can say (e.g.) of a particular man "This is a man." If G is in F, we cannot say (e.g.) "This is a thin"; we need to say something further, such as "This is a thin man."

3. **an individual . . . knowledge:** This might be understood

but is not said of any subject; and an individual [instance of] white is in a subject, the body (for all color is in body), but is not said of any subject. Some
1b things are both said of a subject and in a subject; knowledge, for instance, is in a subject, the soul, and is said of a subject, grammatical knowledge. Some things are neither in a subject nor said of a subject. This is true, for instance, of an individual man or horse; for nothing of this sort is either in a subject or said of a subject.

Things that are individual and numerically one are, without exception, not said of any subject. But nothing prevents some of them from being in a subject; for an individual [instance of] grammatical knowledge is one of the things in a subject.

3

Whenever one thing is predicated of another as of a subject, everything said of what is predicated is also said of the subject. Man, for instance, is predicated of an individual man, and animal of man; and so animal will also be predicated of an individual man, since an individual man is both a man and an animal.

Genera which are different and not subordinate to one another have differentiae that are different in species—for instance, the differentiae of animal and of knowledge. For footed, winged, aquatic, and biped are differentiae of animal, but none of them is a differentia of knowledge; for one sort of knowledge is not differentiated from another by being biped. But if one genus is subordinate to another, nothing prevents them from having the same differentiae; for the higher genera are predicated of those below them, so that the subject will also have all the differentiae of the thing predicated.

as either (1) the unique instance found in (e.g.) Socrates, which differs numerically (but not necessarily qualitatively) from the unique instance found in Callias; or (2) the most fully determinate type falling under some determinable (e.g., this completely determinate-shade of green in contrast to the color green). According to (2), one and the same instance of red is in two traffic lights if they are exactly the same shade of red; according to (1), there will be two instances of red.

4

Of things said without combination, each signifies either substance or quantity or quality or relative or where or when or being in a position or having or acting on or being affected. To describe these in outline, here are some examples:

Substance:	man, horse	
Quantity:	two feet long, three feet long	
Quality:	white, grammatical	
Relative:	double, half, larger	
Where:	in the Lyceum, in the marketplace	2a
When:	yesterday, last year	
Being in a position:	is lying; is sitting	
Having:	has shoes on, has armor on	
Acting on:	cutting, burning	
Being affected:	being cut, being burned	

None of the things just mentioned is said all by itself in any affirmation; an affirmation results from the combination of these things with one another. For every affirmation seems to be either true or false, whereas nothing said without combination—for instance, man, white, runs, wins—is either true or false.

5

What is called substance most fully, primarily, and most of all, is what is neither said of any subject nor in any subject—for instance, an individual man or horse. The species in which the things primarily called substances belong are called secondary substances, and so are their genera. An individual man, for instance, belongs in the species man, and animal is the genus of the species; these things, then (for instance, man and animal), are called secondary substances.

It is evident from what has been said that if something is said of a subject, then both its name and its account must be predicated of the subject. For instance, man is said of a subject, an individual man, and the name is predicated (since you will predicate man of an individual man); moreover, the account of man will also be predicated of an individual man (since an individual man is also a man). And so both the name and the account will be predicated of the subject.

On the other hand, if something is in a subject, in most cases neither its name nor its account is predicated of the subject.[4] In some cases the name may well be predicated of the subject, but the account still cannot be predicated. White, for instance, is in a subject, body, and is predicated of the subject (for body is said to be white); but the account of white is never predicated of body.[5]

All other things are either said of the primary substances as subjects or in them as subjects. This is evident if we examine particular cases. Animal, for instance, is predicated of man, and so also of an individual man; for if it is not predicated of any individual man, neither is it predicated of man at all. Again, color is in body, and so also in an individual body; for if it is not in any of the particular bodies, neither is it in body at all.

Hence all the other things are either said of the primary substances as subjects or in them as subjects. If, then, the primary substances did not exist, neither could any of the other things exist. For all the other things are either said of these as subjects or are in these as subjects, so that if the primary substances did not exist, neither could any of the other things exist.

Among secondary substances, the species is more a substance than the genus, since it is nearer to the primary substance; for if someone says what the primary substance is, it will be more informative and more appropriate if he mentions the species than if he mentions the genus. It will be more informative, for instance, to say that an individual man is a man than to say that he is an animal, since man is more distinctive of an individual man, while animal is more common; and it will be more informative to say that an individual tree is a tree than that it is a plant.

Further, the primary substances are subjects for all the other things, and all the other things are predicated of them or are in them; this is why they, most of all, are called substances. But as the primary substances are related to other things, so also is the species related to the genus; for the species is a subject for the genus, since the genera are predicated of the species, whereas the species are not reciprocally predicated of the genera. And so for this reason too the species is more a substance than the genus.

Among species that are not themselves genera, however, one is no more a substance than another; for it is no more appropriate to say that an individual man is a man than it is to say that an individual horse is a horse. And, similarly, among primary substances one is no more a substance than another; for an individual man is no more a substance than an individual ox is.

It is not surprising that, after the primary substances, only their species and genera are said to be secondary substances; for they are the only things predicated that reveal the primary substance. For if one says what an individual man is, it will be appropriate to mention the species or the genus, though it will be more informative to mention man than animal. But it would be inappropriate to mention anything else—for instance, white or runs or any other such thing. It is not surprising, then, that species and genera are the only other things said to be substances.

Further, it is because the primary substances are subjects for everything else that they are said to be substances most fully. But as the primary substances are related to everything else, so also the species and genera of primary substances are related to all the other [species and genera]; for all the others are predicated of them. For you will call an individual man grammatical, and so you will call both man and animal grammatical; and the same is true in the other cases.

A feature common to every substance is not being in a subject; for a primary substance is neither said of nor in a subject. In the same way, it is evident that secondary substances are not in a subject either; for man is said of a subject—an individual man—but is not in a subject, since man is not in an individual man. Similarly, animal is said of a subject—an individual man—but animal is not in an individual man.

Further, while things in a subject may sometimes have their name predicated of the subject, their account can never be predicated of it. Secondary substances, on the other hand, have both their account and their name predicated of the subject; for you will predicate both the account of man and the

4. **On the other . . . of the subject:** If Electra is brave, then bravery is in her, and neither the name nor the account of bravery can be predicated of her; we cannot say either "Electra is bravery" or "Electra is the virtue that controls fear."

5. **White, for instance . . . of body:** If the table is white then the color white (= whiteness) is in the table, and in this case the name of the color can be predicated of the table, though the account of the color cannot be.

account of animal of an individual man. Hence no substance is in a subject.

This, however, is not distinctive of substance. The differentia is not in a subject either; for footed and biped are said of a subject—man—but are not in a subject, since neither footed nor biped is in man. Again, the account of the differentia is predicated of whatever subject the differentia is said of; for instance, if footed is said of man, the account of footed will also be predicated of man, since man is footed.

We need not be worried that we will ever be compelled to say that the parts of substances, being in a subject (the whole substance), are not substances. For when we spoke of things in a subject, we did not mean things belonging in something as parts.

It is a feature of substances and differentiae that everything called from them is so called synonymously; for all the predications from these are predicated of either the individuals or the species. (For there is no predication from a primary substance—since it is not said of any subject—and among secondary substances the species is predicated of an individual, and the genus is predicated both of the species and of an individual. Similarly, differentiae are also predicated both of the species and of the individuals.) Now the primary substances receive the account both of the species and of the genera, and the species receives the account of the genus; for whatever is said of what is predicated will also be said of the subject. Similarly, both the species and the individuals receive the account of the differentiae; and we saw that synonymous things are those that both have the name in common and also have the same account. Hence everything called from substances and differentiae is so called synonymously.

Every substance seems to signify a this. In the case of primary substances, it is indisputably true that each of them signifies a this; for what is revealed is an individual and is numerically one. In the case of secondary substances, it appears from the character of the name, whenever one speaks of man or animal, that they also signify a this. But this is not true. Rather, each signifies a sort of thing; for the subject is not one, as the primary substance is, but man and animal are said of many things. On the other hand, it does not unqualifiedly signify a sort of thing, as white does. For white signifies nothing other than a sort of thing, whereas the species and the genus demarcate a sort of substance; for they signify a substance of a certain sort. One demarcates more with the genus than with the species; for in speaking of animal one encompasses more than in speaking of man.

It is also a feature of substances that nothing is contrary to them. For what could be contrary to a primary substance? Nothing is contrary, for instance, to an individual man; nor is anything contrary to man or animal. This is not distinctive of substance, however, but is also true of many other things—of quantity, for instance, since nothing is contrary to two feet long, nor to ten, nor to anything else of this kind. One might say that many is contrary to few, or large to small; but no definite quantity is contrary to any other.

Substance does not seem to admit of more or less. By this I do not mean that one substance is no more a substance than another; for we have said that one type of substance is more a substance than another. Rather, I mean that no substance is said to be more or less what it is. For example, if this substance is a man, it will not be more or less a man either than itself or than another. For one man is no more a man than another, in the way that one white thing is whiter than another, or one beautiful thing is more beautiful than another. In some cases a thing is called more or less something than itself—for example, the body which is white is said to be more white now than it was before, and the body which is hot is said to be more or less hot [than it was]. But substance is not spoken of in this way; for a man is not said to be more a man now than before, nor is this said of any other substance. Thus substance does not admit of more or less.

It seems most distinctive of substance that numerically one and the same thing is able to receive contraries. In no other case could one cite something numerically one that is able to receive contraries. For example, the color that is numerically one and the same will not be pale and dark, nor will the action that is numerically one and the same be bad and good, and the same is true of anything else that is not a substance. But a substance that is numerically one and the same is able to receive contraries. An individual man, for instance, being one and the same, becomes at one time pale, at another time dark, and hot and cold, and bad and good; nothing of this sort appears in any other case.

Someone might object, however, that statements and beliefs are like this, since the same statement seems to be both true and false. If, for instance, the statement that someone is seated is true, when he has stood up this same statement will be false. The same is true of belief; for if someone were to believe truly that someone is seated, he will believe falsely if he has the same belief about the same person when he has stood up.

But even if one were to accept this, the way in which these receive contraries is still different. For in the case of substances, a thing is able to receive contraries by itself changing; for it changed when it became cold from hot (since it altered), or dark from pale, or good from bad, and similarly in the other cases it is able to receive contraries by itself changing. But statements and beliefs themselves remain completely unchanged in every way; it is because the object [they are about] changes that the contrary comes to be about them. For the statement that some-
4b one is seated remains the same, but it comes to be true at one time, false at another time, when the object has changed. The same is true of belief. Hence at least the way in which substance is able to receive contraries—by a change in itself—is distinctive of it, if indeed one were to accept it as true that beliefs and statements are also able to receive contraries.

In fact, however, this is not true. For a statement and a belief are said to be able to receive contraries not because they themselves receive something, but because something else has been affected. For it is because the object is or is not some way that the statement is said to be true or false, not because the statement itself is able to receive contraries; for without exception, no statement or belief is changed by anything. And so, since nothing comes to be in them, they are not able to receive contraries. But substance is said to be able to receive contraries, because it receives them itself. For it receives sickness and health, or paleness and darkness; and because it itself receives each thing of this sort, it is said to be able to receive contraries.

Hence it is distinctive of substance that numerically one and the same thing is able to receive contraries. So much, then, about substance.

De Interpretatione

1

16a We must first establish what names and verbs are, then what negations, affirmations, statements, and sentences are.

Spoken sounds are symbols of affections in the soul, and written marks are symbols of spoken sounds; and just as written marks are not the same for everyone, neither are spoken sounds. But the primary things that these signify (the affections in the soul) are the same for everyone, and what these affections are likenesses of (actual things) are also the same for every one. We have discussed these questions in *On the Soul;* they belong to another inquiry.

Some thoughts in the soul are neither true nor false, while others must be one or the other; the same is true of spoken sounds. For falsity and truth involve combination and division. Names and verbs by themselves, when nothing is added (for instance, 'man' and 'pale') are like thoughts without combination and separation, since they are not yet either true or false. A sign of this is the fact that 'goatstag' signifies something but is not yet true or false unless 'is' or 'is not' is added, either without qualification or with reference to time.

2

A name is a spoken sound that is significant by convention, without time, of which no part is significant in separation. For in 'Grancourt', the 'court' does not signify anything in itself, as it does in the phrase 'a grand court'. But complex names are not the same as simple ones; for in simple names the part is not at all significant, whereas in complex names the part has some force but does not signify anything in separation—for instance, 'fact' in 'artifact'. I say 'by convention' because nothing is a name by nature something is name only if it becomes a symbol. For even inarticulate noises—of beasts, for example—reveal something, but they are not names.

'Not-man' is not a name, nor is any established name rightly applied to it since neither is it a sentence or a negation. Let us call it an indefinite name.

'Philo's', 'to-Philo', and the like are not names but inflections of names. The same account applies to them as to names, except that a name with 'is' or 'was' or 'will be' added is always true or false, whereas an inflection with them added is neither true nor false. For example, in 'Philo's is' or 'Philo's is not' nothing is yet either true or false.

3

A verb is [a spoken sound] of which no part signifies separately, and which additionally signifies time; it is a sign of things said of something else. By 'additionally signifies time', I mean that, for instance, 'recovery' is a name but 'recovers' is a verb; for it additionally signifies something's holding now. And it is always a sign of something's holding, i.e. of something's holding of a subject.

I do not call 'does not recover' and 'does not ail' verbs; for, although they additionally signify time and always hold of something, there is difference for which there is not established name. Let us call them indefinite verbs, since they hold of anything whether it is or is not.[1]

Similarly, 'recovered' and 'will-recover' are not verbs, but inflections of verbs. They differ from verbs because verbs additionally signify the present time, whereas inflections of verbs signify times outside the present.

A verb said just by itself is a name and signifies something, since the speaker fixes his thought and the hearer pauses; but it does not yet signify whether something is or is not. For 'being' or 'not being' is not a sign of an object (not even if you say 'what is' without addition);[2] for by itself it is nothing, but it additionally signifies some combination, which cannot be thought of without the components.

4

A sentence is a significant spoken sound, of which some part is significant in separation as an expression, not as an affirmation. I mean the 'animal', for instance, signifies something, but not that it is or is not (but if something is added, there will be an affirmation or negation), whereas the single syllables of 'animal' signify nothing. Nor is the 'ice' in 'mice' significant; here it is only a spoken sound. In the case of double names, as was said, a part signifies, but not by itself.

Every sentence is significant, not because it is a [naturally suitable] instrument but, as we said, by convention. But not every sentence is a statement; only those sentences that are true or false are statements. Not every sentence is true or false; a prayer for instance, is a sentence but it is neither true nor false. Let us set aside these other cases, since inquiry into them is more appropriate for rhetoric or poetics; our present study concerns affirmations. . . .

7

Some things are universals, others are particulars. By 'universal' I mean what is naturally predicated of more than one thing; by 'particular', what is not. For example, man is a universal, and Callias is a particular.

Necessarily, then, when one says that something does or does not hold of something, one sometimes says this of a universal, sometimes of a particular. Now if one states universally of a universal that something does or does not hold, there will be contrary statements. (By 'stating universally of universal' I mean, for instance, 'Every man is pale', 'No man is pale'.) But when one states something of a universal, but not universally, the statement are not contrary, though contrary things may be revealed. (By 'stating of a universal but not universally', I mean, for instance, 'A man is pale', 'A man is not pale'. For although man is a universal, it is not used universally in the statement; for 'every' does not signify the universal, but rather signifies that it is used universally.)

In the case of what is predicated, it is not true to predicate a universal universally; for there will be no affirmation in which the universal is predicated

---

1. **is or is not:** Perhaps "exists or does not exist," or "is the case or is not the case."

2. **For being . . . without addition:** (1) Aristotle may be using the verb "to be" to stand for any verb and pointing out that the verb "run" (e.g.) uttered by itself does not say *what* runs or does not run. (2) Alternatively, he may be taking the verb "to be" as his example, because it would be most tempting to suppose that this verb all by itself could say that something is or is not.

universally of what is predicated, as in, for instance, 'Every man is every animal'.

I call an affirmation and a negation contradictory opposites when what one signifies universally the other signifies not universally—for instance, 'Every man is pale' and 'Not every man is pale', or 'No man is pale' and 'Some man is pale'. But the universal affirmation and the universal negation—for instance, 'Every man is just' and 'No man is just'—are contrary opposites. That is why they cannot both be true at the same time, but their [contradictory] opposites may both be true about the same thing—for instance, 'Not every man is pale' and 'Some man is pale'.

Of contradictory universal statements about a universal, one or the other must be true or false; similarly if they are about particulars—for instance, 'Socrates is pale' and 'Socrates is not pale'. But if they are about universals, but are not universal [statements], it is not always the case that one is true, the other false. For it is true to say at the same time that a man is pale and that a man is not pale, and that a man is handsome and that a man is not handsome; for if ugly, then not handsome. And if something is becoming *F*, it is not *F*. This might seem strange at first sight, since 'A man is not pale' might appear to signify at the same time that no man is pale; but it does not signify the same, nor does it necessarily hold at the same time.

It is clear that a single affirmation has a single negation. For the negation must deny the same thing that the affirmation affirms, and deny it of the same [subject]—either of a particular or of a universal either universally or not universally, as, for instance, in 'Socrates is pale' and 'Socrates is not pale'. (But if something else is denied, or the same thing is denied of different [subject], that will not be the opposite statement but a different one.) The opposite of 'Every man is pale' is 'Not every man is pale'; of 'Some man is pale', 'No man is pale'; of 'A man is pale', 'A man is not pale'.

We have explained, then, that a single affirmation has a single negation as its contradictory opposite, and which these are; that contrary statements are different, and which these are; and that not all contradictory pairs are true or false, and why and when they are true or false.

9

In the case of what is and what has been, then, it is necessary that the affirmation or negation be true or false. And in the case of universal statements about universals, it is always [necessary] for one to be true and the other false; and the same is true in the case of particulars, as we have said. But in the case of universals not spoken of universally, this is not necessary; we have also discussed this. But in the case of particulars that are going to be, it is not the same.

For if every affirmation or negation is true or false, then it is also necessary that everything either is the case or is not the case. And so if someone says that something will be and another denies the same thing, clearly it is necessary for one of them to speak truly, if every affirmation is true or false. For both will not be the case at the same time in such cases.

For if it is true to say that something is pale or not pale, it is necessary for it to be pale or not pale; and if it is pale or not pale, it was to affirm or deny this. And if it is not the case, one speaks falsely; and if one speaks falsely, it is not the case. Hence it is necessary for the affirmation or the negation to be true or false.

Therefore nothing either is or happens by chance or as chance has it; nor will it be nor not be [thus]. Rather, everything [happens] from necessity and not as chance has it, since either the affirmer or the denier speaks truly. For otherwise, it might equally well happen or not happen; for what happens as chance has it neither is nor will be any more this way than that.

Further, if something is pale now, it was true to say previously that it would be pale, so that it was always true to say of any thing that has happened that it would be. But if it was always true to say that it was or would be, it could not not be, or not to going to be. But if something cannot not happen, it is impossible for it not to happen; and what cannot not happen necessarily happens. Everything, then, that will be will be necessarily. Therefore, nothing will be as chance has it or by chance; for if it is by chance it is not from necessity.

But it is not possible to say that neither is true—that, for example, it neither will be nor will not be. For, first, [if this is possible, then] though the affirmation is false, the negation is true; and though the negation is false, it turns out [on this view] that the affirmation is not true.

Moreover, if it is true to say that it is pale and dark, both must be the case; and if [both] will be the case tomorrow, [both] must be the case tomorrow. But if it neither will nor will not be tomorrow, even so, the sea battle for instance, will not happen as chance has it; for in this case, the sea battle would have to neither happen nor not happen.

These and others like them are the absurd consequences if in every affirmation and negation (either about universals spoken of universally or about particulars) it is necessary that one of the opposites be true and the other false, and nothing happens as chance has it, but all things are and happen from necessity. Hence there would be no need to deliberate or to take trouble, thinking that if we do this, that will be, and if we do not, it will not be; for it might well be that ten thousand years ago one person said that this would be and another denied it, so that whichever it was true to affirm at that time will be so from necessity.

Nor does it make a difference whether or not anyone made the contradictory statements; for clearly things are thus even if someone did not affirm it and another deny it. For it is not because of the affirming
19a or denying that it will be or will not be the case, nor is this any more so for ten thousand years ago than for any other time.

Hence if in the whole of time things were such that one or the other statement was true, it was necessary for this to happen, and each thing that happened was always such as to happen from necessity. For if someone has said truly that something will happen, it cannot not happen; and it was always true to say of something that has happened that it would be.

But surely this is impossible. For we see that both deliberation and action originate things that will be; and, in general, we see in things that are not always in actuality that there is the possibility both of being and of not being; in these cases both being and not being, and hence both happening and not happening, are possible.

We find that this is clearly true of many things. It is possible, for instance, for this cloak to be cut up, though [in fact] it will not be cut up but will wear out first instead. Similarly, its not being cut up is also possible; for its wearing out first would not have been the case unless its not being cut up were possible. Hence the same is true for other things that happen, since this sort of possibility is ascribed to many of them.

Evidently, then, not everything is or happens from necessity. Rather some things happen as chance has it, and the affirmation is no more true than the negation. In other cases, one alternative [happens] more than the other and happens usually, but it is still possible for the other to happen and for the first not to happen.

It is necessary for what is, whenever it is, to be, and for what is not, whenever it is not, not to be. But not everything that is necessarily is; and not everything that is not necessarily is not. For everything's being from necessity when it is is not the same as everything's being from necessity without qualification; and the same is true of what is not.

The same argument also applies to contradictories. It is necessary for everything either to be or not to be, and indeed to be going to be or not be going to be. But one cannot divide [the contradictories] and say that one or the other is necessary. I mean that, for instance, it is necessary for there to be or not to be a sea battle tomorrow, but it is not necessary for a sea battle to happen tomorrow, nor is it [necessary] for one not to happen. It is necessary, however, for it either to happen or not to happen.

And so, since the truth of statements corresponds to how things are, it is clear that, for however many things are as chance has it and are such as to admit contraries, it is necessary for the same to be true of the contradictories. This is just what happens with things that neither always are nor always are not. For in these cases it is necessary for one of the contradictories to be true and the other false. It is not, however, [necessary] for this or that one [more than the other one to be true or false]. Rather, [it is true or false] as chance has it; or [in the case of things that happen usually] one is more true than the other, but not thereby true or false [without qualification].

Clearly, then, it is not necessary that of every affir- 19b
mation and negation of opposites, one is true and one false. For what holds for things that are [always] does not also hold for things that are not [always] but are capable of being and of not being; in these cases it is as we have said.

Topics

Book 1

1

100a The purpose of our discussion is to discover a line of inquiry that will allow us to reason deductively from common beliefs on any problem proposed to us, and to give an account ourselves without saying anything contradictory. First, then, we must say what a deduction is and what different types of it there are, so that we can grasp what dialectical deduction is—for this is what we are looking for in our proposed discussion.

A deduction, then, is an argument in which, if p and q are assumed, then something else r, different from p and q, follows necessarily through p and q. It is a demonstration whenever the deduction proceeds from true and primary premisses or our knowledge of the premisses is originally derived from primary and true premisses. A dialectical deduction is the one that proceeds from common beliefs.

100b The premisses that are true and primary are those that produce conviction not through other things, but through themselves. For in the principles of knowledge we must not search further for the reason why; rather, each of the principles must be credible itself in its own right.

The common beliefs are the things believed by everyone or by most people or by the wise (and among the wise by all or by most or by those most known and commonly recognized[1]). A contentious deduction is one proceeding from apparent common beliefs that are not really common beliefs, or one apparently proceeding from real or apparent common beliefs. [We speak of 'apparent' common beliefs,] because not everything that appears to be a common belief really is one; for none of the things called common beliefs has the appearance entirely on the surface. On this point they differ from what happens in the case of the principles of contentious arguments. For in the latter case the nature of the falsity is especially clear straightaway to those with even a little ability to trace consequences. The first kind of
101a deduction that we have called contentious, then, should indeed count as a genuine deduction, whereas the other kind is a contentious deduction, but not a genuine deduction, since it appears to make a deduction, but does not actually do so.

Further, besides all the types of deduction just mentioned, there are fallacious arguments that start from premisses that are proper to a given science, as happens in the case of geometry and cognate sciences. For this type of argument would seem to be different from the types of deduction previously mentioned; for someone who draws the wrong diagram deduces a conclusion neither from true and primary premisses nor from common beliefs. He does not fall into either class, since he does not accept what is believed by all, or by most people, or by the wise (either all or most or the most commonly recognized of these), but produces his deduction by accepting things that are proper to the science but are not true. For example he produces his fallacious argument either by describing the semicircles wrongly or by drawing lines wrongly.

These, then, are, in outline, the types of deduction. In general, both in all the cases we have discussed and in all those to be discussed later, this degree of determinateness is to be taken as adequate. For [in undertaking this discussion] the account we decide to give on any subject is not an exact account, but enough for us to describe it in outline. We assume that the ability to recognize these things in some way is entirely adequate for the proposed line of inquiry.

2

Our next task is to say what areas, and how many, there are in which our discussion is useful. It is useful, then, for three purposes—for training, for encounters, and for the philosophical sciences.

Its usefulness for training is immediately evident; for if we have a line of inquiry, we will more easily be able to take on a question proposed to us. It is useful for encounters, because once we have catalogued the beliefs of the many, our approach to them will begin from their own views, not from other people's, and we will redirect them whenever they appear to us to be wrong. It is useful for the philosophical sciences, because the ability to survey the puzzles on each side

---

1. **commonly recognized:** *endoxos.* "Common beliefs" translates *endoxa.*

of a question makes it easier to notice what is true and false. Moreover it is useful for finding the primary things in each science. For from the principles proper to the science proposed for discussion nothing can be derived about the principles themselves, since the principles are primary among all [the truths con- 101b tained in the science]; instead they must be discussed through the common beliefs in a given area. This is distinctive of dialectic, or more proper to it than to anything else; for since it cross-examines, it provides a way towards the principles of all lines of inquiry.

5

We must say, then, what a definition, a distinctive property, a genus, and a coincident are.

102a A definition is an account that signifies the essence. One provides either an account to replace a name or an account to replace an account—for it is also possible to define some of the things signified by an account. Those who merely provide a name, whatever it is, clearly do not provide the definition of the thing, since every definition is an account. Still, this sort of thing—for example, 'the fine is the fitting'—should also be counted as definitory. In the same way one should also count as definitory a question such as 'Are perception and knowledge the same or different?' for most of the discussion about definition is occupied with whether things are the same or different. Speaking without qualification, we may count as definitory everything that falls under the same line of inquiry that includes definition.

It is clear immediately that all the things just mentioned meet this condition. For if we are able to argue dialectically that things are the same and that they are different, we will in the same way be well supplied to take on definitions; for once we have shown that two things are not the same, we will have undermined that [attempted] definition. The converse of this point, however, does not hold; for showing that two things are the same is not enough to establish a definition, whereas showing that two things are not the same is enough to destroy a definition.

A distinctive property is one that does not reveal what the subject is, though it belongs only to that subject and is reciprocally predicated of it. It is distinctive of man, for instance, to be receptive of grammatical knowledge; for if someone is a man, he is receptive of grammatical knowledge and if someone is receptive of grammatical knowledge, he is a man. For no one counts as a distinctive property what admits of belonging to something else—for instance, no one counts being asleep as a distinctive property of a man, even if at some time it happens to belong only to him. If, then, something of this sort were to be called a distinctive property, it would be called distinctive not without qualification, but at a time, or in relation to something; being on the right, for instance, is distinctive of something at a particular time, while being a biped is distinctive of one thing in relation to another—of man, for instance, in relation to horse and dog. It is clear that nothing that admits of belonging to something else is reciprocally predicated of its subject; it is not necessary, for instance, that what is asleep is a man.

A genus is what is essentially predicated of a plurality of things differing in species. Let us count as essentially predicated whatever it is appropriate to mention if we are asked what a given thing is; when we are asked what man is, for instance, it is appropriate to say that it is an animal. It is also relevant to the genus to say whether two things are in the same genus or each is in a different genus, since this also falls under the same line of inquiry as the genus. If, for instance, we argue dialectically that animal is the genus of man, and also of ox, we will have argued that they are in the same genus; and if we prove that 102b something is the genus of one thing but not of another, we will have argued that these two things are not in the same genus.

A coincident is what though it is none of these things—neither a definition nor a distinctive property nor a genus—belongs to the subject. Again, it is whatever admits both of belonging and of not belonging to one and the same subject. Being seated, for instance, admits both of belonging and of not belonging to one and the same subject, and so does being pale, since the same subject may easily be pale at one time and not pale at another. The second of these two definitions of coincident is better. For if the first is stated, we will not understand it unless we first know what a definition, a distinctive property, and a genus are; the second, however, is sufficient in its own right for our knowing what is meant.

Let us also add to the [class of] coincidents the comparisons between things whose descriptions are derived in some way from the coincident. These include, for instance, the question whether the fine or the advantageous is more choiceworthy, or whether the life of virtue or the life of gratification is pleasanter, and any other questions similar to these. For in all such cases the question proves to be about whether the thing predicated is more [properly] a coincident of the one subject or of the other.

It is immediately clear that a coincident may easily be distinctive of a subject at a particular time and in relation to a particular thing. Whenever, for instance, someone is the only one seated, being seated, which is a coincident, is distinctive at that time; and when he is not the only one seated, being seated is distinctive of him in relation to those not seated. Hence a coincident may easily turn out to be distinctive in relation to a particular thing and at a particular time, but it is not a distinctive property without qualification.

Posterior Analytics

Book 1

1

71a All teaching and all intellectual learning result from previous cognition. This is clear if we examine all the cases; for this is how the mathematical sciences and all crafts arise. This is also true of both deductive and inductive arguments, since they both succeed in teaching because they rely on previous cognition: deductive arguments begin with premisses we are assumed to understand, and inductive arguments prove the universal by relying on the fact that the particular is already clear. Rhetorical arguments also persuade in the same way, since they rely either on examples (and hence on induction) or on argumentations (and hence on deduction).

Previous cognition is needed in two ways. In some cases we must presuppose that something is (for example, that it is true that everything is either asserted or denied truly [of a given subject]). In other cases we must comprehend what the thing spoken of is (for example, that a triangle signifies this); and in other cases we must do both (for example, we must both comprehend what a unit signifies and presuppose that there is such a thing). For something different is needed to make each of these things clear to us.

We may also recognize that *q* by having previously recognized that *p* and acquiring recognition of *q* at the same time [as we acquire recognition of r]. This is how, for instance, we acquire recognition of the cases that fall under the universal of which we have cognition; for we previously knew that, say, every triangle has angles equal to two right angles, but we recognize that this figure in the semicircle is a triangle at the same time as we perform the induction [showing that this figure has two right angles]. For in some cases we learn in this way, (rather than recognizing the last term though the middle); this is true when we reach particulars, i.e. things not said of any subject.

Before we perform the induction or the deduction, we should presumably be said to know in one way but not in another. For if we did not know without qualification whether [a given triangle] is, how could we know without qualification that it has two right angles? But clearly we know it insofar as we know it universally, but we do not know it without qualification. Otherwise we will face the puzzle in the *Meno*, since we will turn out to learn either nothing or else nothing but what we [already] know.[1]

For we should not agree with some people's attempted solution to this puzzle. Do you or do you not know that every pair is even? When you say you do, they produce a pair that you did not think existed and hence did not think was even. They solve this puzzle by saying that one does not know that every pair is even, but rather one knows that what one knows to be a pair is even. In fact, however, [contrary to this 71b
solution], one knows that of which one has grasped and still possesses the demonstration, and the demonstration one has grasped is not about whatever one knows to be a triangle or a number, but about every number or triangle without qualification; for [in a

1. **Otherwise we . . . [already] know:** Plato presents the puzzle at *Meno* 80a–d.

demonstration] a premiss is not taken to say that what you know to be a triangle or rectangle is so and so, but, on the contrary, it is taken to apply to every case.

But, I think, it is quite possible for us to know in one way what we are learning, while being ignorant of it in another way. For what is absurd is not that we [already] know in some way the very thing we are learning; the absurdity arises only if we already know it to the precise extent and in the precise way in which we are learning it.

2

We think we know a thing without qualification, and not in the sophistic, coincidental way, whenever we think we recognize the explanation[2] because of which the thing is [so], and recognize both that it is the explanation of that thing and that it does not admit of being otherwise. Clearly, then, knowing is something of this sort; for both those who lack knowledge and those who have it think they are in this condition, but those who have the knowledge are really in it. So whatever is known without qualification cannot be otherwise.

We shall say later whether there is also some other way of knowing; but we certainly say that we know through demonstration. By 'demonstration' I mean a deduction expressing knowledge; by 'expressing knowledge' I mean that having the deduction constitutes having knowledge.

If, then, knowing is the sort of thing we assumed it is, demonstrative knowledge must also be derived from things that are true, primary, immediate, better known than, prior to, and explanatory of the conclusion; for this will also ensure that the principles are proper to what is being proved. For these conditions are not necessary for a deduction, but they are necessary for a demonstration, since without them a deduction will not produce knowledge.

[The conclusions] must be true, then, because we cannot know what is not [true] (for example, that the diagonal is commensurate). They must be derived from [premisses] that are primary and indemonstrable, because we will have no knowledge unless we have a demonstration of these [premisses]; for to have non-coincidental knowledge of something demonstrable is to have demonstration of it.

They must be explanatory, better known, and prior. They must be explanatory, because we know something whenever we know its explanation. They must be prior if they are indeed explanatory. And they must be previously cognized not only in the sense that we comprehend them, but also in the sense that we know that they are [true]. Things are prior and better known in two ways; for what is prior by nature in not the same as what is prior to us, nor is what is better known [by nature] the same as what is better known to us. By 'what is prior and better known to us' I mean what is closer to perception, and by 'what is prior and better known without qualification' I mean what is further from perception. What is most universal is furthest from perception, and particulars are closest to it; particular and universal are opposite to each other.

Derivation from primary things is derivation from proper principles. (I mean the same by 'primary things' as I mean by 'principles'.) A principle of demonstration is an immediate premiss, and a premiss is immediate if on others are prior to it. A premiss is one or the other part of a contradiction, and it says one thing of one thing. It is dialectical if it takes either part indifferently, demonstrative if it determinately takes one part because it is true. A contradiction is an opposition which, in itself, has nothing in the middle. The part of the contradiction that asserts something of something is an affirmation, and the part that denies something of something is a denial.

By 'thesis' I mean an immediate principle of deduction that cannot be proved, but is not needed if one is to learn anything at all. By 'axiom' I mean a principle one needs in order to learn anything at all; for there are some things of this sort, and it is especially these to which we usually apply the name.

If a thesis asserts one or the other part of a contradiction—for example, that something is or that something is not—it is an assumption; otherwise it is a definition. For a definition is a thesis (since the arithmetician, for example, lays it down that a unit is what is indivisible in quantity), but it is not an assumption (since what it is to be a unit and that a unit is are not the same).

Since our conviction and knowledge about a thing must be based on our having the sort of deduction we

2. **explanation:** or "cause," *aitia*. Aristotle is thinking not only of an explanatory statement, but also of the event or state of affairs that the statement refers to.

call a demonstration, and since we have this sort of deduction when its premisses obtain, not only must we have previous cognition about all or some of the primary things, but we must also know them better. For if *x* makes *y F*, *x* is more *F* than *y*; if, for instance, we love *y* because of *x*, *x* is loved more than *y*. Hence if the primary things produce knowledge and conviction, we must have more knowledge and conviction about them, since they also produce it about subordinate things.

Now if we know *q*, we cannot have greater conviction about *p* than about *q* unless we either know *p* or are in some condition better than knowledge about *p*. This will result, however, unless previous knowledge [of the principles] is the basis of conviction produced by demonstration; for we must have greater conviction about all or some of the principles than about the conclusion.

If we are to have knowledge through demonstration, then not only must we know the principles better and have greater conviction about them than about what is proved, but we must also find anything more convincing or better known that is opposed to the principles and allows us to deduce a mistaken conclusion contrary [to the correct one]. For no one who has knowledge without qualification can be persuaded out of it.

3

Some people think that because [knowledge through demonstration] requires knowledge of the primary things, there is no knowledge; others think that there is knowledge, and that everything [knowable] is demonstrable. Neither of these views is either true or necessary.

The first party—those who assume that there is no knowledge at all—claim that we face an infinite regress. They assume that we cannot know posterior things because of prior things, if there are no primary things. Their assumption is correct, since it is impossible to go through an infinite series. If, on other hand, the regress stops, and there are principles, these are, in their view, unrecognizable, since these principles cannot be demonstrated, and, in these people's view, demonstration is the only way of knowing. But if we cannot know the primary things, then neither can we know without qualification or fully the things derived from them; we can know them only conditionally, on the assumption that we can know the primary things.

The other party agree that knowledge results only from demonstration, but they claim that it is possible to demonstrate everything, since they take circular and reciprocal demonstration to be possible.

We reply that not all knowledge is demonstrative, and in fact knowledge of the immediate premisses is indemonstrable. Indeed, it is evident that this must be so; for if we must know the prior things (i.e. those from which the demonstration is derived), and if eventually the regress stops, these immediate premisses must be indemonstrable. Besides this, we also say that there is not only knowledge but also some origin of knowledge, which gives us cognition of the definitions.

Unqualified demonstration clearly cannot be circular, if it must be derived from what is prior and better known. For the same things cannot be both prior and posterior to the same things at the same time, except in different ways (so that, for example, some things are prior relative to us and others are prior without qualification—this is the way induction makes something known). If this is so, our definition of unqualified knowledge will be faulty, and there will be two sort of knowledge; or [rather] perhaps the second sort of demonstration is not unqualified demonstration, since it is derived from what is [merely] better known to us.

Those who allow circular demonstration must concede not only the previous point, but also that they are simply saying that something is if it is. On these terms it is easy to prove anything. This is clear if we consider three terms—for it does not matter whether we say the demonstration turns back through many or few terms, or through few or two. For suppose that if A is, necessarily B is, and that if B is, necessarily C is; it follows that if A is, C will be. Suppose, then, that if A is, then B necessarily is, and if B is, A is (since this is what circular argument is), and let A be C. In that case, to say that if B is, A is is to say that [if B is,] C is; this [is to say] that if A is, C is. But since C is the same as A, it follows that those who allow circular demonstration simply say that if A is, then A is. On these terms it is easy to prove anything.

But not even this is possible, except for things that are reciprocally predicated, such as distinctive properties. If, then, one thing is laid down, we have proved that it is never necessary for anything else to be the case. (By 'one thing' I mean that neither one term nor one thesis is enough; two theses are the fewest [needed for a demonstration], since they are also the fewest needed for a deduction.) If, then, A follows from B and C, and these follow from each other and from A, then in this way it is possible to prove all the postulates from each other in the first figure, as we proved in the discussion of deduction. We also proved that in the other figures, the result is either no deduction or none relevant to the things assumed. But it is not at all possible to give a circular proof of things that are not reciprocally predicated. And so, since there are few things that are reciprocally predicated in demonstrations, it is clearly empty and impossible to say that demonstration is reciprocal and that for this reason everything is demonstrable .

4

Since what is known without qualification cannot be otherwise, what is known by demonstrative knowledge will be necessary. Demonstrative knowledge is what we have by having a demonstration; hence a demonstration is a deduction from things that are necessary. We must, then, find from what and from what sorts of things demonstrations are derived. Let us first determine what we mean by '[belonging] in every case', 'in its own right', and 'universal'.

By '[belonging] in every case' I mean what belongs not [merely] in some cases, or at some times, as opposed to others. If, for example, animal belongs to every man, it follows that if it is true to say that this is a man, it is also true to say that he is an animal, and that if he is a man now, he is also an animal now. The same applies if it is true to say that there is a point in every line. A sign of this is the fact that when are asked whether something belongs in every case, we advance objections by asking whether it fails to belong either in some cases or at some times.

A belongs to B in its own right in the following cases:

(a) A belongs to B in what B is, as, for example, line belongs to triangle and point to line; for here the essence of B is composed of A, and A is present in the account that says what B is.

(b) A belongs to B, and B itself is present in the account revealing what A is. In this way straight and curved, for instance, belong to line, while odd and even, prime and compound, equilateral and oblong, belong in this way to number. In all these cases either line or number is present in the account saying what [straight or odd, for example,] is. Similarly in other cases, this is what I mean by saying that A belongs to B in its own right. What belongs in neither of these ways I call coincidental—as, for instance, musical or pale belongs to animal.

(c) A is not said of something else B that is the subject of A. A walker or a pale thing, for example, is a walker or a pale thing by being something else; but a substance—i.e. whatever signifies a this—is not what it is by being something else. I say, then, that what is not said of a subject is [a thing] in its own right, whereas what is said of a subject is a coincident.

(d) Moreover, in another way, if A belongs to B because of B itself, then A belongs to B in its own right; if A belongs to B, but not because of B itself, then A is coincidental to B. If, for example, lightning flashed while you were walking, that was coincidental; for the lightning was not caused by your walking but, as we say, was a coincidence. If however, A belongs to B because of B itself, then it belongs to B in its own right. If, for example, an animal was killed in being sacrificed, the killing belongs to the sacrificing in its own right, since the animal was killed because it was sacrificed, and it was not a coincidence that the animal was killed in being sacrificed.

Hence in the case of unqualified objects of knowledge, whenever A is said to belong to B in its own right, either because B is present in A and A is predicated of B, or because A is present in B, then A belongs to B because of B itself and necessarily. [It belongs necessarily] either because it is impossible for A not to belong to B or because it is impossible for neither A nor its opposite (for example; straight and crooked, or odd and even) to belong to B (for example, a line or a number). For a contrary is either a privation or a contradiction in the same genus; even, for example, is what is not odd among numbers, insofar as this follows. Hence, if it is necessary either to affirm or to deny, then what belongs to a subject in its own right necessarily belongs to that subject.

Let this, then, be our definition of what belongs in every case and of what belongs to something in its own right.

By 'universal' I mean what belongs to its subject in every case and in its own right, and insofar as it is itself. It is evident, then, that what is universal belongs to things necessarily. What belongs to the subject in its own right is the same as what belongs to it insofar as it is itself. A point and straightness, for instance, belong to a line in its own right, since they belong to a line insofar as it is a line. Similarly, two right angles belong to a triangle insofar as it is a triangle, since a triangle is equal in its own right to two right angles.

A universal belongs [to a species] whenever it is proved of an instance that is random and primary. Having two right angles, for instance, is not universal to figure; for though you may prove that some figure has two right angles, you cannot prove it of any random figure, nor do you use any random figure in proving it, since a quadrilateral is a figure but does not have angles equal to two right angles. Again, a random isosceles triangle has angles equal to two right angles, but it is not the primary case, since the triangle is prior. If, then, a random triangle is the primary case that is proved to have two right angles, or whatever it is, then that property belongs universally to this case primarily, and the demonstration holds universally of this case in its own right. It holds of the other cases in a way, but not in their own right; it does not even hold universally of the isosceles triangle, but more widely.

Book 2

19

It is evident, then, what deduction and demonstration are and how they come about; the same holds for demonstrative knowledge, since it is the same [as demonstration]. But how do we come to recognize principles, and what state recognizes them? This will be clear from the following argument, if we first state the puzzles.

We said before that we cannot know through demonstration without recognizing the first, immediate principles. But one might be puzzled about whether cognition of the immediate principles is or is not the same [as knowledge of truths derived form them]; whether there is knowledge of each, or knowledge of one but something else of the other; and whether the states are acquired rather than [innately] present in us without our noticing them.

It would be absurd if we had the principles [innately]; for then we would possess cognition that is more exact than demonstration, but without noticing it. If, on the other hand, we acquire the principles and do not previously possess them, how could we recognize and learn them from no prior knowledge? That is impossible, as we also said in the case of demonstration. Evidently, then, we can neither possess the principle [innately] nor acquire them if we are ignorant and possess no state [of knowledge]. Hence we must have some [suitable] potentiality, but not one that is at a level of exactness superior to that of the knowledge we acquire.

All animals evidently have [such a potentiality], since they have the innate discriminative potentiality called perception.[3] Some animals that have perception (though not all of them) also retain [in memory] what they perceive; those that do not retain it have no cognition outside perception (either none at all or none about what is not retained), but those that do retain it keep what they have perceived in their souls even after they have perceived. When this has happened many times a [further] difference arises: in some, but not all, cases, a rational account arises from the retention of perceptions.

From perception, then, as we say, memory arises, and from repeated memory of the same thing experience arises; for a number of memories make up one experience. From experience, or [rather] from the whole universal that has settled in the soul—the one apart from the many, whatever is present as one and the same in all of them—arises a principle of craft (if it is about what comes to be) or of science (if it is about what is).

3. In what follows Aristotle may mean to explain (1) the acquisition of universal concepts (e.g., the concept of horse) from perception (e.g., of particular horses) or (2) the acquisition of knowledge of universal truth (e.g., that horses have four legs) from perception (e.g., that this horse has four legs, that horse . . . etc.) or (3) both (1) and (2).

Hence the relevant states are not [innate] in us in any determinate character and do not arise from states that have a better grasp on cognition; rather, they arise from perception. It is like what happens in a battle when there is a retreat: first one soldier makes a stand, then a second, then another, until they reach a starting point. The soul's nature gives it a potentiality to be affected in this way.

Let us state again, then, what we stated, but not perspicuously, before. When one of the undifferentiated things makes a stand, that is the first universal in the soul; for though one perceives the particular, perception is of the universal—of man, for instance, not of Callias the man. Again, in these [universals something else] makes a stand, until what has no parts and is universal makes a stand—first, for example, a certain sort of animal makes a stand, until animal does, and in this [universal] something else make a stand in the same way. Clearly, then, we must recognize the first things by induction; for that is also how perception produces the universal in us.

Among our intellectual states that grasp the truth, some—knowledge and understanding—are always true, whereas others—for example, belief and reasoning—admit of being false; and understanding is the only sort of state that is more exact than knowledge. Since the principles of demonstration are better known [than the conclusions derived from them], and since all knowledge requires an account, it follows that we can have no knowledge of the principle. Since only understanding can be truer than knowledge, we must have understanding of the principles.

The same conclusion follows from the further point that since the principle of a demonstration is not a demonstration, the principle of knowledge is not knowledge. If, then, the only sort of state besides knowledge that is [always] true is understanding, understanding must be the principle of knowledge. The principle, then, will grasp the principle, and, similarly, all knowledge will grasp its object.

Physics, De Anima, and Metaphysics

The *Physics*, *De Anima*, and *Metaphysics* all concern the study and knowledge of beings, a class that includes more than material objects.

The *Physics* discusses the study of natural phenomena in general, beginning with a characterization of scientific knowledge (Book 1) and then moving to Aristotle's doctrine of the four causes, a discussion of chance and necessity, and arguments for the existence of ends (or "final causes") in nature (Book 2).

The *De Anima* continues the investigation of natural phenomena with a study of the soul, which Aristotle takes to belong at least in part to the biology, since he identifies the soul (though not perhaps all of the human soul) with the form of a living thing. He defines the soul and discusses its parts and organization in Book 2, and then considers the characteristic activity of the highest level of the soul—thinking—in Book 3.

The *Metaphysics*, generally regarded as the most difficult work in the Aristotelian corpus, concerns the subject matter that Aristotle refers to as "first philosophy," or "the science of being." He discusses the history of the notion of causes (Book 1); the nature of the study of being qua being (Book 4); substance, matter, form, essence, and universals (Book 7); and the unmoved mover (Book 12).

Physics

Book 1

1

184a In every line of inquiry into something that has principles or causes of elements, we achieve knowledge—that is, scientific knowledge—by cognizing them; for we think we cognize a thing when we know its primary causes and primary principles, all the way to its elements. Clearly, then is also true in the science of nature that our first task is to determine the principles.

The natural path is to start from what is better known and more perspicuous to us, and to advance to what is more perspicuous and known by nature; for what is better known to us is not the same as what better known without qualification. We must advance in this way then, from what is less perspicuous by nature but more perspicuous to what is more perspicuous and better known by nature.

The things that, most of all, are initially clear and perspicuous to us are inarticulate wholes; later, as we articulate them, the elements and principles come to be known from them. We must, then, advance from universals to particulars; for the whole is better known in perception, and the universal is a sort of whole, 184b since it includes many things as parts. The same is true, in a way, of names in relation to their accounts. For a name—for instance, 'circle'—signifies a sort of whole and signifies indefinitely, whereas the definition [of a circle] articulates it by stating the particular [properties]. Again, children begin by calling all men 'father' and all women 'mother'; only later do they distinguish different men and different women.

Book 2

1

192b Some existing things are natural, while others are due to other causes. Those that are natural are animals and their parts, plants, and the simple bodies, such as earth, fire, air and water; for we say that these things and things of this sort are natural. All these things evidently differ from those that are not naturally constituted, since each of them has within itself a principle of motion and stability in place, in growth and decay, or in alteration.

In contrast to these, a bed, a cloak, or any other [artifact]—insofar as it is described as such, [i.e. as a bed, a cloak, or whatever], and to the extent that it is a product of a craft—has no innate impulse to change; but insofar as it is coincidentally made of stone or earth or a mixture of these, it has an innate impulse to change, and just to that extent. This is because a nature is a type of principle and cause of motion and stability within those things to which it primarily belongs in their own right and not coincidentally. (By 'not coincidentally' I mean, for instance, the following: Someone who is a doctor might cause himself to be healthy, but it is not insofar as he is being healed that he has the medical science; on the contrary it is coincidental that the same person is a doctor and is being healed, and that is why the two characteristics are sometimes separated from each other.)

The same is true of everything else that is produced, since no such thing has within itself the principle of its own production. In some things (for instance, a house or any other product of handicraft) the principle comes from outside, and it is within other things. In other things (those that might turn out to be coincidental causes for themselves) the principle is within them, but not in their own right.

A nature, then, is what we have said; and the things that have a nature are those that have this sort of principle. All these things are substances; for [a substance] is a sort of subject, and a nature is invariably in a subject. The things that are in accordance with nature include both these and whatever belongs to them in their own right, as traveling upwards belongs to fire—for this neither is nor has a nature, but is 193a natural and in accordance with nature. We have said, then, what nature is, and what is natural and in accordance with nature.

To attempt to prove that there is such a thing as nature would be ridiculous; for it is evident that there are many things of the sort we have described. To prove what is evident from what is not evident betrays an inability to discriminate what is known because of itself from what is not. (It is clearly possible to suffer from this inability: someone blind from birth might still make deductions about colors.) And so such people are bound to argue about [mere] names and to understand nothing.

Some people think that the nature and substance of a natural thing is the primary constituent present in it, having no order in its own right, so that the nature of a bed, for instance, [would be] the wood, and the nature of a statue [would be] the bronze. A sign of this, according to Antiphon is the fact that, if you were to bury a bed and the rotting residue were to become able to sprout, the result would be wood, not a bed. He thinks that this is because the conventional arrangement, i.e. the craft [making the wood into a bed], is a [mere] coincident of the wood, whereas the substance is what remains continuously while it is affected in these ways And if each of these things is related to something else in the same way (bronze and gold, for instance, to water; bones and wood to earth; and so on with anything else), that thing is their nature and substance.

This is why some people say that fire or earth or air or water is the nature of the things that exist; some say it is some of these, others say it is all of them. For whenever any of these people supposed one, or more than one, of these things to be [the primary constituent], he takes this or these to be all the substance there is, and he takes everything else to be attributes, states, and conditions of these things; and each of these is held to be everlasting, since they do not change from themselves, but the other things come to be and are destroyed an unlimited number of times.

This, then, is one way we speak of a nature: as the primary matter that is a subject for each thing that has within itself a principle of motion and change.

In another way the nature is the shape, i.e. the form in accordance with the account. For just as we speak of craftsmanship in what is in accordance with craft and is crafted, so also we speak of nature in what is in accordance with nature and is natural. But if something were only potentially a bed and still lacked the form of a bed, we would not yet speak of craftmanship or of a product in accordance with craft; nor would we say the corresponding thing about anything that is constituted naturally. For what is only potentially flesh or bone does not have its *193b* nature, and is not naturally flesh or bone, until it acquires the form in accordance with the account by which we define flesh or bone and say what it is. In another way then, the nature is the shape and form of things that have within themselves a principle of motion; this form is not separable except in account. (What is composed of form and matter—for instance, a man—is not a nature, but is natural.)

Indeed, the form is the nature more than the matter is. For something is called [flesh, bone, and so on] when it is actually so, more than when it is only potentially so. Further, a man comes to be from a man, but not a bed from a bed. In fact that is why some say that the nature of the bed is not the shape but the wood, because if it were to sprout the result would be wood, not a bed. If this shows that the wood is the nature, then the shape is also the nature, since a man comes to be from a man. Further, nature, as applied to coming to be, is really a road towards nature; it is not like medical treatment, which is a road not towards medical science, but towards health. For medical treatment necessarily proceeds *from* medical science, not *towards* medical science. But nature [as coming to be] is not related to nature in this way; rather, what is growing, insofar as it is growing, proceeds from something towards something [else]. What is it, then, that grows? Not what it is growing from, but what it is growing into. Therefore, the shape is the nature.

Shape and nature are spoken of in two ways; for the privation is also form in a way. We must consider later whether or not there is a privation and a contrary in unqualified coming to be.

2

Since we have distinguished the different ways we speak of nature, we should next consider how the mathematician differs from the student of nature; for natural bodies certainly have surfaces, solids, lengths, and points, which are what the mathematician studies. We should also consider whether astronomy is different from or a part of the study of nature; for it would be absurd if a student of nature ought to know what the sun or moon is but need not know any of their coincidents in their own right—especially since it is evident that students of nature also discuss the shape of the sun and moon, and specifically whether or not the earth and heaven are spherical.

These things are certainly the concern of both the mathematician and the student of nature. But the mathematician is not concerned with them insofar as each is the limit of a natural body, and he does not study the coincidents of a natural body insofar as they belong to a natural body. That is why he also separates these coincidents; for they are separable in thought from motion, and his separating them makes no difference and results in no falsehood.

Those who say there are Ideas do not notice that
194a they do this too; for they separate natural objects, though these are less separable than mathematical objects. This would be clear if one tried to state the formulae of both natural and mathematical objects—of the things themselves and of their coincidents. For odd and even, straight and curved, and also number, line and point do not involve motion, whereas flesh, bones, and man do—we speak of them as we speak of the snub nose, not as we speak of the curved.[1]

This is also clear from the parts of mathematics that are more related to the study of nature—for instance, optics, harmonics, and astronomy. These are in a way the reverse of geometry; for geometry investigates natural lines, but not insofar as they are natural, whereas optics investigates mathematical lines, but insofar as they are natural, not insofar as they are mathematical.

Since we speak of nature in two ways—both as form and as matter—we should study it as though we were investigating what snubness is and so we should study natural objects neither independently of their matter nor [simply] insofar as they have matter. For indeed, since there are these two types of nature, there might be a puzzle about which one the student of nature should study. Perhaps the compound of the two? It so, then also each of them. Then is it the same or a different discipline that knows each one of them?

If we judge by the early thinkers, the student of nature would seem to study [only] matter, since Empedocles and Democritus touched only slightly on form and essence. Craft, however, imitates nature, and the same science knows both the form and the matter up to a point. The doctor, for instance, knows health, and also the bile and phlegm in which health [is realized]; similarly, the housebuilder knows both the form of the house and that its matter is bricks and wood; and the same is true in the other cases. The science of nature, therefore, must also know both types of nature.

Moreover the same discipline studies both what something is for—i.e. the end—and whatever is for the end. Nature is an end and what something is for; for whenever a continuous motion has some end this sort of terminus is also what the motion is for. That is why it was ludicrous for the poet to say 'He has reached the end he was born for'; it was ludicrous because by 'end' we mean not every terminus but only the best one.

For crafts produce their matter (some by producing it without qualification, others by making it suitable for their work); and we use all [matter] as being for our sake, since we are also on end in a way. (For what something is for is of two sorts, as we said in *On Philosophy*.[2])

There are two crafts that control the matter and 194b
involve knowledge: the craft that uses [the matter] and the craft that directs this productive craft. Hence the using craft also directs in a way with the difference that the directing craft knows the form, whereas the productive craft knows the matter. For instance, the pilot knows what sort of form the rudder has, and he prescribes [how to produce it], whereas the boatbuilder knows what sort of wood and what sorts of motions are needed to make it. With products of a craft, then, we produce the matter for the sake of the product; with natural things, the matter is already present.

Further, matter is relative; for there is one [sort of] matter for one form, and another for another.

How much, then, must the student of nature know about form and what-it-is? Perhaps as much as the doctor knows about sinews, or the smith about bronze—enough to know what something is for. And he must confine himself to things that are separable in form but are in matter—for a man is born from a man and the sun. But it is a task for first philosophy to determine what is separable and what the separable is like.

1. **we speak . . . the curved:** To speak of them as we speak of the snub nose is to talk of them as involving matter.

2. ***On Philosophy:*** A work of Aristotle's that survives only in fragments.

3

Now that we have determined these points, we should consider how many and what sorts of causes there are. For our inquiry aims at knowledge; and we think we know something only when we find the reason why it is so, i.e. when we find its primary cause. Clearly, then, we must also find the reason why in the case of coming to be, perishing, and every sort of natural change, so that when we know their principles we can try to refer whatever we are searching for to these principles.

In one way, then, that from which, as a [constituent] present in it, a thing comes to be is said to be that thing's cause—for instance, the bronze and silver, and their genera, are causes of the statue and the bowl.

In another way, the form—i.e. the pattern—is a cause. The form is the account (and the genera of the account) of the essence (for instance, the cause of an octave is the ratio two to one, and in general number), and the parts that are in the account.

Further, the source of the primary principle of change or stability is a cause. For instance, the adviser is a cause [of the action], and a father is a cause of his child; and in general the producer is a cause of the product, and the initiator of the change is a cause of what is changed.

Further, something's end—i.e. what it is for—is its cause, as health is of walking. For why does he walk? We say, 'To be healthy'; and in saying this we think we have provided the cause. The same is true of all the intermediate steps that are for the end, where something else has initiated the motion, as, for example, slimming, purging, drugs, or instruments are for health; all of these are for the end, though they differ in that some are activities, while other are instruments.

We may take these, then, to be the ways we speak of causes.

Since causes are spoken of in many ways, there are many non-coincidental causes of the same thing. Both the sculpting craft and the bronze, for instance, are causes of the statue, not insofar as it is something else, but insofar as it is a statue. But they are not causes in the same way: the bronze is a cause as matter, the sculpting craft as the source of the motion. Some things are causes of each other: hard work, for instance, is the cause of fitness, and fitness of hard work. But they are not causes in the same way: fitness is what the hard work is for, whereas hard work is the principle of motion. Further, the same thing is the cause of contraries; for sometimes if a thing's presence causes *F*, that thing is also, by its absence, taken to cause the contrary of *F*, so that, for instance, if a pilot's presence would have caused the safety of a ship, we take his absence to have caused the shipwreck.

All the causes just mentioned are of four especially evident types: (1) Letters are the cause of syllables, matter of artifacts, fire and such things of bodies, parts of the whole, and the assumptions of the conclusion as that out of which. In each of these cases one thing—for instance, the parts—is cause as subject, while (2) the other thing—the whole, the composition, and the form—is cause as essence. (3) The seed, the doctor, the adviser and, in general, the producer, are all sources of the principle of change or stability. (4) In other cases, one thing is a cause of other things by being the end and the good. For what the other things are for is taken to be the best and their end—it does not matter [for present purposes] whether we call the good or the apparent good. These, then, are the number of kinds of causes there are.

Although there are many types of causes, they are fewer when they are arranged under heads. For causes are spoken of in many ways and even among causes of the same type, some are prior and others posterior. For example, the cause of health is a doctor and [speaking more generally] a craftsman, and the cause of an octave is the double and [speaking more generally] number; in every case the inclusive causes are posterior to the particular.

Further, some things and their genera are coincidental causes. Polycleitus and the sculptor, for instance, are causes of the statue in different ways, because being Polycleitus is coincidental to the sculptor. What includes the coincident is also a cause—if, for example, the man or, quite generally, the animal is a cause of the statue. Some coincidental causes are more remote or more proximate than others; if, for instance, the pale man or the musician were said to be the cause of the statue [it would be a more remote cause than Polycleitus is].

We may speak of any [moving] cause, whether proper or coincidental, either as having a potentiality or as actualizing it; for instance, we may say either that the housebuilder, or that housebuilder actually building, is causing the house to be built.

Similar things may also be said about the things of which the causes are causes. For example, we may speak of the cause of this statue, or of a statue, or of an image in general; or of this bronze, or of bronze, or of matter in general. The same is true of coincidents. We may speak in this same way of combinations—of Polycleitus the sculptor, for instance, instead of Polycleitus or a sculptor.

Still all these ways amount to six, each spoken of in two ways. For there is (1) the particular and (2) the genus, and (3) the coincident and (4) the genus of the coincident; and these may be spoken of either (5) in combination or (6) simply. Each of these may be either active or potential. The difference is the following. Active and particular causes exist and cease to exist simultaneously with the things they cause, so that, for instance, this one practicing medicine exists simultaneously with this one being made healthy, and in the same way this one housebuilding exists simultaneously with this thing being built into a house.[3] But this is not true of every cause that is potential; for the house and the housebuilder do not perish simultaneously.

Here as elsewhere, we must always seek the most precise cause. A man, for example, is building because he is a builder, and he is a builder insofar as he has the building craft; his building craft, then, is the prior cause, and the same is true in all cases. Further, we must seek genera as causes of genera, and particulars as causes of particulars; a sculptor, for instance, is the cause of a statue, but this sculptor of this statue. And we must seek a potentiality as the cause of a potential effect, and something actualizing a potentiality as the cause of an actual effect.

This, then, is an adequate determination of the number of causes, and of the ways in which they are causes.

4

Luck and chance are also said to be causes, and many things are said to be and to come to be because of them. We must, then, investigate how luck and chance are included in the causes we have mentioned, whether luck is or is not the same as chance, and, in general, what they are.

196a Some people even wonder whether luck and chance exist. For they say that nothing results from luck; rather, everything that is said to result from chance or luck has some definite cause. If, for instance, as a result of luck someone comes to the marketplace and finds the person he wanted to meet but did not expect, they say the cause is his wanting to go to market. Similarly, for every other supposed result of luck, they say it is possible to find some cause other than luck. For if there were such a thing as luck, it would appear truly strange and puzzling that none of the early philosophers who discussed the causes of coming to be and perishing ever determined anything about luck; in fact it would seem that they also thought that nothing results from luck. But this too is surprising; for surely many things come to be and exist as a result of luck and chance. Though people know perfectly well that everything that comes to be can be referred to some cause, as the old argument doing away with luck says, everyone nonetheless says that some of these things result from luck and that others do not.

That is why the early philosophers should have mentioned luck in some way or other. But they certainly did not think luck was among the causes they recognized—for instance, love or strife or mind or fire or anything else of that sort. In either case, then, it is strange, whether they supposed there was no such thing as luck, or supposed there was such a thing but omitted to discuss it. It is especially strange considering that they sometimes appeal to luck. Empedocles, for example, appeals to luck when he says that air is separated out on top, not always but as luck has it; at least, he says in his cosmogony that 'it happened to run that way at that time, but often otherwise.[4] And he says that most of the parts of animals result from luck.

Other people make chance the cause of our heaven and of all worlds. For they say that the vortex, and the motion that dispersed and established everything in its present order, resulted from chance. And this is certainly quite amazing. For animals and plants, they say,

3. **Active and . . . a house:** Aristotle thinks of an active cause as a substance in a particular condition (e.g., the builder in the condition of building), not as an event (the building engaged in by the builder) or a fact (the fact that the builder is building).

4. **it happened . . . otherwise:** Empedocles DK 31B53.

neither are nor come to be from luck, but rather nature or mind or something of that sort is the cause, since it is not just any old thing that comes to be from a given type of seed, but an olive-tree comes from one type, and a man from another; and yet they say that the heaven and the most divine of visible things result from chance and have no cause of the sort that animals and plants have.

If this is so, it deserves attention, and something might well have been said about it. For in addition to the other strange aspects of what they say, it is even stranger to say all this when they see that nothing in the heavens results from chance, whereas many things happen as a result of luck to things whose existence is not itself a result of luck. Surely the contrary would have been likely.

Other people suppose that luck is a cause, but they take it to be divine and superhuman, and therefore obscure to the human mind.

And so we must consider chance and luck, and determine what each is, and whether they are the same or different, and see how they fit into the causes we have distinguished.

5

First, then, we see that some things always, others usually, come about in the same way. Evidently neither luck nor anything that results from luck is said to be the cause of either of these things—either of what is of necessity and always or of what is usually. But since besides these there is a third sort of event which everyone says results from luck, it is evident that there is such a thing as luck and chance; for we know that this third sort of event results from luck and that the results of luck are of this sort.

Further, some events are for something and others are not. Among the former, some are in accordance with a decision while others are not, but both sorts are for something. And so it is clear that even among events that are neither necessary nor usual there are some that admit of being for something. (Events that are for something include both the actions that result from thought and also the results of nature.) This, then, is the sort of event that we regard as a result of luck, whenever an event of that sort comes about coincidentally. For just as some things are something in their own right, and others are something coincidentally, so also it is possible for a cause to be of either sort. For example, the cause of a house is, in its own right, the housebuilder, but coincidentally the pale or musical thing. Hence the cause in its own right is determinate, but the coincidental cause is indeterminate, since one thing might have an unlimited number of coincidents.

As has been said, then, whenever this [coincidental causation] occurs among events of the sort that are for something the events [that have these coincidental causes] are said to result from chance and luck. The difference between chance and luck will be determined later; we may take it as evident for the moment that both are found among events of the sort that are for something.

For instance, A would have come when B was collecting subscriptions, in order to recover the debt from B, if A had known [B would be there]. In fact, however, A did not come in order to do this; it was a coincidence that A came [when B happened to be there], and so met B in order to collect the debt—given that A neither usually nor of necessity frequents the place [for that purpose]. The end—collecting the debt—is not a cause [of A's action] in A, but it is the sort of thing that one decides to do and that results from thought. And in this case A's coming is said to result from luck; but if A always or usually frequented the place because he had decided to and for the purpose of collecting the debt, then [A's being there when B was there] would not result from luck.

Clearly, then, luck is a coincidental cause found among events of the sort that are for something, and specifically among those of the sort that are in accordance with a decision. Hence thought (since decision requires thought) and luck concern the same things.

Now the causes whose results might be matters of luck are bound to be indeterminate. That is why luck also seems to be something indeterminate and obscure to human beings, and why, in one way, it might seem that nothing results from luck. For, as we might reasonably expect, all these claims are correct. For in one way things do result from luck, since they are coincidental results and luck is a coincidental cause. But luck is not the unqualified [and hence non-coincidental] cause of anything. The [unqualified] cause of a house, for instance, is a housebuilder, and the coincidental cause a flute-player; and the man's coming and collecting the debt, without having come to collect it, has an indefinite number of coincidental causes—he might have come because he wished to see someone, or was going to court or to the theater.

It is also correct to say that luck is contrary to reason. For rational judgment tells us what is always or usually the case, whereas luck is found in events that happen neither always nor usually. And so since causes of this sort are indeterminate, luck is also indeterminate.

Still, in some cases one might be puzzled about whether just any old thing might be a cause of a lucky outcome. Surely the wind or the sun's warmth, but not someone's haircut, might be the cause of his health; for some coincidental causes are closer than others to what they cause.

Luck is called good when something good results, bad when something bad results; it is called good and bad fortune when the results are large. That is why someone who just misses great evil or good as well [as someone who has it is] fortunate or unfortunate; for we think of him as already having [the great evil or good], since the near miss seems to us to be no distance. Further, it is reasonable that good fortune is unstable; for luck is unstable, since no result of luck can be either always or usually the case.

As we have said, then, both luck and chance are coincidental causes, found in events of the sort that are neither without exception nor usual, and specifically in events of this sort that might be for something.

6

Chance is not the same as luck, since it extends more
197b widely; for results of luck also result from chance, but not all results of chance result from luck. For luck and its results are found in things that are capable of being fortunate and in general capable of action, and that is why luck must concern what is achievable by action. A sign of this is the fact that good fortune seems to be the same or nearly the same as being happy, and being happy is a sort of action, since it is doing well in action. Hence what cannot act cannot do anything by luck either. Hence neither inanimate things nor beasts nor children do anything by luck, because they are incapable of decision. Nor do they have good or bad fortune, except by a [mere] similarity—as Protarchus[5] said that the stones from which altars are made are fortunate, because they are honored, while their fellows are trodden underfoot. Still, even these things are affected by the results of luck in a way, whenever an agent affects them by some lucky action; but otherwise they are not.

Chance, on the other hand, applies both to animals other than man and to many inanimate things. We say, for instance, that the horse came by chance, since it was saved because it came but did not come in order to be saved. And the tripod fell by chance, because it did not fall in order to be sat on, although it was left standing in order to be sat on.

Hence it is evident that among types of events that are for something (speaking without qualification), we say that a particular event of such a type results from chance if it has an external cause and the actual result is not what it is for; and we say that it results from luck if it results from chance and is an event of the sort that is decided on by an agent who is capable of decision. A sign of this is the fact that we say an event is pointless if it [is of the sort that] is for some result but [in this case] that result is not what it is for. If, for instance, walking is for evacuating the bowels, but when he walked on this occasion it was not [for that reason] then we say that he walked pointlessly and that his walking is pointless. We assume that an event is pointless if it is naturally for something else, but does not succeed in [being for] what it is naturally for. For if someone said that his washing himself was pointless because the sun was not eclipsed, he would be ridiculous, since washing is not for producing eclipses. So also, then, an event happens by chance (as the name suggests) whenever it is pointless. For the stone did not fall in order to hit someone; it fell by chance, because it might have fallen because someone threw it to hit someone.

The separation of chance from luck is sharpest in natural events. For if an event is contrary to nature, we regard it as a result of chance, not of luck. But even this is different from [other cases of chance; the other cases] have an external cause, but [events contrary to nature] have an internal cause.

We have said, then, what chance and luck are and 198a
how they differ. Each of them falls under the sort of cause that is the source of the principle of motion. For in every case they are either among natural causes or among those resulting from thought, and the number of these is indeterminate.

5. **Protarchus:** An orator and pupil of Gorgias.

Chance and luck are causes of events [of the sort] that mind or nature might have caused, in cases where [particular] events [of this sort] have some coincidental cause. Now nothing coincidental is prior to anything that is in its own right; hence clearly no coincidental cause is prior to something that is a cause in its own right. Chance and luck are therefore posterior to mind and nature. And so however true it might be that chance is the cause of the heavens, still it is necessary for mind and nature to be prior causes of this universe and of many other things.

7

It is clear, then, that there are causes, and that there are as many different types as we say there are; for the reason why something is so includes all these different types [of causes]. For we refer the ultimate reason why (1) in the case of unmoved things, to the what-it-is (for instance, in mathematics; for there we refer ultimately to the definition of straight or commensurate or something else), or (2) to what first initiated the motion (for instance, why did they go to war?—because the other side raided them), or (3) to what it is for (for instance, in order to set themselves up as rulers), or (4) in the case of things that come to be, to the matter.

It is evident, then, that these are the causes and that this is their number. Since there are four of them, the student of nature ought to know them all; and in order to give the sort of reason that is appropriate for the study of nature; he must trace it back to all the causes—to the matter, the form, what initiated the motion, and what something is for. The last three often amount to one; for what something is and what it is for are one, and the first source of the motion is the same in species as these, since a man generates a man; and the same is true generally of things that initiate motion by being in motion.

Things that initiate motion without being in motion are outside the scope of the study of nature. For although they initiate motion, they do not do so by having motion or a principle of motion within themselves, but they are unmoved. Hence there are three inquiries: one about what is unmoved, one about what is in motion but imperishable, and one about what is perishable.

And so the reason why is given by referring to the matter, to the what-it-is, and to what first initiated the motion. For in cases of coming to be, this is the normal way of examining the causes—by asking what comes to be after what, and what first acted or was acted on, and so on in order in every case.

Two sorts of principles initiate motion naturally. One of these principles is not itself natural, since it has no principles of motion within itself; this is true of *198b* whatever initiates motion without itself being in motion—for instance what is entirely without motion (i.e. the first of all beings) and also the what-it-is (i.e. the form), since this is the end and what something is for. And so, since natural processes are for something, this cause too must be known.

The reason why should be stated in all these ways. For instance, (1) this necessarily results from that (either without exception or usually); (2) if this is to be (as the conclusion from the premisses); (3) that this is the essence; and (4) because it is better thus—not unqualifiedly better but better in relation to the essence of a given thing.

8

We must first say why nature is among the causes that are for something and then how necessity applies to natural things. For everyone refers things to necessity, saying that since the hot, the cold, and each element have a certain nature, certain other things are and come to be of necessity. For if they mention any cause other than necessity (as one thinker mentions love or strife, and another mentions mind), they just touch on it, then let it go.

A puzzle now arises: why not suppose that nature acts not for something or because it is better, but of necessity? Zeus's rain does not fall in order make the grain grow, but of necessity. For it is necessary that what has been drawn up is cooled, and that what has been cooled and become water comes down, and it is coincidental that this makes the grain grow. Similarly, if someone's grain is spoiled on the threshing-floor, it does not rain in order to spoil the grain, and the spoilage is coincidental.

Why not suppose, then, that the same is true of the parts of natural organisms? On this view, it is of necessity that, for example, the front teeth grow sharp and well adapted for biting, and the back ones broad and useful for chewing food; this [useful] result was coincidental, not what they were for. The same will be true of all the other parts that seem to be for something. On this view, then, whenever all the parts came about coincidentally as though they were for something, these animals survived, since their constitution, though coming about by chance, made them suitable [for survival]. Other animals, however, were differently constituted and so were destroyed; indeed they are still being destroyed as Empedocles says of the man-headed calves.[6]

This argument, then, and others like it, might puzzle someone. In fact, however, it is impossible for things to be like this. For these [teeth and other parts] and all natural things come to be as they do either always or usually, whereas no result of luck or chance
199a comes to be either always or usually. (For we do not regard frequent winter rain or a summer heat wave, but only summer rain or a winter heat wave, as a result of luck or coincidence.) If, then, these seem either to be coincidental results or to be for something, and they cannot be coincidental or chance results, they are for something. Now surely all such things are natural, as even those making these claims [about necessity] would agree. We find, then, among things that come to be and are by nature, things that are for something.

Further, whenever [some sequence of actions] has an end, the whole sequence of earlier and later actions is directed towards the end. Surely what is true of action[7] is also true of nature, and what is true of nature is true of each action, if nothing prevents it. Now actions are for something; therefore, natural sequences are for something. For example, if a house came to be naturally, it would come to be just as it actually does by craft, and if natural things came to be not only naturally but also by craft, they would come to be just as they do naturally; one thing, then, is what the other is for. In general, craft either completes the work that nature is unable to complete or imitates nature. If, then, the products of a craft are for something, clearly the products of nature are also for something; for there is the same relation of later stages to earlier in productions of a craft and in productions of nature.

This is most evident in the case of animals other than man, since they use neither craft nor inquiry nor deliberation in producing things—indeed this is why some people are puzzled about whether spiders, ants, and other such things operate by understanding or in some other way. If we advance little by little along the same lines, it is evident that even in plants things come to be that promote the end—leaves, for instance, grow for the protection of the fruit. If, then, a swallow makes its nest and a spider its web both naturally and for some end, and if plants grow leaves for the sake of the fruit, and send roots down rather than up for the sake of nourishment, it evidently follows that this sort of cause is among things that come to be and are by nature. And since nature is of two sorts, nature as matter and nature as form, and the form is the end, and since everything else is for the end, the form must be what things are for.

Errors occur even in productions of craft; grammarians, for instance, have written incorrectly, and doctors have given the wrong medicine. Clearly, then, errors are also possible in productions of nature. 199b

In some productions by crafts, the correct action is for something, and in cases of error the attempt is for something but misses the mark. The same will be true, then, of natural things; freaks will be errors, missing what they are for. Hence in the original formations of things, a defective principle would also have brought the [man-headed] calves into being, if they were unable to reach any definite term and end—just as, in the actual state of things, [freaks] come to be when the seed is defective. Further, it is necessary for the seed to come into being first, and not the animal straightaway; in fact the 'all-natured first'[8] was seed.

Further, in plants as well as in animals things happen for something, though in a less articulate way. Then what about plants? Did olive-headed vines keep coming into being, as he says [man-headed] calves did? Surely not—that is absurd—but surely they would have to have come into being if the animals did.

Further, [on Empedocles' view] coming to be would also have to be merely a matter of chance among seeds. But whoever says this does away entirely with nature and natural things. For things are natural when they are moved continuously from

6. **man-headed calves:** Empedocles DK 31B61.

7. **action:** Aristotle is not thinking of all sequences of movements, but only of those rational human actions (including productions) that have an end (*telos*), i.e., are goal-directed.

8. **all-natured first:** Empedocles DK 31B61–2.

some principle in themselves and so arrive at some end. From each principle comes, not the same thing in each case, but not just any old thing either; in every case it proceeds to the same [end], if nothing prevents it.

Now certainly both the end that a process is for and the process that is for this end might also result from luck. We say, for instance, that a friend in a foreign country came by luck and paid the ransom and then went away, when he did the action as though he had come in order to do it, though in fact that was not what he came to do. This end is achieved coincidentally, since (as we said before) luck is one of the coincidental causes. But whenever the end results always or usually, it is neither coincidental nor a result of luck. And in natural things that is how it is in every case, unless something prevents it.

Besides, it is strange for people to think there is no end unless they see an agent initiating the motion by deliberation. Even crafts do not deliberate. Moreover, if the shipbuilding craft were in the wood, it would produce a ship in the same way that nature would. And so if what something is for is present in craft, it is also present in nature. This is clearest when a doctor applies medical treatment to himself—that is what nature is like.

It is evident, then, that nature is a cause, and in fact the sort of cause that is for something.

9

Is the necessity present [in nature only] conditional or is it also unqualified?

The sort of necessity that is ascribed nowadays to things that come to be is the sort there would be if someone supposed that a wall came into being of necessity. On this view, heavy things naturally move downwards, and light things upwards, and that is why the stones and the foundations are below, while the earth is above because of its lightness, and the wooden logs are on the very top because they are lightest of all.

Nonetheless, though the wall certainly requires these things, it did not come to be because of them (except insofar as they are its material cause) but in order to give shelter and protection.

The same is true in all other cases that are for something: although they require things that have a necessary nature, they do not come to be because of these things (except insofar as they are the material cause) but for some end. For instance, why does a saw have such and such features? In order to perform this function, and for this end. But this end cannot come to be unless the saw is made of iron; and so it is necessary for it to be made of iron if there is to be a saw performing its function. What is necessary, then, is conditional, but not [necessary] as an end; for necessity is in the matter, whereas the end is in the form.

Necessity is found both in mathematics and in things that come to be naturally, and to some extent the two cases are similar. For instance, since the straight is what it is, it is necessary for a triangle to have angles equal to two right angles. It is not because the triangle has angles equal to two right angles that the straight is what it is; but if the triangle does not have angles equal to two right angles, the straight will not be what it is either.

The reverse is true in the case of things that come to be for an end: if the end is or will be, then the previous things are or will be too. Just as, in the mathematical case, if the conclusion [about the triangle] is false, the principle [about the straight] will not be true either, so also in nature if the [materials] do not exist, the end that the process is for will not come out either. For the end is also a principle; it is a principle not of the action, but of the reasoning. (In the mathematical case [also] the principle is the principle of the reasoning, since in this case there is no action.)

And so, if there is to be a house, it is necessary for these things to come to be or to be present; and in general, the matter that is for something must exist (for example, bricks and stones if there is to be a house). The end, however, does not exist because of these things, except insofar as they are the material cause, nor will it come about because of them; still, in general, the end (the house or the saw) requires them (the stones or the iron). Similarly, in the mathematical case the principles require the triangle to have two right angles.

Evidently, then, necessity in natural things belongs to the material cause and to the motions of matter. The student of nature should mention both causes, but more especially what something is for, since this is the cause of the matter, whereas the matter is not the cause of the end. The end is what something is for, and the principle comes from the definition and the form.

200b The same is true in productions of craft. For instance, since a house is this sort of thing, these things must come to be and be present of necessity. In the same way, if a man is this, these things must come to be and be present of necessity; and if these, then these.

But presumably necessity is present in the form as well [as in the matter]. Suppose, for instance, that we define the function of sawing as a certain sort of cutting; this sort of cutting requires a saw with teeth of a certain sort and these require a saw made of iron. For the form, as well as the matter, has parts in it as matter of the form.

De Anima

Book 1

1

402a We suppose that knowing is fine and honorable, and that one type of knowing is finer and more honorable than another either because it is more exact or because it is concerned with better and more wonderful things. On both grounds, we might reasonably place inquiry into the soul in the first rank. Moreover, knowledge of it seems to make an important contribution to [knowledge of] the truth as a whole, and especially to the [knowledge of] nature, since the soul is a sort of principle of animals. We seek to study and know the nature and essence of the soul, and then all of its coincidental properties; some of these seem to be distinctive attributes of the soul, while others also seem to belong to animals because they have souls.

And yet it is altogether in every way a most difficult task to reach any conviction about the soul. For, as in many other areas of study, we are seeking the essence and the what-it-is; and so someone might perhaps think some single line of inquiry is appropriate for every case where we want to know the substance—just as demonstration suits all coincidental properties that are distinctive of a given subject. On this view, then, we should seek this single line of inquiry. If, however, no single line of inquiry is suitable for the what-it-is, our task turns out to be still more difficult, since in that case we must discover how to study each area. But even if it is evident whether demonstration or division or some further line of inquiry is the right one, the question of where to begin our investigation causes many puzzles and confusions; for different things—for instance, numbers and surfaces—have different principles.

First of all, presumably, we must determine the soul's genus and what it is. Is it, in other words, a this and a substance, or a quality, or a quantity, or something in one of the other predications that we have distinguished? Further, is it something potential or is 402b it more of an actuality? That makes quite a bit of difference. We should also examine whether it is divisible into parts or has no parts. Do all souls belong to the same species or not? If not, do they differ in species, or in genus? As things are, those who discuss and inquire into the soul would seem to examine only the human soul. Nor should we forget to ask whether there is just one account of the soul, as there is of animal, or a different account for each type of soul—for instance, of horse, dog, man, god—so that the universal animal either is nothing or else is posterior to these. The same will apply to any other common thing predicated.

Further, if there are not many types of soul, but [one type of soul with many] parts, must we begin by inquiring into the whole soul, or by inquiring into the parts? It is also difficult to determine which parts differ in nature from each other and whether we should begin by inquiring into the parts or for their functions. Should we, for instance, begin with understanding, perceiving, and so on, or with the part that understands and the part that perceives? And if we should begin with the functions, we might be puzzled anew about whether we should investigate the corresponding objects before the functions—the object of perception, for instance, before perceiving, and the object of understanding before understanding.

It would indeed seem useful to know the what-it-is, in order to study the causes of the coincidental properties of substances. In mathematics, for instance, it is useful to know what straight and curved are or what a line and a surface are, in order to notice how many right angles the angles of a triangle are equal to. Conversely, however, the [knowledge of the] coincidental properties also is also very important for knowing the what-it-is. For we can state the essence best once we can describe how all or most of the coincidental properties appear to be; for since the what-it-is is the principle of all demonstration, a definition will clearly be dialectical and empty unless it results in knowledge, or at least in ready conjecture, about the coincidental properties.

A further puzzle arises about whether all the affections of the soul also belong to what has the soul or there is also some affection that is distinctive of the soul itself. We must find the answer, but it is not easy.

In most cases (for instance, being angry or confident, having an appetite, or perceiving in general), it appears that without the body the soul neither is affected nor acts. Understanding, more than the other affections, would seem to be distinctive [of the soul]; but if it is also some sort of appearance or requires appearance, then understanding also requires a body. And so if some function or affection of the soul is distinctive of it, then the soul would be separable; but if not, then it would not be separable. Similarly, the straight, insofar as it is straight, has many coincidental properties—for instance, that it touches a bronze sphere at a point—but if it is separated, it will not touch the sphere in this way; for it is inseparable, given that in every case it requires some body.

In fact, all the affections of the soul—emotion, gentleness, fear, pity, confidence, and, further, joy, loving, and hating—would seem to require a body, since whenever we have them the body is affected in some way. An indication of this is the fact that sometimes, though something severe and obvious affects us, we are not provoked or frightened; and sometimes we are moved by something small and faint, if the body is swelling and in the condition that accompanies anger. It is still more evident that sometimes, though nothing frightening is happening people are affected just as a frightened person is.

If this is so, then clearly affections are forms that involve matter. Hence the formulae will be, for instance: 'Being angry is a certain motion of this sort of body or part or capacity by this agency for this end'. Hence study of the soul—either every sort or this sort—turns out to be a task for the student of nature.

The student of nature and the dialectician would give different definitions of each of these affections—of anger, for instance. The dialectician would define it as a desire to inflict pain in return for pain, or something of that sort, whereas the student of nature would define it as a boiling of the blood and of the hot [element] around the heart. The student of nature describes the matter, whereas the dialectician describes the form and the account: for desire, for instance, is the form of the thing, but its existence requires this sort of matter. Similarly, the account of a house is of this sort—that it is a shelter preventing destruction by wind, rain, or heat; someone else will say that it is stones, bricks, and timber; and someone else will say that it is the form in these [stones, for instance,] for the sake of this end. Who, then, is the [real] student of nature—the one who is concerned with the matter but is ignorant of the account, or the one who is concerned only with the account? Or is the [real] student of nature more properly the one who mentions both form and matter? If so, then what is each of the first two?

Perhaps in fact there is no one who is concerned with the inseparable affections of matter but not concerned with them insofar as they are separable. Rather, the student of nature is concerned with all the actions and affections of this sort of body and this sort of matter; what is not of this sort concerns someone else, perhaps a craftsman (for instance, a carpenter or a doctor). Inseparable affections, insofar as they are not affections of this sort of body but [are considered] by abstraction, concern the mathematician; insofar as they are separated, they concern first philosophy.

We should return to where our discussion began. We were saying, then, that the affections of the soul (for instance, emotion and fear) are, insofar as they are affections of the soul, inseparable[1] (unlike surface and line) from the natural matter of animals.

4

We say that the sould feels pain or enjoyment, and confidence or fear, and also that it is angry or perceives or thinks; and all of these seem to be motions.

---

1. **inseparable:** They cannot exist without matter, though they are separable in account and definition.

Hence one might infer that the soul is in motion; but this does not necessarily follow.

For let us by all means grant that feeling pain, feeling enjoyment, and thinking are motions, and that to be in these conditions is to be moved, and that the soul intiates the motion—so that to be angry or afraid, for instance, is for the heart to undergo this motion, while thinking is presumably a motion of this part or of something else, and this comes about in some cases by the local motion of some things, in other cases by alteration (to say which things and what sort of motion requires another discussions). Still, to say that the soul is angry is like saying that the soul weaves or builds houses. For presumably it is better to say, not that the soul feels pity or learns or thinks, but that the human being does so by the soul. And this is true not because the motion is in the soul, but because sometimes it reaches as far as the soul, and sometimes it begins from the soul. Perception, for instance, begins from these [external] things [and reaches as far as the soul], while recollection begins from the soul and extends to the motions or to the traces remaining in the sense-organs. . . .

Book 2

1

412a So much for the views on the soul that our predecessors have handed down. Let us now return and make a new start, trying to determine what the soul is and what account of it best applies to all souls in common.

We say, then, that one kind of being is substance. One sort of substance is matter, which is not a this in its own right; another sort is shape or form, which makes [matter] a this; and the third sort is the compound of matter and form. Matter is potentiality, and form is actuality; actuality is either, for instance, [the state of] knowing or [the activity of] attending [to what one knows].

What seem to be substances most of all are bodies, and especially natural bodies, since these are the sources of the others. Some natural bodies are alive and some are not—by 'life' I mean self-nourishment, growth, and decay.

It follows that every living natural body is a substance and, [more precisely] substance as compound. But since every such body is also this sort of body—i.e. the sort that is alive—the soul cannot be a body, since the body [is substance] as subject and matter and is not said of a subject. The soul, then, must be substance as the form of a natural body that is potentially alive. Now, substance is actuality; hence the soul will be the actuality of this specific sort of body.

Actuality is spoken of in two ways—one corresponding to [the state of] knowing and the other to attending to [what one knows]. Evidently, then, the soul is the same sort of actuality that knowing is. For both being asleep and being awake require the presence of the soul; being awake corresponds to attending and being asleep to the state of inactive knowing. Moreover, in the same subject the state of knowing precedes the activity. Hence the soul is the first actuality of a natural body that is potentially alive.

412b The sort of natural body that is potentially alive is an organic one. The parts of plants are also organs, though altogether simple ones; the leaf, for instance, is a shelter for the shell, and the shell for the fruit, and similarly the roots correspond to a mouth, since both draw in food. And so, if we must give an account common to every sort of soul, we will say that the soul is the first actuality of a natural organic body.

Hence we need not ask whether the soul and body are one, any more than we need to ask this about the wax and the seal or, in general,about the matter and the thing of which it is the matter. For while one and being are spoken of in several ways, the actuality [and what it actualizes] are fully one.

We have said in general, then, that the soul is substance that corresponds to the account; and this [sort of substance] is the essence of this sort of body. Suppose some instrument—an axe, for instance—were a natural body; then being an axe would be its substance, and its soul would also be this [i.e. being an axe]; and if this substance were separated from it, it would no longer be an axe, except homonymously. In fact, however, it is an axe; for the soul is not the essence and form of this sort of body but of the specific sort of natural body that has in itself a principle of motion and rest.

We must also study this point by applying it to the parts [of living things]. If the eye, for instance, were an animal, sight would be its soul. For sight is the eye's substance that corresponds to the account, while the eye is the matter of sight; if an eye loses its sight, it is no longer an eye, except homonymously, as a stone eye or a painted eye is. We must apply this point about the part to the whole living body; for what holds for the relation of part [of the faculty of perception] to part [of the body] holds equally for the relation of the whole [faculty of] perception to the whole perceptive body, insofar as it is perceptive. The sort of body that is potentially alive is not the one that has lost its soul but the one that has it; and the seed or the fruit is potentially this sort of body.

Being awake, then, is [a second] actuality, corre- 413a sponding to cutting or seeing. The soul is [a first] actuality, corresponding to [the faculty of] sight and to the potentiality of the instrument [to cut]; and the body is potentially this. And as an eye is the pupil plus sight, so an animal is soul plus body.

It is clear, then, that the soul is not separable from the body. At least, some parts of it are not, if it is divisible into parts; for the actuality of some [parts of the soul] is [the actuality] of the parts [of the body] themselves. Still, some [parts of the soul] might well not be actualities of any body and might therefore be separable. Moreover, it is still unclear whether the soul is the actuality of the body in the way a sailor is of a ship.

Let this, then, be our outline definition and sketch of the soul.

2

Since what is perspicuous and better known from the point of view of reason emerges from what is less perspicuous but more evident, we must start again and apply this approach to the soul. For the defining account must not confine itself, as most definitions do, to showing the fact; it must also contain and indicate its cause. The accounts that are customarily stated in formulae are like conclusions, so that if we ask, for instance, what squaring is, we are told that it is making an equilateral rectangle equal to an oblong rectangle. This sort of formula is an account of the conclusion, whereas the one that defines squaring as the finding of the mean states the cause of the fact.

To begin our inquiry, then, we say that living is what distinguishes things with souls from things without souls. Living is spoken of in several ways—for instance, understanding, perception, locomotion and rest, and also the motion involved in nourishment, and decay and growth. And so whatever has even one of these is said to be alive.

This is is why all plants as well [as animals] seem to be alive, since they evidently have an internal potentiality and principle through which they both grow and decay in contrary directions. For they grow up and down and in all directions alike, not just up rather than down; they are continually nourished, and they stay alive as long as they can absorb nourishment. This [sort of life] can be separated from the others, but in mortal things the others cannot be separated from it. This is evident in the case of plants, since they have no other potentiality of the soul.

This principle, then, is what makes something 413b alive. What makes something an animal is primarily perception; for whatever has perception, even without motion or locomotion, is said to be an animal, not simply to be alive. Touch is the primary type of perception belonging to all animals, and it can be separated from the other senses, just as the nutritive [potentiality] can be separated from touch and the other senses.

The part of the soul that belongs to plants as well as to animals is called nutritive; and all animals evidently have the sense of touch. Later we will state the explanation of each of these facts. For now let us confine ourselves to saying that the soul is the principle of the [potentialities] we have mentioned—for nutrition, perception, understanding, and motion—and is defined by them.

Is each of these a soul or a part of a soul? And if a part, is it the sort that is separable only in account, or is it also separable in place? In some cases the answer is easily seen, but some parts raise a puzzle For some plants are evidently still alive when they are cut [from one plant] and are separated from each other; for, we assume, the soul in each plant is actually one but potentially more than one. And we see that the same is also true of other differentiae of the soul. [This is clear] in the case of insects that are cut in two. For each part has both perception and locomotion; if it has perception, then it also has appearance and desire. For if it has perception, then it has pain and pleasure, and if it has these, then it necessarily also has appetite.

So far, however, nothing is evident about understanding and the potentiality for theoretical study. It would seem to be a different kind of soul, and the only part that can be separated, in the way in which the everlasting can be separated from the perishable.

It evidently follows, however, that the other parts of the soul are not separable, as some say they are. But they evidently differ in account; for perceiving is different from believing, and hence being the perceptive part is different from being the believing part, and so on for each of the other parts mentioned.

Further, animals are differentiated by the fact that some of them have all of these parts, some have some of them, and some have only one; we should investigate the reason for this later. Practically the same is true of the senses; some animals have all of them, some have some of them, and some have only the most necessary one, touch.

When we say we live and perceive by something, we speak in two ways, just as we do when we say we know by something. For we say we know either by knowledge or by the soul, since we say we know by each of these; and similarly, we are healthy in one way by health, in another way by some part or the whole of the body. In these cases, knowledge or health is a sort of shape and form, i.e. an account and a sort of actuality of what is receptive of knowledge or health; for the actuality of the agent seems to occur in the thing that is acted on and suitably disposed.

Now the soul is that by which we primarily live, perceive, and think, and so it will be an account and a form, not matter and subject. For substance, as we said, is spoken of in three ways, as form, matter, and the compound of both; of these, matter is potentiality, form actuality. Since, therefore, the compound of body and soul is ensouled, body is not the actuality of soul, but the soul is the actuality of some sort of body. This vindicates the view of those who think that the soul is not a body but requires a body; for it is not a body, but it belongs to a body, and for that reason it is present in a body, and in this sort of body. Our predecessors were wrong, then, in trying to fit the soul into a body without further determining the proper sort of body, even though it appears that not just any old thing receives any old thing. Our view, however, is quite reasonable, since a thing's actuality naturally comes to be in what has the potentiality for it, i.e. in the proper matter.

It is evident from this, then, that the soul is a certain sort of actuality and form of what has the potentiality to be of this sort.

3

As we said, some things have all the potentialities of the soul that were previously mentioned, while other things have some of these potentialities, and others have only one. The potentialities we mentioned were those for nutrition, perception, desire, locomotion, and understanding. Now, plants have only the nutritive part. Other things have the nutritive part and also the perceptive part, and if they have the perceptive part, they also have the desiring part. For desire includes appetite, emotion, and wish; but all animals have at least the sense of touch, and whatever has any perception has pleasure and pain and finds things pleasant or painful. Whatever finds things pleasant and painful also has appetite, since appetite is desire for what is pleasant.

Further, animals have the perception of nourishment; for touch is perception of nourishment, since all living things are nourished by things that are dry and wet and hot and cold, and touch is the perception of these. Animals are nourished by other objects of perception only coincidentally, since neither sound nor color nor smell contributes anything to nourishment, and flavor is an object of touch. Now, hunger and thirst are appetites for the dry and hot, and the wet and cold, respectively, while flavor is a sort of pleasant relish belonging to these.

We must make these points clear later on. For now let us confine ourselves to saying that living things that have touch also have desire. Whether they all have appearance is not clear, and must be considered later.

Besides these parts, some things have the locomotive part. Others—human beings, for instance, and any thinking being that is different from, or superior to, a human being—also have the thinking part and intellect.

Clearly, then, soul will have one single account in the same way that figure has; for just as figure is nothing besides the triangle and the figures that follow in order, so equally the soul is nothing besides those [potentialities] we have mentioned. Still, in the case of figures we can find a common account that fits all of them and is distinctive of none; the same is true for the souls we have mentioned. It is ridiculous, then, in these and other such cases, to seek a common account that is not distinctive of any being and does not fit the proper and indivisible species, if we neglect this [distinctive] account. Hence we must ask what the soul of each particular [kind of thing]—for instance, a plant, a human being, or a beast—is.

What is true of the soul is similar to what is true of figure; for in both cases the earlier is invariably present potentially in its successor—for instance, the tri- *415a* angle in the square, and the nutritive in the perceptive. We must consider why they are in this order. For the perceptive part requires the nutritive, but in plants the nutritive is separated from the perceptive. Again, each of the other senses requires touch, whereas touch is found without the other senses, since many animals lack sight, hearing, and smell. Among things that perceive, some but not all have the locomotive part. Finally and most rarely, some have reasoning and understanding. For perishable things that have reasoning also have all the other parts of the soul; but not all of those that have each of the other parts also have reasoning—on the contrary, some animals lack appearance, while some live by appearance alone. Theoretical intellect requires a different account.

Clearly, then, the account of each of these parts of the soul is also the most proper account of [each type of] soul.

4

If we are to investigate these [parts of the soul] we must find what each of them is and then inquire into the next questions and those that follow. And if we ought to say what, for instance, the understanding or the perceptive or the nutritive part is, we should first say what it is to understand or perceive, since actualities and actions are prior in account to potentialities If this is so, and if in addition the objects corresponding to the actualities are prior to them and so must be studied first, then we must, for the same reason, begin by determining the objects corresponding to nutrition, sense, and understanding. And so we should first discuss nourishment and generation; for the nutritive soul belongs to other living things as well as [to plants], and it is the first and most widely shared potentiality of the soul, the one that makes all living things alive.

Its functions are generation and the use of nourishment. For the most natural of all functions for a living thing, if it is complete and not defective and does not come to be by chance, is to produce another thing of the same sort as itself (an animal, if it is an animal, and a plant, if it is a plant), in order to share as far as it can in the everlasting and divine. For this *415b* is the end they all strive for, and for its sake they do every action that accords with nature. (What something is for is of two types—the goal and the beneficiary.) These living things cannot share in the everlasting and divine by continuously existing, since no perishable thing can remain numerically one and the same; hence they share in it as far as they can, to different degrees, and what remains is not the [parent] itself, but something else of the same sort as [the parent]—something that is specifically, not numerically, one with [the parent].

The soul is the cause and principle of the living body. Now, causes are spoken of in many ways, and the soul is a cause in three of the ways distinguished—as the source of motion, as what something is for, and as the substance of ensouled bodies.

It is clearly the cause as substance; for a thing's substance is the cause of its being, and the being of living things is their living, the cause and principle of which is soul. Moreover, the actuality is the form of what is potentially.

The soul is evidently also a cause by being what something is for. For just as productive thought aims at something, so does nature, and what it aims at is its end. In living things the natural end is the soul; for all natural bodies, of plants no less than of animals, are organs of the soul, since they are for the sake of the soul. (The end for the sake of which is of two types, either the goal or the beneficiary.)

Moreover, the soul is also the source of locomotion, though not all living things have this potentiality. Alteration and growth also depend on the soul; for perception seems to be some kind of alteration, and nothing that lacks a soul perceives. The same applies to growth and decay; for nothing either decays or grows naturally without being nourished, and nothing that has no share of life is nourished.

Empedocles is wrong when he adds that plants grow by putting down roots because earth naturally *416a* moves downwards, and that plants grow by extending upwards because fire naturally moves upwards. His conception of up and down is wrong. For up and down are not the same for each particular [sort of] thing as they are for the universe as a whole; in fact, if we ought to call organs the same or different in accordance with their functions, a plant's roots correspond to an animal's head. Besides, what is it that holds the fire and earth together when they are moving in contrary directions? For they will be torn apart unless something prevents it; whatever prevents it will be the soul, the cause of growing and being nourished.

Some think the nature of fire is the unqualified cause of nourishment and growth, since it is the only body that is evidently nourished and grows, and hence one might suppose that it also performs this function in both plants and animals. In fact, however, fire is a sort of joint cause, but not the unqualified cause; it is the soul, rather than fire, that is the unqualified cause. For while fire grows without limit, as long as there is fuel, the size and growth of everything naturally constituted has a limit and form, which are characteristic of soul, not of fire—i.e., of the form rather than of the matter.

Since one and the same potentiality of the soul is both nutritive and generative, we must first determine the facts about nutrition; for this is the function that distinguishes the nutritive potentiality from others.

Contrary seems to nourish contrary, not in every case, but only when they not only come to be but also grow from each other; for many things come to be from each other (healthy from sick, for instance) without gaining any quantity. And not even those contraries that grow seem to nourish each other in the same way; water, for instance, nourishes fire, but fire does not nourish water. It seems to be true, then, of the simple bodies more than of other things, that one thing nourishes and the other is nourished.

A puzzle arises: while some say that like nourishes like, just as (they say) like grows by like, others, as we have said, hold the opposite view, that contrary nourishes contrary; for, they say, like is unaffected by like, but nourishment changes and is digested, and everything changes into its opposite or into the intermediate. Moreover, nourishment is affected by the thing nourished, whereas the thing nourished is unaffected
416b by the nourishment—just as the matter is affected by the carpenter, who is unaffected by it and merely changes from inactivity to activity.

It matters for this question whether nourishment is the first or last thing added. Perhaps it is both, if undigested nourishment is added first, and digested nourishment last. If so, then it would be possible to speak of nourishment in both ways; for insofar as nourishment is undigested, contrary nourishes contrary, and insofar as it has been digested, like nourishes like. Evidently, then, each view is in a way both correct and incorrect.

Since nothing is nourished except what has a share of life, the ensouled body, insofar as it is ensouled, is what is nourished. Nourishment, therefore, is also relative, not coincidentally, to an ensouled thing. However, nourishing something is not the same as making it grow; for an ensouled thing is caused to grow insofar as it has some quantity, but it is nourished insofar as it is a this and a substance. For it preserves its substance and exists as long as it is nourished; and what it generates is not itself, but something else of the same sort—for its own substance already exists, and a thing does not generate, but preserves, itself.

Hence this sort of principle in the soul is a potentiality of the sort that preserves the ensouled thing, insofar as it is ensouled, and nourishment equips it for its actuality; and so if it has been deprived of nourishment it cannot exist. Further, since a thing's end rightly determines what we should call it, and in this case the end is the generation of another thing of the same sort, this first soul will be the generative soul, generating another thing of the same sort.

We must distinguish three things—what is nourished, what it is nourished by, and what nourishes. What nourishes is this first soul, what is nourished is the ensouled body, and what it is nourished by is the nourishment. What the soul nourishes by is of two types—just as what we steer by is both the hand and the rudder: The first both initiates motion and undergoes it, and the second simply undergoes it. Since all nourishment must be digestible and the hot element produces digestion, every ensouled thing contains heat.

This, then, is an outline of what nutrition is; we should describe it more clearly later in the discussions proper to it.

Book 3

3

428a . . . If appearance is that in virtue of which some object appears to us, in contrast to what is so called metaphorically, then is it one of those potentialities or states in virtue of which we discriminate and attain truth or falsity? These are perception, belief, knowledge, and understanding.

It is clear as follows that appearance is not the same as perception. For perception is either a potentiality, such as sight, or an actuality, such as seeing; but we have appearances when we have neither of these—in dreams, for instance. Moreover, perception is present in every [animal] but appearance is not. If they were the same in actuality, then it would be possible for all beasts to have appearance, whereas in fact it does not seem possible [for all]; ants or bees, for instance, and grubs [do not have it]. Further, perceptions are always true, whereas most appearances are false. Again, whenever we are actually perceiving accurately, we do not say that this appears to us [to be] a man; we are more inclined to say [that something appears to be so] in cases where we do not see clearly whether something is true or false. Further, as we were saying before, sights appear to us even when we have our eyes closed.

The remaining question is whether appearance is belief; for belief may also be either true or false. Belief, however, implies conviction—since one cannot believe things if one does not find them convincing—whereas no beasts have conviction, though many have appearance. Further, belief implies conviction, conviction implies being persuaded, and persuasion implies reason, whereas no beasts have reason, though some have appearance.

It is evident, then, that appearance is neither belief that involves perception, nor belief that is produced through perception, nor a combination of belief and perception. This is so both for the reasons given and also because [on this view] belief will not be about anything other than the thing, if there is one, that is the object of perception.

I mean, for instance, that the combination of a belief about the pale and a perception of the pale will turn out to be appearance; for surely it will not be the combination of a belief about the good and a perception of the pale—for appearance will be hav- 428b
ing a belief non-concidentally about the very thing one perceives. In fact, however, we sometimes have false appearances about the same things at the same time as we have a true supposition about them, as when, for instance, the sun appears a foot across even though we are convinced that it is bigger than the inhabited world.

It turns out, then, [on the view being considered] that either we have lost the true belief we had, even though the thing still exists and we have neither forgotten our belief nor been persuaded to change it, or else, if we still have the true belief, the same belief must at the same time be both true and false. But in fact it could have become false only if the thing changed without our noticing it. It follows, then, that appearance cannot be any of these things, nor a product of them.

It is possible, however, when one thing has been set in motion, for a second thing to be set in motion by the first. Moreover, appearance seems to be a sort of motion, to involve perception, to be present in things that have perception, and to be about the objects of perception. Now, it is also possible for motion to result from actual perception, and this motion must be similar to the perception.

Hence this motion cannot occur without perception or in things that do not have perception. Things that have appearance act and are affected in many ways in accordance with it, and it can be either true or false. . . .

4

Now we must consider the part by which the soul has 429a
knowledge and intelligence, and ask whether it is separable, or it is not separable in magnitude but only in account; and what its differentia is, and how understanding comes about.

Now, if understanding[2] is like perceiving, it consists either in being affected by the object of intellect or in something else of the same sort. Hence the

---

2. **understanding:** In this chapter *noein* is rendered "understand," and the term for the relevant faculty, *nous*, by "intellect." Probably Aristotle (in this chapter) is primarily treating *noein* as a form of knowledge, not simply as thinking about things; but it is not always clear which he has in mind.

intellect must be unaffected, but receptive of the form; it must have the quality [of the object] potentially, not actually; and it must be related to its object as the perceiving part is related to the objects of perception.

Hence the intellect, since it understands all things, must be unmixed, in order, as Anaxagoras says, to 'master' them (i.e. to know them); for the intrusion of any foreign thing would hinder and obstruct it. And so it has no nature except this—that it is potential. Hence the part of the soul called intellect (by which I mean that by which the soul thinks and supposes) is not actually, before it understands, any of the things there are. It is also unreasonable, then, for intellect to be mixed with the body, since it would then acquire some quality (for instance, hot or cold) or even, like the perceiving part, have some organ, whereas in fact it has none.

And so those who say that the soul is a place of forms are right, except that it is the intellectual soul, not the whole soul, which is—potentially, not actually—the forms.

The condition of the sense-organ and of the faculty of perception makes it evident that the perceiving part and the intellectual part are unaffected in different ways. For after a sense perceives something very perceptible, it cannot perceive; after hearing very loud sounds, for instance, it cannot hear sound, and after seeing vivid colors or smelling strong odors, it cannot see or smell. But whenever intellect understands something that is very intelligible, it understands more, not less, about inferior objects; for intellect is separable, whereas the perceiving part requires a body.

When the intellect becomes each thing [that it understands], as it does when someone is said to have actual knowledge (this comes about whenever someone is able to actualize his knowledge through himself), even then it is still potential in a way, though not in the same way as before it learnt or discovered; and then it is capable of understanding itself.

Magnitude is different from being magnitude and water from being water; and the same applies in many other cases too, though not in all, since in some cases the thing is the same as its being. It follows that to discriminate being flesh we use something different, or something in a different state, from what we use in discriminating flesh; for flesh requires matter, and, like the snub, it is this [form] in this [matter]. Hence to discriminate the hot and the cold and the things of which flesh is some sort of form, we use the perceptive part; but to discriminate being flesh, we use something else that is either separable [from body] or related to it as a formerly bent line is related to the straight line it has become.

Further, if we turn to things whose being depends on abstraction, the straight is similar to the snub, since it requires something continuous. But if being straight is different from the straight, then so is the essence of straight (duality, let us say) different from the straight, and therefore to discriminate it we use something different, or something in a different state. In general, then, the [separability] of intellect corresponds to the way in which objects are separable from matter.

A puzzle arises. If intellect is simple and unaffected, having, as Anaxagoras says, nothing in common with anything, then how can it understand, if understanding consists in being affected? For it seems that two things must have something in common if one is to affect the other. Again, is intellect itself an object of intellect? For if nothing other [than itself] makes it an object of intellect, and if all objects of intellect are one in species, then the other objects of intellect will also be intellect; alternatively, it will need something mixed into it, to make it an object of intellect in the same way as the other objects of intellect are.

On the other hand, our previous discussion of ways of being affected because of something in common has shown that the intellect is in a way potentially the objects of intellect, but before it understands them, it is none of them actually. Its potentiality is that of a writing tablet with nothing actually written on it—which is also true of intellect.

Further, intellect itself is an object of intellect in the same way as its objects are. For in the case of things without matter, the understanding part and its object are one, since actual knowledge and its object are the same. (We should investigate why it is not [engaged in the activity of] understanding all the time.) In things that have matter, each object of intellect is potentially present; hence intellect will not be in them (since it is a potentiality for being such things without their matter), but it will be an object of intellect.

5

In the whole of nature each kind of thing has something as its matter, which is potentially all the things in the kind, and something else as the cause and producer, which produces them all—for instance, the craft in relation to its matter. These differences, then, must also be found in the soul. One sort of intellect corresponds to matter, since it becomes all things. Another sort corresponds to the producer by producing all things in the way that a state, such as light, produces things—for in a way light makes potential colors into actual colors. This second sort of intellect is separable, unaffected, and unmixed, since its essence is actuality.

For in every case the producer is more valuable than the thing affected, and the principle is more valuable than the matter. Actual knowledge is the same as its object; potential knowledge is temporally prior in an individual [knower], but in general it is not even temporally prior. But [productive intellect] does not understand at one time and not at another.

Only when it has been separated is it precisely what it is, all by itself. And this alone is immortal and everlasting. But [when it is separated] we do not remember, because this [productive intellect] is unaffected, whereas the intellect that is affected is perishable. And without this [productive intellect] nothing understands. . . .

10

433a There are apparently two parts that move us—both intellect and desire, if we take appearance to be a kind of understanding. For many people follow their appearances against their knowledge, and the other animals have appearance but lack understanding and reasoning. Both intellect and desire, then, move us from place to place. This is the intellect that reasons for some goal and is concerned with action; its [concern with an] end distinguishes it from theoretical intellect. All desire also aims at some goal; for the object of desire is the starting point of intellect concerned with action, and the last stage [of our reasoning] is the starting point of action.

Hence it is reasonable to regard these two things—desire, and thought concerned with action—as the movers. For the object of desire moves us, and thought moves us because its starting point is the object of desire. Moreover, whenever appearance moves us, it requires desire.

And so there is one mover, the desiring part. For if there were two—intellect and desire—they would move us insofar as they had a common form. In fact, however, intellect evidently does not move anything without desire, since wish is desire, and any motion in accordance with reasoning is in accordance with wish; desire, on the other hand, also moves us against reasoning, since appetite is a kind of desire. Now, intellect is always correct, but desire and appearance may be either correct or incorrect. Hence in every case the mover is the object of desire, but the object of desire is either the good or the apparent good—not every sort of good, but the good that is achievable in action. What is achievable in action admits of being otherwise.

Evidently, then, the potentiality of the soul that moves us is the one called desire. People who divide 433b
the soul into parts, if they divide it into separate parts corresponding to the different potentialities, will find very many of them—the nutritive, perceptive, intellectual, and deliberative parts, and, moreover, the desiring part; for the difference between these parts is wider than the one between the appetitive and emotional parts.

Desires that are contrary to each other arise, however, when reason and appetite are contrary, which happens in subjects that perceive time. For intellect urges us to draw back because of what is to come, while appetite [urges us on] because of what is present; for the pleasant thing that is present appears both unqualifiedly pleasant and unqualifiedly good, because we do not see what is to come.

Hence the mover is one in species—the desiring part, insofar as it is desiring. Indeed, the first mover of all is the object of desire, since it moves us without being moved, by being present to understanding or appearance. But the movers are numerically more than one.

We must distinguish three things—the mover, its instrument, and the subject moved. There are two types of movers: the unmoved mover and the moved mover. The unmoved mover is the good achievable in action, and the moved mover is the desiring part; for the thing that is moved is moved insofar as it desires, and desire, insofar as it is actual, is a sort of motion.

The thing moved is the animal. When we reach the instrument by which desire moves, we reach something bodily, and so we should study it when we study the functions common to soul and body.

To summarize for the present: What moves something as an instrument is found where the same thing is both the starting point and the last stage. In the hinge-joint, for instance, the convex is last, and hence at rest, while the concave is the starting point, and hence is moved. These are different in account, though they are spatially inseparable. For since everything is moved by pushing and pulling, something must remain at rest, as in a circle, and the motion must originate from this.

In general, then, as we have said, an animal moves itself insofar as it has desire. For desire it needs appearance; and appearance is either rational appearance or the perceptual appearance that other animals share [with human beings].

11

434a We should also consider what it is that moves incomplete animals, whose only form of perception is touch. Can they have appearance and appetite, or not? For they evidently have pleasure and pain; if they have these, they must have appetite. But how could they have appearance? Well, perhaps, just as they are moved indeterminately, so also they have appearance and appetite, but have them indeterminately.

Now, the other animals as well [as man] also have perceptual appearance, as we have said, but [only] reasoning animals have deliberative appearance. For when we come to the question whether one is to do this or that, we come to a task for reasoning. And [in this case] one must measure by one [standard], since one pursues the greater [good]. And so one is able to make one object of appearance out of many. And this is why [non-rational animals] do not seem to have belief; it is because they lack the [appearance] resulting from reasoning.

That is why desire lacks the deliberative part. And sometimes one desire overcomes and moves another, while sometimes the second overcomes and moves the first, like one sphere moving another, whenever incontinence occurs. By nature the [desire] that is superior is dominant in every case and moves [the agent], and so it turns out that three motions are initiated [in the agent]. The part that has knowledge stays at rest and is not moved.

Now, one sort of supposition and statement is universal, while another is about what is particular; for the first says that this sort of agent ought to do this sort of thing, and the second says that this is this sort of thing and I am this sort of agent. Hence the second belief, not the universal belief, initiates motion; or [rather] both initiate motion, but the first does so by being more at rest, in contrast to the second.

Metaphysics

Book 1

1

980a All human beings by nature desire to know. A sign of this is our liking for the senses; for even apart from their usefulness we like them for themselves especially the sense of sight, since we choose seeing above practically all the others, not only as an aid to action, but also when we have no intention of acting. The reason is that sight, more than any of the other senses, gives us knowledge of things and clarifies many differences between them.

Animals possess sense-perception by nature at
980b birth. In some but not all of these, perception results in memory, making them more intelligent and better at learning than those that cannot remember. Some animals that cannot hear sounds (for instance, bees and similar kinds of animals) are intelligent but do not learn; those that both perceive sounds and have memory also learn.

Non-human animals live by appearances and memories but have little share in experience, whereas human beings also live by craft and reasoning. In human beings experience results from memory, since many memories of the same thing result in
the capacity for a single experience. Experience *981a*
seems to be quite like science and craft, and indeed human beings attain science and craft through

experience; for as Polus[1] correctly says, experience has produced craft, but inexperience only luck.

A craft arises when many thoughts that arise from experience result in one universal judgment about similar things. For the judgment that in this illness this treatment benefited Callias, Socrates, and others, in many particular cases, is characteristic of experience, but the judgement that it benefited everyone of a certain sort (marked out by a single kind) suffering from a certain disease (for instance, phlegmatic or bilious people when burning with fever) is characteristic of craft.

For practical purposes, experience seems no worse than craft; indeed we even see that experienced people are actually more successful than those who have a rational account but lack experience. The reason is that experience is cognition of particulars, whereas craft is cognition of universals. Moreover, each action and event concerns a particular; in medical treatment, for instance, we do not heal man (except coincidentally) but Callias or Socrates or some other individual who is coincidentally a man.[2] If, then, someone has a rational account but lacks experience, and recognizes the universal but not the particular falling under it, he will often give the wrong treatment, since treatment is applied to the particular.

Nonetheless, we attribute knowing and comprehending to craft more than to experience, and we judge that craftsmen are wiser than experienced people, on the assumption that in every case knowledge, rather than experience, implies wisdom. This is because craftsmen know the cause, but [merely] experienced people do not; for experienced people know the fact that something is so but not the reason why it is so, whereas craftsmen recognize the reason why, i.e. the cause.

That is why we believe that the master craftsmen
981b in a given craft are more honorable, know more, and
are wiser than the manual craftsmen, because they know the causes of what is produced. The manual craftsmen, we think, are like inanimate things that produce without knowing what they produce, in the way that, for instance, fire burns; the latter produce their products by a natural tendency, while the manual craftsmen produce theirs because of habit. We assume, then, that some craftsmen are wiser than others not because they are better in practice, but because they have a rational account and recognize the causes.

And in general, a sign that distinguishes those who know from those who do not is their ability to teach. Hence we think craft, rather than experience, is knowledge, since craftsmen can teach, while merely experienced people cannot.

Further, we do not think any of the senses is wisdom, even though they are the most authoritative ways of recognizing particulars. They do not tell us why anything is so; for instance, they do not tell us why fire is hot, but only that it is hot.

It is not surprising, then, that in the earliest times anyone who discovered any craft that went beyond the perceptions common to all was admired not only because he discovered something useful, but also for being a wise person, superior to others. Later on, as more crafts were discovered—some related to necessities, others to [leisuretime] pursuits—those who discovered these latter crafts were in every case judged to be wiser than the others, because their sciences did not aim at practical utility. Hence, finally, after all these crafts had been established, the sciences that aim neither at pleasure nor at necessities were discovered, initially in the places where people had leisure. This is why mathematical crafts arose first in Egypt; for there the priestly class were allowed to be at leisure.

The difference between craft and science and other similar sorts of things has been discussed in the *Ethics*.[3] The point of our present discussion is to show that in everyone's judgment any discipline deserving the name of wisdom must describe the first causes, i.e. the principles. And so as we said earlier, the experienced person seems to be wiser than those who have just any old perception; the craftsman seems to be wiser than those with nothing more than
experience; the master craftsman wiser than the 982a
manual craftsman; and the purely theoretical sciences wiser than the productive sciences. It is clear, then, that wisdom is knowledge of certain sorts of principles and causes.

---

1. **Polus:** a rhetorical theorist of the mid-fifth century BCE and a pupil of Gorgias.

2. **coincidentally a man:** i.e., coincidentally from the point of view of healing.

3. **the *Ethics*:** See *Nicomachean Ethics* 4.2.

2

Since this is the science we are looking for, we should consider what sorts of causes and principles wisdom is the science of. Perhaps this will become clearer if we consider our judgements about the wise person. First, we judge that he has knowledge about all things as far as possible, without, however having it about each particular [kind of thing]. Next, the one who is capable of knowing difficult things, i.e. things not easily known by human beings, is the wise person; for sense-perception is common to everyone, and that is why it is easy and not characteristic of wisdom. Further, someone is wiser in a given science if he is more exact, and a better teacher of the causes. Again, if one of two sciences is choiceworthy for itself—[purely] for the sake of knowing it—and the other is choiceworthy [only] for the sake of its results, the first has a better claim to be wisdom than the second. Moreover, the superior science has a better claim than the subordinate science; for the wise person must give orders, not take them, and those who are less wise must follow his orders, not he theirs. These, then, are our judgements about wisdom and wise people.

Of these features, we judge that knowledge about everything necessarily belongs to the one who has the best claim to universal science; for he in a way knows everything that is a subject for a science. These most universal things are also just about the most difficult for human beings to know, since they are furthest from perceptions. Further, the most exact sciences are those that, more than the others, study the first things; for the sciences that are derived from fewer principles—for instance, arithmetic—are more exact than those—for instance, geometry—that require further principles. Moreover, the science that studies the causes is more of a teacher, since teachers are those who state something's causes. Besides, knowledge and science for their own sake are most characteristic of the science of the most appropriate object of knowledge. For one who chooses knowledge for its 982*b* own sake will choose above all the science that is a science to the highest degree. This science is the science of the most appropriate objects of knowledge; these objects are the first things, i.e. the causes, since we know the subordinate things because of these and from these, not the other way round. Further, the most superior science—the one that is superior to any subordinate science—is the one that knows the end for which a given thing should be done; this end is something's good, and in general the end is what is best in every sort of nature.

From everything that has been said, then, we find that the name under discussion, [i.e. 'wisdom'], applies to the same science; for we find that wisdom must study the first principles and causes, and the good, the end, is one of the causes.

The fact that this science is not productive is also clear from those who first engaged in philosophy. For human beings originally began philosophy, as they do now, because of wonder, at first because they wondered at the strange things in front of them, and later because, advancing little by little, they found greater things puzzling—what happens to the moon, the sun and the stars, how the universe comes to be. Someone who wonders and is puzzled thinks he is ignorant (this is why the myth-lover is also a philosopher in a way, since myth is composed of wonders); since, then, they engaged in philosophy to escape ignorance, they were evidently pursuing scientific knowledge [simply]; for the sake of knowing, not for any further use.

What actually happened is evidence for this view. For it was only when practically everything required for necessities and for ease and [leisuretime] pursuits was supplied that they began to seek this sort of understanding; clearly, then, we do not seek it for some further use. Just as we describe a free person as one who exists for his own sake and not for someone else's, so we also describe this as the only free science, since it is the only one that exists for its own sake.

Hence the possession of this science might justifiably be thought to be beyond human capacity. For in many ways human nature is in slavery, so that, as Simonides says, 'the god alone would have this privilege', and it is unfitting for human beings to transgress their own level in their search for the science. If there actually is something in what the poets say, and the divine nature is spiteful, divine spite would be likely in 983*a* this case, and all those who go too far would suffer misfortunes. The divine nature, however cannot be spiteful: as the proverb says, 'Poets tell many lies'.

Nor ought we to take any science to be more honorable than this one since the most divine science is also the most honorable, and this science that we are describing is the most divine. It alone is most divine in two ways: for the divine science [may be understood] as (i) the one that a god more than anyone else would be expected to have, or as (ii) the science of divine things. Only this science [of first causes] satisfies both conditions [for being divine]. For (i) the god seems to be among the causes of all things, and to be some sort of principle, and (ii) this is the sort of science that the god, alone or more than anyone else, would be expected to have. Hence all the other sciences are more necessary than this one, but none is better.

However, the possession of this science must in a way leave us in a condition contrary to the one we were in when we began our search. For as we said, everyone begins from wonder that something is the way it is, as they wonder at toys that move spontaneously, or the turnings of the sun, or the incommensurability of the diagonal (for people who have not yet studied the cause are filled with wonder that there is something that is not measured by the smallest length). But we must end up in the contrary and (according to the proverb) the better state, the one that people achieve by learning [the cause] in these other cases as well—for nothing would be more amazing to a geometer than if the diagonal turned out to be commensurable.

We have described, then, the nature of the science we are seeking, and the goal that our search and our whole line of inquiry must reach.

3

It is evident, then, that we must acquire knowledge of the original causes since we say we know a thing whenever we think we recognize its primary cause. Causes are spoken of in four ways. One of these, we say, is the being and essence; for the reason why is traced back ultimately to the account, and the primary reason why is the cause and principle. Another is the matter and subject. A third is the source of the principle of motion. The fourth is what something is for, i.e. the good—the opposite to the third cause, since it is the end of all coming to be and motion.

983b We have studied these causes adequately in our work on nature. Still, let us also enlist those who previously took up the investigation of beings and pursued philosophical study about the truth; for it is clear that they also mention causes and principles of some sort. A discussion of their views, then, will advance our present line of inquiry; for either we shall find some other kind of cause or we shall be more convinced about those we have just mentioned.

Most of the first philosophers, then, thought that the only principles of all things were material. For, they say, there is some [subject] that all beings come from, the first thing they come to be from and the last thing they perish into, the substance remaining throughout but changing in respect of its attributes. This, they say, is the element and the principle of beings. And for this reason they think that nothing either comes to be or is destroyed, on the assumption that this nature [that is the subject] persists in every change, just as we say that Socrates does not come to be without qualification when he comes to be good or musical, and he is not destroyed when he loses these states (because the subject, Socrates himself, remains)—so also they say that nothing else either comes to be or perishes without qualification (for there must be some nature, either one or more than one, that persists while everything else comes to be from it).

But they do not all agree about the number or type of this material principle. Thales, the originator of this sort of philosophy, says it is water (that is why he also declared that the earth rests on water). Presumably he reached this judgment from seeing that what nourishes all things is wet and that the hot itself comes from the wet and is kept alive by it (and what all things come to be from is their principle). He also reached this judgment because he thought that the seeds of all things have a wet nature (and water is the principle of the nature of wet things).

Some people think that even those who first gave accounts of the gods in very ancient times, long before the present, accepted this judgment about nature. For the ancients made Oceanus and Tethys the parents of coming to be and described the oath of the gods as water, which they called Styx; for what is oldest is most honored, and what is most honored is the oath. It is perhaps unclear whether this belief 984a about nature is in fact old or even ancient, but at any rate this is what Thales is said to have declared about the first cause. (No one would think of including Hippon among these philosophers, given the triviality of his thought.)

Anaximenes and Diogenes take air to be both prior to water and also the primary principle of all the simple bodies, while Hippasus of Metapontium and Heraclitus of Ephesus say this about fire. Empedocles takes the four bodies to be principles, adding earth as a fourth to the ones mentioned. These, he says, always remain, and do not come to be, except insofar as they come to be more or fewer, being combined into one and dispersed from one into many.

Anaxagoras of Clazomenae, who was older than Empedocles but wrote later, says that the principles are unlimited; for he says that practically all the uniform things[4] (for instance, water or fire) come to be and are destroyed only in the ways we have mentioned, by being combined and dispersed; they do not come to be or get destroyed in any other way but always remain.

If one went by these views, one might judge that the material cause is the only sort of cause. But as people thus advanced, reality itself showed them the way and compelled them to search. For however true it might be that all coming to be and perishing is from one (or more than one) thing, still, why does this happen, and what is the cause? For certainly the subject does not produce change in itself. I mean, for instance, neither the wood nor the bronze causes itself to change, nor does the wood itself produce a bed or the bronze a statue, but something else causes the change. And to search for this is (in our view) to search for the second principle—the source of the principle of motion.

Those who were the very first to undertake this line of inquiry into nature, who said that the subject is one, were quite satisfied with this. But at least some of those who said that the subject is one, as though defeated by this search [for an explanation of change], said that the one, i.e. nature as a whole, is immobile, not only as regards coming to be and perishing (that was an old belief agreed on by all), but
984b also as regards every other sort of change. This view is distinctive of them.

Of those who said that the universe is one element, none managed to notice this [second] cause, unless Parmenides did; he noticed it only insofar as he posited not only one cause, but also in a way two causes. Indeed those who recognize more than one element—for instance, hot and cold, or fire and earth—make it easier to state [the cause that initiates motion] since they regard fire as having a nature that initiates motion, and water, earth, and other such things as having natures contrary to this.

After these sorts of principles were proposed by these people, other people found them inadequate to generate the nature of beings; once again as we said, it was as though the truth itself compelled them, and so they began to search for the next sort of principle. For presumably it is unlikely that fire or earth or anything else of that sort would cause some things to be in a good and fine state and would cause other things to come to be in that state, and unlikely that people would think so; still, it was unsatisfactory to entrust so great a result to chance and luck. And so when one of them said that mind is present (in nature just as in animals) as the cause of the world order and of all its arrangement, he seemed like a sober person, and his predecessors seemed like babblers in comparison. We know that Anaxagoras evidently made a start on giving such accounts, but an earlier statement of them is ascribed to Hermotimus of Clazomenae. Those who held this view posited a principle of beings that is at once both the cause of things' turning out well and the sort of cause that is the sources of motion for beings.

4

One might suspect that the first to search for this sort of cause was Hesiod and anyone else who counted desire or appetite among beings as a principle, as Parmenides, for instance, also did. For he too, in describing the coming to be of the whole universe, says: 'Desire was the first of all the gods she devised'. And Hesiod says: 'Before everything else that came to be, there was chaos, and then the broad-fronted earth, and desire, preeminent among all the immortals.'[5] He assumes that there must be some cause among beings to initiate motion in things and to bring them together. Let us leave it till later to determine which of these people was the first [to discover this sort of cause].

---

4. **uniform things:** lit. "things with parts similar to the wholes," *homoiomerē*.

5. **Before . . . immortals:** an inaccurate quotation (probably, like many of Aristotle's quotations, from memory) of Hesiod, *Theogony* 116–20.

Moreover, the contraries of good things (i.e. disorder 985a and ugliness no less than order and beauty) were also apparent in nature, and bad things were apparently more numerous than good things, and base things more numerous than beautiful things. For this reason someone else introduced love and strife so that each of them would be the cause of one of these two sorts of things. For if we follow Empedocles' argument, and do not confine ourselves to his mumbling way of expressing it, but attend to what he has in mind, we will find that love is the cause of good things, and strife of bad. And so, if one were to claim that in a way Empedocles said—indeed was the first to say—that the good and the bad are principles, one would perhaps be right, if the cause of all goods is the good itself.

These people, then, as we say, evidently made this much progress in fastening on two of the four causes that we distinguished in our work on nature—the matter and the principle of motion. But they did so dimly and not at all perspicuously. They were like unskilled boxers in fights, who, in the course of moving around, often land good punches, but are not guided by knowledge; in the same way these thinkers would seem not to know what they are saying, since they evidently make practically no use of these causes, except to a slight degree.

Anaxagoras, for instance, uses mind[6] as an ad hoc device for the production of the universe; it is when he is puzzled about the cause of something's being necessarily as it is that he drags in mind, but in other cases he recognizes anything but mind as the cause of things that come to be Empedocles, admittedly, uses these causes more than Anaxagoras does, but he too still makes insufficient use of them, and he does not succeed in using them consistently. At any rate, he often makes love draw things apart and strife draw them together. For whenever strife scatters the universe into its elements, all the fire is gathered into one, and so is each of the other elements; and whenever love brings things back together again into one, the parts from each element are necessarily scattered again.

Empedocles, then, went beyond his predecessors. He was the first to distinguish this cause and to introduce it; he did not take the principle of motion to be one, but assumed different and contrary principles. Moreover, he was the first to say that there are four material elements. In fact, though, he does not use 985b all four, but treats them as two, treating fire in its own right as one nature, and its opposites—earth, air, and water—as together constituting another; this may be gathered from studying his poems. As we say, then, this is how many principles he recognized, and this is what he said about them.

Leucippus and his colleague Democritus, on the other hand, say that the elements are the full and the empty, and that, of these, the full and solid is what is, and the empty is what is not. That is why they also say that what is is no more of a being than what is not, because body is no more of a being than the empty is. They take these to be the material causes of beings.

Those who take the substance that is the subject to be one explain how everything else comes to be by referring to the ways in which the subject is affected, taking the rare and the dense to be the principle of the ways it is affected. In the same way, Leucippus and Democritus take the differentiae[7] to be the causes of the other things. They say, however, that there are three of these differentiae—shape, order, and position. For they say that what is is differentiated only by rhythm, touching, and turning.[8] Of these rhythm is shape, touching is order, and turning is position; for A differs from N in shape, AN from NA in order, and Z from N in position. Like the other people, however, they were too lazy to take up the question about motion and to ask from what source and in what way it arises in beings.

This, then, would seem to be the extent, as we say, of the earlier thinkers' search for these two causes.

6

Plato's work came after the philosophical views we 987a have mentioned;[9] it agreed with them in most ways,

---

6. **mind:** *nous.*

7. **differentiae:** i.e., of the atoms, the solid bodies referred to in general terms as "the full."

8. **rhythm, touching, and turning:** These are the Atomists' own terms, which Aristotle explains; the illustration using letters (*stoicheia*, also translated "elements") is probably theirs too.

9. **views we have mentioned:** Aristotle has been discussing the Eleatics and Pythagoreans, whom he calls the "Italians."

but it also had distinctive features setting it apart from the philosophy of the Italians. For in his youth Plato first became familiar with Cratylus and with the Heraclitean beliefs that all perceptible things are always flowing and that there is no knowledge of them; he 987b held these views later too. Socrates, on the other hand, was concerned with ethics and not at all with nature as a whole; he was seeking the universal in ethics and was the first to turn his thought to definitions. Plato agreed with Socrates, but because of his Heraclitean views he took these definitions to apply not to perceptible things but to other things; for, he thought, the common formula could not be of any of the perceptible things, since they are always changing. Beings of this sort [that definitions are of], then, he called Ideas, and he said that perceptible things are apart from these, and are all called after them, since the things with the same names as the Forms are what they are by participation in them.

In speaking of 'participation' he changed only the name; for the Pythagoreans say that things are what they are by imitating numbers, and Plato (changing the name) said they are what they are by participating [in Forms]. But they left it to others to investigate what it is to participate in or to imitate Forms.

Further, he says that, apart from perceptible things and Forms, there are also mathematical objects in between. These differ from perceptible things in being everlasting and immobile; they differ from Forms in that there are many of the same kind, whereas there is only one Form for each kind of thing.

Since the Forms are the causes of other things, he thought that their elements are the elements of all beings. The great and the small, then, as matter, and the one, as substance, are principles; for Forms come from these, by participating in the one. And yet he said, agreeing with the Pythagoreans, that the one is substance, and that it is not said to be one by being something else. He also agreed with them in saying that numbers are the causes of the being of other things; but in positing a duality instead of treating the indeterminate as one, and in taking the great and small to constitute the indeterminate, he held a distinctive view of his own. Moreover, in his view numbers exist apart from perceptible things; whereas the Pythagoreans take the objects themselves to be numbers, and do not place mathematical objects between perceptible things and Forms.

His claim that the one and numbers exist apart from the other objects (in contrast to the Pythagorean view) and his introduction of the Forms were the result of his investigation of arguments; for none of his predecessors engaged in dialectic. He made the other nature [besides the One] a duality because he thought that numbers (except the primes) could be neatly produced from the duality, as though from 988a something malleable.

What actually happens, though, is the contrary of this, and it is implausible to think it would happen in the way they [the Platonists] say. For in their view many things are made out of the matter, but the Form generates only once; in fact, however, only one table is apparently made out of one [bit of] matter, whereas the agent who applies the form, though he is one makes many tables. Similarly, in the case of male and female, the female is impregnated from one copulation, whereas the male impregnates many females. And yet these things are imitations of those principles [that they believe in].

This, then, was what Plato determined about the questions we are investigating. It is evident from what has been said that he used only two causes the cause involving the what-it-is and the material cause; for the Forms are causes of the what-it-is of other things, and the one is the cause of the what-it-is of Forms. The nature of the matter that is the subject for the Forms (in the case of perceptible things) and for the one (in the case of Forms) is also evident: it is the duality, the great and the small. Further, he has assigned the cause of good and bad to the elements, one to each, as we say some earlier philosophers, such as Empedocles and Anaxagoras, also sought to do.

9

. . . As for those who posited Ideas, the first objection is that in seeking to grasp the causes of the beings in 990b this world, they introduced different things, equal in number to them. It is as though someone wanted to count things and though he could not do it if there were fewer of them, but could do it if he added more. For the Forms they resorted to in their search for the causes of things in this world are practically equal in number to—or at any rate are no fewer than—the things in this world. For take each [kind of] thing that has a one over many, both substances and non-substances, both things in this world and everlasting things; in each case there is some [one over many] that has the same name [as the many].

Further, none of the proofs we[10] offer to show that there are Forms appears to succeed; for some of them are invalid, while some also yield Forms of things that we think have no Forms. For the arguments from the sciences yield Forms of all the things of which there are sciences; the one over many yields Forms even of negations; and the argument from thinking about something that has perished yields Forms of things that perish, since there is an appearance of these. Further, among the more accurate arguments, some produce Ideas of relatives, whereas we deny that these are a kind of things that are in their own right; others introduce the Third Man.

And in general the arguments for Forms undermine the existence of things that matter more to us than the existence of the Ideas does. For they imply that number, not duality, is first and that what is relative is prior to what is in its own right, and they lead to all the other [unacceptable] conclusions that some people have been led to believe by following the beliefs about the Ideas, even though these beliefs conflict with their own principles.

Further, the reasoning that leads us to say that there are Ideas also yields Forms of many other things as well as of substances. For a thought is one not only in the case of substances but also in other cases; there are sciences of other things as well as of substance; and thousands of other such difficulties arise.

On the other hand, it is necessary, and follows from the beliefs about Forms, that if things can participate in Forms, only substances can have Ideas; for a thing does not participate in a Form coincidentally, but insofar as it is not said of a subject. (If, for instance, something participates in the Double itself, it also participates in the Everlasting, but coincidentally, since it is coincidental that the Double is everlasting). Hence the Forms will be substances. But the
991a same things signify substances among the Forms as in this world—otherwise what will the claim that there is something apart from these things, the one over many, amount to? And if the Idea and the things participating in it have the same form, they will have something in common—for why should [what it is to be] two be one and the same thing in all the perishable twos and in all the many everlasting twos, but not one and the same thing in the Two itself and in some particular two? But if they do not have the same form, they will be [merely] homonymous; it will be like calling both Callias and a wooden [statue] a man, when one has observed no common [nature] that they share.

One might be especially puzzled about what on earth Forms contribute to perceptible things, either to those that are everlasting or to those that come to be and perish; for they cause neither motion nor any change in them. Nor do they contribute to knowledge of other things, since they are not their substance—if they were, they would be in the other things. Nor do they contribute to the being of other things, since Forms are not present in the things that participate in them. For if they were present, they might perhaps be thought to be causes, as white is if it is mixed in a white object. This argument was first stated by Anaxagoras and then by Eudoxus and certain others. It is easily upset, since it is easy to collect many impossible consequences that challenge such a belief.

Nor can the other things be from Forms in any of the ways things are normally said to be from something. And to say that Forms are patterns and that other things participate in them is empty talk, mere poetic metaphors. For what is it that looks to the Ideas when it produces things? And it is possible for one thing to be, or to come to be, like another without being copied form it, so that whether or not Socrates exists, someone like Socrates might come to be; and clearly the same would be true even if Socrates were everlasting. Further, there will be many patterns of same thing, hence many Forms; the Forms of man, for instance, will be Animal and Biped as well as Man-itself. Further, the Forms will be patterns not only of perceptible things, but also of themselves—the genus, for instance, of its species—
so that same thing will be both pattern and copy. *991b*

Further, it would seem impossible for a substance to be separate from what it is the substance of. How, then, if the Ideas are the substances of things, could they be separate from them?

10. **we:** Aristotle thinks of himself as one of the Platonic school—though he does not endorse their position. In the rest of this chapter "we" and "our" also refer to the Platonists, not to Aristotle's independent views.

According to the *Phaedo*,[11] the Forms are the causes both of being and of coming to be. But what participates in the Forms does not come to be, even if the Forms exist, unless something initiates the motion. And in addition to these [natural things], many things—for instance, a house or a ring—which in our view have no Forms, come to be. Hence it is clearly also possible for the [natural] things to be and to come to be because of causes of the sort just mentioned.

Further, if the Forms are numbers, how can they be causes? Is it because beings are other numbers, so that one number, for instance, is man, another is Socrates, and another is Callias? If so, why are one lot of numbers causes of the other lot? It makes no difference if the Forms are everlasting and the other things are not. But if it is because things in this world—for instance, a harmony—are ratios of numbers, it is clear that the things of which they are ratios are some one [kind of] thing. But if there is this one thing, i.e. the matter, then evidently the numbers themselves will also be ratios of one thing to another. If, for instance, Callias is numerical ratio of fire, earth, water, and air, then his Idea will also be the number of certain other subjects. And Man-itself, even if it is in some way numerical will nonetheless be a numerical ratio of certain things, not [properly] a number. This argument, then, does not show that any Idea is number.

992b . . . In general, it is impossible to find the elements of beings without distinguishing the ways they are spoken of, since in fact beings are spoken of in many ways. It is especially impossible to find them if we search in this way for the sorts of elements that compose beings. For what elements compose acting or being affected or the straight? Presumably these cannot be found; at most the elements of substances can be found. Hence it is incorrect either to seek the elements of all beings or to think one has found them.

And how could one even learn the elements of all things? For clearly one cannot begin with previous cognition. If, for instance, we are learning geometry, we many have previous knowledge of other things [outside geometry], but we have no previous cognition about the subject matter of the science we are to learn about; the same is true in other cases. Hence if there is some science of all things, such as some say there is, we could not have previous cognition of anything before we learn this science. And yet all learning, either through demonstration or through definitions, relies on previous cognition of either all or some things; for one must previously know the elements of the definition, and they must be well known; the same is true for learning through induc- 993a
tion. Then is this science actually innate? If so, it is remarkable that we manage not to notice that we possess the supreme science.

Further, how is one to acquire recognition of the elements, and how is this knowledge to be made clear? For there is a puzzle here too, since our answers might be disputed, as in the case of certain syllables; for some say that ZA is from S, D, and A, while others say it is a different sound, and none of the well-known ones.

Further, how could one recognize perceptible things without perception? And yet one would have to, if the elements composing all things are indeed the same, as complex sounds are [composed of] their proper elements.

Book 4

1

There is a science that studies being insofar as it is 1003a
being,[12] and also the properties of being in its own right. It is not the same as any of the so-called special sciences. For none of them considers being quite generally, insofar as it is being; rather, each of them cuts off some part of being and studies the relevant coincident of that part, as, for instance, the mathematical sciences do.

Since we are seeking the principles, i.e. the highest causes, clearly they must be the causes of the nature of some subject as it is in its own right. If, then, those who were seeking the elements of beings were also

11. ***Phaedo:*** See Plato, *Phaedo* 100a–105c.

12. **insofar as:** or "qua," *hē(i)*. Aristotle is not referring to some special kind of being (as though something had the properties of being qua being, but not the properties of any specific sort of being). He is thinking of ordinary beings studied with reference to the properties that belong to them as beings.

seeking these highest principles, the elements must also be the elements of being not coincidentally, but insofar as it is being. That is why we also ought to find the first causes of being insofar as it is being.

2

Being is spoken of in many ways, but always with reference to one thing—i.e. to some one nature—and not homonymously. Everything healthy, for instance, is spoken of with reference to health—one thing because it preserves health, another because it produces health, another because it indicates health, 1003b another because it can receive health. Similarly, the medical is spoken of with reference to medical science; for one thing is called medical because it has the medical science, another because it is naturally suited to medical science, another because it is the function of medical science, and we shall find other things spoken of in ways similar to these.

Similarly, then, being is spoken of in many ways, but in all cases it is spoken of with reference to one principle. For some things are called beings because they are substances, others because they are attributes of substance, others because they are a road to substance, or because they are perishing or privations or qualities of substance, or productive or generative of substance or of things spoken of with reference to it, or because they are negations of one of these or of substance. This is why we also say that not being is—i.e. is not being.

A single science studies all healthy things, and the same applies in the other cases. For it is not only things that are spoken of in accordance with one [common property] that are studied by a single science; the same is true of things that are spoken of with reference to one nature, since these things are also, in a way, spoken of in accordance with one [common property]. Clearly, then, it is also the task of a single science to study beings insofar as they are beings.

In every case the dominant concern of a science is with its primary object, the one on which the others depend and because of which they are spoken of as they are. If, then, this primary object is substance, the philosopher must grasp the principles and causes of substances.[13]

There are as many parts of philosophy as there are 1004a [types of] substances, and so there must be a first philosophy, and a second philosophy following it; for being is divided immediately into genera, which is why the sciences will also conform to these. For the philosopher is spoken of in the same way as the mathematician is; for mathematical science also has parts, and in mathematics there is a first and a second science and others succeeding in order.

For every single genus there is a single [sort of] per- 1003b ception and a single science; there is, for instance, a single grammatical science, and it studies all the [types of] sounds. Hence it is also the task of a science that is one in genus to study all the species of being insofar as it is being; it is the task of the species of that science to study the species [of being].

Being and unity are the same and a single nature, since they imply each other, as principle and cause do, though they are not one and the same in the sense of being revealed by the same account (though indeed it does not matter if we take them to have the same account; that would be even more suitable for our purpose). For one man is the same as man, and moreover a man who is is the same a man, and 'he is man and a man who is' reveals nothing different by the repetition in what is said, since clearly a man and a man who is are separated neither in coming to be nor in perishing. The same also applies to unity. It is evident, then, that in these cases the addition [of 'one'] reveals the same thing [as 'is' reveals], and that unity is nothing different from being. Moreover, the substance of a thing is non-coincidentally one thing; and similarly it is essentially some being.

It follows that there are as many species of being as of unity. Hence it is a task for a science that is the same in genus to study the what-it-is about these species—for instance, about same, similar and other such things. Practically all the contraries are referred 1004a to this principle; our study of these in the Selection of Contraries[14] will suffice.

It is the task of one science to study opposites, and plurality is the opposite of unity. It is also the task of one science to study negation and privation, since in

13. The following paragraph consists of 1004a2–9 transposed to an apparently more suitable place.

14. **Selection of Contraries:** Perhaps this is a separate treatise, now lost.

both cases we study the one thing of which it is the negation or the privation. For either we say without qualification that something does not belong to the subject, or we say that it does not belong to some genus of the subject. In the latter case a differentia is added besides what is in the negation—for the negation is the absence of that property, but the privation also involves some nature that is the subject of which the privation is said.

And so it is also the task of the science we have mentioned to know about the contraries of the things we have mentioned—different, unlike, unequal, and everything else that is spoken of either with respect to these or with respect to plurality and unity. Contrariety is also one of these; for it is a type of difference, and difference is a type of otherness. And so, since unity is spoken of in many ways, these will also be spoken of in many ways; but still it is the task of a single science to know them all. For the mere fact that things are spoken of in many ways does not imply that they cannot be studied by one and the same science; different sciences are required only if it is true both that the things have no one [common property] and that their accounts are not referred to one thing.

Since in each case everything is referred to the primary thing (for instance, everything that is called one is referred to the primary unity), this is also what we ought to say about same, different, and contraries. And so we should first distinguish how many ways each thing is spoken of, and then show how each of the things we have distinguished is spoken of with reference to the primary thing in each predication; for some things will be spoken of as they are because they have that primary thing, others because they produce it, others in other such ways.

Evidently, then, it is the task of a single science to take account both of these things and of substance (this was one of the questions that raised puzzles), and it is the philosopher's task to be able to study all [these] things. For if this is not his task, who will consider whether Socrates is the same as seated Socrates, or whether one thing has [just] one contrary, or what contrariety is, or how many ways it is spoken of? And the same is true for other questions of that sort.

We have found, then, that these are attributes of unity insofar as it is unity, and of being insofar as it is being; each is an attribute of unity and being in their own right, not insofar as they are numbers or lines or fire. Hence it is clearly the task of that science [of being] to know both what being and unity are, and also their coincidents. The mistake of those who currently consider these questions is not that they fail to practice philosophy but that, although substance is prior, they comprehend nothing about it.

There are attributes distinctive of number insofar as it is number (for instance, oddness and evenness, commensurability and inequality, being more and being less), and these belong to numbers both in their own right and in relation to one another. Likewise there are other attributes distinctive of the solid, both moved and unmoved, and [of the moved], both weightless and having weight. In the same way, then, there are also some attributes distinctive of being insofar as it is being, and it is the philosopher's task to investigate the truth about these.

Here is a sign [to show that it is his task]. Dialecticians and Sophists assume the same guise as the philosopher. For sophistic has the appearance of wisdom, though nothing more, and dialecticians practice dialectic about all things; being is common to all things, and clearly they practice dialectic about all things because all things are proper to philosophy. For sophistic and dialectic treat the same genus as philosophy, but philosophy differs from dialectic in the type of power it has, and it differs from sophistic in its decision about how to live. Dialectic tests in the area where philosophy achieves knowledge, while sophistic has the appearance [of knowledge], but not the reality.

Further, one column of contraries is privation, and all contraries are referred to being and not being, and to unity and plurality—for instance, stability belongs to unity, motion to plurality. And practically everyone agrees that beings and substance are composed of contraries. At any rate, they all say that the principles are contrary; for some say that they are the odd and even, some that they are the hot and cold, some that they are the determinate and indeterminate, others that they are love and strife. All the other contraries are also evidently referred to unity and plurality (let us assume this referral), and the principles recognized by others fall completely under unity and plurality as their genera.

This also makes it evident, then, that it is the task of a single science to study being insofar as it is being; for all things are either contraries or composed of contraries, and unity and plurality are principles of the contraries. Unity and plurality belong to one science, whether or not they are spoken of as having one [common property] (and presumably in fact they are not). Even if unity is indeed spoken of in many ways, still the nonprimary unities will be spoken of with reference to the primary unity; the same applies to the contraries. This is true even if being or unity is neither universal and the same over them all nor separable; and presumably it is neither of these, but rather some [beings and unities] are spoken of with reference to one thing, and others in succession. That is why it is not the geometer's task to study what a contrary is or what completeness is, or to study unity, or being; or same, or different, but only to study them on the basis of an assumption.

Clearly, then, it is the task of a single science to study both being insofar as it is being and also the things that belong to it insofar as it is being. And clearly the same science studies not only substances but also their attributes—both those we have mentioned and also prior and posterior, genus and species, whole and part, and the other things of this sort.

3

We ought to say whether it is the task of one and the same science or of different sciences to study both the axioms (as they are called in mathematics) and substance. Evidently it is also the task of one and the same, science—the philosopher's—to examine these, since these belong to all beings and are not distinctive of one genus in separation from the others.

Every scientist uses the axioms because they belong to being insofar as it is being, and each genus is a being. But each uses them to the extent he needs them, and that is however far the genus about which he presents his demonstrations extends. Clearly, then, the axioms belong to all things insofar as they are beings (for this is what all things have in common); and so it is also the task of the one who knows being insofar as it is being to study the axioms.

This is why none of those who investigate a special area—for instance; a geometer or an arithmetician—undertakes to say anything about whether or not the axioms are true. The ones who did so were some of the students of nature; and it is not surprising that they did this, since they were the only ones who thought they were examining the whole of nature and examining being. In fact, however, there is someone still higher than the student of nature, since nature is only one kind of being; and so investigating these axioms will also be a task of this universal scientist, the one who studies primary 1005b substance. The study of nature is also a type of wisdom but not the primary type.

Now, some of those who argue about when a conclusion should properly be accepted as true object that one should not accept [principles that have not been demonstrated]. They do this because they lack education in analytics;[15] for someone who comes [to the science of being] must already know about analytics and not ask about it when he studies [the science of being].

Clearly, then, study of the principles of deductions is also a task for the philosopher—i.e. for the one who studies the nature of all substance. Whoever has the best claim to knowledge of a given genus ought to be able to state the firmest principles of his subject matter; hence whoever has the best claim to knowledge of beings insofar as they are beings should be able to state the firmest principles of all things—and this person is the philosopher.

The firmest principle of all is one about which it is impossible to be mistaken. For this sort of principle must be known best (for what we make mistakes about is invariably what we do not know), and it cannot be an assumption. For a principle that we must already possess in order to understand anything at all about beings is not an assumption; and what we must know in order to know anything at all is a principle we must already possess. Clearly, then, this sort of principle is the firmest of all.

Let us next say what this principle is: that it is impossible for the same thing both to belong and not to belong at the same time to the same thing and in the same respect (and let us assume we have drawn all the further distinctions that might be drawn to meet logical complaints). This, then, is the firmest principle of all, since it has the distinguishing feature previously mentioned.

For it is impossible for anyone to suppose that the same thing is and is not, though some people take

---

15. **Now, some. . . . in analytics:** The translation includes supplementation derived from 1006a5–8, to make the point clearer.

Heraclitus to say this; for what one says need not be what one supposes to be true. For it is impossible for contraries to belong at the same time to the same thing (and let us assume that the customary further distinctions are added to this statement). But what is contrary to a belief is the belief in its contradictory. Hence evidently it is impossible for the same person at the same time to suppose that the same thing is and is not, since someone who makes this mistake would have contrary beliefs at the same time. This is why all those who demonstrate refer back to this belief as ultimate; for this is by nature the principle of all the other axioms as well.

Book 7

1

Being is spoken of in many ways, which we distinguished previously in the work on how many ways things are spoken of. For one [type of being] signifies what-it-is and a this; another signifies quality, or quantity, or any of the other things predicated in this way. But while being is spoken of in this number of ways, it is evident that among these the primary being is the what-it-is, which signifies substance. For whenever we say what quality this has, we call it good or bad, not three cubits long or a man, whereas whenever we say what it is, we call it man or god, not pale or hot or three cubits long; and the other things are called beings by belonging to this type of being—some as quantities, some as qualities, some as affections, some in some other such way.

That is why someone might actually be puzzled about whether walking, flourishing, or sitting signifies a being; for none of these either is in its own right or is capable of being separated from substance, but it is more true that the walking or sitting or flourishing thing is a being—if indeed it is a being. This latter type of thing is apparently more of a being because it has some definite subject—the substance and the particular—which is discerned in such a predication; for this subject is implied in speaking of the good or sitting thing. Clearly, then, it is because of substance that each of those other things is also a being, so that what is in the primary way, what is not something,[16] but is without qualification a being, is substance.

Now the primary is so spoken of in many ways, but still, substance is primary in every way: in nature, in account, and in knowledge. For none of the other things predicated is separable, but only substance. Subtance is also primary in account, since its account is necessarily present in the account of each thing. Moreover, we think we know a thing most of all whenever we know what, for instance, man or fire is, rather than when we know its quality or quantity or place; for indeed we know each of these only when we know *what* the quantity or quality *is*.

Indeed, the old question—always pursued from long ago till now, and always raising puzzles—'What is being?' is just the question 'What is substance?' For it is substance that some say is one and others say is more than one, some saying that it is limited in number, others that it is unlimited. And so we too must make it our main, our primary, indeed practically our only, task to study what it is that is in this way.

2

The most evident examples of substances seem to be bodies. That is why we say that animals and plants and their parts are substances, and also natural bodies, such as fire, water, earth, and all such things, and whatever is either a part of these or composed of all or some of them—for instance, the universe and its parts, the stars, moon, and sun. But we ought to consider: Are these the only substances there are, or are there also others? Or are only some of these things substances and also some other things? Or are none of these things substances, but only some other things?

Some people think that the limits of a body—for instance, surface, line, point, and unit—are substances, and are so to a higher degree than a body and a solid. Further, some think there are no substances apart from perceptible things, while to others it seems that there are also everlasting substances, which are more numerous and are beings to a higher degree. Plato, for example, thinks that Forms and mathematicals are two types of substances, and that the substances of perceptible bodies is a third type. Speusippus posits even more substances, beginning with the one, and posits a principle for each type of substance—one for numbers, another

16. **what is not something:** i.e., what is not something *else*, as the sitting thing is something else, e.g., a man.

for magnitudes, and then another for soul; and in this way he multiplies the substances. Some say that Forms and numbers have the same nature, and that everything else comes after them—lines, planes, and everything else, extending to the substances of the universe and to perceptible things.

We must consider, then, which of these views are correct or incorrect; what substances there are; whether or not there are any substances besides perceptible substances, and in what way these perceptible substances are [substances]; and whether or not there is any separable substance besides perceptible ones, and, if there is, why there is, and in what way it is [substance]. But before doing this, we must first sketch what substance is.

3

Substance is spoken of, if not in several ways, at any rate in four main cases. For the essence, the universal and the genus seem to be the substance of a given thing, and the fourth of these cases is the subject.

Now, the subject is that of which the other things
1029a are said, but which is not itself in turn said of any other thing; hence we must first determine what it is, since the primary subject seems to be substance most of all.

What is spoken of in this way [as the primary subject] is in one way the matter, in another way the form, and in a third way the thing composed of these. (By the matter I mean, for example, the bronze, by the form I mean the arrangement of the figure, and by the thing composed of them I mean the statue, i.e., the compound.) And so if the form is prior to the matter, and more of a being, it will also, by the same argument, be prior to the thing composed of both.

We have now said in outline, then, what substance is: it is what is not said of a subject but has the other things said of it.

However, we must not confine ourselves to this answer. For it is inadequate: for, first, it is itself unclear; and further, the matter turns out to be substance. For if the matter is not substance, it is hard to see what other substance there is; for when all the other things are removed, nothing [but the matter] evidently remains. For the other things are affections, products, and potentialities of bodies; and length, breadth, and depth[17] are kinds of quantities but not substances (for quantity is not substance), but the primary [subject] to which these belong is more of a substance than they are. But when length, breadth, and depth are abstracted, we see that nothing is left, except whatever is determined by these. And so, if we examine it in this way, the matter necessarily appears as the only substance.

By matter I mean what is spoken of in its own right neither as being something, nor as having some quantity, nor as having any of the other things by which being is determined. For there is something of which each of these is predicated, something whose being is different from that of each of the things predicated; for the other things are predicted of the substance, and the substance is predicated of the matter. And so the last thing is in its own right neither something nor of some quantity nor any other [of the thing mentioned]; nor is it [in its own right] the negations of these, since what we have said implies that the negations as well [as the positive properties] belong to it [only] coincidentally.

And so, if we study it from this point of view, the result is that the matter is substance; but that is impossible. For being separable and being a this seem to belong to substance most of all; that is why the form and the [compound] of both [matter and form] would seem to be substance more than the matter is.

And so the substance composed of both—I mean composed of the matter and the form—should be set aside, since it is posterior to the other two, and clear. The matter is also evident in a way. We must, then, consider the third type of substance, since it is the most puzzling.

Since some of the perceptible substances are 1029b
agreed to be substances, we should begin our search with these.

Book 12

6

Since we have found that there are three types of 1071b
substance, two of them natural and one unmoved, we must discuss the third kind, to show that there must be an everlasting unmoved substance. For substances are the primary beings, and if all substances

17. **length, breadth, and depth:** These are the essential properties of bodies.

are perishable, then everything is perishable. But motion cannot come to be or perish (since it has always been), nor can time (since there cannot be a before and an after if there is no time). Motion is also continuous, then, in the same way that time is, since time is either the same as motion or an attribute of it. But the only continuous motion is local motion—specifically, circular motion.

Now if there is something that is capable of initiating, motion or of acting, but it does not actually do so, there will be no motion; for what has a potentiality need not actualize it. It will be no use, then, to assume everlasting substances, as believers in Forms do, unless these include some principle capable of initiating change. And even this, or some other type of substance besides the Forms, is not sufficient; for if it does not actualize its potentiality, there will be no motion. Nor yet is it sufficient if it actualizes its potentiality, but its essence is potentiality; for there will be no everlasting motion, since what has a potentiality need not actualize it. There must, then, be a principle of the sort whose essence is actuality. Further, these substances must be without matter; for they must be everlasting if anything else is to be everlasting, and hence they must be actuality.

Now a puzzle arises. For it seems that whatever actualizes a potentiality must have it, but not everything that has a potentiality also actualizes it; and so potentiality is prior. But now, if this is so, nothing that exists will exist, since things can have the potentiality to exist without actualizing it. And yet, if those who have written about the gods are right to generate everything from night,[18] or if the natural philosophers are right to say that 'all things were together'[19] the same impossibility results. For how will things be moved if there is no cause [initiating motion] in actuality? For surely matter will not initiate motion in itself, but carpentry, [for instance, must initiate the motion]; nor will the menstrual fluid or the earth initiate motion in themselves, but the semen and the seeds [must initiate the motion].

Hence some people—Leucippus and Plato, for instance—believe in everlasting actuality; for they say that there is always motion. But they do not say why there is this motion, or what kind of motion it is, and neither do they state the cause of something's being moved in this way or that. For nothing is moved at random, but in every case there must be some [cause]—as in fact things are moved in one way by nature and in another by force or by the agency of mind[20] or something else. Further, what sort of motion is primary? For that makes an enormous difference. Nor can Plato say that the principle is of the sort that he sometimes thinks it is—what initiates its own motion. For he also says that the soul is later [than motion] and comes into being at the same time as the universe.[21]

The view that potentiality is prior to actuality is in a way correct and in a way incorrect—we have explained how this is so. The priority of actuality is attested by Anaxagoras (since mind is actuality), and by Empedocles (who makes love and strife prior), and by those who say that there is always motion, as Leucippus does. And so chaos or night did not exist for an infinite time, but the same things have always existed (either in a cycle or in some other way), if actuality is prior to potentiality.

If, then, the same things always exist in a cycle, something must always remain actually operating in the same way. And if there is to be coming to be and perishing, then there must be something else that always actually operates, in one way at one time and in another way at another time. This [second mover], then, must actually operate in one way because of itself, and in another way because of something else, and hence either because of some third mover or because of the first mover. Hence it must be because of first mover; for [otherwise] the first mover will cause the motion of both the second and the third. Then surely it is better if the first mover is the cause. For we have seen that it is the cause of what is always the same, and a second mover is the cause of what is different at different times. Clearly both together cause this everlasting succession. Then surely this is also how the motions occur. Why, then, do we need to search for any other principles?

---

18. **from night:** Hesiod.

19. **all things were together:** Anaxagoras.

20. **mind:** *nous*, usually "understanding".

21. **Nor can Plato . . . universe:** Aristotle is probably thinking of *Timaeus* 34b. Plato identifies what moves itself with soul, but he describes soul as coming into existence when some sort of motion already exists.

7

Since it is possible for things to be as we have said they are, and since the only alternative is for everything to come to be from night and from all things being together and from what is not, this may be taken as the solution of the puzzles. There is something, then, that is always being moved in a ceaseless motion, and this motion is circular (this is clear not only from argument but also from what actually happens); and so the first heaven is everlasting. Hence there is also something that initiates motion. And since whatever both is moved and initiates motion is an intermediary there is something that initiates motion without being moved, something that is everlasting and a substance and actuality.

This is how an object of understanding or desire initiates motion; it initiates motion without being moved. The primary objects of desire and of understanding are the same. For what appears fine is the object of appetite, and what is fine is the primary object of wish; and we desire something because it seems [fine], rather than its seeming [fine] because we desire it—for understanding is the principle.

Understanding is moved by its object, and the first column [of opposites] is what is understood in its own right. In this column substance is primary; and the primary substance is the substance that is simple and actually operating. (Being one and being simple are not the same; for being one signifies a measure, while being simple signifies that something is itself in a particular condition.) Further, what is fine and what is choiceworthy for itself are in the same column; and what is primary is in every case either the best or what is analogous to the best.

Division shows that what something is for is among the things that are unmoved. For it is either the end for some [beneficiary] or the end [aimed at] in some [process]; the first of these is moved, and the second is unmoved. The [end] initiates motion by being an object of love, and it initiates motion in the other things by [something else's] being moved.

If, then, something is moved, it can be otherwise. And so, if something's actuality is the primary type of local motion, it follows that insofar as it is in motion, in this respect it admits of being otherwise, in place if not in substance. But since there is something that initiates motion without itself being moved, and this is actually operating, it cannot be otherwise in any respect at all. For local motion is the primary type of motion, and the primary type of local motion is circular motion; and this is the sort of motion that the primary mover initiates. Hence the primary mover exists necessarily; and insofar as it exists necessarily, its being is fine, and insofar as its being is fine, it is a principle. For what is necessary is spoken of in a number of ways—as what is forced because it is contrary to the subject's impulse, as that without which the good cannot be, and as what cannot be otherwise but is necessary without qualification.

This, then, is the sort of principle on which the heaven[22] and nature depend. Its way of life has the same character as our own way of life at its best has for a short time. For the primary mover is always in this state [of complete actuality], whereas we cannot always be in it; for its actuality is also pleasure (that is why being awake, perceiving, and thinking are pleasantest, while expectations and memories are pleasant because of these).

Understanding in its own right is of what is best in its own right, and the highest degree of understanding is of what is best to the highest degree in its own right. And understanding understands itself by sharing the character of the object of understanding; for it becomes an object of understanding by being in contact with and by understanding its object, so that understanding and its object are the same.[23] For understanding is what is capable of receiving the object of understanding and the essence, and it is actually understanding when it possesses its object; and so it is this [actual understanding and possession] rather than [the potentiality to receive the object] that seems to be the divine aspect of understanding, and its actual attention to the object of understanding is pleasantest and best.

If, then, the god is always in the good state that we are in sometimes, that deserves wonder; if he is in a better state, that deserves still more wonder. And that is indeed the state he is in. Further, life belongs to the god. For the actuality of understanding is life, and the god is that actuality; and his actuality in its own right is the best and everlasting life. We say, then, that

---

22. **the heaven:** Aristotle uses "heaven," *ouranos*, both for the upper universe in contrast to the earth and for the universe including the earth.

23. **understanding and its object are the same:** Cf. *De Anima* 430a3.

the god is the best and everlasting living being, so that continuous and everlasting life and duration belong to the god; for that is what the god is.

Some, however, suppose, as the Pythagoreans and Speusippus do, that what is finest and best is not present in the principle, claiming that the principles of plants and animals are their causes, whereas what is fine and complete is found in what results from these. Their view is mistaken. For the seed comes from other [principles] that are prior and complete; and what is primary is not the seed, but the complete [organism]; for instance, one would say that the man is prior to the seed (not the man who comes into being from the seed, but another one, from whom the seed comes).

It is evident from what has been said, then, that there is an everlasting, unmoved substance that is separated from perceptible things. It has also been proved that this substance cannot have any magnitude, but must be without parts and indivisible; for it initiates motion for an infinite time, but nothing finite has infinite potentiality. And since every magnitude is either infinite or finite, [the primary mover] cannot have a finite magnitude, and it cannot have an infinite magnitude, because there is no infinite magnitude at all. Besides, it has also been proved that this substance is not affected or altered, since all other motions depend on local motion. It is clear, then, why these things are so.

8

We must also consider, however, whether we should take there to be one such substance, or more than one, and, if more than one, how many; and we must remember that, on the question about how many there are, other people's views have contributed nothing that can be perspicuously stated. The views about the Ideas, for instance, include no special discussion of the question. For those who speak of Ideas say that the Ideas are numbers, but when they speak of numbers, they sometimes speak as though numbers were infinite, sometimes as though they were finite and went only as far as the number ten; and they make no serious effort to demonstrate the reason why there should be just this many numbers. Let us, however, take what has been laid down and determined as a basis for discussion.

The principle and primary being is unmoved both in its own right and coincidentally, and it initiates the everlasting and single primary motion. Now, what is moved must be moved by something, but the primary mover is unmoved in its own right. Further, an everlasting motion is initiated by an everlasting mover, and a single motion is initiated by a single mover; but we see that besides the simple local motion of the whole, which we say is initiated by the primary and unmoved substance, there are also the everlasting local motions of the planets (for a body that moves in a circle has an everlasting and unceasing motion, as was shown in our work on nature). Hence it necessarily follows that each of these motions is also initiated by the agency of some substance that is unmoved in its own right and everlasting. For the nature of the stars is everlasting and is a type of substance; and what initiates motion is everlasting and prior to what is moved; and what is prior to a substance must be a substance. It is evident, then, that there must be this number of substances that are everlasting in their nature and unmoved in their own right, and (for the reason given above) without magnitude.

It is evident, then, that there are substances, and that one of them is first and another second, in an order corresponding to the motions of the stars. But when we come to the number of these motions, we must examine it on the basis of the mathematical science that is closest to philosophy, i.e. astronomy. For astronomy studies a kind of substance that is perceptible, but still everlasting, whereas the other mathematical sciences—those concerned with numbers and with geometry, for instance—do not study any substance at all.

Now it is evident, even on moderate acquaintance, that there are more motions than there are bodies moved, since each of the planets has more than one motion. On the question of how many motions there are, we now state what some of the mathematicians say, in order to form some conception [of an answer], so that we can suppose some definite number in our thinking. Beyond this [provisional answer] we must on some points inquire ourselves and on other points find out from other people's inquiries. If something different from what is now said appears correct to later students, we must be friends to both sides, but must follow the more exact investigators.

Eudoxus thought that the motion of the sun and the moon in each case involves three spheres. The first is the sphere of the fixed stars; the second moves in the circle along the middle of the zodiac; the third moves in the circle inclined across the breadth of the zodiac; and the moon's circle is inclined at a greater angle than the sun's circle. The motion of each planet involves four spheres. The first and second of these are the same as for the sun and the moon; for the sphere of the fixed stars is the one that moves all the spheres, and the sphere placed under this, moving in the circle along the middle of the zodiac, is also common to all the spheres. But the third sphere of each of the planets has its poles in the circle along the middle of the zodiac; and the fourth moves along the circle inclined at an angle to the equator of the third sphere. And the poles of the third sphere are different for each of the planets, except that for Venus and Mercury they are the same.

Callippus agreed with Eudoxus about the position of the spheres. On their number, he agreed with Eudoxus for Jupiter and Saturn, but for the sun and the moon he thought two further spheres must be added in order to yield the appearances, and that one must be added for each of the other planets.

1074a In fact, however, it is necessary, if all the combined spheres together are to yield the appearances, to admit further spheres (one fewer [than those mentioned]) that counteract [the previous spheres], and in each case restore to the same position the first sphere of the star that is placed beneath the given star. For only in that way is it possible for all the combined spheres to produce the motions of the planets.

And so the spheres in which the planets themselves move are eight and twenty-five; and only the spheres in which the lowest-placed planet moves need no counteracting spheres. Hence the spheres counteracting the spheres of the first two planets will be six, and those counteracting the spheres of the next four will be sixteen. Hence the total number of the [forward-] moving and counteracting spheres will be fifty-five. If we do not add to the moon and sun the motions we mentioned, then the total number of the spheres will be forty-seven.

Let this, then, be the number of the spheres. In that case the supposition that this is also the number of unmoved substances and principles is reasonable—we can leave talk of necessity to stronger people.

And if every local motion [in the heaven] must contribute to the motion of a star, and if every nature and every substance that is unaffected and that in its own right has achieved the best must be regarded as an end, it follows that there can be no other natures besides these, and that this must be the number of substances. For if there were other substances, they would have to initiate motions by being the end of local motion; but there cannot be any other local motion besides those mentioned above. It is reasonable to infer this from the bodies that are moved. For if everything that initiates local motion is for the sake of what is moved, and if every motion is the motion of something that is moved, then no motion is for its own sake or for the sake of some other motion, but every motion is for the sake of the stars. For if every motion were for the sake of some further motion, then that further motion would have to be for the sake of something else; and so, since it cannot go on to infinity, one of the divine bodies, that is moved in the heaven must be the end of every motion.

It is evident that there is only one heaven. For if there were a number of heavens, as there are a number of men, then the principle—one for each heaven—would be specifically one but numerically many. Now, things that are numerically many all have matter; for many [particulars] have one and the same account—that of man, for instance—but Socrates is one [particular]. But the primary essence has no matter, since it is actuality. Hence the primary and unmoved mover is one in number and account; so also, then, is what is always and continuously moved; and so there is only one heaven.

There is a tradition handed down from the distant *1074b* past to later generations, that these stars are gods and that the whole of nature is divine. The rest of the tradition is a mythical accretion, added to persuade the many and to use in upholding what is lawful and advantageous; for those who handed it down say that the gods have human form or are similar to other animals, and they add other features following from these and similar to them. But if we separate the first point—that they thought the primary substances were gods—from these accretions, and consider it alone, we will regard it as a divine insight, on the assumption that every craft and philosophical discipline has probably often been discovered, as far as people could manage it, and has often been forgotten, and that this belief has survived like remains from earlier generations until the present. And so [the truth of] the ancestral beliefs coming from the earliest times is evident to us only to this extent.

9

The nature of [divine] understanding raises a number of puzzles. For understanding seems to be the most divine of the things we observe, but many difficulties arise about what state it must be in if it is to be so divine. For if it understands nothing, what is so impressive about it? It would be like someone asleep. If, on the other hand, it does understand, but something else controls whether it understands (since its essence is not actual understanding, but the potentiality for it), it is not the best substance; for what makes it valuable comes from [actual] understanding.

And in any case, whether its essence is potential or actual understanding, what does it understand? It must understand either itself or something else; if something else, then either always the same thing or else different things at different times. Then does it make any difference whether the object of its understanding is fine or is just any old thing? Surely there are some things that it would be absurd for it to think about. Clearly, then, it understands what is most divine and most valuable, and it does not change; for the change would be to something worse, and it would thereby also be a motion.

First, then, if it is potential, not actual, understanding, it is a reasonable to expect that the continuous [exercise of] understanding would be tiring for it. Moreover, clearly something other than understanding—namely the object of understanding—would be more valuable. For indeed both the potentiality and the activity of understanding will belong even to someone who understands the worst thing; and if this is to be avoided (since there are also some things it is better not to see than to see), then the activity of understanding is not the best thing.

[The divine understanding,] then, must understand itself, so that its understanding is an understanding of understanding. In every case, however, knowledge, perception, belief, and thought have something other than themselves as their object; each has itself as its object as a by-product. Further, if to understand and to be understood are different, which is responsible for the presence of the good? For to be an act of understanding is not the same as to be understood.

Well, perhaps in some cases the knowledge is the object. In the productive [sciences, the knowledge is] the substance and essence [of the product] without the matter, and in the theoretical sciences, the account is both the object and the understanding. In these cases, then, where the object of understanding does not differ from understanding—i.e. in cases where the object has no matter—the object and the understanding will be the same, and the activity of understanding will be one with its object.

One puzzle still remains: Is the object of understanding composite? If it were composite, understanding would change in [understanding different] parts of the whole. Perhaps we should say that whatever has no matter is indivisible. [On this view, the condition of actual understanding is] the condition that human understanding (or rather, the understanding of any composite beings) reaches over a certain length of time; for it does not possess the good at this or that time, but achieves the best, which is something other than it, in some whole [period of time]. And this is the condition the understanding that understands itself is in throughout all time.

Nicomachean Ethics and Politics

The *Nicomachean Ethics* is one of the greatest works in all of moral philosophy, representing the culmination of Aristotle's mature thought. Likewise, Aristotle's *Politics* is considered, along with Plato's *Republic*, to be one of the greatest works of political philosophy.

In the excerpts of the *Nicomachean Ethics* presented here, Aristotle discusses happiness and human good (Book 1); the nature of moral virtue (Book 2); moral responsibility, deliberation, and praise and blame (Book 3); justice (Book 5); the intellectual virtues and practical wisdom (Book 6); weakness of the will (Book 7); and happiness and contemplation (Book 10).

In the excerpts of the *Politics* presented later, Aristotle discusses the definition and structure of the state (Book 1); the classification of constitutions and forms of government (Book 3); the desirability of the middle class in nonideal political conditions (Book 4); and his own account of the best state (Book 7).

Nicomachean Ethics

Book 1

1

1094a Every craft and every investigation, and likewise every action and decision, seems to aim at some good; hence the good has been well described as that at which everything aims.

However, there is an apparent difference among the ends aimed at. For the end is sometimes an activity, sometimes a product beyond the activity; and when there is an end beyond the action, the product is by nature better than activity.

Since there are many actions, crafts and sciences, the ends turn out to be many as well; for health is the end of medicine, a boat of boatbuilding, victory of generalship, and wealth of household management.

But whenever any of these sciences are subordinate to some one capacity—as e.g. bridlemaking and every other science producing equipment for horses are subordinate to horsemanship, while this and every action in warfare are in turn subordinate to generalship, and in the same way other sciences are subordinate to further ones—in each of these the end of the ruling science is more choiceworthy than all the ends subordinate to it since it is the end for which those ends are also pursued. And here it does not matter whether the ends of the actions are the activities themselves, or some product beyond them, as in the sciences we have mentioned.

2

Suppose, then, that (a) there is some end of the things we pursue in our actions which we wish for because of itself, and because of which we wish for the other things; and (b) we do not choose everything because of something else, since (c) if we do, it will go on without limit, making desire empty and futile; then clearly (d) this end will be the good, i.e. the best good.

Then surely knowledge of this good is also of great importance for the conduct of our lives, and if, like archers, we have a target to aim at, we are more likely to hit the right mark. If so, we should try to grasp, in outline at any rate, what the good is, and which science or capacity is concerned with it.

It seems to concern the most controlling science, the one that, more than any other, is the ruling science. And political science apparently has this character.

(1) For it is the one that prescribes which of the sciences ought to be studied in cites, and which ones each class in the city should learn, and how far. 1094b

(2) Again, we see that even the most honored capacities, e.g. generalship, household management and rhetoric, are subordinate to it.

(3) Further, it uses the other sciences concerned with action, and moreover legislates what must be done and what avoided.

Hence its end will include the ends of the other sciences, and so will be human good.

[This is properly called political science;] for though admittedly the good is the same for a city as for an individual, still the good of the city is apparently a greater and more complete good to acquire and preserve. For while it is satisfactory to acquire and preserve the good even for an individual, it is finer and more divine to acquire and preserve it for a people and for cities. And so, since our investigation

---

aims at these [goods, for an individual and for a city], it is a sort of political science.

3

Our discussion will be adequate if its degree of clarity fits the subject matter; for we should not seek the same degree of exactness in all sorts of arguments alike, any more than in the products of different crafts.

Moreover, what is fine and what is just, the topics of inquiry in political science, differ and vary so much that they seem to rest on convention only, not on nature. Goods, however, also vary in the same sort of way, since they cause harm to many people; for it has happened that some people have been destroyed because of their wealth, others because of their bravery.

Since these, then, are the sorts of things we argue from and about, it will be satisfactory if we can indicate the truth roughly and in outline; since [that is to say] we argue from and about what holds good usually [but not universally], it will be satisfactory if we can draw conclusions of the same sort.

Each of our claims, then, ought to be accepted in the same way [as claiming to hold good usually], since the educated person seeks exactness in each area to the extent that the nature of the subject allows; for apparently it is just as mistaken to demand demonstrations from a rhetorician as to accept [merely] persuasive arguments from a mathematician.

Further, each person judges well what he knows,
1095a and is a good judge about that; hence the good judge in a particular area is the person educated in that area, and the unconditionally good judge is the person educated in every area.

This is why a youth is not a suitable student of political science; for he lacks experience of the actions in life which political science argues from and about.

Moreover, since he tends to be guided by his feelings, his study will be futile and useless; for its end is action, not knowledge. And here it does not matter whether he is young in years or immature in character, since the deficiency does not depend on age, but results from being guided in his life and in each of his pursuits by his feelings; for an immature person, like an incontinent person, gets no benefit from his knowledge.

If, however, we are guided by reason in forming our desires and in acting, then this knowledge will be of great benefit.

These are the preliminary points about the student, about the way our claims are to be accepted, and about what we intend to do.

4

Let us, then, begin again. Since every sort of knowledge and decision pursues some good, what is that good which we say is the aim of political science? What [in other words] is the highest of all the goods pursued in action?

As far as its name goes, most people virtually agree [about what the good is], since both the many and the cultivated call it happiness, and suppose that living well and doing well are the same as being happy. But they disagree about what happiness is, and the many do not give the same answer as the wise.

For the many think it is something obvious and evident, e.g. pleasure, wealth or honor, some thinking one thing, others another; and indeed the same person keeps changing his mind, since in sickness he thinks it is health, in poverty wealth. And when they are conscious of their own ignorance, they admire anyone who speaks of something grand and beyond them.

[Among the wise,] however, some used to think that besides these many goods there is some other good that is something in itself, and also causes all these goods to be goods.

Presumably, then, it is rather futile to examine all these beliefs, and it is enough to examine those that are most current or seem to have some argument for them.

We must notice, however, the difference between arguments from origins and arguments towards origins. For indeed Plato was right to be puzzled about this, when he used to ask if [the argument] set out from the origins or led towards them—just as on a race course the path may go from the starting-line to 1095
the far end,[1] or back again.

For while we should certainly begin from origins that are known, things are known in two ways; for some are known to us, some known unconditionally

1. **far end:** lit. "limit." Aristotle thinks of a Greek stadium, in which the midpoint of the race is at the end farthest from the starting line.

[but not necessarily known to us]. Presumably, then, the origin *we* should begin from is what is known to *us*.

This is why we need to have been brought up in fine habits if we are to be adequate students of what is fine and just, and of political questions generally. For the origin we begin from is the belief that something is true, and if this is apparent enough to us, we will not, at this stage, need the reason why it is true in addition; and if we have this good upbringing, we have the origins to begin from, or can easily acquire them. Someone who neither has them nor can acquire them should listen to Hesiod: 'He who understands everything himself is best of all; he is noble also who listens to one who has spoken well; but he who neither understands it himself nor takes to heart what he hears from another is a useless man.'

5

But let us begin again from [the common beliefs] from which we digressed. For, it would seem, people quite reasonably reach their conception of the good, i.e. of happiness, from the lives [they lead]; for there are roughly three most favored lives—the lives of gratification, of political activity, and, third, of study.

The many, the most vulgar, would seem to conceive the good and happiness as pleasure, and hence they also like the life of gratification. Here they appear completely slavish, since the life they decide on is a life for grazing animals; and yet they have some argument in their defense, since many in positions of power feel the same way as Sardanapallus[2] [and also choose this life].

The cultivated people, those active [in politics], conceive the good as honor, since this is more or less the end [normally pursued] in the political life. This, however, appears to be too superficial to be what we are seeking, since it seems to depend more on those who honor than on the one honored, whereas we intuitively believe that the good is something of our own and hard to take from us.

Further, it would seem, they pursue honor to convince themselves that they are good; at any rate, they seek to be honored by intelligent people, among people who know them, and for virtue. It is clear, then, that in the view of active people at least, virtue is superior [to honor].

Perhaps, indeed, one might conceive virtue more than honor to be the end of the political life. However, this also is apparently too incomplete [to be the good]. For, it seems, someone might possess virtue but be asleep or inactive throughout his life; or, further, *1096a* he might suffer the worst evils and misfortunes; and if this is the sort of life he leads, no one would count him happy, except to defend a philosopher's paradox. Enough about this, since it has been adequately discussed in the popular works[3] also.

The third life is the life of study, which we will examine in what follows.

The money-maker's life is in a way forced on him [not chosen for itself]; and clearly wealth is not the good we are seeking, since it is [merely] useful, [choiceworthy only] for some other end. Hence one would be more inclined to suppose that [any of] the goods mentioned earlier is the end, since they are liked for themselves. But apparently they are not [the end] either; and many arguments have been presented against them. Let us, then, dismiss them.

7

But let us return once again to the good we are looking for, and consider just what it could be, since it is apparently one thing in one action or craft, and another thing in another; for it is one thing in medicine, another in generalship, and so on for the rest.

What, then, is the good in each of these cases? Surely it is that for the sake of which the other things are done; and in medicine this is health, in generalship victory, in house-building a house, in another case something else, but in every action and decision it is the end, since it is for the sake of the end that everyone does the other things.

And so, if there is some end of everything that is pursued in action, this will be the good pursued in action; and if there are more ends than one, these will be the goods pursued in action.

Our argument has progressed, then, to the same conclusion [as before, that the highest end is the good]; but we must try to clarify this still more.

---

2. **Sardanapallus:** An Assyrian king who lived in legendary luxury.

3. **the popular works:** (*enkuklia*) Probably these are by Aristotle himself.

Though apparently there are many ends, we choose some of them, e.g. wealth, flutes and, in general, instruments, because of something else; hence it is clear that not all ends are complete. But the best good is apparently something complete. Hence, if only one end is complete, this will be what we are looking for; and if more than one are complete, the most complete of these will be what we are looking for.

An end pursued in itself, we say, is more complete than an end pursued because of something else; and an end that is never choiceworthy because of something else is more complete than ends that are choiceworthy both in themselves and because of this end; and hence an end that is always [choiceworthy, and also] choiceworthy in itself, never because of something else, is unconditionally complete.

Now happiness more than anything else seems unconditionally complete, since we always [choose it, and also] choose it because of itself, never because of something else.

Honor, pleasure, understanding and every virtue we certainly choose because of themselves, since we would choose each of them even if it had no further result, but we also choose them for the sake of happiness, supposing that through them we shall be happy. Happiness, by contrast, no one ever chooses for their sake, or for the sake of anything else at all.

The same conclusion [that happiness is complete] also appears to follow from self-sufficiency, since the complete good seems to be self-sufficient.

Now what we count as self-sufficient is not what suffices for a solitary person by himself, living an isolated life, but what suffices also for parents, children, wife and in general for friends and fellow-citizens, since a human being is a naturally political [animal], Here, however, we must impose some limit; for if we extend the good to parents' parents and children's children and to friends of friends, we shall go on without limit; but we must examine this another time.

Anyhow, we regard something as self-sufficient when all by itself it makes a life choiceworthy and lacking nothing; and that is what we think happiness does.

Moreover, we think happiness is most choiceworthy of all goods, since it is not counted as one good among many. If it were counted as one among many, then, clearly, we think that the addition of the smallest of goods would make it more choiceworthy; for [the smallest good] that is added becomes an extra quantity of goods [so creating a good larger than the original good], and the larger of two goods is always more choiceworthy. [But we do not think any addition can make happiness more choiceworthy; hence it is most choiceworthy.]

Happiness, then, is apparently something complete and self-sufficient, since it is the end of the things pursued in action.

But presumably the remark that the best good is happiness is apparently something [generally] agreed, and what we miss is a clearer statement of what the best good is.

Well, perhaps we shall find the best good if we first find the function of a human being. For just as the good, i.e. [doing] well, for a flautist, a sculptor, and every craftsman, and, in general, for whatever has a function and [characteristic] action, seems to depend on its function, the same seems to be true for a human being, if a human being has some function.

Then do the carpenter and the leatherworker have their functions and actions, while a human being has none, and is by nature idle, without any function? Or, just as eye, hand, foot and, in general, every [bodily] part apparently has its functions, may we likewise ascribe to a human being some function besides all of theirs?

What, then, could this be? For living is apparently shared with plants, but what we are looking for is the special function of a human being; hence we should set aside the life of nutrition and growth. The life next in order is some sort of life of sense-perception; but this too is apparently shared with horse, ox and every animal. The remaining possibility, then, is some sort of life of action of the [part of the soul] that has reason.

Now this [part has two parts, which have reason in different ways], one as obeying the reason [in the other part], the other as itself having reason and thinking. [We intend both.] Moreover, life is also spoken of in two ways [as capacity and as activity], and we must take [a human being's special function to be] life as activity, since this seems to be called life to a fuller extent.

(a) We have found, then, that the human function is the soul's activity that expresses reason [as itself having reason] or requires reason [as obeying reason]. (b) Now the function of *F*, e.g. of a harpist, is the same in kind, so we say, as the function of an excellent *F*, e.g. an excellent harpist. (c) The same is true unconditionally in every case, when we add to the function the superior achievement that expresses the virtue; for a harpist's function, e.g. is to play the harp, and a good harpist's is to do it well. (d) Now we take the human function to be a certain kind of life, and take this life to be the soul's activity and actions that express reason. (e)[Hence by (c) and (d)] the excellent man's function is to do this finely and well. (f) Each function is completed well when its completion expresses the proper virtue. (g) Therefore [by (d), (e) and (f)] the human good turns out to be the soul's activity that expresses virtue.

And if there are more virtues than one, the good will express the best and most complete virtue. Moreover, it will be in a complete life. For one swallow does not make a spring, nor does one day; nor similarly does one day or a short time make us blessed and happy.

This, then, is a sketch of the good; for, presumably, the outline must come first, to be filled in later. If the sketch is good, then anyone, it seems, can advance and articulate it, and in such cases time is a good discoverer or [at least] a good co-worker. That is also how the crafts have improved, since anyone can add what is lacking [in the outline].

However, we must also remember our previous remarks, so that we do not look for the same degree of exactness in all areas, but the degree that fits the subject-matter in each area and is proper to the investigation. For the carpenter's and the geometer's inquiries about the right angle are different also; the carpenter's is confined to the right angle's usefulness for his work, whereas the geometer's concerns what, or what sort of thing, the right angle is, since he studies the truth. We must do the same, then, in other areas too, [seeking the proper degree of exactness], so that digressions do not overwhelm our main task.

1098b Nor should we make the same demand for an explanation in all cases. Rather, in some cases it is enough to prove that something is true without explaining why it is true. This is so, e.g. with origins, where the fact that something is true is the first principle, i.e. the origin.

Some origins are studied by means of induction, some by means of perception, some by means of some sort of habituation, and others by other means. In each case we should try to find them out by means suited to their nature, and work hard to define them well. For they have a great influence on what follows; for the origin seems to be more than half the whole,[4] and makes evident the answer to many of our questions.

8

However, we should examine the origin not only from the conclusion and premises [of a deductive argument], but also from what is said about it; for all the facts harmonize with a true account, whereas the truth soon clashes with a false one.

Goods are divided, then, into three types, some called external, some goods of the soul, others goods of the body; and the goods of the soul are said to be goods to the fullest extent and most of all, and the soul's actions and activities are ascribed to the soul. Hence the account [of the good] is sound, to judge by this belief anyhow—and it is an ancient belief agreed on by philosophers.

Our account is also correct in saying that some sort of actions and activities are the end; for then the end turns out to be a good of the soul, not an external good.

The belief that the happy person lives well and does well in action also agrees with our account, since we have virtually said that the end is a sort of living well and doing well in action.

Further, all the features that people look for in happiness appear to be true of the end described in our account. For to some people it seems to be virtue; to others intelligence; to others some sort of wisdom; to others again it seems to be these, or one of these, involving pleasure or requiring its addition; and others add in external prosperity as well.

Some of these views are traditional, held by many, while others are held by a few reputable men; and it is reasonable for each group to be not entirely in error, but correct on one point at least, or even on most points.

First, our account agrees with those who say happiness is virtue [in general] or some [particular] virtue; for activity expressing virtue is proper to virtue. Presumably, though, it matters quite a bit whether we suppose that the best good consists in possessing or in using, i.e. in a state or in an activity

4. **the origin seems . . .** : A Greek proverb—i.e., "well begun is more than half done."

[that actualizes the state]. For while someone may be in a state that achieves no good, if, e.g., he is asleep
1099a or inactive in some other way, this cannot be true of the activity; for it will necessarily do actions and do well in them. And just as Olympic prizes are not for the finest and strongest, but for contestants, since it is only these who win; so also in life [only] the fine and good people who act correctly win the prize.

Moreover, the life of these [active] people is also pleasant in itself. For being pleased is a condition of the soul, [hence included in the activity of the soul]. Further, each type of person finds pleasure in whatever he is called a lover of, so that a horse, e.g. pleases the horse-lover, a spectacle the lover of spectacles, and similarly what is just pleases the lover of justice, and in general what expresses virtue pleases the lover of virtue. Hence the things that please most people conflict, because they are not pleasant by nature, whereas the things that please lovers of what is fine are things pleasant by nature; and actions expressing virtue are pleasant in this way; and so they both please lovers of what is fine and are pleasant in themselves.

Hence their life does not need pleasure to be added [to virtuous activity] as some sort of ornament; rather, it has its pleasure within itself. For besides the reasons already given, someone who does not enjoy fine actions is not good; for no one would call him just; e.g., if he did not enjoy doing just actions, or generous if he did not enjoy generous actions, and similarly for the other virtues. If this is so, then actions expressing the virtues are pleasant in themselves.

Moreover, these actions are good and fine as well as pleasant; indeed, they are good, fine and pleasant more than anything else, since on this question the excellent person has good judgement, and his judgement agrees with our conclusions.

Happiness, then, is best, finest and most pleasant, and these three features are not distinguished in the way suggested by the Delian inscription: 'What is most just is finest; being healthy is most beneficial; but it is most pleasant to win our heart's desire.' For all three features are found in the best activities, and happiness we say is these activities, or [rather] one of them, the best one.

Nonetheless, happiness evidently also needs external goods to be added [to the activity], as we said, since we cannot, or cannot easily, do fine actions if we lack the resources.

For, first of all, in many actions we use friends, 1099b
wealth and political power just as we use instruments. Further, deprivation of certain [externals]—e.g. good birth, good children, beauty—mars our blessedness; for we do not altogether have the character of happiness if we look utterly repulsive or are ill-born, solitary or childless, and have it even less, presumably, if our children or friends are totally bad, or were good but have died.

And so, as we have said, happiness would seem to need this sort of prosperity added also; that is why some people identify happiness with good fortune, while others [reacting from one extreme to the other] identify it with virtue.

9

This [question about the role of fortune] raises a puzzle: Is happiness acquired by learning, or habituation, or by some other form of cultivation? Or is it the result of some divine fate, or even of fortune?

First, then, if the gods give any gift at all to human beings, it is reasonable for them to give happiness also; indeed, it is reasonable to give happiness more than any other human [good], insofar as it is the best of human [goods]. Presumably, however, this question is more suitable for a different inquiry.

But even if it is not sent by the gods, but instead results from virtue and some sort of learning or cultivation, happiness appears to be one of the most divine things, since the prize and goal of virtue appears to be the best good, something divine and blessed.

Moreover [if happiness come in this way] it will be widely shared; for anyone who is not deformed [in his capacity] for virtue will be able to achieve happiness through some sort of learning and attention.

And since it is better to be happy in this way than because of fortune, it is reasonable for this to be the way [we become] happy. For whatever is natural is naturally in the finest state possible, and so are the products of crafts and of every other cause, especially the best cause; and it would be seriously inappropriate to entrust what is greatest and finest to fortune.

The answer to our question is also evident from our account [of happiness]. For we have said it is a certain sort of activity of the soul expressing virtue, [and hence not a product of fortune]; and some of the other goods are necessary conditions [of happiness], others are naturally useful and cooperative as instruments [but are not parts of it].

Further, this conclusion agrees with our opening remarks. For we took the goal of political science to be the best good; and most of its attention is devoted to the character of the citizens, to make them good people who do fine actions, [which is reasonable if happiness depends on virtue, not on fortune].

It is not surprising, then, that we regard neither ox nor horse nor any other kind of animal as happy, since none of them can share in this sort of activity. *1100a* And for the same reason a child is not happy either, since his age prevents him from doing these sorts of actions; and if he is called happy, he is being congratulated because of anticipated blessedness, since, as we have said, happiness requires both complete virtue and a complete life.

[Happiness needs a complete life.] For life includes many reversals of fortune, good and bad, and the most prosperous person may fall into a terrible disaster in old age, as the Trojan stories tell us about Priam; but if someone has suffered these sorts of misfortunes and comes to a miserable end, no one counts him happy.

13

Since happiness is an activity of the soul expressing complete virtue, we must examine virtue; for that will perhaps also be a may to study happiness better.

Moreover, the true politician seems to have spent more effort on virtue than on anything else, since he wants to make the citizens good and law-abiding. We find an example of this in the Spartan and Cretan legislators and in any others with their concerns. Since, then, the examination of virtue is proper for political science, the inquiry clearly suits our original decision [to pursue political science].

It is clear that the virtue we must examine is human virtue, since we are also seeking the human good and human happiness. And by human virtue we mean virtue of the soul, not of the body, since we also say that happiness is an activity of the soul. If this is so, then it is clear that the politician must acquire some knowledge about the soul, just as someone setting out to heal the eyes must acquire knowledge about the whole body as well. This is all the more true to the extent that political science is better and more honorable than medicine—and even among doctors the cultivated ones devote a lot of effort to acquiring knowledge about the body. Hence the politician as well [as the student of nature] must study the soul.

But he must study it for the purpose [of inquiring into virtue], as far as suffices for what he seeks; for a more exact treatment would presumably take more effort than his purpose requires. [We] have discussed the soul sufficiently [for our purpose] in [our] popular works as well[5] [as our less popular], and we should use this discussion.

We have said, e.g., that one [part] of the soul is nonrational, while one has reason. Are these distinguished as parts of a body and everything divisible into parts are? Or are they two only in account, and inseparable by nature, as the convex and the concave are in a surface? It does not matter for present purposes.

Consider the nonrational [part]. One [part] of it, i.e. the cause of nutrition and growth, is seemingly plant-like and shared [with other living things]: for we can ascribe this capacity of soul to everything that *1102b* is nourished, including embryos, and the same one to complete living things, since this is more reasonable than to ascribe another capacity to them.

Hence the virtue of this capacity is apparently shared, not [specifically] human. For this part and capacity more than others seem to be active in sleep, and here the good and the bad person are least distinct, which is why happy people are said to be no better off than miserable people for half their lives.

And this lack of distinction is not surprising, since sleep is inactivity of the soul insofar as it is called excellent or base, unless to some small extent some movements penetrate [to our awareness], and in this way the decent person comes to have better images [in dreams] than just any random person has. Enough about this, however, and let us leave aside the nutritive part, since by nature it has no share in human virtue.

Another nature in the soul would also seem to be nonrational, though in a way it shares in reason.

[Clearly it is nonrational.] For in the continent and the incontinent person we praise their reason, i.e. the [part] of the soul that has reason, because it

---

5. **in [our] . . . as well:** or perhaps "even in the popular works," on which see note to 1096a3.

exhorts them correctly and towards what is best; but they evidently also have in them some other [part] that is by nature something besides reason, conflicting and struggling with reason.

For just as paralysed parts of a body, when we decide to move them to the right, do the contrary and move off to the left, the same is true of the soul; for incontinent people have impulses in contrary directions. In bodies, admittedly, we see the part go astray, whereas we do not see it in the soul; nonetheless, presumably, we should suppose that the soul also has a [part] besides reason, contrary to and countering reason. The [precise] way it is different does not matter.

However, this [part] as well [as the rational part] appears, as we said, to share in reason. At any rate, in the continent person it obeys reason; and in the temperate and the brave person it presumably listens still better to reason, since there it agrees with reason in everything.

The nonrational [part], then, as well [as the whole soul] apparently has two parts. For while the plantlike [part] shares in reason not at all, the [part] with appetites and in general desires shares in reason in a way insofar as it both listens to reason and obeys it.

It listens in the way in which we are said to 'listen to reason' from father or friends, not in the way in which we ['give the reason'] in mathematics.

The nonrational part also [obeys and] is persuaded
1103a in some way by reason, as is shown by chastening, and by every sort of reproof and exhortation.

If we ought to say, then, that this [part] also has reason, then the [part] that has reason, as well [as the nonrational part] will have two parts, one that has reason to the full extent by having it within itself, and another [that has it] by listening to reason as to a father.

The distinction between virtues also reflects this difference. For some virtues are called virtues of thought, others virtues of character; wisdom, comprehension and intelligence are called virtues of thought, generosity and temperance virtues of character.

For when we speak of someone's character we do not say that he is wise or has good comprehension, but that he is gentle or temperate. [Hence these are the virtues of character.] And yet, we also praise the wise person for his state, and the states that are praiseworthy are the ones we call virtues. [Hence wisdom is also a virtue.]

Book 2

1

Virtue, then, is of two sorts, virtue of thought and virtue of character. Virtue of thought arises and grows mostly from teaching, and hence needs experience and time. Virtue of character [i.e. of *ēthos*] results from habit [*ethos*]; hence its name 'ethical', slightly varied from '*ethos*'.

Hence it is also clear that none of the virtues of character arises in us naturally.

For if something is by nature [in one condition], habituation cannot bring it into another condition. A stone, e.g., by nature moves downwards, and habituation could not make it move upwards, not even if you threw it up ten thousand times to habituate it; nor could habituation make fire move downwards, or bring anything that is by nature in one condition into another condition.

Thus the virtues arise in us neither by nature nor against nature. Rather, we are by nature able to acquire them, and reach our complete perfection through habit.

Further, if something arises in us by nature, we first have the capacity for it, and later display the activity. This is clear in the case of the senses; for we did not acquire them by frequent seeing or hearing, but already had them when we exercised them, and did not get them by exercising them.

Virtues, by contrast, we acquire, just as we acquire crafts, by having previously activated them. For we learn a craft by producing the same product that we must produce when we have learned it, becoming builders, e.g., by building and harpists by playing the harp; so also, then, we become just by doing just actions, temperate by doing temperate actions, brave 1103b
by doing brave actions.

What goes on in cities is evidence for this also. For the legislator makes the citizens good by habituating them, and this is the wish of every legislator; if he fails to do it well he misses his goal. [The right] habituation is what makes the difference between a good political system and a bad one.

Further, just as in the case of a craft, the sources and means that develop each virtue also ruin it. For playing the harp makes both good and bad harpists, and it is analogous in the case of builders and all the rest; for building well makes good builders, building badly, bad ones. If it were not so, no teacher would be needed, but everyone would be born a good or a bad craftsman.

It is the same, then, with the virtues. For actions in dealings with [other] human beings make some people just, some unjust; actions in terrifying situations and the acquired habit of fear or confidence make some brave and others cowardly. The same is true of situations involving appetites and anger; for one or another sort of conduct in these situations makes some people temperate and gentle, others intemperate and irascible.

To sum up, then, in a single account: A state [of character] arises from [the repetition of] similar activities. Hence we must display the right activities, since differences in these imply corresponding differences in the states. It is not unimportant, then, to acquire one sort of habit or another, right from our youth; rather, it is very important, indeed all-important.

2

Our present inquiry does not aim, as our others do, at study; for the purpose of our examination is not to know what virtue is, but to become good, since otherwise the inquiry would be of no benefit to us. Hence we must examine the right way to act, since, as we have said, the actions also control the character of the states we acquire.

First, then, actions should express correct reason. That is a common [belief], and let us assume it; later we will say what correct reason is and how it is related to the other virtues.

1104a But let us take it as agreed in advance that every account of the actions we must do has to be stated in outline, not exactly. As we also said at the start, the type of accounts we demand should reflect the subject-matter; and questions about actions and expediency, like questions about health, have no fixed [and invariable answers].

And when our general account is so inexact, the account of particular cases is all the more inexact. For these fall under no craft or profession, and the agents themselves must consider in each case what the opportune action is, as doctors and navigators do.

The account we offer, then, in our present inquiry is of this inexact sort; still, we must try to offer help.

First, then, we should observe that these sorts of states naturally tend to be ruined by excess and deficiency. We see this happen with strength and health, which we mention because we must use what is evident as a witness to what is not. For both excessive and deficient exercises ruin strength; and likewise, too much or too little eating or drinking ruins health, while the proportionate amount produces, increases and preserves it.

The same is true, then, of temperance, bravery and the other virtues. For if, e.g., someone avoids and is afraid of everything, standing firm against nothing, he becomes cowardly, but if he is afraid of nothing at all and goes to face everything, he becomes rash. Similarly, if he gratifies himself with every pleasure and refrains from none, he becomes intemperate, but if he avoids them all, as boors do, he becomes some sort of insensible person. Temperance and bravery, then, are ruined by excess and deficiency but preserved by the mean.

The same actions, then, are the sources and causes both of the emergence and growth of virtues and of their ruin; but further, the activities of the virtues will be found in these same actions. For this is also true of more evident cases, e.g. strength, which arises from eating a lot and from withstanding much hard labor, and it is the strong person who is most able to do these very things. It is the same with the virtues. Refraining from pleasures makes us become temperate, and when we have become temperate we are most able to refrain from pleasures. And it is similar *1104b* with bravery; habituation in disdaining what is fearful and in standing firm against it makes us become brave, and when we have become brave we shall be most able to stand firm.

3

But [actions are not enough]; we must take as a sign of someone's state his pleasure or pain in consequence of his action. For if someone who abstains from bodily pleasures enjoys the abstinence itself, then he is temperate, but if he is grieved by it, he is intemperate. Again, if he stands firm against terrifying situations and enjoys it, or at least does not find it painful, then he is brave, and if he finds it painful, he is cowardly.

[Pleasures and pains are appropriately taken as signs] because virtue of character is concerned with pleasures and pains.

(1) For it is pleasure that causes us to do base actions, and pain that causes us to abstain from fine ones. Hence we need to have had the appropriate upbringing—right from early youth, as Plato says—to make us find enjoyment or pain in the right things; for this is the correct education.

(2) Further, virtues are concerned with actions and feelings; but every feeling and every action implies pleasure or pain; hence, for this reason too, virtue is concerned with pleasures and pains.

(3) Corrective treatment [for vicious actions] also indicates [the relevance of pleasure and pain], since it uses pleasures and pains; it uses them because such correction is a form of medical treatment, and medical treatment naturally operates through contraries.

(4) Further, as we said earlier, every state of soul is naturally related to and concerned with whatever naturally makes it better or worse; and pleasures and pains make people worse, from pursuing and avoiding the wrong ones, at the wrong time, in the wrong ways, or whatever other distinctions of that sort are needed in an account.

These [bad effects of pleasure and pain] are the reason why people actually define the virtues as ways of being unaffected and undisturbed [by pleasures and pains]. They are wrong, however, because they speak [of being unaffected] unconditionally, not of being unaffected in the right or wrong way, at the right or wrong time, and the added specifications.

We assume, then, that virtue is the sort of state [with the appropriate specifications] that does the best actions concerned with pleasures and pains, and that vice is the contrary. The following points will also make it evident that virtue and vice are concerned with the same things.

(5) There are three objects of choice—fine, expedient and pleasant—and three objects of avoidance—their contraries, shameful, harmful and painful. About all these, then, the good person is correct and the bad person is in error, and especially about pleasure. For pleasure is shared with animals and implied by every object of choice, since what is fine and what is expedient appear pleasant as well.

(6) Further, since pleasure grows up with all of us from infancy on, it is hard to rub out this feeling that is dyed into our lives; and we estimate actions as well [as feelings], some of us more, some less, by pleasure and pain. Hence, our whole inquiry must be about these, since good or bad enjoyment or pain is very important or our actions.

(7) Moreover, it is harder to fight pleasure than to fight emotion, [though that is hard enough], as Heraclitus says. Now both craft and virtue are concerned in every case with what is harder, since a good result is even better when it is harder. Hence, for this reason also, the whole inquiry, for virtue and political science alike, most consider pleasures and pains; for if we use these well, we shall be good, and if badly, bad.

In short, virtue is concerned with pleasures and pains; the actions that are its sources also increase it or, if they are done differently, ruin it; and its activity is concerned with the same actions that are its sources.

4

However, someone might raise this puzzle: 'What do you mean by saying that to become just we must first do just actions and to become temperate we must first do temperate actions? For if we do what is grammatical or musical, we must already be grammarians or musicians. In the same way, then, if we do what is just or temperate, we must already be just or temperate'.

But surely this is not so even with the crafts, for it is possible to produce something grammatical by chance or by following someone else's instructions. To be a grammarian, then, we must both produce something grammatical and produce it in the way in which the grammarian produces it, i.e. expressing grammatical knowledge that is in us.

Moreover, in any case what is true of crafts is not true of virtues. For the products of a craft determine by their own character whether they have been produced well; and so it suffices that they are in the right state when they have been produced. But for actions expressing virtue to be done temperately or justly [and hence well] it does not suffice that they are themselves in the right state. Rather, the agent must also be in the right state when he does them. First, he must know [that he is doing virtuous actions]; second, he must decide on them, and decide on them for themselves; and, third, he must also do them from a firm and unchanging state.

As conditions for having a craft these three do not count, except for the knowing itself. As a condition for having a virtue, however, the knowing counts for nothing, or [rather] for only a little, whereas the other two conditions are very important, indeed all-important. And these other two conditions are achieved by the frequent doing of just and temperate actions.

Hence actions are called just or temperate when they are the sort that a just or temperate person would do. But the just and temperate person is not the one who [merely] does these actions, but the one who also does them in the way in which just or temperate people do them.

It is right, then, to say that a person comes to be just from doing just actions and temperate from doing temperate actions; for no one has even a prospect of becoming good from failing to do them.

The many, however, do not do these actions but take refuge in arguments, thinking that they are doing philosophy, and that this is the way to become excellent people. In this they are like a sick person who listens attentively to the doctor, but acts on none of his instructions. Such a course of treatment will not improve the state of his body; any more than will the many's way of doing philosophy improve the state of their souls.

5

Next we must examine what virtue is. Since there are three conditions arising in the soul—feelings, capacities and states—virtue must be one of these.

By feelings I mean appetite, anger, fear, confidence, envy, joy, love, hate, longing, jealousy, pity, in general whatever implies pleasure or pain.

By capacities I mean what we have when we are said to be capable of these feelings—capable of, e.g., being angry or afraid or feeling pity.

By states I mean what we have when we are well or badly off in relation to feelings. If, e.g., our feeling is too intense or slack, we are badly off in relation to anger, but if it is intermediate, we are well off; and the same is true in the other cases.

First, then, neither virtues nor vices are feelings. (a) For we are called excellent or base insofar as we have virtues or vices, not insofar as have feelings. (b) We are neither praised nor blamed insofar as we have feelings; for we do not praise the angry or the frightened person, and do not blame the person who is simply angry, but only the person who is angry in a particular way. But we are praised or blamed insofar as we have virtues or vices. (c) We are angry and afraid without decision; but the virtues are are decisions of some kind, or [rather] require decision. (d) Besides, insofar as we have feelings, we are said to be moved; but insofar as we have virtues or vices, we are said to be in some condition rather than moved.

For these reasons the virtues are not capacities either; for we are neither called good nor called bad insofar as we are simply capable of feelings. Further, while we have capacities by nature, we do not become good or bad by nature; we have discussed this before.

If, then, the virtues are neither feelings nor capacities, the remaining possibility is that they are states. And so we have said what the genus of virtue is.

6

But we must say not only, as we already have, that it is a state, but also what sort of state it is.

It should be said, then, that every virtue causes its possessors to be in a good state and to perform their functions well; the virtue of eyes, e.g., makes the eyes and their functioning excellent, because it makes us see well; and similarly, the virtue of a horse makes the horse excellent, and thereby good at galloping, at carrying its rider and at standing steady in the face of the enemy. If this is true in every case, then the virtue of a human being will likewise be the state that makes a human being good and makes him perform his function well.

We have already said how this will be true, and it will also be evident from our next remarks, if we consider the sort of nature that virtue has.

In everything continuous and divisible we can take more, less and equal, and each of them either in the object itself or relative to us; and the equal is some intermediate between excess and deficiency.

By the intermediate in the object I mean what is equidistant from each extremity; this is one and the same for everyone. But relative to us the intermediate is what is neither superfluous nor deficient; this is not one, and is not the same for everyone.

If, e.g., ten are many and two are few, we take six as intermediate in the object, since it exceeds [two] and is exceeded [by ten] by an equal amount, [four]; this is what is intermediate by numerical proportion. 1106b But that is not how we must take the intermediate that is relative to us. For if, e.g., ten pounds [of food] are a lot for someone to eat, and two pounds a little, it does not follow that the trainer will prescribe six, since this might also be either a little or a lot for the person who is to take it—for Milo [the athlete] a little, but for the beginner in gymnastics a lot; and the same is true for running and wrestling. In this way every scientific expert avoids excess and deficiency and seeks and chooses what is intermediate—but intermediate relative to us, not in the object.

This, then, is how each science produces its product well, by focusing on what is intermediate and making the product conform to that. This, indeed, is why people regularly comment on well-made products that nothing could be added or subtracted, since they assume that excess or deficiency ruins a good [result] while the mean preserves it. Good craftsmen also, we say, focus on what is intermediate when they produce their product. And since virtue, like nature, is better and more exact than any craft, it will also aim at what is intermediate.

By virtue I mean virtue of character; for this [pursues the mean because] it is concerned with feelings and actions, and these admit of excess, deficiency and an intermediate condition. We can be afraid, e.g., or be confident, or have appetites, or get angry, or feel pity, in general have pleasure or pain, both too much and too little, and in both ways not well; but [having these feelings] at the right times, about the right things, towards the right people, for the right end, and in the right way, is the intermediate and best condition, and this is proper to virtue. Similarly, actions also admit of excess, deficiency and the intermediate condition.

Now virtue is concerned with feelings and actions, in which excess and deficiency are in error and incur blame, while the intermediate condition is correct and wins praise, which are both proper features of virtue. Virtue, then, is a mean, insofar as it aims at what is intermediate.

Moreover, there are many ways to be in error, since badness is proper to what is unlimited, as the Pythagoreans pictured it, and good to what is limited; but there is also one way to be correct. That is why error is easy and correctness hard, since it is easy to miss the target and hard to hit it. And so for this reason also excess and deficiency are proper to vice, the mean to virtue; 'for we are noble in only one way, but bad in all sorts of ways'.

Virtue, then, is (a) a state that decides, (b) [consisting] in a mean, (c) the mean relative to us, (d) 1107a which is defined by reference to reason, (e) i.e. to the reason by reference to which the intelligent person would define it. It is a mean between two vices, one of excess and one of deficiency.

It is a mean for this reason also: Some vices miss what is right because they are deficient, others because they are excessive, in feelings or in actions, while virtue finds and chooses what is intermediate.

Hence, as far as its substance and the account stating its essence are concerned, virtue is a mean; but as far as the best [condition] and the good [result] are concerned, it is an extremity.

But not every action or feeling admits of the mean. For the names of some automatically include baseness, e.g. spite, shamelessness, envy [among feelings], and adultery, theft, murder, among actions. All of these and similar things are called by these names because they themselves, not their excesses or deficiencies, are base.

Hence in doing these things we can never be correct, but must invariably be in error. We cannot do them well or not well—e.g. by committing adultery with the right woman at the right time in the right way; on the contrary it is true unconditionally that to do any of them is to be in error.

[To think these admit of a mean], therefore, is like thinking that unjust or cowardly or intemperate action also admits of a mean, an excess and a deficiency. For then there would be a mean of excess, a mean of deficiency, an excess of excess and a deficiency of deficiency.

Rather, just as there is no excess or deficiency of temperance or of bravery, since the intermediate is a sort of extreme [in achieving the good], so also there is no mean, and no excess or deficiency, of these [vicious actions] either, but whatever may anyone does them, he is in error. For in general there is no mean of excess or of deficiency, and no excess or deficiency of a mean.

Book 3

1

1109b Virtue, then, is about feelings and actions. These receive praise or blame when they are voluntary, but pardon, sometimes even pity, when they are involuntary. Hence, presumably, in examining virtue we must define the voluntary and the involuntary. This is also useful to legislators, both for honors and for corrective treatments.

1110a What comes about by force or because of ignorance seems to be involuntary. What is forced has an external origin, the sort of origin in which the agent or victim contributes nothing—if, e.g., a wind or human beings who control him were to carry him off.

But now consider actions done because of fear of greater evils, or because of something fine. Suppose, e.g., a tyrant tells you to do something shameful, when he has control over your parents and children, and if you do it, they will live, but if not, they will die. These cases raise dispute about whether they are voluntary or involuntary.

However, the same sort of thing also happens with throwing cargo overboard in storms; for no one willingly throws cargo overboard, unconditionally, but anyone with any sense throws it overboard [under some conditions] to save himself and the others.

These sorts of actions, then, are mixed. But they would seem to be more like voluntary actions. For at the time they are done they are choiceworthy, and the goal of an action reflects the occasion; hence also we should call the action voluntary or involuntary with reference to the time when he does it. Now in fact he does it willingly; for in these sorts of actions he has within him the origin of the movement of the limbs that are the instruments [of the action], and when the origin of the actions is in him, it is also up to him to do them or not to do them. Hence actions of this sort are voluntary, though presumably the actions without [the appropriate] condition are involuntary, since no one would choose any action of this sort in itself.

For such [mixed] actions people are sometimes actually praised, whenever they endure something shameful or painful as the price of great and fine results; and if they do the reverse, they are blamed, since it is a base person who endures what is most shameful for nothing fine or for only some moderately fine result.

In some cases there is no praise, but there is pardon, whenever someone does a wrong action because of conditions of a sort that overstrain human nature, and that no one would endure. But presumably there are some things we cannot be compelled to do, and rather than do them we should suffer the most terrible consequences and accept death; for the things that [allegedly] compelled Euripides' Alcmaeon to kill his mother appear ridiculous.

It is sometimes hard, however, to judge what [goods] should be chosen at the price of what [evils], and what [evils] should be endured as the price of what [goods]. And it is even harder to abide by our judgment, since the results we expect [when we endure] are usually painful, and the actions we are compelled [to endure, when we choose] are usually shameful. That is why those who have been com- 1110b
pelled or not compelled receive praise and blame.

What sorts of things, then, should we say are forced? Perhaps we should say that something is forced unconditionally whenever its cause is external and the agent contributes nothing. Other things are involuntary in themselves, but choiceworthy on this occasion and as the price of these [goods], and their origin is in the agent. These are involuntary in themselves, but, on this occasion and as the price of these [goods], voluntary. Still, they would seem to be more like voluntary actions, since actions involve particular [conditions], and [in mixed actions] these [conditions] are voluntary. But what sort of thing should be chosen as the price of what [good] is not easy to answer, since there are many differences in particular [conditions].

But suppose someone says that pleasant things and fine things force us, since they are outside us and compel us. It will follow that for him everything is forced, since everyone in every action aims at something fine or pleasant.

Moreover, if we are forced and unwilling to act, we find it painful; but if something pleasant of fine is its cause, we do it with pleasure.

It is ridiculous, then, for [our opponent] to ascribe responsibility to external [causes] and not to himself, when he is easily snared by such things; and ridiculous to take responsibility for fine actions himself, but to hold pleasant things responsible for his shameful actions.

What is forced, then, would seem to be what has its origin outside the person forced, who contributes nothing.

Everything caused by ignorance is non-voluntary, but what is involuntary also causes pain and regret. For if someone's action was caused by ignorance, but he now has no objection to the action, he has done it neither willingly, since he did not know what it was, nor unwillingly, since he now feels no pain. Hence, among those who act because of ignorance, the agent who now regrets his action seems to be unwilling, while the agent with no regrets may be called non-willing, since he is another case—for since he is different, it is better if he has his own special name.

Further, action caused by ignorance would seem to be different from action done in ignorance. For if the agent is drunk or angry, his action seems to be caused by drunkenness or anger, not by ignorance, though it is done in ignorance, not in knowledge.

[This ignorance does not make an action involuntary.] Certainly every vicious person is ignorant of the actions he must do or avoid, and this sort of error makes people unjust, and in general bad. But talk of involuntary action is not meant to apply to [this] ignorance of what is beneficial.

For the cause of involuntary action is not [this] ignorance in the decision, which cause of vice; it is not [in other words] ignorance of the universal, since
1111a that is a cause for blame. Rather, the cause is ignorance of the particulars which the action consists in and is concerned with; for these allow both pity and pardon, since an agent acts involuntarily if he is ignorant of one of these particulars.

Presumably, then, it is not a bad idea to define these particulars, and say what they are, and how many. They are: (1) who is doing it; (2) what he is doing; (3) about what or to what he is doing it; (4) sometimes also what he is doing it with, e.g. the instrument; (5) for what result, e.g. safety; (6) in what way, e.g. gently or hard.

Now certainly someone could not be ignorant of *all* of these unless he were mad. Nor, clearly, (1) could he be ignorant of who is doing it, since he could hardly be ignorant of himself. But (2) he might be ignorant of what he is doing, as when someone says that [the secret] slipped out while he was speaking, or, as Aeschylus said about the mysteries, that he did not know it was forbidden to reveal it; or, like the person with the catapult, that he let it go when he [only] wanted to demonstrate it. (3) Again, he might think that his son is an enemy, as Merope did; or (4) that the barbed spear has a button on it, or that the stone is pumice-stone. (5) By giving someone a drink to save his life we might kill him; (6) and wanting to touch someone, as they do in sparring, we might wound him.

There is ignorance about all of these [particulars] that the action consists in. Hence someone who was ignorant of one of these seems to have done an action unwillingly, especially when he was ignorant of the most important of them; these seem to be (2) what he is doing, and (5) the result for which he does it.

Hence it is action called involuntary with reference to *this* sort of ignorance [that we meant when we said that] the agent must, in addition, feel pain and regret for his action.

Since, then, what is involuntary is what is forced or is caused by ignorance, what is voluntary seems to be what has its origin in the agent himself when he knows the particulars that the action consists in.

[Our definition is sound.] For, presumably, it is not correct to say that action caused by emotion or appetite is involuntary.

For, first of all, on this view none of the other animals will ever act voluntarily; nor will children. [But clearly they do.]

Next, among all the actions caused by appetite or emotion do we do none of them voluntarily? Or do we do the fine actions voluntarily and the shameful involuntarily? Surely [the second answer] is ridiculous when one and the same thing [i.e. appetite or emotion] causes [both fine and shameful actions]. And presumably it is also absurd to say [as the first answer implies] that things we ought to desire are involuntary; and in fact we ought both to be angry at some things and to have an appetite for some things, e.g. for health and learning.

Again, what is involuntary seems to be painful, whereas what expresses our appetite seems to be pleasant.

Moreover, how are errors that express emotion any less voluntary than those that express rational calculation? For both sorts of errors are to be avoided; and 111
since nonrational feelings seems to be no less human [than rational calculation], actions resulting from

emotion or appetite are also proper to a human being; it is absurd, then, to regard them as involuntary.

2

Now that we have defined what is voluntary and what involuntary, the next task is to discuss decision; for decision seems to be most proper to virtue, and to distinguish characters from one another better than actions do.

Decision, then, is apparently voluntary, but not the same as what is voluntary, which extends more widely. For children and the other animals share in what is voluntary, but not in decision; and the actions we do on the spur of the moment are said to be voluntary, but not to express decision.

Those who say decision is appetite or emotion or wish or some sort of belief would seem to be wrong.

For decision is not shared with nonrational [animals], but appetite and emotion are shared with them.

Further, the incontinent person acts on appetite, not on decision, but the continent person does the reverse and acts on decision, not on appetite.

Again, appetite is contrary to decision, but not to appetite.

Further, appetite's concern is what is pleasant and what is painful, but neither of these is the concern of decision.

Still less is emotion decision; for actions caused by emotion seem least of all to express decision.

But further, it is not wish either, though it is apparently close to it.

For, first, we do not decide to do what is impossible, and anyone claiming to decide to do it would seem a fool; but we do wish for what is impossible, e.g. never to die, as well [as for what is possible].

Further, we wish [not only for results we can achieve], but also for results that are [possible, but] not achievable through our own agency, e.g. victory for some actor or athlete. But what we decide to do is never anything of that sort, but what we think would come about through our own agency.

Again, we wish for the end more [than for what promotes it], but we decide to do what promotes the end. We wish, e.g. to be healthy, but decide to do what will make us healthy; and we wish to be happy, and say so, but could not appropriately say we decide to be happy, since in general what we decide to do would seem to be what is up to us.

Nor is it belief.

For, first, belief seems to be about everything, no less about what is eternal and what is impossible [for us] than about what is up to us.

Moreover, beliefs are divided into true and false, not into good and bad, but decisions are divided into good and bad more than into true and false.

Now presumably no one even claims that decision is the same as belief in general. But it is not the same as any kind of belief either.

For it is our decisions to do what is good or bad, not our beliefs, that make the characters we have.

Again, we decide to take or avoid something good or bad. We believe what it is, whom it benefits or how; but we do not exactly believe to take or avoid.

Further, decision is praised more for deciding on what is right, whereas belief is praised for believing rightly.

Moreover, we decide on something [even] when we know most completely that it is good; but [what] we believe [is] what we do not quite know.

Again, those who make the best decisions do not seem to be the same as those with the best beliefs; on the contrary, some seem to have better beliefs, but to make the wrong choice because of vice.

We can agree that decision follows or implies belief. But that is irrelevant, since it is not the question we are asking; our question is whether decision is the *same* as some sort of belief.

Then what, or what sort of thing, is decision, since it is none of the things mentioned? Well, apparently it is voluntary, but not everything voluntary is decided. Then perhaps what is decided is the result of prior deliberation. For decision involves reason and thought, and even the name itself would seem to indicate that [what is decided, *prohaireton*] is chosen [*haireton*] before [*pro*] other things.

3

But do we deliberate about everything, and is everything open to deliberation, or is there no deliberation about some things? By 'open to deliberation', presumably, we should mean what someone with some sense, not some fool or madman, might deliberate about.

Now no one deliberates about eternal things, e.g. about the universe, or about the incommensurability of the sides and the diagonal; nor about things that are in movement but always come about the same way, either form necessity or by nature or by some other cause, e.g. the solstices or the rising of the stars; nor about what happens different ways at different times, e.g. droughts and rains; nor about what results from fortune, e.g. the finding of a treasure. For none of these results could be achieved through our agency.

We deliberate about what is up to us, i.e. about the actions we can do; and this is what is left [besides the previous cases]. For causes seem to include nature, necessity and fortune, but besides them mind and everything [operating] through human agency.

However, we do not deliberate about all human affairs; no Spartan, e.g., deliberates about how the Scythians might have the best political system. Rather, each group of human beings deliberates about the actions *they* can do.

1112b
Now there is no deliberation about the sciences that are exact and self-sufficient, e.g. about letters, since we are in no doubt how to write them [in spelling a word]. Rather, we deliberate about what results through our agency, but in different ways on different occasions, e.g. about questions of medicine and money-making; more about navigation than about gymnastics, to the extent that it is less exactly worked out, and similarly with other [crafts]; and more about beliefs than about sciences, since we are more in doubt about them.

Deliberation concerns what is usually [one way rather than another], where the outcome is unclear and the right way to act is undefined. And we enlist partners in deliberation on large issues when we distrust our own ability to discern [the right answer].

We deliberate not about ends, but about what promotes ends; a doctor, e.g., does not deliberate about whether he will cure, or an orator about whether he will persuade, or a politician about whether he will produce good order, or any other [expert] about the end [that his science aims at].

Rather, we first lay down the end, and then examine the ways and means to achieve it. If it appears that any of several [possible] means will reach it, we consider which of them will reach it most easily and most finely; and if only one [possible] means reaches it, we consider how that means will reach it, and how the means itself is reached, until we come to the first cause, the last thing to be discovered.

For a deliberator would seem to inquire and analyse in the way described, as though analysing a diagram. [The comparison is apt, since], apparently, all deliberation is inquiry, though not all inquiry, e.g. in mathematics, is deliberation. And the last thing [found] in the analysis is the first that comes to be.

If we encounter an impossible step—e.g. we need money but cannot raise it—we desist; but if the action appears possible, we undertake it. What is possible is what we could achieve through our agency [including what our friends could achieve for us]; for what our friends achieve is, in a way, achieved through our agency, since the origin is in us. [In crafts] we sometimes look for instruments, sometimes [for the way] to use them; so also in other cases we sometimes look for the means to the end, sometimes for the proper use of the means or for the means to that proper use.

As we have said, then, a human being would seem to originate action; deliberation is about the actions he can do; and actions are for the sake of other things; hence we deliberate about what promotes an end, not about the end.

Nor do we deliberate about particulars, e.g. about 1113a
whether this is a loaf or is cooked the right amount; for these are questions for perception, and if we keep on deliberating at each stage we shall go on without end.

What we deliberate about is the same as what we decide to do, except that by the time we decide to do it, it is definite; for what we decide to do is what we have judged [to be right] as a result of deliberation. For each of us stops inquiring how to act as soon as he traces the origin to himself, and within himself to the dominant part; for this is the part that decides. This is also clear from the ancient political systems described by Homer; there the kings would first decide and then announce their decision to the people.

We have found, then, that what we decide to do is whatever action among those up to us we deliberate about and desire to do. Hence also decision will be deliberative desire to do an action that is up to us; for when we have judged [that it is right] as a result of deliberation, our desire to do it expresses our wish.[6]

---

6. **expresses our wish:** reading *boulēsin* rather than *bouleusin*, "deliberation."

So much, then, for an outline of the sort of thing decision is about; it is about what promotes the end.

4

Wish, we have said, is for the end. But to some it seems that wish is for the good, to others that it is for the apparent good.

For those who say the good is what is wished, it follows that what someone wishes if he chooses incorrectly is not wished at all. For if it is wished, then [on this view] it is good; but what he wishes is in fact bad, if it turns out that way. [Hence what he wishes is not wished, which is self-contradictory.]

For those, on the other hand, who say the apparent good is wished, it follows that there is nothing wished by nature. To each person what is wished is what seems [good to him]; but different things, and indeed contrary things, if it turns out that way, appear good to different people, [Hence contrary things will be wished and nothing will be wished by nature.]

If, then, these views do not satisfy us, should we say that, unconditionally and in reality, what is wished is the good, but to each person what is wished is the apparent good?

To the excellent person, then, what is wished will be what is wished in reality, while to the base person what is wished is whatever it turns out to be [that appears good to him]. Similarly in the case of bodies, really healthy things are healthy to sickly people, and the same is true of what is bitter, sweet, hot, heavy and so on.

For the excellent person judges each sort of thing correctly, and in each case what is true appears to him. For each state [of character] has its own special [view of] what is fine and pleasant, and presumably the excellent person is far superior because he sees what is true in each case, being a sort of standard and measure of what is fine and pleasant.

In the many, however, pleasure would seem to
1113b cause deception since it appears good when it is not; at any rate, they choose what is pleasant because they assume it is good, and avoid pain because they assume it is evil.

5

We have found, then, that we wish for the end, and deliberate and decide about what promotes it; hence the actions concerned with what promotes the end will express a decision and will be voluntary. Now the activities of the virtues are concerned with [what promotes the end]; hence virtue is also up to us, and so is vice.

For when acting is up to us, so is not acting, and when No is up to us; so is Yes. Hence if acting, when it is fine, is up to us, then not acting, when it is shameful, is also up to us; and if not acting, when it is fine, is up to us, then acting, when it is shameful, is also up to us. Hence if doing, and likewise not doing, fine or shameful actions is up to us; and if, as we saw, [doing or not doing them] is [what it is] to be a good or bad person; then it follows that being decent or base is up to us.

The claim that no one is willingly bad or unwillingly blessed would seem to be partly true but partly false. For while certainly no one is unwillingly blessed, vice is voluntary. If it is not, we must dispute the conclusion just reached, that a human being originates and fathers his own actions as he fathers his children. But if our conclusion appears true, and we cannot refer [actions] back to other origins beyond those in ourselves, then it follows that whatever has its origin in us is itself up to us and voluntary.

There would seem to be testimony in favor of our views not only in what each of us does as a private citizen, but also in what legislators themselves do. For they impose corrective treatments and penalties on anyone who does vicious actions, unless his action is forced or is caused by ignorance that he is not responsible for; and they honor anyone who does fine actions; they assume that they will encourage the one and restrain the other. But no one encourages us to do anything that is not up to us and voluntary; people assume it is pointless to persuade us not to get hot or distressed or hungry or anything else of that sort, since persuasion will not stop it happening to us.

Indeed, legislators also impose corrective treatments for the ignorance itself, if the person seems to be responsible for the ignorance. A drunk, e.g., pays a double penalty; for the origin is in him, since he controls whether he gets drunk, and his getting drunk is responsible for his ignorance.

They also impose corrective treatment on someone who [does a vicious action] in ignorance of some provision of law that he is required to know and that
is not hard [to know]. And they impose it in other 1114a

cases likewise for any other ignorance that seems to be caused by the agent's inattention; they assume it is up to him not to be ignorant, since he controls whether he pays attention.

But presumably his character makes him inattentive. Still, he is himself responsible for having this character, by living carelessly, and similarly for being unjust by cheating, or being intemperate by passing his time in drinking and the like; for each type of activity produces the corresponding character. This is clear from those who train for any contest or action, since they continually practice the appropriate activities. [Only] a totally insensible person would not know that each type of activity is the source of the corresponding state; hence if someone does what he knows will make him unjust, he is willingly unjust.

Moreover, it is unreasonable for someone doing injustice not to wish to be unjust, or for someone doing intemperate action not to wish to be intemperate. This does not mean, however, that if he is unjust and wishes to stop, he will stop and will be just.

For neither does a sick person recover his health [simply by wishing], nonetheless, he is sick willingly, by living incontinently and disobeying the doctors, if that was how it happened. At that time, then, he was free not to be sick, though no longer free once he has let himself go, just as it was up to us to throw a stone, since the origin was in us, though we can no longer take it back once we have thrown it.

Similarly, then, the person who is [now] unjust or intemperate was originally free not to acquire this character, so that he has it willingly, though once he has acquired the character, he is longer free not to have it [now].

It is not only vices of the soul that are voluntary; vices of the body are also voluntary for some people, and we actually censure them. For we never censure someone if nature causes his ugliness; but if his lack of training or attention causes it, we do censure him. The same is true for weakness or maiming; for everyone would pity, not reproach someone if he were blind by nature or because of a disease or a wound, but would censure him if his heavy drinking or some other form of intemperance made him blind.

Hence bodily vices that are up to us are censured, while those not up to us are not censured. If so, then in the other cases also the vices that are censured will be up to us.

But someone may say, 'Everyone aims at the apparent good, and does not control how it appears; on the 1114b contrary, his character controls how the end appears to him.'

First, then, if each person is in some way responsible for his own state [of character], then he is also himself in some way responsible for how [the end] appears.

Suppose, on the other hand, that no one is responsible for acting badly but one does so because one is ignorant of the end, and thinks this is the way to gain what is best for oneself. One's aiming at the end will not be one's own choice, but one needs a sort of natural, inborn sense of sight, to judge finely and to choose what is really good. Whoever by nature has this sense in a fine condition has a good nature. For this sense is the greatest and finest thing, and one cannot acquire it or learn it from another; rather its natural character determines his later condition, and when it is naturally good and fine, that is true and complete good nature.

If all this is true, then, surely virtue will be no more voluntary than vice? For how the end appears is laid down, by nature or in whatever way, for the good and the bad person alike, and they trace all the other things back to the end in doing whatever actions they do.

Suppose, then, that it is not nature that makes the end appear however it appears to each person, but something also depends on him; or, alternatively, suppose that [how] the end [appears] is natural, but virtue is voluntary because the virtuous person does the other things voluntarily. In either case vice will be no less voluntary than virtue; for the bad person, no less than the good, is responsible for his own actions, even if not for [how] the end [appears].

Now the virtues, as we say, are voluntary, since in fact we are ourselves in a way jointly responsible for our states of character, and by having the sort of character we have we lay down the sort of end we do. Hence the vices will also be voluntary, since the same is true of them.

We have now discussed the virtues in general. We have described their genus in outline; they are means, and they are states. Certain actions produce them, and they cause us to do these same actions, expressing the virtues themselves, in the way that correct reason prescribes. They are up to us and voluntary.

Actions and states, however, are not voluntary in the same way. For we are in control of actions from the origin to the end, when we know the particulars.
1115a With states, however, we are in control of the origin, but do not know, any more than with sicknesses, what the cumulative effect of particular actions will be; nonetheless, since it was up to us to exercise a capacity either this way or another way, states are voluntary.

Let us now take up the virtues again, and discuss each singly. Let us say what they are, what sorts of thing they are concerned with, and how they are concerned with them; it will also be clear at the same time how many virtues there are.

Book 5

1

1129a The questions we must examine about justice and injustice are these: What sorts of actions are they concerned with? What sort of mean is justice? What are the extremes between which justice is intermediate? Let us examine them by the same type of investigation that we used in the topics discussed before.

We see that the state everyone means in speaking of justice is the state that makes us doers of just actions, that makes us do justice and wish what is just. In the same way they mean by injustice the state that makes us do injustice and wish what is unjust. Let us also, then, [follow the common beliefs and] begin by assuming this in outline.

For what is true of sciences and capacities is not true of states. For while one and the same capacity or science seems to have contrary activities, a state that is a contrary has no contrary activities. Health, e.g., only makes us do healthy actions, not their contraries; for we say we are walking in a healthy way if [and only if] we are walking in the way a healthy person would.

Often one of a pair of contrary states is recognized from the other contrary; and often the states are recognized from their subjects. For if, e.g., the good state is evident, the bad state becomes evident too; and moreover the good state becomes evident from the things that have it, and the things from the state. For if, e.g., the good state is thickness of flesh, then the bad state will necessarily be thinness of flesh, and the thing that produces the good state will be what produces thickness of flesh.

It follows, usually, that if one of a pair of contraries is spoken of in more ways than one, so is the other; if, e.g., what is just is spoken of in more ways than one, so is what is unjust.

Now it would seem that justice and injustice are both spoken of in more ways than one, but since the different ways are closely related, their homonymy is unnoticed, and is less clear than it is with distant homonyms where the distance in appearance is wide (e.g., the bone below an animals neck and what we lock doors with are called keys homonymously).

Let us, then, find the number of ways an unjust person is spoken of. Both the lawless person and the greedy and unfair person seem to be unjust; and so, clearly, both the lawful and the fair person will be
just. Hence what is just will be both what is lawful 1129b
and what is fair, and what is unjust will be both what is lawless and what is unfair.

Since the unjust person is greedy, he will be concerned with goods—not with all goods, but only with those involved in good and bad fortune, goods which are, [considered] unconditionally, always good, but for this or that person not always good. Though human beings pray for these and pursue them, they are wrong; the right thing is to pray that what is good unconditionally will also be good for us, but to choose [only] what is good for us.

Now the unjust person [who chooses these goods] does not choose more in every case; in the case of what is bad unconditionally he actually chooses less. But since what is less bad also seems to be good in a way, and greed aims at more of what is good, he seems to be greedy. In fact he is unfair; for unfairness includes [all these actions], and is a common feature [of his choice of the greater good and of the lesser evil].

Since, as we saw, the lawless person is unjust and the lawful person is just, it clearly follows that whatever is lawful is in some way just; for the provisions of legislative science are lawful, and we say that each of them is just. Now in every matter they deal with the laws aim either at the common benefit of all, or at the benefit of those in control, whose control rests on virtue or on some other such basis. And so in one way what we call just is whatever produces and maintains happiness and its parts for a political community.

Now the law instructs us to do the actions of a brave person—not to leave the battle-line, e.g., or to flee, or to throw away our weapons; of a temperate person—not to commit adultery or wanton aggression; of a mild person—not to strike or revile another; and similarly requires actions that express the other virtues, and prohibits those that express the vices. The correctly established law does this correctly, and less carefully framed one does this worse.

This type of justice, then, is complete virtue, not complete virtue unconditionally, but complete virtue in relation to another. And this is why justice often seems to be supreme among the virtues, and 'neither the evening star nor the morning star is so marvellous', and the proverb says 'And in justice all virtue is summed up'.

Moreover, justice is complete virtue to the highest degree because it is the complete exercise of complete virtue. And it is the complete exercise because the person who has justice is able to exercise virtue in relation to another, not only in what concerns himself; for many are able to exercise virtue in their own concerns but unable in what relates to another.

1130a And hence Bias seems to have been correct in saying that ruling will reveal the man, since a ruler is automatically related to another, and in a community. And for the same reason justice is the only virtue that seems to be another person's good, because it is related to another; for it does what benefits another, either the ruler or the fellow-member of the community.

The worst person, therefore, is the one who exercise his vice towards himself and his friends as well [as towards others]. And the best person is not the one who exercises virtue [only] toward himself, but the one who [also] exercises it in relation to another, since this is a difficult task.

This type of justice, then, is the whole, not a part, of virtue, and the injustice contrary to it is the whole, not a part, of vice.

At the same time our discussion makes clear the difference between virtue and this type of justice. For virtue is the same as justice, but what it is to be virtue is not the same as what it is to be justice. Rather, insofar as virtue is related to another, it is justice, and insofar as it is a certain sort of state unconditionally it is virtue.

2

But we are looking for the type of justice, since we say there is one, that consists in a part of virtue, and correspondingly for the type of injustice that is a part [of vice].

Here is evidence that there is this type of justice and injustice:

First, if someone's activities express the other vices—if, e.g., cowardice made him throw away his shield, or irritability made him revile someone, or ungenerosity made him fail to help someone with money—what he does is unjust, but not greedy. But when one acts from greed, in many cases his action expresses none of these vices—certainly not all of them; but it still expresses some type of wickedness, since we blame him, and [in particular] it expresses injustice. Hence there is another type of injustice that is a part of the whole, and a way for a thing to be unjust that is a part of the whole that is contrary to law.

Moreover, if A commits adultery for profit and makes a profit, while B commits adultery because of his appetite, and spends money on it to his own loss, B seems intemperate rather than greedy, while A seems unjust, not intemperate. Clearly, then, this is because A acts to make a profit.

Further, we can refer every other unjust action to some vice—to intemperance if he committed adultery, to cowardice if he deserted his comrade in the battle-line, to anger if he struck someone. But if he made an [unjust] profit, we can refer it to no other vice except injustice.

Hence evidently (a) there is another type of injustice, special injustice, besides the whole of injustice; and (b) it is synonymous with the whole; since the definition is in the same genus. For (b) both have 1130b
their area of competence in relation to another. But (a) special injustice is concerned with honor or wealth or safety, or whatever single name will include all these, and aims at the pleasure that results from making a profit; but the concern of injustice as a whole is whatever concerns the excellent person.

Clearly, then, there is more than one type of justice, and there is another type besides [the type that is] the whole of virtue; but we must still grasp what it is, and what sort of thing it is.

What is unjust is divided into what is lawless and what is unfair, and what is just into what is lawful and what is fair. The [general] injustice previously described, then, is concerned with what is lawless. But what is unfair is not the same as what is lawless, but related to it as part to whole, since whatever is unfair is lawless, but not everything lawless is unfair. Hence also the type of injustice and way for a thing to be unjust [that expresses unfairness] are not the same as the type [that expresses lawlessness], but differ as parts from wholes. For this injustice [as unfairness] is a part of the whole of injustice, and similarly justice [as fairness] is a part of the whole of justice.

Hence we must describe special [as well as general] justice and injustice, and equally this way for a thing to be just of unjust.

Let us, then, set to one side the type of justice and injustice that corresponds to the whole of virtue, justice being the exercise of the whole of virtue, and injustice of the whole of vice, in relation to another.

And it is evident how we must distinguish the way for a thing to be just or unjust that expresses this type of justice and injustice; for the majority of lawful actions, we might say, are the actions resulting from virtue as a whole. For the law instruct us to express each virtue, and forbids us to express each vice, in how we live. Moreover, the actions producing the whole of virtue are the lawful actions that the laws prescribe for education promoting the common good.

We must wait till later, however, to determine whether the education that makes an individual an unconditionally good man is a task for political science or for another science; for, presumably, being a good man is not the same as being every sort of good citizen.

Special justice, however, and the corresponding way for something to be just [must be divided].

One species is found in the distribution of honors or wealth or anything else that can be divided among members of a community who share in a political system; for here it is possible for one member to have a share equal or unequal to another's.

1131a Another species concerns rectification in transactions. This species has two parts, since one sort of transaction is voluntary, and one involuntary. Voluntary transactions include selling, buying, lending, pledging, renting, depositing, hiring out—these are called voluntary because the origin of these transactions is voluntary. Some involuntary ones are secret, e.g. theft, adultery, poisoning, pimping, slave-deception, murder by treachery, false witness; others are forcible, e.g. assault, imprisonment, murder, plunder, mutilation, slander, insult.

Book 6

1

Since we have said previously that we must choose *1138b* the intermediate condition, not the excess or the deficiency, and that the intermediate condition is as correct reason says, let us now determine this, [i.e. what it says].

For in all the states of character we have mentioned, as well as in the others, there is a target which the person who has reason focuses on and so tightens or relaxes; and there is a definition of the means, which we say are between excess and deficiency because they express correct reason.

To say this is admittedly true, but it is not at all clear. For in other pursuits directed by a science it is equally true that we must labour and be idle neither too much nor too little, but the intermediate amount prescribed by correct reason. But knowing only this, we would be none the wiser, e.g. about the medicines to be applied to the body, if we were told we must apply the ones that medical science prescribes and in the way that the medical scientist applies them.

Similarly, then, our account of the states of the soul must not only be true up to this point; we must also determine what correct reason is, i.e. what its definition is.

After we divided the virtues of the soul we said that some are virtues of character and some of thought. *1139a* And so, having finished our discussion of the virtues of character, let us now discuss the others as follows, after speaking first about the soul.

Previously, then, we said there are two parts of the soul, one that has reason, and one nonrational. Now we should divide in the same way the part that has reason.

Let us assume there are two parts that have reason; one with which we study beings whose origins do not admit of being otherwise than they are and one with which we study beings whose origins admit of being otherwise. For when the beings are of different kinds, the parts of the soul naturally suited to each of them are also of different kinds, since the parts possess knowledge by being somehow similar and appropriate [to their objects].

Let us call one of these the scientific part, and the other the rationally calculating part, since deliberating is the same as rationally calculating, and no one deliberates about what cannot be otherwise. Hence the rationally calculating part is one part of the soul that has reason.

Hence we should find the best state of the scientific and the best state of the rationally calculating part; for this state is the virtue of each of them. And since something's virtue is relative to its own proper function [we must consider the function of each part].

2

There are three [capacities] in the soul—perception, understanding, desire—that control action and truth. Of these three perception clearly originates no action, since beasts have perception, but no share in action.

As assertion and denial are to thought, so pursuit and avoidance are to desire. Now virtue of character is a state that decides; and decision is a deliberative desire. If, then, the decision is excellent, the reason must be true and the desire correct, so that what reason asserts is what desire pursues.

This, then, is thought and truth concerned with action. By contrast, when thought is concerned with study, not with action or production, its good or bad state consists [simply] in being true or false. For truth is the function of whatever thinks; but the function of what thinks about action is truth agreeing with correct desire.

Now the origin of an action—the source of the movement, not the action's goal—is decision, and the origin of decision is desire together with reason that aims at some goal. Hence decision requires understanding and thought, and also a state of character, since doing well or badly in action requires both thought and character.

Thought by itself, however, moves nothing; what moves us is thought aiming at some goal and concerned with action. For this is the sort of thought that also originates productive thinking; for every producer in his production aims at some [further] goal, and the unconditional goal is not the product, which is only the [conditional] goal of some [production], and aims at some [further] goal. [An unconditional goal is] what we achieve in *action*, since doing well in action is the goal.

Now desire is for the goal. Hence decision is either understanding combined with desire or desire combined with thought; and what originates movement in this way is a human being.

We do not decide to do what is already past; no one decides, e.g. to have sacked Troy. For neither do we deliberate about what is past, but only about what will be and admits [of being or not being]; and what is past does not admit of not having happened. Hence Agathon is correct to say 'Of this alone, even a god is deprived—to make what is all done to have never happened.'

Hence the function of each of the understanding parts is truth; and so the virtue of each part will be the state that makes that part grasp the truth most of all.

5

To grasp what intelligence is we should first study the sort of people we call intelligent.

It seems proper, then, to an intelligent person to be able to deliberate finely about what is good and beneficial for himself, not about some restricted area—e.g. about what promotes health or strength—but about what promotes living well in general.

A sign of this is the fact that we call people intelligent about some [restricted area] whenever they calculate well to promote some excellent end, in an area where there is no craft. Hence where [living well] as a whole is concerned, the deliberative person will also be intelligent.

Now no one deliberates about what cannot be otherwise or about what cannot be achieved by his action. Hence, if science involves demonstration, but there is no demonstration of anything whose origins admit of being otherwise, since every such thing itself admits of being otherwise; and if we cannot deliberate about what is by necessity; it follows that intelligence is not science nor yet craft-knowledge. It is not science, because what is done in action admits of being otherwise; and it is not craft-knowledge because action and production belong to different kinds.

The remaining possibility, then, is that intelligence is a state grasping the truth, involving reason, concerned with action about what is good or bad for a human being.

For production has its end beyond it; but action does not, since its end is doing well itself, [and doing well is the concern of intelligence].

Hence Pericles and such people are the ones whom we regard as intelligent, because they are able to study what is good for themselves and for human beings; and we think that household managers and politicians are such people.

This is also how we come to give temperance [*sōphrosunē*] its name, because we think that it preserves intelligence [*sōzousan tēn phronēsin*]. This is the sort of supposition that it preserves. For the sort of supposition that it corrupted and perverted by what is pleasant or painful is not every sort—not, e.g., the supposition that the triangle does or does not have two right angles—but suppositions about what is done in action.

For the origin of what is done in action is the goal it aims at; and if pleasure or pain has corrupted someone, it follows that the origin will not appear to him. Hence it will not be apparent that this must be the goal and cause of all his choice and action; for vice corrupts the origin.

Hence [since intelligence is what temperance preserves, and what temperance preserves is a true supposition about action], intelligence must be a state grasping the truth, involving reason, and concerned with action about human goods.

Moreover, there is virtue [or vice in the use] of craft, but not [in the use] of intelligence. Further, in a craft, someone who makes errors voluntarily is more choiceworthy; but with intelligence, as with the virtues, the reverse is true. Clearly, then, intelligence is a virtue, not craft-knowledge.

There are two parts of the soul that have reason. Intelligence is a virtue of one of them, of the part that has belief; for belief is concerned, as intelligence is, with what admits of being otherwise.

Moreover, it is not only a state involving reason. A sign of this is the fact that such a state can be forgotten, but intelligence cannot.

7

1141a We ascribe wisdom in crafts to the people who have the most exact expertise in the crafts, e.g. we call Pheidias a wise stone-worker and Polycleitus a wise bronze-worker, signifying nothing else by wisdom than excellence in a craft. But we also think some people are wise in general, not wise in some [restricted] area, or in some other [specific] way, as Homer says in the *Margites*: 'The gods did not make him a digger or a plowman or wise in anything else'. Clearly, then, wisdom is the most exact [form] of scientific knowledge.

Hence the wise person must not only know what is derived form the origins of a science, but also grasp the truth about the origins. Therefore wisdom is understanding plus scientific knowledge; it is scientific knowledge of the most honorable things that has received [understanding as] its coping-stone.

For it would be absurd for someone to think that political science or intelligence is the most excellent science, when the best thing in the universe is not a human being [and the most excellent science must be of the best things].

Moreover, what is good and healthy for human beings and for fish is not the same, but what is white or straight is always the same. Hence everyone would also say that the content of wisdom is always the same, but the content of intelligence is not. For the agent they would call intelligent is the one who studies well each question about his own [good], and he is the one to whom they would entrust such questions. Hence intelligence is also ascribed to some of the beasts, the ones that are evidently capable of forethought about their own life.

It is also evident that wisdom is not the same as political science. For if people are to say that science about what is beneficial to themselves [as human beings] counts as wisdom, there will be many types of wisdom [corresponding to the different species of animals]. For if there is no one medical science about all beings, there is no one science about the good of all animals, but a different science about each specific good. [Hence there will be many types of wisdom, contrary to our assumption that it has always the same content].

And it does not matter if human beings are the best among the animals. For there are other beings of a far more divine nature than human beings; e.g., most evidently, the beings composing the universe. 1141b

What we have said makes it clear that wisdom is both scientific knowledge and understanding about what is by nature most honorable. That is why people say that Anaxagoras or Thales or that sort of person is wise, but not intelligent, when they see that he is ignorant of what benefits himself. And so they say that what he knows is extraordinary, amazing, difficult and divine, but useless, because it is not human goods that he looks for.

Intelligence, by contrast, is about human concerns, about what is open to deliberation. For we say that deliberating well is the function of the intelligent person more than anyone else; but no one deliberates about what cannot be otherwise, or about what lacks a goal that is a good achievable in action. The unconditionally good deliberator is the one whose aim expresses rational calculation in pursuit of the best good for a human being that is achievable in action.

Nor is intelligence about universals only. It must also come to know particulars, since it is concerned with action and action is about particulars. Hence in other areas also some people who lack knowledge but have experience are better in action than others who have knowledge. For someone who knows that light meats are digestible and healthy, but not which sorts of meats are light, will not produce health; the one who knows that bird meats are healthy will be better at producing health. And since intelligence is concerned with action, it must possess both [the universal and the particular knowledge] or the [particular] more [than the universal]. Here too, however, [as in medicine] there is a ruling [science].

12

1143b Someone might, however, be puzzled about what use they are.

For wisdom is not concerned with any sort of coming into being, and hence will not study any source of human happiness.

Admittedly intelligence will study this; but what do we need it for?

For knowledge of what is healthy or fit—i.e. of what results from the state of health, not of what produces it—makes us no readier to act appropriately if we are already healthy; for having the science of medicine or gymnastic makes us no readier to act appropriately. Similarly, intelligence is the science of what is just and what is fine, and what is good for a human being; but this is how the good man acts; and if we are already good, knowledge of them makes us no readier to act appropriately, since virtues are states[activated in actions].

If we concede that intelligence is not useful for this, should we say it is useful for becoming good? In that case it will be no use to those who are already excellent. Nor, however, will it be any use to those who are not. For it will not matter to them whether they have it themselves or take the advice of others who have it. The advice of others will be quite adequate for us, just as it is with health: we wish to be healthy, but still do not learn medical science.

Besides, it would seem absurd for intelligence, inferior as it is to wisdom, to control it [as a superior. But this will be the result], since the science that produces also rules and prescribes about its product.

We must discuss these questions; for so far we have only gone through the puzzles about them.

First of all, let us state that both intelligence and 1144a
wisdom must be choiceworthy in themselves, even if neither produces anything at all; for each is the virtue of one of the two [rational] parts [of the soul].

Second, they do produce something. Wisdom produces happiness, not in the way that medical science produces health, but in the way that health produces [health]. For since wisdom is a part of virtue as a whole, it makes us happy because it is a state that we possess and activate.

Further, we fulfil our function insofar as we have intelligence and virtue of character; for virtue makes the goal correct, and intelligence makes what promotes the goal [correct]. The fourth part of the soul, the nutritive part, has no such virtue [related to our function], since no action is up to it to do or not to do.

To answer the claim that intelligence will make us no readier to do fine and just actions, we must begin from a little further back [in our discussion].

Here is where we begin. We say that some people who do just actions are not yet thereby just, if, e.g., they do the actions prescribed by the laws, either unwillingly or because of ignorance or because of some other end, not because of the actions themselves, even though they do the right actions, those that the excellent person ought to do. Equally, however, it would seem to be possible for someone to do each type of action in the state that makes him a good person, i.e. because of decision and for the sake of the actions themselves.

Now virtue makes the decision correct; but the actions that are naturally to be done to fulfil the decision are the concern not of virtue, but of another capacity. We must get to know them more clearly before continuing our discussion.

There is a capacity, called cleverness, which is such as to be able to do the actions that tend to promote whatever goal is assumed and to achieve it. If, then, the goal is fine, cleverness is praiseworthy, and if the goal is base, cleverness is unscrupulousness; hence both intelligent and unscrupulous people are called clever.

Intelligence is not the same as this capacity [of cleverness], though it requires it. Intelligence, this eye of the soul, cannot reach its fully developed state without virtue, as we have said and as is clear. For inferences about actions have an origin: 'Since the end and the best good is this sort of thing', whatever it actually is—let it be any old thing for the sake of argument. And this [best good] is apparent only to the good person; for vice perverts us and produces false views about the origins of actions.

1144b Evidently, then, we cannot be intelligent without being good.

13

We must, then, also examine virtue over again. For virtue is similar [in this way] to intelligence; as intelligence is related to cleverness, not the same but similar, so natural virtue is related to full virtue.

For each of us seems to possess his type of character to some extent by nature, since we are just, brave, prone to temperance, or have another feature, immediately from birth. However, we still search for some other condition as full goodness, and expect to possess these features in another way.

For these natural states belong to children and to beasts as well [as to adults], but without understanding they are evidently harmful. At any rate, this much would seem to be clear: just as a heavy body moving around unable to see suffers a heavy fall because it has no sight, so it is with virtue. [A naturally well-endowed person without understanding will harm himself]. But if someone acquires understanding, he improves in his actions; and the state he now has, though still similar [to the natural one], will be virtue to the full extent.

And so, just as there are two sorts of conditions, cleverness and intelligence, in the part of the soul that has belief, so also there are two in the part that has character, natural virtue, and full virtue. And of these full virtue cannot be acquired without intelligence.

This is why some say that all the virtues are [instances of] intelligence, and why Socrates' inquiries were in one way correct, and in another way in error. For in that he thought all the virtues are [instances of] intelligence, he was in error; but in that he thought they all require intelligence, he was right.

Here is a sign of this: Whenever people now define virtue, they all say what state it is and what it is related to, and then add that it is the state that expresses correct reason. Now correct reason is reason that expresses intelligence; it would seem, then, that they all in a way intuitively believe that the state expressing intelligence is virtue.

But we must make a slight change. For it is not merely the state expressing correct reason, but the state involving correct reason, that is virtue. And it is intelligence that is correct reason in this area. Socrates, then, thought, that the virtues are [instances of] reason because he thought they are all [instances of] knowledge, whereas we think they involve reason.

What we have said, then, makes it clear that we cannot be fully good without intelligence, or intelligent without virtue of character.

In this way we can also solve the dialectical argument that someone might use to show that the virtues are separated from each other. For, [it is argued], since the same person is not naturally best suited for all the virtues, someone will already have one virtue before he has got another.

This is indeed possible with the natural virtues. It is not possible, however, with the [full] virtues that someone must have to be called unconditionally good; for as soon as he has intelligence, which is a *1145a*
single state, he has all the virtues as well.

And clearly, even if intelligence were useless in action, we would need it because it is the virtue of this part of the soul, and because the decision will not be correct without intelligence or without virtue. For virtue makes us reach the end in our action, while intelligence makes us reach what promotes the end.

Moreover, intelligence does not control wisdom or the better part of the soul, just as medical science does not control health. For it does not use health, but only aims to bring health into being; hence it prescribes for the sake of health, but does not prescribe to health. Besides, [saying that intelligence controls wisdom] would be like saying that political science rules the gods because it prescribes about everything in the city.

Book 7

1

Next we should make a new beginning, and say that there are three conditions of character to be avoided—vice, incontinence and bestiality. The contraries of two of these are clear; we call one virtue and the other continence.

The contrary to bestiality is most suitably called virtue superior to us, a heroic, indeed divine, sort of virtue. Thus Homer made Priam say that Hector was remarkably good; 'nor did he look as though he were the child of a mortal man, but of a god.' Moreover, so they say, human beings become gods because of exceedingly great virtue.

Clearly, then this is the sort of state that would be opposite to the bestial state. For indeed, just as a beast has neither virtue nor vice, so neither does a god, but the god's state is more honorable than virtue, and the beast's belongs to some kind different from vice.

Now it is rare that a divine man exists. (This is what the Spartans habitually call him; whenever they very much admire someone, they say he is a divine man.) Similarly, the bestial person is also rare among human beings. He is most often found in foreigners; but some bestial features also result from diseases and deformities. We also use 'bestial' as a term of reproach for people whose vice exceeds the human level.

We must make some remarks about this condition later. We have discussed vice earlier. We must now discuss incontinence, softness and self-indulgence,
1145b and also continence and resistance; for we must not suppose that continence and incontinence are concerned with the same states as virtue and vice, or that they belong to a different kind.

As in the other cases we must set out the appearances, and first of all go through the puzzles. In this way we must prove the common beliefs about these ways of being affected—ideally, all the common beliefs, but if not all, then most of them, and the most important. For if the objections are solved, and the common beliefs are left, it will be an adequate proof.

Continence and resistance seem to be good and praiseworthy conditions, while incontinence and softness seem to be base and blameworthy conditions.

The continent person seems to be the same as one who abides by his rational calculation; and the incontinent person seems to be the same as one who abandons it.

The incontinent person knows that his actions are base, but does them because of his feelings, while the continent person knows that his appetites are base, but because of reason does not follow them.

People think the temperate person in continent and resistant. Some think that every continent and resistant person is temperate, while others do not. Some people say the incontinent person is intemperate and the intemperate incontinent, with no distinction; others say they are different.

Sometimes it is said that an intelligent person cannot be incontinent; but sometimes it is said that some people are intelligent and clever, but still incontinent.

Further, people are called incontinent about emotion, honor and gain.

These, then, are the things that are said.

2

We might be puzzled about the sort of correct supposition someone has when he acts incontinently.

First of all, some say he cannot have knowledge [at the time he acts]. For it would be terrible, Socrates thought, for knowledge to be in someone, but mastered by something else, and dragged around like a slave. For Socrates fought against the account [of incontinence] in general, in the belief that there is no incontinence; for no one, he thought, supposes while he acts that his action conflicts with what is best; our action conflicts with what is best only because we are ignorant [of the conflict].

This argument, then, contradicts things that appear manifestly. If ignorance causes the incontinent person to be affected as he is, then we must look for the type of ignorance that it turns out to be; for it is evident, at any rate, that before he is affected the person who acts incontinently does not think [he should do the action he eventually does].

Some people concede some of [Socrates' points], but reject some of them. For they agree that nothing is superior to knowledge, but deny that no one's action conflicts with what has seemed better to him. Hence they say that when the incontinent person is overcome by pleasure he has only belief, not knowledge.

In that case, however, if he has belief, not knowledge, and what resists is not a strong supposition, but only a mild one, such as people have when they are in doubt, we will pardon failure to abide by these beliefs against strong appetites. In fact, however, we do not pardon vice, or any other blameworthy condition [and incontinence is one of these].

Then is it intelligence that resists, since it is the strongest? This is absurd. For on this view the same person will be both intelligent and incontinent; and no one would say that the intelligent person is the sort to do the worst actions willingly.

Besides, we have shown earlier that the intelligent person acts [on his knowledge], since he is concerned with the last things, [i.e. particulars], and that he has the other virtues.

Further, if the continent person must have strong and base appetites, the temperate person will not be continent nor the continent person temperate. For the temperate person is not the sort to have either excessive or base appetites; but [the continent person] must have both.

For if his appetites are good, the state that prevents him from following them must be base, so that not all continence is excellent. If, on the other hand, the appetites are weak and not base, continence is nothing impressive; and if they are base and weak, it is nothing great.

Besides, if continence makes someone prone to abide by every belief, it is bad, if, e.g., it makes him abide by false as well [as a true] belief.

And if incontinence makes someone prone to abandon every belief, there will be an excellent type of incontinence. Neoptolemus, e.g., in Sophocles' *Philoctetes* is praiseworthy when, after being persuaded by Odysseus, he does not abide by his resolve, because he feels pain at lying.

Besides, the sophistical argument is a puzzle. For [the Sophists] wish to refute an [opponent, by showing] that his views have paradoxical results, so that they will be clever in encounters. Hence the inference that results is a puzzle; for thought is tied up, since it does not want to stand still because the conclusion is displeasing, but it cannot advance because it cannot solve the argument.

A certain argument, then, concludes that foolishness combined with incontinence is virtue. For incontinence makes someone act contrary to what he supposes [is right]; but since he supposes that good things are bad and that it is wrong to do them, he will do the good actions, not the bad.

Further, someone who acts to pursue what is pleasant because this is what he is persuaded and decides to do, seems to be better than someone who acts not because of rational calculation, but because of incontinence.

For the first person is the easier to cure, because he might be persuaded otherwise; but the incontinent person illustrates the proverb 'If water chokes us, what must we drink to wash it down?' For if he had been persuaded to act otherwise; but in fact, though already persuaded to act otherwise, he still acts [wrongly].

Further, is there incontinence and continence about everything? If so, who is the simply incontinent? For no one has all the types of incontinence, but we say that some people are simply incontinent.

These, then, are the sorts of puzzles that arise. We must undermine some of these claims, and leave others intact; for the solution of the puzzle is the discovery [of what we are seeking].

3

First, then, we must examine whether the incontinent has knowledge or not, and in what way he has it. Second, what should we take to be the incontinent and the continent person's area of concern—every pleasure and pain, or some definite subclass? Are the continent and the resistant person the same or different? Similarly we must deal with the other questions that are relevant to this study.

We begin the examination with this question: Are the continent and the incontinent person distinguished [from others] (i) by their concerns, or (ii) by their attitudes to them? In other words, is the incontinent person incontinent (i) only by having these concerns, or instead (ii) by having this attitude; or instead (iii) by both?

[Surely (iii) is right]. For [(i) is insufficient] since the simple incontinent is not concerned with everything, but with the same things as the intemperate person. Moreover, [(ii) is insufficient] since he is not incontinent simply by being inclined towards these things—that would make incontinence the same as intemperance. Rather, as [(iii) implies], he is incontinent by being inclined towards them in this way. For the intemperate person acts on decision when he is led on, since he thinks it is right in every case to pursue the pleasant thing at hand; but the incontinent person thinks it is wrong to pursue it, yet still pursues it.

It is claimed that the incontinent person's action conflicts with true belief, not with knowledge. But whether it is knowledge or belief that he has does not matter for this argument. For some people with belief are in no doubt, but think they have exact knowledge.

If, then, it is the weakness of their conviction that makes people with belief, not people with knowledge, act in conflict with their supposition, it follows that knowledge will [for these purposes] be no different from belief; for, as Heraclitus makes clear, some people's convictions about what they believe are no weaker than other people's convictions about what they know.

But we speak of knowing in two ways, and ascribe it both to someone who has it without using it and to someone who is using it. Hence it will matter whether someone has the knowledge that his action is wrong, without attending to his knowledge, or both has and attends to it. For this second case seems extraordinary, but wrong action when he does not attend to his knowledge does not seem extraordinary.

1147a Besides, since there are two types of premisses, someone's action may well conflict with his knowledge if he has both types of premisses, but uses only the universal premiss and not the particular premiss.[7] For [the particular premiss states the particulars and] it is particular actions that are done.

Moreover, [in both types of premisses] there are different types of universal,[8] (a) one type referring to the agent himself, and (b) the other referring to the object. Perhaps e.g., someone knows that (a1) dry things benefit every human being, and that (a2) he himself is a human being, or that (b1) this sort of thing is dry; but he either does not have or does not activate the knowledge that (b2) this particular thing is of this sort.

Hence these ways [of knowing and not knowing] make such a remarkable difference that it seems quite intelligible [for someone acting against his knowledge] to have the one sort of knowledge [i.e. without (b2)], but astounding if he has the other sort [including (b2)].

Besides, human beings may have knowledge in a way different from those we have described. For we see that having without using includes different types of having; hence some people, e.g. those asleep or mad or drunk, both have knowledge in a way and do not have it.

Moreover, this is the condition of those affected by strong feelings. For emotions, sexual appetites and some conditions of this sort clearly [both disturb knowledge and] disturb the body as well, and even produce fits of madness in some people.

Clearly, then [since incontinents are also affected by strong feelings], we should say that they have knowledge in a way similar to these people.

Saying the words that come from knowledge is no sign [of fully having it]. For people affected in these ways even recite demonstrations and verses of Empedocles. Further, those who have just learnt something do not yet know it, though they string the words together; for it must grow into them, and this needs time.

Hence we must suppose that incontinents say the words in the way that actors do.

Further, we may also look at the causes in the following way, referring to [human] nature. One belief (a) is universal; the other (b) is about particulars, and because they are particulars perception controls them. And in the cases where these two beliefs result in (c) one belief, it is necessary in purely theoretical beliefs for the soul to affirm what has been concluded, and in beliefs about production (d) to act at once on what has been concluded.

If, e.g., (a) everything sweet must be tasted, and (b) this, some one particular thing, is sweet, it is necessary (d) for someone who is able and unhindered also to act on this at the same time.

7. **particular premise:** lit. "partial" (*kata meros*), mentioning particulars (*kath'hekasta*).

8. **types of universal:** not universal premises, but universal terms or concepts (e.g., "healthy" or "dry").

Suppose, then, that someone has (a) the universal belief, and it hinders him from tasting; he has (b) the second belief, that everything sweet is pleasant and this is sweet, and this belief (b) is active; and he also has appetite. Hence the belief (c) tells him to avoid this, but appetite leads him on, since it is capable of moving each of the [bodily] parts.

1147b The result, then, is that in a way reason and belief make him act incontinently. The belief (b) is contrary to correct reason, (a), but only coincidentally, not in itself. For it is the appetite, not the belief, that is contrary [in itself to correct reason].

Hence beasts are not incontinent, because they have no universal supposition, but [only] appearance and memory of particulars.

How is the ignorance resolved, so that the incontinent person recovers his knowledge? The same account that applies to someone drunk or asleep applies here too, and is not special to this way of being affected. We must hear it from the natural scientists.

And since the last premiss (b) is a belief about something perceptible, and controls action, this must be what the incontinent person does not have when he is being affected. Or rather the way he has it is not knowledge of it, but, as we saw, [merely] saying the words, as the drunk says the words of Empedocles.

Further, since the last term does not seem to be universal, or expressive of knowledge in the same way as the universal term, even the result Socrates was looking for would seem to come about. For the knowledge that is present when someone is affected by incontinence, and that is dragged about because he is affected, is not the sort that seems to be knowledge to the full extent [in (c)], but only perceptual knowledge [in (b)].

So much, then, for knowing and not knowing, and for how it is possible to know and still to act incontinently.

Book 10

6

1176a We have now finished our discussion of the types of virtue; of friendship; and of pleasure. It remains for us to discuss happiness in outline, since we take this to be the end of human [aims]. Our discussion will be shorter if we first take up again what we said before.

We said, then, that happiness is not a state. For if it were, someone might have it and yet be asleep for his whole life, living the life of a plant, or suffer the greatest misfortunes. If we do not approve of this, we count happiness as an activity rather than a state, as we said before.

Some activities are necessary, i.e. choiceworthy for some other end, while others are choiceworthy in themselves. Clearly, then, we should count happiness as one of those activities that are choiceworthy in themselves, not as one of those choiceworthy for some other end. For happiness lacks nothing, but is self-sufficient; and an activity is choiceworthy in itself when nothing further beyond it is sought from it.

This seems to be the character of actions expressing virtue; for doing fine and excellent actions is choiceworthy for itself.

But pleasant amusements also [seem to be choiceworthy in themselves]. For they are not chosen for other ends, since they actually cause more harm than benefit, by causing neglect of our bodies and possessions.

Moreover, most of those people congratulated for their happiness resort to these sorts of pastimes. Hence people who are witty participants in them have a good reputation with tyrants, since they offer themselves as pleasant [partners] in the tyrant's aims, and these are the sort of people the tyrant requires. And so these amusements seem to have the character of happiness because people in supreme power spend their leisure in them.

However, these sorts of people are presumably no evidence. For virtue and understanding, the sources of excellent activities, do not depend on holding supreme power. Further, these powerful people have had no taste of pure and civilized pleasure, and so they resort to bodily pleasures. But that is no reason to think these pleasures are most choiceworthy, since boys also think that what they honor is best. Hence, just as different things appear honorable to boys and to men, it is reasonable that in the same way different things appear honorable to base and to decent people.

As we have often said, then, what is honorable and pleasant is what is so to the excellent person; and to each type of person the activity expressing his own proper state is most choiceworthy; hence the activity expressing virtue is most choiceworthy to the excellent person [and hence is most honorable and pleasant].

Happiness, then, is not found in amusement; for it would be absurd if the end were amusement, and our lifelong efforts and sufferings aimed at amusing ourselves. For we choose practically everything for some other end—except for happiness, since it is [the] end; but serious work and toil aimed [only] at amusement appears stupid and excessively childish. Rather, it seems correct to amuse ourselves so that we can do something serious, as Anacharsis says; for amusement would seem to be relaxation, and it is because we cannot toil continuously that we require relaxation. Relaxation, then, is not [the] end, since we pursue it
1177a [to prepare] for activity.

Further, the happy life seems to be a life expressing virtue, which is a life involving serious actions, and not consisting in amusement.

Besides, we say that things to be taken seriously are better than funny things that provide amusement, and that in each case the activity of the better part and the better person is more serious and excellent; and the activity of what is better is superior, and thereby has more the character of happiness.

Moreover, anyone at all, even a slave, no less than the best person, might enjoy bodily pleasures; but no one would allow that a slave shares in happiness, if one does not [also allow that the slave shares in the sort of] life [needed for happiness]. Happiness, then, is found not in these pastimes, but in the activities expressing virtue, as we also said previously.

7

If happiness, then, is activity expressing virtue, it is reasonable for it to express the supreme virtue, which will be the virtue of the best thing.

The best is understanding, or whatever else seems to be the natural ruler and leader, and to understand what is fine and divine, by being itself either divine or the most divine element in us.

Hence complete happiness will be its activity expressing its proper virtue; and we have said that this activity is the activity of study. This seems to agree with what has been said before, and also with the truth.

For this activity is supreme, since understanding is the supreme element in us, and the objects of understanding are the supreme objects of knowledge.

Besides, it is the most continuous activity, since we are more capable of continuous study than of any continuous action.

We think pleasure must be mixed into happiness; and it is agreed that the activity expressing wisdom is the pleasantest of the activities expressing virtue. At any rate, philosophy seems to have remarkably pure and firm pleasures; and it is reasonable for those who have knowledge to spend their lives more pleasantly than those who seek it.

Moreover, the self-sufficiency we spoke of will be found in study above all.

For admittedly the wise person, the just person and the other virtuous people all need the good things necessary for life. Still, when these are adequately supplied, the just person needs other people as partners and recipients of his just actions; and the same is true of the temperate person and the brave person and each of the others.

But the wise person is able, and more able the wiser he is, to study even by himself; and though he presumably does it better with colleagues, even so he is more self-sufficient than any other [virtuous person]. 1177b

Besides, study seems to be liked because of itself alone, since it has no result beyond having studied. But from the virtues concerned with action we try to a greater or lesser extent to gain something beyond the action itself.

Happiness seems to be found in leisure, since we accept trouble so that we can be at leisure, and fight wars so that we can be at peace. Now the virtues concerned with action have their activities in politics or war, and actions here seem to require trouble.

This seems completely true for actions in war, since no one chooses to fight a war, and no one continues it, for the sake of fighting a war; for someone would have to be a complete murderer if he made his friends his enemies so that there could be battles and killings.

But the actions of the politician require trouble also. Beyond political activities themselves these actions seek positions of power and honors; or at least they seek happiness for the politician himself and for his fellow-citizens, which is something different from political science itself, and clearly is sought on the assumption that it is different.

Hence among actions expressing the virtues those in politics and war are preeminently fine and great; but they require trouble, aim at some [further] end, and are choiceworthy for something other than themselves.

But the activity of understanding, it seems, is superior in excellence because it is the activity of study, aims at no end beyond itself and has its own proper pleasure, which increases the activity. Further, self-sufficiency, leisure, unwearied activity (as far as is possible for a human being), and any other features ascribed to the blessed person, are evidently features of this activity.

Hence a human being's complete happiness will be this activity, if it receives a complete span of life, since nothing incomplete is proper to happiness.

Such a life would be superior to the human level. For someone will live it not insofar as he is a human being, but insofar as he has some divine element in him. And the activity of this divine element is as much superior to the activity expressing the rest of virtue as this element is superior to the compound. Hence if understanding is something divine in comparison with a human being, so also will the life that expresses understanding be divine in comparison with human life.

We ought not to follow the proverb-writers, and 'think human, since you are human', or 'think mortal, since you are mortal'. Rather, as far as we can, we
1178a ought to be pro-immortal,[9] and go to all lengths to live a life that expresses our supreme element; for however much this element may lack in bulk, by much more it surpasses everything in power and value.

Moreover, each person seems to be his understanding, if he is his controlling and better element; it would be absurd, then, if he were to choose not his own life, but something else's.

And what we have said previously will also apply now. For what is proper to each thing's nature is supremely best and pleasantest for it; and hence for a human being the life expressing understanding will be supremely best and pleasantest, if understanding above all is the human being. This life, then, will also be happiest.

8

The life expressing the other kind of virtue [i.e. the kind concerned with action] is [happiest] in a secondary way because the activities expressing this virtue are human.

For we do just and brave actions, and the others expressing the virtues, in relation to other people, by abiding by what fits each person in contracts, services, all types of actions, and also in feelings; and all these appear to be human conditions.

Indeed, some feelings actually seem to arise from the body; and in many ways virtue of character seems to be proper to feelings.

Besides, intelligence is yoked together with virtue of character, and so is this virtue with intelligence. For the origins of intelligence express the virtues of character; and correctness in virtues of character expresses intelligence. And since these virtues are also connected to feelings, they are concerned with the compound. Since the virtues of the compound are human virtues, the life and the happiness expressing these virtues is also human.

The virtue of understanding, however, is separated [from the compound]. Let us say no more about it, since an exact account would be too large a task for our present project.

Moreover, it seems to need external supplies very little, or [at any rate] less than virtue of character needs them. For grant that they both need necessary goods, and to the same extent, since there will be only a very small difference even though the politician labors more about the body and such-like. Still, there will be a large difference in [what is needed] for the [proper] activities [of each type of virtue].

For the generous person will need money for generous actions; and the just person will need it for paying debts, since wishes are not clear, and people who are not just pretend to wish to do justice. Similarly, the brave person will need enough power, and the temperate person will need freedom [to do intemperate actions], if they are to achieve anything that the virtue requires. For how else will they, or any other virtuous people, make their virtue clear?

Moreover, it is disputed whether it is decision or actions that is more in control of virtue, on the assumption that virtue depends on both. Well, certainly it is clear that what is complete depends on 1178b
both; but for actions many external goods are needed, and the greater and finer the actions the more numerous are the external goods needed.

---

9. **pro-immortal:** (*athanatizein*) Perhaps it means "make oneself immortal."

But someone who is studying needs none of these goods, for that activity at least; indeed, for study at least, we might say they are even hindrances.

Insofar as he is a human being, however, and [hence] lives together with a number of other human beings, he chooses to do the actions expressing virtue. Hence he will need the sorts of external goods [that are needed for the virtues], for living a human life.

In another way also it appears that complete happiness is some activity of study. For we traditionally suppose that the gods more than anyone are blessed and happy; but what sorts of actions ought we to ascribe to them? Just actions? Surely they will appear ridiculous making contracts, returning deposits and so on. Brave actions? Do they endure what [they find] frightening and endure dangers because it is fine? Generous actions? Whom will they give to? And surely it would be absurd for them to have currency or anything like that. What would their temperate actions be? Surely it is vulgar praise to say that they do not have base appetites. When we go through them all, anything that concerns actions appears trivial and unworthy of the gods.

However, we all traditionally suppose that they are alive and active, since surely they are not asleep like Endymion. Then if someone is alive, and action is excluded, and production even more, what is left but study? Hence the gods' activity that is superior in blessedness will be an activity of study. And so the human activity that is most akin to the gods' will, more than any others, have the character of happiness.

A sign of this is the fact that other animals have no share in happiness, being completely deprived of this activity of study. For the whole life of the gods is blessed, and human life is blessed to the extent that it has something resembling this sort of activity; but none of the other animals is happy, because none of them shares in study at all. Hence happiness extends just as far as study extends, and the more someone studies, the happier he is, not coincidentally but insofar as he studies, since study is valuable in itself. And so [on this argument] happiness will be some kind of study.

However, the happy person is a human being, and so will need external prosperity also; for his nature is not self-sufficient for study, but he needs a healthy body, and needs to have food and the other services provided.

Still, even though no one can be blessedly happy 1179a
without external goods, we must not think that to be happy we will need many large goods. For self-sufficiency and action do not depend on excess, and we can do fine actions even if we do not rule earth and sea; for even from moderate resources we can do the actions expressing virtue. This is evident to see, since many private citizens seem to do decent actions no less than people in power do—even more, in fact. It is enough if moderate resources are provided; for the life of someone whose activity expresses virtue will be happy.

Solon surely described happy people well, when he said they had been moderately supplied with external goods, had done what he regarded as the finest actions, and had lived their lives temperately. For it is possible to have moderate possessions and still to do the right actions.

And Anaxagoras would seem to have supposed that the happy person was neither rich nor powerful, since he said he would not be surprised if the happy person appeared an absurd sort of person to the many. For the many judge by externals, since these are all they perceive.

Hence the beliefs of the wise would seem to accord with our arguments.

These considerations do indeed produce some confidence. The truth, however, in questions about action is judged from what we do and how we live, since these are what control [the answers to such questions]. Hence we ought to examine what has been said by applying it to what we do and how we live; and if it harmonizes with what we do, we should accept it, but if it conflicts we should count it [mere] words.

The person whose activity expresses understanding and who takes care of understanding would seem to be in the best condition, and most loved by the gods. For if the gods pay some attention to human beings, as they seem to, it would be reasonable for them to take pleasure in what is best and most akin to them, namely, understanding; and reasonable for them to benefit in return those who most of all like and honor understanding, on the assumption that these people attend to what is beloved by the gods, and act correctly and finely.

Clearly, all this is true of the wise person more than anyone else; hence he is most loved by the gods. And it is likely that this same person will be happiest;

hence the wise person will be happier than anyone else on this argument too.

9

We have now said enough in outlines about happiness and the virtues, and about friendship and pleasure also. Should we then think that our decision [to 1179b study these] has achieved its end? On the contrary, the aim of studies about action, as we say, is surely not to study and know about each thing, but rather to act on our knowledge. Hence knowing about virtue is not enough, but we must also try to possess and exercise virtue, or become good in any other way.

Now if arguments were sufficient by themselves to make people decent, the rewards they would command would justifiably have been many and large, as Theognis says, and rightly bestowed. In fact, however, arguments seem to have enough influence to stimulate and encourage the civilized ones among the young people, and perhaps to make virtue take possession of a well-born character that truly loves what is fine; but they seem unable to stimulate the many towards being fine and good.

For the many naturally obey fear, not shame; they avoid what is base because of the penalties, not because it is disgraceful. For since they live by their feelings, they pursue their proper pleasures and the sources of them, and avoid the opposed pains, and have not even a notion of what is fine and [hence] truly pleasant, since they have had no taste of it.

What argument could reform people like these? For it is impossible, or not easy, to alter by argument what has long been absorbed by habit; but, presumably, we should be satisfied to achieve some share in virtue when we already have what we seem to need to become decent.

Some think it is nature that makes people good; some think it is habit; some that it is teaching.

The [contribution] of nature clearly is not up to us, but results from some divine cause in those who have it, who are the truly fortunate ones.

Arguments and teaching surely do not influence everyone, but the soul of the student needs to have been prepared by habits for enjoying and hating finely, like ground that is to nourish seed. For someone whose life follows his feelings would not even listen to an argument turning him away, or comprehend it [if he did listen]; and in that state how could he be persuaded to change? And in general feelings seem to yield to force, not to argument.

Hence we must already in some way have a character suitable for virtue, fond of what is fine and objecting to what is shameful.

But it is hard for someone to be trained correctly for virtue form his youth if he has not been brought up under correct laws, since the many, especially the young, do not find it pleasant to live in a temperate and resistant way. Hence laws must prescribe their upbringing and practices; for they will not find these things painful when they get used to them.

Presumably, however, it is not enough to get the 1180a correct upbringing and attention when they are young; rather, they must continue the same practices and be habituated to them when they become men. Hence we need laws concerned with these things also, and in general with all of life. For the the many yield to compulsion more than to argument, and to sanctions more than to what is fine.

This, some think, is why legislators should urge people towards virtue and exhort them to aim at what is fine, on the assumption that anyone whose good habits have prepared him decently will listen to them, but should impose corrective treatments and penalties on anyone who disobeys or lacks the right nature, and completely expel an incurable. For the decent person, it is assumed, will attend to reason because his life aims at what is fine, while the base person, since he desires pleasure, has to receive corrective treatment by pain, like a beast of burden; that is why it is said that the pains imposed must be those most contrary to the pleasures he likes.

As we have said, then, someone who is to be good must be finely brought up and habituated, and then must live in decent practices, doing nothing base either willingly or unwillingly. And this will be true if his life follows some sort of understanding and correct order that has influence over him.

A father's instructions, however, lack this influence and compelling power; and so in general do the instructions of an individual man, unless he is a king or someone like that. Law, however, has the power that compels; and law is reason that proceeds from a sort of intelligence and understanding. Besides, people become hostile to an individual human being who opposes their impulses even if he is correct in opposing them; whereas a law's prescription of what is decent is not burdensome.

And yet, only in Sparta, or in a few other cities as well, does the legislator seem to have attended to upbringing and practices. In most other cities they are neglected, and each individual citizen lives as he wishes, 'laying down the rules for his children and wife', like a Cyclops.

It is best, then, if the community attends to upbringing, and attends correctly. If, however, the community neglects it, it seems fitting for each individual to promote the virtue of his children and his friends—to be able to do it, or at least to decide to do it.

From what we have said, however, it seems he will be better able to do it if he acquires legislative science. For, clearly, attention by the community works through laws, and decent attention works through excellent laws; and whether the laws are written or unwritten, for the education of one or of many, seems unimportant, as it is in music, gymnastics and other practices. For just as in cities the provisions of law and the [prevailing] types of character have influence, similarly a father's words and habits have influence, and all the more because of kinship and because of the benefits he does; for his children are already fond of him and naturally ready to obey.

Moreover, education adapted to an individual is actually better than a common education for everyone, just as individualized medical treatment is better. For though generally a feverish patient benefits from rest and starvation, presumably some patient does not; nor does the boxing instructor impose the same way of fighting on everyone. Hence it seems that treatment in particular cases is more exactly right when each person gets special attention, since he then more often gets the suitable treatment.

Nonetheless a doctor, a gymnastics trainer and everyone else will give the best individual attention if they also know universally what is good for all, or for these sorts. For sciences are said to be, and are, of what is common [to many particular cases].

Admittedly someone without scientific knowledge may well attend properly to a single person, if his experience has allowed him to take exact note of what happens in each case, just as some people seem to be their own best doctors, though unable to help anyone else at all. Nonetheless, presumably, it seems that someone who wants to be an expert in a craft and a branch of study should progress to the universal, and come to know that, as far as possible; for that, as we have said, is what the sciences are about.

Then perhaps also someone who wishes to make people better by his attention, many people or few, should try to acquire legislative science, if we will become good through laws. For not just anyone can improve the condition of just anyone, or the person presented to him; but if anyone can it is the person with knowledge, just as in medical science and the others that require attention and intelligence.

Next, then, should we examine whence and how someone might acquire legislative science? Just as in other cases [we go to the practitioner], should we go to the politicians? For, as we saw, legislative science seems to be a part of political science.

But is the case of political science perhaps apparently different from the other sciences and capacities? For evidently in others the same people, e.g. doctors or painters, who transmit the capacity to others actively practice it themselves. By contrast, it is the Sophists who advertise that they teach politics but none of them practices it. Instead, those who practice it are the political activists, and they seem to act on some sort of capacity and experience rather than thought.

For evidently they neither write nor speak on such questions, though presumably it would be finer to do this than to compose speeches for the law courts or the Assembly; nor have they made politicians out of their own sons or any other friends of theirs. And yet it would be reasonable for them to do this if they were able; for there is nothing better than the political capacity that they could leave to their cities, and nothing better that they could decide to produce in themselves, or, therefore, in their closest friends.

Certainly experience would seem to contribute quite a lot; otherwise people would not have become better politicians by familiarity with politics. Hence those who aim to know about political science would seem to need experience as well.

By contrast, those of the Sophists who advertise [that they teach political science] appear to be a long way from teaching; for they are altogether ignorant about the sort of thing political science is, and the sorts of things it is about. For if they had known what it is, they would not have taken it to be the same as rhetoric, or something inferior to it, or thought it an easy task to assemble the laws with good reputations and then legislate. For they think they can select the best laws, as though the selection itself did not require comprehension, and as though correct judgment were not the most important thing, as it is in music.

It is those with experience in each area who judge the products correctly and who comprehend the method or way of completing them, and what fits with what; for if we lack experience, we must be satisfied with noticing that the product is well or badly made, as with painting. Now laws would seem to be
1181b the products of political science; how, then, could someone acquire legislative science, or judge which laws are best, from laws alone? For neither do we appear to become experts in medicine by reading textbooks.

And yet doctors not only try to describe the [recognized] treatments, but also distinguish different [physical] states, and try to say how each type of patient might be cured and must be treated. And what they say seems to be useful to the experienced, though useless to the ignorant.

Similarly, then, collections of laws and political systems might also, presumably, be most useful if we are capable of studying them and of judging what is done finely or in the contrary way, and what sorts of [elements] fit with what. Those who lack the [proper] state [of experience] when they go through these collections will not manage to judge finely, unless they can do it all by themselves [without training], though they might come to comprehend them better by going through them.

Since, then, our predecessors have left the area of legislation uncharted, it is presumably better to examine it ourselves instead, and indeed to examine political systems in general, and so to complete the philosophy of human affairs, as far as we are able.

First, then, let us try to review any sound remarks our predecessors have made on particular topics. Then let us study the collected political systems, to see from them what sorts of things preserve and destroy cities, and political systems of different types; and what causes some cities to conduct politics well, and some badly.

For when we have studied these questions, we will perhaps grasp better what sort of political system is best; how each political system should be organized so as to be best; and what habits and laws it should follow.

Let us discuss this, then, starting from the beginning.

Politics

Book 1

1

1252a We see that every city is some sort of community, and that every community is constituted for the sake of some good, since everyone does everything for the sake of what seems good. Clearly, then, while all communities aim at some good, the community that aims most of all at the good—at the good that most of all controls all the goods—is the one that most of all controls and includes the others; and this is the one called the city, the political community.

It is wrong, then, to suppose, as some do, that the character of the politician, the king, the household manager, and the slave-master is the same. People suppose this because they think the difference is not a difference in kind, but only in the number who are ruled, so that the ruler of a few is a master, the ruler of more people is a household-manager, and the ruler of still more people is a politician or a king—on the assumption that a large household is no different from a small city. And all they can say to distinguish a king from a politician is that someone who directs things himself is a king, whereas someone who follows the principles of political science, ruling and being ruled in turn, is a politician. These views are not true.

What we mean will be clear if the investigation follows our recognized line of inquiry. Just as an in other cases we must divide the composite into incomposites,

---

From Aristotle, *Selections*, translated by Terence Irwin and Gail Fine (Indianapolis: Hackett Publishing Company, 1995). Copyright © 1995. Reprinted by permission of the publisher.

since these are the smallest parts of the whole, so also in this case we must investigate the components of the city; for then we will also see better the difference between these rulers, and the prospect of finding any sort of scientific treatment of the questions we have mentioned.

2

The best way to study this as well as other matters is to trace things back to their beginnings and observe their growth. First, then, those who cannot exist without each other have to form pairs, as female and male do for reproduction. And they do this not because of any decision, but from the natural impulse that they share with other animals and with plants to leave behind another of the same kind as oneself.

Self-preservation [rather than reproduction] is the basis of the natural division between ruler and subject. For the capacity for rational foresight makes one a natural ruler and natural master, and the capacity to execute this foresight by bodily labor makes another a subject and a natural slave; that is why the interests of master and slave coincide.

1252b Now there is a natural distinction between the female and the slave. For nature makes nothing stingily, like a smith making a Delphic knife,[1] but makes one thing for one function, since the best instrument for a particular function is made exclusively for it, not for many others. Among foreigners, however, female and slave have the same rank; the reason is that no foreigners are natural rulers, and so their community consists of a female slave and a male slave. Hence the poets say 'It is to be expected that Greeks rule over foreigners', assuming that the foreigner and the slave are naturally the same.

And so from these two communities [between female and male and between slave and master] the first community that results is the household. Hesiod[2] was right when he said 'Get first of all a house, a wife, and a plow-ox'—for the poor use an ox in place of a slave. Hence the community naturally formed for every day is a household of 'breadbin-mates' (as Charondas calls them) or (as Epimenides the Cretan says) 'manger-mates'.

The first community formed from a number of households for long-term advantage is a village, and the most natural type of village would seem to be an extension of a household, including children and grandchildren, sometimes called 'milkmates'. That is why cities were also originally ruled by kings and some nations are ruled by kings even at present; they were formed from communities ruled by kings—for in every household the oldest member rules as its king, and the same is true in its extensions, because the villagers are related by kinship. Homer[3] describes this when he says 'Each rules over his children and wives', because they were isolated, as households were in ancient times. And for the same reason everyone says the gods are ruled by a king; it is because we were all ruled by kings in ancient times, and some still are, and human beings ascribe to the gods a human way of life, as well as a human form.

The complete community, formed from a number of villages, is a city. Unlike the others, it has the full degree of practically every sort of self-sufficiency; it comes to be for the sake of living, but remains in being for the sake of living well. That is why every city is natural, since the previous communities are natural. For the city is their end, and nature is an end; for we say that something's nature (for instance, of a human being, a horse, or a household) is the character it has when its coming to be is complete. Moreover, the final cause and end is the best [good], and 1253a
self-sufficiency is both the end and the best [good].

It is evident, then, that the city exists by nature, and that a human being is by nature a political animal. Anyone without a city because of his nature rather than his fortune is either worthless or superior to a human being. Like the man reviled by Homer,[4] 'he has no kin, no law, no home'. For his natural isolation from a city gives him an appetite for war, since, like [a solitary piece] in a game of checkers, he has no partner.

It is evident why a human being is more of a political animal than is any bee or any gregarious animal; for nature, we say, does nothing pointlessly, and a human being is the only animal with rational discourse. A voice signifies pleasure and pain, and so the

1. **a Delphic knife:** like a Swiss army knife, with several different functions.

2. **Hesiod . . . :** *Works and Days* 406.

3. **Homer:** *Odyssey* 9.114, referring to the Cyclopes.

4. **Homer:** *Iliad* 9.63.

other animals, as well as human beings, have it, since their nature is far enough advanced for them to perceive pleasure and pain and to signify them to one another. But rational discourse is for making clear what is expedient or harmful, and hence what is just or unjust. For this is distinctive of human beings in contrast to the other animals, that they are the only ones with a perception of good and evil, and of just and unjust, and so on; and it is community in these that produces a household and a city.

Further, the city is naturally prior to the household and to the individual, since the whole is necessarily prior to the part. For if the whole animal is dead, neither foot nor hand will survive, except homonymously, as if we were speaking of a stone hand—for that is what a dead hand will be like. Now everything is defined by its function and potentiality; and so anything that has lost them should not be called the same thing, but a homonymous thing.

Clearly, then, the city is also natural and is prior to the individual. For if the individual separated from the city is not self-sufficient, his relation to it corresponds to that of parts to wholes in other cases; and anyone who is incapable of membership in a community, or who has no need of it because he is self-sufficient, is no part of a city, and so is either a beast or a god.

Everyone has a natural impulse, then, towards this sort of community, and whoever first constituted it is the cause of the greatest goods. For just as a human being is the best of the animals if he has been completed, he is also the worst of them if he is separated from law and the rule of justice. For injustice is most formidable when it is armed, and a human being naturally grows up armed and equipped for intelligence and virtue, but can most readily use this equipment for ends that are contrary to intelligence and virtue; hence without virtue he is the most unscrupulous and savage of animals, the most excessive in pursuit of sex and food. Justice, however, is political; for the rule of justice is an order in the political community, and justice is the judgment of what is just.

Book 3

6

1278b The next question to investigate is whether we should suppose there is one type or several types of political systems, and, if there are several, what and how many they are, and what features differentiate them.

A political system is the ordering in a city of the various ruling offices, and especially of the one that controls everything. For in every city the controlling element is the political body,[5] and the political body is the political system. I mean, for instance, that in democracies the common people are in control, and, by contrast, in oligarchies the few are in control, and we take the political systems of these cities to be different—and we will give the same account of the other political systems as well.

First, then, we should state our assumption about what end the city is constituted for, and how many types of rule are concerned with human beings and with community of life.

In our first discussions, when we determined the features of rule over households and over slaves, we also said that a human being is by nature a political animal. That is why, even when they have no need of mutual help, they desire nonetheless to live together; at the same time common advantage draws them together, to the extent that it contributes something to living finely for each person. Living finely, then, most of all is the goal of a city, both for all the citizens in common and for each separately. Still, they also combine and maintain the political community for the sake of life itself. For presumably even life itself includes something fine in it, as long as its adversities are not overwhelming; and, clearly, most human beings still cling to life even if they must endure much suffering, finding that simply being alive is a source of some well-being and natural delight.

Further, it is easy to distinguish the types of rule we have mentioned—indeed we often distinguish them in popular discussions. First comes the rule of master over slave, where the advantage of the natural slave and of the natural master are in fact the same, but nonetheless the master rules for his own advantage, and for the slave's advantage [only] coincidentally (since the master cannot maintain his rule if the slave is being ruined).

By contrast, rule over children and wife and the whole household—called household-rule—is for the benefit of the ruled, or [coincidentally] for some

5. **political body:** *politeuma*. "Government" would also be a suitable rendering; cf.1279a27f.

benefit common to ruler and ruled, but in itself for 1279a the benefit of the ruled. In the same way we see that the crafts—medicine and gymnastics, for instance—may also be coincidentally for the benefit of the craftsman as well as the subject, since the gymnastics trainer may sometimes be one of the people in training, just as the pilot is always one of the sailors; and so the trainer or pilot considers the good of those he rules, but whenever he turns out to be one of them, he shares coincidentally in the benefit since the pilot is a sailor, and the trainer is at the same time in training.

Hence, when a city is constituted on the basis of equality and similarity among the citizens, they think it right to take turns at ruling. In the past each did this in the naturally suitable way, thinking it right to take his turn in public service, and then in return to have someone else consider his advantage afterwards, just as he previously was a ruler and considered the other's advantage. These days, however, people want to be rulers continuously, to gain the benefits of ruling and holding public office, and so they pursue it as eagerly as they would if they were all sick and would all invariably recover their health if they became rulers.

It is evident, then, that all the political systems that consider the common advantage are correct types, conforming to what is just without qualification, whereas all those that consider only the advantage of the rulers are erroneous types, deviations from the correct political systems—for these are the types of rule that a master exercises over slaves, whereas a city is a community of free citizens.

7

Now that this has been determined, the next task is to investigate how many political systems there are and what they are. First we consider the correct systems; for when we have determined these, we will have made the deviant systems evident.

A political system and a political body signify the same thing; the political body controls a city, and either one person or a few of the many must be in control. If, then, the one person or the few or the many rule for the common advantage, these political systems must be correct; and the systems that aim at the special advantage of the one or the few or the mass of people[6] must be deviations—for either those who do not participate [in the political system] should not be called citizens, or they must [at least] share in the advantage.

The type of monarchy that considers the common advantage is usually called kingship. The corresponding type of rule by a few people, but more than one, is called aristocracy, either because the best people are the rulers or because it aims at what is best for the city and those associated in it. Whenever the masses conduct political life for the common advantage, that system is called a polity—the name that is common to all the political systems. And this [name] is reasonable; for while one person or a few people may excel in virtue, it is not easy for a larger number to be 1279b accomplished in every virtue, but they are accomplished in the virtue of war, since that requires a mass of people. That is why the controlling element in the political system consists of those who fight in wars, and those who own their own weapons are those who participate in the political system.

The deviations from these systems are tyranny, a deviation from kingship; oligarchy, a deviation from aristocracy; and democracy, a deviation from polity. For tyranny is rule by one person, aiming at the advantage of the ruler himself; oligarchy aims at the advantage of the prosperous; and democracy aims at the advantage of the disadvantaged; and none of these aims at what benefits the community.

8

We must spend a little longer, however, in saying what each of these political systems is. For the question raises some puzzles: and if we approach a line of inquiry from a philosophical point of view, not simply focussing on what is useful for action, it is appropriate not to overlook or omit any point, but to make clear the truth about each question.

A tyranny, as we have said, is rule by one person who rules the political community as a master rules slaves. There is an oligarchy whenever possessors of property control the political system, and a democracy, by

---

6. **mass of people:** *plēthos*, or "the majority." The term normally refers (as *dēmos* does, in one of its uses) to the lower clases, not necessarily with any unfavorable suggestion.

contrast, whenever those in control are the disadvantaged, those possessing no large property.

The first puzzle arises about this distinction. For suppose that the majority are prosperous and that they control the city, and it is a democracy whenever the masses are in control; and again suppose that in some city the disadvantaged are fewer in number than the prosperous, but are stronger and control the political system, and there is said to be an oligarchy whenever a small number are in control. In these cases we do not seem to have drawn the right distinction between these political systems.

We might, then, combine being prosperous with small numbers, and being disadvantaged with large numbers, and hence classify the political systems by saying that an oligarchy is the system in which the prosperous are few in number and hold the ruling offices, and that a democracy is the system in which the disadvantaged are many and hold the ruling offices. But these definitions raise another puzzle; what are we to call the systems we have just mentioned—the one in which the prosperous are in control of the system and are more numerous, and the one in which the disadvantaged are in control but are fewer in number—if there is no other political system apart from the ones we listed?

This argument, then, would seem to show that control by the few is coincidental to oligarchies, and control by the many to democracies, because in every city the prosperous are few in number and the disadvantaged are many. Hence the reason we mentioned do not turn out to be reasons for distinguishing the systems [by the number in the ruling group]. What really differentiates democracy from oligarchy is
1280a poverty and wealth. If the rulers rule because they are wealthy, whether they are few or many, the system must be an oligarchy, and if the disadvantaged rule, it must be a democracy; it comes about coincidentally, as we said, that the prosperous are few and the disadvantaged are many. For only a few are well off, but all [wealthy and poor] alike share free citizenship; wealth and freedom cause the struggle between the two [groups] for control of the political system.

9

First we must understand the received formulae of oligarchy and democracy, and the oligarchic and democratic [views of] justice; for everyone touches on some sort of justice, but they make only limited progress and do not describe the whole of what is fully just. Justice seems to be equality, for instance, and indeed it is—but for equals, not for everyone. Again, inequality seems to be just; and so it is—but for unequals, not for everyone. But these [partisans of each view] omit this part—equality or inequality for whom—and so make the wrong judgment. The reason is that they are giving judgment in their own case, and most people are practically always bad judges in their own cases.

Justice is justice *for* certain people, and the division in the things [to be distributed] corresponds to the division in those to whom [they are distributed], as we have said before in the *Ethics*. Hence all sides agree about the equal amount of the thing [to be distributed] but dispute about who should receive it. They do this mainly for the reason we have just given, that people are bad judges in their own cases, but also because each side makes some progress in describing a sort of justice and so thinks it describes unqualified justice. For [supporters of oligarchy] think that if they are unequal in some aspects—wealth, for instance—they are altogether unequal, whereas [supporters of democracy] think that if they are equal in some aspect—free status, for instance—they are altogether equal.

But they fail to mention the most important aspect. For if people combined and formed a [political] community in order to acquire possessions, then someone's share in the city would correspond to his possessions, and the supporters of oligarchy would seem to have a strong argument; for, they say, if A has contributed one out of 100 minas and B has contributed the other 99, it is not just for A to get the same return as B, either of the original sum or of any later profits.

In fact, however, the [political] community does not aim simply at staying alive, but aims predominantly at a good life. For if it aimed simply at staying alive, then slaves and non-human animals would be members of a city, whereas in fact they are not, since they do not participate in happiness or in a life guided by decision.

Nor does the city aim at an alliance, to prevent anyone from doing injustice to anyone; or at exchange and dealings between its members. For it this were the aim, then the Etruscans and the

Carthaginians—and any other peoples related by treaty—would all count as citizens of a single city; at any rate, these have made conventions about imports, treaties to prohibit doing injustice, and written 1280b articles of alliance. These people, however, have no common government, but each has its own government. Moreover, neither people is concerned about the right character to form in the citizens of the other city, or about how to remove injustice or any other vice from the other city that is bound by the agreements; each is concerned only to prevent the other city from doing injustice to it. By contrast, those who are concerned with good government consider the virtues and vices of citizens.

Hence it is evident that whatever is correctly called a city, not just for the sake of argument, must be concerned with virtue. For [otherwise] the community turns out to be [merely] an alliance, differing only in the proximity of its members from the other alliances with more distant members. In that case law turns out to be an agreement and, as Lycophron the Sophist said, a mutual guarantor of just treatment, but unable to make the citizens good and just.

To make it evident that we are right, suppose that we actually joined the territories [of two allied states], so that the cities of the Megarians and the Corinthians had their walls adjacent; even so, they would not be one single city, even if their citizens intermarried—though that is one sort of community that is distinctive of a city. Similarly, suppose people lived apart, though not too far to prevent community, but had laws prohibiting unjust treatement in exchanges (if, for instance, one was a carpenter, another a farmer, another a cobbler, and so on), and there were ten thousand of them, but their community extended no further than such matters as commerce and alliance; that would still not be enough to make a city.

Why is this? Surely it is not because their community is scattered. For if they even lived closer together but in the same sort of community, each treating his own household as a city, and they formed a purely defensive alliance agaisnt unjust actions—even so, an exact study would not count this as a city, if their intercourse when they live closer together is no different from what it was when they lived apart.

Evidently, then, a city is not a community for living in the same place, for preventing the unjust treatement of one member by another, and for exchange. All these are necessary conditions for a city, but their presence does not make a city. Rather, the city is a community for living well for both households and families, aiming at a complete and self-sufficient life (but this requires them to live in the same place and to intermarry). That is why kinship-groups, brotherhoods, religious societies, and pursuits that involve living together have developed in cities; these are the product of friendship, since the decision to live together is friendship.

The end of a city, then, is living well, and these [pursuits] are for the sake of the end. A city is the com- 1281a munity of families and villages in a complete and self-sufficient life. This sort of life, as we say, is a happy and fine life; hence we should suppose that a city aims at fine actions, not [merely] at living together.

That is why someone who contributes most to this sort of community has a greater share in the city than that of someone who is equal or superior in free status or in family, but unequal in a citizen's virtue, and a greater share than that of someone who excels in wealth but is excelled in virtue.

It is evident, then, from what we have said that each of the parties disputing about political systems is describing a part of justice.

Book 4

11

What is the best political system, and the best way of 1295a life for most cities and for most human beings? We are not judging by reference to a type of virtue that is beyond a private citizen's capacity, or by reference to a type of education that requires [a suitable] nature and a level of resources that depends on good fortune, or by reference to a political system that is the best we could aspire to, but by reference to a way of life that most people are able to share and a political system that most cities can achieve. For the so-called aristocracies we discussed just now are in some ways beyond the capacity of most cities, and some ways are close to the so-called polity, so that we can treat [this type of aristocracy and the polity] as one.

A judgment on all these questions depends on the same elementary principles. For if we were right to say in the *Ethics* that the happy life is the one that conforms to unimpeded virtue, and that virtue is a mean, then the intermediate life—achieving the mean that is possible for a given type of person—is the best. Moreover, these same formulae that apply to the virtue and vice [of an individual] must also 1295b apply to a city and a political system, since the political system is a sort of way of life of a city.

Now, in every city there are three parts—the extremely prosperous, the extremely disadvantaged, and, third, those intermediate between them. And so, since it is agreed that what is moderate and what is intermediate is best, it is also evident that the possession of an intermediate amount of goods of fortune is best of all; for it is easiest in this condition to obey reason. But if one is exceedingly handsome, strong, well born, or rich, or, on the contrary, exceedingly poor or feeble or extremely dishonored, it is hard to follow reason. For [the exceedingly well-favored] turn out to be wantonly aggressive and wicked on a grand scale, while the exceedingly ill-favored turn out crooked and excessively wicked on a small scale; and wanton aggression causes some acts of injustice, while crookedness causes others. Further, the intermediate people are least prone either to shirk or to covet ruling offices; and each of these two tendencies is harmful to cities.

Besides, those who have exceedingly good fortune—strength, wealth, friends, and so on—neither wish nor know how to submit to being ruled—indeed, this begins even when they are children at home, since their luxurious upbringing makes them unused to being ruled even at school. On the other hand, the exceedingly needy are excessively abased. And so the needy do not know how to rule but only how to submit to being ruled as slaves, while the fortunate do not know how to submit to any kind of rule but only how to rule as masters over slaves. The result is a city of masters and slaves, not of free citizens, and, moreover, of slaves looking spitefully on their masters and of masters despising their slaves. And this is furthest of all from friendship and a political community. For community involves friendship; people are unwilling even to share the road with their enemies.

Now, the city aims to consist as far as possible of citizens who are equal and similar; these features are most frequent in the intermediate people. And so the city composed of these people, who we say are the naturally [appropriate] constituents of cities, is bound to have the best political system.

Moreover, these are the citizens who most frequently survive in cities. For they do not covet other people's possessions, as the poor do, nor do others covet theirs, as the poor covet those of the rich. And since they are neither victims of plots nor plotters themselves, they pass their lives without danger. And so Phocyclides was right in his wish, 'Many things go best for the intermediate people; I want to be an intermediate in the city.'

Clearly, then, the political community that is in the hands of the intermediate people is best, and the cities capable of having a good system are those in which the intermediate [part] is numerous and superior, preferably to both the other [parts] together, but at least to either one of them—for if it is added [to either one] it tips the balance and tends to prevent the contrary excesses.

Hence it is the greatest good fortune [for a city] if the politically active citizens have intermediate and 1296a adequate property. For if some possess an extremely large amount and others possess nothing, the result is either an extreme democracy or an unmitigated oligarchy, or a tyranny resulting from either of these excesses; for tyranny arises from the most thorough democracy or oligarchy, but far less often from the the intermediate systems and those that are close to them. We will explain this in our account of changes in political systems.

Evidently, then, the intermediate system is best. For it is the only one free from civil conflicts, since the cities that have a large intermediate [part] are least likely to have civil conflicts and divisions among the citizens. And for the same reason large cities are less prone to civil conflict, since their intermediate [part] is numerous; in small cities, by contrast, it is easy to divide all the citizens into two groups, so as to leave no intermediate [part], and they are virtually all either prosperous or disadvantaged.

Moreover, the intermediate people make democracies more secure and lasting than oligarchies; for they are more numerous and more likely to share in honors in democracies than they are oligarchies. For whenever the disadvantaged overcome by weight of numbers, without the intermediate people; things turn out badly, and [the city is] soon ruined.

And we must see further evidence [for our claim] in the fact that the best legislators have come from the intermediate citizens. For Solon was one of them, as he shows in this poetry; so was Lycurgus, since he was not a king; so was Charondas; and so were virtually most of the other legislators.

From this it is also evident why most political systems are either democratic or oligarchic; for since the intermediate [part] is often small in these cities, those outside the intermediate [part] who are on top at the time (either those with property or the common people) lead the system in the direction they prefer, so that the result is either a democracy or an oligarchy.

Besides, civil conflicts and struggles arise between the common people and the prosperous. The result is that the side that happens to beat the opposition does not establish a system that all can share in fairly, but grabs the top places in the political system as a prize of victory, so that one side establishes a democracy, and the other side an oligarchy.

Further, the same applies to those cities[7] that once achieved leadership over Greece. Each city was guided by its own political system, so that one of them set up democracies in the cities, and the other set up oligarchies; each considered its own advantage, not the advantage of the cities.

For these reasons, then, the intermediate system has either never been established or only on a few occasions in a few cities. For only one man in earlier times among those who reached a position of leader-
1296b ship was persuaded to introduce this sort of order; and by now it has become a habit in cities not even to wish for a fair system, but either to seek to rule or to submit to domination by others.

It is evident, then, from this what the best political system is, and why it is best. But among the other systems, since we say there are several types of democracy and of oligarchy, which should we put first, which second, and which next in the order of better and worse? This is not hard to see once we have determined the best system. For in each case the system that is nearer to the best must be better, and the one further from the intermediate must be worse, unless our judgment is relative to an assumption. By 'relative to an assumption' I mean that though one system may be preferable [in general], a different system may well be more beneficial for some cities.

7. **those cities:** Athens and Sparta. They also regarded control over the political system as a prize for the winning side.

Book 7

1

Anyone who is inquiring along the appropriate lines 1323a
into the best political system must first determine what the most choiceworthy life is. If it is left unclear what this is, it must also be unclear what the best political system is; for those who have the best political system in their circumstances will characteristically be best-off, if nothing unexpected happens. That is why we must first agree on what sort of life is most choiceworthy for (we may say) everyone, and then agree on whether such a life is or not the same for an individual as for a community. We may take it then, that the best life is discussed at sufficient length even in [our] popular discussions; and so we should use those now.

For certainly no one would dispute one classification [of goods], at least, into external goods, goods in the body, and goods in the soul, or would deny that blessedly happy people ought to possess them all. For no one would count a person blessedly happy if he had no part of bravery, temperance, justice, or wisdom, but was afraid of every passing fly, sank to any depth to satisfy his appetite for food or drink, ruined his closest friends for some trivial gain, and had his mind as full of senseless illusion as a child's or a madman's.

Everyone would agree with these statements, but people disagree about how much [of each good is needed] and about large amounts of them. For whereas they think any slight degree of virtue is quite enough, they seek extreme abundance of wealth, valuables, power, reputation, and all such things, without limit. We will tell them, on the contrary, that it is easy to reach a confident belief about these questions, by simply attending to the facts.

For we see that people possess and keep external goods by having the virtues, not the other way round. 1323b
Further, as we see, a happy life—whether such a life for human beings consists in enjoyment or in virtue or in both—belongs to those who go to extremes in well-ordered character and intellect, but possess a moderate level of external goods, rather than to those who have more external goods than they can use, but are deficient in character and intellect.

Moreover, the same point is easy to notice if we approach the question by argument. For externals, like instruments, and everything useful for some purpose, have a limit, and excess of them is bound to harm, not to benefit, the possessor; but each good of the soul become more useful as it exceeds (if we are to attribute usefulness as well as fineness even to these goods).

And in general, clearly we will say that the best condition of one thing surpasses the best condition of another in proportion to the superiority of the first thing over the second. And so, if the soul is more honorable, both without qualification and in relation to us, than possessions and the body, it follows that its best condition must be proportionately better than theirs. Further, these other things are naturally choiceworthy for the sake of the soul, and every intelligent person must choose them for its sake, not the soul for their sake.

Let us, then, take it as agreed that each person achieves happiness to the extent that he achieves virtue and intelligence, and acts in accordance with them. We appeal to the god as evidence; for he is happy and blessed, because of himself and the character that is naturally his, not though any external good. Indeed this is also why good fortune cannot be the same as happiness; for chance and fortune produce goods external to the soul, whereas no one is just or temperate from fortune or because of fortune.

The next point, relying on the same arguments, is that the happy city is also the best one, the one that acts finely. But no one can act finely without doing fine actions, and neither a man nor a city does any fine actions without virtue and intelligence. Moreover, the bravery, justice, intelligence, and temperance of a city have the same capacity and form that belongs to a human being who is called brave, just, intelligent, and temperate.

So much, then, for a preface to our argument; for we can neither leave these questions untouched nor go through all the appropiate arguments, since this is a task for another discipline. For now, let us simply assume that the best life for an individual by himself, and the best common life for cities, is the
1324a life involving virtue that has sufficient [external] resources to share in actions expressing virtue. In our present line of inquiry we must leave aside objections, and consider them later, if someone turns out to be unpersuaded by what we have said.

2

It remains to be said, however, whether we should or should not take happiness to be the same for an individual human being and for a city. But the answer to this is also evident; for everyone would agree that it is the same. For those who think an individual lives well in being rich also count a whole city blessed if it is rich, whereas those who honor the tyrant's way of life above all others would say that the happiest city is the one that rules over the most people; and if anyone thinks that virtue makes an individual happy, he will also say that the more excellent city is happier.

But now there are two questions to be investigated. First, which of these two lives is more choiceworthy—the one that involves taking part in political activities and sharing in the city, or the life of an alien, released from the political community? Second, what political system and what condition of the city should we regard as best (no matter whether we decide that participation in the city is choiceworthy for everyone, or only for most people, not for everyone)? This second question—not the question about what is choiceworthy for the individual—is task of political thought and study; and since we have decided to undertake a political investigation now, that first question will be a side-issue, and the second will be the main issue for this line of inquiry.

First, then, it is evident that the best political system must be the order that guides the life of anyone at all who does best and lives blessedly. But even those who agree that the life involving virtue is the most choiceworthy disagree about whether the active life of the citizen is choiceworthy, or the life of someone released from all externals—some life of study, which some people think is the only life for a philosopher—is more choiceworthy. For practically all those, both in the past and now, who have most eagerly pursued virtue have evidently decided on one or other of these two lives, the political and the philosophical; and it is quite important to decide which view is correct, since the intelligent individual, and the intelligent political system no less, will necessarily order life to aim at the best goal.

Some people, however, think that ruling over one's neighbors as a master over slaves involves one of the worst injustices, and that even rule as a citizen over citizens, though it has nothing unjust about it, still interferes with the ruler's well-being. Others take just about the contrary view, supposing that the only life for a man is the life of political activity, since, in their 1324b view, the actions resulting from each virtue are open to those who undertake political action for the community, no less than to a private individual.

Some, then, hold this view. But still others say that only the from of political system that rules as a master and a tyrant is happy. And so in some cities the very aim of the political system and laws is to rule over neighboring peoples as slaves.

And so, while most laws in most cities are pretty haphazard, still any city that has laws aiming to any extent at some end has them all aiming at domination, as in Sparta and Crete both the education and most of the laws are organized for war. Moreover, all the [non-Greek] nations that have the power to get more [at the expense of others] honor this sort of power. For in some places there are even laws that incite them to this sort of virtue. The Carthaginians, for example, so it is said, decorate soldiers with bracelets for the number of campaigns they have served in. Once the Macedonians had a law that someone who had not killed an enemy should wear a rope around his waist instead of a belt. The Scythians used to pass around a cup at feasts and forbade it to anyone who had not killed an enemy. And the warlike Iberian nation place around someone's grave a number of stakes to mark the number of enemies he has killed. Many peoples have many similar practices established by laws or customs.

If we are willing to examine this question, however, we will find it utterly absurd to suppose that the politician's task is the ability to study ways of ruling over neighboring peoples as willing or unwilling slaves. For how could this be a politician's or lawgiver's task, since it is not even lawful? It is unlawful to rule without regard to justice or injustice, and domination may quite possibly be unjust. Moreover, we never see this in the other sciences; it is not the doctor's or pilot's task to force his patients or passengers if he fails to persuade them.

Most people, however, would seem to think the science of mastery over slaves is political science; and they are not ashamed to treat other peoples in ways that they reject as unjust and harmful among individuals. For among themselves they seek to rule justly, but in relations with other peoples they are indifferent to justice.

It is absurd, however, to deny that some creatures are, and some are not, naturally suited to be ruled by masters. And so, if this is true, we must try to rule as masters only over those suited to be ruled, not over everyone, just as we must not try to hunt human beings for a feast or sacrifice, but only animals that are suitable to be hunted; these are the wild animals 1325a that are suitable to eat.

Besides, a single city even by itself—if it has a fine political system, of course—can be happy, if it is possible for a city to live in isolation somewhere, governed by excellent laws. The organization of this political system will not aim at war or at domination over enemy states, since it is assumed to have no enemies or wars.

Clearly, then, all the ways of training for war should be regarded as fine—not, however, as the ultimate end of everything, but as promoting that end. The excellent legislator's task is to consider how a city, or people, or any other community, is to participate in a good life and in the happiness available to it. However, some prescriptions of law will vary; and it is the task of legislative science, if a city has neighbors, to see what practices should be cultivated in relations with different sorts of neighbors and how to apply the suitable ones to dealings with each neighboring city.

This question, however, about the right aim for the best political system, will receive the proper discussion later.

3

We must reply to the two sides who agree that the life involving virtue is the most choiceworthy but differ about the right way to practice it. For those on one side refuse to hold any rule over citizens, since they suppose that the free person's way of life is both different from the life of political activity and the most choiceworthy of all lives. Those on the other side, on the contrary, hold that the politically active life is the best of all, since, in their view, someone who is inactive cannot possibly be acting well, and good action is the same as happiness. In reply we say the each side is partly right and partly wrong.

The one side is right to say that the free person's way of life is better than the life of a master ruling slaves. This is true; for employing a slave, insofar as he is a slave, is quite unimpressive, since there is nothing fine about giving orders for the provision of necessities. But to suppose that every sort of rule is the rule of a master over slaves is wrong. For there is just as great a difference between rule over free people and rule over slaves as there is between being naturally free and being naturally a slave. We have determined this sufficiently in the first discussions. Moreover, it is incorrect to praise inactivity over activity; for happiness is activity, and, further, the actions of just and temperate people achieve many fine goals.

And yet, someone might perhaps take this conclusion to imply that control over everyone is the best thing, thinking that this is the way to be in control of the largest number of the finest actions. And so, on this view, anyone capable of ruling must not resign rule to his neighbor, but must seize it from him; a father must have no consideration for his sons, nor sons for their father, nor in general one friend for another, nor consider them at all in comparison to this goal [of ruling], since what is best is most choiceworthy, and good action is best.

1325b Now, presumably this claim [about ruling] is true, if brigands who rob and use force get the most choiceworthy thing there is. But presumably they cannot, and this assumption is false. For [the actions of an absolute ruler] cannot be fine if he is not as far superior to his subjects as a man is to his wife, or a father is to his children, or a master to his slaves. And so someone who deviates from virtue can never achieve a great enough success thereby to outweigh his previous deviation.

For what is fine and just for people who are similar is [holding office] in turn. For this is equal and similar treatment, whereas unequal treatment for equal people and dissimilar treatment for similar people are against nature, and nothing that is against nature is fine. That is why, if another person is superior in virtue and in the capacity for the best actions, it is fine to follow him, and just to obey him; but he must have not only virtue but also the capacity for the actions.

If this is right, and we should take happiness to be good action, then the life of action is best both for a whole city in common and for the individual.

However, the life of action need not, as some think, involve relations to others, and the thoughts concerned with action need not be only those carried out for the sake of the results of the action. On the contrary, the studies and thoughts that include their own end and are carried out for their own sakes must be far more concerned with action; for [their] end is good action, and hence it is a kind of action. And in fact, even in the case of external actions, those whom we regard as acting most fully are the master craftsmen whose plans [direct production].

Nor, moreover, are cities necessarily inactive if their position is isolated and they have decided to live in isolation. For a city can still have activities involving parts of itself, since the parts of the city have many communities with each other. And the same is also true of any individual human being; otherwise the god and the whole universe would hardly be in a fine condition, since they have no actions directed outside them, but only their own proper actions involving themselves.

It is evident, then, that the same sort of life must be the best one both for an individual human being and for cities and human beings in common. . . .

13

We should now discuss the political system itself and
say which people, and of what character, must con- *1331b*
stitute a city if it is to be blessedly happy and to have a fine political system.

Everyone's welfare depends on two conditions; the goal and end of actions must be correctly laid down, and the actions promoting the end must be found. For these may either conflict or harmonize with each other. Sometimes the goal has been finely laid down, but we fail to obtain it in our actions; sometimes we attain everything that promotes our end, but have laid down a bad end; and sometimes we fail on both counts (as in medicine, for instance, when sometimes they neither make a correct judgment about the character of a healthy body nor manage to find the right productive process relative to the standard that has been laid down). In crafts and sciences we must master both the end and the actions advancing towards it.

It is evident, then, that everyone aims at living well
and at happiness. In fact, however, these are open to *1332a*

some and not to others, because of something in fortune or nature—for living finely also needs resources, fewer if our condition is better, and more if it is worse. Others again, though happiness is open to them, seek it in the wrong way from the start. Our task is to see the best political system, the one that will result in the best political life in the city; this will be the one that most of all results in happiness for the city. Hence we must not be ignorant of what happiness is.

We say, then—as we define it in the *Ethics*,[8] if those discussions are of any benefit—that happiness is complete activity and exercise of virtue, complete. without qualification, not conditionally. By 'conditionally' I mean what is necessary, and by 'without qualification' I mean what is done finely. For in the case of just actions, for instance, penalties and corrective treatments result from virtue, but are necessary, and are done finely only to the extent that is possible for necessary actions, since it is more choiceworthy if neither a man nor a city needs any such thing. By contrast, actions leading to honors and prosperity are the finest actions without qualification; for while the other type of action involves merely the removal of some evil, these, on the contrary, construct and generate goods.

Now, certainly the excellent man will act finely in response to poverty or disease or any other ill fortune. Still, blessedness consists in the contrary of these. For we have determined this also in our ethical discussions, that the excellent person is the sort whose virtue makes unqualified goods good for him; and clearly the ways in which he uses them must also be excellent and fine without qualification. Indeed this is why human beings think external goods cause happiness; it is as though they took the lyre rather than the performer's craft to be the cause of a splendidly fine performance.

It follows, then from what has been said, that some conditions must be presupposed, but some must be provided by the legislator. That is why, in establishing the city, we assume that the goods we want that are controlled by fortune (since we take fortune to control [externals]) are provided at the level we aspire to, but when we come to making the city excellent, it is a task not for fortune, but for science and decision.

8. ***Ethics:*** cf. *Nicomachean Ethics* 1098a16.

Moreover, a city is excellent because the citizens who participate in the political system are excellent; and in our city all the citizens participate in the political system. Hence we must consider how an excellent man comes to be; for even if it is possible for the citizens to be excellent all together without being so individually, still it is more choiceworthy for each to be excellent individually, since being excellent individually also implies being excellent all together [but the converse is not true].

Now, people come to be good and excellent through three means—nature, habit, and reason. For, first of all, we must be born with the nature of a human being, not of some other animal; and then we
must have the appropriate sort of body and soul. But 1332b
in some cases being born with a given quality is no help, since habits alter it; for nature makes some things able to go either way, and habits change them for the worse or the better.

Now, whereas the other animals live mostly by nature, while some live to some slight extent by habit, a human being also lives by reason, since he is the only animal who has it. And so these three ought to be in accord; for people do many actions contrary to habituation and nature because of reason, if they are persuaded that another way is better.

We have previously defined, then, the sort of nature that is needed if people are to be easily handled by the legislator. Thereafter the task falls to education, since some things are learnt by habituation, others by instruction. . . .

15

The goal appears to be the same for a community of 1334a
human beings as for an individual, and the best political system must conform to the same standard that the best man conforms to. Evidently, then, it must possess the virtues applying to leisure; for, as we have often said, the goal of war is peace, and the goal of labor is leisure.

The virtues that are useful for leisure and for spending one's leisure time are those whose function applies to leisure and those whose function applies to labor; for many necessary [goods] must be presupposed if leisure is to be open to us. Hence it is fitting for the city to be temperate, brave, and resistant; for, as the proverb says, slaves have no leisure, and those who cannot face dangers bravely are slaves of their attackers.

Now, bravery and resistance are needed for labor, philosophy for leisure, and temperance and justice in both circumstances—indeed, even more in peace and leisure. For war compels us to be just and temperate, but enjoyment of good fortune and of peacetime makes people insolently aggressive instead. Much justice and temperance, then, are needed by those who seem to do best and to enjoy the [external] goods that bring congratulation for blessedness. This will be true for instance, of the people in the Isles of the Blessed, if there are any, as the poets say there are; for these will have most need of philosophy, temperance, and justice, to the extent that they more than anyone else are at leisure, with abundance of all those [external] goods.

It is evident, then, why the city that is to be happy and excellent needs to share in the virtues. For it is shameful to be incapable of using goods [properly]; it is even more shameful to be incapable of using them in leisure, so that we appear good when we are laboring and fighting wars, but slavish when we are at leisure in time of peace.

1334b That is why we must not cultivate virtue as Sparta does. For the Spartans are superior to other people not by rejecting other people's view that the [externals] are the greatest goods, but by believing that a particular virtue is the best way to secure these goods. But since they esteem these goods and the enjoyment of them more highly than the enjoyment of the virtues[9] . . . and that [virtue is to be cultivated] for itself, is evident from this. The next thing to attend to, then, is the means and method of acquiring virtue.

We have previously determined, then, that the acquisition of virtue depends on nature, habit, and reason; and among these we have previously determined the sort of natural characteristics people should have. The remaining question to study is whether education by reason or by habit should come first.

For reason and habit must achieve the best sort of harmony, since it is possible both for reason to fall short of the best basic assumption and for upbringing by habits to fail similarly. This at least, then, is evident first of all, as in other cases, that coming to be has some starting point, and the end resulting from one starting point is itself the starting point of another end. Now, the goal of nature for us is reason and understanding; hence the coming to be and the practice of habits must be arranged to aim at these.

Further, just as soul and body are two, so also we see that the soul has two parts, the non-rational and the rational, and these have two [characteristic] states, desire and understanding [respectively]. And just as the body comes to be before the soul, so also the non-rational part of the soul comes to before the rational. This also is evident from the fact that emotion, wish, and also appetite are present in children as soon as they are born, whereas reasoning and understanding naturally arise in the course of growth.

First of all, then, attention to the body must precede attention to the soul, and, next, attention to desire must precede attention to understanding. Nonetheless, attention to desire must be for the sake of understanding, just as attention to the body must be for the sake of the soul.

9. **virtues . . .** : There seems to be a passage missing from the manuscripts at this point.

HELLENISTIC PHILOSOPHY

Epicurus

Epicurus was born in 341 BCE on Samos, the island of Pythagoras and Melissus. His most important teacher was a follower of Democritus, and Epicurus was espousing a version of Democritean philosophy by the time he moved to Athens in 307. Because his friends and students gathered in the garden of his house, his school became known as "The Garden." Philosophical conversation amid natural beauty became the Epicureans' model of the best life.

Among the most prolific writers of antiquity, Epicurus wrote dozens of books. Little more of them survives than the letters and maxims printed here, all of which are drawn from Diogenes Laertius (second century CE), our primary source for Hellenistic philosophy. These condensed the essentials of his teachings for the benefit of his followers, who were often eager to memorize their teacher's words. Indeed, the Epicurean motto was, "Act always as if Epicurus is watching," and a bust of him stood in many of their homes, supervising their discussions.

The first letter, to Herodotus, outlines Epicurean physics, which largely follows the atomism of Democritus, while nonetheless allowing for the possibility of free will. Among other matters, Epicurus discusses perception and language, which remain difficult to reconcile with a meaningless world of imperceptible atoms and void. These abstract physical speculations serve an ethical aim: to dispel the anxiety produced by false beliefs about the world. It was fear of death, indeed, and especially of punishment at the hand of vindictive gods, that Epicurus sought above all to eliminate from his followers. Death is not to be feared, he argued, since in it there is no perception. Moreover, the gods are indifferent, so that providence, with its punishments for wrongdoing, is an erroneous fable.

The second letter, to Menoeceus, outlines Epicurean ethics, according to which the goal of life is pleasure. This is found not in ecstasy or license, which disturb the mind and bring pain in their wake, but in health of the soul, particularly "freedom from disturbance." Epicurus thus recommended natural, simple pleasures. "Send me a little pot of cheese," he told a friend, "so that I can indulge in extravagance when I wish." Hostile rivals for philosophical converts—especially the Stoics and the Christians, who shared a belief in providence—nevertheless associated the name of Epicurus with indulgence, a calumny which persists in the English meaning of the word *epicure*.

In antiquity, Epicureanism never gained the widespread influence enjoyed by these rivals, but its few adherents remained fiercely devoted. The most famous of these adherents was the great Roman poet Lucretius, whose poem is excerpted in the next chapter of this volume. Just as impressive, however, is the giant stone inscription of Diogenes of Oenoanda (in modern-day Turkey), which summarized Epicurean philosophy for the benefit of his countrymen five centuries after the founder's death in 271.

Letter to Herodotus (Diogenes Laertius 10.34–83)

Epicurus to Herodotus, greetings:

For the sake of those, Herodotus, who are unable to work out with precision each and every detail of what we have written on nature and who lack the ability to work through the longer books I have composed, I have myself prepared an adequate summary of the entire system, to facilitate the firm memorization of the most general doctrines, in order that at each and every opportunity they may be able to help themselves in the most important issues, to the degree that they retain their grasp on the study of nature. Even those well advanced in the examination of the universe must recall the outline of the entire system; and this outline is structured according to basic principles. For we frequently need the overall application [of the intellect], but not so often the detailed application.

We must, then, approach those [general points] continually, and get into our memory an amount [of doctrine] sufficient to permit the most vital application [of the intellect] to the facts; moreover, complete precision on detailed points will be discovered if the general outlines are comprehensively grasped and remembered. For even the fully expert [student of physics] gets as the most vital benefit of complete precision the ability to make nimble use of his applications, and [this would happen if every point] were united in [a set of] simple principles and maxims. For it is not possible to know the concentrated result of our continuous overview of the universe unless one can have in oneself a comprehensive grasp by means of brief maxims of all that might also be worked out in detail with precision.

Since this kind of method is useful to *all* those who are concerned with the study of nature, I recommend constant activity in the study of nature; and with this sort of activity more than any other I bring calm to my life. That is why I have composed for you this type of summary statement of the basic principles of the entire set of doctrines.

First, Herodotus, we need to have grasped what is denoted by our words, so that by referring to what they denote we can make decisions about the objects of opinion, investigation, or puzzlement and so that all of these things will not remain undecided, [as they would] if we tried to give an infinitely long demonstration, and so that our words will not be empty. For it is necessary that we look to the primary conception corresponding to each word and that it stand in no need of demonstration, if, that is, we are going to have something to which we can refer the object of search or puzzlement and opinion. Again, it is also necessary to observe all things in accordance with one's sense-perceptions, i.e., simply according to the present applications, whether of the intellect or of any other of the criteria, and similarly [to observe everything] in accordance with our actual feelings, so that we can have some sign by which we may make inferences both about what awaits confirmation and about the non-evident.

After distinguishing these points we must next arrive at a general view about the things which are non-evident. The first point is that nothing comes into being from what is not; for [in that case] everything would be coming into being from everything, with no need of seeds. And if that which disappears were destroyed into what is not, all things would have been destroyed, since that into which they were dissolved does not exist. Further, the totality [of things] has always been just like it is now and always will be. For there is nothing for it to change into. For there exists nothing in addition to the totality, which could enter into it and produce the change.

Moreover, the totality is [made up of] [bodies and void]; for in all cases sense-perception itself testifies that bodies exist, and it is by sense-perception that we must infer by reasoning what is non-evident, as I already said. And if there did not exist that which we call void and space and intangible nature, bodies would not have any place to be in or move through, as they obviously do move. Beyond these two things [viz., bodies and void] nothing can be conceived, either by a comprehensive grasp or analogously to things so grasped, [at least not if we mean] grasped as

---

From *Hellenistic Philosophy*, second edition, translated by Brad Inwood and L. P. Gerson (Indianapolis: Hackett Publishing Company, 1997).

complete natures rather than as what are termed properties or accidents of these [two] things.

Further, among bodies, some are compounds, and some are those things from which compounds have been made. And these are atomic and unchangeable, if indeed they are not all going to be destroyed into not being but will remain firmly during the dissolutions of compounds, being full by nature and not being subject to dissolution in any way or fashion. Consequently the principles of bodies must be atomic natures.

Moreover, the totality is unlimited. For what is limited has an extreme; but an extreme is seen in contrast to something else, so that since it has no extreme it has no limit. But since it has no limit it would be unlimited and not limited.

Further, the totality is unlimited in respect of the number of bodies and the magnitude of the void. For if the void were unlimited and bodies limited, bodies would not come to a standstill anywhere but would move in scattered fashion throughout the unlimited void, since they would lack anything to support them or check them by collision. But if the void were limited, the unlimited bodies would not have a place to be in.

In addition, the bodies which are atomic and full, from which compounds both come to be and into which they are dissolved, are ungraspable when it comes to the differences among their shapes. For it is not possible that so many differences [in things] should come to be from the same shapes having been comprehensively grasped. And for each type of shape there is, quite simply, an unlimited number of similar [atoms], but with respect to the differences they are not quite simply unlimited but only ungraspable.

And the atoms move continuously for all time, some recoiling far apart from one another [upon collision], and others, by contrast, maintaining a [constant] vibration when they are locked into a compound or enclosed by the surrounding [atoms of a compound]. This is the result of the nature of the void which separates each of them and is not able to provide any resistance; and their actual solidity causes their rebound vibration to extend, during the collision, as far as the distance which the entanglement [of the compound] permits after the collision.

There is no principle for these [entities], since the atoms and the void are eternal. If all these points are remembered, a maxim as brief as this will provide an adequate outline for [developing] our conceptions about the nature of what exists.

Moreover, there is an unlimited number of cosmoi, and some are similar to this one and some are dissimilar. For the atoms, which are unlimited (as was shown just now), are also carried away to very remote distances. For atoms of the sort from which a world might come to be or by which it might be made are not exhausted [in the production] of one world or any finite number of them, neither worlds like this one nor worlds unlike them. Consequently, there is no obstacle to the unlimitedness of worlds.

Further, there exist outlines [i.e., images, *eidola*] which are similar in shape to solids, only much finer than observed objects. For it is not impossible for such compounds to come into being in the surrounding environment, nor that there should be favourable opportunities for the production of hollow and thin [films], nor that effluences should retain the relative position and standing [i.e., order] that they had in the solid objects. These outlines we call 'images'. Further, since their movement through the void occurs with no conflict from [atoms which] could resist them, it can cover any comprehensively graspable distance in an inconceivably [short] time. For the presence and absence of resistance take on a similarity to slowness and speed.

The moving body itself, however, cannot reach several places at the same time, speaking in terms of time contemplated by reason; for that is unthinkable. Yet when considered as arriving in perceptible time from any point at all in the unlimited, it will not be departing from the place from which we comprehensively grasp its motion as having come from. For it will be like resistance even if to this point we leave the speed of the movement free from resistance. The retention of this basic principle too is useful.

Next, none of the appearances testifies against [the theory] that the images have an unsurpassed fineness; and that is why they have unsurpassed speed too, since they find every passage suitably sized for there being no or few [bodies] to resist their flow, whereas there is some [body] to resist a large or infinite number of atoms.

In addition, [none of the facts testifies against the claim] that the production of images occurs as fast as thought. For there is a continuous flow from the surface of bodies, though it is not obvious from any reduction in bulk because the [objects are] refilled [by other atoms]; [and this flow] preserves for quite some time the position and order of the atoms which it had in the solid, even if it is sometimes disrupted; and [two-dimensional] compounds are quickly produced in the surrounding environment, since they do not need to be filled out with depth—and there are certain other ways in which such natures [i.e., compound images] can be produced. None of these [claims] is testified against by the senses, providing one considers the clear facts in a certain way; one will also refer to [the senses] the [fact that] harmonious sets [of qualities] come to us from external objects.

One must also believe that it is when something from the external objects enters into us that we see and think about their shapes. For external objects would not stamp into us the nature of their own colour and shape via the air which is between us and them, nor via the rays or any kind of flows which move from us to them, as well as [they would] by means of certain outlines which share the colour and shape of the objects and enter into us from them, entering the vision or the intellect according to the size and fit [of the effluences] and moving very quickly; then, for this reason, they give the presentation of a single, continuous thing, and preserve the harmonious set [of qualities] generated by the external object, as a result of the coordinate impact from that object [on us], which [in turn] originates in the vibration of the atoms deep inside the solid object. And whatever presentation we receive by a form of application, whether by the intellect or by the sense organs, and whether of a shape or of accidents, this *is* the shape of the solid object, produced by the continuous compacting or residue of the image. Falsehood or error *always* resides in the added opinion [in the case of something which awaits] testimony for or against it but in the event receives neither supporting testimony [nor opposing testimony].

For the similarity of appearances (which are like what are grasped in a representational picture and occur either in dreams or in some other applications of the intellect or the other criteria) to what are called real and true things would never occur if some such thing were not added [to the basic experience]. And error would not occur if we did not have some other motion too in ourselves which is linked [to the application to presentations] but is distinct; falsehood occurs because of this, if it is not testified for or is testified against; but if it is testified for or is not testified against, truth occurs.

One must, then, keep this doctrine too quite firmly in mind, in order to avoid destroying the criteria of clear facts and to avoid having error placed on an equal basis with that which has been established, which would confound everything.

Moreover, hearing too occurs when a flow moves from that object which makes an utterance or produces a sound or makes a noise or in any other way causes the auditory experience. This flow is broken into small masses which are homogeneous with the whole which at the same time preserve an harmonious set [of qualities] relative to each other and also a unique kind of unity which extends back to the originating source and, usually, produces the perceptual experience occasioned by the flow; and if not, it only makes the external object apparent. For without some harmonious set [of qualities] coming from there, this sort of perceptual experience could not occur. So one must not think that the air itself is shaped by the emitted voice or even by things of like character—for it is far from being the case that it [i.e., air] is affected in this way by that [i.e., voice]—but rather when we emit voice the blow which occurs inside us precipitates the expulsion of certain masses which produce a flow similar to breath, and which causes in us the auditory experience.

Further, one must also believe that the [sense of] smell, like hearing too, would never have produced any experience if there were not certain masses moving from the object and being commensurate for the stimulation of this sense organ, some of them of one sort, i.e., disturbing and uncongenial, and some of another, i.e., non-disturbing and congenial [to the organ of smell].

Further, one must believe that the atoms bring with them none of the qualities of things which appear except shape, weight, and size and the [properties] which necessarily accompany shape. For every quality changes, while the atoms do not change in any respect; for it is necessary that during the dissolution of compounds something should remain solid and undissolved, which will guarantee that the changes are not into what is not nor from what is not, but come about by rearrangements in many cases, and in some cases too by additions and subtractions [of atoms from the compound]. That is why it is necessary that the things which are rearranged should be indestructible and not have the nature of what changes, but rather their own masses and configurations. For it is also necessary that these things should remain [unchanged].

For even with things in our experience which change their shapes by the removal [of matter], the shape is grasped as inhering in the object which changes, while its qualities do not so inhere. The shape remains, but the qualities are eliminated from the entire body. So these features which are left behind [after a change] are sufficient to produce the differences in compounds, since it *is* necessary that some things be left behind and that there not be a destruction into what is not.

Moreover, one should not believe that atoms have every [possible] magnitude, so that one may avoid being testified against by the appearances. But one should believe that there are some differences in magnitude. For if this [doctrine] is added, then it will be easier to account for what, according to our feelings and sense-perceptions, actually happens. But [to suppose] that *every* magnitude exists is not useful for [accounting for] the differences of qualities, and at the same time it would be necessary that some atoms reach the point of being visible to us—which is not seen to occur nor can one conceive how an atom could become visible.

In addition to these points, one must not believe that there can be an unlimited number of masses—no matter how small—in any finite body. Consequently, not only must one eliminate unlimited division into smaller pieces (to avoid making everything weak and being forced in our comprehensive grasps of compound things to exhaust the things which exist by reducing them to non-existence), but one must also not believe that within finite bodies there is an unlimited movement, not even by smaller and smaller stages.

For as soon as one says that there is in some thing an unlimited number of masses, no matter how small, then one cannot think how this magnitude could any longer be limited. For obviously these unlimited masses must be of some size or other; and no matter how small they might be, the magnitude [of the whole object] would for all that be unlimited. And since the limited has an extreme which can be distinguished even if it cannot be observed on its own, it is impossible not to conceive that the thing next to it is of the same character and that by moving forward from one point to the next in this fashion it turns out that one will in this fashion reach the unlimited conceptually.

And we must conceive that the minimal perceptible [part] is neither such as to be traversible nor is it totally and altogether unlike this. It has something in common with things which permit of being traversed, but [unlike them] it does not permit the distinguishing of parts [within it]; but whenever, because of the resemblance created by what they have in common, we think that we are going to distinguish some [part] of it—one part here, another over there—it must be that we encounter something of equal size. We observe these one after another, starting from the first, and not [as being] in the same place nor as touching each other's parts with their own, but rather we [see] them measuring out magnitudes in their own unique way, more of them measuring out a larger magnitude and fewer of them a smaller.

One must believe that the minimal part in the atom also stands in this relation. It is obvious that it is only in its smallness that it differs from what is observed in the case of perception, but it does stand in the same relation. For indeed it is because of this relation that we have already asserted that the atom has magnitude, and have merely extended it far beyond [perceptible things] in smallness. And again we must believe that the minimal and indivisible parts are limits which provide from themselves as primary [units] a standard of measurement for the lengths of larger and smaller [atoms], when we contemplate invisible things with reason. For what they have in common with things which do not permit of movement [across themselves] is enough to get us this far; but it is not possible for these [minimal parts] to possess motion and so move together [into compounds].

Further, one must not assert that the unlimited has an up and a down in the sense of an [absolutely] highest and lowest point. We know, however, that what is over our heads from wherever we stand, or what is below any point which we think of—it being possible to project both indefinitely—will never appear to us as being at the same time and in the same respect both up and down. For it is impossible to conceive of this. Consequently, it is possible to grasp as one motion the one conceived of as indefinitely [extended] upwards and the one conceived of as indefinitely [extended] downwards, even if a thousand times over a thing moving from us towards the places over our heads should arrive at the feet of those above us or a thing moving from us downwards should arrive at the head of those below us.

Furthermore, it is necessary that the atoms move at equal speed, when they move through the void and nothing resists them. For heavy things will not move faster than small and light ones, *when*, that is, nothing stands in their way; nor do small things move faster than large ones, since they all have a passage commensurate to them, when, that is, nothing resists these atoms either; nor is upward [movement] faster; neither is the sideways [movement] produced by collisions faster; nor is the downward [movement] caused by their own weight faster either. For as long as either [of them] prevails, the motion will continue as fast as thought, until it meets with resistance, either from an external source or from its own weight counteracting the force of a colliding body.

Moreover, with respect to compounds, some will move faster than others, though the atoms [by themselves] move at equal speed, because the atoms in aggregates are moving towards one place [i.e., in the same direction] in the shortest continuous time, even if they do not do so in the [units of] time which reason can contemplate; but they frequently collide, until the continuity of the motion becomes perceptible. For the added opinion concerning the invisible—i.e., that the [units of] time which reason can contemplate will allow for continuous motion—is not true in such cases. For everything that is observed or grasped by the intellect in an [act of] application is true.

Next, one must see, by making reference to our sense-perceptions and feelings (for these will provide the most secure conviction), that the soul is a body [made up of] fine parts distributed throughout the entire aggregate, and most closely resembling breath with a certain admixture of heat, in one way resembling breath and in another resembling heat. There is also the [third] part which is much finer than even these [components] and because of this is more closely in harmony with the rest of the aggregate too. All of this is revealed by the abilities of the soul, its feelings, its ease of motion, its thought processes, and the things whose removal leads to our death.

Further, one must hold firmly that the soul is most responsible for sense-perception. But [the soul] would not have acquired this [power] if it were not somehow enclosed by the rest of the aggregate. But the rest of the aggregate, though it provides for the soul this cause [of sense-perception], itself has a share in this property because of the soul; still it does not share in all the features [of sense-perception] which the soul has. That is why, when the soul has departed, it does not have sense-perception. For it could not have acquired this power all by itself, but something else which came into being with it provided body [with this power]; and this other thing, through the power actualized in itself by its motion, immediately produced for itself a property of sense-perception and then gave it (because of their close proximity and harmonious relationship) to the body too, as I said.

That is why the soul, as long as it is in [the body], will never lack sense-perception even if some other part has departed; but no matter what [parts] of it are destroyed along with the container's dissolution (whether entire or partial), *if* the soul survives it will be able to perceive. But the rest of the aggregate—whole or part—is not able to perceive even if it survives, when the number of atoms, however small it be, which makes up the nature of the soul, has departed.

Furthermore, when the entire aggregate is destroyed, the soul is scattered and no longer has the same powers, nor can it move; consequently, it does not then [in fact] have [the power of] sense-perception. For it is not possible to conceive of it as perceiving if it is not in this complex and not executing these movements, [i.e.,] when the containing and surrounding [parts] are not such as now contain it and make possible these motions.

Moreover, one must also think of this, that we apply the term 'incorporeal', in the most common meaning of the term, to what could be conceived of as independently existing. But the incorporeal cannot be thought of as independently existing, except for the void. And the void can neither act nor be acted upon but merely provides [the possibility of] motion through itself for bodies. Consequently, those who say that the soul is incorporeal are speaking to no point. For if it were of that character, it could neither act nor be acted upon at all. But in fact both of these properties are clearly distinguished as belonging to the soul.

So, if one refers all of these calculations concerning the soul to the feelings and sense-perceptions, and remembers what was said at the outset, one will see the points comprehended in the outline with sufficient clarity to be able to work out the details from this basis with precision and certainty.

Further, the shapes and colours and sizes and weights and all the other things which are predicated of body as accidents, either of all [bodies] or of visible ones, and are known by sense-perception itself, these things must not be thought of as independent natures (for that is inconceivable). Nor [must it be thought] that they are altogether non-existent, nor that they are distinct incorporeal entities inhering in [the body], nor that they are parts of it. But [one should think] that the whole body throughout derives its own permanent nature from all of these [properties]—though not in such a way as to be a compound [of them], just as when a larger aggregate is produced from the masses themselves, whether the primary ones or magnitudes smaller than the whole object in question—but only, as I say, deriving its own permanent nature from all of these. But all of these [are known by] their own peculiar forms of application and comprehension, always in close accompaniment with the aggregate and in no way separated from it, which is given the predicate 'body' by reference to the aggregate conception.

Further, it often happens that some impermanent properties, which are neither invisible nor incorporeal, accompany bodies. Consequently, using this term in the commonest sense, we make it clear that the[se] properties neither have the nature of an entire thing, which we call a body when we grasp it in aggregate, nor the nature of the permanent accompaniments without which it is not possible to conceive of a body. They would all be referred to according to certain applications of the aggregate which accompanies [them]—but [only] when they are observed to inhere [in bodies], since the properties are not *permanent* accompaniments [of those bodies]. And we should not eliminate this clear evidence from what exists just because [the properties] do not have the nature of an entire thing which happens to be what we also call a body, nor the nature of the permanent accompaniments; but neither are they to be regarded as independent entities, since this is not conceivable either in their case or in the case of permanent accidents; but one must think that they are all, just as they appear [to be], properties somehow [related to] the bodies and not permanent accompaniments nor things which have the status of an independent nature. But they are observed just as sense-perception itself presents their peculiar traits.

Moreover, one must also think of this very carefully: one should not investigate time as we do the other things which we investigate in an object, [i.e.,] by referring to the basic grasps which are observed within ourselves, but we must reason [on the basis of] the clear experience according to which we utter [the phrases] "for a long time" or "for a short time" interpreting it in a manner closely connected [to our experience]. Nor must we alter the terms we use in order to 'improve' them, but we must apply the current terms to [time]; nor must one predicate anything else of it, as though it had the same substance as this peculiar thing—for there are people who do this. But the best policy is to reason solely by means of that which we associate with this peculiar thing and by which we measure it. For this needs no demonstration, but [only] reasoning, because we associate it with days and nights and their parts, and similarly with the feelings too and with the absence of them, and with motions and states of rest, again, having in mind in connection with them precisely and only this peculiar property according to which we apply the term "time."

On top of what has been said, one must believe that the cosmoi, and every finite compound which is similar in form to those which are frequently seen, have come into being from the unlimited, all these things having been separated off from particular conglomerations [of matter], both larger and smaller; and that they are all dissolved again, some more quickly and some more slowly, and some undergoing this because of one kind of cause, some because of others.

Again, one must not believe that the cosmoi necessarily have one kind of shape. . . . For no one could demonstrate that a cosmos of one sort would not have included the sort of seeds from which animals, plants, and the rest of the observable things are formed as compounds, or that a [cosmos of a] different sort *could not* have [included the same things].

Further, one must suppose that [human] nature was taught a large number of different lessons just by the facts themselves, and compelled [by them]; and that reasoning later made more precise what was handed over to it [by nature] and made additional discoveries—more quickly among some peoples, and more slowly among others and in some periods of time [making greater advances] and in others smaller ones.

Hence, names too did not originally come into being by convention, but the very natures of men, which undergo particular feelings and receive particular presentations according to the tribes they live in, expelled air in particular ways as determined by each of their feelings and presentations, in accordance too with the various local differences among their tribes. And later [the names] were established by a general convention in each tribe, in order that their meanings might be less ambiguous for each other and might be expressed more succinctly. And those who were aware of certain previously unobserved things introduced them [to their tribes] and with them handed over certain words [for the things], some being forced to utter them, others choosing them by reasoning, following the commonest [mode of causation], and communicated [their meaning] in this fashion.

Moreover, when it comes to meteorological phenomena, one must believe that movements, turnings, eclipses, risings, settings, and related phenomena occur without any [god] helping out and ordaining or being about to ordain [things] and at the same time having complete blessedness and indestructibility; for troubles and concerns and anger and gratitude are not consistent with blessedness, but these things involve weakness and fear and dependence on one's neighbors. Nor again can they be in possession of blessedness if they [the heavenly bodies] are at the same time balls of fire and adopt these movements by deliberate choice; rather, we must preserve the complete solemnity implied in all the terms applied to such conceptions, so that we do not generate from these terms opinions inconsistent with their solemnity; otherwise, the inconsistency itself will produce the greatest disturbance in our souls. Hence, one must hold the opinion that it is owing to the original inclusion of these compounds in the generation of the cosmos that this regularly recurring cycle too is produced.

Moreover, one must believe that it is the job of physics to work out precisely the cause of the most important things, and that blessedness lies in this part of meteorological knowledge and in knowing what the natures are which are observed in these meteorological phenomena, and all matters related to precision on this topic.

And again, [one must accept] that in such matters there is no room for things occurring in several ways and things which might occur otherwise, but that anything which suggests conflict or disturbance simply cannot occur in the indestructible and divine nature. And it is possible to grasp with the intellect that this is unqualifiedly so.

And what falls within the ambit of investigation into settings and risings and turnings, and eclipses and matters related to these, makes no further contribution to the blessedness which comes from knowledge; but people who know about these things, if they are ignorant of what the natures [in question] are and what the most important causes are, have fears just the same as if they did not have this special knowledge— and perhaps even more fears, since the wonderment which comes from the prior consideration of these phenomena cannot discover a resolution or the orderly management of the most important factors.

That is why even if we discover several causes for turnings and settings and risings and eclipses and things of this sort (as was also the case in [the investigation] of detailed occurrences) we must not believe that our study of these matters has failed to achieve a degree of accuracy which contributes to our undisturbed and blessed state. Consequently, we should account for the causes of meteorological phenomena and everything which is non-evident, observing in how many different ways similar phenomena occur in our experience; and [we should] disdain those who fail to recognize what exists or comes to be in a single manner and what occurs in many different ways, because they overlook the [fact that the] presentation [comes] from great distances and are, moreover, ignorant of the circumstances in which one cannot achieve freedom from disturbance and those, similarly, in which one can achieve freedom from disturbance. So if we think that [a phenomenon] might also occur in some particular way and recognize the very fact that it [might] happen in many different ways, we shall be as free from disturbance as if we *knew* that it occurred in some particular way.

In addition to all these points in general, one must also conceive that the worst disturbance occurs in human souls because of the opinion that these things [the heavenly phenomena] are blessed and indestructible and that they have wishes and undertake actions and exert causality in a manner inconsistent with those attributes, and because of the eternal expectation and suspicion that something dreadful [might happen] such as the myths tell about, or even because they fear that very lack of sense-perception which occurs in death, as though it were relevant to them, and because they are not in this state as a result of their opinions but because of some irrational condition; hence, not setting a limit on their dread, they suffer a disturbance equal to or even greater than what they would suffer if they actually held these opinions. And freedom from disturbance is a release from all of this and involves a continuous recollection of the general and most important points [of the system].

Hence, one must attend to one's present feelings and sense-perceptions, to the common sense-perceptions for common properties and to the individual sense-perceptions for individual properties, and to every immediately clear fact as revealed by each of the criteria. For if we attend to these things, we will give a correct and complete causal account of the source of our disturbance and fear, and [so] dissolve them, by accounting for the causes of meteorological and other phenomena which we are constantly exposed to and which terrify other men most severely.

Here, Herodotus, in summary form are the most important points about the nature of the universe; consequently, I think that this account, if mastered with precision, would be able to make a man incomparably stronger than other men, even if he does not go on to all of the precise details of individual doctrines. For he will also be able to clarify, by his own efforts, many of the precise details of individual doctrines in our entire system, and these points themselves, when lodged in memory, will be a constant aid.

For [these doctrines] are such that even those who have already worked out the details of individual doctrines sufficiently well or even completely, can, by analysing them into [intellectual] applications of this sort, acquire most of the [elements of the] survey of nature as a whole. But those who are not among the completely accomplished [students of nature] can, on the basis of these points and following the method which does not involve verbal expression, with the speed of thought achieve an overview of the doctrines most important for [achieving] tranquillity.

Letter to Menoeceus (Diogenes Laertius 10.121–35)

Epicurus to Menoeceus, greetings:

Let no one delay the study of philosophy while young nor weary of it when old. For no one is either too young or too old for the health of the soul. He who says either that the time for philosophy has not yet come or that it has passed is like someone who says that the time for happiness has not yet come or that it has passed. Therefore, both young and old must philosophize, the latter so that although old he may stay young in good things owing to gratitude for what has occurred, the former so that although young he too may be like an old man owing to his lack of fear of what is to come. Therefore, one must practise the things which produce happiness, since if that is present we have everything and if it is absent we do everything in order to have it.

Do and practise what I constantly told you to do, believing these to be the elements of living well. First, believe that god is an indestructible and blessed animal, in accordance with the general conception of god commonly held, and do not ascribe to god anything foreign to his indestructibility or repugnant to his blessedness. Believe of him everything which is able to preserve his blessedness and indestructibility. For gods do exist, since we have clear knowledge of them. But they are not such as the many believe them to be. For they do not adhere to their own views about the gods. The man who denies the gods of the many is not impious, but rather he who ascribes to the gods the opinions of the many. For the pronouncements of the many about the gods are not basic grasps but false suppositions. Hence come the greatest harm from the gods to bad men and the greatest benefits [to the good]. For the gods always welcome men who are like themselves, being congenial to their own virtues and considering that whatever is not such is uncongenial.

Get used to believing that death is nothing to us. For all good and bad consists in sense-experience, and death is the privation of sense-experience. Hence, a correct knowledge of the fact that death is nothing to us makes the mortality of life a matter for contentment, not by adding a limitless time [to life] but by removing the longing for immortality. For there is nothing fearful in life for one who has grasped that there is nothing fearful in the absence of life. Thus, he is a fool who says that he fears death not because it will be painful when present but because it is painful when it is still to come. For that which while present causes no distress causes unnecessary pain when merely anticipated. So death, the most frightening of bad things, is nothing to us; since when we exist, death is not yet present, and when death is present, then we do not exist. Therefore, it is relevant neither to the living nor to the dead, since it does not affect the former, and the latter do not exist. But the many sometimes flee death as the greatest of bad things and sometimes choose it as a relief from the bad things in life. But the wise man neither rejects life nor fears death. For living does not offend him, nor does he believe not living to be something bad. And just as he does not unconditionally choose the largest amount of food but the most pleasant food, so he savours not the longest time but the most pleasant. He who advises the young man to live well and the old man to die well is simpleminded, not just because of the pleasing aspects of life but because the same kind of practice produces a good life and a good death. Much worse is he who says that it is good not to be born, "but when born to pass through the gates of Hades as quickly as possible."[1] For if he really believes what he says, why doesn't he leave life? For it is easy for him to do, if he has firmly decided on it. But if he is joking, he is wasting his time among men who don't welcome it. We must remember that what will happen is neither unconditionally within our power nor unconditionally outside our power, so that we will not unconditionally expect that it will occur nor despair of it as unconditionally not going to occur.

One must reckon that of desires some are natural, some groundless; and of the natural desires some are necessary and some merely natural; and of the necessary, some are necessary for happiness and some for freeing the body from troubles and some for life itself. The unwavering contemplation of these enables one to refer every choice and avoidance to the health of the body and the freedom of the soul from disturbance, since this is the goal of a blessed life. For we do everything for the sake of being neither in pain nor in terror. As soon as we achieve this state every storm in the soul is dispelled, since the animal is not in a position to go after some need nor to seek something else to complete the good of the body and the soul. For we are in need of pleasure only when we are in pain because of the absence of pleasure, and when we are not in pain, then we no longer need pleasure.

And this is why we say that pleasure is the starting-point and goal of living blessedly. For we recognized this as our first innate good, and this is our starting point for every choice and avoidance and we come to this by judging every good by the criterion of feeling. And it is just because this is the first innate good that we do not choose every pleasure; but sometimes we pass up many pleasures when we get a larger amount of what is uncongenial from them. And we believe many pains to be better than pleasures when a greater pleasure follows for a long while if we endure the pains. So every pleasure is a good thing, since it has a nature congenial [to us], but not every one is to be chosen. Just as every pain too is a bad thing, but not every one is such as to be always avoided. It is, however, appropriate to make all these decisions by comparative measurement and an examination of the advantages and disadvantages. For at some times we treat the good thing as bad and, conversely, the bad thing as good.

And we believe that self-sufficiency is a great good, not in order that we might make do with few things under all circumstances, but so that if we do not have a lot we can make do with few, being genuinely

1. Theognis 425, 427.

convinced that those who least need extravagance enjoy it most; and that everything natural is easy to obtain and whatever is groundless is hard to obtain; and that simple flavours provide a pleasure equal to that of an extravagant life-style when all pain from want is removed, and barley cakes and water provide the highest pleasure when someone in want takes them. Therefore, becoming accustomed to simple, not extravagant, ways of life makes one completely healthy, makes man unhesitant in the face of life's necessary duties, puts us in a better condition for the times of extravagance which occasionally come along, and makes us fearless in the face of chance. So when we say that pleasure is the goal we do not mean the pleasures of the profligate or the pleasures of consumption, as some believe, either from ignorance and disagreement or from deliberate misinterpretation, but rather the lack of pain in the body and disturbance in the soul. For it is not drinking bouts and continuous partying and enjoying boys and women, or consuming fish and the other dainties of an extravagant table, which produce the pleasant life, but sober calculation which searches out the reasons for every choice and avoidance and drives out the opinions which are the source of the greatest turmoil for men's souls.

Prudence is the principle of all these things and is the greatest good. That is why prudence is a more valuable thing than philosophy. For prudence is the source of all the other virtues, teaching that it is impossible to live pleasantly without living prudently, honourably, and justly, and impossible to live prudently, honourably, and justly without living pleasantly. For the virtues are natural adjuncts of the pleasant life and the pleasant life is inseparable from them.

For who do you believe is better than a man who has pious opinions about the gods, is always fearless about death, has reasoned out the natural goal of life and understands that the limit of good things is easy to achieve completely and easy to provide, and that the limit of bad things either has a short duration or causes little trouble?

As to [Fate], introduced by some as the mistress of all, [he is scornful, saying rather that some things happen of necessity,] others by chance, and others by our own agency, and that he sees that necessity is not answerable [to anyone], that chance is unstable, while what occurs by our own agency is autonomous, and that it is to this that praise and blame are attached. For it would be better to follow the stories told about the gods than to be a slave to the fate of the natural philosophers. For the former suggests a hope of escaping bad things by honouring the gods, but the latter involves an inescapable and merciless necessity. And he [the wise man] believes that chance is not a god, as the many think, for nothing is done in a disorderly way by god; nor that it is an uncertain cause. For he does not think that anything good or bad with respect to living blessedly is given by chance to men, although it does provide the starting points of great good and bad things. And he thinks it better to be unlucky in a rational way than lucky in a senseless way; for it is better for a good decision not to turn out right in action than for a bad decision to turn out right because of chance.

Practise these and the related precepts day and night, by yourself and with a like-minded friend, and you will never be disturbed either when awake or in sleep, and you will live as a god among men. For a man who lives among immortal goods is in no respect like a mere mortal animal.

The Principal Doctrines (Diogenes Laertius 10.139–54)

1. What is blessed and indestructible has no troubles itself, nor does it give trouble to anyone else, so that it is not affected by feelings of anger or gratitude. For all such things are a sign of weakness.

2. Death is nothing to us. For what has been dissolved has no sense-experience, and what has no sense-experience is nothing to us.

3. The removal of all feeling of pain is the limit of the magnitude of pleasures. Wherever a pleasurable feeling is present, for as long as it is present, there is neither a feeling of pain nor a feeling of distress, nor both together.

4. The feeling of pain does not linger continuously in the flesh; rather, the sharpest is present for the shortest time, while what merely exceeds the feeling of pleasure in the flesh lasts only a few days. And diseases which last a long time involve feelings of pleasure which exceed feelings of pain.

5. It is impossible to live pleasantly without living prudently, honourably, and justly and impossible to live prudently, honourably, and justly without living pleasantly. And whoever lacks this cannot live pleasantly.

6. The natural good of public office and kingship is for the sake of getting confidence from [other] men, [at least] from those from whom one *is* able to provide this.

7. Some men want to become famous and respected, believing that this is the way to acquire security against [other] men. Thus if the life of such men is secure, they acquire the natural good; but if it is not secure, they do not have that for the sake of which they strove from the beginning according to what is naturally congenial.

8. No pleasure is a bad thing in itself. But the things which produce certain pleasures bring troubles many times greater than the pleasures.

9. If every pleasure were condensed and were present, both in time and in the whole compound [body and soul] or in the most important parts of our nature, then pleasures would never differ from one another.

10. If the things which produce the pleasures of profligate men dissolved the intellect's fears about the phenomena of the heavens and about death and pains and, moreover, if they taught us the limit of our desires, then we would not have reason to criticize them, since they would be filled with pleasures from every source and would contain no feeling of pain or distress from any source—and that is what is bad.

11. If our suspicions about heavenly phenomena and about death did not trouble us at all and were never anything to us, and, moreover, if not knowing the limits of pains and desires did not trouble us, then we would have no need of natural science.

12. It is impossible for someone ignorant about the nature of the universe but still suspicious about the subjects of the myths to dissolve his feelings of fear about the most important matters. So it is impossible to receive unmixed pleasures without knowing natural science.

13. It is useless to obtain security from men while the things above and below the earth and, generally, the things in the unbounded remained as objects of suspicion.

14. The purest security is that which comes from a quiet life and withdrawal from the many, although a certain degree of security from other men does come by means of the power to repel [attacks] and by means of prosperity.

15. Natural wealth is both limited and easy to acquire. But wealth [as defined by] groundless opinions extends without limit.

16. Chance has a small impact on the wise man, while reasoning has arranged for, is arranging for, and will arrange for the greatest and most important matters throughout the whole of his life.

17. The just life is most free from disturbance, but the unjust life is full of the greatest disturbance.

18. As soon as the feeling of pain produced by want is removed, pleasure in the flesh will not increase but is only varied. But the limit of mental pleasures is produced by a reasoning out of these very pleasures [of the flesh] and of the things related to these, which used to cause the greatest fears in the intellect.

19. Unlimited time and limited time contain equal [amounts of] pleasure, if one measures its limits by reasoning.

20. The flesh took the limits of pleasure to be unlimited, and [only] an unlimited time would have provided it. But the intellect, reasoning out the goal and limit of the flesh and dissolving the fears of eternity, provided us with the perfect way of life and had no further need of unlimited time. But it [the intellect] did not flee pleasure, and even when circumstances caused an exit from life it did not die as though it were lacking any aspect of the best life.

21. He who has learned the limits of life knows that it is easy to provide that which removes the feeling of pain owing to want and make one's whole life perfect. So there is no need for things which involve struggle.

22. One must reason about the real goal and every clear fact, to which we refer mere opinions. If not, everything will be full of indecision and disturbance.

23. If you quarrel with all your sense-perceptions you will have nothing to refer to in judging even those sense-perceptions which you claim are false.

24. If you reject unqualifiedly any sense-perception and do not distinguish the opinion about what awaits confirmation, and what is already present in the sense-perception, and the feelings, and every application of the intellect to presentations, you will also disturb the rest of your sense-perceptions with your pointless opinion; as a result you will reject every criterion. If, on the other hand, in your conceptions formed by opinion, you affirm everything that awaits confirmation as well as what does not, you will not avoid falsehood, so that you will be in the position of maintaining every disputable point in every decision about what is and is not correct.

25. If you do not, on every occasion, refer each of your actions to the goal of nature, but instead turn prematurely to some other [criterion] in avoiding or pursuing [things], your actions will not be consistent with your reasoning.

26. The desires which do not bring a feeling of pain when not fulfilled are not necessary; but the desire for them is easy to dispel when they seem to be hard to achieve or to produce harm.

27. Of the things which wisdom provides for the blessedness of one's whole life, by far the greatest is the possession of friendship.

28. The same understanding produces confidence about there being nothing terrible which is eternal or [even] long-lasting and has also realized that security amid even these limited [bad things] is most easily achieved through friendship.

29. Of desires, some are natural and necessary, some natural and not necessary, and some neither natural nor necessary but occurring as a result of a groundless opinion.

30. Among natural desires, those which do not lead to a feeling of pain if not fulfilled and about which there is an intense effort, these are produced by a groundless opinion and they fail to be dissolved not because of their own nature but because of the groundless opinions of mankind.

31. The justice of nature is a pledge of reciprocal usefulness, [i.e.,] neither to harm one another nor to be harmed.

32. There was no justice or injustice with respect to all those animals which were unable to make pacts about neither harming one another nor being harmed. Similarly, [there was no justice or injustice] for all those nations which were unable or unwilling to make pacts about neither harming one another nor being harmed.

33. Justice was not a thing in its own right, but [exists] in mutual dealings in whatever places there [is] a pact about neither harming one another nor being harmed.

34. Injustice is not a bad thing in its own right, but [only] because of the fear produced by the suspicion that one will not escape the notice of those assigned to punish such actions.

35. It is impossible for someone who secretly does something which men agreed [not to do] in order to avoid harming one another or being harmed to be confident that he will escape detection, even if in current circumstances he escapes detection ten thousand times. For until his death it will be uncertain whether he will continue to escape detection.

36. In general outline justice is the same for everyone; for it was something useful in mutual associations. But with respect to the peculiarities of a region or of other [relevant] causes, it does not follow that the same thing is just for everyone.

37. Of actions believed to be just, that whose usefulness in circumstances of mutual associations is supported by the testimony [of experience] has the attribute of serving as just whether it is the same for everyone or not. And if someone passes a law and it does not turn out to be in accord with what is useful in mutual associations, this no longer possesses the nature of justice. And if what is useful in the sense of being just changes, but for a while fits our basic grasp [of justice], nevertheless it was just for that length of time, [at least] for those who do not disturb themselves with empty words but simply look to the facts.

38. If objective circumstances have not changed and things believed to be just have been shown in actual practice not to be in accord with our basic grasp [of justice], then those things were not just. And if objective circumstances do change and the same things which had been just turn out to be no longer useful, then those things were just as long as they were useful for the mutual associations of fellow citizens; but later, when they were not useful, they were no longer just.

39. The man who has made the best arrangements for confidence about external threats is he who has made

the manageable things akin to himself, and has at least made the unmanageable things not alien to himself. But he avoided all contact with things for which not even this could be managed and he drove out of his life everything which it profited him to drive out.

40. All those who had the power to acquire the greatest confidence from [the threats posed by] their neighbors also thereby lived together most pleasantly with the surest guarantee; and since they enjoyed the fullest sense of belonging they did not grieve the early death of the departed, as though it called for pity.

The Greek Stoics: Zeno, Cleanthes, and Chrysippus

In the Athenian marketplace there was a long colonnade—in Greek, a *stoa*—where the first proponents of the most influential philosophical school of the Hellenistic period met. Unlike the Epicureans, who retreated to a private garden, preferring the quiet life of intimate conversation to the bustle of the city, these "Stoics" met in public and had more ambitious aims. According to them, the universe was not a random concatenation of atoms in a void, but instead a rational order, a divine cosmos that we can understand and should obey with our own share of divine reason.

The first Stoic was Zeno of Citium, born in 333 BCE. Arriving in Athens around 311—two decades after the death of Aristotle, and several years before the arrival of Epicurus—he studied with a group known as "Cynics," which in Greek meant "doglike," and thus "shameless." Disdaining social convention, the Cynics tried to live a natural life, which variously meant foregoing hygiene and clothing, or permitting incest and cannibalism. Joining their asceticism, and occasionally their contrarianism, to Socrates' faith in reason and Heraclitus' notion of the cosmos as fire or *logos*, Zeno forged a philosophy that he began to teach in the Athenian stoa around 300.

As was common during this period, he divided philosophy into three related subjects: logic, which encompassed not only formal logic but also semantics, grammar, stylistics, and epistemology; physics, which studied beings (living, nonliving, and divine); and finally, ethics, which was supreme. The goal of this ethics was harmony with nature or reason, which the Stoics also called Providence or Zeus, especially after Cleanthes succeeded Zeno as head of the Stoa. He developed their theology in writings like the *Hymn to Zeus*, which is included here after an excerpt from Diogenes Laertius' summary of Stoic teachings. Evident in both selections is a cosmopolitanism that disregards the allegiance to city so prominent in the ethics of Plato and Aristotle. *Kosmo-politēs*, in fact, means "citizen of the cosmos." Neither Zeno nor Cleanthes was a citizen of Athens.

The next leader of the Stoa, Chrysippus, was also a foreigner. He had studied in the Academy before his conversion to Stoicism, and thus brought dialectical sophistication to the defense of his predecessors' doctrines. Head of the school from 232 BCE until his death in 208, and author of more than 300 treatises, he so eclipsed his predecessors that many later said "without Chrysippus there would have been no Stoa." Few writings of the Greek Stoics remain, and yet their influence has nonetheless persisted. For example, in the next chapter of this volume are selections of the Roman Stoics, whose writings shaped the ethical thought of the early Christian philosophers, as well as that of Baruch Spinoza and Immanuel Kant. Even today, the adjective "philosophical" can mean dispassionate, a distant nod to Stoicism's signature virtue, *apatheia*.

Introduction
(Diogenes Laertius 7.39–40, excerpts)

They say that philosophical theory [*logos*] is tripartite. For one part of it concerns nature [i.e., physics], another concerns character [i.e., ethics] and another concerns rational discourse [i.e., logic].

They compare philosophy to an animal, likening logic to the bones and sinews, ethics to the fleshier parts and physics to the soul. Or again they compare it to an egg. For the outer parts [the shell] are logic, the next part [the white] is ethics and the inmost part [the yolk] is physics. Or to a productive field, of which logic is the wall surrounding it, ethics the fruit and physics is the land and trees. Or to a city which is beautifully fortified and administered according to reason. And, as some Stoics say, no part [of philosophy] is separate from another, but the parts are mixed. And they taught [the three parts] mixed together. Others put logic first, physics second and ethics third; Zeno (in his *On Rational Discourse*) and Chrysippus and Archedemus and Eudromus are in this group.

Physics
(Diogenes Laertius 7.132–60)

They divide the account of physics into topics on bodies and on principles and elements and gods and limits and place and void. And this is the detailed division; the general division is into three topics, concerning the cosmos, concerning the elements, and the third on causal explanation.

They say that the topic concerning the cosmos is divided into two parts; for the mathematicians share in one branch of its investigations, the one in which they investigate the fixed stars and the planets, for example, [to ascertain] whether the sun is as big as it appears to be, and similarly if the moon is; and concerning the revolution [of the cosmos] and similar enquiries.

The other branch of the investigation of the cosmos is the one which pertains *only* to natural scientists, the one in which the substance [of the cosmos] is investigated and whether it is generated or ungenerated and whether it is alive or lifeless and whether it is destructible or indestructible and whether it is administered by providence; and so forth.

The topic concerning causal explanations is itself also bipartite. For medical investigation shares in one branch of its investigations, the one in which they investigate the leading part of the soul, what happens in the soul, the [generative] seeds, and questions like these. The mathematicians also lay claim on the other, for example, [investigation into] how we see, into the cause of how things appear in a mirror, how clouds are formed, and thunder and rainbows and the halo and comets and similar topics.

They believe that there are two principles of the universe, the active and the passive. The passive, then, is unqualified substance, i.e., matter, while the active is the rational principle [*logos*] in it, i.e., god. For he, being eternal and [penetrating] all of matter, is the craftsman of all things. Zeno of Citium propounds this doctrine in his *On Substance*, Cleanthes in his *On Atoms*, Chrysippus towards the end of book one of his *Physics*, Archedemus in his *On Elements* and Posidonius in book two of his *Account of Physics*. They say that there is a difference between principles and elements. For the former are ungenerated and indestructible, while the elements are destroyed in the [universal] conflagration. And the principles are bodies and without form, while the elements are endowed with form.

According to Apollodorus in his *Physics*, body is that which is extended in three [dimensions], length, breadth and depth; this is also called solid body; surface is the limit of a body or that which has only length and breadth, but no depth; Posidonius, in book 5 of his *On Meteorological Phenomena*, says that it exists both in conception and in reality. A line is the limit of a surface or a length with no breadth, or that which has only length. A point is the limit of a line, and it is the smallest [possible] mark.

God and mind and fate and Zeus are one thing, but called by many different names. In the beginning, then, he was by himself and turned all substance into water via air; and just as the seed is contained in the seminal fluid, so this, being the spermatic principle of the cosmos, remains like this in the fluid and makes the matter easy for itself to work with in the generation of subsequent things. Then, it produces first the four elements, fire, water, air, earth.

And Zeno discusses this in his *On the Universe* and Chrysippus [does so] in book one of his *Physics* and Archedemus in some work entitled *On Elements*.

An element is that from which generated things are first generated and that into which they are dissolved in the end. The four elements together are unqualified substance, i.e., matter; and fire is the hot, water the wet, air the cold, and earth the dry. Nevertheless, there is still in the air the same part. Anyway, fire is the highest, and this is called *aither*; in this is produced first the sphere of the fixed stars, and then the sphere of the planets. Next comes the air, then the water, and, as the foundation for everything, the earth, which is in the middle of absolutely everything.

They use the term 'cosmos' in three senses: the god himself who is the individual quality consisting of the totality of substance, who is indestructible and ungenerated, being the craftsman of the organization, taking substance as a totality back into himself in certain [fixed] temporal cycles, and again generating it out of himself; they also call the organization itself of the stars cosmos; and thirdly, that which is composed of both.

And the cosmos in the sense of the individual quality of the substance of the universe is either, as Posidonius says in his *Elements of the Study of Meteorological Phenomena*, a complex of heaven and earth and the natures in them, or a complex of gods and men and the things which come to be for their sake. Heaven is the outermost periphery in which everything divine is located.

The cosmos is administered by mind and providence (as Chrysippus says in book five of his *On Providence* and Posidonius in book thirteen of his *On Gods*), since mind penetrates every part of it just as soul does us. But it penetrates some things more than others. For it penetrates some as a condition [*hexis*], for example, bones and sinews, and others as mind, for example, the leading part of the soul. In this way the entire cosmos too, being an animal and alive and rational, has aither as its leading part, as Antipater of Tyre [says] in book eight of his *On the Cosmos*. Chrysippus in book one of his *On Providence* and Posidonius in his *On Gods* say that the heaven is the leading part of the cosmos, while Cleanthes says it is the sun. Chrysippus, however, in the same work, again somewhat differently, says it is the purest part of the aither, which they also call the first god in a perceptible sense, [saying also] that it, as it were, penetrates the things in the air and all the animals and plants; and [it penetrates] even the earth in the form of a condition.

[They say] that the cosmos is one, and limited at that, having a spherical shape; for that sort of thing is most fit for movement, as Posidonius, in book five of his *Account of Physics*, and the followers of Antipater, in their treatises on the cosmos, say.

Spread around the outside of it is the unlimited void, which is incorporeal. And the void is what can be occupied by bodies but is not occupied. Inside the cosmos there is no void, but it is [fully] unified. For this is necessitated by the sympathy and common tension of heavenly things in relation to earthly things. Chrysippus speaks about the void in his *On Void* and in the first of his *Arts of Physics* and [so do] Apollophanes in his *Physics* and Posidonius in book two of his *Account of Physics*.

Things said [*lekta*] are incorporeal in the same way. Again, so too is time an incorporeal, being the interval of the movement of the cosmos. Of time, the past and future are unlimited, while the present is limited. They believe too that the cosmos is destructible, on the grounds that it is generated; [and] on the basis of [this] argument: in the case of things conceived of by sense-perception, that whose parts are destructible is also destructible as a whole; but the parts of the cosmos are destructible, since they change into each other; therefore, the cosmos is destructible. And if something is capable of change for the worse, it is destructible; and the cosmos is [capable of such change], since it is dried out and flooded.

The cosmos comes into being when substance turns from fire through air to moisture, and then the thick part of it is formed into earth and the thin part is rarefied and this when made even more thin produces fire. Then by a mixing from these are made plants and animals and the rest of the [natural] kinds. Zeno, then, speaks about the generation and destruction in his *On the Universe*, Chrysippus in book one of the *Physics*, Posidonius in book one of his *On the Cosmos*, and [so does] Cleanthes and [also] Antipater in book ten of his *On the Cosmos*. Panaetius, though, claims that the cosmos is indestructible.

Chrysippus in book one of *On Providence*, Apollodorus in his *Physics*, and Posidonius say that the cosmos is also an animal, rational and alive and intelligent; an animal in the sense that it is a substance which is alive and capable of sense-perception. For an animal is better than a non-animal; and nothing is better than the cosmos; therefore, the cosmos is an animal. And [it is] alive, as is clear from the fact that the soul of [each of] us is a fragment derived from it. Boethus says that the cosmos is not an animal. And Zeno says that it is one in his *On the Universe*, and so do Chrysippus and Apollodorus in his *Physics* and Posidonius in book one of his *Account of Physics*. According to Apollodorus, the totality is said to be the cosmos, and in another sense it is said to be the composite system of the cosmos and the void outside it. Anyway, the cosmos is limited and the void is unlimited.

God is an animal, immortal, rational, perfect in happiness, immune to everything bad, providentially [looking after] the cosmos and the things in the cosmos; but he is not anthropomorphic. [God] is the craftsman of the universe and as it were a father of all things, both in general and also that part of him which extends through everything; he is called by many names in accordance with its powers.[1] They say that *Dia* [a grammatical form of the name Zeus] is the one 'because of whom' all things are; they call [god] *Zena* [a grammatical form of the name Zeus] insofar as he is cause of life or because he penetrates life; and Athena by reference to the fact that his leading part extends into the *aither*; Hera because he extends into the air; Hephaestus because he extends into craftsmanlike fire; Poseidon because he extends into the fluid; and Demeter because he extends into the earth. Similarly they also assign the other titles [to god] by fastening onto one [of his] peculiarities.

Zeno says that the entire cosmos and the heaven are the substance of god, and so does Chrysippus in book one of his *On Gods* and Posidonius in book one of *On Gods*. And Antipater, in book seven of *On the Cosmos*, says that his substance is airy. Boethus [says] in his *On Nature* that the sphere of the fixed stars is the substance of god.

Sometimes they explain 'nature' as that which holds the cosmos together, and other times as that which makes things on earth grow. And nature is a condition which moves from itself, producing and holding together the things it produces at definite times, according to spermatic principles, and making things which are of the same sort as that from which they were separated. They say that this [i.e., nature] aims at both the advantageous and at pleasure, as is clear from the craftsmanlike [structure or activity] of man.

Chrysippus says, in his *On Fate*, that everything happens by fate, and so does Posidonius in book two of *On Fate*, and Zeno, and Boethus in book one of *On Fate*. Fate is a continuous string of causes of things which exist, or a rational principle according to which the cosmos is managed. Moreover, they say that all of prophecy is real, if providence too exists; and they even declare that it is a craft, on the grounds that sometimes it turns out [true], as Zeno says, and Chrysippus in book two of his *On Prophecy* and Athenodorus and Posidonius in book twelve of his *Account of Physics* and in book five of his *On Prophecy*. Panaetius, though, denies the reality of prophecy.

They say that primary matter is the substance of all things which exist, as Chrysippus says in book one of his *Physics* and [so too does] Zeno. Matter is that from which anything at all can come into being. And it has two names, 'substance' and 'matter', both as the matter of all things [as a whole], and as the matter of individual things. The matter of all things [as a whole] does not become greater or smaller, but the matter of the individual things does. Substance is, according to the Stoics, body, and it is limited, according to Antipater in book two of *On Substance* and Apollodorus in his *Physics*. And it is capable of being affected, as the same man says; for if it were immune to change, the things generated from it would not be generated. From this it follows that [matter] can be divided to infinity. Chrysippus says that this division is infinite, [but not to infinity]; for there is no infinity for the division to reach; rather, the division is unceasing.

As Chrysippus says in book three of the *Physics*, mixtures are total and not a matter of being surrounded or being juxtaposed. For a bit of wine thrown into the sea is for a certain time extended through it reciprocally; but then it is destroyed into it.

And they say that there also exist daimons who have a sympathy with men and are overseers of

1. The etymologies which follow involve untranslatable word plays.

human affairs; and the surviving souls of virtuous men are heroes.

They believe that nature is a craftsmanlike fire, proceeding methodically to generation, i.e., a fiery and craftsmanly *pneuma*. And soul is a [nature] capable of sense-perception. And this [soul] is the inborn *pneuma* in us. Therefore, it is a body and lasts after death. It is destructible, but the soul of the universe, of which the souls in animals are parts, is indestructible. Zeno of Citium and Antipater in their treatises *On the Soul* and Posidonius [say] that the soul is a warm *pneuma*. For by means of this we live and breathe and by this we are moved. So Cleanthes says that all [souls] last until [the] conflagration, but Chrysippus says that only those of the wise do so.

They say that there are eight parts of the soul, the five senses, the spermatic principles in us, the vocal part and the reasoning part. We see when the light which is the medium between the [power of] vision and the external object is tensed in a conical fashion, as Chrysippus, in book two of his *Physics*, and Apollodorus say. The conical part of the [tensed] air meets our visual organ, and its base meets the object seen. So the observed object is 'announced' [to us] by the tensed air, just as [the ground is revealed to a blind man] by his walking stick. We hear when the air which is the medium between the speaker and the hearer is struck in spherical fashion, and then forms waves and strikes our auditory organs, just as the water in a cistern forms circular waves when a stone is thrown into it. Sleep occurs when the perceptual tension is relaxed in the region of the leading part of the soul. They say that alterations of the *pneuma* are the causes of the passions. They say that a seed is that which is able to generate other things which are of the same sort as that from which it itself [the seed] was separated. Human seed, which a human emits together with a moist [carrier], is blended with the parts of the soul in a mixture of the [spermatic or rational] principles of his ancestors. In book two of his *Physics* Chrysippus says that it is *pneuma* in its substance, as is clear from seeds which are sown in the earth: when they get old they no longer germinate, obviously because their potency has evaporated. And the followers of Sphaerus say that the seed is derived from the whole body; at any rate, [the seed] is able to generate all the parts of the body. But they claim that the [seed] of the female is sterile; for it lacks tension, is limited in quantity, and is watery, as Sphaerus says. And the leading part is the most authoritative [or: dominant] part in the soul; in it occur the presentations and impulses, and from it rational discourse is emitted. It is in the heart.

These are their physical doctrines, as far as seems sufficient for us [to relate], keeping in view [the need for] due symmetry in [the plan of] my work.

Ethics
(Diogenes Laertius 7.84–131)

They divide the ethical part of philosophy into these topics: on impulse, on good and bad things, on passions, on virtue, on the goal, on primary value, on actions, on appropriate actions, on encouragements and discouragements to actions. This is the subdivision given by the followers of Chrysippus, Archedemus, Zeno of Tarsus, Apollodorus, Diogenes, Antipater and Posidonius. For Zeno of Citium and Cleanthes, as might be expected from earlier thinkers, made less elaborate distinctions in their subject matter. But they did divide both logic and physics.

They say that an animal's first [or primary] impulse is to preserve itself, because nature made it congenial to itself from the beginning, as Chrysippus says in book one of *On Goals*, stating that for every animal its first [sense of] congeniality is to its own constitution and the reflective awareness of this. For it is not likely that nature would make an animal alienated from itself, nor having made the animal, to make it neither congenial to nor alienated from itself. Therefore, the remaining possibility is to say that having constituted the animal she made it congenial to itself. For in this way it repels injurious influences and pursues that which is congenial to it.

The Stoics claim that what some people say is false, viz. that the primary [or first] impulse of animals is to pleasure. For they say that pleasure is, if anything, a byproduct which supervenes when nature itself, on its own, seeks out and acquires what is suitable to [the animal's] constitution. It is like the condition of thriving animals and plants in top condition. And nature, they say, did not operate differently in the cases of plants and of animals; for it directs the life of plants too, though without impulse and sense-perception, and even in us some processes are plant-like. When, in the case of animals, impulse is added (which they use in the pursuit of things to which they have an affinity), then for them what is natural is governed by what is according to impulse. When reason has been given to rational animals as a more perfect governor [of life], then for them the life according to reason properly becomes what is natural for them. For reason supervenes on impulse as a craftsman. Thus Zeno first, in his book *On the Nature of Man*, said that the goal was to live in agreement with nature, which is to live according to virtue. For nature leads us to virtue. And similarly Cleanthes in *On Pleasure* and Posidonius and Hecaton in their books *On the Goal*.

Again, "to live according to virtue" is equivalent to living according to the experience of events which occur by nature, as Chrysippus says in book one of his *On Goals*. For our natures are parts of the nature of the universe. Therefore, the goal becomes "to live consistently with nature", i.e., according to one's own nature and that of the universe, doing nothing which is forbidden by the common law, which is right reason, penetrating all things, being the same as Zeus who is the leader of the administration of things. And this itself is the virtue of the happy man and a smooth flow of life, whenever all things are done according to the harmony of the daimon in each of us with the will of the administrator of the universe. So Diogenes says explicitly that the goal is reasonable behaviour in the selection of things according to nature, and Archedemus [says it is] to live carrying out all the appropriate acts.

By nature, in consistency with which we must live, Chrysippus understands both the common and, specifically, the human nature. Cleanthes includes only the common nature, with which one must be consistent, and not the individual. And virtue is a disposition in agreement. And it is worth choosing for its own sake, not because of some fear or hope or some extrinsic consideration. And happiness lies in virtue, insofar as virtue is the soul [so] made [as to produce] the agreement of one's whole life.

And the rational animal is corrupted, sometimes because of the persuasiveness of external activities and sometimes because of the influence of companions. For the starting points provided by nature are uncorrupted.

Virtue in one sense is generally a sort of completion [or: perfection] for each thing, for example, of a statue. And there is also non-intellectual virtue, for example, health; and intellectual virtue, for example, prudence. For in book one of his *On Virtues* Hecaton says that those virtues which are constituted out of theorems are knowledge-based and intellectual, for example prudence and justice; but those which are understood by extension from those which are constituted out of theorems are non-intellectual, for example health and strength. For it turns out that health follows on and is extended from temperance, which is intellectual, just as strength supervenes on the building of an arch. They are called non-intellectual because they do not involve assent, but they supervene even in base people, as health and courage do.

Posidonius (in book one of his *Ethical Discourse*) says that a sign that virtue exists is the fact that the followers of Socrates, Diogenes, and Antisthenes were making [moral] progress; and vice exists because it is the opposite of virtue. And that it is teachable (virtue, I mean) Chrysippus says in book one of his *On the Goal*, and so do Cleanthes and Posidonius in their *Protreptics* and Hecaton too. It is clear that it is teachable because base men become good.

Panaetius, anyway, says that there are two [kinds of] virtues, theoretical and practical; others [divide virtue into] logical, physical and ethical. Posidonius' followers [say there are] four, and those of Cleanthes and Chrysippus and Antipater [say there are even] more. But Apollophanes says there is one virtue, viz. prudence.

Of virtues, some are primary and some are subordinate to these. The primary are these: prudence, courage, justice and temperance.

The virtues—prudence, justice, courage, temperance and the others—are good; and their opposites—imprudence, injustice and the others—are bad; neither good nor bad are those things which neither benefit nor harm, such as life, health, pleasure, beauty, strength, wealth, good reputation, noble birth, and their opposites death, disease, pain, ugliness, weakness, poverty, bad reputation, low birth and such things, as Hecaton says in book seven of his *On the Goal*, and Apollodorus in his *Ethics* and Chrysippus. For these things are not good, but things indifferent in the category of preferred things. For just as heating, not cooling, is a property of the hot, so benefitting, not harming, is a property of the good; but wealth and health do not benefit any more than they harm; therefore, neither wealth nor health is good. Again, they say that what can be used [both] well and badly is not good; but it is possible to use wealth and health [both] well and badly; therefore, wealth and health are not good. Posidonius, however, says that these things too are in the class of goods. But Hecaton in book nine of *On Goods* and Chrysippus in his *On Pleasure* deny even of pleasure that it is a good; for there are also shameful pleasures, and nothing shameful is good. To benefit is to change or maintain something in accordance with virtue, while to harm is to change or maintain something in accordance with vice.

Things indifferent are spoken of in two senses; in the simple sense, those things which do not contribute to happiness or unhappiness [are indifferent], as is the case with wealth, reputation, health, strength and similar things. For it is possible to be happy even without these things, since it is a certain kind of use of them which brings happiness or unhappiness. But in another sense things indifferent are what do not stimulate an impulse either towards or away from something, as is the case with having an odd or even number of hairs on one's head, or with extending or retracting one's finger; the first sort [of indifferents] are no longer called indifferent in this sense; for they do stimulate impulses towards or away from [themselves]. That is why some of them are selected [and some] are rejected, while those others leave one equally balanced between choice and avoidance.

Of things indifferent, they say that some are preferred and some rejected; preferred are those which have value, rejected are those which have disvalue. They say that one sort of value is a contribution to the life in agreement, which applies to every good; but another sort is a certain intermediate potential or usefulness which contributes to the life according to nature, as much as to say, just that [value] which wealth and health bring forward for [promoting] the life according to nature. And another sense of value is the appraiser's value, which a man experienced in the facts would set, as when one says that wheat is exchanged for barley with a mule thrown in.

Preferred things are those which also have value; for example, among things of the soul, natural ability, skill, [moral] progress and similar things; among bodily things life, health, strength, good condition, soundness, beauty and the like; among external things wealth, reputation, noble birth, and similar things. Rejected are, among things of the soul, natural inability, lack of skill and similar things; among bodily things death, disease, weakness, bad condition, being maimed, ugliness and similar things; among external things poverty, lack of reputation, low birth and the like. Those things which are in neither category are neither preferred nor rejected.

Again, of preferred things, some are preferred for themselves, some because of other things, and some both for themselves and because of other things. For themselves, natural ability, [moral] progress and similar things; because of other things, wealth, noble birth, and similar things; for themselves and because of other things, strength, good perceptual abilities, soundness. [Those which are preferred] for themselves [are preferred] because they are according to nature; [those which are preferred] because of other things, [are preferred] because they produce a significant amount of utility; the same applies to the rejected conversely.

As there are said to be ailments in the body, such as gout and arthritis, so too in the soul there are love of reputation and love of pleasure and the like. For an ailment is a disease coupled with weakness and a disease is a strong opinion about something which seems to be worth choosing. And as in the body there are certain predispositions [to disease], for example catarrh and diarrhoea, so too in the soul there are tendencies, such as proneness to grudging, proneness to pity, quarrelsomeness and the like.

There are also three good states [of the soul], joy, caution, and wish. And joy is opposite to pleasure, being a reasonable elation; and caution to fear, being a reasonable avoidance. For the wise man will not be afraid in any way, but will be cautious. They say that wish is opposite to desire, being a reasonable striving. So just as there are certain passions which are forms of the primary ones, so too there are good states subordinate to the primary; forms of wish are good will, kindliness, acceptance, contentment; forms of caution are respect, sanctity; forms of joy are enjoyment, good spirits, tranquillity.

They say the wise man is also free of passions, because he is not disposed to them. And the base man is 'free of passions' in a different sense, which means the same as hard-hearted and cold. And the wise man is free of vanity, since he is indifferent to good and ill repute. And there is another type of freedom from vanity, i.e., heedlessness; such is the base man. And they say that all virtuous men are austere because they do not consort with pleasure nor do they tolerate hedonistic [actions and attitudes] from others; and there is another kind of austerity, in the same sense that wine is said to be 'austere' [harsh] (which is used medicinally, but not much for drinking).

The virtuous are sincere and protective of their own improvement, by means of a preparation which conceals what is base and makes evident the good things which are there. And they are not phony; for they have eliminated phoniness in their voice and appearance. And they are uninvolved; for they avoid doing anything which is not appropriate. And they will drink wine, but not get drunk. Again, [the wise man] will not go mad, although he will get strange presentations because of an excess of black bile or delirium—not in accordance with the account of what is worth choosing, but rather contrary to nature. Nor indeed will the wise man feel pain (since pain is an irrational contraction of the soul), as Apollodorus says in his *Ethics*.

And they are godly; for they have in themselves a kind of god. And the base man is godless. And the godless are of two kinds, the one opposite to him who is godly, and the one who denies that the godly exists [i.e., the atheist]—and this is not a feature of every base man. The virtuous are also pious, for they have experience of what is lawful with respect to the gods and piety is a knowledge of how to serve the gods. And indeed they will also sacrifice to the gods and be sanctified, since they will avoid [moral] mistakes concerning the gods. And the gods admire them, since they are holy and just towards the divine. And only wise men are priests, for they have conducted an investigation into sacrifices, foundations, purifications and the other matters which are proper for the gods.

The [Stoics] think that he [the wise man] will honour his parents and brothers in the second place, after the gods. They also say that love for one's children is natural to them and does not exist among the base. They also see fit to believe that [moral] mistakes are equal, according to Chrysippus, in book four of his *Ethical Investigations*, and Persaeus and Zeno. For if one truth is not more [true] than another, then neither is one falsehood [falser] than another. So, neither is one deception [more of a deception] than another nor is one [moral] mistake more [of a moral mistake] than another. For he who is a hundred stades from Canopus and he who is one stade away are [both] equally not in Canopus. So too he who makes a larger [moral] mistake and he who makes a smaller one are [both] equally not acting correctly. But Heracleides of Tarsus, the student of Antipater of Tarsus, and Athenodorus say that [moral] mistakes are not equal.

They say that the wise man will participate in politics unless something prevents him, according to Chrysippus in book one of *On Ways of Life*; for he will restrain vice and promote virtue. And he will marry, as Zeno says in his *Republic*, and have children. Again, the wise man will not hold opinions, that is, he will not assent to anything which is false. And he will live like a Cynic. For the Cynic, life is a short road to virtue, as Apollodorus says in his *Ethics*. And he will even taste human flesh in special circumstances. He alone is free, and the base men are slaves; for freedom is the authority to act on one's own, while slavery is the privation of [the ability] to act on one's own. There is also another kind of slavery, in the sense of subordination [to another]; and a third, in the sense of subordination [to] and possession [by another]; its opposite is mastery [or: despotism], and this too is base. Not only are the wise free, but they are also kings, since kingship is a form of rule not subject to review, which only the wise could have, as Chrysippus says in his book *On the Fact That Zeno Used Terms in Their Proper Senses*. For he says that the ruler must know about good and bad things and that none of the base understands these things. Similarly they alone are fit for office or for jury duty, and [they alone are] public speakers, but none of the base are. Again, they are also free of [moral] mistakes, since they are not subject to making [moral] mistakes. And they do no harm; for they harm neither others nor themselves. But they are not prone to pity and forgive no one. For they do not relax the penalties which the law fixes as relevant, since giving in and pity and equity itself are the vapidity of a soul which aims to substitute niceness for punishment; nor does he think that [such punishments] are too severe. Again, the wise man is astonished at none of the things which appear to be wonders, such as the caves of Charon or tidal ebbs or hot springs or fiery exhalations [from the earth]. Moreover, the virtuous man will not, they say, live in solitude; for he is naturally made for [living in a] community and for action. He will, moreover, submit to training for the sake of [building] bodily endurance.

They say that the wise man will pray, asking for good things from the gods, according to Posidonius in book one of his *On Appropriate Actions* and Hecaton in book three of *On Paradoxes*. And they say that friendship exists only among virtuous men, because of their similarity. They say that it is a sharing [or: community] of things needed for one's life, since we treat our friends as ourselves. They declare that one's friend is worth choosing for his own sake and that having many friends is a good thing. And there is no friendship among base men and that no base man has a friend. And all the imprudent are mad; for they are not prudent, but do everything in accordance with madness, which is equivalent to imprudence.

The wise man does everything well, as we also say that Ismenias plays all the flute tunes well. And everything belongs to wise men; for the law has given them complete authority. Some things are *said* to belong to the base, just as things are also *said* to belong to men who are unjust; in one sense we say they belong to the state, in another sense to those who are using them.

They say that the virtues follow on each other and that he who has one has them all. For their theoretical principles are common, as Chrysippus says in book one of his *On Virtues*, and Apollodorus in his *Physics in the Old Stoa*, and Hecaton in book three of *On Virtues*. For he who has virtue has a theoretical knowledge of what is to be done and also practises it. And what one is to do and choose is also what one is to endure for and stand firmly by and distribute, so that if he does some things by way of choosing and others by way of enduring and others by way of distributing and others by standing firmly by [something], one will be prudent and courageous and just and temperate. Each of the virtues is demarcated by a particular sphere of relevance, such as courage which is concerned with what is to be endured for, prudence with what is to be done and what not and what is neither; similarly, the other virtues revolve around their proper objects. Deliberative excellence and understanding follow on prudence, organization and orderliness on temperance, even-handedness and fairness on justice, constancy and vigour on courage.

They believe that there is nothing in between virtue and vice, while the Peripatetics say that [moral] progress is between virtue and vice. For, they say, just as a stick must be either straight or crooked, so must a man be either just or unjust and neither 'more just' nor 'more unjust'; and the same for the other virtues. And Chrysippus says that virtue can be lost, while Cleanthes says that it cannot be lost; [Chrysippus says] that it can be lost owing to drunkenness and an excess of black bile, while [Cleanthes says it] cannot, because [it consists in] secure [intellectual] grasps; and it is worth choosing for its [own] sake. At any rate, we are ashamed at things we do badly, as though we knew that only the honourable is good. And it is sufficient for happiness, as Zeno says, and Chrysippus in book one of *On Virtues* and Hecaton in book two of *On Goods*. "For if," he says, "magnanimity is sufficient for making one superior to everything and if it is a part of virtue, virtue too is sufficient for happiness, holding in contempt even those things which seem to be bothersome." Panaetius, however, and Posidonius say that virtue is not sufficient [for happiness], but that there is a need for health and material resources and strength.

They think that one employs virtue constantly, as the followers of Cleanthes say. For it cannot be lost and the virtuous man always employs a soul which is in perfect condition. And justice is natural and not conventional, as are the law and right reason, as Chrysippus says in *On the Honourable*. They think that one [should] not give up philosophy because of disagreement [among philosophers], since by this argument one would give up one's whole life, as Posidonius too says in his *Protreptics*. And Chrysippus says that general education is very useful.

Again, they think that there is no justice between us and the other animals, because of the dissimilarity [between us and them], as Chrysippus says in book one of *On Justice* and Posidonius in book one of *On Appropriate Action*. And that the wise man will fall in love with young men who reveal through their appearance a natural aptitude for virtue, as Zeno says in the *Republic* and Chrysippus in book one of *On Ways of Life* and Apollodorus in his *Ethics*.

And sexual love is an effort to gain friendship resulting from the appearance of beauty; and it is not directed at intercourse, but at friendship. At any rate Thrasonides, although he had his beloved in his power, kept his hands off her because she hated him. So sexual love is directed at friendship, as Chrysippus says in his *On Sexual Love*; and it is not to be blamed; and youthful beauty is the flower of virtue.

There being three ways of life, the theoretical, the practical, and the rational, they say that the third is to be chosen; for the rational animal was deliberately made by nature for theory and action. And they say that the wise man will commit suicide reasonably [i.e., for a good reason], both on behalf of his fatherland and on behalf of his friends, and if he should be in very severe pain or is mutilated or has an incurable disease.

They think the wise men should have their wives in common, so that anyone might make love to any woman, as Zeno says in the *Republic* and Chrysippus says in his *On the Republic*; and again, so do Diogenes the Cynic and Plato. And we shall cherish all the children equally, like fathers, and the jealousy occasioned by adultery will be removed. The best form of government is that which is a blend of democracy and monarchy and aristocracy.

And this is the sort of thing they say in their ethical opinions, and even more than this, together with the accompanying proofs. But let this be our summary and elementary account.

CLEANTHES' *HYMN TO ZEUS*
(STOBAEUS *ANTHOLOGY* 1.1.12 P. 25.3–27.4; SVF 1.537)

Most glorious of the immortals, called by many names, ever all-mighty
Zeus, leader of nature, guiding everything with law,
Hail! For it is right that all mortals should address you,
since all are descended from you and imitate your voice,
alone of all the mortals which live and creep upon the earth.
So I will sing your praises and hymn your might always.
This entire cosmos which revolves around the earth obeys you,
wherever you might lead it, and is willingly ruled by you;
such is [the might of] your thunderbolt, a two-edged helper
in your invincible hands, fiery and everliving;
for by its blows all deeds in nature are [accomplished].
By it you straighten the common rational principle which penetrates
all things, being mixed with lights both great and small.
By it you have become such a lofty power and king forever.
Nor does any deed occur on earth without you, god,
neither in the aithereal divine heaven nor on the sea,
except for the deeds of the wicked in their folly.
But you know how to set straight what is crooked,
and to put in order what is disorderly; for you, what is not dear is dear.
For thus you have fitted together all good things with the bad,
so that there is one eternal rational principle for them all—
and it is this which the wicked flee from and neglect,
ill-fated, since they always long for the possession of good things
and do not see the common law of god, nor do they hear it;
and if they obeyed it sensibly they would have a good life.
But fools they be, impelled each to his own evil,
some with a strife-torn zeal for glory,
others devoted to gain in undue measure,
others devoted to release and the pleasures of the body.
. . . they are swept off in pursuit of different things at different times
while rushing to acquire the exact opposites of these things above all.
But Zeus, giver of all, you of the dark clouds, of the blazing thunderbolt,
save men from their baneful inexperience

and disperse it, father, far from their souls; grant that they may achieve
the wisdom with which you confidently guide all with justice
so that we may requite you with honour for the honour you give us
praising your works continually, as is fitting
for mortals; for there is no greater prize, neither for mortals
nor for gods, than to praise with justice the common law for ever.

Pyrrho of Elis

Born in 365 BCE, Pyrrho of Elis was an older contemporary of Epicurus, who—despite their philosophical differences—admired him. Each had studied with a Democritean, after all. In Pyrrho's case this was Anaxarchus, court philosopher of Macedon, whom Pyrrho joined on Alexander the Great's Asian campaign, traveling as far as the Indus river. Along the way, they met Persian magi and an assortment of Indian philosophers that included Buddhists and Jains.

On the death of Alexander in 323, Pyrrho returned to a quiet life in Elis, where he taught, though without founding an official school or committing any of his skeptical philosophy to writing. From his student Timon, and much later accounts of his thought—such as the one included here from Diogenes Laertius—we know that he promised "freedom from disturbance" (*ataraxia*) by the "suspension of judgment" (*epochē*). Pyrrho compared this philosophical strategy to the experience of Apelles, court painter of Macedon. Frustrated by his failure to depict the foam of a horse's mouth, Apelles desperately threw his sponge at the canvas, achieving the perfect effect inadvertently. So too, philosophers frustrated by their failure to discover the true nature of the world can achieve the peace of mind they seek by suspending their judgments about it.

Beginning with Xenophanes, many Greek philosophers raised skeptical concerns of one sort or another: Heraclitus, Parmenides, Anaxagoras, Protagoras, the author of the *Dissoi Logoi*, and Socrates. The Democritean world of atoms and void, moreover, rendered everyday experience entirely illusory. With so many skeptical techniques at hand, Pyrrho aimed to juxtapose to any argument an equally plausible counterargument, thereby fostering suspension of judgment and, he hoped, equanimity. In later centuries, Pyrrho's admirers systematized these techniques, calling them "modes." In the meantime, his greatest influence was on Plato's Academy. For in 265, not a decade after Pyrrho's death, Arcesilaus became its head and turned it in a skeptical direction.

Skepticism
(Diogenes Laertius 9.74–108, excerpts)

The skeptics, then, spent their time overturning all the dogmas of the schools, whereas they themselves make no dogmatic pronouncements, and while they presented and set out in detail the views of others, they themselves expressed no determinate opinions, not even this itself [that they had no determinate opinions]. Thus, they even abolished the position of holding no determinate opinion, saying, for example, "we determine nothing" since otherwise they would be determining something; but, they say, they produce the pronouncements [of others] to display their absence of rashness, so that they could show this even if they inclined [to the view]. Thus, by means of the utterance "we determine nothing," they indicate the state of equilibrium [in their souls] and similarly, by means of the utterance "no more this than that" and the utterance "for every argument there is an opposing argument" and similar utterances.

. . . The very utterance "for every argument there is an opposing argument" also concludes to suspension of judgement, for when the facts are disputed, but there is equal force in the [opposing] arguments, ignorance of the truth follows. Even this argument [i.e., that every argument has an opposing argument] has an opposing argument, [namely, there is an argument which has no opposing argument] so that when it has destroyed every other argument it turns on itself and is destroyed by itself, just like purges which first purge the foreign matter and then themselves are purged and destroyed. . . .

The Pyrrhonian strategy, according to Aenesidemus in his *Outline for Pyrrhonian Topics*, is a kind of display of appearances or thoughts according to which they are all juxtaposed and when compared are found to have much inconsistency and confusion. As for the contradictions found in their investigations, first they show the modes by which things persuade us and then how confidence is eliminated by the same modes. For they say that we are persuaded when things are consistently perceived, when they never or at least rarely change, when they become familiar to us and when they are determined by customs and when they are delightful and marvellous. They thus showed that on the basis of indications contrary to those that persuaded in the first place, [conclusions] opposite to those we accepted were equally plausible.

The problems which they raised for the [supposed] agreement of appearances or thoughts were set down according to ten modes [or dialectical moves, *tropoi*], corresponding to the ways in which the facts appeared to differ. These are the ten modes they laid down:

The first mode is based on the differences among animals with respect to pleasure and pain and harm and benefit. By this mode it is inferred that animals do not receive the same presentations from the same things, and that for this reason suspension of judgement follows upon this conflict. For among animals some are conceived without intercourse, such as the animals that live in fire, the Arabian phoenix, and worms; whereas some are conceived through intercourse, such as men and other animals. Further, some are structured in one way, some in another. Therefore, they differ in sense-experience; for example, hawks have the keenest sight, whereas dogs have the most acute sense of smell. It is reasonable, then, that animals whose eyes are different should receive different appearances. So, for example, the shoot of a tree is edible for a goat, but bitter for a man; hemlock is nourishing for a quail, but fatal for a man; excrement is edible for a pig, but not for a horse.

The second mode is based on the natures of men and their idiosyncracies. For example, Demophon, the table-servant of Alexander, used to get warm in the shade, but shivered in the sun. Andron the Argive, according to Aristotle, went across the Libyan desert without drinking anything. Again, one man desires to be a doctor, another a farmer, and still another a businessman; and the same things that harm some benefit others. From these facts, suspension of judgement ought to follow.

The third mode is based on the differences in the sensory passages. For example, the apple strikes sight as pale yellow, taste as sweet, and smell as fragrant. And something with the same shape appears different corresponding to the differences in mirrors that reflect it. Therefore, it follows that that which appears is no more one way than another.

The fourth mode is based on dispositions and, in general, changes; for example, health, sickness, sleep, waking, joy, sorrow, youthfulness, old age, courage, fear, emptiness, fullness, hatred, love, heat, cold; besides these, breathing [freely] and constriction of the passages. Things that strike the observer appear different corresponding to the quality of the dispositions. Even madmen do not have dispositions contrary to nature, for why should theirs be more so than ours? After all, we see the sun as standing still. Theon, the Tithorean Stoic, after going to bed, walked in his sleep and the slave of Pericles [sleepwalked] on the roof.

The fifth mode is based on ways of life, customs, mythical beliefs, agreements among various peoples, and dogmatic assumptions. In this mode are included views about things honourable and shameful, true and false, good and bad, the gods, and the generation and destruction of all phenomena. For the same thing is held to be just by some but unjust by others; good to some and bad to others. The Persians, for example, do not regard it as out of place for a father to have intercourse with his daughter; whereas for the Greeks, this is monstrous. The Massagetae, according to Eudoxus in the first book of his *Travels*, hold wives in common; the Greeks do not.

The Cilicians delighted in being pirates, but not the Greeks. Different people believe in different gods; some believe in providence, some do not. The Egyptians mummify their dead; the Romans cremate them; the Paeonians throw them into lakes. From these facts, suspension of judgement about the truth [ought to follow].

The sixth mode is based on mixtures and combinations according to which nothing appears purely by itself, but only together with air, light, moisture, solidity, heat, cold, motion, vapours and other powers. For example, purple appears different in its shade of colour in sunlight, moonlight and lamplight. Our own complexion appears different in the middle of the day and [at dusk]. Further, a rock which requires two men to lift it in the air, is easily shifted in the water, whether [the rock] is in its nature heavy but buoyed by the water, or light and weighed down by the air. So we are ignorant of properties, as we are of the oil [which is the base for] perfumes.

The seventh mode is based on distances, kinds of positions, places and things in places. According to this mode, things that are held to be large now appear small, square things round, level things bumpy, straight things crooked, pale things differently coloured. The sun, at any rate, appears small from a distance, mountains appear misty and smooth from far away but jagged up close. Further, the sun appears one way when rising but a different way when it is in the middle of the heavens and the same body appears one way in a grove and another in a clearing. Further, the image varies according to the sort of position [of the object], for example, the neck of a dove, depending on the way it is turned. Since these things are never observed outside of some place and position, their nature is not known to us.

The eighth mode is based on quantities and [qualities of things, whether these be] hotness or coldness, swiftness or slowness, paleness or variety of colour. For example, wine drunk in moderate amount fortifies us but in excessive amount weakens; similarly, with food and the like.

The ninth mode is based on that which is unceasing, odd, or rare. At any rate, in those places where earthquakes happen continuously, they occasion no wonder, nor, for that matter, does [the presence of] the sun, because it is seen daily. (The ninth mode is eighth in the list of Favorinus and tenth in the lists of Sextus and Aenesidemus. And the tenth is eighth in Sextus and ninth in Favorinus.)

The tenth mode is based on the comparison of things with each other, for example, the light in comparison with the heavy, the strong in comparison with the weak, the larger in comparison with the smaller, up in comparison with down. At any rate, right is not by nature right, but is so understood in relation to something else; at any rate if it moves, it won't be to the right any more. Similarly, "father" and "brother" are relational terms and "day" is so designated in relation to the sun and, in general, everything in relation to the intellect. Therefore, things relative are, in themselves, unknowable.

These are the ten modes.

The school of Agrippa introduces, in addition to these, five other modes, one based on disagreement, one forcing an infinite regress, one based on relativity, one based on hypothesis and one based on circular reasoning.

The one based on disagreement demonstrates that whatever question is advanced by philosophers or by everyday life is a matter of the greatest contention and full of confusion.

The one based on infinite regress forbids that that which has been sought has been firmly established because confidence in it is based on establishing something else which is in turn based on establishing something else, and so on to infinity.

The one based on relativity says that nothing is understood just by itself, but always with something else; for which reason things are unknowable.

The mode constructed on hypothesis is used when people think that the principles of things should be assumed as immediately plausible and not questioned. But this is in vain, for someone will hypothesize the opposite.

The mode based on circularity occurs whenever that which ought to provide support for some claim needs to have its own establishment based on the plausibility of the claim, as, for example, if someone based the existence of pores on the occurrence of emanations and took the existence of pores as establishing the occurrence of emanations.

They also used to abolish all demonstration, criterion, sign, cause, motion, learning, generation and something being good or bad by nature. For every demonstration, they say, is constructed out of things [claimed to be] previously demonstrated or things not demonstrated. If the former, then they will need to produce the demonstration [for the things used as support], and this will go on indefinitely. If the latter, then if either all [of the undemonstrated supports], or some, or even a single one, is in doubt, then the whole argument is undemonstrated. If it is held that they say there are things in need of no demonstration, then those who hold this are mental marvels if they don't grasp that there must be a demonstration of the fact that these things are self-confirming.

. . . Further they abolish the criterion with this sort of argument. Either the criterion has been judged or it has not. If it has not been judged, then it is untrustworthy and it errs with respect to the true and the false. If it has been judged, it [the criterion] will become one of the particulars being judged, so that the same thing would [have to] judge and be judged, and that which has served as a criterion will have to be judged by something else, which itself will have to be judged by yet another and so on to infinity.

The dogmatists, responding to them, say that they themselves [the skeptics] grasp things and dogmatize. For, insofar as they believe they have refuted someone, they are grasping [something], since by the same act they are confirming [their belief] and dogmatizing. Moreover, when they say that they determine nothing and that for every argument there is an opposing argument, they determine something and dogmatize about these very things. The skeptics reply: "We concede the point about what we experience qua human; for we acknowledge that it is daytime, that we are alive, and many other appearances in life. But concerning the things the dogmatists assert definitely with argument, saying that they have grasped them, we suspend judgement because of their being non-evident, acknowledging only the states which we find ourselves in. We concede that we see and acknowledge that we think, but as for how we see or think, we are ignorant. That this appears white we say colloquially without asserting definitely that it is really so. Regarding the utterance 'I determine nothing' and the like, we say that these are uttered but not as dogmas. For they are unlike the utterance 'the cosmos is round.' The latter is non-evident, whereas the former are mere admissions. So, when we say 'we determine nothing' we are not determining this very thing."

Again, the dogmatists say that they [the skeptics] abolish life, in the sense that they throw out everything that goes to make up a life. But the skeptics say that these charges are false. For they do not abolish, say, sight, but only hold that we are ignorant of its explanation. "For we do posit the phenomenon, but not as being what it appears to be. We do sense that fire burns, but we suspend judgement as to whether it is fire's nature to burn. Further, we do see that someone is moving, that someone perishes; but as for how these things occur, we do not know. We only object," they say, "to the non-evident things added on to the phenomena. . . .

Against this criterion of appearances, the dogmatists say that different presentations coming from the same things strike us; for example, from a tower which presents itself as round or square; and if the skeptic does not prefer one to the other, he will be unable to act; but if he gives credence to one or the other, they say, he will no longer be assigning equal force to each appearance. In reply to them, the skeptics say that when various presentations strike them, we say that each one appears; and for this reason, we posit that the appearances appear.

The skeptics say the goal is suspension of judgement, upon which freedom from anxiety follows like a shadow, as Timon and Aenesidemus and their followers put it. For we shall neither choose this nor avoid that in matters which are up to us; as for matters not up to us, but which happen of necessity, like hunger, thirst, and pain, these we cannot avoid, for they cannot be removed by argument. And when the dogmatists say that the skeptic's position is such that he will live a life in which, were he commanded, he would not shrink from cannibalizing his father, the skeptics reply that he will be able to live so that he can suspend judgement about dogmatic questions, but not about matters of everyday life and of observance. So, we can choose and avoid something according to habit, and we can follow customs. Some say that the skeptics say that the goal is freedom from passions; others say that they say it is gentleness.

ROMAN PHILOSOPHY

Cicero

"You are teaching philosophy in Latin, and, so to speak, making it a Roman citizen." Cicero wrote these words in a dialogue, but they described his own vocation perfectly. He was a poet, a statesman, and the greatest orator of his time, and yet his most lasting contribution was to convey Hellenistic thought to the Romans, inventing a Latin idiom for the translation, adaptation, and transmission of Greek philosophy. Many of the works he adapted have been lost, but his own works have survived, becoming standard texts in the philosophical education first of Rome and then later of modern Europe.

Born in 106 BCE, between Rome and Naples, Marcus Tullius Cicero received an excellent education in rhetoric and philosophy, thanks to the hopes of his ambitious father. His first teacher was an Epicurean. But while still young he heard Philo of Larissa speak when the last head of the Skeptical Academy visited Rome. No longer content with the philosophers of Italy, Cicero traveled to Greece in 79. Antiochus of Ascalon, one of the more dogmatic Academics, taught him while he was in Athens; on Rhodes, he met Posidonius, the Platonizing Stoic. Returning to Rome, finally, he adopted one last teacher, Diodotus the Stoic. With so varied a training, it is no wonder that Cicero's own philosophy was eclectic.

Cicero turned his dialectical and rhetorical skills first to the courts, where he won several difficult cases, earning himself both powerful friends and dangerous enemies. Despite the fact that he was a *novus homo*, or "new man," lacking the noble lineage usually required for political success in fiercely aristocratic Rome, he rose through the ranks as quickly as the laws permitted—an achievement of which he was very proud. Reaching the highest office, that of consul, in 63 BCE, he then thwarted the conspiracy of Catiline, which threatened both a revolution and his own life. His retribution was swift and severe: the chief conspirators were executed without trial, although a trial was their right as Roman citizens. Cicero's illegal action emboldened his political enemies, who five years later forced him into exile.

During his first hiatus in political life, he began to write philosophical works, primarily on politics and law. Throughout his life he also wrote letters, many of which have survived, giving us a more intimate portrait of Cicero than of any other ancient philosopher. This portrait is not always flattering, since Cicero was quite vain, but it is always fascinating and sometimes poignant. The letters were collected by Tiro, his former slave, and in one letter Cicero says that he freed Tiro "to be our friend rather than our slave." In another, he laments the death of his beloved daughter Tullia. This loss and his second hiatus in politics—a result of Julius Caesar becoming dictator in 46 BCE—spurred more philosophical writing. Between 45 and 44, in fact, Cicero wrote more than a dozen works, including those excerpted here.

Often taking the form of dialogues between Epicureans, Stoics, and Sceptics, these works exhibit the mind of an advocate at work, presenting the best case for each position and then subjecting it to a thorough and often rhetorical cross-examination. Cicero himself was a partisan of the Academy, believing that certain knowledge was unattainable, but that appearances nonetheless offer a positive guide to living. He included the conventions of Roman politics and religion among these appearances, and found that Stoicism, with its doctrines of universal citizenship and divine providence, approximated these conventions most closely. His sympathies with Stoicism were matched by his disdain for Epicureanism—he makes its case alongside the others, if only to subject it to more decisive objections.

This last period of intense writing came to an end on the Ides of March, with the assassination of Caesar. As a champion of republican politics, Cicero returned to public life more popular than ever. Seeing Caesar's subordinate Mark Antony as a threat to the restored but fragile republic, he composed a series of speeches (the *Philippics*) vilifying him and lionizing his rival, Caesar's adopted son, Octavian (later Augustus). These speeches earned more hatred from Antony than affection from Octavian: when the two generals made an alliance in 43 BCE, Octavian allowed Antony to assassinate Cicero. Henchmen found him on his seaside estate, first making a half-hearted attempt to escape in a rowboat, then surrendering bravely. They decapitated him. To mock the orator whose speeches had stung him so deeply, Antony fixed Cicero's severed head and hands to the speaker's platform in the Roman forum.

ACADEMICA (2.7–9, 2.96–8)

. . . Still, our case at least is straightforward; all we want to do is to discover the truth without strife, and this we pursue with the greatest care and enthusiasm. For although all knowledge is beset by many hardships and although there is so much unclarity in the things themselves and so much weakness in our faculty of judgement that the most ancient and wise thinkers were justified in doubting that they could discover what they wished to, still, they did not give up and neither shall we weary and abandon our enthusiasm for uncovering [what we seek]. The sole aim of our discussions is to tease out—or, as it were, squeeze out—something which is either true or comes as close to it as possible, by speaking on both sides of the issue and listening [to our opponents]. The only difference between us and those who think that they know something is that they do not doubt that the positions which they defend are true, while we say that many things are plausible, those which we can easily follow [in practice] but can hardly affirm.

But we are freer and more flexible just insofar as our ability to decide lies wholly in our own hands; we are not compelled by any necessity to defend a whole set of positions which are laid down like orders. For the others are tied down and committed before they can decide what is best; furthermore, it is when they are at the most vulnerable time of life that they either follow some friend or become captivated by one speech given by the first person they happen to hear and so make decisions about things which are unknown to them. Having been carried off to whatever school it might be as though by a storm, they then cling to it as though to a rock. For I would approve of their saying that they believe in all respects him whom they judge to be a wise man, if they had been able to make such a judgement while so inexperienced and uneducated. To settle who is wise seems to be more than any other thing a job for the wise man. But grant that they were capable of making that assessment; either they made that judgement after hearing all the arguments and understanding the positions of the rest of the philosophical schools, or they delivered themselves into the authority of one man after one quick hearing. But for some reason or other most people prefer going astray and defending most aggressively that position which they have fallen in love with to the job of searching without stubbornness for what can most consistently be claimed.

So what do you make of how this argument works? 'If you say that it is now light and you speak the truth, then it is light; but you say that it is now light and you speak the truth; therefore it is light.' Surely you

---

approve of the general form of argument and say that it is a completely valid argument; that is why you treat it as the first argument form in your teaching of logic. So, either you will approve of every argument which uses the same form, or the entire craft [of logic] is nullified. So see whether you are going to approve of this argument: 'if you say you are lying and you speak the truth, then you are lying; but you do say that you are lying and you speak the truth; therefore, you are lying.' How can you avoid approving of this argument when you have approved of the previous one which has the same form? These problems were put by *Chrysippus*, but even he did not solve them. For what would he make of this argument: 'if it is light, it is light; but it is light; therefore, it is light.' Surely he would allow it; for the very nature of the conditional is such that when you have granted the antecedent you are compelled to grant the consequent. How then does this argument differ from the following? 'If you are lying, you are lying; but you are lying; therefore, you are lying.' You say that you can neither approve of this nor disapprove of it; so how can you do any better with the other? If craft, reason, method, if rational inference itself have any force, then they are all found equally in both arguments.

Their final position is this: they demand that these [arguments] be excepted as inexplicable. I think they had better appeal to a tribune for their exception; they will certainly never get it from me. Further, they cannot get Epicurus, who disdains and scoffs at dialectic as a whole, to grant that statements of this form are true, 'either Hermarchus will be alive tomorrow or he will not,' despite the declaration of the dialecticians that every utterance with this form, '*p* or not-*p*' is not just true but necessary; but notice the cleverness of the man whom those dialecticians think is slow-witted: 'if I grant that one of the two is necessary, then it will be necessary tomorrow for Hermarchus either to live or not to live; but there is no such necessity in the nature of things.'

So let your dialecticians, i.e., Antiochus and the Stoics, quarrel with Epicurus; for he undermines all of dialectic, since if a disjunction of contradictories (by contradictories I mean two statements, one of which says *p* and the other not-*p*)—if such a disjunction can be false then none is true. So what is their quarrel with me, who follow their own teaching on the matter? When this sort of problem arose, Carneades used to tease them as follows: 'if my argument is sound, then I will stick to it; but if it is unsound, then Diogenes should give me my mina back.' For he had studied dialectic with this Stoic, and that was the fee which dialecticians used to charge. So I follow the methods which I learned from Antiochus; and therein I do not find any reason to judge that 'if it is light, it is light' is true (for the reason that I learned that every doubled conditional is true) and not to judge that 'if you are lying, you are lying' is a conditional of the same form. Either, then, I will make both judgements, or if I should not make the one, then I should not make the other either.

On Fate (22–48)

Epicureanism Attacked

But Epicurus thinks that the necessity of fate can be avoided by the swerve of an atom. And so a third kind of motion appears, in addition to weight and collision, when an atom swerves by a minimal interval (he calls it an *elachiston* [smallest]); and he is forced to concede, in fact if not in his words, that this swerve is uncaused. For an atom does not swerve because it is struck by another atom. For how can one be struck by another if the atomic bodies are moving, owing to their weight, downward in straight lines, as Epicurus thinks? It follows that, if one atom is never displaced by another, then one atom cannot even contact another. From which it is also concluded that if an atom exists and it does swerve, it does so without cause. Epicurus introduced this line of reasoning because he was afraid that if an atom always moved by its natural and necessary heaviness, we would have no freedom, since our mind would be moved in such a way that it would be compelled by the motion of atoms. Democritus, the founder of atomism, preferred to accept that all things happened by necessity than to tear from the atomic bodies their natural motions. Carneades was even more acute and showed that the Epicureans could defend their case without this fictitious swerve. For since they taught that there could be a voluntary motion of the mind, it was better to defend that claim than to introduce the swerve, especially since they could not find a cause for it. And if they defended this [the possibility of a voluntary motion of the mind] they could easily resist Chrysippus' attack. For although they conceded that there was no motion without a cause, they did not concede that everything which occurred occurred by antecedent causes. For there are no external and antecedent causes for our will. Thus we [merely] exploit the common linguistic convention when we say that someone wills or does not will something without cause. For we say "without cause" in order to indicate "without external and antecedent cause," not "without any cause at all"; just as when we refer to an "empty jar" we do not speak as the physicists do, who do not believe that there is a genuinely empty space, but to indicate that the jar is without water or wine or oil, for example. Thus when we say that the mind is moved without cause, we say that it is moved without an external and antecedent cause, not without any cause at all. It can even be said of the atom itself that it moves without a cause when it moves through the void because of weight and heaviness, since there is no external cause.

But again, to avoid being mocked by the physicists if we say that anything occurs without a cause, one must make a distinction and say that the nature of the atom itself is such that it moves because of weight and heaviness and that exactly this is the cause of its moving the way it does. Similarly, no external cause is needed for the voluntary motions of the mind; for voluntary motion itself contains within it a nature such that it is in our power and obeys us, but not without a cause. Its very nature is the cause of this fact.

. . . . But from all eternity this proposition was true: "Philoctetes will be abandoned on the island," and this was not able to change from being true to being false. For it is necessary, when you have two contradictories—and here I call contradictories statements one of which affirms something and the other of which denies it—of these, then, it is necessary that one be true and the other false, though Epicurus disagrees. For example, "Philoctetes will be wounded" was true during all previous ages, and "he will not be wounded" was false. Unless, perhaps, we want to accept the view of the Epicureans, who say that such propositions are neither true nor false, or, since they are ashamed of that, say what is [in fact] even more outrageous: that disjunctions of such contradictories are true, but that neither of the propositions contained in them is true. What an amazing audacity and what a wretched ignorance of logic! For if in speech there is something which is neither true nor false, certainly it is not true. But how can what is not true not be false? Or how can what is not false not be true? So the principle defended by Chrysippus will be retained, that every proposition is either true or false. Reason itself will require that certain things be true from all eternity, that they not have been bound by eternal causes, and that they be free from the necessity of fate. . . .

This is how this matter should be discussed, rather than seeking help from wandering atoms which swerve from their [natural] course. He says, "an atom swerves." First of all, why? Democritus had already given them another kind of force, that of collision, which he called a "blow"; and you, Epicurus, had given them the force of heaviness and weight. What new cause, then, is there in nature which would make the atom swerve? Or surely you don't mean that they draw lots with each other to see which ones will swerve and which not? Or why do they swerve by the minimal interval, and not by a larger amount? Or why do they swerve by one minimal interval, and not by two or three? This is wishful thinking, not argument. For you do not say that the atom moves from its place and swerves because it is struck from outside, nor that there is in the void through which the atom moves any trace of a cause for it not to move in a straight line, nor is there any change in the atom itself which would cause it not to maintain the natural motion of its weight. So, although he adduced no cause to produce that swerve, he still thinks that he is making sense when he makes the claim which everyone's mind rejects and recoils from. And I do not think that there is anyone who does more to confirm, not just fate, but even a powerful necessity governing all things, or who has more effectively abolished voluntary motions of the mind, than [Epicurus], who concedes that he could not have resisted fate in any other way than by taking refuge in these fictitious swerves. For even supposing that there were atoms, which can in no way be proven to my satisfaction, nevertheless, those swerves will remain unexplained. For if it is by natural necessity that atoms move [downward] owing to their weight, since it is necessary that every heavy body should move and be carried along when there is nothing to prevent it, then it is also necessary for certain atoms (or, if they prefer, all atoms) to swerve, . . . naturally. . . .

On Fate (28–44, excerpts)

Stoicism Defended

. . . Nor will the so-called "Lazy Argument" stop us. For a certain argument is called the *argos logos* by the philosophers, and if we listened to it we would never do anything at all in life. For they argue in the following fashion: "if it is fated for you to recover from this illness whether you call the doctor or not, you will recover; similarly, if it is fated for you not to recover from this illness whether you call the doctor or not, you will not recover. And one of the two is fated. Therefore, there is no point in calling the doctor." It is right to call this kind of argument "lazy" and "slothful," because on the same reasoning all action will be abolished from life. One can also change the form of it, so that the word "fate" is not included and still keep the same sense, in this way: "if from eternity this has been true, 'you will recover from that disease whether you call a doctor or not,' you will recover; similarly, if from eternity this has been false, 'you will recover from that disease whether you call the doctor or not' you will not recover. Et cetera."

Chrysippus criticizes this argument. "For," he says, "some things are simple, some conjoined. 'Socrates will die on that day' is simple. Whether he does anything or not, the day of death is fixed for him. But if it is fated, 'Oedipus will be born to Laius,' it cannot be said 'whether Laius lies with a woman or not.' For the events are conjoined and co-fated." For that is how he refers to it, since it is fated thus, *both* that Laius will lie with his wife *and* that Oedipus will be produced by her. Just as, if it had been said, "Milo will wrestle at the Olympics" and someone reported "therefore, he will wrestle whether or not he has an opponent," he would be wrong. For "he will wrestle" is conjoined, because there is no wrestling match without an opponent. "Therefore, all the sophistries of that type are refuted in the same way. 'Whether you call a doctor or not, you will recover' is fallacious; for calling the doctor is fated just as much as recovering." Such situations, as I said, he calls co-fated.

Carneades [the Academic] did not accept this entire class [co-fated events] and thought that the above argument had been constructed with insufficient care. And so he approached the argument in another way, not using any fallacious reasoning. This was the result: if there are antecedent causes for everything that happens, then everything happens within a closely knit web of natural connections. If this is so, then necessity causes everything. And if this is true there is nothing in our power. There is, however, something in our power. But if everything happens by fate, everything happens as a result of antecedent causes. Therefore, it is not the case that whatever happens happens by fate. This argument cannot be made tighter. For if someone wished to turn the argument around and say: "if every future event is true from eternity so that whatever should happen would certainly happen, then everything happens within a closely knit web of natural connections," he would be speaking nonsense. For there is a great difference between a natural cause making future events true from eternity and future events which might be understood to be true, without natural [cause] from eternity. Thus Carneades said that not even Apollo is able to pronounce on any future events unless it were those the causes of which are already contained in nature, so that they would happen necessarily. On what basis could even a god say that Marcellus, who was three times a consul, would die at sea? This was indeed true from eternity, but it did not have efficient causes. Thus [Carneades] was of the opinion that if not even past events of which no trace existed would be known to Apollo, how much less would he know future events, for only if the efficient causes of any thing were known would it then be possible to know what would happen in the future. Therefore, Apollo could not predict anything regarding Oedipus, there not being the requisite causes in nature owing to which it was necessary that he would kill his father, or anything of this sort.

Since there were two opinions of the older philosophers, one belonging to those men who believed that everything occurred by fate in such a way that the fate in question brought to bear the force of necessity (this was the view of Democritus, Heraclitus, Empedocles and Aristotle), the other of those who held that there were voluntary motions of the mind without fate, Chrysippus, it seems to me, wanted to strike a middle path, like an informal arbitrator, but attached himself more to the group which wanted the motions of the mind to be free of necessity. But while employing his own terms he slipped into such difficulties that he wound up unwillingly confirming the necessity of fate.

And, if you please, let us see how this occurs in the case of assent, which we discussed at the start of our discourse. For the older philosophers who held that everything occurred by fate said that it occurred by force and necessity. Those who disagreed with them freed assent from fate and denied that if fate applied to assent it could be free of necessity and so they argued thus: "if everything happens by fate, everything occurs by an antecedent cause, and if impulse [is caused], then also what follows from impulse [is caused]; therefore, assent too. But if the cause of impulse is not in us then impulse itself is not in our own power; and if this is so, not even what is produced by impulse is in our power; therefore, neither assent nor action is in our power. From which it follows that neither praise nor blame nor honours nor punishments are fair." Since this is wrong, they think that it is a plausible conclusion that it is not the case that whatever happens happens by fate.

Chrysippus, however, since he both rejected necessity and wanted that nothing should occur without prior causes, distinguished among the kinds of causes in order both to escape from necessity and to retain fate.

"For," he said, "some causes are perfect and principal, while others are auxiliary and proximate. Therefore, when we say that all things occur by fate by antecedent causes, we do not want the following to be understood, viz. that they occur by perfect and principal causes; but we mean this, that they occur by auxiliary and proximate causes." And so his response to the argument which I just made is this: if everything occurs by fate it does indeed follow that everything occurs by antecedent causes, but not by principal and perfect causes. And if these are not themselves in our power it does not follow that not even impulse is in our power. But this would follow if we were saying that everything occurred by perfect and principal causes with the result that, since these causes are not in our power, "not even [impulse] would be in our power." Therefore, those who introduce fate in such a way that they connect necessity to it are subject to the force of that argument; but those who will not say that antecedent causes are perfect and principal will not be subject to the argument at all.

As to the claim that assents occur by antecedent causes, he says that he can easily explain the meaning of this. For although assent cannot occur unless it is stimulated by a presentation, nevertheless since it has that presentation as its proximate cause and not as its principal cause, it can be explained in the way which we have been discussing for some time now, just as Chrysippus wishes. It is not the case that the assent could occur if it were not stimulated by a force from outside (for it is necessary that an assent should be stimulated by a presentation); but Chrysippus falls back on his cylinder and cone. These cannot begin to move unless they are struck; but when that happens, he thinks that it is by their own natures that the cylinder rolls and the cone turns.

"Therefore," he says, "just as he who pushed the cylinder gave it the start of its motion, he did not, however, give it its "rollability," so a presentation which strikes will certainly impress its object and as it were stamp its form on the mind, but our assent will be in our own power and the assent, just as was said in the case of the cylinder, when struck from without, will henceforth be moved by its own force and nature. But if something were produced without an antecedent cause, then it would be false that everything occurs by fate. But if it is probable that a cause precedes all things which occur, what could block the conclusion that all things occur by fate? Let it only be understood what difference and distinction there is among causes."

Since Chrysippus has clarified this, if his opponents who say that assents do not occur by fate were nevertheless to concede that they do not occur without a presentation as antecedent [cause]—then that is a different argument; but if they grant that presentations precede and nevertheless that assents do not occur by fate, on the grounds that it is not that proximate and immediate [kind of] cause which moves the assent, note that they are really saying the same thing [as Chrysippus]. For Chrysippus, while granting that there is in the presentation a proximate and immediate cause of assent, will not grant that this cause necessitates assent in such a way that, if all things occur by fate, all things would occur by antecedent and *necessary* causes. And similarly the opponents, who disagree with him while conceding that assents do not occur without prior presentations, will say that, if everything occurs by fate in the sense that nothing occurs without a prior cause, it must be granted that all things occur by fate.

From this it is easy to understand, since both sides get the same result once their opinions are laid out and clarified, that they disagree verbally but not in substance.

On the Nature of the Gods (1.43–56, excerpts)

Epicureanism Defended

43. . . . For he [Epicurus] is the only one who saw, first, that the gods exist, because nature herself has impressed a conception of them on the souls of everyone. For what people or race of men is there which does not have, even without being taught, a basic grasp of the gods, which is what Epicurus calls a *prolepsis*, i.e., a kind of outline of the thing [in question], which is antecedently grasped by the mind, and without which nothing can be either understood or investigated or debated? We have learned the force and utility of this line of inference from that divine book of Epicurus on the canon or standard [of truth]. 44. You see, then, that the point which is the foundation of this investigation has been laid very well indeed. For since the opinion is established not on the basis of some convention or custom or law, but is and remains a solid and harmonious consensus of all men, it is necessary to understand that there are gods, because we have implanted, or rather innate, conceptions of them. For what all men by nature agree about must necessarily be true. So one must concede that the gods exist. Since this point is accepted by virtually everyone, philosophers and laymen alike, let us admit that the following point too is established, that we have this basic grasp, as I said before, or preconception about the gods—for new names must be assigned to new things, just as Epicurus himself referred to a *prolepsis*, which no one had previously designated by this term—45. we have, then, this basic grasp, that we consider the gods to be blessed and immortal. And the same nature which gave us an outline of the gods themselves has also inscribed in our minds the notion that they are eternal and blessed. And if this is so, that was a true maxim expounded by Epicurus, that what is blessed and eternal neither has any troubles of its own nor provides them to others, and so is subject to neither anger nor gratitude, since everything of this nature is weak.[1]

Enough would have been said already, if all we were looking for were pious worship of the gods and freedom from superstition; for the excellent nature of the gods would be worshipped by pious men because of that nature's blessedness and eternity (for whatever is excellent is justifiably the object of reverence), and all fears of the anger or power of the gods would have been expelled (for it is understood that anger and gratitude are banned from a blessed and immortal nature, and when these are removed no fears about the beings above hang over us). But in order to confirm this opinion, the mind enquires into the form of god, the kind of activity which characterizes his life, and the mode of operation of his intellect.

46. Nature tells us part of what we need to know about the form of the gods, and the rest is the

1. Principal Doctrines 1.

instruction of reason. For by nature all of us, men of all races, have no other view of the gods but that they have human form; for what other form ever appears to anyone either waking or sleeping? But so that every point will not be referred to the primary notions, reason herself reveals the same thing. 47. For it seems appropriate that the most excellent nature, excellent either for its blessedness or for its eternity, should also be the most beautiful. So what configuration of the limbs, what arrangement of features, what shape, what general appearance can be more beautiful than the human? . . . 48. But if the human shape is superior to the form of all living things, and a god is a living thing, then certainly he has that shape which is most beautiful of all. And since it is agreed that the gods are most blessed, but no one can be blessed without virtue, nor can virtue exist without reason, nor can reason exist except in a human form, one must concede that the gods have human appearance. 49. But that appearance is not [really] a body, but a quasi-body, nor does a god have blood, but quasi-blood.

Although Epicurus was so acute in the discovery of these truths and expounded them so subtly that not just anyone could grasp them, still I can rely on your intelligence and expound them more briefly than the subject matter actually demands. Epicurus, then, who not only has a mental vision of hidden and deeply abstruse matters but even manipulates them as though they were tangible, teaches us that the force and nature of the gods is as follows. First, they are perceived not by the senses but by the intellect, and not in virtue of some solidity or numerical identity (like those things which because of their resistance he calls 'solids' [*steremnia*]), but rather because the images [of the gods] are perceived by virtue of similarity and transference; and since an unlimited series of very similar images arises from innumerable atoms and flows from the gods, our intellect attends to those images and our intelligence is fixed on them with the greatest possible pleasure, and so it grasps the blessed and eternal nature [of the gods]. 50. It is most worthwhile to reflect long and hard on the tremendous power of infinity, which we must understand is such as to make it possible that all [classes of] things have an exact and equal correspondence with all other [classes of] things. Epicurus calls this *isonomia*, i.e., equal distribution. In virtue of this it comes about that if there is such and such a number of mortal beings, there is no less a number of immortal beings, and if there is an innumerable set of forces which destroy, there ought also to be an infinite set of forces which preserve.

Balbus, you [Stoics] often ask us what the life of the gods is like and how they pass their time. 51. Well, they spend their time in such a manner that nothing can be conceived which is more blessed or better supplied with all kinds of good things. For a god is idle, is entangled with no serious preoccupations, undertakes no toilsome labour, but simply rejoices in his own wisdom and virtue, being certain that he will always be in the midst of pleasures which are both supreme and eternal. 52. This god we could properly call blessed, but your [i.e., the Stoic] god is assigned to very hard labour. For if god is the world itself, what can be less restful than to be revolving around the heaven's axis at amazing speed, with not even a moment of rest? But nothing is blessed if it is not at rest. But if there is some god *in* the world to rule and guide it, to maintain the orbits of the heavenly bodies, the changes of the seasons and the ordered variations of [natural] events, to oversee land and sea to ensure that men have lives full of advantages, then surely that god is entangled with burdensome and laborious obligations. 53. But we claim that happiness is a matter of freedom from disturbance in the mind and leisure from all duties. For the same person who taught us the rest [of this theory] also taught us that the world was produced by nature and that there was no need for someone to make it, and that the task which you say cannot be carried out without divine wisdom is so easy that nature has produced, is producing and will produce an unlimited number of worlds. Since you do not see how nature can do so without [the use of] intelligence, you take refuge like tragedians in [the agency of] god when you cannot work out the conclusion of the plot. 54. You would certainly not need the assistance of god if you realized the unlimited magnitude of space which is unbounded in all directions; the intellect casts itself into and contemplates this [infinity] and travels so far and wide that it can see no final boundary at which it might stop. So, in this immense length, breadth, and height there flies about an infinite quantity of innumerable atoms, which (despite the interspersal of void) cling to each other and are linked together by their mutual contacts. From this are produced those forms and shapes which you think cannot be produced without the use of a veritable blacksmith's shop! And so you have burdened us with the yoke of an eternal master whom we are to fear by day and by night; for who would not fear an inquisitive and busy god who foresees everything, thinks about and notices everything, and supposes that everything is his own business? 55. This is the origin of that fated necessity which you call *heimarmenē*, and which leads you to say that whatever happens has flowed from an eternal [set of] truth[s] and a continuous chain of causes. But how much is your philosophy worth, if it thinks, like old women—and uneducated ones at that—that everything occurs by fate. Your *mantikē* follows too, which is called 'divination' in Latin, because of which we would be drenched in such superstition (if we were prepared to listen to you [Stoics]) that we would have to worship the soothsayers and augurs, the oracular priests and the prophets, and even the diviners! 56. We are freed from these terrifying fears by Epicurus; we are liberated from them! We do not fear [gods] whom we know do not create trouble for themselves nor for anyone else, and we worship in piety and holiness their excellent and supreme nature.

On the Nature of the Gods (1.69–104, 2.12–86, excerpts)

Epicureanism Attacked

69. You [Epicureans] do this all the time. You say something implausible and want to avoid criticism, so you adduce something which is absolutely impossible to support it! It would be better to give up the point under attack than to defend it in such a brazen manner. For example, when Epicurus saw that, if the atoms moved by their own weight straight down, nothing would be in our power, since the atoms' movements would be certain and necessitated, he found a way to avoid necessity—a point which had escaped Democritus' notice. He says that an atom, although it moves downward in a straight line because of its weight and heaviness, swerves a little bit. 70. This claim is more shameful than the inability to defend the point he is trying to support. He does the same thing in his debate with the dialecticians. They have an accepted teaching to the effect that, in all disjunctions which have the form "either this or not this," one of the two disjuncts must be true; but Epicurus was afraid that if a statement such as "Epicurus will either be alive tomorrow or he will not" were admitted, then one of the two disjuncts would be necessary. So he denied that all statements of the form "either this or not this" were necessary. What could be more stupid than this?

Arcesilaus attacked Zeno because, while he himself said that all sense-perceptions were false, Zeno said that some were false, but not all. Epicurus was afraid that, if one sense-perception were false, none would be true; so he said that all sense-perceptions were messengers of the truth. None of these cases shows great cleverness; in order to ward off a minor blow, he opened himself up to a more serious one.

71. He does the same thing with the nature of the gods. While trying to avoid saying that [the gods are] a dense compound of atoms, so that he will not have to admit that they perish and dissipate, he says that the gods do not have a body, but only a quasi-body, and that they do not have blood, but only quasi-blood. It is taken to be remarkable if one soothsayer can see another without laughing, but it is even more remarkable, that you [Epicureans] can restrain your laughter when you are by yourselves. "This is not a body, but a quasi-body"; I could understand what this would be like if we were talking about waxen images and earthenware figurines. But I cannot understand what quasi-body and quasi-blood are supposed to be in the case of a god. . . .

But suppose that I believe in things which I cannot even understand. Now show me the outlines and shapes of those shadowy gods of yours! 76. Here you suffer from no lack of arguments designed to show that the gods have human form. First [is the argument that] our minds contain an outline and basic grasp of such a nature that when a man thinks about a god, a human form appears to him; second, that since the divine nature is better than everything else, it ought also to have the most beautiful form, and none is more beautiful than the human form; the third argument you adduce is that no other shape can house an intellect. . . .

103. Let us suppose it true, then, as you wish, that god is an image and semblance of man: What home, what dwelling, what place does he have? What, indeed, are his activities? In virtue of what is he, as you claim, happy? For he who is going to be happy ought to both use and enjoy his own goods. And even inanimate natures have each their own proper place; for example, earth occupies the lowest place, water floods the earth, air is above it, and the highest reaches [of the cosmos] are set aside for the fires of the heavens. Some animals are terrestrial, some aquatic, some are 'double', as it were, living in both environments; there are even some which are thought to be born in fire and which often appear flying about in blazing furnaces! 104. So I ask, first, where does this god of yours live? Next, what cause motivates him to move spatially—if, that is, he ever does move? Then, since it is characteristic of animals that they pursue what is adapted to their nature, what does god pursue? To what, pray tell, does he apply his mind and reason? Finally, *how* is he happy, *how* is he eternal?

Whichever of these issues you touch on, it is a weak spot. A theory with such a bad foundation cannot come to a successful conclusion. . . .

Stoicism Defended

2.12 (excerpt)–22

. . . And so the general issue is agreed upon by all people of all nations; for in the minds of all there is an inborn and, as it were, engraved [conviction] that there are gods. 13. There is disagreement about what they are like, but no one denies that they exist. Cleanthes, [a leader of] our [school] said that four causes accounted for the formation of conceptions of the gods in the minds of men. First, he cited the cause I was just mentioning, which is derived from the premonition of future events; second, one we have derived from the magnitude of the benefits we receive from our temperate climate, the fertility of the land and the bounty of many other benefits; 14. third, one which strikes fear into our minds because of thunderbolts, storms, cloudbursts, snowstorms, hail, natural devastation, plagues, earthquakes and underground rumblings, showers of stones and blood-coloured raindrops, and monstrosities which violate nature, whether human or animal, and flashes of light seen in the sky, and the stars which the Greeks call 'comets' and we [Romans] call 'curly-haired' [stars] . . . when frightened by these men came to believe that there is a certain divine power in the heavens; 15. the fourth cause, and also the most effective, is the regularity of the motions and revolutions of the heaven, and the distinctive and varied, yet orderly beauty of the sun, moon and all the stars; just looking at them indicates clearly enough that these things are not the result of chance. When someone goes into a house or gymnasium or public forum and sees the orderliness of everything, and its regularity and systematic character, he cannot judge that these things happen with no cause, but he understands that there is someone who is in charge and runs things; in the same way, but much more so, in the midst of so many motions and changes, and the orderly patterns of so many things of such great size which since the beginning of time have never belied themselves, one must decide that natural motions on such a scale are governed by some intelligence.

16. For all his intellectual acuity, Chrysippus nevertheless puts these points in such a way that they seem to be the teachings of nature and not his own discoveries. "If," he says, "there is something in nature which the human mind, reason, strength and power cannot accomplish, then certainly that which does accomplish it is better than man; but the heavenly bodies and everything which is part of the eternal natural order cannot be created by man; therefore, that by which they are created is better than man; but what would you call this thing if not god? Indeed, if there are no gods, what can there be in nature which is better than man? For reason exists in man alone, and there is nothing more splendid than that; but it is arrogant lunacy for there to be a man who supposes that there is nothing in the whole cosmos better than he; therefore, there is something better; therefore, obviously, there is a god."

17. If you see a large and beautiful house, you could not be induced to think that it was built by

mice and polecats, even if you do not see the master of the house. If, then, you were to think that the great ornament of the cosmos, the great variety and beauty of the heavenly bodies, the great power and vastness of the sea and land, were your own house and not that of the immortal gods, would you not seem to be downright crazy? Or do we not understand even this, that everything above is better and that the earth is in the lowest position and is surrounded by the densest form of air? As a result, for the same reason that applies when we observe that some regions and cities have duller-witted inhabitants because of the more congested nature of their climatic conditions, the human race too is afflicted by this because men are located on the earth, i.e., in the densest part of the universe. 18. And yet, we ought to infer from the very cleverness of man that there is some intelligence [in the universe as a whole], indeed one which is more acute and divine. For where did man 'snatch' his own intelligence from (as Socrates puts it in Xenophon)?[2] Indeed, if someone were to inquire about the source of the moisture and heat which is distributed throughout our bodies, and of the earthy solidity of our organs, and finally about [the source of] the air-like spirit [i.e., *pneuma*] which we have, it appears that we derived one from the earth, another from the moisture, another from fire, and another from the air which we inhale as we breathe. But the most important of these, I mean reason and (if it is all right to use a number of words) intelligence, planning, thought and prudence, where did we find this? Where did we derive it from? Or does earth have all the rest and not have this one thing which is of the highest value? And yet, it is certain that nothing at all is superior to or more beautiful than the cosmos; and not only *is* there nothing better, but nothing can even be conceived of which is better. And if nothing is better than reason and wisdom, it is necessary that these be present in that which we have granted to be the best.

19. What? Who is not compelled to accept what I say by [consideration of] the tremendous sympathy, agreement and interconnected relationships [of the cosmos]? Could the earth bloom at one time, and be barren at another in turn? Could the approach and retreat of the sun at the summer and winter solstices be known by the manifold changes of things? Could the sea tides in channels and straits be moved by the risings and settings of the moon? Or could the variable orbits of the heavenly bodies be maintained despite the uniform revolution of the entire heavens? These things, and the mutual harmony of the parts of the cosmos, certainly could not happen as they do unless they were bound together by one divine and continuously connected *pneuma*.[3]

20. When these doctrines are expounded in a fuller and more flowing fashion, as I intend to do, they more easily escape the captious criticisms of the Academy; but when they are demonstrated in the manner of Zeno, in shorter and more cramped syllogisms, then they are more open to attack; for just as a flowing river is virtually free of the risk of pollution while a confined body of water is polluted quite readily, in the same way the reproaches of a critic are diluted by a flowing oration while a cramped syllogistic demonstration cannot easily protect itself. Zeno used to compress the arguments which we expand upon, in the following manner. 21. "That which is rational is better than that which is not rational; but nothing is better than the cosmos; therefore, the cosmos is rational." It can be proven in a similar manner that the cosmos is wise, happy and eternal, since all of these are better than things which lack them, and nothing is better than the world. From all of this it will be proven that the cosmos is a god. Zeno also used this argument: 22. "If something lacks the ability to perceive, no part of it can have the ability to perceive; but some parts of the cosmos have the ability to perceive; therefore, the cosmos does not lack the ability to perceive." He goes on and presses his point even more compactly. He says, "nothing which lacks life and reason can produce from itself something which is alive and rational; but the cosmos produces from itself things which are alive and rational; therefore, the cosmos is alive and rational." He also argues by means of a comparison, as he often does, as follows: "If flutes playing tunefully grew on olive trees, surely you would not doubt that the olive tree possessed some knowledge of flute-playing? What if

2. *Memorabilia* 1.4.8.

3. Cicero uses the term *spiritus*, but the Greek term he has in mind is obviously *pneuma*, which has been transliterated where it occurs in Greek sources. Similarly, Cicero's *mundus* has been rendered by "cosmos" for the sake of uniformity with the Greek sources.

plane trees bore lyres playing melodiously? Surely you would also decide that there was musical ability in plane trees. Why, then, is the cosmos not judged to be alive and wise, when it produces from itself creatures which are alive and wise?"

2.86 (excerpt)

. . . The cosmos is the sower and planter and (if I may so put it) the parent and nurse and nourisher of all things governed by nature; the cosmos nourishes and holds together everything as though those things were its limbs and parts of itself. But if the parts of the cosmos are governed by nature, it is necessary that the cosmos itself be governed by nature. And the governance of the cosmos contains nothing which is subject to criticism; the best possible result which could be produced from those natures which existed was indeed produced. Let someone, then, show that something better could have been produced! But no one will ever show this. And if someone wants to improve on something [in the cosmos], either he will make it worse or he will be longing for something which simply could not have happened.

But if all parts of the cosmos are so constituted that they could neither have been more useful nor more beautiful, let us see whether they are the products of chance or of such a character that they could never even have held together if not for the control exerted by a perceptive and divine providence. If, therefore, the products of nature are better than those of the crafts and if the crafts do nothing without the use of reason, then nature too cannot be held to be devoid of reason. When you look at a statue or a painting, you know that craftsmanship was applied; and when you see from afar the course steered by a ship, you do not doubt that it is moved by rational craftsmanship; when you gaze on a sundial or waterclock, you understand that the time is told as a result of craft and not as a result of chance. So what sense does it make to think that the cosmos, which contains these very crafts and their craftsmen and all else besides, is devoid of deliberative ability and reason? . . .

Lucretius

Titus Lucretius Carus was probably born in the nineties BCE, wrote *On the Nature of Things*, arguably the greatest philosophical poem of all time, and died in the fifties. Nothing more is known with certainty about him. According to the only surviving ancient account of his life, recorded by St. Jerome, Lucretius drank a love potion, went mad, wrote his poetry between periods of insanity, and then killed himself. But since Jerome wrote over four centuries after Lucretius' death and no doubt shared in the hostility that characterized Christian accounts of Epicureanism, we should take his claims with a grain of salt.

Lucretius' poem is a systematic introduction to the Epicurean philosophy that flourished during the turbulent final years of the Roman Republic. A series of powerful generals, most notably Julius Caesar, made Italy a battleground in one civil war after another. Not surprisingly, some Roman intellectuals chose to retreat from public life into the philosophy of the "The Garden." "Sweet it is," wrote Lucretius, "to watch the mighty battles of war, armies drawn up on the battlefields, without yourself sharing in the danger." This sweetness is not *schadenfreude*, but the true pleasure of equanimity that Epicurus promised to those who prefer philosophical quietism to the luxuries and glories that inevitably bring pain in their wake.

By teaching the real nature of things—that is to say, Epicurean orthodoxy—Lucretius hoped to encourage pursuit of this pleasure and to dispel the irrational fears that spoiled it. Adducing dozens of arguments that are not to be found in any other extant Epicurean source, Lucretius defends Atomism and offers naturalistic explanations of the soul, heavenly phenomena, and the origin of human civilization. Above all, death is no more to be feared than are the gods, who become simultaneously models of Epicurean equanimity and reproaches to the superstitions of traditional Greek and Roman religion.

It may appear odd, then, that Lucretius begins his poem with an invocation of Venus. Not only a goddess of traditional religion, she is the goddess of sexual passion, which Lucretius later condemns as a soul-destroying wound. As much a poet as he is a philosopher, however, he must pay homage to his predecessors in verse. Lucretius is thus adapting for a Roman audience both the conventions of Greek poetry and the wisdom of Greek philosophy, synthesizing the style of Empedocles with the substance of Epicurus. He artfully puts his humble position thus: "Why should the swallow [*hirundo*] compete with swans [*cycnis*]." *Hirundo* is a good Latin word; *cycnis*, however, Lucretius has borrowed from Greek.

On the Nature of Things

1

1 Mother of Aeneas' people, delight of human beings and the gods, Venus,[1] power of life, it is you who beneath the sky's sliding stars inspirit the ship-bearing sea, inspirit the productive land. . . .

21 Since you and you alone stand at the helm of nature's ship, and since without your sanction nothing springs up into the shining shores of light, nothing blossoms into mature loveliness, it is you whom I desire to be my associate in writing this poem *On the Nature of Things*, which I am attempting to compose for my friend Memmius. Through your will, goddess, he is always endowed outstandingly with all fine qualities. So with all the more justification, Venus, give my words charm that will ensure their immortality.

265 Now then, I have taught that things cannot be produced from nothing, and also that, once born, they cannot be reduced to nothing. But in case you are beginning to treat my words with skepticism because the elements of things are imperceptible to our eyes, let me draw your attention to other particles that, though invisible, have undeniable reality.

In the first place, the wild wind awakened whips the waves of the sea, capsizes huge ships, and sends the clouds scudding; sometimes it swoops and sweeps across the plains in tearing tornado, strewing them with great trees, and hammers the heights of mountains with forest-splitting blasts. Such is the frenzied fury of the wind, when it shrieks shrill, rages, and menacingly murmurs. Undoubtedly, therefore, there are invisible particles of wind that sweep the sea, sweep the lands, sweep the clouds in the sky, buffeting and battering them with swirling suddenness. The flow of their current and the devastation they deal is no different from that of a river in sudden spate: water is by nature soft, but when swollen by a great deluge racing down from high mountains after heavy rains, it rams together debris of forests and whole trees; even sturdy bridges cannot withstand the sudden shock of the advancing flood, so furious is the force with which the river, made to boil by bulk of rain, dashes against the piles; with thundering roar it deals destruction, rolling big boulders beneath its waves and sweeping away all that obstructs its course. This, then, is the way in which currents of wind also must operate: when, with the strength of a river, they have pounced in any direction, they chase things before them and sweep them away in attack after attack and sometimes, swooping upon them in swirling eddy, whirl them around and carry them off in a swift tornado. So I insist that there are invisible particles of wind, since in their effects and behavior they are found to rival great rivers, whose substance is manifest.

From Lucretius, *On the Nature of Things*, translated by Martin Ferguson Smith (Indianapolis: Hackett Publishing Company, 2001).

1. Venus is the goddess of love and fertility from whose union with Anchises Aeneas, the legendary ancestor of the Romans, was born, and she is the lover of Mars, god of war and father of Romulus and Remus.

Then again, we smell the various odors of things, even though we never see them approaching our nostrils; we do not observe seething heat, nor can we discern cold with our eyes, nor do we see sounds; and yet all these must be of a corporeal nature, since they have the power to act upon our sensory organs. For nothing can touch or be touched, unless it is corporeal.

Moreover, garments hung up on a wave-plashed shore grow damp, and the same garments spread out in the sun grow dry. Yet we do not see how the moisture has soaked them through, nor again how it has withdrawn under the influence of the heat. Therefore the moisture is sprayed out in the form of tiny particles that are completely invisible to our eyes.

Furthermore, as the sun completes many annual circuits, a finger ring is worn thin on the inside; the fall of water drop by drop hollows a stone; the curved plowshare, though made of iron, imperceptibly suffers attrition in the fields; we see the stone pavements of streets worn away by the feet of the crowd; and the bronze statues by city gates display right hands rubbed thin by the frequent reverential touch of passersby. We observe, then, that all these objects, being worn away, are losing substance; but our inadequate faculty of sight has debarred us from being shown what particles are departing at any particular moment.

Lastly, whatever increase nature in course of time apportions little by little to things, duly curbing their growth, cannot be perceived by straining the keenest eyesight. Likewise, whenever things waste away, decayed by age, or cliffs beetling over the sea are devoured by the corroding brine, you cannot see what they lose at any single moment. Therefore it is by means of invisible particles that nature does her work.

Yet it is not true that everything is packed solid and confined on every side by corporeal substance; for there is void in things. Knowledge of this fact will stand you in good stead in many connections; it will prevent you from straying in uncertainty, from continually questioning about the universe, and from treating my words with skepticism. There is, then, intangible space, void, and vacuity. Otherwise, movement would be absolutely impossible. For the obvious province of matter, namely to prevent and obstruct, would operate against all things all the time, with the result that nothing could advance because nothing would begin to give way. But as it is, throughout the seas and lands and heights of heaven we plainly perceive countless things moving in countless different ways; whereas if void did not exist, things would not so much be robbed and deprived of restless motion, as could never under any circumstances have been produced at all, since on every side matter would be packed solid in a motionless mass.

Moreover, no matter how solid things may appear to be, they are in fact of a porous consistency, as you may perceive from the following examples. In caverns moist streams of water seep through, making the rocks all weep with an abundance of drops. Food distributes itself into every part of an animal's body. Trees grow and produce a profusion of fruit in season, because their sustenance is diffused right through them from the deepest roots, up through the trunks, and into every branch. Sounds penetrate partitions and wing their way through the walls of houses. Numbing cold permeates to our very bones. But you could not possibly perceive these things happening if there were no empty spaces that the various particles could use as passages.

Lastly, why, in the case of objects of identical bulk, do we observe that some weigh more than others? If a ball of wool and a lump of lead contain an equal quantity of matter, the two ought to be of equal weight, because it is the function of matter to press everything downward, whereas void by nature is invariably weightless. So an object which is evidently lighter than another of equal bulk without doubt shows plainly that it contains more void; conversely, the heavier object indicates that it contains more matter and much less vacuity. Therefore it is indisputable that, as I have been seeking to prove by penetrative reasoning, what we term void exists as an ingredient in things.

In this connection, I feel obliged to anticipate the false view of certain theorists, for fear it should divert you from the truth. They claim that waters yield to the pressure of squamous creatures and open liquid paths for them, because the fish leave behind them spaces into which the waters that yield can stream together; and they maintain that other things are able to move by the same reciprocal process and so exchange position, even though the universe is a plenum. Be sure that credence has been given to this theory on totally false grounds. For how in the world can the squamous fish advance when the waters have not given them room? And again, how can the waters withdraw when the fish are unable to move? So we have a choice of two alternatives: either we must deny motion to all bodies, or we must say that void is an ingredient in things and that this is what enables each thing to begin to move.

So, no matter how many objections you offer, you are only delaying the time when you must admit that things contain void.

You will find that all predicable things are either properties or accidents of matter and void. A property is what cannot under any circumstances be severed and separated from a body without the divorce involving destruction: such is the relationship of heaviness to rocks, heat to fire, liquidity to water, touch to all matter, intangibility to void. On the other hand, to slavery, poverty and wealth, freedom, war, concord, and all other things whose coming and going does not impair the essential nature of a thing, we regularly apply the appropriate term "accidents." Likewise time has no independent existence: rather from events themselves is derived a sense of what has occurred in time past, of what is happening at present, and of what is to follow in the future; and it must be admitted that no one has a sense of time as an independent entity, but only as something relative to the movement of things and their restful calm.

Doctors who try to give children foul-tasting wormwood first coat the rim of the cup with the sweet juice of golden honey; their intention is that the children, unwary at their tender age, will be tricked into applying their lips to the cup and at the same time will drain the bitter draught of wormwood—victims of beguilement, but not of betrayal, since by this means they recover strength and health. I have a similar intention now: since this philosophy of ours often appears somewhat off-putting to those who have not experienced it, and most people recoil back from it, I have preferred to expound it to you in harmonious Pierian poetry and, so to speak, coat it with the sweet honey of the Muses. My hope has been that by this means I might perhaps succeed in holding your attention concentrated on my verses, while you fathom the nature of the universe and the form of its structure.

Certainly the primary elements did not intentionally and with acute intelligence dispose themselves in their respective positions, nor did they covenant to produce their respective motions; but because throughout the universe from time everlasting countless numbers of them, buffeted and impelled by blows, have shifted in countless ways, experimentation with every kind of movement and combination has at last resulted in arrangements such as those that created and compose our world; and the world, guaranteed preservation through many long years once it had been directed into harmonious movements, in its turn ensures that the rivers replenish the insatiable sea with plentiful streams of water, that the earth, warmed by the sun's fostering heat, renews her produce, that the family of animals springs up and thrives, and that the gliding ethereal fires have life.

2

It is comforting, when winds are whipping up the waters of the vast sea, to watch from land the severe trials of another person: not that anyone's distress is a cause of agreeable pleasure; but it is comforting to see from what troubles you yourself are exempt. It is comforting also to witness mighty clashes of warriors embattled on the plains, when you have no share in the danger. But nothing is more blissful than to occupy the heights effectively fortified by the teaching of the wise, tranquil sanctuaries from which you can look down upon others and see them wandering everywhere in their random search for the way of life, competing for intellectual eminence, disputing about rank, and striving night and day with prodigious effort to scale the summit of wealth and to secure power. O minds of mortals, blighted by your blindness! Amid what deep darkness and daunting dangers life's little day is passed! To think that you should fail to see that nature importunately demands only that the body may be rid of pain, and that the mind, divorced from anxiety and fear, may enjoy a feeling of contentment!

And so we see that the nature of the body is such that it needs few things, namely those that banish pain and, in so doing, succeed in bestowing pleasures in plenty. Even if the halls contain no golden figures of youths, clasping flaring torches in their right hands to supply light for banquets after dark, even if the house lacks the luster of silver and the glitter of gold, even if no gold-fretted ceiling rings to the sound of the lyre, those who follow their true nature never feel cheated of enjoyment when they lie in friendly company on velvety turf near a running brook beneath the branches of a tall tree and provide their bodies with simple but agreeable refreshment, especially when the weather smiles and the season of the year spangles the green grass with flowers. Fiery fevers quit your body no quicker, if you toss in embroidered attire of blushing crimson, than if you must lie sick in a common garment.

Therefore, since neither riches nor rank nor the pomp of power have any beneficial effect upon our bodies, we must assume that they are equally useless to our minds. Or when you watch your legions swarming over the spacious Plain[2] in vigorous imitation of war, reinforced with numerous reserves and powerful cavalry, uniform in their armor, uniform in their spirit, can it be that these experiences strike terror into your irrational notions, causing them to flee in panic from your mind? Can it be that the fears of death leave your breast disburdened and eased of care? But if we recognize that these suppositions are absurd and ridiculous, because in reality people's fears and the cares at their back dread neither the din of arms nor cruel darts, and strut boldly among kings and potentates, respecting neither the glitter of gold nor the brilliant luster of purple raiment, how can you doubt that philosophy alone possesses the power to resist them? All the more so, because life is one long struggle in the gloom. For, just as children tremble and fear everything in blinding darkness, so we even in daylight sometimes dread things that are no more terrible than the imaginary dangers that cause children to quake in the dark. This terrifying darkness that enshrouds the mind must be dispelled not by the sun's rays and the dazzling darts of day, but by study of the superficial aspect and underlying principle of nature.

217 In this connection, I am anxious that you should grasp a further point: when the atoms are being drawn downward through the void by their property of weight, at absolutely unpredictable times and places they deflect slightly from their straight course, to a degree that could be described as no more than a shift of movement. If they were not apt to swerve, all would fall downward through the unfathomable void like drops of rain; no collisions between primary elements would occur, and no blows would be effected, with the result that nature would never have created anything.

Anyone who happens to believe that heavier atoms are carried straight through the void more swiftly than lighter ones, fall on them from above, and so cause the blows capable of producing the movements necessary for creation, is diverging far from the path of sound judgment. Everything that drops through water and unsubstantial air falls with a velocity proportional to its weight, because the body of water and air with its fine nature are unable to retard all bodies equally, but yield more quickly to the superior power of heavier objects. On the other hand, empty void cannot offer any resistance to any object in any part at any time: it must give way at once in conformity to its own nature. Thus all the atoms, despite their unequal weights, must move with equal velocity as they shoot through the unresisting void. The heavier will therefore never be able to fall on the lighter from above, or of themselves cause the blows determining the varied movements that are the instruments of nature's work.

So I insist that the atoms must swerve slightly, but only to an infinitesimal degree, or we shall give the impression that we are imagining oblique movements—a hypothesis that would be contradicted by the facts. For it is a plain and manifest matter of observation that objects with weight, left to themselves, cannot travel an oblique course when they plunge from above—at least not perceptibly; but who could possibly perceive that they do not swerve at all from their vertical path? Moreover, if all movements are invariably interlinked, if new movement arises from the old in unalterable succession, if there is no atomic swerve to initiate movement that can annul the decrees of destiny and prevent the existence of an endless chain of causation, what is the source of this free will possessed by living creatures all over the earth? What, I ask, is the source of this power of will wrested from destiny, which enables each of us to advance where pleasure leads us, and to alter our movements not at a fixed time or place, but at the

2. **41:** The Campus Martius, or "Plain of Mars," beside the Tiber was used by the Romans for assemblies, recreation, and military exercises.

direction of our own minds? For undoubtedly in each case it is the individual will that gives the initial impulse to such actions and channels the movements through the limbs.

Have you not observed too that, at the very moment when the starting gates are opened, the horses, despite their strength and impatience, cannot burst forward as suddenly as their minds desire? The reason is that the whole mass of matter throughout the whole body must be actuated: only when the whole frame has been actuated can it respond with energy to the eagerness of the mind. So you can see that the initial movement is produced by the mind: it originates from the act of mental will, and is then diffused through every part of the body.

But it is a quite different matter when we are thrust forward by a blow delivered with formidable force and powerful pressure by another person; for in that event it is transparently clear that the whole bulk of our body moves and is swept along involuntarily until the will has reined back all our limbs. So do you now see that, even though an external force pushes a crowd of us, often compelling us to move forward against our will and sweeping us along precipitately, there is in our breasts something with the ability to oppose and resist it? At its bidding the mass of matter through every member and limb at times is compelled to change direction or, when thrown forward, is reined back and brought back to rest.

Thus you are obliged to acknowledge that the seeds have the same ability, and that, besides blows and weight, they have another cause of motion from which this innate power of ours is derived, since we see that nothing can come into being from nothing. Weight ensures that all movements are not caused by blows, that is to say by external force. But the factor that saves the mind itself from being governed in all its actions by an internal necessity, and from being constrained to submit passively to its domination, is the minute swerve of the atoms at unpredictable places and times.

And so the destructive motions cannot hold sway eternally and bury existence forever; nor again can the motions that cause life and growth preserve created things eternally. Thus, in this war that has been waged from time everlasting, the contest between the elements is an equal one: now here, now there, the vital forces conquer and, in turn, are conquered; with the funeral dirge mingles the wail that babies raise when they reach the shores of light; no night has followed day, and no dawn has followed night, which has not heard mingled with those woeful wails the lamentations that accompany death and the black funeral.

Death does not destroy things so completely that it 1003
annihilates the constituent elements: it merely dissolves their union. Then it joins them in fresh combinations and so causes all things to alter their forms and change their colors, to acquire sensation and resign it in an instant. It all goes to show that it is important in what groupings and positions the same primary elements are combined, and what motions they reciprocally impart and receive. You must not imagine that the fluctuating qualities that we perceive on the surfaces of things, sporadically appearing and suddenly disappearing, are permanently inherent in the ultimate particles. Why, even in these verses of mine it is important in what groupings and order all the letters are placed. For the same letters denote sky, sea, lands, rivers, and sun, the same denote crops, trees, and animals; although not all the letters are alike, the great majority are so,
and it is their position that is the distinguishing factor. 1021
It is the same with physical objects: when the concurrences, motions, order, position, and shapes of the atoms are changed, the objects too must change.

3

Well, now that I have demonstrated the nature of the 34
primary elements of all things, the diversity of their forms, the spontaneous manner in which they fly about under the impulse of incessant movement, and their ability to create everything, it is obvious that my next task is to illuminate in my verses the nature of the mind and the spirit, and send packing that fear of Acheron[3] which disturbs human life from its deepest depths, suffusing all with the darkness of death, and allows no pleasure to remain unclouded and pure.

In the first place, I declare that the mind, or the intelligence as we often term it, in which the reasoning and governing principle of life resides, is part of a person

---

3. **39:** The souls of the dead were thought to be ferried across this river into Hades.

no less than the hand and foot and eyes are seen to be parts of a whole living creature.

[Some theorists imagine] that the sensibility of the mind is not located in any specific part, but that it is a sort of vital condition of the body—a "harmony"[4] as the Greeks call it; this, they suppose, endows us with life and sensation, without the mind residing in any part of the body, in the same way that one commonly speaks of the good health of the body, even though this health is not an organ of the strong person. Thus they do not locate the sensibility of the mind in any specific part; and here I consider that they go far astray. Often, although the plainly perceptible parts of the body are sick, elsewhere in some hidden part we feel pleasure; often too quite the opposite happens: a person who is miserable in mind may feel pleasure throughout the body. The situation is no different from that when a sick person has a painful foot, but happens to have no pain in the head at the same time. Moreover, even when we have resigned our limbs to gentle slumber and our sprawling body lies heavy and insensible, there is something within us that at that time is stirred by many kinds of emotion, experiencing all the movements of pleasure and the heart's unreal anxieties.

Now, what follows will enable you to grasp that the spirit too resides in the limbs, and that the body does not owe its power of sensation to a "harmony." In the first place, even when a considerable portion of the body has been removed, it is a common occurrence for life to linger in our limbs. On the other hand, when a few particles of heat have escaped from the body and a little air has been exhaled through the mouth, this same life at once abandons the veins and quits the bones. You may gather from this that not all particles have equal functions or safeguard the body to an equal degree; it is mainly these seeds of wind and warm heat that ensure that life lingers in our limbs. The body itself, then, contains vital heat and wind, which abandon our frame at the moment of death.

4. **100:** The Greek *harmonia* means "attunement" rather than what we call "harmony." The origin of the theory that the soul is an attunement of the bodily constituents, a theory presented by Simmias and refuted by Socrates in Plato's *Phaedo* (85e–86d, 91c–95a), is uncertain. It is likely to have been influenced by Pythagoreanism.

So, since the mind and spirit have been found to be a natural part of the human body, repudiate this term "harmony," which was brought down to musicians from lofty Helicon—or maybe the musicians themselves borrowed it from some other source and transferred it to that quality that previously had no distinctive name. In any case, let them keep it; as for you, listen to the rest of my arguments.

Next I declare that, although mind and spirit are intimately connected and together form a single substance, the head, so to speak, and supreme ruler of the whole body is the reason, which we term the mind or intelligence; and this has its seat fixed in the middle region of the breast. Here we feel the palpitation of throbbing fear, here the soothing touch of joy: here, then, is the intelligence and mind. The rest of the soul is disseminated through all the body and moves in obedience to the will and impulse of the mind. The mind quite independently possesses intelligence and experiences joy at times when no stimulus affects either the body or the spirit. And in the same way that the head or eye can smart under a painful attack without our whole body being agonized as well, so our mind sometimes by itself suffers pain or is animated with joy, when the rest of the soul, scattered through the limbs of the body, is not roused by any new stimulus. But when the mind is disturbed by a more intense fear, we observe that the whole spirit throughout the limbs sympathizes with it: sweating and pallor break out all over the body; the tongue stutters and the voice falters; the eyes grow blear, the ears buzz, and the limbs give way: in fact we often see people collapse in consequence of the mind's terror. It is a simple matter for anyone to infer from this that the spirit is intimately linked with the mind, and that the spirit, once shaken by the mind's force, in its turn strikes the body and sets it in motion.

The same method of argument teaches us that the mind and spirit have a material nature. For it is an observable fact that they impel the limbs, wrench the body from sleep, transform the countenance, and pilot and steer the whole person; and since we perceive that all these operations imply touch, and touch in its turn implies matter, are we not bound to acknowledge that the mind and spirit consist of material substance?

Moreover, you notice that the mind suffers in concert with the body and sympathizes with it. Even if a spear fails to strike the vitals when it is driven into the body with quivering force and severs bones and sinews, it induces faintness and a blissful sinking to the ground, and on the ground a dizziness of mind and now and then a vacillating inclination to rise up again. So the mind must have a material nature, since it is affected by the painful blows of material spears.

Now, the substance of the soul is encased by the whole body and is in its turn the custodian of the body and the cause of its safety; for the two are twined together by common roots and evidently cannot be disentangled without being destroyed. It is no easier matter to extricate the substance of the mind and spirit from the whole body without causing general disintegration than it is to extract the scent from lumps of incense without destroying the substance in the process. Having their constituent atoms inextricably intertwined from the moment of their creation, body and soul are copartners in life; and it is evident that neither of them is capable of experiencing sensation independently, without the help of the other: rather it is by the united motions of both together that sensation is kindled and fanned into flame in every part of our flesh. Besides, the body is never born without the soul, never grows up without it, and manifestly never lives on without it after death. For, unlike water, which often releases the heat that has been imparted to it without undergoing dissolution or diminution in consequence, never, I say, never can the limbs survive when they are divorced from the spirit and abandoned by it: they suffer decomposition, dissolution, and total destruction. So from the beginning of their existence, even when they are nestling in the mother's womb, body and spirit in mutual association learn the motions necessary to life; and this is why they cannot be divorced without meeting with disaster and destruction. You may see then that, since their lives are bound up together, their substances also are firmly bound together.

Now then, to enable you to grasp that the minds and light spirits of living creatures are subject to birth and death, I will proceed to set forth verses that are the product of long research and the fruit of joyful labor—verses worthy of your manner of life. See to it that you couple spirit and mind together under one name, and when, for example, I proceed to speak of the spirit and demonstrate its mortality, assume that my words apply to the mind as well, since the two are identical in structure and constitute a unity.

Now therefore, since, when vessels containing water are shattered, you perceive that the liquid flows out on all sides and disperses, and since mist and smoke dissolve into the breezy air, you must assume that the spirit too is dissipated, perishing much more quickly and being resolved more speedily into its ultimate particles, once it has been dislodged from the limbs and has withdrawn. For if the body, which is, as it were, the vessel of the spirit, is shattered by some force and made porous by the withdrawal of blood from the veins, so that it is no longer able to retain it, how can you believe that the spirit can ever be retained by air, which is a more porous container than our body?

Moreover, we are aware that the mind is born with the body, develops with it, and declines with it. A toddling child possesses a feeble intellect that matches the weakness and delicacy of its body. Then, when maturity is attained and strength is robust, judgment and mental power are correspondingly more fully developed. Later, when the body is shaken by the stern strength of time and the frame droops with forces dulled, the intellect halts, the tongue raves, the mind staggers; everything fades and fails at once. So it is natural to infer that the substance of the spirit too is all dissolved, like smoke, into the breezy air aloft, since we observe that it is born with the body, develops with it, and, as I have shown, succumbs with it to the stress and strain of age.

There is the further point that, just as the body suffers dreadful diseases and pitiless pain, so the mind manifestly experiences the gripe of cares, grief, and fear; so the natural inference is that it has an equal share in death.

Even during the body's sicknesses the mind often wanders from the path of reason: patients are demented and mutter deliriously and sometimes, severely comatose, sink with drooping eyelids and nodding head into a deep and endless sleep, from which they do not hear the voices and cannot recognize the features of those who, with faces and cheeks bedewed with tears, stand around and implore them to return to life. Therefore, seeing that the mind is susceptible to the infection of disease, you are bound to admit that it suffers dissolution like the body. For pain and disease are the architects of death—a lesson that the fate of millions in the past has inculcated upon us.

Again, when the piercing potency of wine has penetrated into people, and its warmth has been distributed and channeled into the veins, the limbs become heavy; they reel about with staggering steps; the tongue drawls, the mind is sodden, and the eyes swim; they bawl, belch, and brawl more and more violently. What is the reason for these and all the other similar symptoms of drunkenness, if it is not that the potent punch of the wine invariably has the effect of confounding the spirit within the body? And the very fact that things can be confounded and crippled always signifies that, if a slightly stronger force were to insinuate itself into them, the result would be destruction and debarment from further life.

Moreover, the fact that the mind, like the body, manifestly can be cured of sickness and can respond to the influence of medicine is another intimation of its mortality. For it is fair to assume that every endeavor to transform the mind, and indeed every attempt to alter any other substance, entails the addition of parts or the transposition of the existing parts or the subtraction of at least some tittle from the sum. But an immortal substance does not allow its parts to be transposed, nor does it permit one jot to be added or to steal away. For every change that involves a thing outstepping its own limits means the instantaneous death of what previously existed. Therefore, as I have shown, whether the mind falls sick or responds to the influence of medicine, it betrays its mortal nature. So firmly is true fact seen to confront false reasoning and cut off its retreat, proving the falsehood by a two-pronged refutation.

Furthermore, the body and mind as vital forces owe their energy and enjoyment of life to their interconnection: divorced from the body, the substance of the mind cannot by itself produce vital motions; and the body, once abandoned by the spirit, cannot live on and experience sensation. The fact is that, just as an eye, ripped from its roots and detached from the rest of the body, is unable to see anything, so the spirit and mind evidently have no power by themselves. Doubtless the reason is that, in their interpenetration of the veins and flesh and sinews and bones, their elements are confined by the whole body and are unable to spring apart freely to considerable distances; and because they are thus pent in, they perform sensory motions—motions that, after death and their expulsion from the body into the breezy air, they cannot perform, since they are not then confined in the same manner. Indeed air would be an animate body, if the spirit could maintain its cohesion and restrict itself to those motions that it performed previously in the sinews and in the body itself. So I insist that, when the whole bodily encasement has disintegrated and the vital breath has been expelled, you must acknowledge that the mind and the spirit with their powers of sensation suffer dissolution, since body and soul are interdependent.

Moreover, if the substance of the spirit is immortal and retains sentient power when separated from our body, presumably we must assume that it is provided with the five senses. In no other way can we visualize spirits roaming in the infernal realms of Acheron. That is why painters and writers of generations past have represented spirits as endowed with senses. But, divorced from the body, the soul cannot have either eyes or nose or hands or tongue or ears and therefore cannot possess either sentience or life.

Moreover, if the substance of the spirit is immortal and stealthily enters the body at the moment of birth, why do we have no recollection of our earlier existence, and why do we retain no vestiges of past actions? If the faculties of the mind are so totally transformed that all memory of past events has been obliterated, such a state, in my opinion, is not far removed from death. Therefore you must admit that the previous spirit has perished, and that the present spirit is a new creation.

Furthermore, if the living power of the mind is imported into our already completed bodies at the moment of birth, when we are crossing the threshold of life, one would not then expect to see it grow with the body and the limbs in the very blood; rather one would expect it to live in total isolation, as in a cage, while still managing to flood the whole body with sensibility. So I insist that spirits must not be considered either uncreated or exempt from the law of death. For it must not be supposed that they could be so intimately connected with our bodies if they were insinuated into them from without; and yet the existence of this intimate connection is a patent fact: indeed the spirit's interpenetration of the body through the veins, flesh, sinews, and bones is so complete that even the teeth are given a share in sensation, as is shown by toothache, or the twinge caused by icy water, or the crunching of rough grit concealed in a piece of bread. What is more, since the spirit is so closely interwoven with the tissue of the body, it is evident that it cannot depart in its integrity and disentangle itself intact from all the sinews, bones, and joints.

But if by chance you imagine that the spirit insinuates itself into the body from without and then permeates our limbs, it is all the more certain that it will perish through fusion with the body, because permeation implies dissolution and therefore destruction. The spirit is diffused through all the pores in the body; and just as food, when it is channeled into all the members and limbs, disintegrates and converts itself into a new substance, so the mind and spirit, even if intact when they pass into the newly formed body, suffer dissolution in the process of permeation: their particles are channeled through all the pores into the limbs, and form this new mind that is the present ruler of our body and the offspring of the original mind that perished when it was diffused through the frame. It is obvious therefore that the substance of the spirit is neither without a birthday nor exempt from death.

Again, why is cruel ferocity a permanent characteristic of the sullen breed of lions, and cunning of foxes? Why, in the case of deer, is the instinct of flight transmitted from generation to generation, so that their limbs are spurred by inherited timidity? Indeed, why are all other such qualities implanted in the constitution of body and mind from life's first dawn? Surely the explanation must be that a mind, whose nature is determined by its own seed and breed, develops along with the body of each individual animal. But if the mind were immortal and in the habit of transmigrating, the characters of living creatures would be topsy-turvy: often the hound of Hyrcanian stock[5] would flee before the onset of the antlered stag; the hawk would flee trembling through the breezy air at the swoop of the dove; human beings would be irrational, while the species of brute beasts would be rational. The argument that an immortal soul undergoes alteration when it changes its body is advanced on false grounds. For change implies dissolution and therefore destruction. The parts of the soul are subject to transposition and rearrangement, and therefore must be liable also to suffer dissolution throughout the limbs, so that ultimately they all perish with the body. If it is claimed that human souls always migrate into human bodies, I will still want to know why a wise soul can become foolish, why a child never possesses prudence, and why a foal is less well trained than a horse of powerful strength. No doubt my opponents will take refuge in the supposition that in a weak body the mind becomes weak. But if this supposition is true, you must admit that the soul is mortal, since it is so totally transformed throughout the body that it loses its former vitality and sensibility. Moreover, how will the mind be able to grow strong in concert with any particular body and attain with it the coveted bloom of maturity, if it is not its partner from the moment of conception? And what prompts it to abandon the decrepit limbs? Is it afraid of remaining cooped up in the crumbling body, in case its home, worn out by long lapse of years, collapses and crushes it? But an immortal thing has no dangers to fear.

Again, a tree cannot exist in the sky, or clouds in the depths of the sea; fish cannot live in fields; blood is not found in timber, or sap in stones. The place where each thing may grow and exist is fixed and determined. Thus the substance of the mind cannot come to birth alone without the body or exist separated from sinews and blood. But even if this were possible, the mind could far more easily reside in the head or the shoulders or the base of the heels, or be born in any other part of the body, and so at least remain within the same person, within the same vessel. However, since even within our body it is evident that a special place is firmly fixed and reserved for the existence and growth of the spirit and mind, it is all the more necessary for us to deny that they could survive or come to birth wholly outside the body. Therefore, when the body has died, you must acknowledge

5. **750**: The Hyrcani, who lived on the southeast shore of the Caspian Sea, had an extremely fierce breed of dogs.

that the soul too has perished, torn to pieces all through the body.

807 Furthermore, all things that subsist eternally must either be composed of solid substance, so that they repel blows and are impenetrable to anything that might destroy the close cohesion of their parts from within—like the elements of matter, whose nature I have already demonstrated; or their ability to survive throughout all time must be due to their immunity from blows—as is the case with void, which is always intangible and never experiences any impact; or else the cause of their indestructibility must be the absence of any surrounding space into which their substance might disperse and dissolve—as is the case with the totality of the universe: for outside the universe there is no space into which its substance can escape, and no matter capable of striking it and shattering it with a powerful blow.

830 Death, then, is nothing to us and does not affect us in the least, now that the nature of the mind is understood to be mortal. And as in time past we felt no distress when the advancing Punic hosts were threatening Rome on every side, when the whole earth, rocked by the terrifying tumult of war, shudderingly quaked beneath the coasts of high heaven, while the entire human race was doubtful into whose possession the sovereignty of the land and the sea was destined to fall;[6] so, when we are no more, when body and soul, upon whose union our being depends, are divorced, you may be sure that nothing at all will have the power to affect us or awaken sensation in us, who shall not then exist—not even if the earth be confounded with the sea, and the sea with the sky.

And even supposing that the mind and the spirit retain their power of sensation after they have been wrenched from our body, it is nothing to us, whose being is dependent upon the conjunction and marriage of body and soul. Furthermore, if in course of time all our component atoms should be reassembled after our death and restored again to their present positions, so that the light of life was given to us a second time, even that eventuality would not affect us in the least, once there had been a break in the chain of consciousness. Similarly at the present time we are not affected at all by any earlier existence we had, and we are not tortured with any anguish concerning it. When you survey the whole sweep of measureless time past and consider the multifariousness of the movements of matter, you can easily convince yourself that the same seeds that compose us now have often before been arranged in the same order that they occupy now. And yet we have no recollection of our earlier existence; for between that life and this lies an unbridged gap—an interval during which all the motions of our atoms strayed and scattered in all directions, far away from sensation.

People evidently are aware that their minds are carrying a heavy load, which wearies them with its weight; and if only they could also understand what causes it, and why such a mass of misery occupies their breasts, they would not live in the manner in which we generally see them living, ignorant of what they want for themselves, and continually impatient to move somewhere else as if the change could relieve them of their burden. Often a man leaves his spacious mansion, because he is utterly bored with being at home, and then suddenly returns on finding that he is no better off when he is out. He races out to his country villa, driving his Gallic ponies hell-for-leather. You would think he was dashing to save a house on fire. But the moment he has set foot on the threshold, he gives a yawn or falls heavily asleep in search of oblivion or even dashes back to the city. In this way people endeavor to run away from themselves; but since they are of course unable to make good their escape, they remain firmly attached to themselves against their will, and hate themselves because they are sick and do not understand the cause of their malady. If only they perceived it distinctly, they would at once give up everything else and devote themselves first to studying the nature of things; for the issue at stake is their state not merely for one hour, but for eternity—the state in which mortals must pass all the time that remains after their death. 1054

4

Well, now that I have demonstrated the nature of the soul, its constitution, the way in which it develops 27

6. **832–7**: The reference is to the Punic Wars, fought between Rome and Carthage, and especially to the Second Punic War (218–201 BCE) during which Hannibal invaded Italy and defeated the Romans in several battles.

with the body, and the manner in which it is disaggregated and resolved into its component elements, I will begin to explain to you a matter that has an important bearing on these questions—namely, the existence of what we term images of things. Images are a sort of membranes stripped from the surfaces of objects and float this way and that through the air. It is these that visit us when we are awake or asleep, and terrify our minds each time we see the weird forms and phantoms of people bereft of the light of life—visions that often make us start from our heavy slumber and tremble with terror. We must not imagine that spirits escape from Acheron, or that shades of the dead flit among the living, or that any part of us can survive after death, when both the body and the substance of the soul have been destroyed and dissolved into their respective elements. I contend, then, that things emit filmy forms and images from their surfaces; and the proofs that follow will enable even the dullest wit to understand that I am right.

324 It is a fact that our eyes shrink from glaring objects and avoid looking at them. Indeed the sun blinds us if we try to gaze straight at it. This is because its own strength is great, and the images radiated by it, descending from a great height through pure air, move so impetuously that, when they impinge on our eyes, they disturb their atomic composition. Moreover, any object of glaring brightness is apt to burn the eyes, because it contains numerous seeds of fire that penetrate into the eyes and cause them pain.

Again, the reason why all looks yellow to jaundiced people is that many seeds of this color stream from their bodies to meet the images emitted by objects; many too are mingled in their eyes, and these tinge everything with their contagious paleness.

354 The square towers of a city, viewed by us from a distance, often appear round. This is because every angle surveyed from afar is seen as obtuse—or rather is not seen at all. The image loses its sharpness before it can deliver a blow to our eyes, because the images, during their long journey through the air, are constantly buffeted and so become blunted. In this way every angle eludes our vision, with the result that the stone structures appear as though they were shaped on a lathe. Even so, they do not look like objects close at hand that really are round, but vaguely resemble them in a shadowy fashion.

However, in this connection we do not allow that the eyes are in any way deceived. Their business is to observe the areas of light and shadow. But the question of whether the light is the same or not, and whether it is the same shadow passing from place to place, or whether the position is rather as I have stated it above—this can be decided only by the reasoning of the mind: the eyes cannot take cognizance of the real nature of things. Refrain, then, from foisting on the eyes the shortcomings of the mind.

448 Again, if we chance to place our hand beneath one of our eyes and press the eyeball, it happens, by a certain sensory impression, that, wherever we look, we appear to see everything double—double the light of each lamp flowering with flame, double the furniture throughout the house, double the faces of people, double their bodies.

Lastly, even when our limbs are prisoners of balmy slumber and our whole body is sunk in sound repose, we imagine that we are awake and moving our limbs; though enveloped by the blind blackness of night, we have the illusion of seeing the sun and daylight; though confined within our room, we fancy that we pass over sky and sea, rivers and mountains, and traverse plains on foot; though encompassed by the solemn stillness of night, we seem to hear sounds; and though quite silent, we imagine that we speak.

We experience an extraordinarily large number of other illusions of this kind. It is as though all of them are conspiring to undermine our confidence in the senses. Their efforts, however, are unavailing, since the majority of these errors are due to inferences added by our own minds, which cause us to imagine that we have seen what our senses have not seen. The truth is that nothing is more difficult than to separate patent facts from the dubious opinions that our mind at once adds of its own accord.

Moreover, if people suppose that knowledge of anything is impossible, they do not even know whether knowledge of the impossibility of knowledge is possible, since, on their own admission, they know nothing. Against such people, who have planted themselves with their head in their own footprints, I disdain to argue. However, if I were to concede that they do have this knowledge, I would put the following questions to them. Since they have never before encountered anything true, how do they recognize knowledge and ignorance? What has given them their conception of truth and falsehood? What proof have they that the doubtful differs from the certain?

You will find that our conception of truth is derived ultimately from the senses, and that their evidence is unimpugnable. You see, what we need is some specially reliable standard which by its own authority is able to ensure the victory of truth over falsehood. Well now, what standard can be regarded as more reliable than sensation? If the senses are false, will reason be competent to impeach them when it is itself entirely dependent upon the senses? If they are not true, all reason also is rendered false. Or can sight be corrected by hearing, or hearing by touch? Can the evidence of touch be challenged by taste, refuted by hearing, or invalidated by sight? Not so, in my opinion. The fact is that each sense has its own special sphere, its own separate function. Thus the discernment of softness, cold, and heat must be the province of one particular sense, while the perception of the various colors and everything connected with colors must be the business of another. Taste too has its own distinct function; smell is produced separately, and so is sound. It necessarily follows therefore that one sense cannot refute another. It is also impossible for any sense to correct itself, since it must always be considered equally reliable. Therefore all sensations at all times are true.

And even if reason fails to resolve the problem of why objects, which close at hand were square, have a round appearance when viewed from a distance, it is better, if one is ignorant of the reason, to give an erroneous explanation of the difference in shape than to let manifest facts slip from one's grasp and to undermine the first principles of belief and tear up all the foundations upon which our life and safety are based. For if you were not prepared to trust the senses, not only would all reason fall in ruin, but life itself would at once collapse, since you would be unable to avoid precipices and other such dangers and keep to places of safety. You may be sure, then, that the arguments that have been marshaled and arrayed against the senses are merely a multitude of empty words.

I conclude with an illustration. If, when you begin to construct a building, your rule is warped, your square not truly rectilinear, and your level the slightest bit inexact in any part, the inevitable result is a structure full of faults—crooked, lopsided, leaning forward here and backward there, and all out of proportion, with some parts seemingly on the verge of collapse and others actually collapsing, all having been betrayed by those erroneous calculations at the outset. In the same way, then, your reasoning about things must of necessity be distorted and false if the senses upon which it is based are themselves false.

5

Now what cause has made belief in the gods universal throughout mighty nations and filled cities with altars and prompted the institution of solemn religious rites—rites that now flourish in great states and places? What is it that even now implants in mortals this shuddering fear that all over the earth raises new shrines to the gods and crowds them with congregations on festal days? The explanation is quite easy to supply.

The truth is that even in remote antiquity the minds of mortals were visited in waking life, and still more in sleep, by visions of divine figures of matchless beauty and stupendous stature. To these beings they attributed sensation, because they saw them move their limbs and speak in a majestic manner appropriate to their splendid appearance and ample strength. They gave them immortal life, because their images presented themselves in constant succession and their forms remained unchanged, but above all because they thought that beings endowed with such mighty strength could not easily be overcome by any force. And they regarded them as consummately happy, because fear of death did not trouble any of them and also because in sleep they saw them perform many marvelous feats without experiencing any fatigue.

Furthermore, they observed the orderly movements of the heavenly bodies and the regular return of the seasons of the year without being able to account for these phenomena. Therefore they took refuge in ascribing everything to the gods and in supposing that everything happens in obedience to their will. And they located the habitations and sacred quarters of the gods in the sky, because it is through the sky that night and the revolving moon are seen to pass, yes the moon, day and night, and night's austere constellations, and the night-roving torches and flying flames of heaven,[7] clouds, sunlight, rains, snow, winds, lightning, hail, and the rapid roars and mighty menacing rumbles of thunder.

O hapless humanity, to have attributed such happenings to the gods and to have ascribed cruel wrath to them as well! What sorrows did they then prepare for themselves, what wounds for us, what tears for generations to come! Piety does not consist in veiling one's head and turning with ostentatious frequency to a stone, or in visiting every altar, or in prostrating oneself on the ground with outstretched palms before the shrines of the gods, or in saturating the sacrificial slabs with the blood of four-footed beasts, or in linking vows to vows, but rather in possessing the ability to contemplate all things with a tranquil mind.

Seneca

Lucius Annaeus Seneca was born around the same time as Jesus of Nazareth, but at the opposite end of the Roman Empire (in the Spanish town of Cordoba), and in very different conditions. His wealthy father and namesake was a considerable author, well-connected in the imperial capital. Educated there as a child, Seneca "the younger" mastered subjects dear to his father, such as rhetoric and history, but also a subject his father despised: philosophy. Falling under the spell of Demetrius the Cynic, Seneca said "I converse with that half-naked man and I admire him—and why not? I have seen that he lacks nothing."

Becoming as much a playwright as a philosopher, Seneca adapted Athenian tragedies for Roman audiences. His Latin versions became more influential than their Greek originals, imitated in turn by Shakespeare and Racine. His philosophical writings carried Stoicism to medieval and Renaissance Europe. These writings include dialogues and treatises, but Seneca is best known for his moral letters. In them he exhorts his young friend, Lucilius—and through him, all his readers—to a life of virtue. This life is broadly Stoic in conception, but Seneca draws liberally on Roman history and the sayings of Epicurus to give it a more practical and appealing character. Of the writings presented here, the first deals with the happy life, and the remainder are moral letters.

In 41 CE, Seneca lost his only son and was exiled to Corsica by Emperor Claudius. Undaunted, however, he returned to Rome eight years later, invited by Nero's mother to tutor the future emperor. When Nero took the throne in 54, Seneca became his chief counselor. For eight years he was able to restrain Nero's vices, but flatterers displaced him in the emperor's favor and then compelled him, along with the poets Lucan and Petronius and many other people, to commit suicide (in 65). Never missing an opportunity for moral instruction, Seneca went to his death like Socrates—philosophizing, consoling his grieving friends, and reminding them of his own example of virtue. Whereas Socrates dismissed his wife (Plato, *Phaedo* 116a–b), however, Seneca allowed his to die with him, as she wished.

7. **1191:** Comets and meteors.

On the Happy Life

I. All people, dear brother Gallio,[1] want to live happy lives but, when it comes to discerning what it is that makes for a happy life, their vision is blurred. So difficult is it to achieve happiness that, once you have lost the track, the more energetically you press on the farther happiness recedes away from you. When the road takes you in the opposite direction, your own speed is the cause of your increasing distance from your destination.

In the first place, therefore, it is necessary to determine what is the result we wish to achieve. Then it is necessary to look around for the quickest route by which to travel there, with the ability to perceive in the course of the journey, provided it is direct, how much of the distance is extinguished each day and how much nearer we are to the goal to which we are impelled by a natural attraction.

For as long as we wander all over the place, following no guide but rather the roar and clamor of discordant voices calling to us from different directions, our short lifespan will be ground out in the midst of delusions; for life is short enough even if we spend it striving day and night for a healthy state of mind. Therefore it needs to be determined where we are headed and by what route; and it is necessary to have an experienced guide who has previously explored those regions we are planning to enter because our predicament is, in one respect, wholly unlike that faced by other travelers. They are prevented from going astray by their access to established roads and opportunities to ask the local inhabitants for directions; but in our case the most well-worn track and most crowded highway are the most deceptive.

Nothing is more important to understand than that we must not, in the manner of sheep, follow the lead of the flock walking ahead of us, going where they go habitually, not where they need to go. Nothing entangles us in greater evils than our propensity to obey public opinion, to regard those things as best that are endorsed by the approval of the majority. Because we are surrounded by the example of so many others, we live our lives not according to reason but by imitation.

III. The life that is happy is in harmony with its own nature. This can only come about when the mind is in a healthy state and in permanent possession of its own sanity, robust and vigorous, capable of the noblest endurance, responsive to circumstances, concerned for the body and all that affects it but not to the point of anxiety, conscientious about the other accoutrements of life without being too enamored of any one thing, ready to make use of the gifts of fortune without being enslaved to them.

IV. You understand, even if I do not spell it out, that, once those things that irk or alarm us have been driven out, the result is lasting tranquility and freedom; and in place of pleasures that were paltry and ephemeral, there comes into being an overwhelming sense of joy, steady and invulnerable, a peace and concord of soul, and a sublimity that is also humane. For cruelty always arises out of weakness.

It is possible to define our idea of the good in different ways, which is to say that the same concept is able to be captured in different verbal formulations. Just as the same army on some occasions is spread out over a wide area and on others pulled back into a compact force or extends its center out into curving wings or is deployed with its front ranks in a straight line, yet its potency remains the same whatever its current formation and its motivation to stand in defense of the same cause remains the same, so also the definition of the highest good can sometimes be opened up and drawn out, at other times condensed and contracted into itself.

Therefore it will amount to the same thing if I say, "The highest good is a mind that takes delight in virtue and looks down on what is merely fortuitous," or, "It is an indomitable force of mind that, strengthened by experience, shows itself in action as calm, profoundly generous and concerned for the welfare of others." One could also define it like this: that we

---

"On the Happy Life" and "Moral Letters to Lucilius," translated by Marcus Wilson, from *The Practice of Virtue*, edited by Jennifer Welchman (Indianapolis: Hackett Publishing Company, 2006).

1. The essay is addressed to Seneca's older brother Annaeus Novatus (who took the name Gallio). Like Seneca, he had a distinguished senatorial career that culminated in appointment as governor of the province of Achaia. When Seneca was implicated in an assassination plot against Emperor Nero, Gallio, too, was obliged to commit suicide.

would call that person happy who counts nothing good or evil but a good or evil soul, who reveres the honorable, is content with virtue alone, who is neither overly exhilarated nor heartbroken by chance events, who is convinced there is no greater good than the good that is self-conferred, for whom true pleasure consists in the disdain of pleasures.

If you want to stretch it out further, it is possible to shift the same thought into one of several other forms while preserving intact its cogency. For what prevents us describing the happy life as the possession of a soul that is free and upright and undaunted and steadfast, standing beyond fear, beyond desire; a soul that treats integrity as the only good, lack of integrity as the only evil, and regards the remaining mass of things as having no significant value, adding nothing to the happy life and subtracting nothing from it, having no power to increase or detract from the highest good as they appear or vanish.

When a life is built on this foundation it is accompanied by constant cheerfulness, whether wished for or not, and a deep-rooted sense of elation stemming from deep within. It rejoices in what is its own and does not hanker after greater rewards than this interior satisfaction. Why should this not outweigh the trivial and frivolous and impermanent sensations of the frail body? On the day we lose our susceptibility to pleasure we lose our susceptibility to pain. You see how those who are possessed alternately by those most fickle and uncontrollable of tyrants, the pleasures and pains, are enslaved in an evil and poisonous system of servitude?

Therefore you must break out to liberty. The only thing that has power to grant this freedom is indifference to fortune. Then that incalculable good will arise, the serenity and majesty of a mind installed in a safe place and, with all delusions ousted, the grand and undying joy that attends the discovery of truth, as well as an ease and affability of soul; and the delight we discover in these comes not from the fact that they are goods but from the fact that they are born out of our own good.

IX. Someone may make the following objection. "The real motivation for your cultivating virtue is because you anticipate it will bring you pleasure." To begin with, if it is true that virtue carries with it pleasure, it does not follow that it is sought for this purpose. For virtue does not confer pleasure but confers pleasure in addition; it does not exert itself for pleasure, but its exertions, although directed at other ends, attain pleasure in the process.

In a field that has been ploughed for the sowing of some crop, certain flowers spring up here and there. The work was not undertaken for the sake of these little plants, although they are pleasing to the eye. A different purpose motivated the person planting the crop, and the flowers are an unintended byproduct. Similarly, pleasure is neither the reward nor cause of virtue, but a bonus. We do not embrace virtue because it delights us, but, if we embrace it, it also delights us.

The ultimate good of virtue resides in the perspicacity of choice and the perfected condition of a mind that has completed its proper journey and contained itself within its own bounds. With this the supreme good is accomplished and the mind needs nothing more. For there is nothing outside the whole nor is there any place farther than the end. Therefore you are mistaken when you ask what it is I hope to gain from striving for virtue. You are asking for something beyond the ultimate. Do you want to know what I want from virtue? Virtue itself. It has nothing better to give and is its own reward. Is this not a big enough reward for you? When I say to you, "The greatest good is the austerity and foresight and magnanimity and sanity and freedom and harmony and beauty of an unbreakable spirit," do you still want something more for which those qualities are just the means to another end? Why do you call my attention to pleasure? I want to know the proper good of the human being, not of the belly, in the magnitude of which even cattle and wild beasts surpass us.

XV. Someone else may ask, "Why can't virtue and pleasure be alloyed so that the highest good is realized when the same actions are both honorable and gratifying?" Because you cannot have any part of the honorable that is not itself honorable, and the supreme good will lose its integrity if it sees something in itself inconsistent with its finer quality.

Even the delight that arises from virtue, though it is a good thing, is no more a constituent part of the absolute good than happiness and serenity, which are also born out of the most exalted causes. For those things are goods but attendant upon the supreme good, not components of it.

The person who allies virtue with pleasure in a partnership, inevitably an unequal partnership, blunts all the force of the one by the fragility of the other, and sends under the yoke that freedom that cannot be defeated so long as it does not recognize anything as being more precious than itself. Such a person falls into a great enslavement by becoming dependent on fortune. The life that follows is worried, suspicious, fearful, ever-alarmed at chance occurrences, uncertain from one moment to the next.

You do not set virtue on solid and immovable foundations but order it to stand on shifting ground. What is so unstable as the reliance on chance events and the continual alteration of the human body and of things that affect the body? How can such a person obey god and accept whatever happens in a sound frame of mind and not complain of fate and react to misfortunes positively, when rocked by every little pinprick of pleasure or pain? Nor can those who incline to pleasure do a good job of protecting or liberating their country or standing up for their friends. So allow the supreme good to occupy a height from which no force can drag it down, a height beyond the reach of pain and hope and fear and anything else that would lessen its authority as the supreme good. Only virtue can stand on that height.

XVI. True happiness, therefore, is founded upon virtue. Of what will this virtue persuade you? That you should consider nothing either good or evil other than what is characterized by virtue or vice. Secondly, that you become immovable from the good and against evil so that, insofar as it is right to do so, you exemplify the divine.

What does virtue promise in return for this outlay? Huge advantages, equivalent even to those of the gods: you will be under no compulsion, you will not be in want of anything, you will be free, secure, unassailable; you will attempt nothing in vain, be excluded from nothing; everything will come out according to your judgment; no setbacks will occur, nothing contrary to your wishes or expectation.

"What are you saying? That virtue is sufficient for living a happy life?" Perfect and divine as virtue is, why would it not be sufficient, or, rather, superabundant? For what can be lacking for someone placed beyond all desires? What need is there of external things if you have gathered all your assets within yourself?[2] For those, however, who are still directing their steps in virtue's direction, even when well advanced, there is a need for a certain leniency on fortune's part as they struggle in the midst of human affairs until the time when they have untangled that knot and loosened every mortal bond. "So how are they any different?" Because some people are hobbled, some are fettered, some are spread-eagled on a rack. Those who have made progress toward betterment and lifted themselves higher drag a loosened chain. They are not yet free but are as good as free.[3]

XVII. One of those who yap at philosophy[4] may make a speech of their usual type: "So why do you talk more boldly than you live? Why do you lower your voice to a superior, consider money a necessary tool for life, get upset when you incur a loss, weep when you learn that your spouse or your friend is dead, have regard for your reputation, and allow yourself to be disturbed by slanders?

Why do you have more land in cultivation than your natural needs require? Why do your dinner parties not abide by your own recommendations? Why is your furniture polished? Why is the wine drunk at your house of a vintage older than yourself? Why is gold on display? Why have you planted trees that will provide you with nothing other than shade? How come your wife wears the price of a house hanging from her affluent ears? How come your servant boys are dressed in costly garments? How come at your place serving at table is raised to the level of an art, and the silver tableware is not set out haphazardly and instinctively but is skillfully arranged and you have a trained expert whose job it is to cut the meat?"

---

2. Recall what Seneca said at the outset: one needs a clear conception of one's goal if one is to improve one's life. Perfect virtue is that goal and for the Stoic sage who achieves it, virtue is sufficient for happiness. Most of us will never attain it. Nevertheless, the quality of our lives hinges on the quality of our character.

3. If we are not yet fully virtuous, our state of character development will not as yet be sufficient for true happiness. Yet in pursuing virtue, we are already better off than those who do not recognize where true happiness is to be found.

4. Unlike early Greek Stoics, such as Zeno, and the Cynics, another Greek philosophical movement that held that nothing but virtue was necessary for happiness, Roman Stoics like Seneca did not argue for the rejection of gifts of fortune, such as wealth, or social status. Critics argued that to fail to do so was hypocritical. In what follows, Seneca considers and replies to such charges.

Add to this, if you wish: "Why do you own property overseas? Why more than you have visited? Why, to your disgrace, are you either so uninterested that your few slaves are completely unknown to you or so extravagant that you have more slaves than your memory can recall?" Later I'll add to your invective and cast more aspersions on myself than you have thought of, but for now I'll reply as follows. I fall far short of sagacity and, to provide food for your malevolence, I will never be a perfect sage. Demand of me, therefore, not that I be on a par with the best but just somewhat better than the depraved. This is enough of an achievement for me, to subtract each day something from my vices and to castigate my failings.

I have not achieved soundness of mind, nor will I ever do so. I am setting out alleviations for my gout, not cures, and am content if the attacks are less frequent and less painful. But compared with the state of your feet, you cripples, I'm a sprinter. I do not say these things on behalf of myself—for I am sunk deep in every kind of vice—but on behalf of those who have improved themselves to some degree.

XXI. "Why is that follower of philosophy living the life of a wealthy man?[5] Why does he say riches need to be scorned and yet he possesses them, and thinks life needs to be scorned but he's still alive, and that health needs to be scorned and still he looks after himself very carefully and prefers to be in peak condition? He maintains exile is a word without substance, asking, 'What evil is there in a change of locality?' and yet, if allowed, he grows old in his homeland. He judges there to be no significant difference between a longer and a shorter lifespan but, if nothing prevents him, he prolongs his life and calmly thrives far into old age."

The philosopher says these things should be scorned not to make the point that he should not have them but that he should not be in a state of anxiety about them. He does not drive them from his presence but when they take their leave he sees them out without regret. Where more securely could fortune deposit its wealth than where it can be recovered without any complaint from the person giving it back.

XXII. There can be no doubt that there is more scope in wealth than in poverty for the expression of a wise person's character, since in poverty there is only one type of virtue, not to be demeaned and ground down by it, but in wealth, moderation, generosity, responsibility, propriety, and nobility all have an open field in which to operate.

Wise people do not scorn themselves if they are short, although they'd like to be tall. If they are in poor health, thin in body or blind in one eye, they will prefer to be physically strong even though they are aware they have something in themselves that is stronger than the body. They will tolerate sickness but choose health.

Certain things, even though they are trivial in the larger context and can be taken away without damage to the primary good, nevertheless add something to the lasting joy that is born of virtue. Wealth encourages and enlivens the wise in the way a favorable wind affects the sailor it propels across the sea, or like a nice day in winter or a sunny spot in a cold place.

Where is the philosopher—I'm speaking of the stoics here, who think virtue is the only good—who does not agree that these things we refer to as "indifferent"[6] also contain some advantage, and that some of these are preferable to others. To a number of these a degree of respect is accorded, and in certain cases a considerable degree of respect. Make no mistake, therefore: wealth is one of the advantageous things.

"You must be trying to make a fool of me," you retort, "because wealth has the same importance for you as for me." Do you want to know how it does not have the same importance? If my wealth should melt away it would deprive me of nothing but itself, but if yours were to depart you would be stunned and feel you were deprived of what makes you yourself. With me, wealth has a certain place; in your case it has the highest place. In short, I own my wealth, your wealth owns you.

---

5. Although the charges of hypocrisy discussed above were leveled generally at Roman Stoics who did not reject worldly goods, here the text seems to become autobiographical. Seneca was himself very wealthy. His spending on behalf of his guests was lavish. And it was known that he had not endured his years of exile on Corsica wholly without complaint. Seneca's response thus seems personal as well as philosophical.

6. *Indifferent* was the Stoics' technical term for "gifts of fortune," such as health, wealth, beauty, or social status. Stoics held that some indifferent things may rationally be preferred to others; e.g., those, like health, that are instrumentally valuable for pursuing a virtuous human life. However, strictly speaking, none are necessary either for virtue or happiness.

Moral Letters to Lucilius[1]

Letter 76

Everything is endowed with its own particular good. The abundance of its grapes and taste of its wine is what we appreciate in a vine; with a deer it is its speed. In pack animals you look for a strong back, since their only task is to transport freight. With dogs, keenness of scent is the prime quality of those whose task it is to track wild animals, swiftness of those that pursue the prey, aggression if their role is to bite and attack. In each thing that faculty should be considered best for which it is born, by which it is judged.

What is best in a human being? Reason. In this the human being surpasses the animals and comes close to the gods. Therefore perfected reason is our own particular good, because everything else we have in common with plants and animals. Someone is strong; so are lions. Someone is strikingly beautiful; so are peacocks. Another is a fast runner; so are horses. I am not saying that in all these abilities the human is eclipsed. I'm not looking to establish what is superior in human nature but what is unique. As humans we have body; so do trees. We have control of our own movement and direction; so do beasts and worms. We have a voice; but the sound made by dogs is much louder, the sound of the eagle is more high-pitched, that of the bull much deeper, and the song of the nightingale is sweeter and more supple.

What is peculiar to humanity? Reason. Right and perfected reason is the fulfillment of human well-being. So, if every thing is esteemed when it has realized its own particular good and has achieved the objective of its own nature, and the particular good of a human being is reason, if a person has perfected this, that person is considered worthy of esteem and has reached the summit of human nature. This perfected reason is called virtue and is identical with the honorable.

So that alone is good in a human being which is uniquely human. We are not investigating here what is good in general but what is good in the case of human beings. Given that there is nothing other than reason unique to human nature, this will be the only true good, but it is one that outweighs all others.

Therefore in the case of human beings, it is wholly beside the point how much land they have under plough, how much money they have invested, how many people pay their respects, how expensive are their couches or translucent their cups, but how good they are.

A person is good whose reason is well developed and right and fitted to what human nature wills. This is called virtue, this is what we refer to as the honorable and is the one and only human good. Since reason alone can perfect a human being, it is only perfected reason that brings happiness. Because it is the only true human good, it is the only source of true human fulfillment. We also talk of other things as goods which are enhanced and conserved by virtue; in other words, all virtue's works. But virtue itself is the only true good because there is no other good without it.

All our actions in every sphere of life are governed by the measuring of what is the honorable thing to do against what is despicable. It is to these values that our reasoning for or against an action is directed. I will spell out the implications of this. A good person who judges an action honorable will do it even if it will involve a lot of trouble, even if it will involve financial loss, even if it involves danger. Similarly, a good person will not do something despicable even if it would bring profit, even if it would bring pleasure, even if it would bring power. Nothing will be able to divert such a person from the honorable course or toward the despicable course.

If you were to admit the idea that there is some good beside what is honorable, no virtue would be left secure. For no virtue can be sustained if it has to pay homage to something beyond itself. If there is some such thing, it is inconsistent with reason from

1. In the last year of his life, probably while living in unofficial retirement outside of Rome, Seneca wrote (for publication) a series of 124 letters on moral and philosophical topics. He addressed them to a younger acquaintance, Lucilius Junior, a Roman civil servant working in Sicily, of whom little else is known. (Significant gaps between excerpts within letters are indicated in the text.)

which the virtues come and with truth, which is nothing without reason. Any idea inconsistent with truth is false.

A good person, I'm sure you will agree, will feel the greatest respect for the gods. Such a person, therefore, would face any eventuality with a calmness of spirit, knowing that it happened in accordance with divine law by which everything in the universe is ordered. If this is so, there will be but one good recognized by the person, namely what is honorable. For it is part of the honorable to submit to the will of the gods, not to be incensed at the unexpected or to bemoan misfortune, but to accept fate patiently and comply with its mandates.

If you admit anything else to be a good besides the honorable, not only will craving for life persecute you but also the craving for life's paraphernalia, a situation that is intolerable, limitless, and unstable. Again, therefore, the only good is the honorable, which has bounds.

Letter 66

So it is Lucilius. Whatever true reason recommends is solid and imperishable. It uplifts and supports the mind so it remains always elevated. Those other things that popular opinion thoughtlessly values and treats as goods pump people up with empty pleasures. Likewise, the things people fear as if they were real evils stir them up with mental panic just as animals are spooked by the mere semblance of danger.

In neither case is there any foundation to the pleasure or distress of mind. The one does not warrant real joy nor the other real fear. Only reason is unalterable and capable of consistency of judgment. It is not the servant but the ruler of the senses. As two straight lines are equally straight, equally right, reason is equal to reason; and so also is virtue to virtue. Virtue is nothing other than right reason. All virtues are instances of reason. They are instances of reason if they are right. If they are right, they are also equal.

As is the case with reason, so is it also with actions. They too, therefore, are all equal. For in that they match reason they also match one another. Actions are equal among themselves, I maintain, insofar as they are honorable and right. But there are also great differences between actions as dictated by varying circumstances, which are sometimes open-ended, at others constrained, either in the public gaze or hidden in obscurity, affecting many other people or very few. Though circumstances are variable, whatever action is best is equal to any other best action; they are all honorable.

Analogously, all good persons are equal in respect of their goodness. Yet they have differences of age: one is older, another younger; of appearance: one is attractive, another ugly; of status: this one is rich, that one poor, this one popular, powerful, known to all the city and population, that one a nonentity to most people and obscure. But in respect of their goodness, they are equals.

About what is good and what is evil the senses are wholly unqualified to judge. They are ignorant of what is useful and what is useless. They cannot offer any opinion unless the thing is placed before them in the present. They cannot see ahead to the future or remember the past. As for consequences, they have no inkling. Yet it is from awareness of these consequences that the order and sequence of actions is interwoven and the unity of a life proceeding in a right direction is created. Therefore it falls to Reason to be the adjudicator of things good and things bad. To alien and extraneous things she assigns no value and treats those which are neither good nor evil as the most trivial and insignificant of trappings. All Reason's good is situated in the mind.

Of goods there is a group Reason thinks of as being in the first rank and with which she designedly associates herself, such as victory, good children, and public well-being. There is a second group that does not make itself known except in bad times, like enduring a painful illness or exile with composure. A third group is neutral, for these goods are no more in accordance with nature than contrary to nature, such as a modest way of walking or an orderly way of sitting. For to sit is no less in keeping with nature than to stand or go for a walk.

The first and second groups of goods are distinct. The first is aligned with nature: to find satisfaction in the affection of one's children or the security of one's homeland. The second group is at odds with nature: to show courage in withstanding torment or enduring thirst as some disease burns your body's organs.

"What's this?" someone will ask. "Can anything that is contrary to nature be a good?" Not at all; but that from which the good springs is sometimes contrary to nature. To be wounded, to have your flesh burnt off in a fire, to be crushed by ill health, these are against nature; but to beat such things with an undefeated spirit—that is to behave according to nature.[2]

To state my point briefly, the material from which good arises is sometimes against nature, but good itself never is. For no good is divorced from reason, and reason always conforms with nature. What therefore is reason? Compliance with nature. What is the highest human good? It is to conduct oneself in harmony with nature's will.

Letter 95

Consider also this question: how we are to behave toward other human beings. How do we act? What principles can we give people to follow? That we should not shed human blood? It is surely an inadequate ideal to avoid harming those one has a duty to assist! What a great thing to pride ourselves on, that one member of the human race is civilized to another! Should we teach, then, that we must stretch out a helping hand to the shipwrecked, show the right road to the bewildered, share our bread with the starving? How long it would take to list everything item by item that ought either to be done for others or not done. I can more briefly impart a general principle to govern all our interactions with human beings.

Everything that you see, everything human and divine, is one. We are all limbs of one all-encompassing body. Nature brought us into existence as creatures related to one another, forming us from the same elements for the same ends. She instilled in us reciprocal affection and made us innately sociable. She also invested us with a sense of fairness and justice. According to her law it is more deplorable to harm another than to be harmed. It is in obedience to her command that our hands are ready to assist those who need assistance.

That line of poetry should ever be in our hearts and on our lips: "I am human and I count nothing human as foreign to me."[3] Let us possess what we possess as members of a community. Into it we were born. Our society is like an arch of stones that will collapse unless each stone lends its weight to the next, allowing the whole structure to support itself.

Letter 50

Harpaste is a female clown[4] belonging to my wife. You'll recall that we inherited the obligation to look after her under the terms of a will and she has continued to live in my house. I myself have little interest in whatever entertainment these freaks of nature afford. If ever I want to be amused by a fool I don't have far to look. I just laugh at myself.

Anyway, this clown has suddenly lost her eyesight. What I'm going to tell you is hard to believe, but it's true: she doesn't realize that she's gone blind and she keeps asking her attendant to change her room. She complains that the house is always too dark.

I think it will be obvious to you that the reason we smile at Harpaste's misunderstanding is that it is somehow typical of all of us. We do not recognize our own greed, our own passion for possessions. At least blind people generally look for a guide, but we wander about without anyone to show us the way and we say: "I'm not driven by ambition; it's just that no one can survive in Rome any other way. I'm not extravagant; it's this city that costs so much to live in. The fact that I lose my temper, that I haven't settled down to any definite way of life, isn't a defect in me; youth is to blame for this." Why do we deceive ourselves? It

2. Seneca is playing with several senses of "nature" in this letter. It is in our nature as animals to flee from what may damage us physically. However, because we are not merely animals but *rational* animals, it is also consistent with our nature to follow reason when it requires us to override animal impulse. Further, it is consistent with nature in a broader sense; i.e., nature as the universal order that determines our specific nature and the course of events in our world. In acting as reason directs, we act in accordance with our own nature and with the universal order of nature.

3. Seneca is quoting from *The Self-Tormentor*, a comedy by Roman playwright Terence (195–159 BCE).

4. Harpaste was a "clown" or "fool"; i.e., a slave or servant kept for the amusement value of her appearance, speech, or mannerisms. Seneca would naturally disapprove of the practice for its exclusive focus on "indifferents" in assigning value to persons.

is not our environment that is responsible for our failings. They are inside us, seated deep within our innermost being, and the reason it is so difficult to achieve a healthy state of mind is because we fail to recognize that it is we ourselves who are sick.

To learn the virtues is to unlearn the vices. As we aim to improve ourselves we should draw confidence from the fact that the possession of goodness, once it has been obtained, is a possession forever. Virtue can't be unlearned. This is because discordant things are only weakly fixed to their mismatched hosts. Consequently they can be detached and expelled. But things that arrive at their true home settle in for the long term. Virtue is in keeping with nature whereas the vices are antagonistic and hostile to it.

But while the virtues, once they have been welcomed in, do not leave and are easy to safeguard; nevertheless, establishing the initial contact with them is hard work because fear of the unfamiliar is typical of a feeble and irresolute mind. So the mind needs to be pushed into taking the first step. From then on the medicine is not bitter. It heartens at the same time as it cures. With other remedies the enjoyment comes after the return to health; philosophy, by contrast, is both therapeutic and sweet from the very first dose. Farewell.

Letter 124

. . . The question is whether the good is grasped with the senses or the mind; connected with this is the fact that the good is not found in dumb animals and infants. Those who make pleasure supreme hold that the good is perceptible, but we on the other hand attribute it to the mind and hold that it is intelligible. If the senses made judgements about the good, we would not reject any pleasure; for no pleasure fails to attract us and every pleasure pleases us; conversely, we would not willingly suffer any pain; for every pain hurts our senses. Moreover, those who are excessively pleased by pleasure and who fear pain more than anything else would not deserve criticism. But in point of fact we do disapprove of those who are devoted to their bellies and to pleasure and we hold in contempt those whose fear of pain prevents them from ever daring to act in a manly fashion. What are they doing wrong if they obey their senses, i.e., the judges of what is good and bad? For you have handed over the decision about what is good and bad to the senses. But surely it is reason which is in charge of that matter; that is what makes the decisions about good and bad, just as it does about the happy life, about virtue and about the honourable. But [the hedonists] let the lowest part [of man] make the decisions about what is better, so that judgement is pronounced on the good by sense perception, which is blunt and lazy, and slower in men than it is in beasts. What [would we think] if someone wanted to discriminate tiny things not by the eyes but by touch? . . .

He says, "Just as every branch of knowledge and every craft takes something which is obvious and is grasped by sense perception as the starting point from which it will develop, similarly, the happy life must take something obvious as its foundation and starting point. Surely you say that the happy life has something obvious as its starting point." We say that those things which are in accordance with nature are happy. And what is in accordance with nature is out in the open and immediately apparent, just as is the case with what is healthy. I do not call the natural, [i.e.,] what immediately affects a newborn [animal], good, but rather the starting point of the good. You give over the highest good, i.e., pleasure, to infancy, so that a newborn starts out from the point which a fully accomplished man [might hope to] reach. You put the top of the tree where the roots ought to be. It would be a blatant error if someone said that the fetus hidden in its mother's womb, still of uncertain sex, immature, unfinished and not yet formed, were already in some good condition. And yet, how small is the difference between one who is just in the act of receiving life and one who lies as a hidden burden inside its mother's body. As far as an understanding of good and bad is concerned, both are equally mature; an infant is no more capable of the good than a tree or some dumb animal! But why is the good not found in a tree or a dumb animal? Because reason is not there either. That is also the reason why it is missing in an infant; for infants too lack reason. It attains the good when it attains reason.

There is such a thing as a non-rational animal; and such a thing as an animal which is not yet rational; and one which is rational but not yet perfect. In none of them can you find the good, which is brought with reason. What is the difference, then, between the [kinds of animal] I have mentioned? In the non-rational the good will never exist; in that which is not yet rational the good cannot exist just then; [in the rational] but imperfect the good is already *able* to [exist], but does not. I maintain, Lucilius, that the good is not found in just any body, nor in just any age; it is as far from the state of infancy as the last is from the first and as the perfect is from its starting point; so it is not found in a young body, still immature and in the process of formation. Of course it is not found there, any more than it is found in the seed!

You could put it like this: we are familiar with the good in a tree or a plant: it does not lie in the first sprouts which are just breaking the soil as they sprout. There is something good in a stalk of wheat, but it is not yet present in the sappy sprout nor when the tender ear [first] emerges from the husk, but when it ripens with the heat of summer and its proper maturity. Just as every nature refuses to bring forth its good until it is finished, so too man's good is not present in man until his reason is perfected. But what is this good? I shall say: a free and upright mind, superior to other things and inferior to nothing. So far is infancy from having this good that childhood does not hope for it, and adolescence is wrong to hope for it. We are lucky if it comes with old age as a result of long and serious effort. If this is what is good, it is also intelligible.

He says, "You said that there was a certain [kind of] good which belongs to a tree and to a plant; so there can also be a certain [kind of] good in an infant." The true good is not in trees or dumb animals; what is good in them is called good by courtesy. "What is this?" you say. [Merely] that which is in accord with the nature of each. But the good can in no way apply to a dumb animal; it belongs to a happier and better nature. Where there is no room for reason, there is no good. There are these four kinds of natures: that of a tree, of an animal, of a man and of a god. The latter two are rational and have the same nature and differ [only] in that the one is immortal and the other mortal. Nature perfects the goodness of one of these, i.e., god, while effort perfects the goodness of the other, i.e., man. The others, which lack reason, are perfect in their own natures, but not really perfect. For in the final analysis the only thing which is perfect is that which is perfect in accordance with universal nature; and universal nature is rational. The other things can [only] be perfect in their own kind. And in this there cannot exist a happy life, nor that which produces a happy life. But a happy life is produced by good things. In a dumb animal the happy life does not exist, [nor does that by which a happy life] is produced: the good does not exist in a dumb animal.

A dumb animal grasps what is present by its senses; it remembers past events when it meets with something which reminds its senses, as a horse is reminded of the road when it is placed at its starting point. But when in the stable he has no recollection of the road, no matter how often he has trodden it. The third [part of] time, i.e., the future, does not apply to dumb animals. So how can their nature seem to be perfect when they cannot make use of the past? For time consists of three parts, past, present and future. For animals the present is the briefest and most transitory time; they rarely recall the past, and then only when it is occasioned by the occurence of something in the present. Therefore, the good of a perfected nature cannot exist in an imperfect nature, or if such a nature has it, so do plants. I do not deny that dumb animals have great and powerful impulses towards achieving what is according to their natures; but they are disorderly and confused. But the good is never disorderly or confused. "What, then?" you say, "Are dumb animals moved in a thoroughly confused and disorganized fashion?" I would say that they are moved in a thoroughly confused and disorganized fashion, if their nature were capable of orderliness; but as it is, each is moved according to his own nature. Disorganized is [a term] reserved for those things which can sometimes move in a non-disorganized fashion; troubled [a term reserved] for that which can be free of care. Nothing has a vice if it cannot have virtue; and such is the motion of dumb animals by their very nature. But to avoid detaining you any longer, there will be a kind of good in a dumb animal, a kind of virtue, and a kind of perfection; but there will not be good or virtue or perfection in an absolute sense, since these properties apply only to rational animals, to whom it has been given to know why, to what extent, and how. So nothing which does not have reason can possess the good. . . .

Epictetus

Epictetus began life as a slave but ended it as one of the Roman Empire's most renowned philosophers. Born in Asia Minor (now Turkey) during the reign of Claudius in the mid-first century CE, he appeared first in Rome as the property of Epaphroditus, a member of Nero's staff and himself a freed slave. Allowed by this sympathetic master to study with the great Stoic of his day, Musonius Rufus, and freed by him after the death of Nero, Epictetus soon became a teacher of philosophy himself. He was expelled from Italy during the reign of Emperor Domitian. Moving to Epirus, in northwestern Greece, he established a philosophical school called The Hospital (*iatreion*). Fashioning himself as a doctor of souls, a *psychiatrist*, Epictetus preferred his students to leave his lectures in pain—as if their limbs had been reset—rather than in pleasure. Despite that, his lectures drew many students, including many sons of noble Roman families.

One of these students, Arrian, published Epictetus' thought in two books: the *Discourses*, which contained his lectures, and the *Handbook* (*Encheiridion*, in Greek), which set out his main doctrines. The most prominent concept in all these writings is freedom. Given Epictetus' origins, this is hardly surprising; what is surprising, though, is that he does not prohibit slavery. In the end, whether your body is free or enslaved is not up to you; neither is the fate of your family, friends, or possessions. According to Epictetus, all that is in your power is your mind—more specifically, your judgment of whether or not to assent to its presentations—and only what is in your power should be of concern to you. You should assent to presentations only when you judge them to be in accord with nature, the *logos*, or God (three names borrowed from the early Stoics for a providential force in the cosmos).

Perfect accord with nature is achieved only by the Sages, who understand the orders of God and remain at their post despite the adversity of circumstances. Socrates was the highest example of this virtue, since he preferred to drink the hemlock rather than surrender his philosophical mission. Epictetus also admired Zeno of Citium, the founder of Stoicism; Heraclitus, the first to teach of the divine *logos*; and Diogenes the Cynic, whom he considered a divine messenger. In the shadows of these Sages, Epictetus' own teachings were more for those who fell short of perfection but were seeking to make progress toward virtue. "This is my task," he said, "and I will not leave this post that has been assigned to me." He died sometime during reign of Hadrian, two generations before he would have witnessed the rule of Marcus Aurelius, a Stoic emperor deeply influenced by his thought.

The Handbook

1. Some things are up to us and some are not up to us. Our opinions are up to us, and our impulses, desires, aversions—in short, whatever is our own doing. Our bodies are not up to us, nor are our possessions, our reputations, or our public offices, or, that is, whatever is not our own doing. The things that are up to us are by nature free, unhindered, and unimpeded; the things that are not up to us are weak, enslaved, hindered, not our own. So remember, if you think that things naturally enslaved are free or that things not your own are your own, you will be thwarted, miserable, and upset, and will blame both gods and men. But if you think that only what is yours is yours, and that what is not your own is, just as it is, not your own, then no one will ever coerce

---

From Epictetus, *The Handbook*, translated by Nicholas White (Indianapolis: Hackett Publishing Company, 1983).

you, no one will hinder you, you will blame no one, you will not accuse anyone, you will not do a single thing unwillingly, you will have no enemies, and no one will harm you, because you will not be harmed at all.

As you aim for such great goals, remember that you must not undertake them by acting moderately, but must let some things go completely and postpone others for the time being. But if you want both those great goals and also to hold public office and to be rich then you may perhaps not get even the latter just because you aim at the former too; and you certainly will fail to get the former, which are the only things that yield freedom and happiness.

From the start, then, work on saying to each harsh appearance,[1] "You are an appearance, and not at all the thing that has the appearance." Then examine it and assess it by these yardsticks that you have, and first and foremost by whether it concerns the things that are up to us or the things that are not up to us. And if it is about one of the things that is not up to us, be ready to say, "You are nothing in relation to me."

2. Remember, what a desire proposes is that you gain what you desire, and what an aversion proposes is that you not fall into what you are averse to. Someone who fails to get what he desires is *un*fortunate, while someone who falls into what he is averse to has met *mis*fortune. So if you are averse only to what is against nature among the things that are up to you, then you will never fall into anything that you are averse to; but if you are averse to illness or death or poverty, you will meet misfortune. So detach your aversion from everything not up to us, and transfer it to what is against nature among the things that are up to us. And for the time being eliminate desire completely, since if you desire something that is not up to us, you are bound to be unfortunate, and at the same time none of the things that are up to us, which it would be good to desire, will be available to you. Make use only of impulse and its contrary, rejection,[2] though with reservation, lightly, and without straining.

3. In the case of everything attractive or useful or that you are fond of, remember to say just what sort of thing it is, beginning with the least little things. If you are fond of a jug, say "I am fond of a jug!" For then when it is broken you will not be upset. If you kiss your child or your wife, say that you are kissing a human being; for when it dies you will not be upset.

4. When you are about to undertake some action, remind yourself what sort of action it is. If you are going out for a bath, put before your mind what happens at baths—there are people who splash, people who jostle, people who are insulting, people who steal. And you will undertake the action more securely if from the start you say of it, "I want to take a bath and to keep my choices in accord with nature;" and likewise for each action. For that way if something happens to interfere with your bathing you will be ready to say, "Oh, well, I wanted not only this but also to keep my choices in accord with nature, and I cannot do that if I am annoyed with things that happen."

5. What upsets people is not things themselves but their judgments about the things. For example, death is nothing dreadful (or else it would have appeared dreadful to Socrates), but instead the judgment about death that it is dreadful—*that* is what is dreadful. So when we are thwarted or upset or distressed, let us never blame someone else but rather ourselves, that is, our own judgments. An uneducated person accuses others when he is doing badly; a partly educated person accuses himself, an educated person accuses neither someone else nor himself.

6. Do not be joyful about any superiority that is not your own. If the horse were to say joyfully, "I am beautiful," one could put up with it. But certainly you, when you say joyfully, "I have a beautiful horse," are joyful about the good of the horse. What, then, is your own? Your way of dealing with appearances. So whenever you are in accord with nature in your way of dealing with appearances, then be joyful, since then you are joyful about a good of your own.

---

1. The word "appearance" translates *phantasia,* which some translators render by "impression" or "presentation." An appearance is roughly the immediate experience of sense or feeling, which may or may not represent an external state of affairs. (The Stoics held, against the Skeptics, that some appearances self-evidently do represent external states of affairs correctly.)

2. Impulse and rejection (*hormē* and *aphormē*) are, in Stoic terms, natural and nonrational psychological movements, so to speak, that are respectively toward or away from external objects.

7. On a voyage when your boat has anchored, if you want to get fresh water you may pick up a small shellfish and a vegetable by the way, but you must keep your mind fixed on the boat and look around frequently in case the captain calls. If he calls you must let all those other things go so that you will not be tied up and thrown on the ship like livestock. That is how it is in life too: if you are given a wife and a child instead of a vegetable and a small shellfish, that will not hinder you; but if the captain calls, let all those things go and run to the boat without turning back; and if you are old, do not even go very far from the boat, so that when the call comes you are not left behind.

8. Do not seek to have events happen as you want them to, but instead want them to happen as they do happen, and your life will go well.

9. Illness interferes with the body, not with one's faculty of choice,[3] unless that faculty of choice wishes it to. Lameness interferes with the limb, not with one's faculty of choice. Say this at each thing that happens to you, since you will find that it interferes with something else, not with you.

10. At each thing that happens to you, remember to turn to yourself and ask what capacity you have for dealing with it. If you see a beautiful boy or woman, you will find the capacity of self-control for that. If hardship comes to you, you will find endurance. If it is abuse, you will find patience. And if you become used to this, you will not be carried away by appearances.

11. Never say about anything, "I have lost it," but instead, "I have given it back." Did your child die? It was given back. Did your wife die? She was given back. "My land was taken." So this too was given back. "But the person who took it was bad!" How does the way the giver[4] asked for it back concern you? As long as he gives it, take care of it as something that is not your own, just as travelers treat an inn.

12. If you want to make progress,[5] give up all considerations like these: "If I neglect my property I will have nothing to live on," "If I do not punish my slave boy he will be bad." It is better to die of hunger with distress and fear gone than to live upset in the midst of plenty. It is better for the slave boy to be bad than for you to be in a bad state. Begin therefore with little things. A little oil is spilled, a little wine is stolen: say, "This is the price of tranquillity; this is the price of not being upset." Nothing comes for free. When you call the slave boy, keep in mind that he is capable of not paying attention, and even if he does pay attention he is capable of not doing any of the things that you want him to. But he is not in such a good position that your being upset or not depends on him.

13. If you want to make progress, let people think you are a mindless fool about externals, and do not desire a reputation for knowing about them. If people think you amount to something, distrust yourself. Certainly it is not easy to be on guard both for one's choices to be in accord with nature and also for externals, and a person who concerns himself with the one will be bound to neglect the other.

14. You are foolish if you want your children and your wife and your friends to live forever, since you are wanting things to be up to you that are not up to you, and things to be yours that are not yours. You are stupid in the same way if you want your slave boy to be faultless, since you are wanting badness not to be badness but something else. But wanting not to fail to get what you desire—*this* you are capable of. A person's master is someone who has power over what he wants or does not want, either to obtain it or take it away. Whoever wants to be free, therefore, let him not want or avoid anything that is up to others. Otherwise he will necessarily be a slave.

15. Remember, you must behave as you do at a banquet. Something is passed around and comes to you: reach out your hand politely and take some. It goes by: do not hold it back. It has not arrived yet: do not stretch your desire out toward it, but wait until it comes to you. In the same way toward your children, in the same way toward your wife, in the same way toward public office, in the same way toward wealth, and you will be fit to share a banquet with the gods. But if when things are set in front of you, you do not take them but despise them, then you will not only share a banquet with the gods but also be a ruler along with them. For by acting in this way Diogenes

3. "Faculty of choice" translates *proairesis*, which designates a rational faculty of the soul.

4. The "giver" can be taken to be nature, or the natural order of the cosmos, or god, which the Stoics identified with each other.

5. "Making progress" (*prokoptein*) is the Stoic expression for movement in the direction of the ideal condition for a human being, embodied by the Stoic "sage."

and Heraclitus and people like them were deservedly gods and were deservedly called gods.

16. When you see someone weeping in grief at the departure of his child or the loss of his property, take care not to be carried away by the appearance that the externals he is involved in are bad, and be ready to say immediately, "What weighs down on this man is not what has happened (since it does not weigh down on someone else), but his judgment about it." Do not hesitate, however, to sympathise with him verbally, and even to moan with him if the occasion arises; but be careful not to moan inwardly.

17. Remember that you are an actor in a play, which is as the playwright wants it to be: short if he wants it short, long if he wants it long. If he wants you to play a beggar, play even this part skillfully, or a cripple, or a public official, or a private citizen. What is yours is to play the assigned part well. But to choose it belongs to someone else.

18. When a raven gives an unfavorable sign by croaking, do not be carried away by the appearance, but immediately draw a distinction to yourself and say, "None of these signs is for me, but only for my petty body or my petty property or my petty judgments or children or wife. For all signs are favorable if I wish, since it is up to me to be benefited by whichever of them turns out correct.

19. You can be invincible if you do not enter any contest in which victory is not up to you. See that you are not carried away by the appearance, in thinking that someone is happy when you see him honored ahead of you or very powerful or otherwise having a good reputation. For if the really good things are up to us, neither envy nor jealousy has a place, and you yourself will want neither to be a general or a magistrate or consul, but to be free. And there is one road to this: despising what is not up to us.

20. Remember that what is insulting is not the person who abuses you or hits you, but the judgment about them that they *are* insulting. So when someone irritates you be aware that what irritates you is your own belief. Most importantly, therefore, try not to be carried away by appearance, since if you once gain time and delay you will control yourself more easily.

21. Let death and exile and everything that is terrible appear before your eyes every day, especially death; and you will never have anything contemptible in your thoughts or crave anything excessively.

22. If you crave philosophy prepare yourself on the spot to be ridiculed, to be jeered at by many people who will say, "Here he is again, all of a sudden turned philosopher on us!" and "Where did he get that high brow?" But don't *you* put on a high brow, but hold fast to the things that appear best to you, as someone assigned by god to this place. And remember that if you hold to these views, those who previously ridiculed you will later be impressed with you, but if you are defeated by them you will be doubly ridiculed.

23. If it ever happens that you turn outward to want to please another person, certainly you have lost your plan of life. Be content therefore in everything to be a philosopher, and if you want to seem to be one, make yourself appear so to yourself, and you will be capable of it.

24. Do not be weighed down by the consideration, "I shall live without any honor, everywhere a nobody!" For if lack of honors is something bad, I cannot be in a bad state because of another person any more than I can be in a shameful one. It is not your task to gain political office, or be invited to a banquet, is it? Not at all. How then is that a lack of honor? And how will you be a nobody everywhere, if you need to be a somebody only in things that are up to you—in which it is open to you to be of the greatest worth? "But your friends will be without help!" What do you mean, "without help?" Well, they will be without a little cash from you, and you will not make them Roman citizens. Who told you, then, that these things are up to you and not the business of someone else? Who can give to someone else what he does not have himself? "Get money," someone says, "so that we may have some." If I can get it while keeping self-respect and trustworthiness and high-mindedness, show me the way and I will get it. But if you demand that I lose the good things that are mine so that you may acquire things that are not good, see for yourselves how unfair and inconsiderate you are. Which do you want more, money or a self-respecting and trustworthy friend? Then help me more toward this, and do not expect me to do things that will make me lose these qualities. "But my country," he says, "will be without help, insofar as it depends on me!" Again, what sort of "help" is this? So it will not have porticos and baths by your efforts. What does that amount to? For it does not have shoes because of the blacksmith or weapons because of the cobbler, but it is enough if each person fulfills his own task. And if you furnished for it another citizen who was trustworthy and self-respecting, would you in no way be helpful to it? "Yes, I would be." Then neither would you yourself be unhelpful to it. "Then what place," he says "will I have in the city?" The one you can have by preserving your trustworthiness and self-respect. And if while wanting to help it you throw away these things, what use will you be to it if you turn out shameless and untrustworthy?

25. Has someone been given greater honor than you at a banquet or in a greeting or by being brought in to give advice? If these things are good, you should be glad that he has got them. If they are bad, do not be angry that you did not get them. And remember, you cannot demand an equal share if you did not do the same things, with a view to getting things that are not up to us. For how can someone who does not hang around a person's door have an equal share with someone who does, or someone who does not escort him with someone who does, or someone who does not praise him with someone who does? You will be unjust and greedy, then, if you want to obtain these things for free when you have not paid the price for which they are bought. Well, what is the price of heads of lettuce? An obol, say. So if someone who has paid an obol takes the heads of lettuce, and you who do not pay do not take them, do not think that you are worse off than the one who did. For just as he has the lettuce, you have the obol that you did not pay. It is the same way in this case. You were not invited to someone's banquet? You did not give the host the price of the meal. He sells it for praise; he sells it for attention. Then give him the balance for which it is sold, if that is to your advantage. But you are greedy and stupid if you want both not to pay and also to take. Have you got nothing, then, in place of the meal? Indeed you do have something; you did not praise someone you did not wish to praise, and you did not have to put up with the people around his door.

26. It is possible to learn the will of nature from the things in which we do not differ from each other. For example, when someone else's little slave boy breaks his cup we are ready to say, "It's one of those things that just happen." Certainly, then, when your own cup is broken you should be just the way you were when the other person's was broken. Transfer the same idea to larger matters. Someone else's child is dead, or his wife. There is no one who would not say, "It's the lot of a human being." But when one's own dies, immediately it is, "Alas! Poor me!" But we should have remembered how we feel when we hear of the same thing about others.

27. Just as a target is not set up to be missed, in the same way nothing bad by nature happens in the world.

28. If someone turned your body over to just any person who happened to meet you, you would be angry. But are you not ashamed that you turn over your own faculty of judgment to whoever happens along, so that if he abuses you it is upset and confused?

29. For each action, consider what leads up to it and what follows it, and approach it in the light of that. Otherwise you will come to it enthusiastically at first, since you have not borne in mind any of what will happen next, but later when difficulties turn up you will give up disgracefully. You want to win an Olympic victory? I do too, by the gods, since that is a fine thing. But consider what leads up to it and what follows it, and undertake the action in the light of that. You must be disciplined, keep a strict diet, stay away from cakes, train according to strict routine at a fixed time in heat and in cold, not drink cold water, not drink wine when you feel like it, and in general you must have turned yourself over to your trainer as to a doctor, and then in the contest "dig in," sometimes dislocate your hand, twist your ankle, swallow a lot of sand, sometimes be whipped, and, after all that, lose. Think about that and then undertake training, if you want to. Otherwise you will be behaving the way children do, who play wrestlers one time, gladiators another time, blow trumpets another time, then act a play. In this way you too are now an athlete, now a gladiator, then an orator, then a philosopher, yet you are nothing wholeheartedly, but like a monkey you mimic each sight that you see, and one thing after another is to your taste, since you do not undertake a thing after considering it from every side, but only randomly and half-heartedly.

In the same way when some people watch a philosopher and hear one speaking like Euphrates[6]

6. Euphrates was a Stoic lecturer noted for his eloquence.

(though after all who can speak like him?), they want to be philosophers themselves. Just you consider, as a human being, what sort of thing it is; then inspect your own nature and whether you can bear it. You want to do the pentathlon, or to wrestle? Look at your arms, your thighs, inspect your loins. Different people are naturally suited for different things. Do you think that if you do those things you can eat as you now do, drink as you now do, have the same likes and dislikes? You must go without sleep, put up with hardship, be away from your own people, be looked down on by a little slave boy, be laughed at by people who meet you, get the worse of it in everything, honor, public office, law courts, every little thing. Think about whether you want to exchange these things for tranquillity, freedom, calm. If not, do not embrace philosophy, and do not like children be a philosopher at one time, later a tax-collector, then an orator, then a procurator of the emperor. These things do not go together. You must be one person, either good or bad. You must either work on your ruling principle,[7] or work on externals, practise the art either of what is inside or of what is outside, that is, play the role either of a philosopher or of a non-philosopher.

30. Appropriate actions[8] are in general measured by relationships. He is a father: that entails taking care of him, yielding to him in everything, putting up with him when he abuses you or strikes you. "But he is a bad father." Does nature then determine that you have a good father? No, only that you have a father.[9] "My brother has done me wrong." Then keep your place in relation to him; do not consider his action, but instead consider what you can do to bring your own faculty of choice into accord with nature. Another person will not do you harm unless you wish it; you will be harmed at just that time at which you take yourself to be harmed. In this way, then, you will discover the appropriate actions to expect from a neighbor, from a citizen, from a general, if you are in the habit of looking at relationships.

31. The most important aspect of piety toward the gods is certainly both to have correct beliefs about them, as beings that arrange the universe well and justly, and to set yourself to obey them and acquiesce in everything that happens and to follow it willingly, as something brought to completion by the best judgment. For in this way you will never blame the gods or accuse them of neglecting you. And this piety is impossible unless you detach the good and the bad from what is not up to us and attach it exclusively to what is up to us, because if you think that any of what is not up to us is good or bad, then when you fail to get what you want and fall into what you do not want, you will be bound to blame and hate those who cause this. For every animal by nature flees and turns away from things that are harmful and from what causes them, and pursues and admires things that are beneficial and what causes them. There is therefore no way for a person who thinks he is being harmed to enjoy what he thinks is harming him, just as it is impossible to enjoy the harm itself. Hence a son even abuses his father when the father does not give him a share of things that he thinks are good; and thinking that being a tyrant was a good thing is what made enemies of Polyneices and Eteocles.[10] This is why the farmer too abuses the gods, and the sailor, and the merchant, and those who have lost their wives and children. For wherever someone's advantage lies, there he also shows piety. So whoever takes care to have desires and aversions as one should also in the same instance takes care about being pious. And it is always appropriate to make libations and sacrifices and give firstfruits according to the custom of one's forefathers, in a manner that is pure and neither slovenly nor careless, nor indeed cheaply nor beyond one's means.

32. When you make use of fortune-telling, remember that you do not know what will turn out and have

---

7. The "ruling principle" (or "governing principle"), the *hēgemonikon*, in the rather complicated psychological theory adopted by the Stoics, is that central part of the soul that can understand what is good and decide to act on that understanding.

8. "Appropriate actions" are *kathēkonta*, which Cicero called *officia*, and are in English translations often called "duties," though the notion is actually somewhat different from that of duty. They are the actions that are of a type generally in accord with nature, or with a particular sort of person's place in it.

9. The idea here is, roughly, that there are certain relationships of affinity established by the natural order, and that having a father represents one of them, but that having a good father is not entailed by it.

10. The story of the conflict between the brothers Polyneices and Eteocles is best known to modern readers from Sophocles' tragedy *Antigone*.

gone to the fortune-teller to find out, but that if you really are a philosopher you have gone already knowing what sort of thing it is. For if it is one of the things that is not up to us, it is bound to be neither good nor bad. Therefore do not bring desire or aversion to the fortune-teller and do not approach him trembling but instead realizing that everything that turns out is indifferent[11] and nothing in relation to you, and that whatever sort of thing it may be, you will be able to deal with it well and no one will hinder that. So go confidently to the gods as advisers, and thereafter when some particular advice has been given to you remember who your advisers are and whom you will be disregarding if you disobey. Approach fortune-telling as Socrates thought a person should, in cases where the whole consideration has reference to the outcome, and no resource is available from reason or any other technique to find out about the matter. So, when it is necessary to share a danger with a friend or with your country, do not use fortune-telling about whether you should share the danger. For if the fortune-teller says that the omens are unfavorable, clearly death is signified or the injury of a part of your body or exile. But reason chooses to stand by your friend and to share danger with your country even under these conditions. For this reason pay attention to the greater fortune-teller, Pythian Apollo, who threw out of the temple the man who did not help his brother when he was being murdered.[12]

33. Set up right now a certain character and pattern for yourself which you will preserve when you are by yourself and when you are with people. Be silent for the most part, or say what you have to in a few words. Speak rarely, when the occasion requires speaking, but not about just any topic that comes up, not about gladiators, horse-races, athletes, eating, or drinking—the things that always come up; and especially if it is about people, talk without blaming or praising or comparing. Divert by your own talk, if you can, the talk of those with you to something appropriate. If you happen to be stranded among strangers, do not talk. Do not laugh a great deal or at a great many things or unrestrainedly. Refuse to swear oaths, altogether if possible, or otherwise as circumstances allow. Avoid banquets given by those outside philosophy. But if the appropriate occasion arises, take great care not to slide into their ways, since certainly if a person's companion is dirty the person who spends time with him, even if he happens to be clean, is bound to become dirty too. Take what has to do with the body to the point of bare need, such as food, drink, clothing, house, household slaves, and cut out everything that is for reputation or luxury. As for sex, stay pure as far as possible before marriage, and if you have it, do only what is allowable. But do not be angry or censorious toward those who do engage in it, and do not always be making an exhibition of the fact that you do not.

If someone reports back to you that so-and-so is saying bad things about you, do not reply to them but answer, "Obviously he didn't know my other bad characteristics, since otherwise he wouldn't just have mentioned these."

For the most part there is no need to go to public shows, but if ever the right occasion comes do not show your concern to be for anything but yourself; that is to say, wish to have happen only what does happen, and for the person to win who actually does win, since that way you will not be thwarted. But refrain completely from shouting or laughing at anyone or being very much caught up in it. After you leave, do not talk very much about what has happened, except what contributes to your own improvement, since that would show that the spectacle had impressed you.

Do not go indiscriminately or readily to people's public lectures, but when you do be on guard to be dignified and steady and at the same time try not to be disagreeable.

When you are about to meet someone, especially someone who seems to be distinguished, put to yourself the question, "What would Socrates or Zeno have done in these circumstances?" and you will not be at a loss as to how to deal with the occasion. When you go to see someone who is important, put to yourself the thought that you will not find him at home, that you will be shut out, that the door will be slammed, that he will pay no attention to you. If it is appropriate to go even under these conditions, go and put up

11. Things that are "indifferent" in the Stoic view are all things that are external and not up to oneself.

12. The idea is that one does not need a fortune-teller to tell one whether one should defend one's country or one's friends, and that this fact was recognized by the oracle of Apollo at Delphi.

with what happens, and never say to yourself, "It wasn't worth all that!" For that is the way of a non-philosopher, someone who is misled by externals.

In your conversations stay away from making frequent and longwinded mention of what you have done and the dangers that you have been in, since it is not as pleasant for others to hear about what has happened to you as it is for you to remember your own dangers. Stay away from raising a laugh, since this manner slips easily into vulgarity and at the same time is liable to lessen your neighbors' respect for you. It is also risky to fall into foul language. So when anything like that occurs, if a good opportunity arises, go so far as to criticize the person who has done it, and otherwise by staying silent and blushing and frowning you will show that you are displeased by what has been said.

34. Whenever you encounter some kind of apparent pleasure, be on guard, as in the case of other appearances, not to be carried away by it, but let the thing wait for you and allow yourself to delay. Then bring before your mind two times, both the time when you enjoy the pleasure and the time when after enjoying it you later regret it and berate yourself; and set against these the way you will be pleased and will praise yourself if you refrain from it. But if the right occasion appears for you to undertake the action, pay attention so that you will not be overcome by its attractiveness and pleasantness and seductiveness, and set against it how much better it is to be conscious of having won this victory against it.

35. When you do something that you determine is to be done, never try not to be seen doing it, even if most people are likely to think something bad about it. If you are not doing it rightly, avoid the act itself; if you are doing it rightly, why do you fear those who will criticize you wrongly?

36. Just as the propositions "It is day" and "It is night" have their full value when disjoined [*sc.*, in "It is day *or* it is night"] but have negative value when conjoined [*sc.*, in "It is day *and* it is night"], in the same way, granted that taking the larger portion has value for one's body, it has negative value for preserving the fellowship of a banquet in the way one should.[13] So when you eat with another, remember not merely to see the value for your body of what lies in front of you, but also to preserve your respect for your host.

37. If you undertake some role beyond your capacity, you both disgrace yourself by taking it and also thereby neglect the role that you were unable to take.

38. Just as in walking about you pay attention so as not to step on a nail or twist your foot, pay attention in the same way so as not to harm your ruling principle. And if we are on guard about this in every action, we shall set about it more securely.

39. The measure of possessions for each person is the body, as the foot is of the shoe. So if you hold to this principle you will preserve the measure; but if you step beyond it, you will in the end be carried as if over a cliff; just as in the case of the shoe, if you go beyond the foot, you get a gilded shoe, and then a purple embroidered one. For there is no limit to a thing once it is beyond its measure.

40. Women are called ladies by men right after they are fourteen. And so when they see that they have nothing else except to go to bed with men, they begin to make themselves up and place all their hopes in that. It is therefore worthwhile to pay attention so that they are aware that they are honored for nothing other than appearing modest and self-respecting.

41. It shows lack of natural talent to spend time on what concerns the body, as in exercising a great deal, eating a great deal, drinking a great deal, moving one's bowels or copulating a great deal. Instead you must do these things in passing, but turn your whole attention toward your faculty of judgment.[14]

42. When someone acts badly toward you or speaks badly of you, remember that he does or says it in the belief that it is appropriate for him to do so. Accordingly he cannot follow what appears to you but only what appears to him, so that if things appear badly to him, he is harmed in as much as he has been

13. Very roughly, the idea is that the value of an action has to be judged from all features of the context. The parallel is that allegedly the meaningfulness of a sentence depends in a way on its context.

14. The claim is in effect that one should be concerned wholly with the state of the ruling part of one's soul, and not with external states of affairs or with those aspects of the soul, such as one's affective feelings or desires, that are directly dependent on external states of affairs. One can see here the Stoic view, which seems paradoxical to many, that one's feelings and nonrational desires are in a crucial sense external to one's true self.

deceived. For if someone thinks that a true conjunctive proposition[15] is false, the conjunction is not harmed but rather the one who is deceived. Starting from these considerations you will be gentle with the person who abuses you. For you must say on each occasion, "That's how it seemed to him."

43. Everything has two handles, one by which it may be carried and the other not. If your brother acts unjustly toward you, do not take hold of it by this side, that he has acted unjustly (since this is the handle by which it may not be carried), but instead by this side, that he is your brother and was brought up with you, and you will be taking hold of it in the way that it can be carried.

44. These statements are not valid inferences: "I am richer than you; therefore I am superior to you," or "I am more eloquent than you; therefore I am superior to you." But rather these are valid: "I am richer than you; therefore my property is superior to yours," or "I am more eloquent than you; therefore my speaking is superior to yours." But you are identical neither with your property nor with your speaking.

45. Someone takes a bath quickly; do not say that he does it badly but that he does it quickly. Someone drinks a great deal of wine; do not say that he does it badly but that he does a great deal of it. For until you have discerned what his judgment was, how do you know whether he did it badly? In this way it will not turn out that you receive convincing appearances of some things but give assent to quite different ones.[16]

46. Never call yourself a philosopher, and do not talk a great deal among non-philosophers about philosophical propositions, but do what follows from them. For example, at a banquet do not say how a person ought to eat, but eat as a person ought to. Remember that Socrates had so completely put aside ostentation that people actually went to him when they wanted to be introduced to philosophers, and he took them. He was that tolerant of being overlooked. And if talk about philosophical propositions arises among non-philosophers, for the most part be silent, since there is a great danger of your spewing out what you have not digested. And when someone says to you that you know nothing and you are not hurt by it, then you know that you are making a start at your task. Sheep do not show how much they have eaten by bringing the feed to the shepherds, but they digest the food inside themselves, and outside themselves they bear wool and milk. So in your case likewise do not display propositions to non-philosophers but instead the actions that come from the propositions when they are digested.

47. When you have become adapted to living cheaply as far as your body is concerned, do not make a show of it, and if you drink water do not say at every opening that you drink water. If you wish to train yourself to hardship, do it for yourself and not for those outside. Do not throw your arms around statues. Instead, when you are terribly thirsty, take cold water into your mouth, and spit it out, and do not tell anyone about it.

48. The position and character of a non-philosopher: he never looks for benefit or harm to come from himself but from things outside. The position and character of a philosopher: he looks for all benefit and harm to come from himself.

Signs of someone's making progress: he censures no one; he praises no one; he blames no one; he never talks about himself as a person who amounts to something or knows something. When he is thwarted or prevented in something, he accuses himself. And if someone praises him he laughs to himself at the person who has praised him; and if someone censures him he does not respond. He goes around like an invalid, careful not to move any of his parts that are healing before they have become firm. He has kept off all desire from himself, and he has transferred all aversion onto what is against nature among the things that are up to us. His impulses toward everything are diminished. If he seems foolish or ignorant, he does not care. In a single phrase, he is on guard against himself as an enemy lying in wait.

49. When someone acts grand because he understands and can expound the works of Chrysippus, say

---

15. A proposition of this sort consists of two component propositions conjoined by "and."

16. A "convincing appearance" is a *katalēptikē phantasia*, the sort of appearance that according to the Stoics is a self-evidently correct representation of the way things actually are. "Assent" is *synkatathēsis*. Correct assent would of course be assent to self-evidently correct appearances. The line of thought here is, however, quite compressed, and the student will find it a difficult exercise to explain it.

to yourself, "If Chrysippus had not written unclearly, this man would have nothing to be proud of."

But what do *I* want? To learn to understand nature and follow it. So I try to find out who explains it. And I hear that Chrysippus does, and I go to him. But I do not understand the things that he has written, so I try to find the person who explains them. Up to this point there is nothing grand. But when I do find someone who explains them, what remains is to carry out what has been conveyed to me. This alone is grand. But if I am impressed by the explaining itself, what have I done but ended up a grammarian instead of a philosopher—except that I am explaining Chrysippus instead of Homer. Instead, when someone says to me, "Read me some Chrysippus," I turn red when I cannot exhibit actions that are similar to his words and in harmony with them.

50. Abide by whatever task is set before you as if it were a law, and as if you would be committing sacrilege if you went against it. But pay no attention to whatever anyone says about you, since that falls outside what is yours.

51. How long do you put off thinking yourself worthy of the best things, and never going against the definitive capacity of reason?[17] You have received the philosophical propositions that you ought to agree to and you have agreed to them. Then what sort of teacher are you still waiting for, that you put off improving yourself until he comes? You are not a boy anymore, but already a full-grown man. If you now neglect things and are lazy and are always making delay after delay and set one day after another as the day for paying attention to yourself, then without realizing it you will make no progress but will end up a non-philosopher all through life and death. So decide now that you are worthy of living as a full-grown man who is making progress, and make everything that seems best be a law that you cannot go against. And if you meet with any hardship or anything pleasant or reputable or disreputable, then remember that the contest is *now* and the Olympic games are *now* and you cannot put things off any more and that your progress is made or destroyed by a single day and a single action. Socrates became fully perfect in this way, by not paying attention to anything but his reason in everything that he met with. You, even if you are not yet Socrates, ought to live as someone wanting to be Socrates.

52. The first and most necessary aspect of philosophy is that of dealing with philosophical propositions, such as "not to hold to falsehood." The second is that of demonstrations, for example, "How come one must not hold to falsehood?" The third is that of the confirmation and articulation of these, for example. "How come this is a demonstration? What is demonstration? What is entailment? What is conflict? What is truth? What is falsity?" Therefore the third is necessary because of the second, and the second because of the first; but the most necessary, and the one where one must rest, is the first. We, however, do it backwards, since we spend time in the third and all of our effort goes into it, and we neglect the first completely. Therefore we hold to falsehood, but we are ready to explain how it is demonstrated that one must not hold to falsehood.

53. On every occasion you must have these thoughts ready:

Lead me, Zeus, and you too, Destiny,
Wherever I am assigned by you;
I'll follow and not hesitate,
But even if I do not wish to,
Because I'm bad, I'll follow anyway.

Whoever has complied well with necessity
Is counted wise by us, and understands divine
affairs.

Well, Crito, if it is pleasing to the gods this way,
then let it happen this way.

Anytus and Meletus can kill me, but they can't
harm me.[18]

---

17. In brief, the capacity of reason here is that of distinguishing different things from each other and defining them.

18. These four bits of poetry have the following origins. The first is by Cleanthes, who was head of the Stoic school at Athens between Zeno and Chrysippus. The second is a fragment of Euripides (*fr.* 965 Nauck). The third is Plato, *Crito* 43d, and the fourth is Plato, *Apology* 30c–d (slightly modified as compared with our manuscript texts), both purporting to be quotations from Socrates.

Marcus Aurelius

Born in 121 CE to a Spanish family that had reached the top of the Roman political ladder, Marcus soon became a favorite of Emperor Hadrian, who had been so interested in Greek culture in his own youth that he had earned the nickname *Graeculus* ("Little Greek"). Before dying, Hadrian ensured that his immediate successor, Aurelius Antoninus Pius, would adopt Marcus, making him next in line for the throne. Marcus Aurelius Antoninus' reign, from 161 to 180, has perhaps been the closest approximation to Plato's ideal of the rule of a philosopher-king. It was, wrote Edward Gibbon in the eighteenth century, the "period in the history of the world during which the condition of the human race was most happy and prosperous."

Even so, it was not without trouble. Parthians threatened from the east, and the armies Marcus sent to fight them returned with a plague that decimated the empire. Germans threatened from the north, and Marcus himself led several difficult campaigns against them. A giant column erected in Rome portrays the official history of these campaigns, but a more intimate portrait of their leader is afforded by the philosophical diary in Greek that Marcus seems to have written by the Danube, perhaps during those harsh winters that eventually killed him. Never intended for publication, and originally given the title *To Himself*, this diary was largely unknown until the sixteenth century, when it acquired a wide readership under the title *Meditations*.

Marcus begins by listing everything for which he is thankful—notably, the favors of Antoninus Pius and, in the first passage selected here, the fact that he was not seduced by Sophists and their subtleties. Like Epictetus, from whom he draws much of his thought, Marcus is less concerned with logic and physics than with ethics. Moral improvement requires conforming oneself to nature, which he often calls "the Whole." Since this Whole is divine and follows a rational plan, the *logos* of Heraclitus, Marcus resigns himself to his many sufferings—which included the loss of four of his five sons—with the reassurance that "nothing is harmful to the part which is advantageous to the Whole," and *everything* is advantageous to the Whole. The old Stoic tensions thus remain: on one hand, an apparently cruel but ultimately benign fate; on the other, the philosopher's moral exhortation—as if character were not fated and could be improved.

Marcus appears unfazed by such tensions. "Do not discuss in general terms the question of what is a good man," he urges: "Be one." Thus the *Meditations'* practical recommendations outweigh their metaphysical speculations. Desires and passions that thwart our conformity with the whole, for example, must be purged by specific spiritual exercises. The ideal soul has achieved *apatheia*, the absence of passions; reason alone determines its approach to the divine and rational cosmos. Living by pure reason, Marcus thus believes, we become more divine ourselves, and even more tolerant of those less pure. They too are part of the whole, after all.

To ensure the survival of philosophy after his death, Marcus endowed four professorships in Athens, one for each of the major philosophies of his day: Stoic, of course, but also Academic, Peripatetic (Aristotelian), and Epicurean. Philosophers occupied these professorships for nearly four centuries, until one of Marcus' successors, the Christian emperor Justinian, disbanded them in 529, as pagan influences. Nonetheless, each of the four schools still has its advocates today, and almost 2,000 years after Marcus wrote, even Christians—whom he criticizes for their passionate enthusiasms, and whose persecution he allowed during his reign—find inspiration in his diary.

MEDITATIONS

1

17. . . . that, though I longed for philosophy, I did not fall in with any Sophist or withdraw from active life to analyze literary compositions or syllogisms, or busy myself with questions of natural science, for all these things need the help of the gods and of Fortune.

2

11. It is possible to depart from life at this moment. Have this thought in mind whenever you act, speak, or think. There is nothing terrible in leaving the company of men, if the gods exist, for they would not involve you in evil. If, on the other hand, they do not exist or do not concern themselves with human affairs, then what is life to me in a universe devoid of gods or of Providence? But they do exist and do care for humanity, and have put it altogether within a man's power not to fall into real evils. And if anything else were evil they would have seen to it that it be in every man's power not to fall into it. As for that which does not make a man worse, how could it make the life of man worse?

Neither through ignorance nor with knowledge could the nature of the Whole have neglected to guard against this or correct it; nor through lack of power or skill could it have committed so great a wrong, namely that good and evil should come to the good and the evil alike, and at random. True, death and life, good and ill repute, toil and pleasure, wealth and poverty, being neither good nor bad, come to the good and the bad equally. They are therefore neither blessings for evils.

16. The human soul violates itself most of all when it becomes, as far as it can, a separate tumor or growth upon the universe; for to be discontented with anything that happens is to rebel against that Nature which embraces, in some part of itself, all other natures. The soul violates itself also whenever it turns away from a man and opposes him to do him harm, as do the souls of angry men; thirdly, whenever it is overcome by pleasure or pain; fourthly, whenever it acts a part and does or says anything falsely and hypocritically; fifthly, when it fails to direct any action or impulse to a goal, but acts at random, without purpose, whereas even the most trifling actions must be directed toward the end; and this end, for reasonable creatures, is to follow the reason and the law of the most honored commonwealth and constitution.

17. In human life time is but a point, reality a flux, perception indistinct, the composition of the body subject to easy corruption, the soul a spinning top, fortune hard to make out, fame confused. To put it briefly: physical things are but a flowing stream, things of the soul dreams and vanity; life is but a struggle and the visit to a strange land, posthumous fame but a forgetting.

What then can help us on our way? One thing only: philosophy. This consist in guarding our inner spirit inviolate and unharmed, stronger than pleasures and pains, never acting aimlessly, falsely or hypocritically, independent of the actions or inaction of others, accepting all that happens or is given as coming whence one came oneself, and at all times awaiting death with contented mind as being only the release of the elements of which every creature is composed. If it is nothing fearful for the elements themselves that one should continually change into another, why should anyone look with suspicion upon the change and dissolution of all things? For this is in accord with nature, and nothing evil is in accord with nature.

3

2. We should also observe things like these: that the incidental results of natural phenomena have some charm and attractiveness. For example, when a loaf of bread is being baked, some parts break open, and these cracks, which are not intended by the baker's craft, somehow stand out and arouse in us a special eagerness to eat; figs, too, burst open when they are

---

From Marcus Aurelius, *The Meditations*, translated by G.M.A. Grube (Indianapolis: Hackett Publishing Company, 1983).

very ripe, and the very closeness of decay adds a special beauty to olives that have ripened on the tree. The same is true of ears of wheat as they bend to the ground, of the wrinkles of a lion's brow, of the foam flowing from a boar's mouth, and of many other things. Looked at in themselves they are far from attractive, but because they accompany natural phenomena they further adorn them and attract us. As a result, the man of feeling and deeper understanding of the phenomena in Nature as a whole will find almost all these incidentals pleasantly contrived. He will look with as much pleasure upon the gaping jaws of actual wild beasts as upon representations of them in painting or sculpture. He will see a kind of fulfillment and freshness in the old, whether man or woman; he will be able to look upon the loveliness of his own slave boys with eyes free from lust.

Many such things will not appeal to everyone, but only to the man who has come to be genuinely at home with Nature and her works.

4

1. The attitude of that which rules within us toward outside events, if it is in accord with nature, is ever to adapt itself easily to what is possible in the given circumstances. It does not direct its affection upon any particular set of circumstances to work upon, but it starts out toward its objects with reservations, and converts any obstacle into material for its own action, as fire does when it overpowers what is thrown upon it. A small flame might be quenched by it, but a bright fire very rapidly appropriates to itself whatever is put upon it, consumes it and rises higher because of these obstacles.

3. Men seek retreats for themselves in country places, on beaches and mountains, and you yourself are wont to long for such retreats, but that is altogether unenlightened when it is possible at any hour you please to find a retreat within yourself. For nowhere can a man withdraw to a more untroubled quietude than in his own soul, especially a man who has within him things of which the contemplation will at once put him perfectly at ease, and by ease I mean nothing other than orderly conduct. Grant yourself this withdrawal continually, and refresh yourself. Let these be brief and elemental doctrines which when present will suffice to overwhelm all sorrows and to send you back no longer resentful of the things to which you return.

For what is it you resent? The wickedness of men? Reflect on the conclusion that rational beings are born for the sake of each other, that tolerance is a part of righteousness, and that men do not sin on purpose. Consider how many men have been hostile and suspicious, have hated and waged war, and then been laid out for burial or reduced to ashes. Desist then. Do you resent the portions received from the whole? Consider the alternatives afresh, namely "Providence or atoms,"[1] and how many proofs there are that the universe is like a city community. Are you still affected by the things of the body? Reflect that the mind, once it has freed itself and come to know its own capacities, is no longer involved in the movements of animal life, whether these be smooth or tumultuous. For the rest, recall all you have heard about pain and pleasure, to which you have given assent.

Does paltry fame disturb you? Look how swift is the forgetting of all things in the chaos of infinite time before and after, how empty is noisy applause, how liable to change and uncritical are those who seem to speak well of us, how narrow the boundaries within which fame is confined. The whole earth is but a point in the universe, and how small a part of the earth is the corner in which you live. And how many are those who there will praise you, and what sort of men are they?

From now on keep in mind the retreat into this little territory within yourself. Avoid spasms and tensions above all; be free and look at your troubles like a man, a citizen, and a mortal creature. Among the foremost things which you will look into are these two: first, that external matters do not affect the soul but stand quietly outside it, while true disturbances come from the inner judgement; second, that everything you see has all but changed already and is no more. Keep constantly in mind in how many things you yourself have witnessed changes already. The universe is change, life is understanding.

---

1. That is, either the universe is directed by Reason and Providence, as Marcus and the Stoics believed, or it is a mechanical conglomeration of atoms which scatter at death, as the Epicureans thought.

4. If we have intelligence in common, so we have reason which makes us reasoning beings, and that practical reason which orders what we must or must not do; then the law too is common to us and, if so, we are citizens; if so, we share a common government; if so, the universe is, as it were, a city—for what other common government could one say is shared by all mankind?

From this, the common city, we derive our intelligence, our reason and our law—from what else? Just as the dry earth-element in me has been portioned off from earth somewhere, and the water in me from the other element, the air or breath from some other source, and the dry and fiery from a source of its own (for nothing comes from what does not exist or returns to it), so also then the intelligence comes from somewhere.

10. "Everything which happens, is right." Examine this saying carefully and you will find it so. I do not mean right merely in the sense that it fits the pattern of events, but in the sense of just, as if someone were giving each his due. Examine this then as you have begun to do, and, whatever you do, do it as a good man should, as the word good is properly understood. Safeguard this goodness in your every action.

14. You exist but as a part of the Whole. You will disappear into the Whole which created you, or rather you will be taken up into the creative Reason when the change comes.

21. If souls live on, how has the air of heaven made room for them through eternity? How has the earth made room for such a long time for the bodies of those who are buried in it? Just as on earth, after these bodies have persisted for a while, their change and decomposition makes room for other bodies, so with the souls which have migrated into the upper air. After they have remained there for a certain time, they change and are dissolved and turned to fire as they are absorbed into the creative Reason, and in this way make room for those additional souls who come to share their dwelling place. Thus might one answer on the assumption that souls live on.

One should not, however, consider only the multitude of bodies that are buried thus, but also take into account the multitude of animals eaten every day by us and by other animals, how great is the number thus consumed and in a manner buried in the bodies of those who eat them. Yet there is room for them nevertheless because they are transformed into blood and changed into air and fire.

Where lies the investigation of the truth in this matter? In distinguishing between the matter and the cause.

24. "Do but little, if you would have contentment." Surely it is better to do what is necessary, as much as the reason of one who is by nature a social creature demands, and in the manner reason requires it to be done. This will not only bring the contentment derived from right conduct, but also that of doing little, since most of our words and actions are unnecessary and whoever eliminates these will have more leisure and be less disturbed. Hence one should on each occasion remind oneself: "Surely this is not one of the necessary actions?" One should eliminate not only unnecessary actions but also unnecessary imaginings, for then no irrelevant actions will follow.

27. Either it is a universe with order and purpose or a medley thrown together by chance, but that too has order. Or can there be order of a kind in your inner world, but no order in the Whole, especially as all things are distinguished from one another, yet intermingle, and respond to each other?

40. One should continually think of the universe as one living being, with one substance and one soul—how all it contains falls under its one unitary perception, how all its actions derive from one impulse, how all things together cause all that happens, and the nature of the resulting web and pattern of events.

46. Always remember the words of Heraclitus that "the death of earth becomes water and the death of water becomes air, and that of air, fire, and so back again." Remember also what he says about the man who has forgotten whither the road leads. And "men are at odds with that with which they are in most constant touch, namely the Reason" which governs all; and again, "those things seem strange to them which they meet every day"; and "we must not act and speak as if asleep," for even then we seem to act and speak. And that one should not accept things "like children from parents" simply because they have been handed down to us.

48. Think continually how many doctors have died who often knit their brows over their dying

patients, how many astrologers who had foretold the deaths of others as a matter of importance, how many philosophers who had discoursed at great length on death and immortality, how many heroic warriors who had killed many men, how many tyrants who had used their power over men's lives with terrible brutality, as if immortal themselves. How often have not whole cities died, if I may use the phrase, Helike, Pompeii, Herculaneum,[2] and innumerable others. Go over in your mind the dead whom you have known, one after the other: one paid the last rites to a friend and was himself laid out for burial by a third, who also died; and all in a short time. Altogether, human affairs must be regarded as ephemeral, and of little worth: yesterday sperm, tomorrow a mummy or ashes.

Journey then through this moment of time in accord with nature, and graciously depart, as a ripened olive might fall, praising the earth which produced it, grateful to the tree that made it grow.

49. Be like a rock against which the waves of the sea break unceasingly. It stands unmoved, and the feverish waters around it are stilled.

"I am unfortunate because this has happened to me." No indeed, but I am fortunate because I endure what has happened without grief, neither shaken by the present nor afraid of the future. Something of this sort could happen to any man, but not every man can endure it without grieving. Why then is this more unfortunate than that is fortunate? Would you call anything a misfortune which is not incompatible with man's nature, or call incompatible with the nature of man that which is not contrary to his nature's purpose? You have learned to know that purpose. What has happened can then in no way prevent you from being just, great-hearted, chaste, wise, steadfast, truthful, self-respecting and free, or prevent you from possessing those other qualities in the presence of which man's nature finds its own fulfillment. Remember in the future, when something happens which tends to make you grieve, to cling to this doctrine: this is no misfortune, but to endure it nobly is good fortune.

2. The city of Helike in Achaea was suddenly destroyed in 373 BCE when it sank into the sea. In 79 BCE the eruption of Vesuvius in Campania destroved Pompeii and Herculaneum.

5

13. I have been made out of that which is cause and that which is matter. Neither of these will be destroyed into nonexistence just as neither was made out of the nonexistent. Therefore when the change comes every part of me will be assigned its place in that which is a part of the universe, and that part again will change into another part, and so on indefinitely. It is by a change of this kind that I came to be, and so with my parents, and so on in another infinite sequence. Nothing prevents one's saying this, even if the world is governed in a sequence of appointed cycles of time.

16. The kind of thoughts you frequently have will make your mind of the same kind, for your mind is dyed by your thoughts. Color your mind therefore with a succession of thoughts like these, for example: Where it is possible to live, it is also possible to live the good life; it is possible to live in a palace, therefore it is also possible to live the good life in a palace. Or again: each thing is made with that in view for the sake of which it was made; it is drawn towards that for which it was made; its end is found in that to which it is drawn; and where its end is, there too the advantage and the good of each is to be found. Now the good of a rational creature lies in a community, and it has long ago been shown that we are born for association in a community. For surely it is clear that the inferior exist for the sake of the better, and the better for the sake each other. Now what is endowed with life is better than what is lifeless, and what is endowed with Reason is better than the merely alive.

26. Your directing mind, the ruler of your soul, must remain unaffected by the activity of your flesh, whether painful or pleasurable. It must not mingle with it but stay within its own frontiers and confine the affections of the body to their own sphere. When, however, these affections reach the mind through the other channel of common feeling, since both exist in a body organically one, then we should not resist this perception of them, since it is natural; but the directing mind should not add to this any judgment of its own as to whether the bodily affections are good or bad.

6

5. The governing Reason knows its own condition, what it creates, and in what material.

10. Either a medley of entangled and dispersed atoms, or a unity of order and Providence. If the former, why am I eager to remain in such a haphazard concatenation and confusion? Why should I even care for anything but how to "return to earth"? Why be disturbed? The dispersal of atoms will come upon me whatever I do. If the latter, however, I worship and am content and derive courage from the governing Reason.

13. How useful, when roasted meats and other foods are before you, to see them in your mind as here the dead body of a fish, there the dead body of a bird or a pig. Or again, to think of Falernian wine as the juice of a cluster of grapes, of a purple robe as sheep's wool dyed with the blood of a shellfish, and of sexual intercourse as internal rubbing accompanied by a spasmodic ejection of mucus. What useful perceptual images these are! They go to the heart of things for what they are. You must do this throughout life; when things appear too enticing, strip them naked, destroy the myth which makes them proud. For vanity is a dangerous perverter of Reason, and it is when you think your preoccupation most worthwhile that you are most enthralled.

14. Most of the objects of popular admiration belong to the general class of things held together by coherence, such as stones and timber, or by a principle of natural growth such as figs, vines, or olives. The things admired by somewhat more temperate men belong to the class of things held together by a principle of life such as flocks, herds, or the simple ownership of crowd of slaves. The things admired by men still more cultured are held together by rational soul, not, however, as rational but as endowed with craftsmanship or some other proficiency. But the man who prizes soul as rational and social is no longer involved with those other things at all, but above all else preserves his own soul's rational disposition and activity, and to this end co-operates with what is akin to himself.

16. We should not greatly value the fact that we breathe through our pores, which plants do, or have a respiratory system like that of the animals, both tame and wild, or are impressed by sensual images, or are jerked this way and that like puppets on the strings of desire, or live in herds, or take nourishment, for this last is on a par with the ejection of food wastes. What then are we to value? Noisy applause? No, not even to be applauded by men's tongues, for the praise of the multitude is only clacking of tongues. You have now also discarded that poor thing, fame. What is there left worthy of esteem? This, I think: to act or not to act in accordance with the way we were made; to this all arts and crafts show the way, for it is the aim of every craft that its product be suited to the task for which it was made; it is also the aim of one who plants and nurses a vine, or tames horses, or trains dogs. What else is the concern of tutors and teachers?

Here then lies what is of value. If you are successful in this you will not esteem anything else as of much value for yourself. Will you then not cease to value many other things? Otherwise you will not be free, self-sufficient, or unperturbed, since the pursuit of those other things will compel you to feel envy and jealousy, to keep a watchful eye on those who have the power to deprive you of them, and to intrigue against those who possess what you esteem. In general, the man who needs any one of those things is inevitably in turmoil and utters many reproaches against the gods.

On the other hand, if you esteem and reverence the mind within you, you will be at peace with yourself, in tune with your fellows, and in harmony with the gods. You will, that is, be satisfied with whatever lot they have given you as your share and prescribed for you.

57. Jaundice makes honey seem bitter, a mad dog's bite makes one fear water, and small boys believe a little round ball to be a thing of beauty. Why should I be angry with them? And do you not think that untrue notions have as much power over men as bile has over the jaundiced or poison over the victim of hydrophobia?

7

22. It is human to love even those who falter, and you will do so if you reflect that people are akin, that they do wrong through ignorance and unwillingly, that

you will both be dead in a little while, and, above all, that he has done you no injury, for he did not make your directing mind worse than it was before.

66. How do we know that Telauges was not a better person than Socrates? It is not enough that Socrates died more gloriously, that he disputed more skillfully with the Sophists, that he showed more hardihood in spending a whole night outside in freezing weather, that, when ordered to bring in the man from Salamis he thought it nobler to refuse, and that he "swaggered in the streets," about which last one might well wonder if it was true. What we need to examine is the nature of Socrates' soul, whether he could find satisfaction in being just toward men and pious toward the gods, in not being heedlessly angry with vice or subservient to anyone's ignorance, whether he accepted any part of the fate allotted to him from the Whole as alien to himself and bore it as an intolerable burden, whether he allowed his intelligence to share the suffering of his paltry flesh.

8

3. Alexander, Caesar, Pompey—what are they compared with Diogenes, Heraclitus, Socrates? The latter men saw the nature of things, its causes and its substances, and their directing minds were their own, while the former had to care for so many things and were enslaved to so many ends.

12. When you wake from sleep with difficulty, remind yourself that it is in accord with your constitution and with your human nature to perform social acts, whereas sleep we share with irrational animals. And what is in accord with the nature of each is more congenial, more his own, and indeed more agreeable.

21. Look at it from all sides and observe what kind of thing it is, what it becomes in old age, in illness, in debauch.

He who praises is a short-lived creature, so is the object of his praise, and so is he who remembers and he who is remembered. Moreover, not even in this your corner of your region of the earth do all men agree, nor is a man in agreement with himself. And the whole earth is only a point in space.

24. Just as taking a bath seems to you a matter of oil, sweat, dirt, scummy water, all of it offensive, so is every part of life and every kind of matter.

28. Pain is either an evil for the body—then let the body prove it so—or for the soul. The soul, however, can preserve its own fair weather and calm, and not accept it as an evil. For every judgment, impulse, desire, and aversion is within the soul, and no evil can penetrate there.

48. Remember that your ruling spirit is invincible when it is withdrawn into itself and satisfied with itself, not doing what it does not wish to do, even if the stand it takes is unreasonable. How will it be then when its judgement is reasonable and prudent? That is why a mind free from passions is a citadel, and man has no more secure refuge to make him safe for the future. He who has not seen this is stupid; he who has seen it and has not taken refuge there is unfortunate.

51. Be not slovenly in action or careless of the company you keep; let not your senses cause you to wander; not once must your soul contract with pain or leap with pleasure; ensure yourself leisure in life. "They kill you, butcher you, drive you away with curses." What matters this compared with your mind remaining pure, sound, temperate, and righteous? Just as if a man standing by a limpid, sweet spring were to curse it, yet the spring would not cease to bubble up fresh water; even if he throws mud or dung into it, the spring soon scatters this and washes it away, and is in no way stained. How then may you posses such an eternally fresh spring rather than a well? By watching yourself at all seasons with a view to attaining freedom, together with kindliness, simplicity, and self-respect.

54. Do not only breathe in unison with the air which surrounds you, but think now in unison with the intelligence which encompasses everything. For the intelligence which spreads everywhere and permeates everything is available to him who wishes to absorb it no less than air is available to him who is able to breathe.

57. The sun appears to be poured down, and its light is poured in all directions, but it does not pour itself out. This pouring is but an extension of itself; indeed its rays are called beams because of this extending in a straight line. You might understand the nature of a sunbeam if you observe the sunlight

making its way into a dark house through a narrow opening, for it extends itself in a straight line, and as it were presses against any solid obstacle in its way which cuts off the air on the other side; it pauses there and does not glide off or fall off. Such must be the pouring and outpouring of thought, not a pouring out of itself but an extension; it does not press violently or furiously against any obstacles in its way, nor does it fall away from them, but it rests there and illuminates that which receives it. And that which does not receive it deprives itself of its light.

9

28. The revolutions of the cosmos are the same, up and down, through the ages. Either the mind of the Whole has an impulse which reaches to each individual—and if this be so, welcomes that which it set in motion—or it had this impulse once, and the rest has followed in consequence. Why then are you anxious? The Whole either is a god, and all is well, or it is without plan—atoms somehow and indivisible particles—but you need not be without plan yourself.

Very soon the earth will cover us all, and then earth itself will change, and what it has changed into will also change indefinitely, and so on to eternity. As a man reflects upon these successive waves of changes and alterations, and their swift passing, he will despise all mortal things.

39. Either all things come from one intelligent source and happen as in one body, and the part must not then complain of what is to the advantage of the Whole, or else all things are atoms and nothing but a medley and a dispersal. Why then are you perturbed? Say to your directing mind: "You are dead, you have decayed, you have been made a beast, you are an actor, you are joining the herd, and feeding like them."

40. Either the gods have no power or they have power. If they have not, why do you pray? If they have, why not rather pray to be rid of fear and passion and grief for any of these things, rather than to have this and not that. In any case, if the gods can cooperate with men, it is with regard to these things. . .

42. When somebody's shameless conduct offends you, ask yourself at once: "Is it possible for there to be no shameless men in the world?" It is not possible. Do not then ask for the impossible. For the man who asks for this is himself one of the shameless who needs must be in the world. Have the same argument at hand for the knavish, the disloyal, indeed for every kind of wrongdoer. And when you remind yourself that such kinds of people must exist, you will also feel more kindly to them as individuals. . .

There is nothing evil or strange in a stupid man behaving stupidly. Ought you not rather to blame yourself for not foreseeing that he would go wrong in this way? Your intelligence gave you every reason to expect that he would probably err in this way, yet you forgot this and wonder that he did.

10

3. Everything happens in such a way that you are by nature either able or unable to endure it. If it happens so that you can by nature endure it, do not complain but endure it as you are by nature able to do. If it happens so that you cannot endure it, do not complain, for it will anticipate your complaint by destroying you. But be sure to remember that it is within your power to endure anything which it is within the power of your thought to make endurable and bearable by representing it as to your advantage or as your duty.

11. Acquire a systematic view of how all things change into one another; consistently apply your mind to, and train yourself in, this aspect of the universe. Nothing is so productive of high-mindedness. The high-minded man has put off the restraints of the body; he realizes he must very soon leave the company of men and leave all these things behind, and he devotes himself to righteousness in his own actions and to the nature of the Whole in dealing with external events; he gives no thought to what anyone may say or think about him, or do against him; he is satisfied with two things: to be just in his present action and to welcome his present lot. He has given up all occupations and concerns which hindered his leisure and has only one desire: to go forward along the straight path according to the law and, in so going forward, to follow the god.

16. Do not discuss in general terms the question of what is a good man. Be one.

26. The father casts his seed into the womb and then goes away; for the rest another causal force takes charge, fashions and perfects the child. From what small beginnings noteworthy things arise! Again, a man swallows food down his throat, and for the rest another causal force takes charge and produces sensation, impulse, life as a whole, and strength, and how many other strange things. Consider these things then which are thus done and hidden from us, and see the force which produces them, as we see that which weighs some things downward and makes others rise. We do not see it with our eyes, but no less vividly for that.

33. . . . Keep before your eyes the ease with which reason can make its way through all obstacles—just as fire rises, a stone falls, a round stone rolls down a slope—and seek for nothing further. The remaining obstacles are either those of the corpse which is our body, or they cannot shatter it or do us any harm without our judgment and the agreement of our reason itself.

Otherwise the man hindered would himself at once become evil. For in the case of all other organisms, whatever is harmed in any way becomes worse itself; but in our case, if one may say so, the man becomes better and more praiseworthy, if he makes the right use of his circumstances. Remember that, to put it in general terms, nothing harms one who is by nature a citizen if it does not harm the city, or harms the city if it does not harm the law, and none of the so-called misfortunes harms the law. And what does not harm the law does not harm either the city or the citizen.

35. A healthy eye must look at all that is to be seen, and not say: "I want soft colors," for so speaks a man suffering from ophthalmia. A healthy faculty of hearing or smelling should be ready for all sounds or smells, and a healthy stomach should be ready for all nourishment, and a millstone for all the things it was constituted to grind. And so, surely, a healthy mind should be prepared for all that happens. The mind which says: "Let my children be safe," or "Let all men praise whatever I do," is like the eye which requires soft colors, or the teeth which require tender food.

38. Remember that what pulls the strings is hidden within. It is the source of speech, it is the principle of life; it is, so to speak, the man himself. In your imagination never put this on a par with the containing vessel or the organs that are fashioned about it. These are but instruments like the ax, differing only in that they are attached. None of these parts is of any more use without the agent who moves or restrains them than the shuttle without the woman weaving, the pen without the writer, or the whip without the charioteer.

11

1. The properties of the rational soul: it sees itself, it shapes itself, it makes itself such as it wishes to be, it gathers its own fruit, whereas the fruit of plants and what animals may be said to produce as fruit is gathered by others. The rational soul achieves its end at whatever point life may be cut off, unlike a dance, a play, and the like, where the whole performance is incomplete if it is interrupted; but in every scene, wherever it is overtaken by death, its intended task is completely fulfilled, so that it can say: "I am in full possession of what is my own."

Moreover, the rational soul travels through the whole universe and the void which surrounds it, and observes its form; it stretches into infinity of time and grasps and understands the periodic rebirth of the Whole; it observes that those who come after us will see nothing new, nothing different from what our predecessors saw, but in a sense a man of forty, if he has any intelligence, has seen all the past and all the future, because they are of the same kind as the present.

It is also characteristic of the rational soul to love its neighbors, to be truthful, to show reverence, and to honor nothing more than itself, which is also characteristic of the law. Thus there is no difference between the right Reason and the Reason embodied in justice.

2. You will come to despise pleasant songs, dances, wrestling and boxing, if you break up the melody into its individual notes and ask yourself in the case of each: Am I overcome by this? You will scorn to admit it. Proceed in the same way with every movement and posture of the dance. Altogether, except for virtue and the results of virtue, remember to look at once at the component parts, analyze them and despise them. And apply this same method to the whole of life.

3. What an admirable soul is that which is ready and willing, if the time has come to be released from

the body, whether that release means extinction, dispersal, or survival. This readiness must be the result of a specific decision; not, as with the Christians, of obstinate opposition, but of a reasoned and dignified decision, and without dramatics if it is to convince anyone else.

8. A branch cut off from its neighboring branch must of necessity be cut off form the whole tree. So a man who severs himself form a single other man falls away from the whole human community. The branch, however, is cut off by an external agent, whereas it is the man himself who separates himself from his neighbor through hatred or indifference, and he does not know that he has also cut himself off form the community of citizens. But there is this gift from Zeus, the founder of the society of men, that we can again grow at one with our neighbor and again help to perfect the Whole. However, if it happens too often, the separation makes the severed part hard to unite and restore again. The branch, too, which grew with the tree form the beginning, shared its vital force, and remained with it, is not altogether like the one that has been separated, whatever gardeners say.

Grow together, but do not share the same doctrines.

12

3. You are a combination of three parts: body, vital breath, and intellect. The first two are yours insofar as you must care for them, but the third alone is yours in the strict sense. Therefore, if you separate from yourself, that is, from your mind, all that other people do or say, all that you have said or done yourself, all that disturbs you as likely to happen, all that belongs to the body which encases you or the life-breath which has grown with it and thus reaches you without choice on your part, and all that the external whirl causes to rotate—if you separate all this from yourself, your power of intelligence will be freed from the bonds of fate, pure and liberated, to live its own life doing what is just, desiring what is happening and saying what is true. If, I say, you separate from your directing mind what is linked to it by passion, what is beyond us in time, and what is past, you will make yourself, like the sphere of Empedocles, "rounded and rejoicing in its solitude." Practice to live only the present which you are now living, and you will be able to live through to the time of your death in imperturbability and kindliness, and at peace with the divinity which is within you.

5. How did the gods, who ordered all things well and in a spirit of kindness toward men, ever overlook this one thing, that some few among men who were especially good, who had made most covenants with the gods, as it were, and become familiars of the divine through pious deeds and the performance of many sacred rites—that when these men died they were not born again but completely extinguished?

If this is indeed the case, know well that if it ought to have been otherwise, then the gods would have done otherwise. For if it had been just, it had also been possible; and if it had been in accord with nature, nature would have brought it about. And if it is not so, then its not being so should lead you to believe that it ought not to be so.

You should yourself see that in these wrongheaded questions you are pleading a case with the god. Now we could not thus be arguing with the gods if they were not very good and very just; and, if they are, they would not overlook anything in the ordered universe being unjustly and unreasonably neglected.

12. The gods must not be blamed, for they do no wrong whether voluntary or involuntary. Nor should men be blamed, for they do no wrong that is not involuntary. So you must blame no one.

14–15. Either there is a Necessity of fate and an unalterable order, or a propitious Providence, or a random and leaderless confusion. If an unalterable Necessity, why do you strain against it? If a Providence which allows itself to be placated, make yourself worthy of divine help. If a leaderless confusion, be glad that in that surging flood you have within yourself a directing intelligence. If the flood is to sweep you away, let it sweep away your flesh, your vital breath, and the rest, but your mind it will not sweep away. The flame of a lamp shines and does not cease to cast its rays of light until it is extinguished; shall then the truth and justice and reasonableness within you be extinguished before your time comes?

20. First, do not act at random, without relating your actions to an end. Second, do not relate them to any end but the common good.

26. When you find something hard to tolerate, you have forgotten that everything happens in accord

with the nature of the Whole; that the wrong done to you is another's concern; and further, that everything which happens has always happened so, and will so happen, and is happening now, everywhere; and again, how close is the kinship between a man and the whole human race, for they are a community, not of blood or seed but of intelligence.

You have also forgotten that the intelligence of any individual is divine, and emanated from yonder; also that nothing is anyone's private property: even his child and his body and his very soul come from yonder; also that every man lives only the present, and this only he loses.

28. To those who inquire: "Where did you see the gods, from what do you deduce that they exist, that you worship them thus?" First, our eyes can in fact see them.[3] Then, I have certainly not seen my soul either, but I prize it. So too with the gods whose power I experience on all occasions; it is from this that I deduce that they exist, and I reverse them.

30. The light of the sun is one, though it is broken by walls, mountains, and countless other things. There is one common substance though it is broken up into countless bodies with individual qualities; one animal-soul, even if broken up into countless natures and individual surfaces; there is one intelligent soul, even though it appears divided. The other parts of the things we have mentioned, such as the life-breath and the objects without sensation, are not related to each other. Nevertheless, they are held together by a certain oneness and by the gravitation of like to like. But the mind has its peculiar tendency toward its own kind, joins with it, and its feeling of community is not broken.

34. What should rouse men most to despise death is that even those who judge pleasure to be good and pain evil nonetheless despise death.

36. Mortal, you have been a citizen in this great city, what matter to you whether for five years or fifty, for what is in accord with the law is equal for all. What then is there to fear if you are sent away from the city not by a dictator or an unjust judge, but by the same nature which brought you to it, as if the magistrate who had chosen a comic actor were to dismiss him. "But I have not played the five acts, but only three." "You have played well, but in your life at any rate the three acts are the whole play." For he sets the limit who was at one time the cause of your creation, and is now the cause of your dissolution. You have no responsibility for either. So depart graciously, for he who dismisses you is also gracious.

Sextus Empiricus

Most of our knowledge of ancient Skepticism—especially the variety taking Pyrrho of Elis as its founder—comes from the surviving texts of Sextus, about whom very little is known. He flourished in the second half of the second century CE, more than 200 years after Aenesidemus revived Pyrrhonism in the waning days of the Roman Republic. Sextus' two extant books, *Outlines of Pyrrhonism* and *Against the Professors,* were written in Greek and show a command of the language that suggests he was himself a Greek. We know that he became the head of a Skeptical school in some major city of the empire, though we do not know which. We know neither where he was born nor where he died. About these matters, it seems, we must suspend judgment.

He was a physician, though of what school it is difficult to say. Three approaches dominated Roman medicine of the time: Dogmatists theorized about the hidden causes of diseases, whereas Empiricists and Methodists studied only the apparent associations between symptoms and remedies. By his name alone, and his frequent association with Empiricists, we would assume that Sextus was one of them. But the Empiricists positively denied that hidden causes could be

3. Marcus means the sun and the heavenly bodies.

known, whereas the Methodists merely suspended judgment about them, an approach more consistent with Pyrrhonism, as Sextus himself observes. For he likewise divided all philosophers into three camps: Dogmatists make assertions about logic, physics, and ethics, matters that are in fact hidden; Academic Skeptics are no less dogmatic because they positively deny such answers can be found; Pyrrhonists, by contrast, avoid dogmatism by recognizing that these matters are hidden, but asserting nothing about them one way or the other. They suspend judgment and achieve, according to Sextus, *ataraxia*, freedom from disturbance, or mental tranquility.

Sextus thus taught the traditional "modes," canonical arguments that encourage the suspension of judgment. Some of these modes may stem from Pyrrho, but most of them can be attributed to Aenesidemus and other Roman Skeptics. Besides these modes, Sextus compiled a treasury of critical arguments—against causes, change, time, induction, anything good by nature, the possibility of self-knowledge, and God's existence, among other topics central to modern as well as ancient philosophy. Variations of these arguments have been used by a host of modern philosophers, such as Montaigne and Hume.

Two objections persistently arose against Pyrrhonism in antiquity, and still bother its critics today. First of all, shouldn't the consistent Skeptic turn his doubt against Pyrrhonism itself? Sextus agreed, comparing his philosophy to an emetic. Skepticism cures the Dogmatist, he wrote, by provoking him to vomit up not only his dogmas but also Skepticism itself. Secondly, isn't such a thoroughgoing Skepticism unlivable? Stories circulated about Pyrrho, for instance, that he survived only because his admirers kept him from falling into wells, whose danger, after all, was hidden. As a physician, Sextus could not have been so oblivious, and he credited four sources of irresistible appearances: nature, our feelings, custom and law, and the arts (or sciences). To become livable, in other words, radical Skepticism became indistinguishable in behavior from conservative surrender to everything considered compelling.

Outlines of Pyrrhonism

Book 1

1. The Basic Difference between Philosophies

It is a fair presumption that when people search for a thing the result will be either its discovery, a confession of non-discovery and of its non-apprehensibility, or perseverance in the search. Perhaps this is the reason why in matters of philosophical research some claim to have discovered the truth, while others declare that finding it is an impossibility, and others are still seeking it. There are some who think they have found the truth, such as Aristotle, Epicurus, the Stoics and certain others. These are, in a special sense of the term, the so-called dogmatists. Clitomachus and Carneades, on the other hand, and other Academics, claim it is a search for inapprehensibles. But the Skeptics go on searching. It is, therefore, a reasonable inference that basically there are three philosophies, the dogmatic, the Academic, and the Skeptic. For the present our task will be to present an outline of the Skeptic discipline, leaving it to such others as it befits to treat of the former two. We declare at the outset that we do not make any positive assertion that anything we shall say is wholly as we affirm it to be. We merely report accurately on each thing as our impressions of it are at the moment.

2. The Arguments of Skepticism

The Skeptic philosophy comprises two types of argument, the general and the special. In the first we undertake an exposition of the character of Skepticism by stating its notion, the principles and methods of reasoning involved, and its criterion and end. We set

---

Unless noted in the text, these selections are reprinted from Sextus Empiricus, *Selections from the Major Writings on Scepticism, Man, and God*, edited by Philip P. Hallie, translated by Sanford P. Etheridge (Indianapolis: Hackett Publishing Company, 1985).

forth also the various modes of suspension of judgement, the manner in which we use the Skeptic formulae, and the distinction between Skepticism and those philosophies which closely approach it. The special argument is that in which we dispute the validity of so-called philosophy in all its parts. Let us, then, first treat of the general argument and begin our sketch with the various appellations of the Skeptic discipline.

3. The Names of Skepticism

Now, the Skeptic discipline is called "zetetic" (searching) from its activity of searching and examining. It is also called the "ephectic" (suspending) from the experience which the inquirer feels after the search. "Aporetic" (doubting) is another name for it, either from the fact that their doubting and searching extends to everything (the opinion of some), or from their inability to give final assent or denial. It is also called "Pyrrhonean," because Pyrrho appears to us to have applied himself to Skepticism more thoroughly and with more distinction than his predecessors.

4. The Meaning of Skepticism

Skepticism is an ability to place in antithesis, in any manner whatever, appearances and judgements, and thus—because of the equality of force in the objects and arguments opposed—to come first of all to a suspension of judgement and then to mental tranquillity. Now, we call it an "ability" not in any peculiar sense of the word, but simply as it denotes a "being able." "Appearances" we take as meaning the objects of sense-perception; hence we set over against them the objects of thought. The phrase "in any manner whatever" may attach itself to "ability," so that we may understand that word (as we have said) in its simple sense, or it may be understood as modifying the phrase "to place in antithesis appearances and judgements." For since the antitheses we make take various forms, appearances opposed to appearances, judgements to judgements, or appearances to judgements, we say "in any manner whatever" in order to include all the antitheses. Or, we may understand it as "any manner of appearances and judgements whatever," in order to relieve ourselves of the inquiry into how appearances appear or how judgements are formed, and thus take them at their face value. When we speak of arguments which are "opposed," we do not at all mean denial and affirmation, but use this word in the sense of "conflicting." By "equality of force" we mean equality in respect of credibility and incredibility, since we do not admit that any of the conflicting arguments can take precedence over another on grounds of its being more credible. "Suspension of judgement" is a cessation of the thought processes in consequence of which we neither deny nor affirm anything. "Mental tranquillity" is an undisturbed and calm state of soul. The question how mental tranquillity enters into the soul along with suspension of judgement we shall bring up in the chapter "On the End."

5. The Skeptic

The definition of the Pyrrhonean philosopher is also virtually included in the concept of the Skeptic discipline. It is, of course, he who shares in the "ability" we have spoken of.

6. The Principles of Skepticism

Skepticism has its inception and cause, we say, in the hope of attaining mental tranquillity. Men of noble nature had been disturbed at the irregularity in things, and puzzled as to where they should place their belief. Thus they were led on to investigate both truth and falsehood in things, in order that, when truth and falsehood were determined, they might attain tranquillity of mind. Now, the principle fundamental to the existence of Skepticism is the proposition, "To every argument an equal argument is opposed," for we believe that it is in consequence of this principle that we are brought to a point where we cease to dogmatize.

7. Does the Skeptic Dogmatize?

We say that the Skeptic does not dogmatize. But in saying this we do not understand the word "dogma" as some do, in the more general sense of "approval of a thing." The Skeptic, of course, assents to feelings which derive necessarily from sense-impressions; he would not, for example, when feeling warm (or cold), say; "I believe I am not warm (or cold)." But some say that "dogma" is "the assent given to one of the non-evident things which form the object of scientific research." It is this meaning of "dogma" that we have in view when we say that the Skeptic does not dogmatize, for concerning non-evident things the Pyrrhonean philosopher holds no opinion. In fact, he does not even dogmatize when he is uttering the Skeptic formulae in regard to non-evident things (these formulae, the "No more," the "I determine nothing," and the others, we shall speak of later). No—for the dogmatizer affirms the real existence of that thing about which he is said to be dogmatizing, whereas the Skeptic does not take the real existence of these formulae wholly for granted. As he understands them, the formula "All things are false," for example, asserts its own falsity together with that of all other things, and the formula "Nothing is true" likewise. Thus also the formula "No more" asserts not only of other things but of itself also that it is "no more" existent than anything else, and hence cancels itself together with the other things. We say the same about the other Skeptic formulae also. However, if the dogmatizer affirms the real existence of the thing about which he is dogmatizing, while the Skeptic, uttering his own formulae, does so in such a way that they virtually cancel themselves, he can hardly be said to be dogmatizing when he pronounces them. The greatest indication of this is that in the enunciation of these formulae he is saying what appears to him and is reporting his own feeling, without indulging in opinion or making positive statements about the reality of things outside himself.

8. Does the Skeptic Have a System?

Our attitude is the same when we are asked whether the Skeptic has a system. For if one defines "system" as "an adherence to a set of numerous dogmas which are consistent both with one another and with appearances," and if "dogma" is defined as "assent to a non-evident thing," then we shall say that we have no system. But if one means by "system" a "discipline which, in accordance with appearance, follows a certain line of reasoning, that line of reasoning indicating how it is possible to seem to live rightly ('rightly' understood not only with reference to virtue, but more simply), and extending also to the ability to suspend judgement," then we say that we do have a system. For we follow a certain line of reasoning which indicates to us, in a manner consistent with appearances, how to live in accordance with the customs, the laws, and the institutions of our country, and with our own natural feelings.

9. Is the Skeptic Concerned with the Study of Physics?

To the inquiry whether the Skeptic should theorize about physics our reply is similar. We do not theorize about physics in order to give firm and confident opinions on any of the things in physical theory about which firm doctrines are held. On the other hand, we do touch on physics in order to have for every argument an equal argument to oppose to it, and for the sake of mental tranquillity. Our approach to the logical and ethical divisions of so-called philosophy is similar.

10. Do the Skeptics Deny Appearances?

Those who say that the Skeptics deny appearance seem to me to be ignorant of what we say. As we said above, we do not deny those things which, in accordance with the passivity of our sense-impressions, lead us involuntarily to give our assent to them; and these are the appearances. And when we inquire whether an object is such as it appears, we grant the fact of its appearance. Our inquiry is thus not directed at the appearance itself. Rather, it is a question of what is predicated of it, and this is a different thing from investigating the fact of the appearance itself. For example, honey appears to us to have a sweetening quality. This much we concede, because it affects us with a sensation of sweetness. The question, however, is whether it is sweet in an absolute sense. Hence not the appearance is questioned, but that which is predicated of the appearance. Whenever we do expound arguments directly against appearances, we do so not with the intention of denying them, but in order to point out the hasty judgement of the dogmatists. For if reason is such a rogue as to all but snatch even the appearances from under our very eyes, should we not by all means be wary of it, at least not be hasty to follow it, in the case of things non-evident?

11. The Criterion of Skepticism

That we pay attention to appearances is clear from what we say about the criterion of the Skeptic discipline. Now, the word "criterion" is used in two senses. First, it is the standard one takes for belief in reality or non-reality. This we shall discuss in our refutation. Second, it is the standard of action the observance of which regulates our actions in life. It is this latter about which we now speak. Now, we say that the criterion of the Skeptic discipline is the appearance, and it is virtually the sense-presentation to which we give this name, for this is dependent on feeling and involuntary affection and hence is not subject to question. Therefore no one, probably, will dispute that an object has this or that appearance; the question is whether it is in reality as it appears to be. Now, we cannot be entirely inactive when it comes to the observances of everyday life. Therefore, while living undogmatically, we pay due regard to appearances. This observance of the requirements of daily life seems to be fourfold, with the following particular heads: the guidance of nature, the compulsion of the feelings, the tradition of laws and customs, and the instruction of the arts. It is by the guidance of nature that we are naturally capable of sensation and thought. It is by the compulsion of the feelings that hunger leads us to food and thirst leads us to drink. It is by virtue of the tradition of laws and customs that in everyday life we accept piety as good and impiety as evil. And it is by virtue of the instruction of the arts that we are not inactive in those arts which we employ. All these statements, however, we make without prejudice.

12. The Goal of Skepticism

The next point to go through would be the goal of Skepticism. A goal is "that at which all actions or thoughts are directed, and which is itself directed at nothing, in other words, the ultimate of desirable things." Our assertion up to now is that the Skeptic's end, where matters of opinion are concerned, is mental tranquillity; in the realm of things unavoidable, moderation of feeling is the goal. His initial purpose in philosophizing was to pronounce judgement on appearances. He wished to find out which are true and which false, so as to attain mental tranquillity. In doing so, he met with contradicting alternatives of equal force. Since he could not decide between them, he withheld judgement. Upon his suspension of judgement there followed, by chance, mental tranquillity in matters of opinion. For the person who entertains the opinion that anything is by nature good or bad is continually disturbed. When he lacks those things which seem to him to be good, he believes he is being pursued, as if by the Furies, by those things which are by nature bad, and pursues what he believes to be the good things. But when he has acquired them, he encounters further perturbations. This is because his elation at the acquisition is unreasonable and immoderate, and also because in his fear of a reversal all his exertions go to prevent the loss of the things which to him seem good. On the other side there is the man who leaves undetermined the question what things are good and bad by nature. He does not exert himself to avoid anything or to seek after anything, and hence he is in a tranquil state.

The Skeptic, in fact, had the same experience as that related in the story about Apelles the artist.[1] They say that when Apelles was painting a horse, he wished to represent the horse's foam in the painting. His attempt was so unsuccessful that he gave it up and at the same time flung at the picture his sponge, with which he had wiped the paints off his brush. As it struck the picture, the sponge produced an image of horse's foam. So it was with the Skeptics. They were in hopes of attaining mental tranquillity, thinking that they could do this by arriving at some rational judgement which would dispel the inconsistencies involved in both appearances and thoughts. When they found this impossible, they withheld judgement. While they were in this state, they made a chance discovery. They found that they were attended by mental tranquillity as surely as a body by its shadow.

Nevertheless, we do not suppose the Skeptic to be altogether free from disturbance; rather, we say that when he is disturbed, it is by things which are unavoidable. Certainly we concede that he is sometimes cold and thirsty, and that he suffers in other such ways. But even here there is a difference. Two circumstances combine to the detriment of the ordinary man: he is hindered both by the feelings

1. Apelles was a contemporary of Alexander the Great and also of Pyrrho, the Skeptic, in the fourth century BCE. He was famous not only for his portrait of Alexander holding a thunderbolt and another picture of Venus rising from the sea but also for his unceasing efforts at self-improvement in his art.

themselves and not less by the fact that he believes these conditions to be evil by nature. The Skeptic, on the other hand, rejects this additional notion that each of these things is evil by nature, and thus he gets off more easily. These, then, are our reasons for saying that the Skeptic's end is mental tranquillity where matters of opinion are concerned, and moderate feeling in the realm of things unavoidable. Some notable Skeptics have, however, added to these a third: suspension of judgement in investigations.

13. General Introduction to the Modes of Suspension of Judgment

We were saying that mental tranquillity follows on suspension of judgement in regard to all things. Next, it would be proper for us to state how we attain suspension of judgement. As a general rule, this suspension of judgment is effected by our setting things in opposition. We oppose appearances to appearances, or thoughts to thoughts, or appearances to thoughts. For example, when we say, "The same tower appears round from a distance, but square from close by," we are opposing appearances to appearances. When a person is trying to prove the existence of providence from the order of the celestial bodies, and we counter him with the observation that the good often fare ill while the evil prosper and then conclude from this that there is no providence, we are opposing thoughts to thoughts. And then appearances may be opposed to thoughts. Anaxagoras, for instance, could oppose to the fact that snow is white his reasoning that "Snow is frozen water, and water is black, snow therefore is black also." And sometimes, from the point of view of a different concept, we oppose present things to present things, as in the foregoing, and sometimes present things to past or future things. An example of this is the following. Whenever someone propounds an argument that we are not able to dispose of, we make this reply: "Before the birth of the founder of the school to which you belong, this argument of your school was not yet seen to be a sound argument. From the point of view of nature, however, it existed all the while as such. In like manner it is possible, as far as nature is concerned, that an argument antithetical to the one now set forth by you is in existence, though as yet unknown to us. This being so, the fact that an argument seems valid to us now is not yet a sufficient reason why we must assent to it."

But for a better understanding of these antitheses, I shall now present also the modes by which suspension of judgement is induced. I cannot, however, vouch for their number or validity, since it is possible that they are unsound, and that there are more of them than the ones to be discussed.

15. The Five Modes

The later Skeptics, however, teach five modes of suspension. These are the following. The first is based on disagreement. The second is that which produces to infinity. Third, that based on relativity. Fourth, that from assumption. And fifth, the argument in a circle.

That based on disagreement is the one in which we find that in regard to a proposed matter there has arisen in the opinions both of people at large and of the philosophers an unresolved dissension. Because of this dissension we are unable either to choose or to reject anything, and thus we end with suspension of judgement. The mode based on the extension to infinity is the one is which we say that proof offered for the verification of a proposed matter requires a further verification, and this one another, and so on to infinity, so that since we lack a point of departure for our reasoning, the consequence is suspension of judgement. That based on relativity is that in which, just as we have already said, the object appears thus or thus in relation to the thing judging and the things perceived along with it, while as to its true nature we suspend judgement. The mode from assumption exists when dogmatists, in their *regressus ad infinitum*, take as their point of departure a proposition which they do not establish by reasoning, but simply and without proof assume as conceded to them. The mode of argument in a circle arises when that which ought itself to be confirmatory of the matter under investigation requires verification from the thing being investigated; at that point, being unable to take either of them to establish the other, we suspend judgement about both.

That it is possible to refer every question to these modes we shall show briefly as follows. The object proposed is either an object of sense or an object of thought; but no matter which it is, it is a disputed point. For some say that the objects of sense alone are true, some say only the objects of thought are true, while others say that some objects of sense and some objects of thought are true. Now, will they assert that the disagreement is resolvable, or irresolvable? If irresolvable, then we have the necessity of suspension granted; for it is not possible to pronounce on things when the disputed about them is irresolvable. But if the dispute is resolvable, then we ask from what quarter the decision is to come. Taking, for example, the object of sense (to fix our argument on this one first), is it to be judged by an object of sense or by an object of thought? If by an object of sense, then, seeing that our inquiry is about objects of sense, that object too will need another as confirmation. And if that other is an object of sense, again it will itself need another to confirm it, and so on to infinity. But if the object of sense will have to be judged by an object of thought, then, since objects of thought also are a matter of dispute, this object, being an object of thought, will require judgement and confirmation. Where, then, is the confirmation to come from? If it is to be confirmed by an object of thought, we shall likewise have an extension *ad infinitum*; but if by an object of sense, the mode of circular reasoning is introduced, because an object of thought was employed for the confirmation of the object of sense and an object of sense for the confirmation of the object of thought.

If, however, our interlocutor should try to escape from these conclusions and claim the right to assume, as a concession without proof, some proposition serving to prove the rest of his argument, then the mode of assumption will be brought in, which leaves him no way out. For if a person is worthy of credence when he makes an assumption, then we shall in each case also be not less worthy of credence if we make the opposite assumption. And if the person making the assumption assumes something which is true, he renders it suspicious by taking it on assumption instead of proving it. But if what he assumes is false, the foundation of what he it trying to prove will be unsound. Moreover, if assumption conduces at all towards proof, let the thing in question itself be assumed and not something else by means of which he will then prove the thing under discussion. But if it is absurd to assume the thing in question, it will also be absurd to assume what transcends it.

But it is evident that all objects of sense are also relative, for they exist as such in relation to those who perceive them. It is clear, then, that whatever sensible object is set before us, it can easily be referred to the five modes. Our reasoning concerning the intelligible object is similar. For if it should be said that it is the subject of an irresolvable disagreement, the necessity of suspending judgement on this matter will be granted us. But in the case of a resolution of the disagreement, if the resolution is reached by means of an object of thought, we shall have recourse to the extension *ad infinitum*; if by means of an object of sense, we shall have recourse to the mode of circular reasoning. For as the sensible again is an object of disagreement, and incapable, because of the extension to infinity, of being decided by means of itself, it will stand in need of the intelligible just as the intelligible also requires the sensible. For these reasons, whoever accepts anything on assumption will again be in an absurd position. But intelligibles are also relative, for they are relative to the intellect in which they appear, whence their name. And if they really were in nature such as they are said to be, there would be no disagreement about them. Thus the intelligible too has been referred to the five modes, so that in any case we must suspend judgement with regard to the object presented.

Such are the five modes taught by the later Skeptics. Their purpose in setting them forth is not to repudiate the ten modes, but to provide for a more diversified exposure of the rashness of the dogmatists by combining these modes with the others.

16. The Two Modes

They also teach two other modes of suspension. Since everything apprehended seems to be apprehended either through itself or through something else, they show us that nothing is apprehended either through itself or through another thing, thus introducing, as they think, doubt about all things. That nothing is apprehended through itself is clear, they say, from the disagreement existing amongst the physicist regarding, I believe, all sensibles and intelligibles. Since we are not able to take either an object of sense or an object of thought as a criterion (any criterion we take, if there is disagreement about it, is unreliable), the disagreement is of course irresolvable. Because of this they do not concede that anything can be apprehended through another thing either. For if that through which something is apprehended must itself always be apprehended through another thing, we fall into the mode of circular reasoning or into the mode of infinity. But if a person should wish to assume a thing (through which another thing is apprehended) as being apprehended through itself, an objection arises in the fact that, by reason of what we have said above, nothing is apprehended through itself. And we are uncertain as to how that which conflicts with itself can be apprehended either though itself or through something else, since no criterion of truth or of apprehension appears and since even signs apart from proof are rejected, as we shall recognize in the next book. So much, then, for the modes of suspension. What we have said will be sufficient for the present.

Outlines of Pyrrhonism

Book 2

15. On Induction

I also think that it is easy to dispense with the method of induction. For since what they [the Dogmatists] want is to establish the universal on the basis of particulars by means of induction, either they do so by surveying all of the particulars or by surveying only some of them. But if they do so by surveying only some of them, then the induction is insecure, since it is possible that some of the remaining particulars covered by the induction contradict the universal. But if they do so by surveying all of the particulars, then they are undertaking impossible labours, since the particulars are unlimited in number and indefinite. Consequently, on both of these assumptions I think that it turns out that induction is undermined [as a mode of reasoning].

(tr. Inwood and Gerson)

Against the Professors (Book 2, 479–81)

Yes, they say, but [the argument] which concludes that there is no demonstration refutes itself by being demonstrative. In response to this we must say that it does not refute itself utterly. For many things are said in a way which implies exceptions; and as we say that Zeus is the father of gods and men with an implied exception of this very point (for he is surely not his own father!), so too when we say that there is no demonstration we say so with an implicit exception for the argument which demonstrates that there is no demonstration. For this alone is a demonstration. And if it refutes itself it is not thereby established that demonstration exists. For there are many things which do to themselves the same thing as they do to other things. For example, just as fire consumes its fuel and then destroys itself along with it, and just as purgative medicines expel fluids from the body and then eliminate themselves as well, in the same way the argument against demonstration is able to wipe itself out after having destroyed all demonstration. And again, just as it is not impossible for someone, after climbing up a ladder to a higher place, to knock down the ladder with his foot after he gets up there, so too it is not unreasonable for the Skeptic, after arriving at the establishment of his point by using the argument which demonstrates that there is is no demonstration as a kind of step-stool, thereupon to destroy this argument itself.

(tr. Inwood and Gerson)

Outlines of Pyrrhonism

Book 3

3. On God

Now, since the majority have declared that God is the most efficient cause, let us first examine the question of God. We premise the remark that we conform to the ordinary view, in that we affirm undogmatically the existence of gods, reverence gods, and affirm that they are possessed of foreknowledge. But in reply to the rashness of the dogmatists we have this to say.

When we form notions of objects, we ought to conceive of their substances—for example, whether they are corporeal or incorporeal—and also of their forms, for no one would be able to conceive of a horse without first learning the form of a horse. And the object conceived must be conceived of as being somewhere. Now, some of the dogmatists assert that God is corporeal, while others say he is incorporeal, and some say he has human form, while others deny it, and some say he exists in a place, while others say he does not. And of those who assert his existence in a place, some place him within the world and others outside it. How then shall we be able to form a conception of God, when neither his substance nor his form nor his whereabouts is agreed upon? Let them first reach agreement and harmony with themselves that God is of such and such a nature, and when they have presented us their sketch of that nature, then they can ask us to form a notion of God. But as long as their disagreement is unresolved, we have from them no agreed basis for forming a conception of God.

But, they say, conceive of something imperishable and blessed, and regard this as the Deity. But this is foolish. For just as the man who does not know Dion is also unable to conceive what properties belong to him qua Dion, so also when we are ignorant of the substance of God we shall be unable to learn and concieve of the properties belonging to him. And apart from this consideration, let them tell us what "the blessed" is, whether it is that which operates according to virtue and which takes thought for the things subject to itself, or that which is inactive and neither troubles itself nor causes any other trouble. For by their unresolved disagreement on this head also, they have rendered inconceivable to us "the blessed" and therefore the Deity as well.

But granted that God can be conceived, it is necessary, as far as the dogmatists are concerned, to suspend judgement on the question of his existence or non-existence. For the existence of God is not self-evident. If the impression of him proceeded from himself, the dogmatists would have been in harmony with one another as to who he is, what he is like, and where he stays. But their unresolved disagreement has caused him to seem to us non-evident and in need of demonstration. Now, he who demonstrates the exsistence of God does so either by means of the self-evident or by means of the non-evident. He certainly cannot do so by means of the self-evident. For since that which is proved is conceived together with that which proves it, and hence is also apprehended together with it (as we have also stated), then, if what proves the existence of God were self-evident, God's existence would also be self-evident, it being apprehended together with the self-evident proof of it. But as we have shown, it is not self-evident. Therefore neither can it be proved by the self-evident. But neither can it be proved by the non-evident. For that non-evident fact which is demonstrative of God's existence requires proof. And if it should be said to be proved by means of something self-evident, it will no longer be non-evident, but self-evident. Therefore the non-evident fact proving his existence is not proved by means of the self-evident. Nor is it proved by the non-evident. For whoever asserts this will be driven to infinity under our constant demands for proof of the non-evident fact brought out as proof of the one exhibited before it. Therefore the existence of God cannot be demonstrated from anything else. But if it is neither spontaneously self-evident nor proved from anything else, the existence of God will be inapprehensible.

One thing more. He who says that God exists either affirms or denies his forethought for the things in the world, and if he affirms it, he affirms it either for all things or for some things. But if he had forethought for all things, there would be neither any bad thing nor any evil in the world. But they say that all things are full of evil. Therefore, God will not be said to have forethought for all things. But if he has forethought for some things, why for some things and not for others? For either he has both the will and the power to think of all things beforehand, or he has the will but not the power, or the power but not the will, or neither the will nor the power. But if he had both the will and the power, he would have forethought for all things; but *ex hypothesi* he does not forethink all things; therefore he does not have both the will and the power to take thought for all things. And if he has the will but not the power, he is weaker than that which is the cause of his inability to extend his forethought to all things. But it is against our conception of God that he should be weaker than anything. But if he has the power of forethought for all things, but not the will, he will be considered malicious. And if he has neither the will nor the power, he is both malicious and weak. But to say this about God is impiety. Therefore God has no forethought for the things in the world.

But if he takes no thought for anything, and no work or product of his exists, a person will not be able to say where we get the idea that God exists, seeing that he neither appears of himself nor is apprehended by means of any of his products. For these reasons, then, it cannot be apprehended whether God exists. And our conclusion from all this is that those who positively assert the existence of God probably are necessarily guilty of impiety. For if they say that he takes thought of all things, they will be saying that God is responsible for what is evil, while if they say he takes forethought for some things, or even for nothing, they will necessarily be saying that God is either malicious or weak, which is manifest impiety.

NEOPLATONISM

Plotinus

"Plotinus seemed ashamed of being in the body." So begins the biography of him written by his foremost student, Porphyry. For a victim of leprosy, which appears to have killed Plotinus in 270 CE, such shame is hardly surprising. But he seems to have felt it from a far earlier age, and for philosophical reasons. Beginning his bodily life in 205, somewhere in Egypt, he did not discover philosophy until he was twenty-seven. Alexandria was a philosophical center, and Plotinus went there to study, finally finding the sort of instruction he sought in the lectures of Ammonius Saccas. This obscure philosopher also taught Origen, the brilliant Christian theologian who became so contemptuous of his own body and its sexual desires that he castrated himself.

Plotinus spent eleven years studying with Ammonius before he joined a Roman expedition against the Parthians. This, he supposed, would acquaint him with the philosophical traditions of the east, especially India. But the expedition failed, the emperor who led it was killed, and Plotinus was lucky to return to the safety of the empire alive. Settling in Rome, he began to teach, attracting a diverse following—senators, women, and physicians, among others—who were attracted by his informal style as well as his erudition. He taught primarily by commenting on the Platonic dialogues, presenting his own philosophy as no more than an exposition of Plato's. Yet many have since regarded Plotinus as an innovator who synthesized authentic Platonic doctrines with those of Aristotle, the Stoics, and others. Scholars of the nineteenth century thus labeled him and his followers "Neoplatonist." Their tradition had a formative influence on the early theology of Christianity, the philosophy of medieval Islam, and the metaphysics of Renaissance Europe.

Waiting until age fifty to record his lectures, Plotinus circulated them only among his intimate students. After his death, Porphyry collected these lectures into six sets of nine (yielding their title, *Enneads*, from the Greek word for "nine"). In these writings, Plotinus developed an ontology of baroque complexity. The highest reality lies "beyond being," a phrase used by Plato to describe the Form of the Good (*Republic* 509b8). From this Good—or Beauty, or the One, as Plotinus preferred to call it—proceed all inferior realities, each of which is mentioned in Plato's *Timaeus*. The first such procession is the Intellect (*Nous*), followed next by the Soul (*Psychē*). Individual souls, Plotinus believed, fall away from this cosmic Soul by a desire for independence that ends in the grief of embodiment. For here on earth the soul becomes complex and divided; its rational part preserves an allegiance with its origins above, while its irrational parts become infected by their association with a body below.

Since matter is farthest of all from the One, and thus almost totally deprived of the One's goodness, it is the source of evil. Our souls thus become better to the extent that we purify ourselves of it. This purification begins with the civic virtues—temperance, courage, justice, and prudence—which Plotinus sought to encourage with a "Platonopolis" on the site of a ruined Pythagorean settlement in southern Italy. (Although he was a cherished friend of Emperor Gallienus, his plan was thwarted by rivals in the imperial court.) But the civic virtues alone are insufficient, and must be consummated in philosophical contemplation. With great effort, he believed, the philosopher can achieve union with the One even while embodied. Plotinus modeled this ascent on Plato's *Symposium*, and Porphyry reports that his teacher reached its mystical summit four times. His dying words: "I try to lead the god in us up to the divine in the cosmos."

Enneads 1.6: On Beauty

1. Chiefly beauty is visual. Yet in word patterns and in music (for cadences and rhythms are beautiful) it addresses itself to the hearing as well. Dedicated living, achievement, character, intellectual pursuits are beautiful to those who rise above the realm of the senses; to such ones the virtues, too, are beautiful. Whether the range of beauty goes beyond these will become clear in the course of this exposition.

What makes bodily forms beautiful to behold and has one give ear to sounds because they are "beautiful"? Why is it that whatever takes its rise directly from the soul is, in each instance, beautiful? Is everything beautiful with the one same beauty, or is there a beauty proper to the bodily and another to the bodiless? What, one or many, is beauty?

Some things, as the virtues, are themselves beautiful. Others, as bodily forms, are not themselves beautiful but are beautiful because of something added to them: the same bodies are seen to be at times beautiful, at other times not, so that to be body is one thing and to be beautiful is something else again.

Now what this something is that is manifest in some bodily forms we must inquire into first. Could we discover what this is—what it is that lures the eyes of onlookers, bends them to itself, and makes them pleased with what they see—we could "mount this ladder" for a wider view.

On every side it is said that visual beauty is constituted by symmetry of parts one with another and with the whole (and, in addition, "goodly coloration"); that in things seen (as, generally speaking, in all things else) the beautiful simply is the symmetrical and proportioned. Of necessity, say those who hold this theory, only a composite is beautiful, something without parts will never be beautiful; and then, they say, it is only the whole that is beautiful, the parts having no beauty except as constituting the whole.

However, that the whole be beautiful, its parts must be so, too; as beautiful, it cannot be the sum of ugliness: beauty must pervade it wholly. Further: colors, beautiful hues as those of the sun, this theory would rule out; no parts, therefore no symmetry, therefore no beauty. But is not gold beautiful? And a single star by night? It is the same with sound: the simple tone would be proscribed, yet how often each of the sounds that contribute to a beautiful ensemble is, all by itself, beautiful. When one sees the same face, constant in its symmetry, now beautiful and now not, is it not obvious that beauty is other than symmetry, that symmetry draws its beauty from something else?

And what of the beauty of dedicated lives, of thought expressed? Is symmetry here the cause? Who would suggest there is symmetry in such lives, or in laws, or in intellectual pursuits?

What symmetry is there in points of abstract thought? That of being accordant with one another? There may be accord, even complete agreement, where there is nothing particularly estimable: the idea that "temperance is folly" fits in with the idea that "justice is naïve generosity"; the accord is perfect.

Then again, every virtue is a beauty of The Soul—more authentically beautiful than anything mentioned so far. The Soul, it is true, is not a simple unity. Yet neither does it have quantitative numerical symmetry. What yardstick could preside over the balancing and interplay of The Soul's potencies and purposes?

Finally, in what would the beauty of that solitary, The Intelligence, consist?

2. Let us, then, go back to the beginning and determine what beauty is in bodily forms.

Clearly it is something detected at a first glance, something that the soul—remembering—names, recognizes, gives welcome to, and, in a way, fuses

---

From *The Essential Plotinus*, translated by Elmer O'Brien, S. J. (Indianapolis: Hackett Publishing Company, 1975).

with. When the soul falls in with ugliness, it shrinks back, repulses it, turns away from it as disagreeable and alien. We therefore suggest that the soul, being what it is and related to the reality above it, is delighted when it sees any signs of kinship or anything that is akin to itself, takes its own to itself, and is stirred to new awareness of whence and what it really is.

But is there any similarity between loveliness here below and that of the intelligible realm? If there is, then the two orders will be—in this—alike. What can they have in common, beauty here and beauty there? They have, we suggest, this in common: they are sharers of the same Idea.

As long as any shapelessness that admits of being patterned and shaped does not share in reason or in Idea, it continues to be ugly and foreign to that above it. It is utter ugliness since all ugliness comes from an insufficient mastery by form and reason, matter not yielding at every point to formation in accord with Idea. When Idea enters in, it groups and arranges what, from a manifold of parts, is to become a unit; contention it transforms into collaboration, making the totality one coherent harmoniousness, because Idea is one and one as well (to the degree possible to a composite of many parts) must be the being it informs.

In what is thus compacted to unity, beauty resides, present to the parts and to the whole. In what is naturally unified, its parts being all alike, beauty is present to the whole. Thus there is the beauty craftsmanship confers upon a house, let us say, and all its parts, and there is the beauty some natural quality may give to a single stone.

3. The beauty, then, of bodily forms comes about in this way—from communion with the intelligible realm. Either the soul has a faculty that is peculiarly sensitive to this beauty—one incomparably sure in recognizing what is kin to it, while the entire soul concurs—or the soul itself reacts without intermediary, affirms a thing to be beautiful if it finds it accordant with its own inner Idea, which it uses as canon of accuracy.

What accordance can there be between the bodily and the prior to the bodily? That is like asking on what grounds an architect, who has built a house in keeping with his own idea of a house, says that it is beautiful. Is it not that the house, aside from the stones, is inner idea stamped upon outer material, unity manifest in diversity? When one discerns in the bodily the Idea that binds and masters matter of itself formless and indeed recalcitrant to formation, and when one also detects an uncommon form stamped upon those that are common, then at a stroke one grasps the scattered multiplicity, gathers it together, and draws it within oneself to present it there to one's interior and indivisible oneness as concordant, congenial, a friend. The procedure is not unlike that of a virtuous man recognizing in a youth tokens of a virtue that is in accord with his own achieved goodness.

The beauty of a simple color is from form: reason and Idea, an invasion of incorporeal light, overwhelm the darkness inherent in matter. That is why fire glows with a beauty beyond all other bodies, for fire holds the rank of Idea in their regard. Always struggling aloft, this subtlest of elements is at the last limits of the bodily. It admits no other into itself, while all bodies else give it entry; it is not cooled by them, they are warmed by it; it has color primally, they receive color from it. It sparkles and glows like an Idea. Bodies unable to sustain its light cease being beautiful because they thus cease sharing the very form of color in its fullness.

In the realm of sound, unheard harmonies create harmonies we hear because they stir to an awareness of beauty by showing it to be the single essence in diversity. The measures in music, you see, are not arbitrary, but fixed by the Idea whose office is the mastering of matter.

This will suffice for the beauties of the realm of sense, which—images, shadow pictures, fugitives—have invaded matter, there to adorn and to ravish wherever they are perceived.

4. But there are beauties more lofty than these, imperceptible to sense, that the soul without aid of sense perceives and proclaims. To perceive them we must go higher, leaving sensation behind on its own low level.

It is impossible to talk about bodily beauty if one, like one born blind, has never seen and known bodily beauty. In the same way, it is impossible to talk about the "luster" of right living and of learning and of the like if one has never cared for such things, never beheld "the face of justice" and temperance and seen it to be "beyond the beauty of evening or morning star." Seeing of this sort is done only with the eye of the soul. And, seeing thus, one undergoes a joy, a wonder, and a distress more deep than any other because here one touches truth.

Such emotion all beauty must induce—an astonishment, a delicious wonderment, a longing, a love, a trembling that is all delight. It may be felt for things invisible quite as for things you see, and indeed the soul does feel it. All souls, we can say, feel it, but souls that are apt for love feel it especially. It is the same here as with bodily beauty. All perceive it. Not all are stung sharply by it. Only they whom we call lovers ever are.

5. These lovers of beauty beyond the realm of sense must be made to declare themselves.

What is your experience in beholding beauty in actions, manners, temperate behavior, in all the acts and intents of virtue? Or the beauty in souls? What do you feel when you see that you are yourselves all beautiful within? What is this intoxication, this exultation, this longing to break away from the body and live sunken within yourselves? All true lovers experience it. But what awakens so much passion? It is not shape, or color, or size. It is the soul, itself "colorless," and the soul's temperance and the hueless "luster" of its virtues. In yourselves or others you see largeness of spirit, goodness of life, chasteness, the courage behind a majestic countenance, gravity, the self-respect that pervades a temperament that is calm and at peace and without passion; and above them all you see the radiance of The Intelligence diffusing itself throughout them all. They are attractive, they are lovable. Why are they said to be beautiful? "Because clearly they are beautiful and anyone that sees them must admit that they are true realities." What sort of realities? "Beautiful ones." But reason wants to know why they make the soul lovable, wants to know what it is that, like a light, shines through all the virtues.

Let us take the contrary, the soul's varied ugliness, and contrast it with beauty; for us to know what ugliness is and why it puts in its appearance may help us attain our purpose here.

Take, then, an ugly soul. It is dissolute, unjust, teeming with lusts, torn by inner discord, beset by craven fears and petty envies. It thinks indeed. But it thinks only of the perishable and the base. In everything perverse, friend to filthy pleasures, it lives a life abandoned to bodily sensation and enjoys its depravity. Ought we not say that this ugliness has come to it as an evil from without, soiling it, rendering it filthy, "encumbering it" with turpitude of every sort, so that it no longer has an activity or a sensation that is clean? For the life it leads is dark with evil, sunk in manifold death. It sees no longer what the soul should see. It can no longer rest within itself but is forever being dragged towards the external, the lower, the dark. It is a filthy thing, I say, borne every which way by the allurement of objects of sense, branded by the bodily, always immersed in matter and sucking matter into itself. In its trafficking with the unworthy it has bartered its Idea for a nature foreign to itself.

If someone is immersed in mire or daubed with mud, his native comeliness disappears; all one sees is the mire and mud with which he is covered. Ugliness is due to the alien matter that encrusts him. If he would be attractive once more, he has to wash himself, get clean again, make himself what he was before. Thus we would be right in saying that ugliness of soul comes from its mingling with, fusion with, collapse into the bodily and material: the soul is ugly when it is not purely itself. It is the same as with gold that is mixed with earthy particles. If they are worked out, the gold is left and it is beautiful; separated from all that is foreign to it, it is gold with gold alone. So also the soul. Separated from the desires that come to it from the body with which it has all too close a union, cleansed of the passions, washed clean of all that embodiment has daubed it with, withdrawn into itself again—at that moment the ugliness, which is foreign to the soul, vanishes.

6. For it is as was said of old: "Temperance, courage, every virtue—even prudence itself—are purifications." That is why in initiation into the mystery religions the idea is adumbrated that the unpurified soul, even in Hades, will still be immersed in filth because the unpurified loves filth for filth's sake quite as swine, foul of body, find their joy in foulness. For what is temperance, rightly so called, but to abstain from the pleasures of the body, to reject them rather as unclean and unworthy of the clean? What else is courage but being unafraid of death, that mere parting of soul from body, an event no one can fear whose happiness lies in being his own unmingled self? What is magnanimity except scorn of earthly things? What is prudence but the kind of thinking that bends the soul away from earthly things and draws it on high?

Purified, the soul is wholly Idea and reason. It becomes wholly free of the body, intellective, entirely of that intelligible realm whence comes beauty and all things beautiful. The more intellective it is, the more beautiful it is. Intellection, and all that comes from intellection, is for the soul a beauty that is its own and not another's because then it is that the soul is truly soul. That is why one is right in saying that the good and the beauty of the soul consist in its becoming godlike because from the divinity all beauty comes and all the constituents of reality. Beauty is genuine reality; ugliness, its counter. Ugliness and evil are basically one. Goodness and beauty are also one (or, if you prefer, the Good and Beauty). Therefore the one same method will reveal to us the beauty-good and the ugliness-evil.

First off, beauty is the Good. From the Good, The Intelligence draws its beauty directly. The Soul is, because of The Intelligence, beautiful. Other beauties, those of action or of behavior, come from the imprint upon them of The Soul, which is author, too, of bodily beauty. A divine entity and a part, as it were, of Beauty, The Soul renders beautiful to the fullness of their capacity all things it touches or controls.

7. Therefore must we ascend once more towards the Good, towards there where tend all souls.

Anyone who has seen it knows what I mean, in what sense it is beautiful. As good, it is desired and towards it desire advances. But only those reach it who rise to the intelligible realm, face it fully, stripped of the muddy vesture with which they were clothed in their descent (just as those who mount to the temple sanctuaries must purify themselves and leave aside their old clothing), and enter in nakedness, having cast off in the ascent all that is alien to the divine. There one, in the solitude of self, beholds simplicity and purity, the existent upon which all depends, towards which all look, by which reality is, life is, thought is. For the Good is the cause of life, of thought, of being.

Seeing, with what love and desire for union one is seized—what wondering delight! If a person who has never seen this hungers for it as for his all, one that has seen it must love and reverence it as authentic beauty, must be flooded with an awesome happiness, stricken by a salutary terror. Such a one loves with a true love, with desires that flame. All other loves than this he must despise and all that once seemed fair he must disdain.

Those who have witnessed the manifestation of divine or supernal realities can never again feel the old delight in bodily beauty. What then are we to think of those who see beauty in itself, in all its purity, unencumbered by flesh and body, so perfect is its purity that it transcends by far such things of earth and heaven? All other beauties are imports, are alloys. They are not primal. They come, all of them, from it. If then one sees it, the provider of beauty to all things beautiful while remaining solely itself and receiving nothing from them, what beauty can still be lacking? This is true and primal beauty that graces its lovers and makes them worthy of love. This is the point at which is imposed upon the soul the sternest and uttermost combat, the struggle to which it gives its total strength in order not to be denied its portion in this best of visions, which to attain is blessedness. The one who does not attain to it is life's unfortunate, not the one who has never seen beautiful colors or beautiful bodies or has failed of power and of honors and of kingdoms. He is the true unfortunate who has not seen this beauty and he alone. It were well to cast kingdoms aside and the domination of the entire earth and sea and sky if, by this spurning, one might attain this vision.

8. What is this vision like? How is it attained? How will one see this immense beauty that dwells, as it were, in inner sanctuaries and comes not forward to be seen by the profane?

Let him who can arise, withdraw into himself, forego all that is known by the eyes, turn aside forever from the bodily beauty that was once his joy. He must not hanker after the graceful shapes that appear in bodies, but know them for copies, for traceries, for shadows, and hasten away towards that which they bespeak. For if one pursues what is like a beautiful shape moving over water—Is there not a myth about just such a dupe, how he sank into the depths of the current and was swept away to nothingness? Well, so too, one that is caught by material beauty and will not cut himself free will be precipitated, not in body but in soul, down into the dark depths loathed by The Intelligence where, blind even there in Hades he will traffic only with shadows, there as he did here.

"Let us flee then to the beloved Fatherland." Here is sound counsel. But what is this flight? How are we to "gain the open sea"? For surely Odysseus is a parable for us here when he commends flight from the sorceries of a Circe or a Calypso, being unwilling to linger on for all the pleasure offered to his eyes and all the delight of sense that filled his days. The Fatherland for us is there whence we have come. There is the Father. What is our course? What is to be the manner of our flight? Here is no journeying for the feet; feet bring us only from land to land. Nor is it for coach or ship to bear us off. We must close our eyes and invoke a new manner of seeing, a wakefulness that is the birthright of us all, though few put it to use.

9. What, then, is this inner vision?

Like anyone just awakened, the soul cannot look at bright objects. It must be persuaded to look first at beautiful habits, then the works of beauty produced not by craftsman's skill but by the virtue of men known for their goodness, then the souls of those who achieve beautiful deeds. "How can one see the beauty of a good soul?" Withdraw into yourself and look. If you do not as yet see beauty within you, do as does the sculptor of a statue that is to be beautified: he cuts away here, he smooths it there, he makes this line lighter, this other one purer, until he disengages beautiful lineaments in the marble. Do you this, too. Cut away all that is excessive, straighten all that is crooked, bring light to all that is overcast, labor to make all one radiance of beauty. Never cease "working at the statue" until there shines out upon you from it the divine sheen of virtue, until you see perfect "goodness firmly established in stainless shrine." Have you become like this? Do you see yourself, abiding within yourself, in pure solitude? Does nothing now remain to shatter that interior unity, nor anything external cling to your authentic self? Are you entirely that sole true light which is not contained by space, not confined to any circumscribed form, not diffused as something without term, but ever unmeasurable as something greater than all measure and something more than all quantity? Do you see yourself in this state? Then you have become vision itself. Be of good heart. Remaining here you have ascended aloft. You need a guide no longer. Strain and see.

Only the mind's eye can contemplate this mighty beauty. But if it comes to contemplation purblind with vice, impure, weak, without the strength to look upon brilliant objects, it then sees nothing even if it is placed in the presence of an object that can be seen. For the eye must be adapted to what is to be seen, have some likeness to it, if it would give itself to contemplation. No eye that has not become like unto the sun will ever look upon the sun; nor will any that is not beautiful look upon the beautiful. Let each one therefore become godlike and beautiful who would contemplate the divine and beautiful.

So ascending, the soul will come first to The Intelligence and will survey all the beautiful Ideas therein and will avow their beauty, for it is by these Ideas that there comes all beauty else, by the offspring and the essence of The Intelligence. What is beyond The Intelligence we affirm to be the nature of good, radiating beauty before it.

Thus, in sum, one would say that the first hypostasis is Beauty. But, if one would divide up the intelligibles, one would distinguish Beauty, which is the place of the Ideas, from the Good that lies beyond the beautiful and is its "source and principle." Otherwise one would begin by making the Good and Beauty one and the same principle. In any case it is in the intelligible realm that Beauty dwells.

Enneads 5.1: The Three Primal Hypostases

1. How is it, then, that souls forget the divinity that begot them so that—divine by nature, divine by origin—they now know neither divinity nor self?

This evil that has befallen them has its source in self-will, in being born, in becoming different, in desiring to be independent. Once having tasted the pleasures of independence, they use their freedom to go in a direction that leads away from their origin. And when they have gone a great distance, they even forget that they came from it. Like children separated from their family since birth and educated away from home, they are ignorant now of their parentage and therefore of their identity.

Our souls know neither who nor whence they are, because they hold themselves cheap and accord their admiration and honor to everything except themselves. They bestow esteem, love, and sympathy on anything rather than on themselves. They cut themselves off, as much as may be, from the things above. They forget their worth. Ignorance of origin is caused by excessive valuation of sense objects and disdain of self, for to pursue something and hold it dear implies acknowledgment of inferiority to what is pursued. As soon as a soul thinks it is worth less than things subject to birth and death, considers itself least honorable and enduring of all, it can no longer grasp the nature and power of the divinity.

A soul in such condition can be turned about and led back to the world above and the supreme existent, The One and first, by a twofold discipline: by showing it the low value of the things it esteems at present, and by informing—reminding!—it of its nature and worth. The second discipline precedes the first and, once made clear, supports the first (which we shall treat elsewhere rather fully).

The second must occupy us now, particularly as it is a prerequisite for the study of that supreme object we desire to know.

It is the soul that desires to know. Therefore the soul must first examine its own nature in order to know itself and decide whether it is capable of such an investigation, has an eye capable of such seeing, and whether such seeking is its function. If the things it seeks are alien to the soul, what good will its seeking do? But, if the soul is akin to them and it seeks them, it can find them.

2. Each should recall at the outset that soul is the author of all living things, has breathed life into them all, on earth, in the air, and in the sea—the divine stars, the sun, the ample heavens. It was soul that brought order into the heavens and guides now its measured revolving. All this it does while yet remaining transcendent to what it gives form, movement, life. Necessarily, it is superior by far to them. They are born or they die to the extent that soul gives or withdraws their life. Soul, because it can "never abandon itself," exists eternally.

Now to understand how life is imparted to the universe and to each individual, the soul must rise to the contemplation of The Soul, the soul of the world. The individual soul, though different from The Soul, is itself no slight thing. Yet it must become worthy of this contemplation: freed of the errors and seductions to which other souls are subject, it must be quiet. Let us assume that quiet too is the body that wraps it round—quiet the earth, quiet the air and the sea, quiet the high heavens. Then picture The Soul flowing into this tranquil mass from all sides, streaming into it, spreading through it until it is luminous. As the rays of the sun lighten and gild the blackest cloud, so The Soul by entering the body of the universe gives it life and immortality; the object it lifts up. The universe, moved eternally by an intelligent Soul, becomes blessed and alive. The Soul's presence gives value to a universe that before was no more than an inert corpse, water and earth, or rather darksome matter and nonbeing, an "object of horror to the gods," as someone has said.

The Soul's nature and power reveal themselves still more clearly in the way it envelops and rules the world in accordance with its will. It is present in every point of the world's immense mass, animating all its segments, great and small. While two bodies cannot be in the same place and are separated from each other both spatially and otherwise, The Soul is not thus extended. It need not divide itself to give life to each particular individual. Although it animates particular things, it remains whole and is present in its wholeness, resembling in this indivisibility and omnipresence its begetter, The Intelligence. It is through the power of The Soul that this world of multiplicity and variety is held within the bonds of unity. It is through its presence that this world is divine: divine the sun because ensouled; so too the stars. And whatever we are, we are on its account, for "a corpse is viler than a dunghill."

The deities owe their divinity to a cause necessarily their superior. Our soul is the same as The Soul which animates the deities: strip it of all things infesting it, consider it in its original purity, and you will see it to be of equal rank with The Soul, superior to everything that is body. The Body, without the soul, is nothing but earth. If one make fire the basic element, one still needs a principle to give life to its flame. It is the same even if one combines earth and fire, or adds to them water and air as well.

If it is soul that makes us lovable, why is it that we seek it only in others and not in ourselves? You love others because of it. Love, then, yourself.

3. So divine and precious is The Soul, be confident that, by its power, you can attain to divinity. Start your ascent. You will not need to search long. Few are the steps that separate you from your goal. Take as your guide the most divine part of The Soul, that which "borders" upon the superior realm from which it came.

Indeed, in spite of the qualities that we have shown it to have, The Soul is no more than an image of The Intelligence. Just as the spoken word is the image of the word in the soul, The Soul itself is the image of the word in The Intelligence and is the act of The Intelligence by which a further level of existence is produced, for the act of The Intelligence has this essence but also radiates heat. Nevertheless, The Soul does not become completely separated from The Intelligence. Partly it remains in it. Although its nature is distinct because it derives from The Intelligence, The Soul is itself an intellective existent: discursive reason is the manifestation of its intellectual capacity. The Soul derives its perfection from The Intelligence, which nourishes it as a father would. But, in comparison with itself, The Intelligence has not endowed The Soul with complete perfection.

Thus The Soul is the hypostasis that proceeds from The Intelligence. Its reason finds its actualization when it contemplates The Intelligence. So contemplating, it possesses the object of its contemplation within itself, as its own, and it is then wholly active. These intellectual and interior activities are alone characteristic of The Soul. Those of a lower kind due to an alien principle and they are passive rather than active experiences for The Soul. The Intelligence makes The Soul more divine because it is its begetter and grants its presence to it. Nothing separates the two but the difference of their natures. The Soul is related to The Intelligence as matter is to Idea. But this "matter" of The Intelligence is beautiful: it has an intellectual form and is partless.

How great, then, must The Intelligence be if it is greater than The Soul!

4. Greatness of The Intelligence may also be seen in this: We marvel at the magnitude and beauty of the sense world, the eternal regularity of its movement, the divinities—visible and invisible—that it contains, its daimons, animals, plants. Let us then rise to the model, to the higher reality from which this world derives, and let us there contemplate the whole array of intelligibles that possess eternally an inalienable intelligence and life. Over them presides pure Intelligence, unapproachable wisdom. That world is the true realm of Cronus, whose very name suggests both abundance [*koros*] and intelligence [*nous*]. There is contained all that is immortal, intelligent, divine. There is the place of every soul. There is eternal rest.

Since it is in a state of bliss, why should The Intelligence seek change? Since it contains everything, why should it aspire to anything? Since it is perfect, what need has it of development? All its content is perfect, too, so that it is perfect throughout. It contains nothing that is not of the nature of thought—of thought, however, that is not a search but possession. Its happiness does not depend on something else. It is eternally all things in that eternity of which time, which abandons one moment for the next, is only a fleeting image upon the level of The Soul. The Soul's action is successive, divided by the various objects that draw its attention—now Socrates, now a horse, always some particular. The Intelligence, however, embraces all, possesses all in unchanging identity. It "is" alone. And it always has this character of presentness. Future it has not; already it is all it could ever later become. Past it has not; no intelligible entity ever passes away. All it contains exist in an eternal present because they remain identical with themselves, contented, you might say, with their present condition. Singly they are both intelligence and being. Together they form the totality of intelligence and the totality of being. The Intelligence gives existence to Being in thinking it. Being, by being object of thought, gives to The Intelligence its thinking and its existence.

But there must still exist something else that make The Intelligence think and Being be—their common cause. It is true that The Intelligence and Being exist simultaneously and together and never part. But their oneness—which is simultaneously intelligence and being, thinking and object of thought—is twofold: The Intelligence inasmuch as it thinks, and Being inasmuch as it is the object of thought. Intellection implies difference as well as identity. Therefore the primary terms are "intelligence," "being," "identity," "difference." And to them must be added "movement" and "rest." Movement is implied in the intellective acitivity of the intelligible realm; rest, in its sameness. Difference is implicit in the distinction between the thinker and the thought because without difference they are reduced to unity and to silence. The objects of thought also require difference in order to be distinguished from one another. Identity is implied in the self-sufficient unity of The Intelligence and in the nature shared in common by all intelligible beings, quite as difference is implied in their being distinguishable. From this multiplicity of these terms come "number" and "quantity," while the proper character of each of them is "quality." From these terms, as from originating principles, everything else proceeds.

5. The Intelligence, manifold and divine, is in The Soul, since The Soul is joined to it, provided The Soul does not will to overstep its bounds and "secede" from it. So close to The Intelligence that it is almost one with it, The Soul is everlastingly vivified.

What established The Intelligence thus?

Its source did, the partless that is prior to plurality, that is the cause both of being and of multiplicity, that is the maker of number.

Number is not the first; one is prior to two and two comes after one. Two, indeterminate in itself, is made determinate by one. When plurality becomes determinate, with a determinacy rather like that of substances, it becomes number. The Soul is number, too, because the primals are not quantitative masses. Masses, the gross in nature, are secondary, for all that sense perception thinks them essences. Nobility of seed or plants consists not in perceptible moisture but in number and seminal reason—both imperceptible.

Number and plurality that are in the intelligible realm are reasons and intelligence. But, in itself, as it were, plurality is indeterminate. The number, however, that comes from it and from The One is form—quite as if all things assumed form in it. The Intelligence is formed differently by The One than it is formed of itself, that is, like sight made actual, for intellection is the seen as seen—the two are one.

6. Some questions remain: How does The Intelligence see? What does it see? How does it exist and issue from The One in order to see?

The Soul accepts what is necessarily so, but now it wishes to resolve the problem so often raised by the ancient philosophers: how multiplicity, duality, and number proceeded from The One. Why did The One not remain by itself? Why did it emanate the multiplicity we find characterizing being and that we strive to trace back to The One?

In approaching this problem let us first invoke the divinity. Let us do so not with words but with a lifting of our souls to it and thus to pray alone to the Alone.

To see The One that remains in itself as if in an inner sanctuary, undisturbed and remote from all things, we must first consider the images in the outer precincts, or rather the first one to appear. This seems to be its message: All that is moved must have a goal towards which it is moved. But The One has no goal towards which it is moved. We must, then, not assume it to be moved. When things proceed from it, it must not cease being turned towards itself. (We have to remove from our minds any idea that this is a process like generation in time because here we are treating of eternal realities. We speak metaphorically, in terms of generation, to indicate the causal relations of things eternal and their systematic order.) What is begotten by The One must be said to be begotten without any motion on the part of The One. If The One were moved, the begotten, because of this movement, would have to be ranked third since the movement would be second. The One therefore produces the second hypostasis without assent, or decree, or movement of any kind. How are we to conceive this sort of generation and its relation to its immovable cause? We are to conceive it as a radiation that, though it proceeds from The One, leaves its selfsameness undisturbed, much in the way the brilliance that encircles and is ceaselessly generated by the sun does not affect its selfsame and unchanging existence. Indeed everything, as existing, necessarily produces of its own substance some further existent dependent on its power and image of its existence. Thus fire radiates heat and snow radiates cold. Perfumes provide an especially striking example: as long as they last they send off exhalations in which everything around them shares. What becomes perfect becomes productive. The eternally perfect is eternally productive, and what it produces is eternal, too, although its inferior.

What, then, are we to say of that which is supremely prefect? It produces only the very greatest of the things that are less than it. What is most perfect after it is the second hypostasis, The Intelligence. The Intelligence contemplates The One and needs nothing but The One. The One, however, has no need of The Intelligence. The One, superior to The Intelligence, produces The Intelligence, the best after The One since it is superior to all the others. The Soul is word and deed of The Intelligence just as the Intelligence is word and deed of the One. But in The Soul the word is obscure, for The Soul is only an image of The Intelligence. Therefore The Soul turns itself to The Intelligence, just as, to be The Intelligence, it must contemplate The One. The Intelligence contemplates The One without being separated from it because there is no other existent between the two of them, just as there is none between The Intelligence and The Soul. Begotten always longs for its begetter and loves it; especially is this so when begetter and begotten are solitaries. But when the begetter is the highest Good, the begotten must be so close to it that its only separateness is its otherness.

7. We call The Intelligence image of The One. This we must explain.

It is its image because what is begotten by The One must possess many of its characteristics, be like it as light is like the sun. But The One is not an intellectual principle. How then can it produce an intellectual principle? In turning towards itself The One sees. It is this seeing that constitutes The Intelligence. For what is seen is different from sensation or intelligence. . . . Sensation as line and so on. . . . But the circle is divisible; The One is not.

In The Intelligence there is unity; The One, however, is the power productive of all things. Thought, apportioning itself in accord with this power, beholds all in the power of The One: did it not, it would not be The Intelligence. The Intelligence is aware of its power to produce and even to limit being through that power derived from The One. It sees that being is part of what belongs to The One and proceeds from it and owes all its force to it, that it achieves being because of The One. The Intelligence sees that, because it becomes multiple when proceeding from The One, it derives from The One (which is indivisible) all the realities it has, such as life and thought, while The One is not any of these things. The totality of beings must come after The One because The One itself has no determinate form. The One simply is one while The Intelligence is what in the realm of being constitutes the totality of beings. Thus The One is not any of the beings The Intelligence contains but the sole source from which all of them are derived. That is why they are "beings"; they are already determined, each with its specific form; a being cannot be indeterminate, but only definite and stable. For intelligible beings such stability consists in the determination and form to which they owe their existence.

The Intelligence of which we speak deserves to be of this lineage and to derive from no other source than the supreme. Once begotten, it begets with it all beings, all the beauty of the Ideas, all the intelligible deities. Full of the things it has begotten, it "devours" them in the sense that it keeps them all, does not allow them to fall into matter or to come under the rule of Rhea. This the mysteries and myths of the gods obscurely hint at: Cronus, the wisest of the gods, was born before Zeus and devoured his children—quite like The Intelligence, big with its conceptions and in a state of satiety. Then, out of his fullness, Cronus begot Zeus. Thus The Intelligence, out of its fullness, begets The Soul. It begets necessarily because it is perfect and, being so great a power, it cannot remain sterile. Here, again, the begotten had to be inferior, an image, and—since it was indeterminate by itself—be determined and formed by the principle that begot it. What The Intelligence begets is a word and substantive reasoning, the being that moves about The Intelligence and is the light of The Intelligence, the ray that springs from it. On the one hand, it is bound to The Intelligence, fills itself with it, enjoys its presence, shares in it, and is itself an intellectual existent. On the other hand, it is in contact with lower beings begetting beings lower than itself. Of these we shall treat later. The sphere of the divine stops here at The Soul.

8. This is the reason why Plato establishes three degrees of reality. He says: "It is in relation to the king of all and on his account that everything exists. . . . In relation to a second, the second class of things exists, and in relation to a third, the third class." Further, he speaks of the "father of the cause," by "cause" meaning The Intelligence because for him The Intelligence is the demiurge. He adds that it is this power

that forms the soul in the mixing bowl. The Good, he says, the existent that is superior to The Intelligence and "superior to Being," is the father of the cause, i.e., of The Intelligence. Several times he says that Idea is Being and The Intelligence. Therefore, he realized that The Intelligence proceeds from the Good and The Soul proceeds from The Intelligence. These, indeed, are not new doctrines; they have been taught from the most ancient times, without, however, being made fully explicit. Our claim is to be no more than interpreters of these earlier doctrines whose antiquity is attested by Plato's writings.

The first philosopher to teach this was Parmenides. He identified Being and The Intelligence and did not place Being among sense objects. "To think," he said, "is the same as to be," and "Being is immobile." Although he adds thought to Being, he denies that Being (since it must remain always the same) has any bodily motion. He compares it to a "well-rounded sphere"; it contains everything and does not draw thought from without but possesses it within. When in his writings he called Being The One, he was criticized because his unity was found to be multiple.

The Parmenides of Plato speaks with greater accuracy. He distinguishes between the first one, which is one in the proper sense, and the second one, which is a multiple one, and a third—The-One-and-the-manifold. Therefore this latter Parmenides also distinguished the three degrees here discussed.

9. Anaxagoras, in teaching the simplicity of pure and unmingled Intelligence, also asserted that The One is primary and separate. But, living too long ago, he did not treat the matter in sufficient detail. Heracleitus also knew The One, eternal and intelligible, for he taught that bodies are in a perpetual process of flux and return. According to Empedocles, "Hate" is the principle of division but "Love" is The One, an incorporeal principle, the elements playing the role of matter.

Aristotle says that the first existent is "separate" and intelligible. But in saying that "it thinks itself," he denies it transcendency. He asserts as well the existence of a plurality of other intelligible entities in a number equal to the heavenly spheres so that each of them has its own principle of motion. He therefore advances a doctrine of intelligible entities that is different from that of Plato. And as he has no valid reason for this change, he appeals to necessity. Even if his reasons were valid, one might well object that it seems more reasonable to suppose that the spheres, as they are coordinated in a single system, are directed towards the one ultimate, the supreme existent. We might also ask whether, for him, intelligible beings derive from one first originating principle or whether there are for them several such principles. If intelligible beings proceed from one principle, their condition will be analogous to that of the sense spheres where one envelops another and one alone—the exterior sphere—dominates all of the others. In this case the primal existent will contain all intelligible entities and be the intelligible realm. The spheres in the realm of sense are not empty, for the first is full of stars and the others, too, have theirs. Similarly, the principles of motion in the intelligible realm will contain many entities, beings that are more real than sense objects. On the other hand, if each of these principles is independent, their interrelation will be subject to chance. How, then, will they unite their actions and converge in producing that single effect which is the harmony of the heavens? Further, what is the basis for the assertion that sense objects in the heavens equal in number their intelligible movers? Finally, why is there a plurality of movers since they are incorporeal and are not separated one from another by matter?

Thus the ancient philosophers who faithfully followed the doctrines of Pythagoras, of his disciples, and of Pherecydes have maintained the existence of the intelligible realm. Some of them have recorded their views in their writing; others orally; others have bothered to do neither.

10. That beyond Being there exists The One we have attempted to prove as far as such an assertion admits of proof. In the second place come Being and The Intelligence; in the third, The Soul.

Now it must be admitted that as these three are in the very nature of things, they also are in us.

My meaning is not that they exist in our sense part (they are separate from sense) but in what is external to sense (understanding "external" in the same way that one says they are "external" to the heavens)—the area, that is, that Plato calls "the man within."

Our soul, too, then, is something divine, its nature different from that of sense. It is essentially like The Soul. Possessing intelligence, it is perfect.

It is necessary to distinguish between the intelligence which reasons and that which furnishes the principles of reasoning. The soul's discursive reasoning needs no bodily organ; it keeps its action pure of the bodily in order to reason purely. Separate from the body, it has no admixture of body. It is no mistake to place it in the first degree of the intelligible. We need not seek to locate it in space; it exists outside space. To be within oneself and exterior to all else and immaterial is to be outside body and the bodily. That is why Plato says, speaking of the cosmos, that the demiurge has The Soul envelop the world "from without." His meaning? A part of The Soul remains in the intelligible realm. Thus, in speaking of the human soul, he says that "it dwells at the top of the body." When he counsels separation of soul from body, he does not mean spatial separation, such as is established by Nature, but that soul must not incline towards body even in imagination but must alienate itself from body. Such separation is achieved by raising to the intelligible realm that lower part of the soul which, established in the realm of sense, is the sole agent that builds up and modifies the body and busies itself with its care.

11. Since discursive reason inquires, "Is this just?" or, "Is that beautiful?" and then decides that a particular object is beautiful or that a certain action is just, there must exist a justice that is immutable and a beauty that is immutable according to which the soul deliberates. Otherwise, how could it reason? Moreover, since the soul reasons only intermittently about such topics, it cannot be discursive reason that continually possesses the idea, say, of justice. Rather must it be intelligence. We must also possess within us the source and cause of intelligence, the divinity, which is not divisible and exists not in a place but in itself. Not in a place, it is found in that multitude of beings capable of receiving it just as if it were divisible—quite as the center of the circle remains in itself while each of the points of the circle contains it and each of the radii touches it. Thus we ourselves, by one of our parts, touch the supreme, unite ourselves to it, and are suspended from it. We establish ourselves in it when we turn towards it.

12. How is it that we who possess in ourselves such great things are not aware of them, that some of us often, and some of us always, fail to actualize these capacities? The realities themselves, The Intelligence and the self-sufficient above it, are "always active." The Soul, too, is always active. As to our own souls, we are not aware of all that goes on in them. Such activities are known only when perceptible by sensation. Unless they attain to sense they are not communicated to the entire soul and thus we are not conscious of them. Yet the faculty of sense perception is only part of man; it is the whole soul with all of its parts that constitutes the man. Each part of the soul is always alert and always engaging in its appropriate function, but we are aware only when there is communication as well as perception.

To grasp what is within us we must turn our perceptive faculties inward, focusing their whole attention there. Just as the person who wants to hear a cherished sound must neglect all others and keep his ears attuned to the approach of the sound he prefers to those he hears about him, so we too must here close our senses to all the noises that assail us (if they are not necessary) and preserve the perceptive power of the soul pure and ready to attend to tones that come from above.

PROCLUS

PROCLUS WAS BORN c. 410 CE to a prominent lawyer in Constantinople, the new capital of the Roman Empire. After studying in Alexandria—first to become a lawyer, but more and more to become a philosopher—he moved to Athens in 430, where he could attend the lectures of the Neoplatonists who now staffed Plato's Academy. A mere seven years later he became its head, a position he held until his death in 485. This headship brought him great renown in Athens, but also inevitable suspicion, since he remained a pagan despite the growing prevalence of Christianity. Once he even endured a voluntary exile, escaping political pressures mounting against him, and using his year abroad to experience various mystery cults.

For although Proclus considered Plato a source of divine truths, he sought these truths elsewhere as well: from oracles and antique sages, mythic and real, barbarian and Greek. While acquiring his encyclopedic knowledge of religion and philosophy, and writing voluminously about both, he also produced treatises on mathematics, physics, astronomy, and Greek literature. Excerpted here is his best-known work, *Elements of Theology*, which presents the Neoplatonic system inherited from Plotinus and his successors in a "geometric" form modeled on Euclid's *Elements*. Beginning with propositions about the One, or Unity, Proclus methodically deduces conclusions about lower levels of reality, through to individual souls and their descent into bodies. Still more intricate and precise than Plotinus' system, Proclus' is no less mystical at its core.

This last great expression of Greek metaphysics was soon appropriated by an influential Christian theologian, pseudo-Dionysius, who helped give it a long afterlife in the medieval period. Two generations later, however, Proclus earned an equally powerful critic in the Christian philosopher John Philoponus. Publishing *Against Proclus on the Eternity of the World* in 529, Philoponus argued against the eternal world favored for a millennium by most Greek philosophers, and for the world's creation in time, a doctrine more congenial to *Genesis*. Fatefully, 529 was also the year in which Emperor Justinian closed the pagan philosophical schools in Athens, marking the end of the philosophical tradition presented in this volume. In the new era, philosophy would become less the supreme guide to life, as it had been to all the pagan Greek and Roman philosophers, and more the handmaiden of religion.

Elements of Theology

Prop. 1. *Every multiplicity participates in some way in unity.*

For if it participated in no way, neither would any given whole be one nor would each of the many elements from which a multiplicity is made up, but each of those also will be a multiplicity, and this will continue to infinity, and each of those infinite elements will in turn be an infinite multiplicity; for a multiplicity that in no way participates in any unity, neither in respect of the whole of itself nor in respect of any of the individual components of it, will be infinite in every way and as a whole, for each of the many entities that exist, no matter which you take, will either be one or not one; and if not one, then either many or nothing. But if each part is nothing, then the sum total of these will be nothing; if many, then each of them is made up of infinites infinitely multiplied. These conclusions, however, are impossible. For neither is it the case that any existent thing is made up of infinite-times-infinite parts (since there is nothing greater than infinity, but that which is the sum of all things will be greater than any given part); nor, on the other hand, that anything can be made up of parts which are nothing. Every multiplicity, therefore, participates in some way in unity.

Prop. 7. *Everything that is productive of something else is superior to the nature of its product.*

For either it is superior or it will be either inferior or equal. But let us first suppose it to be equal. Then that which is produced by it either has power itself to be productive of something else, or it is completely incapable of generation. But if it were incapable of generation, then by this very fact it would be inferior to its producer, and in its unproductiveness it would be unequal to it, which is productive and has the power to create. And if, on the other hand, it is productive of other things, either it will produce something equal to itself—and this will be universally the case, and so all beings will be equal to one another and none will be superior to any

From *Neoplatonic Philosophy*, translated and edited by John Dillon and Lloyd P. Gerson (Indianapolis: Hackett Publishing Company, 2004.

other by reason of the fact that the producer generates what follows upon it as equal to itself—or else it will produce something unequal to it, and so it would no longer be equal to what produced it. For it is a property of equal powers to create what is equal to themselves. But the products of these powers will be unequal to each other, if it is the case that the producer is equal to what is prior to it but that what follows from it is unequal to it. Therefore, it is impossible that the product should be unequal to the producer.

But neither will the producer ever be inferior, for if it gives the product being, it must also provide it with the power that goes with its being. But if it were itself productive of all the power that is in what follows upon it, then it would have the power to make itself such as that is. And if that were the case, then it could make itself more powerful, for it would not be prevented from this by incapacity, since the creative power would be inherent in it; or through lack of will, since by nature all things strive towards their good. So, if it were able to bring about another thing more perfect than itself, it would perfect itself before it did the same for what follows upon it.

Therefore, since the product is neither equal to the producer nor superior to it, it follows that in all cases the producer is superior in nature to the product.

Prop. 11. *All things that exist proceed from a unique cause, the first.*

For otherwise, either no one among things will have a cause; or alternatively, the totality of existence being limited, the sequence of causes will be circular; or else we will be faced with an infinite regress, cause lying behind cause, so that the positing of prior causes will never come to an end.

But if no thing had a cause, there would be no sequence of primary and secondary, perfecting and perfected, regulative and regulated, generative and generated, active and passive; and so there would be no scientific knowledge of anything. For the task of science is the recognition of causes, and only when we recognize the causes of things do we say that we know them.

If, on the other hand, the sequence of causes is circular, the same things will be at once prior and consequent and both more powerful and weaker; for every productive cause is superior in power to its product. (It makes no difference whether we connect cause and effect by deriving the one from the other through a greater or a less number of intermediaries, for the cause of all these will be superior to all of them, and the greater their number, the more powerful a cause will it be.)

But if the accumulation of causes is to be continued to infinity, and one comes before the other forever, once again there can be no scientific knowledge of anything; for there can be no knowledge of anything infinite. And if the causes are unknowable, there can be no scientific knowledge of their consequents.

Since, then, there must be a cause for all things, and causes must be distinguished from effects, and there can be no such thing as an infinite regress, there must be a first cause of all existing things, from which they each proceed as from a root, some closer to it and others more remote (that this principle must be unique, of course, has already been established, inasmuch as the existence of every multiplicity must be secondary to unity).

Prop. 15. *Everything that is capable of reverting on itself is incorporeal.*[1]

For nothing that is a body is of such a nature as to revert on itself, for if that which reverts upon anything is joined to that upon which it reverts, then it is plain that all the parts of any body that reverted upon itself must be joined to every other part; for that is what it means, after all, to revert upon oneself: both elements becoming one—both the reverted subject and that on which it has reverted. But this is impossible for a body and, in general, for any divisible substance. For the whole of a divisible substance cannot be joined with the whole of itself because of the separation of its parts, seeing as they occupy distinct positions in space. No body, therefore, is of such a nature as to revert upon itself in such a way that the whole is reverted upon the whole. If, therefore, there is anything that is capable of reverting upon itself, it is incorporeal and without parts.

---

1. In this proposition and the two following, Proclus wishes to establish the general principle that nothing corporeal can achieve self-reversion and the self-consciousness that goes with it.

Prop. 16. *Everything that is capable of reverting on itself has being separable from all body.*

For if it were inseparable from any body whatsoever, it could not have any activity separable from the body, since it is impossible that, if a given essence be inseparable from bodies, the activity that proceeds from that essence should be separable, for if that were the case, the activity would be superior to the essence in that the latter would need a body while the former would be self-sufficient, being dependent not on bodies but on itself. Anything, then, that is inseparable in its essence is, to the same or an even greater degree, inseparable in its activity. But if that is the case, it cannot revert on itself. For that which reverts on itself, being other than body, has an activity separate from body and not carried on through the body or with its cooperation, since neither the activity itself nor the end to which it is directed requires the body. Therefore, that which reverts on itself is entirely separable from bodies.

Prop. 17. *Everything that is originally self-moving is capable of reverting on itself.*

For if it moves itself, then its motive activity is directed towards itself, and mover and moved exist together as one. For either it moves in respect of one part of itself and is moved in another; or the whole moves and is moved; or the whole originates motion, but it is moved in respect of a part, or the other way about. But if the mover be one part and the moved another, in itself the whole will not be self-moved, since it will be composed of parts that are not self-moved: it will have the appearance of a self-mover, but will not be such in essence. And if the whole originates a motion that occurs in a part, or the other way about, there will be a part common to both that is simultaneously and in the same respect mover and moved, and it is this part that is the primal self-mover. But if one and the same thing moves and is moved, it will have its activity of motion directed towards itself, since it is a self-mover. But to direct activity towards something is to revert on that thing. Therefore, everything that is primarily self-moving is capable of reverting on itself.

Prop. 20. *Beyond all bodies is the essence of the soul; and beyond all souls is the intellectual nature; and beyond all intellectual substances, the One.*[2]

For every body is moved by something other than it: it is not of such a nature as to move itself, but by the presence of soul it is moved from within, and it is through the soul that it has life. When soul is present, the body is in some sense self-moved, but when soul is absent it is moved externally, showing that body is naturally moved from without, while self-movement is the soul's portion; for that in which soul is present is endowed with a degree of self-movement. And that which soul bestows by virtue of its mere existence must belong in a far more basic degree to soul itself. Soul is, therefore, beyond bodies, as it is self-moved in its essence, while they come to be self-moved by participation.

Soul in turn, being self-moved, occupies a rank inferior to the unmoved nature that is unmoved even in its activity, for among all things that are moved, the self-moved holds the dominant rank; and among all movers, the unmoved. If, therefore, soul moves other things through moving itself, there must exist prior to it a cause of motion that is unmoved. Now Intellect is such an unmoved cause of motion, being eternally active without change. It is by means of Intellect that soul participates in constant thinking, even as body partakes in self-movement through soul. For if constant thinking belonged primarily to soul, then it would inhere, like self-movement, in all souls. Therefore, it does not belong primarily to soul. Therefore, prior to soul there must be something that is primarily intellectual. Therefore, Intellect is prior to souls.

But, again, prior to the Intellect there is the One. For the Intellect, even though it is unmoved, is not yet a unity, for it serves as object of knowledge to itself

2. This proposition provides the first exposition within the *Elements* of a logical derivation of the three Neoplatonic hypostases. Proclus sets out to show dialectically that the existence of objects that move without being self-moving demands an entity that is self-moving, and that in turn demands the existence of something that, while causing motion, is superior to spatial motion (though not to "spiritual motion," i.e., self-thought); but that in turn demands a first principle, the unity of which precludes even self-thought.

and is object of its own activity. Moreover, while all things, of whatever level, participate in unity, not all participate in Intellect, for to participate in Intellect is to participate in knowledge, since intuitive knowledge is the beginning and first cause of all knowing. Therefore, the One is beyond Intellect.

Beyond the One, on the other hand, there is no further principle, for the One is identical with the Good,[3] and is, therefore, the principle of all things, as has been shown.[4]

Prop. 25. *Everything that has attained its perfection proceeds to generate those things that it is capable of producing, imitating in this the unique principle of all things.*

For even as that principle, by reason of its own goodness, is by a unitary act constitutive of all beings (for the Good is identical with the One, and action that is performed in accordance with goodness is identical with unitary action), so in like manner the principles consequent upon it are impelled because of their own perfection to generate further principles inferior to their own essence, for perfection is a function of the Good; and the perfect, insofar as it is perfect, imitates the Good. Now we saw that the Good was constitutive of all things. Accordingly, the perfect is by nature productive within the limits of its power. The more perfect is the cause of more, in proportion to the degree of its perfection, for the more perfect participates more fully in the Good. That is, it is nearer to the Good. And that means that it is more nearly akin to the cause of all things; that is, it is the cause of more. And the less perfect, insofar as it is less perfect, is the cause of less; for being further removed from that which produces all things, it is constitutive of fewer things. This is so because that which brings into being—or imposes order or perfection on, or holds together, or gives life to, or creates—all things has a closer kinship to that which does all this to more things, while that which does this to fewer things is more alien to it.

3. Cf. Prop. 13: "Every good is such as to unify what participates in it; and all unification is a good; and the Good is identical with the One."

4. Prop. 12: "All that exists has the Good as its first principle and cause."

On the basis of this, it is clear that that which is most remote from the first principle of all things is unproductive and a cause of nothing. For if it generates something and has something after it, it is plain that it will no longer be the most remote, but what it produces will be more remote than it, and it itself will be nearer by reason of producing something else, whatever that be, thus imitating the cause that is productive of all beings.

Prop. 35. *Every effect both remains in its cause, and proceeds from it, and reverts on it.*

For if it were simply to remain, it will in no way differ from its cause, being without distinction from it; for distinction arises simultaneously with procession. And if it should proceed only, it will be devoid of conjunction or sympathy with its cause, since it will have no means of communication with it. And if it should revert only, how can that which does not derive its being from its cause revert in its being upon a principle that is alien to it? And if it should remain and proceed, but does not revert, how does it come about that each thing has a natural desire in the direction of its well-being and the Good, and an upward striving towards its generative cause? And if it should proceed and revert, but not remain, how does it come about that after being parted from its cause it strives to be conjoined with it, although before being separated there was no conjunction? For if it was conjoined with the cause, it certainly remained in it. Finally, if it should remain and revert, but not proceed, how can something revert that has not undergone distinction, since all reversion, after all, resembles resolution into that source from which it has been divided according to being?

So, then, it is necessary that the effect should either remain simply or revert simply, or proceed simply, or combine the extreme terms, or combine the mean term with one of the other two, or else combine all three. The only possibility remaining, then, is that every effect remains in its cause, proceeds from it, and reverts on it.

Prop. 123. *Everything that is divine is itself, by reason of its superessential unity, ineffable and unknowable to all things secondary to it, but it may be grasped and known from what participates in it.*

For this reason, only the first principle is completely unknowable, as being unparticipated.

For all knowledge that comes through reasoning is of real beings and possesses its grasp of truth in virtue of real beings (for it grasps thoughts and consists in acts of thinking). But the gods are beyond all being. Accordingly, the divine neither is an object of opinion or of discursive reason nor is it intelligible. This is so because all that exists is either sensible, and therefore an object of opinion; or true being, and therefore intelligible; or of intermediate rank, at once being and becoming; and, owing to this, an object of discursive reason. If, then, the gods are superessential, or have an existence prior to beings, we can have neither opinion concerning them nor scientific knowledge nor discursive reason nor yet thinking of them.

Nevertheless, from the beings dependent upon them, their distinctive properties may be cognized, and this with the force of necessity. For it is in accordance with the distinctive properties of the principles participated in that differences within a participant order are determined. And it is not everything that participates in everything (for there can be no conjunction of things that are wholly unlike each other), nor does any chance thing participate in any chance thing, but it is what is akin that is joined to each thing, and from it each proceeds.

Prop. 186. *Every soul is an incorporeal substance and separable from body.*[5]

For if it knows itself, and if anything that knows itself reverts on itself[6] and what reverts on itself is neither body (since all body is incapable of reverting on itself) nor inseparable from body (since, again, what is inseparable from body does not have the ability to revert on itself; for in this way it would be separated from body), the consequence will be that soul is neither a corporeal substance nor inseparable from body. But that it knows itself is plain, for if it has knowledge of principles superior to itself, it is capable that much the more of knowing itself, as it derives self-knowledge from its knowledge of the causes prior to it.

Prop. 187. *Every soul is indestructible and imperishable.*

Anything that can in any way be dissolved or destroyed either is corporeal and composite or has its existence in a substrate; the former kind, being made up of a plurality of elements, is destroyed by being dissolved, while the latter, being capable of existence only in something other than itself, disappears into nonexistence when severed from its substrate.[7] But the soul is both incorporeal and external to any substrate, existing, as it does, in itself and reverting on itself. It is, therefore, indestructible and imperishable.

5. Proclus is here assuming a distinction between the cognitive aspect of soul that is an incorporeal substance and the aspect of soul that is, in fact, inseparable from the body. The latter he calls an "image of soul."

6. This principle is established in Prop. 83: "Everything that is capable of knowing itself is capable of reverting upon itself in every way." And this in turn follows from the earlier Props. 15 and 16, above: "Everything that is capable of reverting upon itself is incorporeal," and "Everything that is capable of reverting upon itself has an existence separable from all body." This proposition and the following one simply relate these more general principles to the case of souls.

7. This is an application of Prop. 48: "Everything that is not eternal either is composite or has its existence in something else."